THE EREZ SERIES

RABBI ADIN
EVEN-ISRAEL
STEINSALTZ

A CONCISE GUIDE TO
HALAKHA

AN OVERVIEW OF JEWISH LAW

A Concise Guide to Halakha
First edition, 2020

Koren Publishers Jerusalem Ltd.
POB 8531, New Milford, CT 06776-8531, USA
& POB 4044, Jerusalem 91040, Israel

www.korenpub.com

Original Hebrew Edition © Adin Even-Israel Steinsaltz, 2018
English translation © Adin Even-Israel Steinsaltz 2020
Koren Tanakh font © 1962, 2020 Koren Publishers Ltd.
Koren Siddur font and text design © 1981, 2020 Koren Publishers Jerusalem Ltd.

This book was published in cooperation with
the Israeli Institute for Talmudic Publication.
All rights reserved for Rabbi Adin Even-Israel Steinsaltz.

The right of Adin Steinsaltz to be identified as the author
of this work has been asserted by him in accordance
with the Copyright, Designs & Patents Act 1988.

Steinsaltz Center is the parent organization of institutions
established by Rabbi Adin Even-Israel Steinsaltz
POB 45187, Jerusalem 91450 ISRAEL
Telephone: +972 2 646 0900, Fax +972 2 624 9454
www.steinsaltz-center.org

ISBN 978-1-59264-563-3, *hardcover*
Printed and bound in the United States

Contents

Shabbat and Festivals

Daily Routine

Various Topics

Foreword

This volume is an up-to-date survey of the commandments, prohibitions, and customs practiced by Jews today. Halakhic literature in general, beyond the commandments stated in the Torah itself, begins with the Mishna, which is in essence a book of *halakha*. After the Mishna, many halakhic rulings appear in the Talmud, as well as in the writings of the Sages of subsequent generations, the *geonim*. Thereafter, numerous halakhic books were written in a variety of styles; throughout the generations, the material was updated from time to time. This includes the *Halakhot Gedolot*, the Rif, and the Rambam, and afterward the *Beit Yosef* and the *Shulḥan Arukh*. Typically, the later books, each in its particular style, were based on the material of the earlier generations, and were updated by the inclusion of all the discussions and rulings of the subsequent generations.

This volume is a brief, modern presentation of practical *halakha*. Although it does not presume to be a book of authoritative halakhic rulings, it nevertheless offers a survey of *halakha* as it is practiced today. Accordingly, it was written not as a commentary on other books but as an independent work, written in a modern style, in a language we hope will be clear and straightforward for every reader. Since we have striven to make the book current, we have dealt as much as possible with contemporary problems, while also attempting to include at least a summary of the various customs practiced by the different ethnic communities inside and outside of contemporary Israel.

Due to the great scope of Jewish law, one small volume could not possibly cover all the important issues, and certainly it could not touch upon all the details and nuances that pertain to the subjects at hand. For this reason, the book is not a substitute either for halakhic works that are defined as such or for those specific problems and questions that should be presented to scholars and rabbis with whom one can speak in person.

The book is divided into several sections:

One section, entitled "Life Cycle," focuses on the major milestones of life, from pregnancy and birth to illness and death. The second section deals with the Jewish calendar year, with its holidays, festivals, fast days, and other special days. Another section discusses the *halakhot* of Shabbat and major festivals. The fourth section analyzes the relationship between man and his fellow man, both with regard to those actions that one should pursue in this regard and those that must be avoided. A further section presents the daily routine of a Jew, from arising in the morning to retiring at night. In addition, there is a section on miscellaneous issues that a Jewish person might encounter, whether in daily life or in special circumstances.

We have aimed to keep the translation as true to the original Hebrew as possible. However, as the Hebrew edition was composed for an Israeli audience, it often was missing *halakhot* that are unique to the Diaspora, such as those relating to the additional day of the festival celebrated outside of Israel. We have therefore added material to address these topics and render this survey relevant also to Jews living in the Diaspora.

We have included the original Hebrew, along with a translation and a transliteration for passages which are ritually recited on various occasions. For texts that one should recite in the language he knows best, transliteration is not included.

A detailed table of contents appears at the beginning of the book, which lists all the topics contained within.

Rabbi Adin Even-Israel Steinsaltz

Introducing the Erez Concise Guides

A Jewish home, at any time or place, cannot be maintained based on the mere identity of its residents as Jews. Whether they conceive of themselves as religious, traditional, or secular, people need to have access to written expression of their tradition through which they can come to know, understand, and "enter" their tradition.

"To enter the tradition" can mean something different for each person. Some are simply curious, others have a particular interest, and there are undoubtedly many Jews who just do not want the worlds of the Jewish spirit to be closed to them. People therefore require bridges and gates to gain access. There is no obligation to use these, but their existence makes it possible for anyone – when that person so desires – to enter, or even to glance within; the way is clear and he or she can do so.

We have thus produced the Erez series which provides different gates by which one can enter the Jewish tradition. Just as it is told about Abraham's tent that it was open from all four directions in order to welcome guests from everywhere, these books allow anyone, whenever he or she feels like it or finds something interesting, to enter into the tradition.

There are thousands of books that cover, in various ways and at different levels, the materials presented here. However, most of them require prior knowledge and no small amount of effort to be understood. In these volumes, we have striven to give anyone who seeks it a paved road into the riches of the Jewish world. More than merely a gate, we hope that these books can be said to offer their readers a "ride" into the tradition. Each person can get off whenever he or she desires and continue traveling when their interest is reawakened.

These volumes contain some of the fundamentals of Judaism. In each of them there are elements that can be considered hors d'oeuvres that can be snacked upon and others that are more comparable to entrees, that require more time for digestion. In either case, the invitation offered by *A Concise Guide to the Sages* in Proverbs (9:5) is relevant: "Come, partake of my bread, and drink of the wine that I have mixed." The books were deliberately designed to be accessible to everyone, whether he or she is highly educated or someone whose source of intellectual stimulation consists in occasionally reading the newspaper. Anyone can enjoy something, whether by means of an occasional taste, or by sitting down to a hearty meal. The way is open and anyone can find the gate appropriate for him or her, without effort.

We have aimed to keep the translation as true to the original Hebrew and Aramaic as possible. As some of these texts are not easy to understand, we have added clarifying comments in square brackets where appropriate. Further explication is appended in notes at the end of certain passages. When we have felt it appropriate to use a transliteration, the term transliterated is first explained and then followed by the transliteration in square brackets. At the end of each book we have provided a glossary of Hebrew terms mentioned in the series. Some of the terms found there may not be found in this book, as we have used the same glossary for all the volumes of the Erez series. *The Reference Guide to the Talmud* has a more extensive glossary as is necessary for that work.

Given the antiquity of the texts collected here, there are many occasions where it was impossible to avoid gendered usage and we have followed the texts themselves in using the male gender as the default.

Each of the volumes in this series stands alone, with only occasional citations connecting them. The first volume, *A Concise Guide to the Torah*, contains the translation of the Torah taken from the *Steinsaltz Humash*; we have abridged the commentary that can be found there. One can take this volume to the synagogue but also peruse it in the comforts of one's home.

The second volume, *A Concise Guide to the Sages*, is an anthology of rabbinic literature, organized by topics. One part includes rabbinic thinking associated with the Torah, while other topics are also addressed: the cycle of the Jewish year, the cycle of life in rabbinic eyes, as well as other topics where a person can find something that fits his or her needs.

The third volume, *A Concise Guide to Mahshava*, addresses spiritual matters. It contains an anthology of non-halakhic literature from the Jewish spiritual tradition: Kabbala, Jewish philosophy, the Musar tradition, and hasidic writings. Here too, the texts are presented in a manner that is accessible to all, in clear English. This volume addresses a broad array of topics: Besides comments and explanations on the Torah, there are sections devoted to the cycle of the Jewish year, the life cycle, and fundamental questions of human life such as parenthood, marriage, and death. There are many other topics addressed in this volume and one can open it at random and find wisdom that touches the soul.

The fourth volume, *A Concise Guide to Halakha*, is a survey of practical *halakha*. It does not delve into the sources of *halakha* and provide an opportunity for intensive study but serves rather as a guidebook to what the *halakha* instructs one to do in various situations. In this way the book offers a summary of the *halakhot* of Shabbat and the holidays, of life cycle events, and of those mitzvot that any Jew is likely to encounter. If one wishes to act in accordance with the *halakha*, he or she will know what to do with the help of this volume. It is written in clear English with a minimum of technical language so that it is accessible to anyone, man, woman, or child. And if he or she decides to act accordingly, may he or she be blessed.

The fifth volume, *Reference Guide to the Talmud*, is a reprint of the work that was issued as a companion to the *Koren Talmud Bavli*. It is an indispensable resource for students of all levels. This fully revised, English-language edition of the *Reference Guide* clearly and concisely explains the Talmud's fundamental structure, concepts, terminology, assumptions, and inner logic; it provides essential historical and biographical information; it includes appendixes, a key to abbreviations, and a comprehensive index.

For improved usability, this completely updated volume has a number of new features: topical organization instead of by Hebrew alphabet, re-edited and revised text to coordinate with the language used in the *Koren Talmud Bavli*, and an index of Hebrew terms to enable one seeking a Hebrew term to locate the relevant entry.

These books are certainly not the entire Torah, but they are beneficial for any Jew to have in his or her home. If one finds something interesting, or is curious about something, these books offer a resource to investigate that topic. Even if one opens one of these volumes by chance, he or she will gain from reading them, both intellectually and spiritually. In short, these are books that it is convenient to have in one's home.

Our thanks are extended to all the people who participated in the project of writing these books, editing them, and finding the sources therein. We likewise would like to thank the publisher, and those first readers who offered helpful criticism and advice, and finally to those good people whose donations made it possible to create these books.

The Editors

Life Cycle

Birth of a Son
First month

The Torah, which literally means "instruction" or "guidance," is sometimes referred to as a "Torah of life," as it leads us through every step of our lives. This is especially true of the momentous occasions in life: birth, circumcision, bar and bat mitzva, weddings, etc.

This chapter, the first in the "Life Cycle" section, deals with the first month of a newborn son. It introduces the laws and customs that apply to the time of birth, continues with the practice of the days before circumcision, moves on to the circumcision itself, and concludes with the ceremony of the redemption of the firstborn [*pidyon haben*].

Birth

Birth is a miraculous event that unfolds before our very eyes. When all goes well, the parents of the newborn are often filled with a fervent desire to thank God for the gift of life and parenthood which He has bestowed upon them.

Prayers and Blessings

During the birthing process, it is commendable, when possible, to read from the book of Psalms, praying for the welfare of the mother and the baby. There are several psalms from which to choose that are especially appropriate for childbirth: 1, 2, 3, 4, 20, 21, 22, 23, 24, 33, 47, 72, 86, 90, 91, 92, 93, 104, and from 112 until the end of Psalms.

Following the birth of a son, the parents give thanks to God and recite the blessing:

בָּרוּךְ אַתָּה אֲדֹנָי, אֱלֹהֵינוּ מֶלֶךְ הָעוֹלָם, הַטּוֹב וְהַמֵּטִיב.

Barukh ata Adonai, Eloheinu, melekh ha'olam, hatov vehametiv.

"Blessed are You, Lord our God, King of the universe, who is good and imparts good."

After the mother has recovered from the birth, it is customary for her to recite the blessing of "...who bestows good" [*HaGomel*], like any other individual who has safely emerged from a position of danger. The *HaGomel* blessing must be recited in the presence of a *minyan*. If she gave birth to a son, it is common practice for the mother to recite the blessing at the circumcision [*brit*] ceremony, after the circumcision itself, as there is usually a *minyan* present.

The blessing is as follows:

בָּרוּךְ אַתָּה אֲדֹנָי, אֱלֹהֵינוּ מֶלֶךְ הָעוֹלָם, הַגּוֹמֵל לְחַיָּבִים טוֹבוֹת, שֶׁגְּמָלַנִי כָּל טוֹב.

Barukh ata Adonai, Eloheinu, melekh ha'olam, hagomel laḥayavim tovot, shegemalani kol tov.

"Blessed are You, Lord our God, King of the universe, who bestows good upon the culpable, who has bestowed all goodness upon me."

Ashkenazim respond:

אָמֵן, מִי שֶׁגְּמָלְךָ כָּל טוֹב, הוּא יִגְמָלְךָ כָּל טוֹב סֶלָה.

Amen. Mi shegemalakh kol tov, Hu yigmalekh kol tov, sela.

"Amen. May He who bestowed all goodness upon you always bestow all goodness upon you, Selah."

Sephardim respond:

אָמֵן, הָאֵל שֶׁגְּמָלְךָ כָּל טוֹב, הוּא יִגְמָלֶךָ כָּל טוֹב סֶלָה.

Ha'El shegemalakh kol tov, Hu yigmalekh kol tov, sela.

"Amen. May the God who bestowed all goodness upon you always bestow all goodness upon you, Selah."

The husband may recite the blessing on behalf of his wife. In such a case, he should do so in his wife's presence, and the blessing is recited in the second person:

בָּרוּךְ אַתָּה אֲדֹנָי, אֱלֹהֵינוּ מֶלֶךְ הָעוֹלָם, הַגּוֹמֵל לְחַיָּבִים טוֹבוֹת, שֶׁגְּמָלֵךְ כָּל טוֹב.

Barukh ata Adonai, Eloheinu, melekh ha'olam, hagomel laḥayavim tovot, shegemalakh kol tov.

"Blessed are You, Lord our God, King of the universe, who bestows good upon the culpable, who bestowed all goodness upon you," and his wife responds: "Amen."

📖 **Further reading:** For the *halakhot* of birth on Shabbat, see the chapter that deals with the laws of medical treatment on Shabbat, p. 439.

Circumcision

The commandment of circumcision was given to Abraham, the first Jew, as it states: "God said to Abraham: And you, you shall observe My covenant, you, and your descendants after you throughout their generations.... You shall circumcise the flesh of your foreskin and it shall be a mark of a covenant between Me and you" (Genesis 17:9–11).

Circumcision is also the first commandment that is experienced by every Jewish male after birth. This commandment, more than any other, symbolizes the eternal bond between the Jewish male and his Creator; it is carved into his flesh and accompanies him everywhere, in all circumstances.

> 📖 **Further reading:** For more on circumcision and its meaning, see *A Concise Guide to the Torah*, pp. 34, 142, 277; *A Concise Guide to the Sages*, p. 144; *A Concise Guide to Mahshava*, p. 9.

Preparations for the Circumcision

It is advisable to contact a certified circumciser, or *mohel*, immediately after the birth, to arrange for the circumcision in a place of the parents' choosing. (A *mohel* is the most skilled person at performing circumcisions, even more than doctors, as this is the *mohel's* specific area of expertise.) In Israel, the website of the Chief Rabbinate has a list of certified *mohalim* who are licensed by the Department of Health. It is also advisable to consult with friends who have used the services of a *mohel* for their sons' circumcision. The *mohel* will keep an eye on the baby's welfare and check to see if he is fit for undergoing circumcision. Sometimes he will wish to examine the boy the day before the circumcision.

There are three minor events that may be held between childbirth and circumcision, in accordance with the customs of the various communities: welcoming the newborn male child [*Shalom Zakhar*], the recitation of *Shema*, and the Covenant of Isaac [*Brit Yitzhak*].

Shalom Zakhar: It is customary, mainly in Ashkenazic communities, to host a *Shalom Zakhar*, a gathering of friends and family on the first Shabbat evening following the birth. Members of the family, along with friends and neighbors, come together in the newborn's home (or in a nearby synagogue) after the Friday night meal and sit around the table for a short while. Light refreshments are served and the guests bless the parents that they shall merit to raise the child to partake of "Torah knowledge, the wedding canopy, and good deeds." It is customary to serve, among other items, cooked chickpeas [commonly called arbes] at this gathering. The event can be held even if the infant has not yet been released from the hospital, or when he and his mother are recovering.

Recitation of *Shema*: On the night preceding the circumcision, it is customary to invite children to come to the home, stand together around the infant's crib, and recite the verses of *Shema*, the text of the priestly blessing, and the verse: "May the angel who delivers me…" (Genesis 48:16). The purpose of this ceremony is to provide increased protection for the infant during the night before his circumcision. The full verses that are recited are as follows:

שְׁמַע יִשְׂרָאֵל, אֲדֹנָי אֱלֹהֵינוּ, אֲדֹנָי אֶחָד:

Shema Yisrael: Adonai Eloheinu, Adonei ehad.

וְאָהַבְתָּ אֵת אֲדֹנָי אֱלֹהֶיךָ, בְּכָל לְבָבְךָ וּבְכָל נַפְשְׁךָ וּבְכָל מְאֹדֶךָ: וְהָיוּ הַדְּבָרִים הָאֵלֶּה אֲשֶׁר אָנֹכִי מְצַוְּךָ הַיּוֹם, עַל לְבָבֶךָ: וְשִׁנַּנְתָּם לְבָנֶיךָ וְדִבַּרְתָּ בָּם, בְּשִׁבְתְּךָ בְּבֵיתֶךָ וּבְלֶכְתְּךָ בַדֶּרֶךְ וּבְשָׁכְבְּךָ וּבְקוּמֶךָ: וּקְשַׁרְתָּם לְאוֹת עַל יָדֶךָ, וְהָיוּ לְטֹטָפֹת בֵּין עֵינֶיךָ: וּכְתַבְתָּם עַל מְזֻזוֹת בֵּיתֶךָ וּבִשְׁעָרֶיךָ:

Ve'ahavta et Adonai Elohekha bekhol levavekha, uvkhol nafshekha, uvkhol me'odekha. Vehayu hadevarim ha'eleh asher anokhi metzavekha hayom al levavekha. Veshinantam levanekha, vedibarta bam beshivtekha beveitekha uvlekhtekha vaderekh uvshokhbekha uvkumekha. Ukshartam le'ot al yadekha vehayu letotafot bein einekha. Ukhtavtam al mezuzot beitekha uvisharekha.

וַיְדַבֵּר אֲדֹנָי אֶל מֹשֶׁה לֵּאמֹר: דַּבֵּר אֶל אַהֲרֹן וְאֶל בָּנָיו לֵאמֹר; כֹּה תְבָרְכוּ אֶת בְּנֵי יִשְׂרָאֵל אָמוֹר לָהֶם: יְבָרֶכְךָ אֲדֹנָי וְיִשְׁמְרֶךָ: יָאֵר אֲדֹנָי פָּנָיו אֵלֶיךָ וִיחֻנֶּךָּ: יִשָּׂא אֲדֹנָי פָּנָיו אֵלֶיךָ וְיָשֵׂם לְךָ שָׁלוֹם: וְשָׂמוּ אֶת שְׁמִי עַל בְּנֵי יִשְׂרָאֵל, וַאֲנִי אֲבָרֲכֵם:

Vaydaber Adonai el Moshe lemor. Daber el Aharon ve'el banav lemor, ko tevarekhu et benei Yisrael, emor lahem: Yevarekhekha Adonai veyishmerekha; ya'er Adonai panav elekha vihuneka; yisa Adonai panav elekha veyasem lekha shalom.

הַמַּלְאָךְ הַגֹּאֵל אֹתִי מִכָּל רָע, יְבָרֵךְ אֶת הַנְּעָרִים וְיִקָּרֵא בָהֶם שְׁמִי וְשֵׁם אֲבֹתַי אַבְרָהָם וְיִצְחָק, וְיִדְגּוּ לָרֹב בְּקֶרֶב הָאָרֶץ:

Hamalakh hagoel oti mikol ra yevarekh et hane'arim, veyikareh vahem shemi veshem avotai Avraham veYitzhak, veyidgu larov bekerev ha'aretz.

"Hear, Israel: The Lord is our God, the Lord is one.

"You shall love the Lord your God with all your heart, and with all your soul, and with all your might. These matters that I command you today shall be upon your heart. You shall inculcate them in your children, and you shall speak of them while you are sitting in your house, and while you are walking on the way, and while you are lying down, and while you are rising. You shall bind them as a sign on your hand, and they shall be for ornaments between your eyes. You shall write them on the doorposts of your house, and on your gates" (Deuteronomy 6:4–9).

"The Lord spoke to Moses, saying: Speak to Aaron and to his sons, saying: So shall you bless the children of Israel, say to them: The Lord shall bless you, and keep you. The Lord shall shine His countenance to you, and be gracious to you. The Lord shall lift His countenance to you, and grant you peace. And they shall place My name upon the children of Israel, and I shall bless them" (Numbers 6:22–27).

"May the angel who delivers me from all evil, bless the lads and let my name and the name of my fathers, Abraham and Isaac, be called upon them and may they proliferate like fish in the midst of the earth" (Genesis 48:16).

Brit Yitzḥak: Sephardic communities have a custom of gathering friends together on the night before the circumcision to recite selected passages from the book of *Zohar* (from *Parashat Lekh Lekha*). For those who follow this practice, it is recommended that the study session be conducted by at least ten males [*minyan*]. The order of the study session can be found in books that deal with circumcision and the preparations for it, or in special prayer books for this night.

The reason for this gathering is twofold: to enhance the honor of the mitzva of circumcision that will be performed the next day, and to provide extra protection for the baby. Even if no gathering can be arranged, it is customary for the father of the son to recite the relevant sections of the *Zohar* himself.

Choosing the Name

Although a child's name is entirely the choice of his parents, according to kabbalistic sources, a name is not merely a technical matter, but a "channel" through which a person receives his life source. Therefore, it is important for parents to select for their child a Hebrew name that has a positive significance, not one that expresses an undesirable message or the name of a negative historical character.

📖 Further reading: For more on the calling of a name and its meaning, see *A Concise Guide to the Sages*, p. 7.

Date of the Circumcision

On which day is the circumcision performed?

The Torah specifies that the circumcision should be performed on the eighth day following the birth of the baby. The day of birth itself is included in the eight days, and therefore, the circumcision is ordinarily performed on the same day of the week as the birth. For example, if the baby was born on a Tuesday, his circumcision would take place on the following Tuesday.

In all matters of *halakha*, nighttime is considered part of the next day. Consequently, a baby born on the night between Tuesday and Wednesday is considered to have been born on Wednesday, and his circumcision will be performed on the Wednesday of the following week.

If a baby is born during the twilight hours, that is, between sunset and the emergence of the stars, his date of circumcision is calculated the same as that of a baby born after dark. The reason is that there is halakhic uncertainty as to whether twilight is part the previous day or the following one, and in a case of doubt the circumcision may be performed a day late, but never earlier than the eighth day. Accordingly, a baby born during twilight on Wednesday, a time which may be considered either Wednesday or Thursday, will be circumcised on Thursday a week later.

A baby born on Shabbat will be circumcised at the regular time, i.e., on the following Shabbat. That is, the commandment of circumcision overrides the prohibition of Shabbat desecration.

Unusual Cases

The circumcision of a baby born during twilight on Friday evening will be postponed until the Sunday of the following week. This is because circumcision supersedes Shabbat only when it is certain that Shabbat is actually the eighth day from birth. If there is any doubt, as there is in the case of a twilight birth, the sanctity of the Shabbat takes precedence and the circumcision is postponed to Sunday.

Even when the baby is born on Shabbat itself, if he was born by Caesarean section the circumcision is not held on the following Shabbat, but is postponed until Sunday. There are halakhic opinions that a baby conceived via artificial insemination is not circumcised on Shabbat either, even if he was delivered by regular birth on Shabbat.

In any case of uncertainty about the date of the circumcision, a rabbi should be consulted.

If the baby is unwell or is jaundiced, and circumcision might endanger his health, the circumcision is postponed until he recovers. Many *mohalim* have extensive experience and a broad understanding of this matter, and therefore it is recommended to consult the *mohel*, together with a doctor.

At What Time?

A circumcision may be performed only in the daytime, between sunrise and sunset. Although the entire day is valid for the performance of a circumcision, it is preferred to try to hold it early in the morning, in accordance with the halakhic principle that "the vigilant perform mitzvot early," that is, it is best to perform a mitzva as soon as possible.

Nevertheless, the *halakha* does take other factors into consideration. For example, if the early hours of the day are inconvenient for the invitees, and they would rather come after work, it is permitted and even advisable to postpone the time of the circumcision, in accordance with the principle that "in the multitude of people is the glory of a king" (Proverbs 14:28). This rule, which applies to other mitzvot as well, means that performing a mitzva in the presence of a large gathering serves to honor the King who has commanded us to perform that mitzva.

The Functionaries at a Circumcision

These are the main roles in a circumcision ceremony:

Mohel: The *mohel* performs the actual circumcision, and is almost always in charge of running the ceremony as well.

Sandak: The *sandak* is the person who holds the baby on his knees while the circumcision is performed. This is an important role that is given to a close relative or a dignitary. It is customary to honor one of the grandparents, a respected member of the family, an important rabbi, or someone of similar status. According to custom, the same person should not serve as *sandak* twice in the same nuclear family. In other words, if a grandfather on the father's side was granted the honor of being the *sandak* for the first child, he should not be given the same role again for the second child. Instead, it would be offered to, say, the maternal grandfather. However, some maintain that a great rabbi can be a *sandak* more than once for the same family.

Kvatter: In Ashkenazic communities, the couple who carries the baby from the mother to the father is called the *kvatter*. The mother hands the baby to the wife, who hands him to her husband, who then passes the baby to the father.

There are other functions with which one can honor family and friends, although the *mohel* or the father of the baby can perform these tasks themselves: (1) Placing the baby on the "chair of Elijah" (see below). (2) Lifting the baby from the "chair of Elijah" and placing him on the lap of the *sandak*. (3) After the circumcision, holding the baby while standing during the recitation of the blessings and the naming of the baby. (4) Reciting the blessings and announcing the baby's name. At times, the blessings and the name are recited by two different honorees.

It is customary that all the functionaries at a circumcision (apart from the couple serving as *kvatter*) should wear a ritual shawl [*tallit*]. Some have the custom for the father of the child and the *sandak* to also don phylacteries [*tefillin*].

Further reading: For how to don a *tallit*, see p. 583; for how to don *tefillin*, see p. 592.

The Ceremony

The circumcision begins when the baby is brought to the place where the ceremony will be performed, with the congregation standing.

The text presented below is the one accepted by most Ashkenazic communities in Israel. There are only minor variations in the Sephardic version, except for one significant change, which involves the recitation of the blessing, "…to bring him into the covenant of Abraham." This difference will be noted below.

The *mohel* announces:

בָּרוּךְ הַבָּא!

"Blessed be the one who has arrived."

The *mohel* then recites:

אַשְׁרֵי תִּבְחַר וּתְקָרֵב יִשְׁכֹּן חֲצֵרֶיךָ (תהילים סה:ה).

"Happy is the one You choose to bring near You to dwell in Your Sanctuary" (Psalms 65:5), and the congregation responds with the conclusion of that verse:

הקהל משיב: נִשְׂבְּעָה בְּטוּב בֵּיתֶךָ קְדֹשׁ הֵיכָלֶךָ (תהילים סה:ה).

"May we be sated by the bounty of Your House, the holiness of Your Temple" (Psalms 65:5).

After the baby has been handed over to his father by the *kvatter*, the father, followed by the congregation, recites these verses out loud. (Ashkenazim outside Israel do not recite these verses):

שְׁמַע יִשְׂרָאֵל, אֲדֹנָי אֱלֹהֵינוּ, אֲדֹנָי אֶחָד (דברים ו:ד).

Shema Yisrael: Adonai Eloheinu, Adonei eḥad.

אֲדֹנָי מֶלֶךְ, אֲדֹנָי מָלָךְ, אֲדֹנָי יִמְלֹךְ לְעוֹלָם וָעֶד. הקהל חוזר.

Adonai melekh, Adonai malakh, Adonai yimlokh le'olam va'ed. Congregation repeats after him.

אֲדֹנָי מֶלֶךְ, אֲדֹנָי מָלָךְ, אֲדֹנָי יִמְלֹךְ לְעוֹלָם וָעֶד. הקהל חוזר.

Adonai melekh, Adonai malakh, Adonai yimlokh le'olam va'ed. Congregation repeats.

אָנָּא אֲדֹנָי הוֹשִׁיעָה נָּא (תהילים קיח:כה). הקהל חוזר.

Ana Adonai, hoshi'a na. Congregation repeats.

אָנָּא אֲדֹנָי הוֹשִׁיעָה נָּא. הקהל חוזר.

Ana Adonai, hoshi'a na. Congregation repeats.

אָנָּא אֲדֹנָי הַצְלִיחָה נָּא (תהילים קיח:כה). הקהל חוזר.

Ana Adonai, hatzliḥa na. Congregation repeats.

אָנָּא אֲדֹנָי הַצְלִיחָה נָּא. הקהל חוזר.

Ana Adonai, hatzliḥa na. Congregation repeats.

"Hear, Israel: The Lord is our God, the Lord is one" (Deuteronomy 6:4). Congregation repeats after him.

"The Lord reigns, the Lord reigned, the Lord will reign forever and ever." Congregation repeats.

"The Lord reigns, the Lord reigned, the Lord will reign forever and ever." Congregation repeats.

"Lord, save us, we beseech You!" (Psalms 118:25). Congregation repeats.

"Lord, save us, we beseech You!" Congregation repeats.

"Lord, grant us success, we beseech You!" (Psalms 118:25). Congregation repeats.

"Lord, grant us success, we beseech You!" Congregation repeats.

Some *mohalim* add the following verses at this point:

וַיְדַבֵּר אֲדֹנָי אֶל מֹשֶׁה לֵּאמֹר: פִּינְחָס בֶּן אֶלְעָזָר בֶּן אַהֲרֹן הַכֹּהֵן הֵשִׁיב אֶת חֲמָתִי מֵעַל בְּנֵי יִשְׂרָאֵל בְּקַנְאוֹ אֶת קִנְאָתִי בְּתוֹכָם וְלֹא כִלִּיתִי אֶת בְּנֵי יִשְׂרָאֵל בְּקִנְאָתִי: לָכֵן אֱמֹר, הִנְנִי נֹתֵן לוֹ אֶת בְּרִיתִי שָׁלוֹם (במדבר כה, י-יב).

"The Lord spoke to Moses, saying: Pinhas, son of Elazar, son of Aaron the priest, has caused My wrath to be withdrawn from the children of Israel, in that he was zealous on My behalf among them, that I did not destroy the children of Israel in My zealotry. Therefore, say: Behold, I am giving him My covenant of peace" (Numbers 25:10–12).

The father places the baby on "the chair of Elijah," which is where the *sandak* will sit while holding the baby on his knees. This chair is dedicated to Elijah the prophet, who according to the Sages is called "the angel of the covenant [of circumcision]," because he is present in spirit at every circumcision.

The *mohel* declares:

זֶה הַכִּסֵּא שֶׁל אֵלִיָּהוּ הַנָּבִיא זָכוּר לַטּוֹב. לִישׁוּעָתְךָ קִוִּיתִי אֲדֹנָי, שִׂבַּרְתִּי לִישׁוּעָתְךָ אֲדֹנָי, וּמִצְוֹתֶיךָ עָשִׂיתִי. אֵלִיָּהוּ מַלְאַךְ הַבְּרִית, הִנֵּה שֶׁלְּךָ לְפָנֶיךָ, עֲמֹד עַל יְמִינִי וְסָמְכֵנִי. שִׂבַּרְתִּי לִישׁוּעָתְךָ אֲדֹנָי, שָׂשׂ אָנֹכִי עַל אִמְרָתֶךָ כְּמוֹצֵא שָׁלָל רָב. שָׁלוֹם רָב לְאֹהֲבֵי תוֹרָתֶךָ וְאֵין לָמוֹ מִכְשׁוֹל. אַשְׁרֵי תִּבְחַר וּתְקָרֵב יִשְׁכֹּן חֲצֵרֶיךָ, נִשְׂבְּעָה בְּטוּב בֵּיתֶךָ, קְדֹשׁ הֵיכָלֶךָ (בראשית מט, יח; תהילים קיט, קסו, קסב, קסה; שם סה, ה).

"This is the chair of Elijah the prophet, may his memory be a blessing. 'For your salvation, I await, Lord' (Genesis 49:18). 'I await Your salvation, Lord, and I have fulfilled Your commandments' (Psalms 119:166). Elijah, angel of the covenant, behold what is yours is before you, stand on my right side and support me. 'I hope for Your salvation, Lord' (Psalms 119:166). 'I rejoice at Your sayings, as one who finds great spoils' (Psalms 119:162). 'Those who love Your teaching know great peace; for them there is no obstacle' (Psalms 119:165). 'Happy is the one You choose to bring near You to dwell in Your Sanctuary. May we be sated by the bounty of Your House, the holiness of Your Temple'" (Psalms 65:5).

At this point the baby is placed on the lap of the *sandak*, and the circumcision is performed while he is lying there. Since the obligation to perform the circumcision is incumbent upon the father of the infant, the father should appoint the *mohel* as his agent to circumcise his son for him. Some have the custom to state this explicitly:

הִנְנִי מְמַנֶּה אוֹתְךָ כִּשְׁלִיחַ מִצְוָה לָמוּל
אֶת בְּנִי.

Hineni memaneh otekha kishliaḥ mitzva lamul et beni.

"I hereby appoint you as an agent for fulfilling my mitzva to circumcise my son."

The *mohel* finishes preparing the baby for the circumcision, and recites the blessing:

בָּרוּךְ אַתָּה אֲדֹנָי אֱלֹהֵינוּ מֶלֶךְ הָעוֹלָם,
אֲשֶׁר קִדְּשָׁנוּ בְּמִצְוֹתָיו וְצִוָּנוּ עַל הַמִּילָה.

Barukh ata Adonai, Eloheinu, melekh ha'olam, asher kideshanu bemitzvotav, vetzivanu al ḥamila.

"Blessed are You, Lord our God, King of the universe, who sanctified us with His commandments and commanded us concerning circumcision."

The *mohel* then cuts the foreskin, and immediately afterward, before the *mohel* starts executing *peri'ah* (the removal of a thin layer of skin), the father recites the blessing:

בָּרוּךְ אַתָּה אֲדֹנָי אֱלֹהֵינוּ מֶלֶךְ הָעוֹלָם,
אֲשֶׁר קִדְּשָׁנוּ בְּמִצְוֹתָיו וְצִוָּנוּ לְהַכְנִיסוֹ
בִּבְרִיתוֹ שֶׁל אַבְרָהָם אָבִינוּ.

Barukh ata Adonai, Eloheinu, melekh ha'olam, asher kideshanu bemitzvotav, vetzivanu lehakhniso bivrito shel Avraham avinu.

"Blessed are You, Lord our God, King of the universe, who sanctified us with His commandments and commanded us to bring him into the covenant of Abraham."

The father then adds the *Sheheḥeyanu* blessing. However, outside of Israel, Ashkenazic custom is not to recite this blessing. In Sephardic communities in Israel, the accepted custom is for the father of the infant to recite this blessing before the baby is placed on the lap of the *sandak*.

בָּרוּךְ אַתָּה אֲדֹנָי, אֱלֹהֵינוּ מֶלֶךְ הָעוֹלָם,
שֶׁהֶחֱיָנוּ וְקִיְּמָנוּ וְהִגִּיעָנוּ לַזְּמַן הַזֶּה.

Barukh ata Adonai, Eloheinu, melekh ha'olam, sheheḥeyanu vekiyemanu vehigi'anu la'zeman hazeh.

"Blessed are You, Lord our God, King of the universe, who has given us life, sustained us, and brought us to this time."

Congregation:

אָמֵן. כְּשֵׁם שֶׁנִּכְנַס לַבְּרִית, כֵּן יִכָּנֵס לְתוֹרָה
וּלְחֻפָּה וּלְמַעֲשִׂים טוֹבִים.

Amen. Keshem shenikhnas la'berit, ken yikanes leTorah ulhupa ulma'asim tovim.

"Amen. Just as he has entered into the covenant, so may he enter into Torah knowledge, the wedding canopy, and good deeds."

The *mohel* continues to care for the baby and soothes him. Meanwhile, the recitation of the blessings resumes. One of the congregants is given the honor to hold the baby while standing, and another is called upon to recite the blessings. The *mohel* himself may be the one who recites the blessings.

The individual who recites the blessings holds a cup of wine in his hand and says:

בָּרוּךְ אַתָּה אֲדֹנָי, אֱלֹהֵינוּ מֶלֶךְ הָעוֹלָם,
בּוֹרֵא פְּרִי הַגָּפֶן.

Barukh ata Adonai, Eloheinu, melekh ha'olam, boreh peri hagafen.

"Blessed are You, Lord our God, King of the universe, who creates the fruit of the vine."

According to the Sephardic custom, he also recites a blessing over spices:

בָּרוּךְ אַתָּה אֲדֹנָי, אֱלֹהֵינוּ מֶלֶךְ הָעוֹלָם,
בּוֹרֵא מִינֵי בְשָׂמִים.

Barukh ata Adonai, Eloheinu, melekh ha'olam, boreh minei vesamim.

"Blessed are You, Lord our God, King of the universe, who creates various spices."

He continues with the following blessing:

בָּרוּךְ אַתָּה אֲדֹנָי, אֱלֹהֵינוּ מֶלֶךְ הָעוֹלָם,
אֲשֶׁר קִדַּשׁ יְדִיד מִבֶּטֶן, וְחֹק בִּשְׁאֵרוֹ שָׂם
וְצֶאֱצָאָיו חָתַם בְּאוֹת בְּרִית קֹדֶשׁ, עַל
כֵּן בִּשְׂכַר זֹאת אֵל חַי חֶלְקֵנוּ צוּרֵנוּ, צַוֵּה
לְהַצִּיל יְדִידוּת שְׁאֵרֵנוּ מִשַּׁחַת לְמַעַן בְּרִיתוֹ
אֲשֶׁר שָׂם בִּבְשָׂרֵנוּ, בָּרוּךְ אַתָּה אֲדֹנָי, כּוֹרֵת
הַבְּרִית.

Barukh ata Adonai, Eloheinu, melekh ha'olam, asher kidash yedid mibeten, vehok bishero sam, vetze'etza'av hatam be'ot berit kodesh. Al ken biskhar zot, El hai, helkenu, tzurenu, tzaveh lehatzil yedidut she'erenu mishahat, lema'an berito asher sam bivsarenu. Barukh ata Adonai, koret ha'berit.

"Blessed are You, Lord our God, King of the universe, who sanctified the beloved one [Isaac] from the womb, marked the decree in his flesh, and gave his descendants the seal and the sign of the holy covenant. Therefore, as a reward for this, the living God, our Portion, commanded to deliver the beloved of our flesh from destruction, for the sake of His covenant that He set in our flesh. Blessed are You, Lord, who establishes the covenant."

The baby is then blessed and named. The one reciting the following blessing pauses after the words: "And his name shall be called in Israel...," at which point the father whispers the name of the baby in his ear or hands him a note on which the name is written. The person reciting the blessing then says the baby's name out loud and continues with the recitation of this paragraph:

אֱלֹהֵינוּ וֵאלֹהֵי אֲבוֹתֵינוּ, קַיֵּם אֶת הַיֶּלֶד הַזֶּה לְאָבִיו וּלְאִמּוֹ וְיִקָּרֵא שְׁמוֹ בְּיִשְׂרָאֵל [הַשֵּׁם שֶׁנִּבְחַר] בֶּן [שֵׁם הָאָב]. יִשְׂמַח הָאָב בְּיוֹצֵא חֲלָצָיו וְתָגֵל אִמּוֹ בִּפְרִי בִטְנָהּ, כַּכָּתוּב: יִשְׂמַח אָבִיךָ וְאִמֶּךָ וְתָגֵל יוֹלַדְתֶּךָ (משלי כג, כה). וְנֶאֱמַר: וָאֶעֱבֹר עָלַיִךְ וָאֶרְאֵךְ מִתְבּוֹסֶסֶת בְּדָמָיִךְ, וָאֹמַר לָךְ בְּדָמַיִךְ חֲיִי, וָאֹמַר לָךְ בְּדָמַיִךְ חֲיִי (יחזקאל טז, ו). וְנֶאֱמַר: זָכַר לְעוֹלָם בְּרִיתוֹ דָּבָר צִוָּה לְאֶלֶף דּוֹר, אֲשֶׁר כָּרַת אֶת אַבְרָהָם וּשְׁבוּעָתוֹ לְיִשְׂחָק, וַיַּעֲמִידֶהָ לְיַעֲקֹב לְחֹק לְיִשְׂרָאֵל בְּרִית עוֹלָם (תהילים קה, ח-י). וְנֶאֱמַר: וַיָּמָל אַבְרָהָם אֶת יִצְחָק בְּנוֹ בֶּן שְׁמֹנַת יָמִים כַּאֲשֶׁר צִוָּה אֹתוֹ אֱלֹהִים (בראשית כא, ד). הוֹדוּ לַאדֹנָי כִּי טוֹב, כִּי לְעוֹלָם חַסְדּוֹ (תהילים קיח, א).

Eloheinu velohei avoteinu: Kayem et hayeled hazeh le'aviv ul'imo, veyikareh shemo BeYisrael [baby's Hebrew name] ben [father's Hebrew name]. Yismaḥ ha'av beyotzeh ḥalatzav vetagel imo bifri bitnah, kakatuv: "Yismaḥ avikha ve'imekha vetagel yoladtekha"; vene'emar: "vae'evor alayikh va'erekh mitboseset bedamayikh, va'omar lakh bedamayikh ḥayi, va'omar lakh bedamayikh ḥayi"; vene'emar: "zakhar le'olam berito davar tziva le'elef dor, asher karat et Avraham ushvuato leYishak vaya'amideha leYa'akov leḥok, leYisrael berit olam"; vene'emar: "Vayamol Avraham et Yitzḥak beno ben shemonat yamim ka'asher tziva oto Elohim." "Hodu ladonai ki tov, ki le'olam ḥasdo."

"Our God and God of our fathers, preserve this child for his father and mother, and his name shall be called in Israel [his Hebrew name], son of [father's Hebrew name]. May the father rejoice in his offspring, and his mother be glad with the fruit of her womb, as it is written: 'Your father and your mother will rejoice, and she who bore you will be happy' (Proverbs 23:25). And it is stated: 'I passed by you and I saw you wallowing in your blood, and I said to you: In your blood, you shall live; I said to you: In your blood, you shall live' (Ezekiel 16:6). And it is stated: 'He remembers His covenant forever, the word that He ordained for a thousand generations, which He made with Abraham; and His oath to Isaac. He set it for Jacob as a statute, for Israel as an everlasting covenant' (Psalms 105:8–10). And it is stated: 'Abraham circumcised his son Isaac when he was eight days old, as God had commanded him' (Genesis 21:4). 'Give thanks to the Lord, for He is good, for His kindness is forever'" (Psalms 118:1).

The congregation repeats:

הוֹדוּ לַאדֹנָי כִּי טוֹב, כִּי לְעוֹלָם חַסְדּוֹ.   *Hodu ladonai ki tov, ki le'olam ḥasdo.*

"Give thanks to the Lord, for He is good, for His kindness is forever."

The one reciting the blessing continues:

[שֵׁם הַתִּינוֹק] בֶּן [שֵׁם הָאָב] זֶה הַקָּטָן גָּדוֹל יִהְיֶה. כְּשֵׁם שֶׁנִּכְנַס לַבְּרִית, כֵּן יִכָּנֵס לַתּוֹרָה וּלְחֻפָּה וּלְמַעֲשִׂים טוֹבִים, אָמֵן.   [Baby's Hebrew name] *ben* [father's Hebrew name], *zeh hakaton gadol yiheye. Keshem shenikhnas la'berit, ken yikanes leTorah ulḥupa ulma'asim tovim.*

"May this small child [baby's name], son of [father's Hebrew name], grow and become great. Just as he has entered into the covenant, so may he enter into Torah knowledge, the marriage canopy, and good deeds."

The one reciting the blessing then drinks from the cup of wine in his hand. The *mohel* proceeds to recite a prayer for the health of the baby and the woman who gave birth. At the conclusion of the circumcision ceremony, many have the custom to recite the *Aleinu* prayer, which can be found in all prayer books at the conclusion of each of the three daily prayers.

After the circumcision, the *mohel* instructs the parents on the proper care for the baby. Many *mohalim* will return in person to examine the circumcision wound and remove the bandage.

Circumcising Two Babies

When two babies are circumcised in immediate succession, as with twin boys, the above blessings need not be recited more than once.

Many have the custom in such cases to perform two completely separate ceremonies. If so, there should be some sort of break between the two circumcisions; they should not be carried out one immediately after the other.

The Redemption of the Firstborn

After the plague of the firstborn on the eve of the Exodus, which afflicted the firstborn sons of Egypt but spared the firstborn of Israel, the Torah states: "Sanctify to Me every firstborn; the first issue of any womb among the children of Israel, from man and animal, is Mine" (Exodus 13:2). This means that a special sanctity applies to firstborn males, similar to the status of priests. They were designated to perform the divine service in the Temple in future generations.

Later, in the wake of the participation of the firstborns in the sin of the Golden Calf, the status of the priesthood was taken away from them and given instead to the descendants of Aaron, but their sanctity was to remain intact. In order to release a firstborn son from this status of holiness, he must be redeemed on the thirtieth day after his birth, as it is stated: "However, the firstborn of man you shall redeem…and its redeemed, from one month old shall you redeem them with a value of five shekels of silver" (Numbers 18:15–16). The redemption money (see below for the modern equivalent) is given to the priest as a gift for the fulfillment of the former role of the firstborn by himself and his fellow priests.

> 📖 **Further reading:** The source for the mitzva of the redemption of the firstborn can be read in *A Concise Guide to the Torah*, pp. 165, 385.

Who Is Redeemed?

The obligation of redeeming the eldest son depends upon a number of conditions:

He must be the firstborn of his mother. If he is the firstborn of his father alone, as for example, when the mother already has a child from a previous marriage, he is not subject to redemption. Consequently, it is possible for a father to need to redeem two or more of his sons, if they were born to different mothers and they were all the firstborn sons of their mothers.

In a case where the mother had experienced a miscarriage prior to the birth of her first child, a rabbi should be consulted, as the question of whether this negates the firstborn status of the later child depends on the stage of pregnancy in which the miscarriage occurred.

The firstborn must be born naturally, not by caesarian section. If the first son is born by caesarian, the son that is born after him is also not redeemed.

If the father is a priest or Levite, the child is not redeemed. Likewise, if the mother of the child is the daughter of a priest or Levite, the child is not redeemed.

The obligation of redemption applies to the oldest son of a woman convert, whether she converted before she became pregnant or during the pregnancy. If the woman had given birth already before converting, the first son born to her after she converts is not redeemed.

A baby born by vacuum extraction is redeemed. With regard to a child born with the aid of forceps, there are opinions that he is redeemed without the recitation of a blessing, but nowadays it is the custom to redeem such a child with a blessing.

The Time of the Redemption

The redemption is performed after the passage of thirty days since the son's birth. There are two disputing opinions about how to calculate this timeframe:

According to one opinion, the day of the baby's birth counts as the first day, regardless of when during the day the baby was born. Upon the completion of twenty-nine additional days, the thirty days have passed, and the redemption can take place even at night, which is the beginning of the thirty-first day.

According to the second opinion, the waiting period is twenty-nine days, twelve hours, and approximately forty-four minutes from the time of birth. This corresponds to the duration of an astronomical month, the time it takes the moon to complete a full circumnavigation of the earth. According to this opinion, apart from the twenty-nine intervening days, one must also wait a further twelve hours and forty-four minutes from the time of birth. Accordingly, if the baby is born in the afternoon, the redemption may not be carried out immediately upon nightfall after the thirtieth day, but only in the morning hours of the following day.

To ensure that the calculation is done properly, it is recommended to consult with a rabbi before setting the date of the redemption. This consultation will also help the parents determine the time of the ceremony, as some communities refrain from performing the redemption at night, while others actually prefer the nighttime.

To Bring Forward or to Postpone?

When the day of the redemption falls on a Shabbat or festival, the ceremony is postponed until the following day.

The ceremony involves drinking a cup of wine and holding a celebratory meal in honor of the performance of this mitzva. Thus, if the day of the redemption falls on a fast day (the Fast of Gedaliah, the Tenth of Tevet, the Fast of Esther, or the Seventeenth of Tamuz), instead of holding the ceremony during the day, when it is forbidden to eat, it is brought forward to the night before the fast, when eating is permitted. But if the day of redemption falls on *Tisha BeAv*, in which case eating is forbidden on the previous night as well, the ceremony is postponed until the conclusion of the fast. In such a case as well, it is recommended to consult a rabbi.

The Sum of the Redemption

The primary aspect of the redemption ceremony is the father's giving a sum of money to a priest. How much is this sum in modern terms?

It is stated in the Torah (Numbers 18:16) that the father must give the priest "five shekels of silver." The weight of five shekels is estimated at about 100 g of silver, which means that the sum to be paid is the value of 100 g of pure silver, according to the market value of silver on the day of the ceremony.

The simplest way to find the exact amount is to ascertain how much a gram of silver is worth on the day of the redemption. Silver is evaluated in terms of an ounce, which is 31 g. Hence, the value of an ounce of silver should be divided by 31 to get the value of a gram, which is then multiplied by a hundred. Some maintain that one must add to this amount the relevant taxes or other fees one might incur if one were to actually purchase 100 g of silver.

It is important to clarify that this sum should not be given to the priest in the form of banknotes or a check. The redemption fee must be given in pure silver coins or in the form of an object equal in value to 100 g of pure silver.

Experienced priests will often have in their possession five coins of pure silver, each weighing 20 g, which together amounts to 100 g. Before the ceremony, the father buys the coins from the priest according to the price of silver on that day, and during the ceremony he gives the coins back to him.

In principle, the priest is permitted to return the redemption fee to the father. Therefore, if the father of the boy has difficult financial circumstances and the priest is willing to perform the ceremony for free, he may return the money. However, the father must give the priest the money wholeheartedly and unconditionally.

In an even more extreme case, when the father wishes in advance to condition his giving of the money on the priest returning it to him, he may do so, but he must tell the priest that the money is being given to him as a "gift given on the condition that it be returned." It is necessary to adhere to this formula precisely, as only in this manner is such a transfer considered a full-fledged "gift"; otherwise the precondition would negate its legal status entirely and the baby would not be considered redeemed.

The Main Roles

The main participants in the redemption ceremony are the father, who redeems his son, and the priest, who receives the redemption fee. It is not necessary for the child himself to be present at the event, although if the ceremony is conducted in the absence of the son there are certain differences in its performance (see below).

The obligation of redeeming the son applies solely to his father, and therefore he alone can and must redeem his son. If the firstborn does not have a father, or if the father has neglected to perform the redemption, the obligation of redemption passes on to the son himself, and as soon as he becomes an adult, he will be obligated to redeem himself. In such a case, there is a dispute between halakhic authorities as to whether the redemption has to be done by the firstborn himself when he reaches adulthood or whether a religious court can also perform the redemption on his behalf as a child. In such a situation, a rabbi should be consulted.

One should choose a priest who has a definitive family lineage of priesthood.

The redemption of the son can be performed only by a Torah-observant priest who is also careful to observe the laws of the priesthood, such as not marrying a woman who is forbidden to a priest and avoiding becoming ritually defiled by contact with the dead. A priest who was born from a union prohibited by the Torah is classified as a *ḥalal*, an illegitimate priest, and cannot redeem firstborns.

The Ceremony according to the Ashkenazic Custom

The redemption ceremony is performed during a festive meal. The occasion is considered a great celebration, as it marks the performance of a mitzva that is not commonly performed due to the conditions stated above. In Ashkenazic communities it is customary to begin the event by starting the meal with the recitation of the *HaMotzi* blessing and eating some bread, and then to proceed with the redemption ceremony itself.

This is the procedure of the ceremony according to the Ashkenazic custom: The father presents the child to the priest. It is customary to place the child on a cushion and to decorate him with the jewelry of the women who are present.

The father says:

אִשְׁתִּי הַיִשְׂרְאֵלִית יָלְדָה לִי בֵּן זֶה הַבְּכוֹר. זֶה בְּנִי בְּכוֹרִי, וְהוּא פֶּטֶר רֶחֶם לְאִמּוֹ הַיִשְׂרְאֵלִית, וְהַקָּדוֹשׁ בָּרוּךְ הוּא צִוָּה לִפְדוֹתוֹ, שֶׁנֶּאֱמַר: וּפְדוּיָו מִבֶּן חֹדֶשׁ תִּפְדֶּה בְּעֶרְכְּךָ כֶּסֶף חֲמֵשֶׁת שְׁקָלִים בְּשֶׁקֶל הַקֹּדֶשׁ עֶשְׂרִים גֵּרָה הוּא (במדבר יח, טז). וְנֶאֱמַר: קַדֶּשׁ לִי כָל בְּכוֹר פֶּטֶר כָּל רֶחֶם בִּבְנֵי יִשְׂרָאֵל בָּאָדָם וּבַבְּהֵמָה לִי הוּא (שמות יג, ב).

Ishti haYisre'elit yalda li ben zeh habekhor. Zeh beni bekhori, vehu peter reḥem le'imo haYisre'elit. VeHakadosh Barukh Hu tziva lifdoto, shene'emar: "Ufduyav miben ḥodesh tifde be'erkekha kesef hameshet shekalim beshekel hakodesh, esrim gera hu"; vene'emar: "Kadesh li khol bekhor, peter kol reḥem bivnei Yisrael, ba'adam uvabehema, li hu."

"My Israelite wife has borne me this firstborn son. This is my firstborn son; he is the first issue of his Israelite mother, and the Holy One, blessed be He, commanded that he be redeemed, as it is stated: 'And its redeemed, from one month old shall you redeem them with a value of five shekels of silver in the sacred shekel; it is twenty gera' (Numbers 18:16) and it is stated: 'Sanctify to Me every firstborn; the first issue of any womb among the children of Israel, from man and animal, is Mine'" (Exodus 13:2).

The priest then asks:

אֵיזֶה תִּרְצֶה יוֹתֵר, בִּנְךָ בְּכוֹרְךָ זֶה אוֹ חֲמִשָּׁה סְלָעִים שֶׁנִּתְחַיַּבְתָּ בְּפִדְיוֹנוֹ?

Eizeh tirtze yoter: Binkha bekhorekha zeh, oh ḥamisha sela'im shenithayavta befidyono?

"Which do you want more, this firstborn son of yours or the five *sela* (another name for shekel) that you are obligated to give for his redemption?"

The father holds the five pure silver shekels (the five *sela*) or their equivalent and replies:

חָפֵץ אֲנִי לִפְדוֹת אֶת בְּנִי, וְהֵא לְךָ דְּמֵי פִּדְיוֹנוֹ שֶׁנִּתְחַיַּבְתִּי מִן הַתּוֹרָה.

Hafetz ani lifdot et beni, vehe lekha demei pidyono shenithayavti min haTorah.

"I want to redeem my son, and here you have the redemption money that I am required by the Torah to give."

The father, while still holding the money, recites the blessing:

בָּרוּךְ אַתָּה אֲדֹנָי, אֱלֹהֵינוּ מֶלֶךְ הָעוֹלָם,
אֲשֶׁר קִדְּשָׁנוּ בְּמִצְוֹתָיו וְצִוָּנוּ עַל פִּדְיוֹן הַבֵּן.

Barukh ata Adonai, Eloheinu, melekh ha'olam, asher kideshanu bemitzvotav, vetzivanu al pidyon haben.

"Blessed are You, Lord our God, King of the universe, who sanctified us with His commandments and commanded us concerning the redemption of the son."

The father recites another blessing:

בָּרוּךְ אַתָּה אֲדֹנָי, אֱלֹהֵינוּ מֶלֶךְ הָעוֹלָם,
שֶׁהֶחֱיָנוּ וְקִיְּמָנוּ וְהִגִּיעָנוּ לַזְּמַן הַזֶּה.

Barukh ata Adonai, Eloheinu, melekh ha'olam, sheheḥeyanu vekiyemanu vehigi'anu la'zeman hazeh.

"Blessed are You, Lord our God, King of the universe, who has given us life, sustained us, and brought us to this time."

At this point, the father gives the redemption fee to the priest. The priest holds the coins, circles them over the baby's head, and says:

זֶה תַּחַת זֶה, זֶה חִלּוּף זֶה, זֶה מָחוּל עַל
זֶה, וְיִכָּנֵס זֶה הַבֵּן לְחַיִּים לְתוֹרָה וּלְיִרְאַת
שָׁמַיִם. יְהִי רָצוֹן שֶׁכְּשֵׁם שֶׁנִּכְנַס לְפִדְיוֹן
כֵּן יִכָּנֵס לְתוֹרָה וּלְחֻפָּה וּלְמַעֲשִׂים טוֹבִים.

Zeh taḥat zeh, zeh ḥiluf zeh, zeh maḥul al zeh, veyikanes zeh haben leḥayim leTorah ulyirat shamayim. Yehi ratzon shekeshem shenikhnas lefidyon, ken yikanes leTorah ulḥupa ulma'asim tovim.

"This shall be instead of this; this shall be a substitute for this; this one shall be forgiven through this. May this boy enter into life, to Torah observance and to the fear of Heaven. May it be [God's] will that just as he has entered [the precept of] redemption, so may he enter into Torah observance, the wedding canopy, and good deeds."

After the redemption, the priest places both hands over the baby's head, and blesses him with the priestly blessing, adding several other scriptural blessings:

יְשִׂמְךָ אֱלֹהִים כְּאֶפְרַיִם וְכִמְנַשֶּׁה (בראשית
מח, כ). יְבָרֶכְךָ אֲדֹנָי וְיִשְׁמְרֶךָ, יָאֵר אֲדֹנָי
פָּנָיו אֵלֶיךָ וִיחֻנֶּךָּ, יִשָּׂא אֲדֹנָי פָּנָיו אֵלֶיךָ

Yesimkha Elohim ke'Efrayim ve-khiMenashe. Yevarekhekha Adonai veyishmerekha; ya'er Adonai panav

וְיָשֵׂם לְךָ שָׁלוֹם (במדבר ו, כד). אֲדֹנָי
שֹׁמְרֶךָ אֲדֹנָי צִלְּךָ עַל יַד יְמִינֶךָ (תהילים
קכא, ה), אֲדֹנָי יִשְׁמָרְךָ מִכָּל רָע יִשְׁמֹר אֶת
נַפְשֶׁךָ (תהילים קכא, ז), כִּי אֹרֶךְ יָמִים
וּשְׁנוֹת חַיִּים וְשָׁלוֹם יוֹסִיפוּ לָךְ (משלי ג, ב).

elekha vihuneka; yisa Adonai panav elekha veyasem lekha shalom. Adonai shomerekha, Adonai tzilekha al yad yeminekha. Adonai yishmorkha mikol ra, yishmor et nafshekha. Ki orekh yamim ushnot ḥayim veshalom yosifu lakh.

"May God make you like Ephraim and like Manasseh" (Genesis 48:20). "The Lord shall bless you, and keep you. The Lord shall shine His countenance to you, and be gracious to you. The Lord shall lift His countenance to you, and grant you peace" (Numbers 6:24). "The Lord is your guardian; the Lord is your shade by your right hand" (Psalms 121:5). "The Lord will guard you from all evil; He will guard your life" (Psalms 121:7). "For they will add length of days, years of life, and peace to you" (Proverbs 3:2).

📖 **Further reading:** For more on the verses of the priestly benediction, see *A Concise Guide to the Sages,* p. 178.

To conclude the ceremony, a cup of wine is poured for the priest, who recites the blessing:

בָּרוּךְ אַתָּה אֲדֹנָי, אֱלֹהֵינוּ מֶלֶךְ הָעוֹלָם,
בּוֹרֵא פְּרִי הַגָּפֶן.

Barukh ata Adonai, Eloheinu, melekh ha'olam, boreh peri hagafen.

"Blessed are You, Lord our God, King of the universe, who creates fruit of the vine."

After the priest has drunk from the cup, he passes it to the other congregants to partake of the wine.

At the end of the ceremony, the guests continue with the festive meal.

The Ceremony according to the Sephardic Custom

According to the Sephardic tradition it is customary to first hold the ceremony, and only afterward to sit down for the meal. The ceremony according to Sephardic custom proceeds as follows:

The priest asks:

בִּנְךָ זֶה בְּכוֹר הוּא? *Binkha zeh bekhor hu?*

"Is this son of yours a firstborn?"

The father answers, "yes" (*ken*)

The priest asks:

אֵיזֶה תִּרְצֶה יוֹתֵר, בִּנְךָ בְּכוֹרְךָ זֶה אוֹ חֲמִשָּׁה סְלָעִים שֶׁנִּתְחַיַּבְתָּ בְּפִדְיוֹנוֹ?

Eizeh tirtze yoter: Binkha bekhorekha zeh, oh ḥamisha sela'im shenithayavta befidyono?

"Which do you want more, this firstborn son of yours or the five sela [another name for shekel] that you are obligated to give for his redemption?"

The father replies:

בִּבְנִי בְּכוֹרִי.

Bivni bekhori.

"My firstborn son."

Now the priest turns to the mother of the baby and asks:

בְּנֵךְ זֶה בְּכוֹר. שֶׁמָּא יָלַדְתְּ בֵּן אַחֵר לְפָנָיו אוֹ שֶׁמָּא הִפַּלְתְּ?

Benekh zeh bekhor. Shema yaladet ben aḥer lefanav oh shema hipalt?

"Is this son of yours a firstborn? Did you perhaps give birth to another child before him, or did you perhaps have a miscarriage [before he was born]?"

The mother answers the priest's questions:

זֶה בְּנִי בְּכוֹרִי. לֹא יָלַדְתִּי וְלֹא הִפַּלְתִּי לְפָנָיו.

Zeh beni bekhori. Lo yaladti velo hipalti lefanav.

"This is my firstborn son; I did not give birth nor have a miscarriage before [giving birth to] him."

The priest recites a formula which includes the Torah verses that pertain to the redemption of the son:

זֶה הַבֵּן בְּכוֹר הוּא, וְהַקָּדוֹשׁ בָּרוּךְ הוּא צִוָּה לִפְדוֹתוֹ, שֶׁנֶּאֱמַר: וּפְדוּיָו מִבֶּן חֹדֶשׁ תִּפְדֶּה בְּעֶרְכְּךָ כֶּסֶף חֲמֵשֶׁת שְׁקָלִים בְּשֶׁקֶל הַקֹּדֶשׁ עֶשְׂרִים גֵּרָה הוּא (במדבר יח, טז). כְּשֶׁהָיִיתָ בִּמְעֵי אִמְּךָ הָיִיתָ בִּרְשׁוּת אָבִיךָ שֶׁבַּשָּׁמַיִם וּבִרְשׁוּת אָבִיךָ וְאִמֶּךָ, עַכְשָׁו אַתָּה בִּרְשׁוּתִי שֶׁאֲנִי כֹּהֵן, וְאָבִיךָ וְאִמְּךָ

Zeh haben bekhor hu, veHakadosh Barukh Hu tziva lifdoto, shene'emar: "Ufduyav miben ḥodesh tifde be'erkekha kesef ḥameshet shekalim beshekel hakodesh, esrim gera hu." Keshehayita bimei imekha hayita birshut avikha shebashamayim uvirshut

מְבַקְשִׁים לִפְדּוֹתְךָ שֶׁאַתָּה בְּכוֹר מְקֻדָּשׁ,
שֶׁכֵּן כָּתוּב: וַיְדַבֵּר אֲדֹנָי אֶל מֹשֶׁה לֵּאמֹר:
קַדֶּשׁ לִי כָל בְּכוֹר, פֶּטֶר כָּל רֶחֶם בִּבְנֵי
יִשְׂרָאֵל בָּאָדָם וּבַבְּהֵמָה – לִי הוּא.

avikha ve'imekha. Akhshav ata birshu-ti, she'ani kohen, ve'avikha ve'imekha mevakshim lifdotekha, she'ata bekhor mekudash, sheken katuv: "Vaydaber Adonai el Moshe lemor: Kadesh li khol bekhor, peter kol reḥem bivnei Yisrael, ba'adam uvabehema, li hu."

"This son is a firstborn, and the Holy One, blessed be He, commanded that he be redeemed, as it is stated: 'Its redeemed, from one month old shall you redeem them with a value of five shekels of silver in the sacred shekel; it is twenty gera' (Numbers 18:16). When you were in your mother's womb you were in the possession of your Father in heaven and in the possession of your father and your mother; but now you are in my possession as I am a priest, and your father and mother wish to redeem you, for you are a sancti-fied firstborn, as it is written: 'And the Lord spoke to Moses, saying: Sanctify to Me every firstborn; first issue of any womb among the children of Israel, from man and animal, is Mine'" (Exodus 13:1–2).

The father holds the redemption money, the five pure silver shekels or their equivalent, and declares:

אֲנִי רוֹצֶה לִפְדּוֹתוֹ, שֶׁכָּךְ כָּתוּב בַּתּוֹרָה: אַךְ
פָּדֹה תִפְדֶּה אֵת בְּכוֹר הָאָדָם, וּפְדוּיָו מִבֶּן
חֹדֶשׁ תִּפְדֶּה בְּעֶרְכְּךָ כֶּסֶף חֲמֵשֶׁת שְׁקָלִים
בְּשֶׁקֶל הַקֹּדֶשׁ, עֶשְׂרִים גֵּרָה הוּא.

Ani rotze lifdoto, shekakh katuv ba-Torah: "Akh pado tifde et bekhor ha'adam, ufduyav miben ḥodesh tifde, be'erkhekha, kesef ḥameshet shekalim beshekel hakodesh, esrim gera hu."

"I want to redeem him, as it is written in the Torah: 'However, the firstborn of man you shall redeem, and the firstborn of the impure animal you shall redeem. Its redeemed, from one month old shall you redeem them with a value of five shekels of silver in the sacred shekel; it is twenty gera'" (Num-bers 18:15–16).

The father then recites the blessing:

בָּרוּךְ אַתָּה אֲדֹנָי, אֱלֹהֵינוּ מֶלֶךְ הָעוֹלָם,
אֲשֶׁר קִדְּשָׁנוּ בְּמִצְוֹתָיו וְצִוָּנוּ עַל פִּדְיוֹן הַבֵּן.

Barukh ata Adonai, Eloheinu, melekh ha'olam, asher kideshanu bemitzvotav, vetzivanu al pidyon haben.

"Blessed are You, Lord our God, King of the universe, who sanctified us with His commandments and commanded us concerning the redemption of the son."

The father further recites:

בָּרוּךְ אַתָּה אֲדֹנָי, אֱלֹהֵינוּ מֶלֶךְ הָעוֹלָם, שֶׁהֶחֱיָנוּ וְקִיְּמָנוּ וְהִגִּיעָנוּ לַזְּמַן הַזֶּה.

Barukh ata Adonai, Eloheinu, melekh ha'olam, sheheheyanu vekiyemanu vehigi'anu la'zeman hazeh.

"Blessed are You, Lord our God, King of the universe, who has given us life, sustained us, and brought us to this time."

At this stage the father gives the redemption fee to the priest, and says:

זֶה פִּדְיוֹן בְּנִי בְּכוֹרִי.   *Zeh pidyon beni bekhori.*

"This is the redemption of my firstborn son."

📖 **Further reading:** For more on the partnership between the parents and God, see *A Concise Guide to the Sages*, p. 407.

The priest holds the coins and says:

קִבַּלְתִּי מִמְּךָ חֲמִשָּׁה סְלָעִים אֵלּוּ בְּפִדְיוֹן בִּנְךָ זֶה, וַהֲרֵי הוּא פָּדוּי בָּהֶן כְּדַת מֹשֶׁה וְיִשְׂרָאֵל.

Kibalti mi'mekha hamisha sela'im elu befidyon binkha zeh, veharei hu padui bahen kedat Moshe veYisrael.

יְהִי רָצוֹן מִלְּפָנֶיךָ, אֲדֹנָי אֱלֹהֵינוּ וֵאלֹהֵי אֲבוֹתֵינוּ, כְּשֵׁם שֶׁזָּכָה הַבֵּן הַזֶּה לַפִּדְיוֹן, כָּךְ יִזְכֶּה לַתּוֹרָה וְלַמִּצְוֹת וְלַחֻפָּה בְּחַיֵּי אָבִיו וּבְחַיֵּי אִמּוֹ, אָמֵן כֵּן יְהִי רָצוֹן.

Yehi ratzon milefanekha, Adonai Eloheinu velohei avoteinu, keshem she-zakha haben hazeh lapidyon, kakh yizke laTorah velamitzvot velahupa behayey aviv uvhayey imo, amen ken yehi ratzon.

"I have received from you these five *sela* for the redemption of this son of yours, and he is hereby redeemed through them in accordance with the law of Moses and Israel.

"May it be Your will, Lord our God, and the God of our fathers, that just as [this boy] entered [the precept of] redemption, so may he enter into Torah observance, the wedding canopy, and good deeds in his father's lifetime and in his mother's lifetime. Amen, so may it be [God's] will."

After the redemption procedure, the priest places both hands over the baby's head, and blesses him with the priestly blessing, adding some other scriptural blessings:

יְשִׂמְךָ אֱלֹהִים כְּאֶפְרַיִם וְכִמְנַשֶּׁה (בראשית מח, כ). יְבָרֶכְךָ אֲדֹנָי וְיִשְׁמְרֶךָ, יָאֵר אֲדֹנָי פָּנָיו אֵלֶיךָ וִיחֻנֶּךָּ, יִשָּׂא אֲדֹנָי פָּנָיו אֵלֶיךָ וְיָשֵׂם לְךָ שָׁלוֹם (במדבר ו, כד). אֲדֹנָי שֹׁמְרֶךָ אֲדֹנָי צִלְּךָ עַל יַד יְמִינֶךָ (תהילים קכא, ה), אֲדֹנָי יִשְׁמָרְךָ מִכָּל רָע יִשְׁמֹר אֶת נַפְשֶׁךָ (שם, ז), כִּי אֹרֶךְ יָמִים וּשְׁנוֹת חַיִּים וְשָׁלוֹם יוֹסִיפוּ לָךְ (משלי ג, ב).

Yesimkha Elohim ke'Efrayim ve-khiMenashe. Yevarekhekha Adonai veyishmerekha; ya'er Adonai panav elekha vihuneka; yisa Adonai panav elekha veyasem lekha shalom. Adonai shomerekha, Adonai tzilekha al yad yeminekha. Adonai yishmorkha mikol ra, yishmor et nafshekha. Ki orekh ya-mim ushnot ḥayim veshalom yosifu lakh.

"May God make you like Ephraim and like Manasseh" (Genesis 48:20). "The Lord shall bless you, and keep you. The Lord shall shine His counte-nance to you, and be gracious to you. The Lord shall lift His countenance to you, and grant you peace" (Numbers 6:24). "The Lord is your guardian; the Lord is your shade by your right hand" (Psalms 121:5). "The Lord will guard you from all evil; He will guard your life" (Psalms 121:7). "For they will add length of days, years of life, and peace to you" (Proverbs 3:2).

At the end of the ceremony, the festive meal is held.

Various *Halakhot*

The following are various laws related to the observance of the mitzva of redeeming one's son:

In any case of uncertainty with regard to the obligation to redeem the baby (for instance: there was a prior miscarriage; there is doubt as to wheth-er the father or mother is of priestly or Levite lineage; the calculation of the proper date for redemption is uncertain), a rabbi should be consulted.

If the parents do not personally know a suitable priest, they can ask a rabbi to help them find one to perform the redemption ceremony.

When it is not possible to bring the baby to the redemption ceremony, it may be performed without his being present. In such a situation, the word-ing of what the father says to the priest at the beginning of the ceremony is adjusted from: "My Israelite wife has borne me this firstborn son. This is my firstborn son...." to: "My Israelite wife has borne me a firstborn son. I have a firstborn son...."

According to Sephardic halakhic authorities, the redemption of the son may also be performed by means of an agent appointed by the father to act in his stead. This can be useful in a situation where the father is abroad or otherwise unavailable on the date of the redemption. In such a case, a rabbi should be consulted.

The redemption may be held on the intermediate days [*Hol HaMoed*] of *Sukkot* and Passover, but not on Shabbat or festivals.

If a woman gives birth to twin boys, who are her first children, the first-born twin is redeemed. If the twins are a boy and girl, and the girl was the first to emerge, her twin brother is not redeemed. When there is uncertainty as to which baby was born first, a rabbi should be consulted.

Redemption of an Adult

An adult who is a firstborn, but whose father did not redeem him as a child, must redeem himself from a priest. He may do so at any age. In such a case the wording of the redemption varies accordingly. The rest of the details are similar to the redemption of a thirty-day-old baby.

Birth of a Daughter
The first stage

There are quite a few laws and customs that apply during birth and to the period of time immediately following the birth of a girl. This chapter will review the rituals, prayers, and blessings associated with childbirth and the giving of a name.

Birth

Birth is an incredible event, like a miracle unfolding before our very eyes. When all goes well, the parents are often filled with a fervent desire to thank God for the gift of life and parenthood which He has bestowed upon them.

Prayers and Blessings

During childbirth, it is considered commendable when possible to read from the book of Psalms, praying for the welfare of the mother and the baby. There are several psalms from which to choose that are especially appropriate for childbirth: 1, 2, 3, 4, 20, 21, 22, 23, 24, 33, 47, 72, 86, 90, 91, 92, 93, 104, and from 112 until the end of Psalms.

Upon seeing their daughter, as soon as it is possible for them to do so, the parents should express their joy and thanks to God by means of the blessing:

בָּרוּךְ אַתָּה אֲדֹנָי, אֱלֹהֵינוּ מֶלֶךְ הָעוֹלָם, שֶׁהֶחֱיָנוּ וְקִיְּמָנוּ וְהִגִּיעָנוּ לַזְּמַן הַזֶּה.

Barukh ata Adonai, Eloheinu, melekh ha'olam, sheheheyanu vekiyemanu vehigi'anu la'zeman hazeh.

"Blessed are You, Lord our God, King of the universe, who has given us life, sustained us, and brought us to this time."

After the mother has recovered from the birth, it is customary for her to recite the blessing of *HaGomel* ("who bestows good"), like any other individual who has safely emerged from a position of danger. The *HaGomel* blessing must be recited in the presence of a quorum of ten men [*minyan*].

The formula of the blessing is as follows:

בָּרוּךְ אַתָּה אֲדֹנָי, אֱלֹהֵינוּ מֶלֶךְ הָעוֹלָם, הַגּוֹמֵל לְחַיָּבִים טוֹבוֹת, שֶׁגְּמָלַנִי כָּל טוֹב.

Barukh ata Adonai, Eloheinu, melekh ha'olam, hagomel laḥayavim tovot, she-gemalani kol tov.

"Blessed are You, Lord our God, King of the universe, who bestows good upon the culpable, who has bestowed all goodness upon me."

Ashkenazim respond:

אָמֵן, מִי שֶׁגְּמָלְךָ כָּל טוֹב, הוּא יִגְמָלְךָ כָּל טוֹב סֶלָה.

Amen. Mi shegemalakh kol tov, Hu yig-malekh kol tov, sela.

"Amen. May He who bestowed all goodness upon you always bestow all goodness upon you, Selah."

Sephardim respond:

אָמֵן, הָאֵל שֶׁגְּמָלְךָ כָּל טוֹב, הוּא יִגְמָלְךָ כָּל טוֹב סֶלָה.

Amen. Ha'El shegemalakh kol tov, Hu yigmalekh kol tov, sela.

"Amen. May the God who bestowed all goodness upon you always bestow all goodness upon you, Selah."

The husband may recite the blessing on behalf of his wife. In such a case, he should do so in his wife's presence, and the blessing is recited in the second person: "Blessed are you, Lord … who bestowed all goodness upon you," and his wife responds: "Amen."

📖 Further reading: For the *halakhot* of birth on Shabbat, see p. 439.

The Giving of a Name

As stated above, after the birth of a boy the naming is delayed until the circumcision. By contrast, in the case of a girl, the birth itself is considered like her "circumcision," and accordingly she is named without delay, commonly during the Torah reading at a service following the birth. In this sense a girl has an advantage over a boy, as she receives at birth the level of soul that a boy receives on the eighth day.

📖 **Further reading:** For more on the calling of a name and its meaning, see *A Concise Guide to Mahshava*, p. 7.

Reading the Torah in the Synagogue

The Torah is read on Shabbat morning, during the afternoon prayer of Shabbat, and in the morning service on Mondays and Thursdays, *Rosh Hodesh*, major and minor festivals, and on fast days. The new father may use any of these opportunities to be called up to the Torah. At the end of the reading of the father's portion, the synagogue sexton [*gabbai*], who oversees the service, recites a blessing for the mother and child, and announces the name of the baby girl. This should be arranged in advance with the *gabbai*.

It is recommended to name the child on the first opportunity the father has to be called to the reading of the Torah, but some name the daughter on the Shabbat after the birth, or shortly thereafter.

Kiddush and *Zeved HaBat*

Since the birth of a daughter does not involve the fulfillment of a specific mitzva, as is the case with circumcision of a boy, various customs have evolved over the years to mark the event in a celebratory manner that expresses one's thanks to God. One possibility is to hold a *kiddush* in the synagogue. This is a light meal that takes place in the synagogue on Shabbat morning after the completion of the morning prayer. It starts with the recitation of *Kiddush* over wine, for which it is named.

During the *kiddush*, it is customary for the guests to express their best wishes and congratulations to the parents, and to wish the baby well. People will also typically deliver words of Torah at the *kiddush*.

This event should of course be arranged in advance with the relevant synagogue officials.

Another possibility is to hold a *Zeved HaBat* party, a celebratory event for the birth of a daughter [*bat*]. The word *zeved* means a gift, expressing the idea that the daughter is a precious gift. The expression comes from the statement of our matriarch Leah after the birth of one of her sons, Zebulun: "God has granted me a fine gift [*zeved*]" (Genesis 30:20).

Some have the practice of giving the girl her name at the *kiddush* or the *Zeved HaBat* party.

Life Cycle

The Recitation of Verses

There are different versions of prayers and verses that can be recited at a *Zeved HaBat*. The following is one of the most common versions:

יוֹנָתִי בְּחַגְוֵי הַסֶּלַע בְּסֵתֶר הַמַּדְרֵגָה הַרְאִינִי
אֶת מַרְאַיִךְ הַשְׁמִיעִנִי אֶת קוֹלֵךְ כִּי קוֹלֵךְ
עָרֵב וּמַרְאֵיךְ נָאוֶה (שיר השירים ב, יד).

Yonati behagvei hasela beseter hamadrega, harini et marayikh, hashmi'ini et kolekh, ki kolekh arev umarekh naveh.

"My dove, in the clefts of the rock, in the covert of the terrace: Show me your appearance, let me hear your voice, for your voice is pleasant, and your appearance is lovely" (Song of Songs 2:14).

In the case of a firstborn daughter, one adds:

אַחַת הִיא יוֹנָתִי תַמָּתִי אַחַת הִיא לְאִמָּהּ
בָּרָה הִיא לְיוֹלַדְתָּהּ רָאוּהָ בָנוֹת וַיְאַשְּׁרוּהָ
מְלָכוֹת וּפִילַגְשִׁים וַיְהַלְלוּהָ (שיר השירים
ו, ט).

Ahat hi yonati tamati, ahat hi le'imah, bara hi leyoladtah, ra'uha banot vayashruha, melakhot ufilagshim vayhaleluha.

"Unique is my faultless dove, unique to her mother, pure to the one who bore her. Girls see her and laud her, queens and concubines, and praise her" (Song of Songs 6:9).

The individual assigned to announce the girl's name at the ceremony says:

מִי שֶׁבֵּרַךְ אִמוֹתֵינוּ שָׂרָה וְרִבְקָה, רָחֵל וְלֵאָה
וּמִרְיָם הַנְּבִיאָה וַאֲבִיגַיִל וְאֶסְתֵּר הַמַּלְכָּה
בַּת אֲבִיחַיִל, הוּא יְבָרֵךְ אֶת הַיַּלְדָּה
הַנְּעִימָה הַזֹּאת וְיִקָּרֵא שְׁמָהּ [השם שנבחר]
בַּת [שם האב]. בְּמַזָּל טוֹב וּבִשְׁעַת בְּרָכָה,
וִיגַדְּלוּהָ בִּבְרִיאוּת, שָׁלוֹם וּמְנוּחָה, וִיזַכֶּה
אֶת אָבִיהָ וְאֶת אִמָּהּ לִרְאוֹת בְּשִׂמְחָתָהּ
וּבְחֻפָּתָהּ, בְּבָנִים וּבְבָנוֹת, עֹשֶׁר וְכָבוֹד.
עוֹד יְנוּבוּן בְּשֵׂיבָה, דְּשֵׁנִים וְרַעֲנַנִים יִהְיוּ,
וְכֵן יְהִי רָצוֹן וְנֹאמַר אָמֵן.

Mi sheberakh imoteinu Sara veRivka, Rahel veLeah, uMiryam hanevia, vaAvigayil, ve'Ester hamalka bat Avihayil, hu yevarekh et hayalda hane'ima hazot veyikareh shemah [girl's Hebrew name] bat [father's Hebrew name], bemazal tov uvishat berakha. Vigadluha bivriut, shalom, umnuha, vizakeh et aviha ve'et imah lirot besimhatah uvhupatah, bevanim uvevanot, osher vekhavod. Od yenuvun beseiva, deshenim vera'ananim yiheyu, vekhen yehi ratzon venomar amen.

"He who blessed our forebears Sarah, Rebecca, Rachel, and Leah, and Miriam the prophetess, and Avigayil, and Queen Esther the daughter of Avihayil, may He bless this lovely child. And let her name be called [chosen name], daughter of [father's name], for good fortune and at a time of blessing. May her parents raise her in health, peace, and tranquility, and may her father and mother merit to see her joy and her wedding canopy, and to see her with sons and daughters, wealth and honor. 'They will continue to yield fruit even in old age; they will remain full and fresh' (Psalms 92:15). So may it be [God's] will, and let us say: 'Amen.'"

Some add the verse:

וַיְבָרְכוּ אֶת רִבְקָה וַיֹּאמְרוּ לָהּ אֲחֹתֵנוּ אַתְּ
הֲיִי לְאַלְפֵי רְבָבָה (בראשית כד, ס).

Vayvarekhu et Rivka vayomeru lah: Aḥoteinu, at hayi le'alfei revava.

"They blessed Rebecca, and said to her: Our sister, may you become thousands and ten thousands" (Genesis 24:60).

Those present proceed with verses of thanksgiving and congratulations:

שִׁיר הַמַּעֲלוֹת אַשְׁרֵי כָּל יְרֵא אֲדֹנָי הַהֹלֵךְ
בִּדְרָכָיו. יְגִיעַ כַּפֶּיךָ כִּי תֹאכֵל אַשְׁרֶיךָ וְטוֹב
לָךְ. אֶשְׁתְּךָ כְּגֶפֶן פֹּרִיָּה בְּיַרְכְּתֵי בֵיתֶךָ, בָּנֶיךָ
כִּשְׁתִלֵי זֵיתִים סָבִיב לְשֻׁלְחָנֶךָ. הִנֵּה כִי כֵן
יְבֹרַךְ גָּבֶר יְרֵא אֲדֹנָי. יְבָרֶכְךָ אֲדֹנָי מִצִּיּוֹן
וּרְאֵה בְּטוּב יְרוּשָׁלָיִם כֹּל יְמֵי חַיֶּיךָ. וּרְאֵה
בָנִים לְבָנֶיךָ, שָׁלוֹם עַל יִשְׂרָאֵל (תהלים
קכח).

Shir hama'alot: Ashrei kol yerei Adonai, haholekh bidrakhav. Yegia kapekha ki tokhel, ashrekha vetov lakh. Eshtekha kegefen poriya beyarketei beitekha, banekha kishtilei zeitim saviv leshulḥanekha. Hinei khi khen yevorakh gaver yerei Adonai. Yevarekhekha Adonai miTziyon, ureh betuv Yerushalayim, kol yemei ḥayekha. Ureh vanim levanekha, shalom al Yisrael.

"A song of ascents. Blessed are all who fear the Lord, who walk in His ways. When you eat of the labor of your hands, you are happy, and it is good for you. Your wife is like a fruitful vine by the side of your house; your children, like young olive trees surrounding your table. Indeed, so shall a man who fears the Lord be blessed. May the Lord bless you from Zion; may you see the prosperity of Jerusalem all the days of your life. And may you see the children of your children. Peace to Israel" (Psalms 128).

It should be noted that the two aforementioned ceremonies, the *kiddush* and the *Zeved HaBat*, are not considered a mitzva or a halakhic obligation. Likewise, they do not have to be performed on a specific date, and therefore one may hold them at any time.

First Haircut
[Halaka]

In many communities it is customary not to cut a boy's hair before the age of three, at which point a ceremonial haircut is held, called a ḥalaka (which means haircut in Arabic) or upsherin (lit., 'shear off' in Yiddish). The reason for the celebration is based on the commandment of the Torah: "You shall not round the edge of your head" (Leviticus 19:27), meaning that a man may not cut the hairs of the head in a full circle, by removing the pe'ot (the hairs that grow alongside and slightly above the ears). Accordingly, it is a mitzva when cutting the hair to leave pe'ot on the two sides of the head, and when this mitzva is fulfilled with a boy for the first time, this is cause for rejoicing and celebration. This chapter presents the customs associated with the first haircut.

A Milestone

The age of three is the official age at which parents must begin to accustom their son to the fulfillment of mitzvot. This is, of course, a very slow and gradual process, which starts with actions that are easy for the child to implement. The first haircut is therefore an important milestone in the education of a son in the Jewish way of life.

The first haircut is performed at the age of three, in accordance with the allegorical comparison of the Sages between a man and a tree (Midrash Tanḥuma, Parashat Kedoshim, ch. 14): Just as the halakha of orla (the prohibition against deriving benefit from the fruit of a tree in its first three years) applies to a tree, we likewise refrain from cutting the child's hair in his first three years.

When?

The haircut is performed on the third birthday. If this date falls on a Shabbat or a festival, the ceremony is conducted after the Shabbat or festival, but it is not moved ahead to a date before the child is three years old.

If his birthday falls between Passover and Lag BaOmer, a period during which haircuts are not taken, in commemoration of twenty-four thousand students of Rabbi Akiva who died during this period, the haircutting ceremony should be held on Lag BaOmer itself. In some communities, it is the custom not to have haircuts between Lag BaOmer and Shavuot either. Accordingly, if the birthday falls during this period, the haircut is postponed until after *Shavuot*. Each person should follow the custom of his community and the instruction of his rabbi in this regard.

Likewise, Ashkenazim do not have a haircut during the three weeks between the fast of the Seventeenth of Tamuz and the fast of the Ninth of Av, *Tisha BeAv*. On these days, called the period "between the straits," we mourn the destruction of the Temple. When the birthday falls during this time, the haircut is postponed until after *Tisha BeAv*.

Where?

The first haircut can be performed anywhere: at home, in a courtyard, a synagogue, or in a hall, but over the generations it has become the practice to hold it in a holy place. In Jerusalem many have the custom of giving their three-year-old son his first haircut near the tomb of Simon the Righteous, located in a cave north of the Old City.

The most common place to hold the ceremony in Israel is by the grave of the *tanna* Rabbi Shimon bar Yohai in Meron. The first individual to follow this practice was the renowned kabbalist Rabbi Yitzhak Luria (the Ari), who lived and flourished in nearby Safed in the sixteenth century. His most prominent disciple, Rabbi Hayim Vital, related that when the Ari's son reached the age of three, "our master led his little son there [to Meron] with all the members of his household, where they shaved his head in accordance with the known custom, and they held there a day of celebration and joy." This tradition persists to this day.

The Ceremony

Family and friends gather together to celebrate the festive event. As part of the ceremony, each person is invited to cut off a few hairs from the boy's head, while of course taking care not to remove the two *pe'ot* themselves. If a rabbi or priest is present, it is customary to honor them first with the hair cutting. Some bring their son to righteous individuals and great Torah scholars, so that they can participate in this facet of the youngster's mitzva education.

Usually the haircut is performed at a festive meal, at which words of Torah are delivered and the attendees bless the child and his parents.

It should be noted that it is not mandatory for the first haircut to be performed at the age of three; it is merely a custom. Some do not do so, but rather cut the child's hair, leaving him with two *pe'ot*, at a time suitable for them.

Bar and Bat Mitzva

When a boy reaches the age of thirteen or a girl reaches the age of twelve, they become formally obligated in mitzvot. Prior to that time, parents train their children to fulfill mitzvot and educate them to live in accordance with Jewish law and values. However, it is only once the child comes of age that he or she bears personal responsibility for his or her actions and becomes legally obligated in all of the Torah's commands. Consequently, reaching the age of bar or bat mitzva is a significant milestone. One should prepare for this transition, and it should be celebrated as a joyous occasion.

Bar Mitzva

On the day he turns thirteen, a boy becomes a bar mitzva. *Bar* is the Aramaic equivalent of the Hebrew word *ben*, which literally means "son," but is also used to indicate the ability to do something, or even more broadly as a general manner of defining a status. Thus, bar mitzva means that the individual is now defined as someone who is subject to mitzvot. This expression reflects the profound connection that is formed between the maturing adolescent and the mitzvot that he will begin to observe.

Obligations and Privileges

As soon as a boy reaches the age of thirteen, he is obligated to fulfill all of the Torah's commandments that apply to him, just like a full-fledged adult. For example, he must fast on public fast days, such as Yom Kippur and *Tisha BeAv*. He is similarly required to dwell in a *sukka* on *Sukkot*, eat matza on Passover, wear ritual fringes [*tzitzit*], and observe Shabbat.

Along with these obligations, the new bar mitzva also acquires the halakhic privileges of adulthood. He may now be counted for a *minyan*, the quorum of ten men required for public prayer and some other ritual matters. He may even serve as the prayer leader [*hazan*] in the synagogue. He may recite *Kiddush* on Shabbat and festivals and thereby facilitate the fulfillment of the mitzva for those who hear him. And of course, he is entitled to be called up to the Torah reading.

The Date

It is important to note that one becomes bar mitzva on his date of birth in the Jewish calendar, not on his birthday according to the Gregorian calendar. These two dates will not coincide, and there is often a gap of days or even weeks between them. One must therefore consider his son's Hebrew birthday when determining the date of the bar mitzva.

In this context, it is important to note that while a new day in the Gregorian calendar begins at midnight, the date in the Jewish calendar begins at nightfall. Consequently, if one is determining the Hebrew birthday by looking it up in a calendar based on the Gregorian date, one must also know the time of day when the child was born. For example, if he was born at night, the Hebrew date that appears on the calendar for that Gregorian date would actually be the day before his birthday, as the date had already changed in the Jewish calendar by the time he was born.

Therefore, one who was born between sunset and midnight must move his birthday one day later, after converting the Gregorian date to the Hebrew date. For example, if he was born on March 23, 2004, a conversion table will give the date of the first of Nisan 5764. Nevertheless, as he was born after nightfall, his birthday is actually the second of Nisan, and he becomes bar mitzva on that date.

There are several websites that help one convert the Gregorian date to the Hebrew one, and they include the option of specifying the time of birth, which helps one find the correct date without difficulty.

Special Circumstances

There are some instances that require special attention when determining the date of a bar mitzva:

In the Jewish calendar, seven of every nineteen years are leap years, in which an additional month is added. In leap years there are two months called Adar. If a child was born in the month of Adar in a regular year and his bar mitzva is in a leap year, he becomes bar mitzva in the second Adar rather than the first. With regard to birthdays, the second Adar is considered the primary month of Adar.

However, if one was born in the first Adar in a leap year and the year of his bar mitzva is also a leap year, he becomes bar mitzva in the first Adar. Similarly, if he was born in the second Adar in a leap year, and he becomes bar mitzva during a leap year, he will be considered a bar mitzva in the second Adar.

If a child was born during either of the two months of Adar in a leap year and the year of his bar mitzva is a regular year with only one Adar, he will become bar mitzva during the month of Adar.

There are two other dates that exist in only some years: the thirtieth of Marheshvan (the first day of *Rosh Hodesh* Kislev) and the thirtieth of Kislev (the first day of *Rosh Hodesh* Tevet). The months of Marheshvan and Kislev can contain twenty-nine or thirty days, depending on the year. If one was born on either of these two dates and it does not exist in the year that he becomes bar mitzva, he is considered a bar mitzva on the following date. Consequently, if he was born on the thirtieth of Marheshvan he will become bar mitzva on the first of Kislev, and if he was born on the thirtieth of Kislev he will become bar mitzva on the first of Tevet.

Bar Mitzva Preparations

Preparations for the bar mitzva should focus on the main significance of the event. People sometimes tend to focus on what is really marginal while ignoring what ought to be primary. In the leadup to a bar mitzva, people may focus on the celebration itself while forgetting the real purpose of the celebration. The preparations for the bar mitzva and the celebration itself should be calibrated according to the true significance of the occasion: A Jewish boy's becoming obligated in mitzvot.

Study

The most important things a boy should study for his bar mitzva are those that will help him fulfill his duties as an adult Jew. As part of his preparations for his bar mitzva, a boy should study the foundations of Judaism and what it means to be Jewish. He must learn the *halakhot* of the mitzvot that he is required to observe. If his school curriculum is insufficient in these areas, his parents should find a way to supplement his education by hiring a private tutor. He must learn how to don phylacteries [*tefillin*]. It is important for him to learn about the sanctity and significance of *tefillin* as well as all the laws that pertain to their use.

The boy should also learn the blessings to recite when one is called up to the Torah reading. It should be noted that there is no obligation for the bar mitzva boy to read the portion of the Prophets read on Shabbat after the Torah reading, the *haftara*. Sometimes too much energy is invested in memorizing the *haftara*, at the expense of far more vital matters. In addition, there is certainly no need for the boy to read the entire Torah reading himself. If he can manage to master the reading without neglecting the other important and necessary preparations, that is a nice initiative, but it is certainly not essential.

The bar mitzva celebration itself should also be focused on the primary significance of the occasion, namely the fact that the boy is now obligated in mitzvot. This should be the dominant theme of the affair and the preparations leading up to it. In this way the boy will internalize the importance of mitzva observance. Conversely, if he sees that the primary focus of the celebration is impressing the guests or other superficial matters, he may well internalize that those are important values.

The Mitzva of *Tefillin*

Upon reaching his thirteenth birthday, the first biblical commandment that every bar mitzva boy is obligated to fulfill is the recitation of *Shema* in the evening prayer service. The next commandment, which is a particularly important and meaningful mitzva, is the mitzva to don *tefillin*, which is fulfilled in the morning.

Although a boy becomes obligated to wear *tefillin* only on the morning of his bar mitzva day, it has become customary in many Jewish communities for him to begin practicing donning *tefillin* a month or two beforehand. According to the custom of some communities, the boy does so at first without reciting the blessings, but as the time of the bar mitzva approaches, he begins to recite the appropriate blessings as he dons the *tefillin*.

Purchasing *Tefillin*

Parents should begin the process of purchasing *tefillin* several months before the bar mitzva.

It should be kept in mind that the production of *tefillin* is quite complex. *Tefillin* contain four passages from the Torah, painstakingly handwritten, letter by letter, by a certified scribe on parchment. The black leather boxes that contain them, which are made of leather that has undergone special processing, are also handmade.

Like any other product, there are *tefillin* of various levels of quality, which are among the determining factors of their price. The quality of *tefillin* depends on, among other things, the type of parchment and leather used, the scribe's level of knowledge and expertise, the appearance and precision of the writing, and various halakhic stringencies that may have been taken into account in producing the boxes. Therefore, it is recommended to consult a knowledgeable person as to where to purchase *tefillin*.

One should keep in mind that *tefillin* are usually bought to last a lifetime, or for decades at the very least. It is worth spending a bit more in order to get good quality *tefillin*.

📖 **Further reading:** For more on the laws of *tefillin*, see p. 589.

The Celebration

It is customary to mark the day of a boy's bar mitzva with a festive meal, together with family and friends. According to several halakhic authorities, this meal has the status of a celebratory meal [*seudat mitzva*] in honor of a mitzva, which is itself considered like a mitzva. This is because it serves to mark and celebrate the boy's becoming obligated in mitzvot.

In this context, it is worthwhile to quote the words of Rabbi Shlomo Luria, known as the Maharshal: "A bar mitzva meal...presumably there is no greater *seudat mitzva* than this, as indicated by its name. One should rejoice and give praise and thanks to God that the boy has merited to become obligated in mitzvot, as [the Sages taught]: 'Greater is one who is commanded and performs [a mitzva than one who does so voluntarily].' The father has merited to raise him to this point, to bring him into the covenant of the entire Torah" (*Yam Shel Shlomo* on tractate *Bava Kama*, chap. 7, section 37). The Maharshal is referring to the Talmud's statement that one who observes mitzvot due to an obligation imposed on him is greater than one who does so voluntarily. Since on this day the young man becomes obligated to perform the commandments, it is a cause for great joy, the joy of doing a mitzva.

The Bar Mitzva Day

If, for whatever reason, it is not possible to hold the main celebration on the exact Hebrew date of the boy's thirteenth birthday, it is nevertheless appropriate to arrange some sort of celebratory meal on that day, in the presence of at least ten adult male Jews.

There is a long-standing tradition in Jewish communities that the bar mitzva boy delivers a Torah discourse to the participants at the celebration.

Being Called Up to the Torah [*Aliya*]

After the boy has become a bar mitzva, he may be called up to the Torah reading for an *aliya*, and it is customary to celebrate his first *aliya*.

Many have the custom that the boy is called up for his first *aliya* on a Shabbat. Others do so on one of the weekdays on which the Torah is read, such as Monday, Thursday, or *Rosh Hodesh*. The advantage of this practice is that it enables the family and friends to arrive from afar by car without violating Shabbat. Similarly, on these days one can take pictures to commemorate the occasion.

Where Is the *Aliya* Held?

Most people opt to have the *aliya* to the Torah in a synagogue close to home, or in the synagogue where the family generally prays. In Israel, some choose the plaza of the Western Wall, which adds a special dimension to the ceremony. In such a case, it is more practical to hold the ceremony on a weekday. The Western Wall Heritage Foundation helps arrange the *aliya* ceremony of bar mitzva boys, free of charge.

Which *Aliya*?
There are several possibilities regarding the boy's *aliya* to the Torah:

(1) He may be called up to the Torah solely to recite the blessings at the beginning and end of a subdivision of that day's Torah reading.

(2) He may be called up to the Torah to recite the blessings and also to read the passage from the Torah that comprises his *aliya*.

(3) On Shabbat, he may be called up last to the Torah, for the *aliya* known as *maftir*, which also includes reading a passage from the Prophets [the *haftara*]. Reading the *haftara* is easier than reading from the Torah scroll, as a Torah scroll has no vowels or cantillation notes, and these must therefore be memorized, whereas the *haftara* is usually read from a book which includes both.

(4) On Shabbat, a boy who enjoys a challenge may read the entire weekly portion of the Torah, serving as the Torah reader for the congregation on that Shabbat.

Further reading: For more on how and when a person is called up to the Torah, see p. 492.

It should once again be emphasized that there is no need to pressure the boy to read from the Torah for his bar mitzva. It takes a lot of preparation and practice, which might come at the expense of more important things. If the boy is motivated and capable, it is a nice practice. But if it is difficult for him, it may be preferable to forego it. It would be unfortunate for him to remember his first *aliya* to the Torah as being a stressful event.

Preparations for the *Aliya*
The bar mitzva boy should be prepared in advance, and he should practice his *aliya* to the Torah, in whichever of the above options was agreed upon. In virtually every Jewish community there are people who specialize in teaching and preparing boys for this event.

If the boy plans to read the *haftara*, he must learn to do so correctly, with the proper pronunciation of the words and rendition of the cantillation notes. If he intends to read from the Torah itself, his preparation must be even more thorough, as the entire congregation will be fulfilling its obligation to hear the weekly Torah portion through his recitation, and he must therefore read it properly.

Everything must be coordinated in advance with the individual who oversees the synagogue services [*gabbai*]: what exactly the bar mitzva boy intends to read, how many guests are expected to come, which guests will be called up to the Torah, and so forth.

Prior consultation with the rabbi or *gabbai* will also ensure that the bar mitzva boy will have prepared the correct Torah portion and/or *haftara*. Sometimes additional sections from the Torah are read on Shabbat, or two adjacent Torah portions are read.

It should be noted that the first Shabbat on which the boy may be called to the Torah is the one after his bar mitzva day, not the one preceding it, though in some congregations a boy may receive the *aliya* for *maftir* even before his bar mitzva.

In many synagogues it is customary for the boy's parents to invite the congregants to a *kiddush* to be held following the services. For this purpose, they provide wine, light refreshments, and drinks. Those present partake and congratulate the boy and his family. It is important to coordinate this event with the *gabbai*, who will provide direction to the family about the appropriate products and the synagogue's *kashrut* standards.

The Blessing Known as *Barukh Shepetarani*

After the boy's *aliya* to the Torah and the conclusion of the blessing after the Torah reading, his father recites the blessing:

בָּרוּךְ שֶׁפְּטָרַנִי מֵעָנְשׁוֹ שֶׁלָּזֶה.   *Barukh shepetarani me'onsho shelazeh.*

"Blessed is He who has released me from the punishment of this [child]."

There are minor variations in the Hebrew formula, which do not affect the meaning.

Some recite it with the formula of a full-fledged blessing:

בָּרוּךְ אַתָּה אֲדֹנָי, אֱלֹהֵינוּ מֶלֶךְ הָעוֹלָם,   *Barukh ata Adonai, Eloheinu, me-*
שֶׁפְּטָרַנִי מֵעָנְשׁוֹ שֶׁלָּזֶה.   *lekh ha'olam, shepetarani me'onsho shelazeh.*

"Blessed are You, Lord our God, King of the universe, who has released me from the punishment of this [child]."

The reason for reciting this blessing is that until the bar mitzva, the father bears responsibility for the sins of his son. From that point onward, the responsibility for the son's actions rests on his own shoulders, and the father is relieved from this liability.

Bat Mitzva

When a girl reaches the age of twelve, she becomes a bat mitzva. From this point forward, she is obligated to fulfill all of the mitzvot, just like any other adult woman.

The age at which girls become obligated in mitzvot is earlier than that of boys, due to their quicker physical and mental maturation. Some connect this *halakha* to the following talmudic statement: "The Holy One, blessed be He, granted a woman a greater level of understanding than that of a man" (*Nidda* 45b).

Obligations and Privileges

From the age of twelve, a girl must observe all the commandments that apply to adult women. She must eat matza on Passover, fast on public fast days such as Yom Kippur and *Tisha BeAv*, refrain from actions that violate the sanctity of Shabbat and festivals, and much more.

Likewise, from now on, her actions have halakhic ramifications for others. For example, until the age of twelve, when baking bread, she may not be the one to fulfill the mitzva of setting aside a portion of the dough [*halla*]. When she turns twelve, she can fulfill this mitzva, which thereby renders the bread permitted for all to eat. She is also permitted to recite *Kiddush* for other women, enabling them to fulfill their obligation by listening to her.

Further reading: For more on the mitzva and procedure of separating *halla*, see p. 547.

Bat Mitzva Celebrations

In the past, it was not customary to mark a girl's bat mitzva with a festive celebration. It seems that this was due to the domestic nature of girls' lives in those days. In modern times, it has become common to hold a bat mitzva celebration. At a bat mitzva celebration it is fitting for the young woman to share some Torah thoughts, and thereby imbue the event with religious content.

Birthdays

Birthdays are typically not taken very seriously. Many people mark the occasion with some sort of celebration, but taking it overly seriously is viewed as childish. This is not correct. A birthday is like a personal Rosh HaShana. Just as Rosh HaShana involves an intriguing combination of joy and solemnity, celebration and seriousness, birthdays likewise include these divergent components. It is a happy day, because one has matured another year and closed another circle in his life. At the same time, a birthday is also a day for reflection, soul-searching, and the acceptance of resolutions so that the next year will be even better.

According to Jewish thought, there is a renewal and reawakening of events each year on the date on which they occurred. A verse from the Book of Esther (9:28) states: "These days are remembered and observed [na'asim]." The kabbalists interpreted this verse to mean that when these days are remembered, on their anniversary, they are "made" [na'asim] and experienced anew. Accordingly, a person's birth is renewed on his birthday. In a certain sense, he is reborn. This accounts for the joy felt on a birthday; on this day the happiness that our arrival brought to the world is rekindled. In addition, together with that joy, the day imposes upon us the responsibility to examine our deeds and our general conduct, and to aspire to improve and mature.

An examination of the rabbinic sources reveals that one's good fortune increases on his birthday. He is accompanied by a special blessing from heaven, which can help him succeed in all his endeavors. He receives unique energy which he can exploit for good ends. It is only natural that such a day should be treated seriously and utilized for positive goals.

Past and Future

A birthday is first and foremost a day to express thanks to God for the gift of life itself. In addition, it is also appropriate to set aside time on this day for reflection on the past and resolutions for the future.

Ideas for Good Resolutions

Over the generations, especially in the hasidic movement, several ideas have been suggested as to how to make one's birthday a meaningful day:

Self-examination: A birthday is a suitable time for reflecting on one's achievements of the past year, which should be developed even further. At the same time, one should examine his shortcomings that can be improved upon in the coming year.

Resolutions: On one's birthday, it is appropriate to undertake to improve one's conduct, both in matters involving other people, as well as those that are between a person and his Creator.

Setting the tone: A birthday has a spiritual influence on the rest of the year. Therefore, one should take advantage of this day to increase his focus in the three main areas of activity in Judaism: Torah study, prayer, and acts of charity.

Celebration: A birthday party, which is celebrated with friends or family members, can become more meaningful if one shares a Torah thought with the participants, or perhaps reveals the resolutions he has accepted upon himself. This will serve to reinforce one's resolutions and will encourage those around him to accept such resolutions upon themselves as well.

***Aliya* to the Torah:** It is appropriate to be called up to the Torah reading on the Shabbat before one's birthday. If the actual birthday falls on a day which includes a Torah reading (Shabbat, festivals, *Rosh Hodesh*, or every Monday and Thursday of the year), it is proper to have an *aliya* on that day as well. An *aliya* to the Torah, which literally means an "ascent" to the Torah, indeed lifts one closer to the Torah and its values.

Special Birthdays

Every birthday is important, but there are unique customs in Jewish communities for certain birthdays (apart, of course, from the thirteenth birthday of a boy and the twelfth of a girl, when they become a bar or bat mitzva).

Thanksgiving to God

Thirty-fifth birthday: It is stated in the Book of Psalms: "You, God, will bring them down to the pit of destruction. Men of bloodshed and deceit will not live out half their days, but I shall trust in You" (Psalms 55:24). Here King David expresses his hope that evil people, "men of bloodshed and deceit," will not reach half of their allotted lifespan. Since one who lives to the age of seventy is considered to have lived a full life, as the verse states: "The days of our lives in it are seventy years" (Psalms 90:10), one who has reached the age of thirty-five and thereby passed the halfway point to seventy should give thanks to God. Some have the custom of holding a festive meal on this day, known as the *lo yehetzu* ("will not live out half") meal, after the aforementioned verse.

Sixtieth birthday: There are certain severe sins that carry a punishment of *karet*, excision. According to one opinion, someone who is liable to receive *karet* will not reach the age of sixty. Consequently, one who has passed this age can be sure that he has not been punished with *karet*. Some hold a celebratory meal of thanksgiving to mark this date, called the "*karet* meal." For this meal it is recommended to bring a new fruit or a new garment, so that one can recite the *Sheheheyanu* blessing on it while having his milestone birthday in mind as well.

Seventieth birthday: Some have the custom of holding a festive meal when they turn seventy, because this age marks the end of the period during which the life of a person who was sentenced to "death at the hands of Heaven" (which is a punishment for certain sins) is supposed to end. Here too, the main feature of the meal is thanksgiving to God.

Weddings

In Judaism, a wedding is a lofty event that lays the foundation for establishing a Jewish home in which the Divine Presence can rest. As the couple enters into the covenant of marriage, God joins them and dwells among them. In this regard, the Sages state: "If a man and woman merit it, the Divine Presence rests between them" (*Sota* 17a). This is the reason for the atmosphere of reverence that prevails during a wedding ceremony.

This ceremony, in which a man and woman stand under the wedding canopy and establish a joint covenant, is a moment of sanctity that marks the creation of a holy union. Therefore, it is crucial that the wedding be conducted in accordance with the sacred traditions and customs of the Jewish people, which are based on profound kabbalistic ideas.

The union between man and woman represents the bonding of two halves into a single, complete unit. The *Zohar* refers to a man and a woman before marriage as "half a body." There is also an allusion to this idea in the Torah's description of the creation of man: "Male and female He created them...and He called their name Man" (Genesis 5:2). Only after the two of them unite are they called "Man."

This section will review the stages leading up to the wedding day, and the wedding ceremony itself, with all its many components.

📖 **Further reading:** For more on the relationship between couples, see *A Concise Guide to Mahshava*, pp. 16, 179.

Background: The Halakhic Marriage Process

Marriage in *halakha* is a two-stage process. The first stage is betrothal, called *kiddushin* or *eirusin* in Hebrew, in which the groom gives the bride a ring. After this has occurred the couple is legally married, although they do not yet begin to live together. If they would decide to split up, a divorce would be required. The second stage is called *nisu'in*, and its primary feature is the ceremony under the wedding canopy. In the period of the Mishna and the Talmud, it was customary to perform these two components of the marriage process at different times, months or even a full year apart. However, over the course of the generations it has become customary to perform the *kiddushin* under the wedding canopy, at the same time as the *nisu'in*.

Engagement

In contemporary times, engagement is a declaration of intent by the bride and groom. This declaration carries no legal or halakhic significance.

In order to distinguish between the binding betrothal [eirusin] of the past and the currently practiced, non-binding engagement, which is also popularly known as eirusin in modern Hebrew, there are some Hebrew speakers who are careful not to use the term eirusin for their engagement party. Instead, some call the event tena'im, which means terms and conditions of an agreement. Jews of European ancestry refer to the party as a vort, which literally means "word," that is, the declaration of commitment to marry which the parties give to each other. At an engagement party, it is proper for the couple to express their thanks to God for enabling them to find their match and to lay the groundwork for establishing their home.

Timing

It is permitted to become engaged and even to hold an engagement party during the intermediate festival days of Sukkot and Passover.

Although the three weeks between the Seventeenth of Tamuz and Tisha BeAv are days of mourning for the destruction of the two Temples, it is permitted to become engaged during this time and to hold a small engagement party without music. One may get engaged during the first nine days of the month of Av, but it is not permitted to hold a celebration at that time. Instead, the festivities should be postponed until after Tisha BeAv.

📖 **Further reading:** For more on the Three Weeks and the customs of mourning that are practiced during this period, see p. 359.

Ceremonial Aspects of Engagement

During the engagement party, it is customary in some Ashkenazic communities to break a plate. There are two main reasons for this:

(1) to commemorate the destruction of the Temple, similar to the breaking of a glass under the wedding canopy, which is described below;

(2) to serve as a symbolic action indicating that just as the broken plate cannot be restored to its former whole state, so too, the two parties will not renounce their decision to marry. It is customary for the mother of the bride and the mother of the groom to hold on to the plate and throw it to the ground together. Alternatively, some break the plate not at the engagement party but when signing the deed of "terms and conditions" known as tena'im, at a later time, as explained below.

Tena'im

When it became accepted in Jewish communities to consolidate the *kiddushin* stage (giving of the ring to the bride) and the *nisu'in* stage (standing together under the wedding canopy) into a single event, there was no halakhic impediment to prevent the parties from calling off the wedding. This situation was a source of concern for many, as a cancelled engagement could lead to great financial loss as well as heartbreak. Therefore, a custom was developed, which has been preserved to this day in some communities, to write a deed of terms and conditions, known as *tena'im*. This document is a statement of commitment not to cancel the engagement, and it includes financial sanctions for such cancellation.

In addition to the commitment not to withdraw from the intention to marry, which is the essence of the *tena'im*, the document obligates the bride and groom and their parents to comply with the monetary agreements upon which they had agreed.

Some write this document at the engagement party. In other communities there is an interest to preserve the custom but not to accept financial penalties, and they therefore write the document at the wedding, just before the ceremony. Others do not write a *tena'im* document at all. When a *tena'im* document is signed on the wedding day, many write the document differently than how it was traditionally formulated: Instead of writing that both sides commit to get married, imposing financial penalties if they renege, they write that the parties have fulfilled their obligations and they do not have any claims against each other.

In the unfortunate circumstance in which a wedding is called off, especially if it is close enough to the wedding that the sides have incurred significant financial expense, it is worthwhile to consult a rabbi to ensure that the process will be done fairly and in accordance with *halakha*, and also to help the sides avoid any further or unnecessary emotional turmoil and ill will.

The Henna Ceremony

In communities of Middle Eastern and North African descent, it is customary to conduct a henna ceremony, which symbolizes the transition of the bride from single life to marriage. During the ceremony, a brown-colored dye produced from the leaves of the henna plant is applied to the bride's hands. It is customary to draw circles on her hands in the form of a coin, symbolizing blessings of abundance and good fortune.

There are two main variations of the henna ceremony:

(1) Henna at a ritual bath [*mikva*]: Every bride immerses in a *mikva* before her wedding. In some communities it is customary for the bride's family and friends to accompany her to the *mikva*, and after the immersion, to distribute sweet foods to the attendees and to paint the palms of the bride's hands with henna. Only women and girls participate in this ceremony.

(2) A henna celebration: Some conduct the henna ceremony earlier than when the bride immerses in the *mikva*. This celebration is held at home or in a hall and is not limited to women. Sweet foods are distributed at the celebration and the palms of the hand of the bride and groom are painted with henna. In addition, a festive meal is held with the participation of the groom and his family.

> **Further reading:** For more on immersing in a *mikva* and the preparations for this ritual, see p. 578.

Instruction

In order to live their married life in accordance with Jewish law, the bride and groom must be knowledgeable in the many mitzvot and *halakhot* that govern married life. It is therefore customary for the bride and groom to receive instruction in these areas before the wedding. In their meetings with their instructors, it is a good idea for them to raise any questions and concerns they may have, not only about the relevant *halakhot* but about the husband-wife relationship and general family life. It is therefore important to choose a counselor with whom one feels comfortable enough to speak openly about any questions or concerns they may have.

In Israel, in accordance with the directives of the Chief Rabbinate of Israel, every bride must undergo a training course with a certified bridal counselor. Upon completing the course, this instructor gives the bride a written confirmation of her training, which the bride will pass on to the office that handles the marriage file. Some religious councils require that grooms as well receive guidance from qualified counselors before the wedding.

Choosing a Wedding Date

When setting the date of the wedding, the woman's menstrual cycle should be taken into consideration. This is done in order to ensure that she will be ritually pure on her wedding night. Nowadays, many brides take pills before the wedding to regulate menstruation, thus enabling the couple to choose any date that suits them. In this regard, it is advisable to consult with the bridal counselor.

When One May Not Get Married

There are specific days of the year on which weddings are not held:

Shabbat and festivals: It is prohibited to get married on Shabbat and festivals. It is halakhically permissible to get married on a Friday. However, this would need to be arranged carefully in order to avoid any violation of the Shabbat or festival.

Purim and Hanukkah are not considered festivals in this regard, and therefore it is permitted to get married on those days.

The intermediate festival days of *Sukkot* and Passover: It is prohibited to get married on the intermediate festival days. The exception to this rule is in the case of a divorced couple who wishes to remarry.

The *omer*: During the period between Passover and *Shavuot*, which is known as the time period of the *omer* (see p. 331), there are certain days on which weddings are not held. Sephardic practice is not to have weddings from Passover until the thirty-fourth day of the *omer*, while Ashkenazic custom is to allow weddings on the thirty-third day of the *omer*. However, some Ashkenazic communities have other customs. Therefore, if a couple is considering getting married during this time of year, the rabbi who will conduct the wedding ceremony should be consulted.

The Three Weeks: The three-week period between the Seventeenth of Tamuz and *Tisha BeAv* is a period of mourning for the destruction of the two Temples. Sephardim refrain from conducting weddings only during the nine days from the first day of Av through *Tisha BeAv*. By contrast, Ashkenazim do not marry throughout the Three Weeks.

The Israeli Chief Rabbinate has established regulations regarding the dates on which it is permissible to have a wedding in Israel, and these can be found on its website. Rabbis are prohibited from conducting weddings at other times. For example, the Rabbinate does not allow weddings to be held on Saturday night or on Friday afternoon, so as to prevent the possible desecration of Shabbat.

It should be noted that in order to be legally married in Israel, one must first open a marriage file in the office of the Chief Rabbinate. According to the regulations of the Rabbinate, this must be done no later than forty-five days before the date of the wedding. All relevant information can be found on the website of the Ministry of Religious Services.

Wedding Preparations

The Ring, *Mikva*, etc.

Before the wedding, the groom must purchase a wedding ring with which to betroth his future wife. (For a discussion of the customs relating to the wedding ring, see p. 61.) The ring must belong to the groom in order for him to betroth his bride with it.

It is stated in the Zohar that the souls of the celebrants' deceased parents come to attend the wedding. Accordingly, some people have the custom to visit the graves of their parents and grandparents and "invite" them to the wedding. Some even place a printed invitation on the grave.

It should be noted that while some have the custom not to visit the grave within the first year after death, it is acceptable for a bride or groom to do so if they wish to invite the deceased to their wedding.

There is a practice, especially in Ashkenazic communities, that the bride and groom do not see each other for a week before the wedding.

On the Shabbat prior to the wedding, which Ashkenazim call the *aufruf* (Yiddish for "calling up") or *Shabbat Hatan*, it is customary to call up the groom to the Torah reading.

If possible, it is appropriate to honor the groom with the final *aliya*, known as the *maftir*, so that in addition to reciting the blessings on the Torah, he can also read the *haftara* for the congregation. Some invite the groom's friends and family members to partake in festive meals together on this Shabbat, in honor of the forthcoming wedding celebration. On Shabbat morning, after prayer services, some have the custom of hosting a *kiddush* for all the worshippers at the synagogue.

The bride must immerse in a *mikva* before the wedding. Ashkenazic practice is for this immersion to take place as close to the wedding as possible, and no more than three days before the wedding.

The Eve of the Wedding

The wedding day is a special time that marks the end of one period of life and the beginning of a new one. According to tradition, one's past transgressions are forgiven on one's wedding day. Consequently, there is an element of seriousness, and even soul searching, on this day.

Escorts

On the day of the wedding, it is customary for the bride and the groom to each be accompanied by an escort, so that they are never left alone. There are two reasons for this custom:

(1) to provide protection against harmful spiritual forces;

(2) on their wedding day, the bride and groom are compared to a queen and a king, who do not go anywhere without an escort.

Fasting

It is a widespread custom, especially among Ashkenazim, for the bride and groom to fast on their wedding day. The reason for this is that the wedding day is considered to be a time of forgiveness and atonement, and so it is appropriate to fast on this day. Another reason is that this ensures that the bride and groom will not drink alcoholic beverages before the ceremony, and they will thus arrive at the wedding in a state of complete mental clarity.

This fast ends immediately after the wedding ceremony, when the bride and groom enter a private room, known as the *yihud* room, where they may eat and drink as they wish. Even if the wedding ceremony is conducted before sunset, the fast ends immediately after the ceremony; there is no need to wait until nightfall.

When a wedding is held on certain dates, the couple does not fast. These days are *Rosh Hodesh*, Hanukkah, Purim, *Tu BeShvat,* and *Tu BeAv.*

On their wedding day, it is customary for a bride and groom to add, at the end of the afternoon silent *Amida* prayer, the confession of sins that is recited on Yom Kippur.

> **Further reading:** For more on the special confession of Yom Kippur, see p. 170; *A Concise Guide to Mahshava*, p. 69.

Many Ashkenazim have the custom for the groom to wear a white garment that is worn on Yom Kippur [*kittel*] at the wedding ceremony, as the color white symbolizes kindness and forgiveness. Furthermore, white is reminiscent of the shrouds of the dead, and the wearing of the *kittel* conveys the message that our time in this world is limited and must be utilized properly.

The Wedding Ceremony

The wedding ceremony is one of the most important occasions in one's life. It marks the union of two individuals into a single unit, with all that this transformation entails. There are many and varied themes to the ceremony, with its sanctity and mitzvot, monetary aspects alongside national and historical motifs. The structure of the Jewish wedding is ancient and takes into account numerous laws and customs. The reasons for some of the customs are known, while others are more obscure. The following is a presentation of the different stages of the ceremony and the ideas they represent.

Basic Components of the Ceremony

The basic components of the ceremony are as follows:

Covering the bride with a veil: Before the ceremony under the wedding canopy, the groom covers the bride's face with a veil, but only if it is the bride's first marriage.

The wedding canopy [*huppa*]: The bride and groom stand together under the wedding canopy.

Kiddushin: The groom gives the bride a ring and betroths her.

The marriage contract [*ketuba*]: During the ceremony, the text of the marriage contract is read aloud. Some have the witnesses sign the document before the ceremony begins while others have them sign it at this point, under the wedding canopy. After it is read, the groom gives the marriage contract to the bride.

The seven blessings [*sheva berakhot*]: Seven blessings are recited as part of the wedding ceremony, in honor of the bride and groom. The blessings are recited by the rabbi who is officiating at the ceremony, or by honored guests who are invited to do so.

Private room: According to Ashkenazic custom, after the ceremony, the bride and groom stay alone together [*yihud*] for a certain period of time in this locked room. This is often referred to as the *yihud* room.

The Marriage

What is the key component in this series of ceremonies that turns the man and woman into a married couple? The Sages state that this process, called *nisu'in*, takes place through the *huppa*. However, there are different opinions among halakhic authorities as to the definition of the term *huppa*. Some maintain that it refers to when the groom covers the bride with a veil. Others claim that the crucial stage is when the bride and groom stand together under the wedding canopy (the canopy itself is commonly referred to as the *huppa*). According to a third opinion, when the groom and the bride spend a few minutes in seclusion in the *yihud* room they become a married couple. Yet others contend that the decisive step is the entry of the bride and groom into their new home at the very end of the evening. The Ashkenazic community stresses the importance of fulfilling all four of these opinions, while many Sephardic couples do not spend time in seclusion at the wedding. Each community should follow its own custom.

The Participants

In addition to the bride and groom, who are of course the main participants, there are several other individuals who serve vital functions at the wedding ceremony:

The officiating rabbi [*mesader kiddushin*]: Every wedding takes place in the presence of a rabbi, who officiates at the ceremony and sees to it that everything is carried out in accordance with *halakha*. The rabbi must ensure that all the details of the marriage contract are filled out correctly, and that valid witnesses sign the document. He then conducts the ceremony, which must be performed "in accordance with the law of Moses and Israel."

When choosing a rabbi to officiate at the ceremony, it is important to be sure of the following two factors:

(1) the rabbi is legally authorized by local authorities to conduct weddings;

(2) the rabbi is aware of the preferred styles and expectations of the bride and groom, and knows how to conduct the ceremony in a pleasant and dignified manner. Some rabbis, for example, will pause to explain the meaning of various components of the wedding ceremony.

Witnesses for the marriage contract: Two valid witnesses are appointed to sign the marriage contract and thereby ratify the husband's obligations to his wife. In some communities the groom also signs the contract. These signings take place before or during the wedding ceremony.

Witnesses for the betrothal: At each wedding, two valid witnesses are chosen from among the invited guests, whose job it is to stand close to the wedding canopy and observe the ceremony as it unfolds. The presence of the witnesses provides halakhic validity to the act of marriage. Most importantly, they must watch the groom betroth the bride by giving her a ring. Additionally, witnesses should observe the groom covering the bride's face with the veil, the transfer of the marriage contract to the bride, and the entrance of the groom and the bride to the *yihud* room (for those who follow this custom).

It is important to bear in mind that without proper witnesses the marriage is not halakhically valid. These witnesses must be two Torah-observant adult males, who are not relatives of the groom or the bride, and are not related to each other.

There is no reason that the two witnesses for the marriage contract cannot also serve as witnesses to the *kiddushin*. Likewise, the officiating rabbi can himself be one of the witnesses. In some cases, the rabbi comes to the wedding with an assistant, and these two men may serve as the witnesses.

Escorts: These are the people who accompany the bride and groom to the wedding canopy.

Ten attendees: At least ten men [*minyan*] must be present at the wedding ceremony. The groom himself counts toward the *minyan*.

The Marriage Contract

Before the wedding ceremony begins, the groom sits with the officiating rabbi and the witnesses for the marriage contract, and together they go through the details of the text. Usually they are joined by the father of the groom and as well as the father of the bride. In the marriage contract, the groom accepts upon himself several obligations toward his future wife. He agrees that he must honor her and take care of her financial needs, as accepted in Jewish tradition. The text of the marriage contract includes various details in this regard; the main point is the husband's financial obligation toward his wife if, Heaven forbid, she is later divorced or widowed from him. In the latter case, his monetary obligation will be realized from the inheritance funds. The amount for which he is liable is stipulated in the marriage contract. Those who sign a document of *tena'im* (see p. 49) just before the wedding ceremony will do so at this stage as well.

The Groom's Financial Liability

The purpose of the groom's financial obligation toward his wife is twofold:

(1) to ensure that the husband will not act in haste before considering the option of divorce;

(2) to help the woman sustain herself after a divorce or after her husband's death.

The sum specified in the marriage contract includes two components: the main sum and the supplementary sum.

The main sum: This is a fixed sum that every husband is obligated to pledge to his wife. The amount established by the Sages and written into the text of the marriage contract is two hundred *zuz*, if it is the bride's first marriage. According to Sephardic tradition, this amount is equivalent to the value of 120 g of pure silver, whereas Ashkenazim consider it to be the value of 960 g of pure silver. There is also an opinion which maintains that two hundred *zuz* should be understood as being the amount of money equal to one year's average wage in the local economy.

The supplement: It is customary for the husband to add a supplementary amount to the primary sum of the marriage contract ordained by the Sages. For Ashkenazic Jews outside of Israel, the document typically specifies a supplement of two hundred *zekukim*, a European silver coin from the seventeenth century, an amount widely understood to be the value of 2784 g of silver. In Israel, it is common to specify a specific sum of the modern currency. This amount depends on the generosity of the groom, but it should not be an exaggerated, unrealistic amount, as the marriage contract is a binding legal document that he or his heirs may someday be required to pay. Experienced rabbinical court judges in Israel recommend that the total sum of the marriage contract be 120,000 NIS, and the Chief Rabbinate of Israel limits the liability to a maximum of one million NIS.

Notwithstanding the above, in a case of divorce, modern law calls for the dividing of assets between the couple. This law reduces the practical importance of the sum of the marriage contract, but it does not eliminate it altogether.

Safekeeping the Marriage Contract

The marriage contract is filled out by the officiating rabbi. After the wedding, this copy is held by the wife. From the moment the couple enter their joint residence, the wife must have a copy of the marriage contract.

In Israel, the Religious Council where the marriage application was filed will supply two copies of the marriage contract for the officiating rabbi to fill out. One copy of the marriage contract is held by the wife, and the second copy is completed and submitted to the Religious Council.

It is advisable to appoint in advance a person to safeguard the marriage contract at the wedding so that it is not lost during the course of the wedding festivities. If the marriage contract is lost, a new one must be filled out and signed with the help of a rabbi and in the presence of witnesses.

Act of Acquisition and Signing

When the rabbi has finished filling out the marriage contract, the groom performs a formal act of acquisition by lifting a pen or some other object that is handed to him by the rabbi. This act has halakhic significance, as it is an official act of acquisition, whereby the groom becomes legally bound to fulfill all the obligations specified in the marriage contract.

The marriage-contract witnesses must see the act of acquisition, and only after that do they sign the document.

Some have a custom to perform the act of acquisition for the marriage contract and the signing of the witnesses under the wedding canopy. The exact stage when this is done will be noted below.

In some Sephardic communities it is customary to record in the marriage contract that the groom has taken an oath to fulfill everything written in the contract. Then, during the reading of the marriage contract, when the reader reaches the words "and I also swear...," he pauses, and the groom affirms the oath by means of a handshake. The reading of the marriage contract then resumes. Some have the custom that the rabbi says to the groom, "I hereby administer an oath to you on all that is written above," whereupon the groom shakes his hand, and they then continue reading the marriage contract.

There is no need for the bride to be present at the signing of the marriage contract. In communities where it is customary for the groom and the bride not to see each other for a week before the wedding, up until the marriage ceremony itself, the bride obviously cannot be in attendance for the signing. It is common practice that during this process the bride stays with her friends and family in a different part of the wedding hall. It is recommended that she use these last moments before the wedding ceremony to recite psalms and personal prayers for the success of the couple's relationship and their forthcoming family life.

📖 **Further reading:** For another occasion on which an act of acquisition is performed, see p. 282.

The Procession

After the signing of the marriage contract, it is time to proceed to the wedding canopy. These are moments of great emotion for the bride and groom and their parents and families. One chapter in life, including many years of childhood, adolescence, and young adulthood, is coming to its conclusion, as a new, meaningful, exciting, and challenging period in life is about to begin.

First the groom is led by his escorts to the wedding canopy. If he is going to wear a *kittel* for the ceremony (see above), he puts it on at this stage. Then the bride is brought to the canopy, accompanied by her escorts. The fact that the bride and groom are brought in separately symbolizes the fact that each of them approaches the wedding canopy as individuals, but will leave together as a united couple.

It is customary for the parents to escort the bride and groom to the canopy. Some have the custom that the bride's parents accompany the bride while the groom's parents walk with him. According to another custom, the two fathers walk with the groom while the two mothers accompany the bride.

In many communities it is customary that only married couples escort the bride and groom to the wedding canopy, as a good omen for the new couple. If the parents of one or both parties are divorced or widowed, one should consult the officiating rabbi as to who should accompany the groom and/or bride to the canopy. Some have the custom that in such a situation a married couple from the family (grandparents or an uncle and aunt) should do so.

Many Ashkenazim have the practice that those accompanying the bride and groom carry lit candles, to enhance the honor and dignity of the ceremony.

Just before he walks to the wedding canopy, the groom, with his escorts, approaches the bride and covers her face with a veil. The bride stays covered with the veil until the end of the wedding ceremony. Two explanations are given for this ancient custom:

(1) the veil symbolizes that the bride reserves her beauty for the groom, and therefore she is covered from the gaze of others;

(2) in this manner the bride follows the path of our matriarch Rebecca, who covered her face with a scarf when she first met our forefather Isaac (see Genesis 24:65).

The witnesses to the *kiddushin* should see the groom covering the bride's face with the veil. If it is not the woman's first marriage, her face is not covered.

These moments are considered to be an auspicious time of heavenly mercy for the bride and groom, when they can pray for the success of the joint home they are about to establish, as well as for the welfare of all those who are in need. Many have the custom of handing notes to the bride, listing names of people suffering from medical or other difficulties so that she can pray for them at this special time.

After the bride's face has been covered with the veil, some have the custom that her parents and grandparents approach her and bless her. Some recite the blessing that Rebecca received from her family: "Our sister, may you become thousands and ten-thousands" (Genesis 24:60).

To the Wedding Canopy

After the groom covers the bride's face with the veil, he is escorted to the canopy and waits for the bride to arrive. This is an appropriate time for the groom to pray for the success of his marriage and for others who are in need.

Now the bride begins her approach to the canopy with her escorts. Some have a custom that as she reaches the wedding canopy, the groom comes out to meet her and to accompany her for the final few steps to the canopy. The wedding canopy symbolizes the groom's house, and the groom is symbolically bringing the bride into his home.

At the beginning of the ceremony, the groom stands at the center of the wedding canopy, and it is customary for the bride, together with her mother and the mother of the groom, to encircle him seven times. Some find an allusion to this custom in a statement of the prophet Jeremiah: "For the Lord has created a novelty on the earth: A woman will court a man" (Jeremiah 31:21), as the literal translation of these words is: A woman will go around a man.

Various Customs

Standing under the wedding canopy is a very significant part of the wedding ceremony. The bride enters and stands with the groom in a place that has been specially designated for the marriage of the couple.

The custom of most Ashkenazim is that the canopy is set up under the open sky, as a symbolic blessing for the couple, that their descendants should be like the stars of heaven. Sephardim do not follow this practice; they maintain that the canopy may be situated even under a roofed structure.

When it is not possible for the canopy to be set up under the open sky, as, for example, when there is inclement weather, Ashkenazim generally conduct the ceremony in an enclosed area. Yet, some are very strict about this matter, and under no circumstances will they perform the ceremony other than under the open sky.

After the bride circles the groom seven times, she stands to his right. During the ceremony, the following individuals stand under the canopy: the bride and groom, their parents, the rabbi, the witnesses, those reciting the blessings (each in turn), and sometimes also the master of ceremonies.

Many have the custom to place ashes on the groom's head before the wedding ceremony, in commemoration of the destruction of the Temple.

Kiddushin

As stated above, nowadays the *kiddushin*, or betrothal, is carried out under the wedding canopy. In order to betroth a woman, a man must give her either money or an object worth at least one *peruta* (the equivalent of 25 mg of pure silver, in accordance with the current price of silver), and stating that this is for the purpose of betrothal. If the bride responds positively by accepting the money or object from his hand, she is betrothed. Although it is permissible to betroth a woman with a coin or any other object that meets the minimum value stated above, it is customary in all Jewish communities to use a ring for this purpose. Following are some of the *halakhot* of this ring and the act of *kiddushin*.

The Ring

The ring must be the groom's personal property. Even if his parents purchased the ring for him, they must give it to their son as a full-fledged gift, so that the ring will belong only to him.

According to *halakha*, the ring must be worth more than one *peruta* (see above), which is halakhically the minimum monetary value of significance. An object worth less than a *peruta* is viewed as being of no importance, and therefore is not considered to have monetary value. A ring, and especially one made of precious metal, certainly meets this requirement.

A problem can arise if the bride mistakenly thinks that the ring is worth much more than its actual value. For example, if a man betroths a woman with a ring worth $100, and the woman believes that it is worth $1000, this raises a problem with the process of acquisition. The woman could later claim to have consented to the betrothal only by means of an expensive ring worth $1000, and not through a ring worth substantially less than that. To avoid significant gaps between the bride's evaluation and the actual value of the wedding ring, it has been established that the *kiddushin* must be performed with a relatively simple ring, without adornments or precious stones.

There are various customs regarding the shape of the ring. Most use a ring that is round on the outside and inside, while others use a ring that is square on the outside and round on the inside. The same applies to the material from which it is made: Some prefer white gold, while others opt for yellow gold, pure silver, or platinum. Each option is acceptable, but it is important that the appearance of the ring corresponds with its true value.

There are some rabbis who show the ring to the witnesses under the wedding canopy and ask them to confirm that it is worth at least one *peruta*, and only after the witnesses answer in the affirmative does the rabbi return the ring to the groom for the betrothal.

Life Cycle

It is customary for the bride to remove all jewelry that she is wearing before the groom gives her the ring, or before she approaches the canopy.

The Blessings and Declaration of Betrothal

The *kiddushin* consists of the groom giving the ring to his bride and declaring: "You are hereby betrothed to me with this ring, in accordance with the law of Moses and Israel." This is a mitzva like any other, and therefore a blessing is recited before its performance, as described in the following paragraph. In addition, due to its importance, the blessing for the betrothal is preceded by a blessing over a cup of wine. Usually the officiating rabbi recites both blessings, but in certain communities it is the groom who recites the blessings.

The one reciting the blessing takes a full cup of wine in his hand and recites the following:

בָּרוּךְ אַתָּה אֲדֹנָי, אֱלֹהֵינוּ מֶלֶךְ הָעוֹלָם, בּוֹרֵא פְּרִי הַגָּפֶן.

Barukh ata Adonai, Eloheinu, melekh ha'olam, borei peri hagafen.

בָּרוּךְ אַתָּה אֲדֹנָי, אֱלֹהֵינוּ מֶלֶךְ הָעוֹלָם, אֲשֶׁר קִדְּשָׁנוּ בְּמִצְוֹתָיו וְצִוָּנוּ עַל הָעֲרָיוֹת, וְאָסַר לָנוּ אֶת הָאֲרוּסוֹת וְהִתִּיר לָנוּ אֶת הַנְּשׂוּאוֹת לָנוּ עַל יְדֵי חֻפָּה וְקִדּוּשִׁין, בָּרוּךְ אַתָּה אֲדֹנָי, מְקַדֵּשׁ עַמּוֹ יִשְׂרָאֵל עַל יְדֵי חֻפָּה וְקִדּוּשִׁין.

Barukh ata Adonai, Eloheinu, melekh ha'olam, asher kideshanu bemitzvotav, vetzivanu al ha'arayot, ve'asar lanu et ha'arusot, vehitir lanu et hanesuot lanu al yedei ḥuppa vekidushin. Barukh ata Adonai, mekadesh amo Yisrael al yedei ḥuppa vekidushin.

"Blessed are You, Lord our God, King of the universe, who creates the fruit of the vine.

"Blessed are You, Lord our God, King of the universe, who sanctified us through His commandments, and commanded us concerning forbidden relationships, and prohibited to us [intimacy with] women who are betrothed, and permitted to us women who are married to us by means of the wedding canopy and betrothal. Blessed are You, Lord, who sanctifies His people Israel by means of the wedding canopy and betrothal."

The meaning of the blessing is as follows: "Who...commanded us concerning forbidden relationships" – God prohibited us from marrying or engaging in marital relations with family members. "And prohibited to us women who are betrothed" – He even forbade us from having marital relations with our fiancées. "And permitted to us women who are married to us by means of the wedding canopy and betrothal" – He permitted us to engage in marital relations only after going through the process of *huppa* and *kiddushin*. "Blessed are You, Lord, who sanctifies His people Israel by means of the wedding canopy and betrothal" – God sanctifies the people of Israel by permitting them to live as couples only through the wedding canopy and betrothal.

📖 **Further reading:** For more on forbidden relatives, see *A Concise Guide to the Torah*, p. 298.

The rabbi then takes a sip of the wine and gives the cup to the groom to drink as well. The groom returns the cup to the rabbi, who hands it over to the bride's mother, and she helps the bride take a sip. Some have the custom that only the bride and groom drink from the cup, not the rabbi.

After tasting the wine, the groom places the ring on the index finger of the bride's right hand, and declares:

הֲרֵי אַתְּ מְקֻדֶּשֶׁת לִי בְּטַבַּעַת זוֹ, כְּדַת מֹשֶׁה וְיִשְׂרָאֵל.   *Harei at mekudeshet li betaba'at zo kedat Moshe veYisrael.*

"You are hereby betrothed to me with this ring, in accordance with the law of Moses and Israel."

It is customary for those present to respond:

מְקֻדֶּשֶׁת, מְקֻדֶּשֶׁת, מְקֻדֶּשֶׁת.   *Mekudeshet, mekudeshet, mekudeshet.*

"Betrothed, betrothed, betrothed!"

The witnesses to the *kiddushin* must watch the groom place the ring on the bride's finger.

The Reading of the *Ketuba*

The *kiddushin* segment has now been concluded, and the ceremony continues with the seven blessings that are recited at the time of *nisu'in*. However, in order to create a break between the blessings recited on the *kiddushin* and those recited on the *nisu'in*, it is customary to read the marriage contract out loud at this point in the ceremony.

The officiating rabbi, or someone else who is invited to do so, reads out the marriage contract, a legal document that is written mostly in Aramaic. There are those who have the custom not to read the entire text but only certain passages from it. This depends on the officiating rabbi and the one charged with the reading of the text.

It was noted earlier that some have the custom for the witnesses to sign the marriage contract under the wedding canopy, and that would take place at this point, after the reading of its main text.

Those who follow this practice proceed as follows: First the groom performs an act of acquisition regarding the obligations laid out in the marriage contract (as detailed above), after which the witnesses sign the document.

Following the reading of the marriage contract, the document is given to the groom who hands it over to the bride and says to her:

הֲרֵי זוֹ כְּתֻבָּתֵךְ.   Harei zo ketubatekh.

"Here is your marriage contract."

She takes the marriage contract from him and then hands it to someone in her family for safekeeping.

A New Prayer Shawl [Tallit]

Some have the custom of putting on a new *tallit* after the reading of the *ketuba*. Among other reasons for this is that while the *Sheheheyanu* blessing is not recited as part of the wedding ceremony itself, the wearing of a new *tallit* enables the groom to recite this blessing.

If the ceremony takes place before sunset, he recites a blessing before donning the *tallit*:

בָּרוּךְ אַתָּה אֲדֹנָי, אֱלֹהֵינוּ מֶלֶךְ הָעוֹלָם,   Barukh ata Adonai, Eloheinu, melekh
אֲשֶׁר קִדְּשָׁנוּ בְּמִצְוֹתָיו וְצִוָּנוּ לְהִתְעַטֵּף   ha'olam, asher kideshanu bemitzvotav,
בְּצִיצִית.   vetzivanu lehitatef betzitzit.

"Blessed are You, Lord our God, King of the universe, who sanctified us through His commandments, and commanded us to wrap ourselves with ritual fringes."

If the ceremony is held after sunset, he does not recite the above blessing. In either event, the *Sheheheyanu* blessing is now recited:

בָּרוּךְ אַתָּה אֲדֹנָי, אֱלֹהֵינוּ מֶלֶךְ הָעוֹלָם,   Barukh ata Adonai, Eloheinu, melekh
שֶׁהֶחֱיָנוּ וְקִיְּמָנוּ וְהִגִּיעָנוּ לַזְּמַן הַזֶּה.   ha'olam, sheheheyanu vekiyemanu
     vehigi'anu la'zeman hazeh.

"Blessed are You, Lord our God, King of the universe, who has given us life, sustained us, and brought us to this time."

When reciting this blessing of joy and thanks over the *tallit*, he should have the wedding in mind as well.

The Seven Blessings [*Sheva Berakhot*]

After the reading of the marriage contract, the ceremony continues with the seven blessings of *nisu'in*. These blessings contain expressions of thanksgiving to God for the joy of the marriage, combined with good wishes for the bride and groom.

The seven blessings are recited while holding a full cup of wine. It is customary to use a different cup of wine, not the one that was already used for the first blessing over the wine and the blessing on the *kiddushin*.

Who Recites the Blessings

The seven blessings may be recited by the officiating rabbi or by any other man present. The blessings can also be divided up, in order to honor various family members, friends, and other guests. The first two blessings are recited by one person, while the five additional blessings may be given to five different people. Thus, a total of six people can participate in the recitation of the blessings.

The Blessings and Their Meanings

The seven blessings are as follows:

בָּרוּךְ אַתָּה אֲדֹנָי, אֱלֹהֵינוּ מֶלֶךְ הָעוֹלָם,   *Barukh ata Adonai, Eloheinu, melekh*
 בּוֹרֵא פְּרִי הַגָּפֶן.   *ha'olam, borei peri hagafen.*

"Blessed are You, Lord our God, King of the universe, who creates the fruit of the vine."

בָּרוּךְ אַתָּה אֲדֹנָי, אֱלֹהֵינוּ מֶלֶךְ הָעוֹלָם,   *Barukh ata Adonai, Eloheinu, melekh*
 שֶׁהַכֹּל בָּרָא לִכְבוֹדוֹ.   *ha'olam, shehakol bara likhvodo.*

"Blessed are You, Lord our God, King of the universe, who has created all for His glory."

The blessing of "who creates the fruit of the vine" is recited over the drinking of the wine itself. The blessing of "who has created all for His glory" is in honor of those who came to rejoice with the bride and groom. Through their very presence, these people give honor to God, who acted as the groomsman, as it were, in his presentation of Eve to Adam, at humankind's first marriage.

בָּרוּךְ אַתָּה אֲדֹנָי, אֱלֹהֵינוּ מֶלֶךְ הָעוֹלָם, יוֹצֵר הָאָדָם.

Barukh ata Adonai, Eloheinu, melekh ha'olam, yotzer ha'adam.

"Blessed are You, Lord our God, King of the universe, Creator of man."

This blessing refers to the creation of Adam, who was fashioned alone, without a partner. It is an appropriate introduction to the next blessing:

בָּרוּךְ אַתָּה אֲדֹנָי, אֱלֹהֵינוּ מֶלֶךְ הָעוֹלָם, אֲשֶׁר יָצַר אֶת הָאָדָם בְּצַלְמוֹ, בְּצֶלֶם דְּמוּת תַּבְנִיתוֹ, וְהִתְקִין לוֹ מִמֶּנּוּ בִּנְיַן עֲדֵי עַד. בָּרוּךְ אַתָּה אֲדֹנָי, יוֹצֵר הָאָדָם.

Barukh ata Adonai, Eloheinu, melekh ha'olam, asher yatzar et ha'adam betzalmo, betzelem demut tavnito, vehitkin lo mimenu binyan adei ad. Barukh ata Adonai, yotzer ha'adam.

"Blessed are You, Lord our God, King of the universe, who created the [first] man in His image, in the image of the likeness of His form, and out of his very self formed an edifice for all eternity. Blessed are You, Lord, Creator of man."

This blessing recalls the creation of Adam and his wife. Adam was initially created alone and only afterward did God take a part of his body to form a spouse for him. Together the couple produced generations of offspring and established the human race – for all eternity.

שׂוֹשׂ תָּשִׂישׂ וְתָגֵל הָעֲקָרָה, בְּקִבּוּץ בָּנֶיהָ לְתוֹכָהּ בְּשִׂמְחָה. בָּרוּךְ אַתָּה אֲדֹנָי, מְשַׂמֵּחַ צִיּוֹן בְּבָנֶיהָ.

Sos tasis vetagel ha'akara, bekibutz baneha letokhah besimha. Barukh ata Adonai, mesame'ah Tziyon bevaneha.

"May the barren one greatly rejoice and delight with the ingathering of her children within her in joy. Blessed are You, Lord, who gladdens Zion through her children."

In this blessing we remember and memorialize the destruction of the Temple and Jerusalem and pray for its restoration, as is customary for Jews to do on every joyous occasion. Alongside the sorrow for the destruction, we wish for "the ingathering of her children within her in joy," in the messianic redemption.

שַׂמֵּחַ (או: שַׂמַּח) תְּשַׂמַּח רֵעִים הָאֲהוּבִים, כְּשַׂמֵּחֲךָ יְצִירְךָ בְּגַן עֵדֶן מִקֶּדֶם. בָּרוּךְ אַתָּה אֲדֹנָי, מְשַׂמֵּחַ חָתָן וְכַלָּה.

Same'aḥ (or: *samaḥ*) *tesamaḥ re'im ha'ahuvim, kesameḥakha yetzirekha began eden mikedem. Barukh ata Adonai, mesame'aḥ ḥatan vekhala.*

"Bring great joy to the loving companions, as You gave joy to Your creation in Eden in ancient times. Blessed are You, Lord, who brings joy to the groom and bride."

"The loving companions" are the bride and groom, and we pray that God will fill their lives with joy and happiness.

בָּרוּךְ אַתָּה אֲדֹנָי, אֱלֹהֵינוּ מֶלֶךְ הָעוֹלָם, אֲשֶׁר בָּרָא שָׂשׂוֹן וְשִׂמְחָה חָתָן וְכַלָּה, גִּילָה רִנָּה דִּיצָה וְחֶדְוָה, אַהֲבָה וְאַחֲוָה וְשָׁלוֹם וְרֵעוּת. מְהֵרָה אֲדֹנָי אֱלֹהֵינוּ יִשָּׁמַע בְּעָרֵי יְהוּדָה וּבְחוּצוֹת יְרוּשָׁלַיִם, קוֹל שָׂשׂוֹן וְקוֹל שִׂמְחָה, קוֹל חָתָן וְקוֹל כַּלָּה, קוֹל מִצְהֲלוֹת חֲתָנִים מֵחֻפָּתָם, וּנְעָרִים מִמִּשְׁתֵּה נְגִינָתָם. בָּרוּךְ אַתָּה אֲדֹנָי, מְשַׂמֵּחַ חָתָן עִם הַכַּלָּה.

Barukh ata Adonai, Eloheinu, melekh ha'olam, asher bara sason vesimḥa, ḥatan vekhala, gila rina ditza veḥedva, ahava ve'ahva, veshalom, vere'ut. Mehera, Adonai Eloheinu, yishama be'arei Yehuda uvḥutzot Yerushalayim: Kol sason vekol simḥa, kol ḥatan vekol kala, kol mitzhalot ḥatanim meḥupatam, unarim mimishteh neginatam. Barukh ata Adonai, mesame'aḥ ḥatan im hakala.

"Blessed are You, Lord our God, King of the universe, who has created joy and gladness, groom and bride, delight, exultation, happiness, jubilation, love, and brotherhood, and peace, and friendship. Soon, Lord our God, may there be heard in the cities of Judea and in the streets of Jerusalem the sound of joy and the sound of gladness, the sound of the groom and the sound of the bride, the joyous sound of grooms from their wedding canopy and of young people from their feast of song. Blessed are You, Lord, who brings joy to the groom together with the bride."

This blessing is for the entire Jewish people. It is a fervent request that we should merit very soon to rejoice in the "wedding" of the Jewish people with God, which will occur with the messianic redemption.

Breaking the Glass

At the conclusion of the seven blessings, the groom breaks a glass to commemorate the destruction of the Temple and Jerusalem. Before breaking the glass, it is customary to recite the following verses:

אִם אֶשְׁכָּחֵךְ יְרוּשָׁלַםִ תִּשְׁכַּח יְמִינִי. תִּדְבַּק
לְשׁוֹנִי לְחִכִּי אִם לֹא אֶזְכְּרֵכִי, אִם לֹא
אַעֲלֶה אֶת יְרוּשָׁלַםִ עַל רֹאשׁ שִׂמְחָתִי.

Im eshkaḥekh Yerushalayim tishkaḥ yemini. Tidbak leshoni leḥiki im lo ezkerekhi, im lo a'aleh et Yerushalayim al rosh simḥati.

"If I forget you, Jerusalem, let my right hand lose its power. Let my tongue cleave to my palate if I do not recall you, if I do not set Jerusalem above my foremost joy" (Psalms 137:5–6).

The breaking of the glass concludes the ceremony under the wedding canopy.

In some communities there are other customs concerning the stage at which the glass is broken, and how it is done.

Seclusion [*Yihud*]

According to Ashkenazic custom, immediately following the conclusion of the ceremony, the bride and groom go to a room known as the *yihud* room, where they spend a short time in seclusion. This also symbolizes the groom bringing his bride into his home. This room is locked, ensuring privacy. There is food available for them to break their fast. This stage ensures that the *nisu'in* stage of the marriage process has been completed according to virtually all opinions, and they are now husband and wife.

It is customary for witnesses to make sure that no one else is in the room before the bride and groom enter. After the bride and groom have enclosed themselves in the room, the witnesses remain outside the door to ensure that they indeed remain in seclusion for a few minutes, and to prevent any interference from those on the outside.

In most Sephardic communities, seclusion in a *yihud* room is not practiced. They follow the halakhic ruling that the marriage process is fully completed at the end of the wedding, when the groom takes the bride to their shared home.

The Week after the Wedding

The seven-day period after the wedding is a time of rejoicing and feasting for the bride and groom. The couple devotes these days to celebrating their marriage. They dress more formally and do not go to work. It is also customary that during these days neither the bride nor the groom leaves their home while unaccompanied. When they go together there is no need for additional accompaniment, but if only one of them leaves the house, he or she requires an escort. The reason is that on these days the bride and groom are likened to a queen and king, and it is not proper for royalty to walk the streets alone.

The Seven Days

The wedding day is included in the seven days of feasting. If the ceremony was held even a few moments before sunset, this short period of time is considered the first day, which is followed by six more days of rejoicing and festivity.

No *Tahanun*

During these seven days, when the groom is in the synagogue, the entire congregation omits the *Tahanun* prayer, which is not recited on days of rejoicing.

Further reading: For more on *Tahanun*, see p. 492.

A Second Marriage

The seven days of rejoicing are observed in celebration of the bride's first marriage. If it is the groom's first marriage but the bride's second marriage, some sources indicate that three days of rejoicing are observed while others indicate that the full seven days are observed. If it is the second marriage for both, only three days of rejoicing are observed, during which the bride and groom wear festive clothing and do not go to work.

The *Sheva Berakhot* Meals

During the seven days of rejoicing it is customary to hold festive meals with the bride and groom, at the end of which Grace after Meals is recited, followed by seven blessings. These are the same blessings that were recited under the wedding canopy (although in a slightly different order, as explained below). These meals are not obligatory, but they are a mitzva designed to enhance the bride and groom's joy, and an opportunity for others to share in their celebration. These meals are colloquially referred to as *sheva berakhot*, literally, seven blessings.

Where Are the Blessings Recited?

The *sheva berakhot* meals are held all week if it is the first marriage for either the groom or the bride. If both sides are remarrying, they recite the seven blessings only under the wedding canopy and at the conclusion of the wedding meal. After this, even though the next three days are days of rejoicing for them (see above), the seven blessings are not recited at the end of the meals.

In times past, it was customary for the bride and groom to remain throughout the seven days after the wedding in a special home that was prepared in honor of the wedding, and their relatives and friends would come to this house to rejoice with them. When this was the custom, the *halakha* was that the seven blessings would be recited only at meals held in the house of the bride and groom. Nowadays, however, it is customary to recite the seven blessings wherever a meal is held in honor of the bride and groom. Nevertheless, there are still some Sephardic communities that maintain the former custom, reciting the seven blessings only at the home of the bride and groom.

New Faces [*Panim Hadashot*]

In order to recite the seven blessings at the end of a meal, there must be a *minyan* present. There must also be a person who did not attend the wedding meal or any previous *sheva berakhot* meals celebrated for this couple. This individual is referred to as *panim hadashot*, literally, a new face. The reason for this is that the participation of a new person at the meal increases the joy of the occasion, justifying the recitation of the seven blessings.

On Shabbat and festivals, there is no need for *panim hadashot*; even if all those present at the meal had already attended previous meals, the seven blessings are recited. The rationale here is that Shabbat and festivals in and of themselves add joy to the occasion.

The above *halakha* applies to the Friday night meal and that of Shabbat morning. With regard to the third meal on Shabbat afternoon, Ashkenazim do not require *panim hadashot* at that meal either, whereas Sephardim maintain that *panim hadashot* is needed in order for the seven blessings to be recited.

If there is no *minyan* present, or if there is no one in attendance as *panim hadashot*, only the last of the special blessings, "who has created joy and gladness," is recited. Even this blessing may be said only if guests were invited and there are at least three men who can recite Grace after Meals with the special introduction [*zimmun*] (see the section dealing with the *halakhot* of Grace after Meals, p. 527). If no guests were invited, or there are not at least three men to perform a *zimmun*, the blessing of "who has created joy and gladness" is not recited either.

Further reading: For more on the *zimmun* before Grace after Meals, see p. 528.

Even in those situations in which only the blessing of "who has created joy and gladness" is said, one should still recite the blessing over wine, as explained below.

Whether all seven blessings are recited, or only the blessing of "who has created joy and gladness," one adds to the introduction to Grace after Meals the phrase, "in whose dwelling there is joy" [*shehasimḥa vimono*]. When the *zimmun* is recited by three men, they recite: "Blessed be He in whose dwelling there is joy, of whose bounty we have eaten." If there are ten males present, the formula is: "Blessed be our God in whose dwelling there is joy, of whose bounty we have eaten...."

The Seven Blessings

For Grace after Meals and the recitation of the seven blessings, two full cups of wine are used. The Grace after Meals is recited over one of the cups, while the second cup is used for the seven blessings.

The procedure is as follows: The person leading the *zimmun* raises a cup of wine in his right hand and starts the *zimmun*, followed by Grace after Meals. Afterward, six blessings are recited over the second cup of wine. These are the same blessings that were recited under the wedding canopy, but without first reciting the blessing on wine. It is customary to honor several guests by passing the cup from one to the other, each man reciting one of the blessings. After the conclusion of six blessings, the one who led the *zimmun* recites the blessing on the wine over the cup in his hand and drinks from it. After he has taken a drink, the wine of the one leading the *zimmun* is mixed with the wine in the cup over which the rest of the blessings were recited. One of the two cups is then served to the groom and the men around him, while the second cup is given to the bride and the women around her.

The Shabbat after the Wedding

The Shabbat after the wedding is called the *Shabbat Hatan*, the "groom's Shabbat," by Sephardim, while Ashkenazim call it the "Shabbat *sheva berakhot*." On this Shabbat, in addition to the seven blessings that are recited at the end of the meal as discussed above, it is customary to call up the groom to the Torah and, if possible, to honor him with the reading of the *haftara*. Some host a *kiddush* or a full meal for the worshippers at the synagogue after the morning prayers.

Acquiring a Grave, Inheritances, and Wills

According to the Jewish view, a person's existence does not end with his departure from this world. Rather, his soul, which is his real self, sheds its attachment to its physical body and moves on to the World to Come, where it receives its reward for all the good deeds it has performed during its years of life in the physical world. It is stated in the Mishna (*Avot* 4:16): "This world is comparable to a vestibule to the World to Come; prepare yourself in the vestibule so that you may enter the palatial chamber." It states further in the same tractate: "At the time of death, a person is accompanied not by his silver or gold or precious stones or gems, but by his Torah and good deeds alone" (*Avot* 6:9).

These two mishnaic statements provide a proper perspective on life and guide us toward the next stage of existence, of which one should always be cognizant, and for which one should constantly be preparing. This emphasis on the World to Come applies both to one's values and to one's behavior, two elements that are always intertwined in Judaism. With this in mind, we move to a discussion of the *halakhot* of buying a grave, inheritances, and wills.

Burial and the Choice of a Burial Place

The last mitzva that is fulfilled with a person's body is his burial, as it is a mitzva to bury the dead. In the book of Genesis, it is written: "By the sweat of your brow shall you eat bread, until you return to the ground; for from it were you taken; for you are dust, and to dust shall you return" (3:19). There is a moral and symbolic aspect to this mitzva: A person completes his role in this world and returns to the point from which everything began, which is dust.

The Talmud (*Sanhedrin* 32b) adds two reasons for burials:

(1) burial provides atonement for the deceased;

(2) burial honors the family of the deceased, who took care to provide a proper grave for him.

Purchasing a Burial Plot during One's Lifetime

Some have the custom of buying a burial plot for themselves. There are both practical and conceptual reasons for this custom.

From a practical perspective: A person may want to be buried in a specific cemetery, or even in a specific plot in a cemetery, in order to be buried close to loved ones. Even in Israel, where each person is entitled to a burial free of charge in his local cemetery, one may wish to be buried outside his hometown. In such a case, he must purchase his chosen burial plot with his own money.

From a halakhic perspective it is preferable for a person to be buried in a grave that belongs to him. Accordingly, it is desirable to purchase a burial plot rather than to receive it.

Another rationale for buying a burial plot during one's lifetime is that this acquisition is considered to be a favorable omen, a *segula*, for longevity.

The Jewish burial practiced for generations involved entombing the body in the ground, without a casket, and this is indeed the general practice in Israel today. Only in certain cases, such as military funerals, are caskets used. Outside of Israel, however, it is common to bury the body in a casket.

Burial in Tiers

Due to the ever-growing shortage of burial space in Israel, some cemeteries have begun burying people in multi-tiered burial structures. Burial societies refer to this method as "the burial of the Sanhedrin," because the graves of the Sanhedrin and similar sites that have been discovered in Jerusalem and elsewhere in the country are not underground, but rather within crypts hewn into the bedrock.

Is the multi-tiered formation a desirable form of burial? The halakhic discussion concerning this issue focuses on the question of whether this is considered burial in the ground. On the one hand, the entire structure is connected to the ground. On the other hand, the deceased is interred above ground level. If one is unsure as to how to proceed, it is recommended to consult a rabbi.

Nowadays, some cemeteries offer other forms of burial, such as the burial of both spouses in one grave in the ground, one above the other, separated by a layer of earth. Here too, if one is uncertain, he should consult a rabbi.

Dividing an Estate

A person obviously does not take his worldly possessions with him after his passing. His estate is inherited by his children in accordance with the relevant *halakhot*, or he can write a will in his lifetime and thereby determine how his estate is divided. It is important to note that the *halakhot* of inheritance do not correspond to the civil laws of inheritance. Advanced planning is advised in order to ensure that the estate is divided peacefully and in a manner that accounts for *halakha*.

The Division

These are the main differences between the laws of inheritance in Jewish law and the inheritance laws of many countries: By Torah law, a father's firstborn son receives a double portion of inheritance compared with the individual portions of each of the other sons; daughters do not inherit unless the deceased had no sons; a wife does not inherit her husband's inheritance. By contrast, according to common civil laws of inheritance, the inheritance is divided equally between the surviving spouse and the children, with the spouse receiving one half, and each of the children, sons and daughters alike, receiving an equal share in the remaining half.

The Solution

According to civil law, a written and signed will overrides the inheritance laws. In his will, one may instruct that his estate be divided however he sees fit. He can bequeath an extra portion to his firstborn son; he can stipulate that only his sons, and not his daughters, will share the property; he can favor a certain son over the others; he can bequeath his assets to his daughters alone; he can even exclude his children from his property entirely and leave everything to a total stranger or an institution.

From a halakhic perspective, if one distributes his assets to others and does not leave his children any inheritance at all, it is stated that "the Sages are displeased with him" (*Bava Batra* 133b), and the general directive to those who are around him is not to cooperate, and not to sign such a will. A document that is not signed by two witnesses is invalid.

Moreover, long ago the rabbis were aware of possible tensions and rivalries that could result from an unequal distribution of an inheritance among family members. They therefore recommended that each person distribute his or her property as equally as possible, by writing a will that does not discriminate against any of the sons or daughters. A written will is an entirely acceptable option by Torah law. Nevertheless, in order not to uproot entirely the laws of inheritance prescribed by the Torah, the rabbis recommended leaving out of the will a symbolic sum of money to be divided according to the Torah's principles of inheritance.

📖 **Further reading:** For statements of the Sages on treating family members equally and the inadvisability of disinheriting a child, see *A Concise Guide to the Sages*, p. 405.

Writing a Will

Writing a will is a complicated matter, both halakhically and legally. In order for a will to be executed according to Jewish law, it must stipulate that the assets are acquired by those to whom they have been bequeathed before the death of the individual writing the will. This is because the halakhic laws of inheritance take effect immediately upon death, and at that point a will is no longer effective to remove assets from the rightful heirs. By contrast, according to secular law, a will can take effect even after death, and it overrides the laws of inheritance. Since the *halakhot* of inheritance do not accord with local inheritance laws, as stated above, it is necessary to write the document in a way that will be binding both legally and halakhically.

In light of this complexity, and to prevent potential conflicts among the heirs, it is recommended to consult with experts in the field who are familiar with all the relevant halakhic and legal aspects of wills and inheritance.

From Death to the Funeral

The Torah encompasses the entire life of a person, from birth until death, and it instructs us how to behave after a person has returned his soul to his Creator. The Sages state: "Against your will you are created, against your will you are born, against your will you live, and against your will you die" (Mishna *Avot* 4:22). In other words, it is not we who determine when we will be born and when our lives will come to an end; rather, these matters are in the hands of God. Our awareness of this fact provides strength in challenging moments. Nonetheless, the loss of a loved one is a painful experience, and often leads to uncertainty and difficult decisions. The Torah stands beside us and illuminates our path even in this emotionally complex time.

This section deals with the laws pertaining to the hours before death, as well as death itself and everything that follows, up to the time of the funeral.

Shortening and Extending Life

A challenging issue that often arises in modern times is the possibility of shortening the life of a terminally ill patient by hours or days. It is important to realize that as long as a person is alive, it is strictly prohibited to hasten his death. The *halakha* even warns against moving a dying person or closing his eyes, as this might hasten his death. The Torah does not distinguish between the murder of an infant, the killing of a person in his prime, or an action that shortens the life of a dying man struggling for his last breaths. Human life is not measured in qualitative terms, but is considered absolutely sacred, and it is strictly prohibited to bring about its termination. Nevertheless, a distinction must be made between shortening a life and artificially prolonging a life, which in some cases does not need to be done.

Early Consultation

The advancement of modern medicine enables the extension of human life by artificial means, and this is certainly a welcome development. But sometimes this entails the suffering of the dying individual as well as his family. When a person is about to die, and he – or his family, in a situation in which the patient himself is unable to respond or make decisions – seeks to avoid prolonging his life, one must consult both a physician and a halakhic authority who is proficient in this area, and only then make a decision.

Organ Donation

Thanks to remarkable recent developments in organ transplantation, it is now possible to save lives by removing organs and tissues from the dead and transplanting them into a patient who needs them. The donation of organs involves the fulfillment of the greatest mitzva of saving lives, but it also entails difficult halakhic questions that require careful investigation.

Brain Death and Cardiac Death

One of the major problems in the field of organ transplantation is the question of determining death. There are organs and tissues that can be removed after a person has died completely and his heart has stopped beating, but many body parts can be successfully transplanted only if they are removed from the donor while the heart is still beating. Organs are harvested from patients who have experienced brain death, but whose hearts are still beating.

This brings to the fore the question of defining the moment of death, for the removal of organs before death would be strictly prohibited according to *halakha*. There is no conformity of opinion between the halakhic authorities and doctors on this issue. Given the gravity and complexity of this matter, it is essential that both medical and halakhic authorities be consulted in determining the death of a person. Together they will establish that the person is indeed dead, which means that the removal of his organs is not considered murder.

Adi Card

In recent years in Israel, there has been a widespread campaign to encourage people to sign an "Adi card." This signature is a declaration of the fundamental willingness of a person to donate his organs after his death, for transplantation into other humans. By law, the family of the deceased can refuse to donate the organs even though the deceased had signed such a card. The converse is also true: Even if a person had not signed a donor card, his family has the right to decide to donate his organs, unless the deceased announced in advance his objection to this.

At the time of the signing of the Adi card in Israel, there is the option of adding the clause: "Provided that a religious authority of the family's choosing will approve the donation after my death." Signing such a card with the above addition should ensure that the procedure, if technically and medically possible, will be performed according to *halakha*, as well as secular law and medical ethics.

The Recitation of Confession

When a person is about to leave this world, he should confess his sins. Confession is an expression of remorse for one's transgressions and a request from God that death itself should serve as atonement for these sins.

Atonement for Sin

When a person is critically ill, a dilemma often arises over the message that should be conveyed to him: Should one offer him words of encouragement and urge him to fight his illness and hope for recovery? Or should the state of affairs be presented to him in a realistic manner, and thereby perhaps help him to prepare properly for his death, which will also aid his soul in its future path? A highly sensitive formulation has been created that should be presented to the patient in such a circumstance:

הַרְבֵּה הִתְוַדּוּ וְלֹא מֵתוּ, וְהַרְבֵּה שֶׁלֹּא הִתְוַדּוּ מֵתוּ, וּבִשְׂכַר שֶׁאַתָּה מִתְוַדֶּה אַתָּה
חַי, וְכָל הַמִּתְוַדֶּה יֵשׁ לוֹ חֵלֶק לָעוֹלָם הַבָּא.

"Many have recited confessions and not died, and many have not recited confessions and have died. In reward for confessing, you shall live, and whoever confesses has a portion in the World to Come."

Formula of the Confession

The following is the translation of the formula of the confession:

אֱלֹהֵינוּ וֵאלֹהֵי אֲבוֹתֵינוּ. תָּבוֹא לְפָנֶיךָ תְּפִלָּתֵנוּ וְאַל תִּתְעַלַּם מִתְּחִנָּתֵנוּ. שֶׁאֵין
אָנוּ עַזֵּי פָנִים וּקְשֵׁי עֹרֶף לוֹמַר לְפָנֶיךָ: אֲדֹנָי אֱלֹהֵינוּ וֵאלֹהֵי אֲבוֹתֵינוּ, צַדִּיקִים
אֲנַחְנוּ וְלֹא חָטָאנוּ, אֲבָל אֲנַחְנוּ וַאֲבוֹתֵינוּ חָטָאנוּ.

אָשַׁמְנוּ, בָּגַדְנוּ, גָּזַלְנוּ, דִּבַּרְנוּ דֹפִי. הֶעֱוִינוּ, וְהִרְשַׁעְנוּ, זַדְנוּ, חָמַסְנוּ, טָפַלְנוּ שֶׁקֶר.
יָעַצְנוּ רָע, כִּזַּבְנוּ, לַצְנוּ, מָרַדְנוּ, נִאַצְנוּ, סָרַרְנוּ, עָוִינוּ, פָּשַׁעְנוּ, צָרַרְנוּ, קִשִּׁינוּ עֹרֶף.
רָשַׁעְנוּ, שִׁחַתְנוּ, תִּעַבְנוּ, תָּעִינוּ, תִּעְתָּעְנוּ.

סַרְנוּ מִמִּצְוֹתֶיךָ וּמִמִּשְׁפָּטֶיךָ הַטּוֹבִים וְלֹא שָׁוָה לָנוּ. וְאַתָּה צַדִּיק עַל כָּל הַבָּא
עָלֵינוּ, כִּי אֱמֶת עָשִׂיתָ, וַאֲנַחְנוּ הִרְשָׁעְנוּ.

"Our God and the God of our fathers, may our prayers come before You, and do not hide Yourself from our supplication, as we are not so arrogant or stubborn as to say before You, Lord, our God and God of our fathers, that we are righteous and have not sinned, but we and our fathers have sinned.

"We have transgressed, we have acted treacherously, we have robbed, we have spoken slander. We have acted perversely, and we have acted wickedly,

Life Cycle

we have acted presumptuously, we have performed violence, we have framed lies. We have given bad advice, we have deceived, we have scorned, we have rebelled, we have provoked, we have turned away, we have committed iniquity, we have transgressed, we have persecuted, we have been obstinate. We have acted wickedly, we have corrupted, we have acted abominably, we have strayed, we have spoken in derision. We have turned away from Your commandments and good laws, to no avail. You are just in all that befalls us, as You have acted faithfully, and we have done wickedly."

If it is not possible to recite the above version, one should say instead:

מוֹדֶה (לאשה: מוֹדָה) אֲנִי לְפָנֶיךָ, אֲדֹנָי אֱלֹהַי וַאלֹהֵי אֲבוֹתַי, שֶׁרְפוּאָתִי וּמִיתָתִי בְּיָדֶךָ. יְהִי רָצוֹן מִלְּפָנֶיךָ, שֶׁתִּרְפָּאֵנִי רְפוּאָה שְׁלֵמָה, וְאִם אָמוּת תְּהֵא מִיתָתִי כַּפָּרָה עַל כָּל חֲטָאִים וַעֲוֹנוֹת וּפְשָׁעִים שֶׁחָטָאתִי וְשֶׁעָוִיתִי וְשֶׁפָּשַׁעְתִּי לְפָנֶיךָ, וְתֵן חֶלְקִי בְּגַן עֵדֶן, וְזַכֵּנִי לָעוֹלָם הַבָּא הַצָּפוּן לַצַּדִּיקִים.

"I acknowledge before You, Lord, my God, God of my fathers, that my recovery and my death are in Your hand. May it be Your will that You heal me completely, but if I die, let my death be atonement for all the sins, transgressions, and rebellious acts with which I have sinned, transgressed, and rebelled before You. Grant me a portion in the Garden of Eden, and grant me the merit to partake of the World to Come, which is stored away for the righteous."

If one does not have the ability or time for even that version, the basic formula of the confession is:

מִיתָתִי תְּהֵא כַּפָּרָה עַל כָּל עֲוֹנוֹתַי.

"May my death be atonement for all my transgressions."

If the patient is able to do so, he should recite the full text of the long confession which appears in the Yom Kippur prayers.

Among some Sephardic communities, it is customary to recite the liturgical poem, "My yearning, God, is to You," which includes the entire text of the confession. The text can be found in Sephardic prayer books.

It is recommended for the individual to also recite the following psalms if he is able: 16, 23, 25, 51, 91, 102, 103, 121, 139, 142.

In the case of a dying man who cannot utter the words verbally, those surrounding him should recite the words to him so that he may contemplate them in his mind.

When it is suggested to a patient that he recite the confession, one should try to make sure that no children or especially sensitive people are present, as their crying could cause the dying man even further discomfort.

The Departure of the Soul

One must ensure that the deceased is not alone when he passes away, and it is a virtuous act to be with him at this hour. Some try to have ten men (a *minyan*) in the room at the time of death.

Immediately after Death

It is customary to light a yahrzeit candle next to the deceased after his departure. This practice is based on the verse: "The soul of man is the lamp of the Lord" (Proverbs 20:27), meaning that one's soul is comparable to a candle, the lamp of God.

After death has definitively been established, the face of the deceased should be covered.

One who is present at the death of a Jew must tear his garment (see below). If the death occurred on a Shabbat, when ripping of clothing is not permitted, some maintain that he must tear his clothes after Shabbat, while others contend that he need not tear them at all.

Nonetheless, the contemporary custom in many places is not to tear one's clothing at the time of death. The reason for this leniency is to prevent people from avoiding being present alongside the deceased at the time of his death.

Relatives of the first degree, meaning spouses, parents, siblings, and children, tear their garments during the funeral (see below). In this regard, half-brothers and half-sisters are also classified as first-degree relatives.

A divorced man or woman is not considered a mourner for an ex-spouse. They do not tear their garments or sit shiva. Likewise, more distant relatives do not tear their garments and do not sit shiva.

Guarding the Dead

From the moment of death until burial, the body of a dead person may not be left alone. Two reasons are given for this:

(1) It is an honor for the deceased, as leaving the body alone gives the impression that no one is interested in him.

(2) There are spiritually harmful beings that seek to reach the person's body between death and burial, in order to harm him. The presence of a living person prevents these beings from approaching the deceased. It is

customary for the person guarding the deceased to sit and recite psalms. This obligation to guard the dead body also applies on Shabbat.

The guard is exempt from the fulfillment of mitzvot (such as the recitation of *Shema*), similar to an *onen* (an acute mourner; see below). In a case where there is another person available to replace him as the guard, he should leave the room, recite *Shema*, and then resume his place by the deceased.

One may not eat or recite blessings in the presence of the deceased, nor may one be in his immediate vicinity while wearing *tefillin* or with his ritual fringes visible. A person who has died is obviously no longer capable of doing mitzvot, so fulfilling mitzvot in his presence is considered like taunting him. To do so would be a violation of the verse, "Whoever mocks the poor blasphemes his Maker" (Proverbs 17:5).

The Start of Mourning

The stages following the death of a close relative are as follows, in chronological order:

(1) Acute mourning [*aninut*]

(2) The funeral

(3) The shiva

(4) The first thirty days [*sheloshim*]

(5) The first year

The following details refer to the period from the time of death until the funeral. The *halakhot* of the funeral itself, the days of the shiva, and the first thirty days will be presented in subsequent chapters.

> **Further reading:** The various stages of mourning correspond to the stages of the separation of the soul from the body; see *A Concise Guide to Mahshava*, p. 26.

Acute Mourning

When someone's first-degree relative dies, he is an called an *onen*, an acute mourner, from the time of death until the burial. The Sages exempted the *onen* from all positive commandments, due to the sorrow he feels over the passing and the need to focus on preparations for the funeral. Among other things, he is exempt from reciting prayers and blessings. Nevertheless, he may not actively violate any prohibitions. Thus, for example, he may not eat non-kosher food.

All the obligations of mourning that are in force during the shiva (see below) apply to the *onen* as well, with the following exceptions: the *onen* may continue to wear his shoes, even if they are of leather; he is not required to sit on a low stool; and he may leave his house freely. However, an *onen* may not eat meat or drink wine.

If a person is an *onen* on Shabbat, e.g., if a relative died on Shabbat or if he died earlier but there was not enough time to bury him before Shabbat, the laws of acute mourning do not apply to him. This means that throughout that Shabbat he is obligated to observe all the mitzvot and he may eat meat and drink wine. In such a case, however, the *onen* does not perform *Havdala* after Shabbat, but waits and does so only after the funeral.

📖 **Further reading:** The full details of the laws of mourning can be found in the next section, p. 85.

Arranging the Funeral

One should contact the local Jewish burial society [*hevra kadisha*] to coordinate a time for the funeral. In most cities and communities in Israel there is only one burial society, which operates on behalf of the local Religious Council. In certain large cities in Israel (Jerusalem, Haifa, B'nei Brak, and a few more), one can choose between different burial societies, which follow the customs of the various segments of the community. These societies take care of the purification and preparation of the body for burial in accordance with their respective custom. Outside of Israel, the burial society is often connected to the synagogue, and is sometimes an independent communal organization.

Time of the Funeral

In determining the time of the funeral, the following considerations should be taken into account:

It is prohibited to leave the dead body overnight without burial when there is no justifiable reason to do so. Yet, it is permitted to delay the burial out of respect for the dead. Examples of this include if there was not enough time to get word of the death and funeral to relatives and acquaintances, if no suitable place has been found yet for the burial, or if one wishes to wait for the arrival of a family member who is abroad.

The *hevra kadisha* might have its own constraints in determining the time of the funeral. For example, if another funeral is already scheduled for a particular time and they do not have enough manpower to conduct a second funeral at the same time, they might adjust the time accordingly. The same applies if there is a fear of overcrowding in the cemetery. Therefore, it is their job to schedule the funerals in a manner that is most comfortable for all.

In Jerusalem, it is prohibited to leave the dead overnight even if it is for the honor of the deceased, although this technically applies only within the Old City walls and a little beyond. Consequently, if a person passes away in other parts of Jerusalem in the evening and the family wants to wait and hold his funeral the next day so that there is time for people to find out about the funeral, this is permitted in principle. Nevertheless, the custom has been established throughout Jerusalem to try to avoid this situation, and therefore in this city, funerals are conducted even late at night.

When a funeral ends before sunset, the time remaining until sunset, even if it is only a few minutes, is considered the first day of the seven days of mourning; only six days of mourning would then remain. This can also be a relevant consideration when deciding whether to hold the funeral in the afternoon or to postpone it to the next day.

The Place of Burial

A *kohen* is prohibited from being in close proximity to graves. Consequently, if the deceased and his family are *kohanim*, the *hevra kadisha* should be informed of this so that they can arrange a burial place that provides access to *kohanim*. There are also other customs that apply specifically to the burial of *kohanim*.

If a burial plot was purchased in advance by the deceased or on his behalf, the *hevra kadisha* should be informed of this as well.

Attending the Funeral

It is considered an honor to the deceased for as many people as possible to attend his funeral. Therefore, it is important to inform the general public of the death and to publicize the time and location of the funeral. In Israel this is often accomplished by means of obituary notices posted in public places, but the use of any kind of media can be equally suitable for this purpose.

The Funeral and Burial

It is a great mitzva to accompany the deceased to his final resting place, this being the last act of kindness performed for a person. The funeral procession is the first step in the separation process of the mourners and the rest of the living from the deceased. They accompany him to the cemetery, where he will be buried in the ground, as it is stated: "For you are dust, and to dust shall you return" (Genesis 3:19). This section details the stages of the funeral process until the completion of the burial.

The Start of the Funeral

Usually the funeral starts at the funeral home, where the deceased is also prepared and purified for the funeral. There are places where there is no funeral home, in which case the funeral procession starts from the synagogue or from some other central location. One can also begin the funeral procession from the home of the deceased. When the family wishes to start the funeral procession from a less standard location, they should coordinate this with the members of the *hevra kadisha*.

Tearing Clothing and Reciting the Blessing

The Ashkenazic custom is for the mourners to tear their garments at the beginning of the funeral and recite this blessing:

בָּרוּךְ אַתָּה אֲדֹנָי, אֱלֹהֵינוּ מֶלֶךְ הָעוֹלָם,
דַּיַּן הָאֱמֶת.

Barukh ata Adonai, Eloheinu, melekh ha'olam, dayan ha'emet.

"Blessed are You, Lord our God, King of the universe, the true Judge."

Through this blessing, the mourners express the belief that death is a common fact of the natural world, which is directed by God, and that the judgment of God is true and just. This attitude, of the justification and acceptance of God's judgment, finds further expression in the continuation of the funeral as well, and also in the specific version of the Kaddish prayer recited by the mourners.

The standard explanation for the tearing of one's garment is that this act demonstrates the deep sorrow that the mourners feel over the death of their loved one. Some explain that on the contrary, tearing the garment helps one deal with the emotionally difficult moments by means of an action that temporarily diverts the mourner's attention.

Sephardic custom is to perform the tearing of the garments and to recite the blessing above after the conclusion of the funeral.

For the passing of siblings, children, and spouses, the mourners tear the garment from the collar down, for the length of roughly eight centimeters on the right side of the chest, and they tear the outer garment only. In the case of the passing of parents, the mourners tear the garment on the left side, down to the place of the heart, and they tear all the upper layers they are wearing (apart from the undershirt). It is customary to start the tear with a knife, and to tear the rest by hand. The tearing should be performed while standing.

Some observe the custom that someone else tears the garment for the mourner, while others have the custom that the mourners themselves tear the garment.

The mourner continues to wear the torn garment throughout the shiva. When mourning for siblings, children, and spouses, the mourners may change their garment during the shiva for a different item of clothing, which need not be torn. When mourning for parents, they must remain with a torn garment until the end of the shiva. If they nevertheless wish to change clothes, they must tear the alternative garment as well.

When a funeral takes place on the intermediate festival days [Hol HaMoed] of Sukkot or Passover, there are different opinions regarding the tearing. The local rabbi or members of the hevra kadisha should be consulted.

If an immediate family member died while the mourner was wearing an important or expensive garment, he may change into a less expensive garment before the funeral so that he can tear the less expensive garment.

If he is mourning for two relatives, the mourner performs only one act of tearing. But if one of the deceased relatives is his father or mother and the other is a sibling, a child, or a spouse, then two tears must be made, one on each side of the garment, in accordance with the aforementioned specifications.

Eulogies

It is customary to eulogize the deceased before the funeral procession. Indeed, it is a mitzva to eulogize him and praise his virtues and good deeds.

The purpose of the eulogy is to honor the deceased and to encourage the living to follow his virtuous actions.

When eulogizing a person, one should not lie or grossly misrepresent who the individual was and what he stood for. However, it is proper to focus on his strengths and to present him in a positive light. One may eulogize briefly or speak at length, but one should try not to overly inconvenience those who have come to pay their respects to the deceased.

If the deceased requested before his death that he should not be eulogized, his wishes should be respected. There are a small number of communities where it is customary that eulogies are not said at all.

In most instances, if the funeral procession starts from a synagogue, the eulogies should be delivered outside, not in the building.

There are certain times of year when it is permitted to bury the dead, but not to eulogize them: *Rosh Hodesh*, Hanukkah, the two days of Purim (fourteenth and fifteenth of Adar), and, in a leap year, "*Purim Katan*" (the fourteenth and fifteenth of Adar I). Some maintain that it is permitted to deliver a eulogy on *Purim Katan*. Eulogies are not given on the intermediate festival days [*Hol HaMoed*] of *Sukkot* and Passover, or at any time during the month of Nisan. According to some opinions, no eulogies are delivered on the fourteenth of Iyar, which is known as "Second *Pesah*." In each of these cases one should ask a rabbi how to proceed.

If the deceased was a great Torah scholar, he is eulogized even if the funeral is held on one of the above dates (with the exception of the intermediate festival days). But even in the case of a Torah scholar, eulogies should be kept short on these dates.

The Funeral Procession

After the eulogies, the funeral procession moves from the funeral home to the gravesite. It is a great mitzva to accompany the dead and join the funeral procession.

Kaddish

During the funeral procession, the rabbi or members of the *hevra kadisha* recite psalms and other verses. In some communities, the procession pauses for the mourners to recite the Kaddish again. Below is the wording of the Kaddish according to the different communities.

Further reading: For more details on the Kaddish recited throughout the year of mourning, see the chapter on Kaddish, p. 500.

Ashkenazim say:

האבלים: יִתְגַּדַּל וְיִתְקַדַּשׁ שְׁמֵהּ רַבָּא.

Mourner: *Yitgadal veyitkadash shemeh raba*

הקהל עונה: אָמֵן.

Congregation: *Amen.*

האבלים: בְּעָלְמָא דִּי בְרָא כִרְעוּתֵהּ, וְיַמְלִיךְ מַלְכוּתֵהּ, (המתפללים בנוסח ספרד מוסיפים: וְיַצְמַח פֻּרְקָנֵהּ, וִיקָרֵב מְשִׁיחֵהּ.

Mourner: *be'alma di vera khiruteh, veyamlikh malkhuteh* (some add: *veyatzmaḥ purkaneh vikarev meshiḥeh*

הקהל עונה: אָמֵן.)

Congregation: *Amen.*)

האבלים: בְּחַיֵּיכוֹן וּבְיוֹמֵיכוֹן וּבְחַיֵּי דְכָל בֵּית יִשְׂרָאֵל, בַּעֲגָלָא וּבִזְמַן קָרִיב, וְאִמְרוּ אָמֵן.

Mourner: *beḥayeikhon uvyomeikhon, uvḥayey dekhol beit Yisrael, ba'agala uvizman kariv, ve'imru amen.*

הקהל עונה: אָמֵן.

Congregation: *Amen.*

ומיד מצטרפים גם האבלים: יְהֵא שְׁמֵהּ רַבָּא מְבָרַךְ לְעָלַם וּלְעָלְמֵי עָלְמַיָּא.

Congregation and mourner: *Yehe shemeh rabba mevarakh le'alam ul'a'lemei a'lemaya.*

האבלים: יִתְבָּרַךְ וְיִשְׁתַּבַּח וְיִתְפָּאַר וְיִתְרוֹמַם וְיִתְנַשֵּׂא וְיִתְהַדָּר וְיִתְעַלֶּה וְיִתְהַלָּל שְׁמֵהּ דְּקֻדְשָׁא, בְּרִיךְ הוּא.

Mourner: *Yitbarakh veyishtabaḥ veyitpa'ar veyitromam veyitnaseh veyit'hadar veyitaleh veyit'hallal shemeh dekudsha berikh hu.*

הקהל עונה: בְּרִיךְ הוּא או אָמֵן.

Congregation: *Berikh hu* or: *Amen.*

האבלים: לְעֵלָּא מִן כָּל (בעשרת ימי תשובה: לְעֵלָּא לְעֵלָּא מִכָּל) בִּרְכָתָא וְשִׁירָתָא, תֻּשְׁבְּחָתָא וְנֶחֱמָתָא, דַּאֲמִירָן בְּעָלְמָא, וְאִמְרוּ אָמֵן.

Mourner: *le'ela min kol* (during the Ten Days of Repentance: *le'ela ul'ela mikol*) *birkhata veshirata tushbeḥata veneḥemata, da'amiran be'a'lema ve'imru amen.*

הקהל עונה: אָמֵן.

Congregation: *Amen.*

הָאֲבֵלִים: יְהֵא שְׁלָמָא רַבָּא מִן שְׁמַיָּא, וְחַיִּים טוֹבִים עָלֵינוּ וְעַל כָּל יִשְׂרָאֵל, וְאִמְרוּ אָמֵן.

Mourner: *Yehe shelama raba min sh-emaya vehayim* (some add: *tovim*) *aleinu ve'al kol Yisrael, ve'imru amen.*

הַקָּהָל עוֹנֶה: אָמֵן.

Congregation: *Amen.*

הָאֲבֵלִים (פּוֹסְעִים שָׁלוֹשׁ פְּסִיעוֹת לְאָחוֹר וְאוֹמְרִים): עֹשֶׂה שָׁלוֹם (בַּעֲשֶׂרֶת יְמֵי תְּשׁוּבָה: הַשָּׁלוֹם) בִּמְרוֹמָיו, הוּא יַעֲשֶׂה שָׁלוֹם עָלֵינוּ וְעַל כָּל יִשְׂרָאֵל, וְאִמְרוּ אָמֵן.

Mourner takes three steps backward and says: *Oseh shalom* (in the Ten Days of Repentance: *hashalom*) *bim-romav, hu* (some add: *verahamav*) *ya'aseh shalom aleinu, ve'al kol Yisrael, ve'imru amen.* Congregation: *Amen.*

Mourner: "May His great name be exalted and sanctified,"

Congregation: "Amen."

Mourner: "in the world He created according to His will, and may He establish His kingdom"

(those who pray in *Nusah Sefarad* add: "bring forth His redemption, and hasten the coming of His messiah,"

Congregation: "Amen.")

Mourner: "in your lifetime and in your days, and in the lifetime of all the house of Israel, swiftly and soon, and say: Amen."

Congregation: "Amen."

Congregation and mourner: "May His great name be blessed forever and for all time."

Mourner: "Blessed and praised, glorified and exalted, raised and honored, uplifted and lauded, be the name of the Holy One, blessed be He,"

Congregation: "Blessed be He," or "Amen."

Mourner: "beyond (during the Ten Days of Repentance: far beyond) all the blessings, songs, praises, and consolations that are spoken in the world, and say: Amen."

Congregation: "Amen."

Mourner: "May there be abundant peace from Heaven and life, for us and all Israel, and say: Amen."

Congregation: "Amen."

Mourner takes three steps backward and says: "May He who makes peace in His high place make peace for us and all Israel, and say: Amen."

Congregation: "Amen."

Sephardim say:

האבלים: יִתְגַּדַּל וְיִתְקַדַּשׁ שְׁמֵהּ רַבָּא.

Mourner: *Yitgadal veyitkadash shemeh raba*

הקהל עונה: אָמֵן.

Congregation: *Amen.*

האבלים: בְּעָלְמָא דִּי בְרָא כִרְעוּתֵהּ, וְיַמְלִיךְ מַלְכוּתֵהּ, וְיַצְמַח פֻּרְקָנֵהּ, וִיקָרֵב מְשִׁיחֵהּ.

Mourner: *be'alma di vera khiruteh, veyamlikh malkhuteh veyatzmaḥ purkaneh vikarev meshiḥeh*

הקהל עונה: אָמֵן.

Congregation: *Amen.*

האבלים: בְּחַיֵּיכוֹן וּבְיוֹמֵיכוֹן וּבְחַיֵּי דְכָל בֵּית יִשְׂרָאֵל, בַּעֲגָלָא וּבִזְמַן קָרִיב וְאִמְרוּ אָמֵן.

Mourner: *behayeikhon uvyomeikhon, uvhayey dekhol beit Yisrael, ba'agala uvizman kariv, ve'imru amen.*

הקהל עונה: אָמֵן.

Congregation: *Amen.*

האבלים: יְהֵא שְׁמֵהּ רַבָּא מְבָרַךְ לְעָלַם וּלְעָלְמֵי עָלְמַיָּא

Mourner: *Yehe shemeh rabba mevarakh le'alam ul'a'lemei a'lemaya.*

יִתְבָּרַךְ וְיִשְׁתַּבַּח וְיִתְפָּאַר וְיִתְרוֹמַם וְיִתְנַשֵּׂא וְיִתְהַדָּר וְיִתְעַלֶּה וְיִתְהַלָּל שְׁמֵהּ דְּקֻדְשָׁא, בְּרִיךְ הוּא.

Mourner: *Yitbarakh veyishtabaḥ veyitpa'ar veyitromam veyitnaseh veyit'hadar veyitaleh veyit'hallal shemeh dekudsha berikh hu,*

הקהל עונה: אָמֵן.

Congregation: *Amen.*

האבלים: לְעֵלָּא מִן כָּל בִּרְכָתָא, שִׁירָתָא, תֻּשְׁבְּחָתָא וְנֶחֱמָתָא דַּאֲמִירָן בְּעָלְמָא, וְאִמְרוּ אָמֵן.

Mourner: *le'ela min kol birkhata veshirata tushbeḥata veneḥemata, da'amiran be'a'lema ve'imru amen.*

הקהל עונה: אָמֵן.

Congregation: *Amen.*

האבלים: יְהֵא שְׁלָמָא רַבָּא מִן שְׁמַיָּא. חַיִּים וְשָׂבָע, וִישׁוּעָה וְנֶחָמָה, וְשֵׁיזָבָא וּרְפוּאָה, וּגְאֻלָּה וּסְלִיחָה וְכַפָּרָה, וְרֶוַח וְהַצָּלָה. לָנוּ וּלְכָל עַמּוֹ יִשְׂרָאֵל, וְאִמְרוּ אָמֵן.

Mourner: *Yehe shelama raba min shemaya ḥayim vesava vishu'a veneḥama veshezava urfu'a ugula u'seliḥa vekhapara vereveḥ vehatzala, lanu ulkhol amo Yisrael, ve'imru amen.*

הקהל עונה: אָמֵן.   Congregation: *Amen.*

הָאֲבֵלִים (פּוֹסְעִים שָׁלוֹשׁ פְּסִיעוֹת לְאָחוֹר   Mourner takes three steps backward
וְאוֹמְרִים): עֹשֶׂה שָׁלוֹם בִּמְרוֹמָיו, הוּא   and says: *Oseh shalom bimromav, hu*
בְּרַחֲמָיו יַעֲשֶׂה שָׁלוֹם עָלֵינוּ וְעַל כָּל עַמּוֹ   *berahamav ya'aseh shalom aleinu, ve'al*
יִשְׂרָאֵל, וְאִמְרוּ אָמֵן.   *kol Yisrael, ve'imru amen.*

הקהל עונה: אָמֵן.   Congregation: *Amen.*

Mourner: "May His great name be exalted and sanctified,"

Congregation: "Amen."

Mourner: "in the world He created according to His will, and may He establish His kingdom, bring forth His redemption, and hasten the coming of His messiah,"

Congregation: "Amen."

Mourner: "in your lifetime and in your days, and in the lifetime of all the house of Israel, swiftly and soon, and say: Amen."

Congregation: "Amen."

Congregation and mourner: "May His great name be blessed forever and for all time."

Mourner: "Blessed and praised, glorified and exalted, raised and honored, uplifted and lauded, be the name of the Holy One, blessed be He,"

Congregation: "Amen."

Mourner: "beyond all the blessings, songs, praises, and consolations that are spoken in the world, and say: Amen."

Congregation: "Amen."

Mourner: "May there be abundant peace from Heaven, life and contentment, salvation and consolation, and help and healing, and redemption and forgiveness and atonement, and relief and deliverance, for us and for all His nation Israel, and say: Amen."

Congregation: "Amen."

Mourner takes three steps backward and says: "May He who makes peace in His high place in His mercy make peace for us and all Israel, and all His people Israel, and say: Amen."

Congregation: "Amen."

Various Customs

There are several customs regarding the number of times that the funeral procession stops in order to recite Kaddish.

In some communities, particularly in Israel, it is customary that if the deceased is a man, his children do not walk after his bier. This practice is designed to spare the soul of the deceased from certain heavenly accusations, but it is not necessary in the case of a woman. In places where this is the custom, in many instances the children walk in front of the bier and arrive at the burial plot before the deceased. In this manner, they do not accompany the deceased but are still present at the burial. Alternatively, in some instances the children do not attend the burial at all, and come to the grave only after the burial has finished.

Burial

The deceased is buried face up and with his hands at his sides. In Israel, members of the *hevra kadisha* place the deceased into the grave. Cinder blocks are then placed on a ledge covering the deceased so that he is surrounded by airspace rather than in the dirt. After the tomb cavity is sealed with the blocks, the grave is then filled in with dirt. It is a mitzva to participate in the burial, and therefore those in attendance will customarily help with shoveling the dirt. While doing so, the shovel is not transferred from one hand to another, but rather the one who has finished shoveling puts it down for the next one to pick it up and continue shoveling.

Justification of the Decree

At the end of the burial, a prayer known as the Justification of the Decree [*Tzidduk HaDin*], is recited, which is an expression of one's acceptance of God's decision. There are different versions of this prayer for Ashkenazim and Sephardim:

Ashkenazim say:

הַצּוּר תָּמִים פָּעֳלוֹ כִּי כָל דְּרָכָיו מִשְׁפָּט, אֵל אֱמוּנָה וְאֵין עָוֶל צַדִּיק וְיָשָׁר הוּא. הַצּוּר תָּמִים בְּכָל פֹּעַל, מִי יֹאמַר לוֹ מַה תִּפְעָל, הַשַּׁלִּיט בְּמַטָּה וּבְמַעַל, מֵמִית וּמְחַיֶּה, מוֹרִיד שְׁאוֹל וַיָּעַל. הַצּוּר תָּמִים בְּכָל מַעֲשֶׂה, מִי יֹאמַר לוֹ מַה תַּעֲשֶׂה, הָאוֹמֵר וְעוֹשֶׂה, חֶסֶד חִנָּם לָנוּ תַעֲשֶׂה, וּבִזְכוּת הַנֶּעֱקַד כְּשֶׂה, הַקְשִׁיבָה וַעֲשֵׂה.

Hatzur, tamim pa'olo, ki khol derakhav mishpat, El emuna ve'ein avel, tzadik veyashar Hu. Hatzur, tamim bekhol po'al, mi yomar Lo ma tifal, hashalit bemata uvma'al, memit umhayeh, morid she'ol vaya'al. Hatzur, tamim bekhol ma'aseh, mi yomar Lo ma ta'aseh, ha'omer ve'oseh, hesed hinam lanu ta'aseh, uvezkhut hane'ekad kaseh, hakshiva va'aseh.

92

צַדִּיק בְּכָל דְּרָכָיו הַצּוּר תָּמִים, אֶרֶךְ אַפַּיִם
וּמָלֵא רַחֲמִים, חֲמָל נָא וְחוּס נָא עַל אָבוֹת
וּבָנִים, כִּי לְךָ, אָדוֹן, הַסְּלִיחוֹת וְהָרַחֲמִים.
צַדִּיק אַתָּה אֲדֹנָי לְהָמִית וּלְהַחֲיוֹת, אֲשֶׁר
בְּיָדְךָ פִּקְדוֹן כָּל רוּחוֹת, חָלִילָה לְךָ זִכְרוֹנֵנוּ
לִמְחוֹת, וְיִהְיוּ נָא עֵינֶיךָ בְּרַחֲמִים עָלֵינוּ
פְּקוּחוֹת, כִּי לְךָ, אָדוֹן, הָרַחֲמִים וְהַסְּלִיחוֹת.

Tzadik bekhol derakhav hatzur tamim, erekh apayim umaleh rahamim, hamal na, vehus na al avot uvanim, ki lekha, Adon, haselihot veharahamim. Tzadik ata Adonai lehamit ulhahayot, asher beya'dekha pikadon kol ruhot, halila lekha zikhronenu limhot, veyiheyu na einekha berahamim aleinu pekuhot, ki lekha, Adon, harahamim vehaselihot.

אָדָם אִם בֶּן שָׁנָה יִהְיֶה, אוֹ אֶלֶף שָׁנִים
יִחְיֶה, מַה יִּתְרוֹן לוֹ, כְּלֹא הָיָה יִהְיֶה, בָּרוּךְ
דַּיַּן הָאֱמֶת, מֵמִית וּמְחַיֶּה.

Adam im ben shana yiheye, oh elef shanim yihye, ma yitron lo, kelo haya yiheye, barukh dayan ha'emet, memit umhayeh.

בָּרוּךְ הוּא, כִּי אֱמֶת דִּינוֹ, וּמְשׁוֹטֵט הַכֹּל
בְּעֵינוֹ, וּמְשַׁלֵּם לְאָדָם חֶשְׁבּוֹנוֹ וְדִינוֹ, וְהַכֹּל
לִשְׁמוֹ הוֹדָיָה יִתֵּנוּ.

Barukh hu, ki emet dino, umsho-tet hakol be'eino, umshalem la'adam heshbono vedino, vehakol lishmo ho-daya yitenu.

יָדַעְנוּ אֲדֹנָי כִּי צֶדֶק מִשְׁפָּטֶךָ, תִּצְדַּק בְּדָבְרֶךָ
וְתִזְכֶּה בְשָׁפְטֶךָ, וְאֵין לְהַרְהֵר אַחַר מִדַּת
שָׁפְטֶךָ, צַדִּיק אַתָּה אֲדֹנָי, וְיָשָׁר מִשְׁפָּטֶיךָ.
דַּיַּן הָאֱמֶת, שׁוֹפֵט צֶדֶק וֶאֱמֶת, בָּרוּךְ דַּיַּן
הָאֱמֶת, כִּי כָל מִשְׁפָּטָיו צֶדֶק וֶאֱמֶת. נֶפֶשׁ
כָּל חַי בְּיָדֶךָ, צֶדֶק מָלְאָה יְמִינֶךָ וְיָדֶךָ, רַחֵם
עַל פְּלֵיטַת צֹאן עֲבָדֶיךָ, וְתֹאמַר לַמַּלְאָךְ
הֶרֶף יָדֶךָ.

Yadanu, Adonai, ki tzedek mish-patekha, titzdak bedovrekha vetizke beshoftekha, ve'ein leharher ahar midat shoftekha, tzadik ata, Adonai, veyashar mishpatekha. Dayan ha'emet, shofet tzedek ve'emet, barukh dayan ha'emet, ki khol mishpatav tzedek ve'emet. Nefesh kol hai beyadekha, tzedek mal'a yeminekha veyadekha, rahem al pelei-tat tzon avadekha, vetomar lamalakh: Heref yadekha.

"The rock, His actions are perfect, as all His ways are justice; a faithful God and there is no injustice, righteous and upright is He" (Deuteronomy 32:4). The rock, perfect in every action, who can tell Him what to do? He rules below and above, brings death and gives life, brings down to the grave and raises up. The rock, perfect in every deed, who can tell Him what to do? You who declares and acts [accordingly], perform undeserved kindness with us;

and in the merit of the one [Isaac] who was bound like a lamb, hearken and act.

"Righteous in all His ways, the perfect rock, slow to anger and full of mercy, please take pity and please spare parents and children, for Yours, Lord, are forgiveness and mercy. Righteous are You, Lord, to bring death and give life, as in Your hand all spirits are entrusted. Far be it from You to erase our remembrance. Let Your eyes please be open for us with mercy, for Yours, Lord, are mercy and forgiveness. Man, whether he is one year old, or whether he lives a thousand years, what did he gain? He is as though he had never been. Blessed be the true Judge, who brings death and gives life.

"Blessed is He, for His judgment is true; He examines everything with His eye, and He repays man according to his account and his sentence, and all give thanksgiving to His name. We know, Lord, that Your judgment is righteous, You are justified in Your word and vindicated in Your judgments, and none may doubt the method of Your judgment. Righteous are You, Lord, and Your judgments are fair, the true Judge, judging with righteousness and truth. Blessed be the true Judge, for all of His judgments are righteous and true. The soul of all the living is in Your hand, Your right hand and Your [left] hand are full of righteousness. Have mercy on the remnant of the flock of Your servants, and say to the angel [of death]: Hold back your hand."

Some add these verses:

גְּדֹל הָעֵצָה וְרַב הָעֲלִילִיָּה, אֲשֶׁר עֵינֶיךָ פְקֻחוֹת עַל כָּל דַּרְכֵי בְּנֵי אָדָם, לָתֵת לְאִישׁ כִּדְרָכָיו וְכִפְרִי מַעֲלָלָיו. לְהַגִּיד כִּי יָשָׁר אֲדֹנָי, צוּרִי וְלֹא עוֹלָתָה בּוֹ. אֲדֹנָי נָתַן, וַאֲדֹנָי לָקָח, יְהִי שֵׁם אֲדֹנָי מְבֹרָךְ. וְהוּא רַחוּם יְכַפֵּר עָוֹן וְלֹא יַשְׁחִית, וְהִרְבָּה לְהָשִׁיב אַפּוֹ, וְלֹא יָעִיר כָּל חֲמָתוֹ.

Gedol ha'etza verav ha'aliliya, asher einekha pekuḥot al kol darkhei venei adam, latet le'ish kidrakhav vekhifri ma'alalav. Lehagid ki yashar Adonai, tzuri velo avlata bo. Adonai natan, vadonai lakaḥ, yehi shem Adonai mev-orakh. Vehu raḥum yekhaper avon velo yashḥit, vehirba lehashiv apo, velo ya'ir kol ḥamato.

"He is great in design and mighty in deed, whose eyes are open upon all the ways of men, to give each man in accordance with his ways and in accordance with the fruit of his actions" (Jeremiah 32:19). "To tell that the Lord is upright. He is my rock, and there is no wrongdoing in Him" (Psalms 92:16). "The Lord gave and the Lord has taken, blessed be the name of the Lord" (Job 1:21). "Yet He, being merciful, forgives iniquity and does not destroy. He has repeatedly restrained His anger and does not kindle all of His wrath" (Psalms 78:38).

Sephardim say:

צַדִּיק אַתָּה אֲדֹנָי, וְיָשָׁר מִשְׁפָּטֶיךָ. צַדִּיק אֲדֹנָי בְּכָל דְּרָכָיו, וְחָסִיד בְּכָל מַעֲשָׂיו. צִדְקָתְךָ צֶדֶק לְעוֹלָם, וְתוֹרָתְךָ אֱמֶת. מִשְׁפְּטֵי אֲדֹנָי אֱמֶת, צָדְקוּ יַחְדָּו. בַּאֲשֶׁר דְּבַר מֶלֶךְ שִׁלְטוֹן, וּמִי יֹאמַר לוֹ מַה תַּעֲשֶׂה.

Tzadik ata, Adonai, veyashar mish-patekha. Tzadik Adonai bekhol derakhav, vehasid bekhol ma'asav. Tzid-katekha tzedek le'olam, vetoratekha emet. Mishpetei Adonai emet, tza'deku yahdav. Ba'asher devar melekh shilton, umi yomar lo ma ta'aseh.

וְהוּא בְאֶחָד וּמִי יְשִׁיבֶנּוּ, וְנַפְשׁוֹ אִוְּתָה וַיָּעַשׂ. קָטֹן וְגָדוֹל שָׁם הוּא, וְעֶבֶד חָפְשִׁי מֵאֲדֹנָיו. הֵן בַּעֲבָדָיו לֹא יַאֲמִין, וּבְמַלְאָכָיו יָשִׂים תָּהֳלָה. אַף כִּי אֱנוֹשׁ רִמָּה, וּבֶן אָדָם תּוֹלֵעָה.

Vehu ve'ehad, umi yeshivenu, venaf-sho ivta vaya'as. Katon vegadol sham hu, ve'eved hofshi me'adonav. Hen ba'avadav lo ya'amin, uvmalakhav yas-im tahola. Af ki enosh rima, uven adam tole'a.

הַצּוּר תָּמִים פָּעֳלוֹ כִּי כָל דְּרָכָיו מִשְׁפָּט, אֵל אֱמוּנָה וְאֵין עָוֶל צַדִּיק וְיָשָׁר הוּא. דַּיַּן הָאֱמֶת, שׁוֹפֵט צֶדֶק וֶאֱמֶת, בָּרוּךְ דַּיַּן הָאֱמֶת, כִּי כָל מִשְׁפָּטָיו צֶדֶק וֶאֱמֶת.

Hatzur, tamim pa'olo, ki khol derakhav mishpat, El emuna ve'ein avel, tzadik veyashar Hu. Dayan ha'emet, shofet tzedek ve'emet, barukh dayan ha'emet, ki khol mishpatav tzedek ve'emet.

בִּלַּע הַמָּוֶת לָנֶצַח, וּמָחָה אֲדֹנָי אֱלֹהִים דִּמְעָה מֵעַל כָּל פָּנִים, וְחֶרְפַּת עַמּוֹ יָסִיר מֵעַל כָּל הָאָרֶץ, כִּי אֲדֹנָי דִּבֵּר.

Bila hamavet lanetzah, umaha Adonai Elohim dim'a me'al kol panim, veherpat amo yasir me'al kol ha'aretz, ki Adonai diber.

יִחְיוּ מֵתֶיךָ נְבֵלָתִי יְקוּמוּן, הָקִיצוּ וְרַנְּנוּ שֹׁכְנֵי עָפָר כִּי טַל אוֹרֹת טַלֶּךָ, וָאָרֶץ רְפָאִים תַּפִּיל. וְהוּא רַחוּם יְכַפֵּר עָוֹן וְלֹא יַשְׁחִית, וְהִרְבָּה לְהָשִׁיב אַפּוֹ, וְלֹא יָעִיר כָּל חֲמָתוֹ. אֲדֹנָי הוֹשִׁיעָה, הַמֶּלֶךְ יַעֲנֵנוּ בְיוֹם קָרְאֵנוּ.

Yihyu metekha nevelati yekumun, hakitzu veranenu shokhenei afar ki tal orot talekha, va'aretz refa'im tap-il. Vehu rahum yekhaper avon velo yashhit, vehirba lehashiv apo, velo ya'ir kol hamato. Adonai hoshi'a, hemelekh ya'anenu veyom korenu.

"Righteous are You, Lord, and upright are Your judgments" (Psalms 119:137). "Just is the Lord in all His ways, and kind in all His deeds" (Psalms 145:17). "Your righteousness is eternal. Your teaching is truth" (Psalms 119:142). "The judgments of the Lord are true and altogether righteous" (Psalms 19:10). "Since governance is by the king's word, and who will say to him: What are you doing?" (Ecclesiastes 8:4).

"He is of one mind, and who can respond to Him? His soul desires and He does" (Job 23:13). "Small or great, he is there [in the grave], and the slave is free from his master" (Job 3:19). "Behold, He does not trust His servants, and to His angels He attributes misconduct" (Job 4:18). "How much less so man, a maggot; the son of man, a worm" (Job 25:6). "The rock, His actions are perfect, as all His ways are justice; a faithful God and there is no injustice, righteous and upright is He" (Deuteronomy 32:4). The true Judge, judging with righteousness and truth. Blessed be the true Judge, as all of His judgments are righteous and true.

"He will eliminate death forever and the Lord God will wipe tears from all faces, and He will remove the disgrace of His people from upon the entire earth, for the Lord has spoken" (Isaiah 25:8). "Your dead will live, my corpses will rise; awaken and sing, dwellers of the dust, for the dew of light is Your dew and You will cause the spirits to fall to the earth" (Isaiah 26:19). "Yet He, being merciful, forgives iniquity and does not destroy. He has repeatedly restrained His anger and does not kindle all of His wrath" (Psalms 78:38). "Deliver us, Lord. The King will answer us on the day we call" (Psalms 20:10).

After the *Tzidduk HaDin* prayer, the "Great Kaddish" is recited. This is a special, expanded version of the Kaddish that is said on special occasions. The following are two formulas of this Kaddish:

Ashkenazim say:

האבלים: יִתְגַּדַּל וְיִתְקַדַּשׁ שְׁמֵהּ רַבָּא.

Mourner: *Yitgadal veyitkadash shemeh raba*

הקהל עונה: אָמֵן.

Congregation: *Amen.*

האבלים: בְּעָלְמָא דְהוּא עָתִיד לְאִתְחַדָּתָא, וּלְאַחְיָאָה מֵתַיָּא, וּלְאַסָּקָא יָתְהוֹן לְחַיֵּי עָלְמָא, וּלְמִבְנֵי קַרְתָּא דִירוּשְׁלֵם, וּלְשַׁכְלֵל

Mourner: *be'alma dehu atid le'ithadata, ulaḥya'a metaya, ulasaka yat'hon leḥayay alma, ulmivnei*

הֵיכְלֵהּ בְּגַוֵּהּ, וּלְמֶעְקַר פֻּלְחָנָא נֻכְרָאָה מֵאַרְעָא, וְלַאֲתָבָא פֻּלְחָנָא דִשְׁמַיָּא לְאַתְרֵהּ, וְיַמְלִיךְ קֻדְשָׁא בְּרִיךְ הוּא בְּמַלְכוּתֵהּ וִיקָרֵהּ,

karta dirushlem, ulshakhlel heikheleh begaveh, ulme'kar palhana nukhra'a me'ara, vela'atava polhana dishmaya le'atreh, veyamlikh Kudsha Berikh Hu bemalkhuteh vikareh,

(הַמִּתְפַּלְלִים בְּנֻסַח סְפָרַד, מוֹסִיפִים: וְיַצְמַח פֻּרְקָנֵהּ וִיקָרֵב מְשִׁיחֵהּ.

(Those who pray in *Nusah Sefarad* add: *veyatzmah purkaneh vikarev meshiheh*

הַקָּהָל עוֹנֶה: אָמֵן.)

Congregation: *Amen.*)

הָאֲבֵלִים: בְּחַיֵּיכוֹן וּבְיוֹמֵיכוֹן וּבְחַיֵּי דְכָל בֵּית יִשְׂרָאֵל בַּעֲגָלָא וּבִזְמַן קָרִיב וְאִמְרוּ אָמֵן.

Mourner: *behayeikhon uvyomeikhon, uvhayey dekhol beit Yisrael, ba'agala uvizman kariv, ve'imru amen*

הַקָּהָל עוֹנֶה: אָמֵן.

Congregation: *Amen.*

וּמִיָּד מְצַטְרְפִים גַּם הָאֲבֵלִים: יְהֵא שְׁמֵהּ רַבָּא מְבָרַךְ לְעָלַם וּלְעָלְמֵי עָלְמַיָּא.

Congregation and mourner: *Yehe she-meh rabba mevarakh le'alam ul'almei almaya*

הָאֲבֵלִים: יִתְבָּרַךְ וְיִשְׁתַּבַּח וְיִתְפָּאַר וְיִתְרוֹמַם וְיִתְנַשֵּׂא וְיִתְהַדָּר וְיִתְעַלֶּה וְיִתְהַלָּל שְׁמֵהּ דְּקֻדְשָׁא, בְּרִיךְ הוּא.

Mourner: *Yitbarakh veyishtabah veyitpa'ar veyitromam veyitnaseh veyit'hadar veyit'aleh veyit'hallal she-meh dekudsha berikh hu,*

הַקָּהָל עוֹנֶה: בְּרִיךְ הוּא אוֹ אָמֵן.

Congregation: *Berikh hu or Amen.*

הָאֲבֵלִים: לְעֵלָּא מִן כָּל (בַּעֲשֶׂרֶת יְמֵי תְשׁוּבָה: לְעֵלָּא לְעֵלָּא מִכָּל) בִּרְכָתָא וְשִׁירָתָא, תֻּשְׁבְּחָתָא וְנֶחֱמָתָא, דַּאֲמִירָן בְּעָלְמָא, וְאִמְרוּ אָמֵן.

Mourner: *le'ela min kol* (during the Ten Days of Repentance: *Le'ela ul'ela mikol*) *birkhata veshirata tushbehata venehemata, da'amiran be'a'lema ve'imru amen.*

הַקָּהָל עוֹנֶה: אָמֵן.

Congregation: *Amen.*

הָאֲבֵלִים: יְהֵא שְׁלָמָא רַבָּא מִן שְׁמַיָּא וְחַיִּים טוֹבִים עָלֵינוּ וְעַל כָּל יִשְׂרָאֵל וְאִמְרוּ אָמֵן.

Mourner: *Yehe shelama raba min she-maya vehayim* (some add: *tovim*) *aleinu ve'al kol Yisrael, ve'imru amen.*

הקהל עונה: אָמֵן. | Congregation: *Amen.*

הָאֲבֵלִים (פּוֹסְעִים שָׁלֹשׁ פְּסִיעוֹת לְאָחוֹר | Mourner takes three steps backward
וְאוֹמְרִים): עֹשֶׂה שָׁלוֹם (בַּעֲשֶׂרֶת יְמֵי | and says: *Oseh shalom* (during the Ten
תְּשׁוּבָה: הַשָּׁלוֹם) בִּמְרוֹמָיו, הוּא יַעֲשֶׂה | Days of Repentance: *hashalom*) *bim-*
שָׁלוֹם עָלֵינוּ וְעַל כָּל יִשְׂרָאֵל וְאִמְרוּ אָמֵן. | *romav, Hu* (some add: *veraḥamav*)
| *ya'aseh shalom aleinu, ve'al kol Yisrael,*
| *ve'imru amen.*

הקהל עונה: אָמֵן. | Congregation: *Amen.*

Mourner: "May His great name be exalted and sanctified,"

Congregation: "Amen."

Mourner: "in the world that He will renew in the future, [when] He will revive the dead and raise them to eternal life, and build the city of Jerusalem and perfect His Sanctuary within it, and uproot idolatry from the land, and restore the divine service to its place, and the Holy One, blessed be He, will reign in His kingdom and in His glory (those who pray in *Nusaḥ Sefarad* add: and bring forth His redemption and hasten the coming of His messiah."

Mourner: "in your lifetime and in your days, and in the lifetime of all the house of Israel, swiftly and soon, and say: Amen."

Congregation: "Amen."

Congregation and mourner: "May His great name be blessed forever and for all time."

Mourner: "Blessed and praised, glorified and exalted, raised and honored, uplifted and lauded, be the name of the Holy One, blessed be He,"

Congregation: "Blessed be He," or "Amen."

Mourner: "beyond (in the Ten Days of Repentance: far beyond) all the blessings, songs, praises, and consolations that are spoken in the world, and say: Amen."

Congregation: "Amen."

Mourner: "May there be abundant peace from Heaven and good life, for us and all Israel, and say: Amen."

Congregation: "Amen."

Mourner takes three steps backward and says: "May He who makes peace (during the Ten Days of Repentance: the peace) in His high place make peace for us and all Israel, and say: Amen."

Congregation: "Amen."

Sephardim say:

האבלים: יִתְגַּדַּל וְיִתְקַדַּשׁ שְׁמֵהּ רַבָּא.

Mourner: *Yitgadal veyitkadash shemeh raba*

הקהל עונה: אָמֵן.

Congregation: *Amen.*

האבלים: בְּעָלְמָא דְּהוּא עָתִיד לְאִתְחַדְתָּא, וּלְאַחֲיָא מֵיתַיָּא, וּלְאַסָּקָא יַתְהוֹן לְחַיֵּי עָלְמָא, וּלְמִבְנֵי קַרְתָּא דִירוּשְׁלֵם, וּלְשַׁכְלֵל הֵיכָלָא בְּגַוַּהּ, וּלְמֶעְקַר פֻּלְחָנָא נֻכְרָאָה מֵאַרְעָא, וּלְאָתָבָא פֻּלְחָנָא דִשְׁמַיָּא לְאַתְרֵהּ, וְיַמְלִיךְ קֻדְשָׁא בְּרִיךְ הוּא בְּמַלְכוּתֵהּ וִיקָרֵהּ, וְיַצְמַח פֻּרְקָנֵהּ וִיקָרֵב מְשִׁיחֵהּ.

Mourner: *be'alma dehu atid le'ithadata, ulahya mitaya, ulasaka yat'hon lehayay alma, ulmivnei karta dirushlem, ulshakhlel heikhela begava, ulmi'kar pulhana nukhra'a me'ara, ul'a'atava pulhana dishmaya le'atreh, veyamlikh Kudsha Berikh Hu bemalkhuteh vikareh, veyatzmah purkaneh vikarev meshiheh*

הקהל עונה: אָמֵן.

Congregation: *Amen.*

האבלים: בְּחַיֵּיכוֹן וּבְיוֹמֵיכוֹן וּבְחַיֵּי דְכָל בֵּית יִשְׂרָאֵל בַּעֲגָלָא וּבִזְמַן קָרִיב וְאִמְרוּ אָמֵן.

Mourner: *behayeikhon uvyomeikhon, uvhayey dekhol beit Yisrael, ba'agala uvizman kariv, ve'imru amen.*

הקהל עונה: אָמֵן.

Congregation: *Amen.*

האבלים: יְהֵא שְׁמֵהּ רַבָּא מְבָרַךְ לְעָלַם וּלְעָלְמֵי עָלְמַיָּא.

Mourner: *Yehe shemeh rabba mevarakh le'alam ul'almei almaya.*

האבלים: יִתְבָּרַךְ וְיִשְׁתַּבַּח וְיִתְפָּאַר וְיִתְרוֹמַם וְיִתְנַשֵּׂא וְיִתְהַדָּר וְיִתְעַלֶּה וְיִתְהַלָּל שְׁמֵהּ דְּקֻדְשָׁא בְּרִיךְ הוּא.

Mourner: *Yitbarakh veyishtabah veyitpa'ar veyitromam veyitnaseh veyit'hadar veyit'aleh veyit'hallal shemeh dekudsha berikh hu,*

הקהל עונה: אָמֵן.

Congregation: *Amen.*

האבלים: לְעֵלָּא מִן כָּל בִּרְכָתָא וְשִׁירָתָא, תֻּשְׁבְּחָתָא וְנֶחֱמָתָא דַּאֲמִירָן בְּעָלְמָא, וְאִמְרוּ אָמֵן.

Mourner: *le'ela min kol birkhata veshirata tushbehata venehemata, da'amiran be'a'lema ve'imru, Amen.*

הקהל עונה: אָמֵן.

Congregation: *Amen.*

האבלים: יְהֵא שְׁלָמָא רַבָּא מִן שְׁמַיָּא וְחַיִּים וְשָׂבָע וִישׁוּעָה וְנֶחָמָה וְשֵׁיזָבָא וּרְפוּאָה וּגְאֻלָּה וּסְלִיחָה וְכַפָּרָה וְרֶוַח וְהַצָּלָה לָנוּ וּלְכָל עַמּוֹ יִשְׂרָאֵל וְאִמְרוּ אָמֵן.

Mourner: *Yehe shelama raba min shemaya ḥayim vesava yeshu'a veneḥama veshezava urfu'a ugula u'seliḥa vekhapara verevaḥ vehatzala, lanu ulkhol amo Yisrael, ve'imru amen.*

הקהל עונה: אָמֵן.

Congregation: *Amen.*

האבלים (פוסעים שלוש פסיעות לאחור ואומרים): עֹשֶׂה שָׁלוֹם בִּמְרוֹמָיו הוּא בְּרַחֲמָיו יַעֲשֶׂה שָׁלוֹם עָלֵינוּ וְעַל כָּל יִשְׂרָאֵל וְאִמְרוּ אָמֵן.

The mourner takes three steps backward and says: *Oseh shalom bimromav, Hu beraḥamav ya'aseh shalom aleinu, ve'al kol Yisrael, ve'imru amen.*

הקהל עונה: אָמֵן.

Congregation: *Amen.*

Mourner: "May His great name be exalted and sanctified,"

Congregation: "Amen."

Mourner: "in the world that He will renew in the future, [when] He will revive the dead and raise them to eternal life, and build the city of Jerusalem and perfect His Sanctuary within it, and uproot idolatry from the land, and restore the divine service to its place, and the Holy One, blessed be He, will reign in His kingdom and in His glory, and bring forth His redemption and hasten the coming of His messiah,"

Congregation: "Amen."

Mourner: "in your lifetime and in your days, and in the lifetime of all the house of Israel, swiftly and soon, and say: Amen."

Congregation: "Amen."

Congregation and mourner: "May His great name be blessed forever and for all time."

Mourner: "Blessed and praised, glorified and exalted, raised and honored, uplifted and lauded, be the name of the Holy One, blessed be He,"

Congregation: "Amen."

Mourner: "beyond all blessings, songs, praises, and consolations that are spoken in the world, and say: Amen."

Congregation: "Amen."

Mourner: "May there be abundant peace from Heaven, life and contentment, salvation and consolation, and help and healing, and redemption and forgiveness and atonement, and relief and deliverance, for us and for all His nation Israel, and say: Amen."

The congregation responds: "Amen."

The mourner takes three steps backward and says: "May He who makes peace in His high place, in His mercy make peace for us and all Israel, and say: Amen."

Congregation: "Amen."

Various Customs

On joyous days when the *Tahanun* prayer is not recited, one does not say the *Tzidduk HaDin* prayer. Psalm 16 is recited instead, followed by a regular Kaddish, not the Great Kaddish.

After the *Tzidduk HaDin* prayer, Sephardim say the *Ashkava* prayer and Ashkenazim say the *El Malei Raḥamim* prayer, while others do not recite these prayers at the funeral, but only later, at the end of the seven days of mourning [shiva].

After the Burial

After the burial, the mourners remove their shoes, in accordance with laws of mourning. From this point onward, the period of mourning begins (see next section).

Upon Exiting the Cemetery

Before leaving the burial plot, it is customary for each of those present to place a small stone on the mound of earth that covers the grave. It is customary to do this every time one visits a grave. Several explanations have been offered for this practice, but it is primarily an indication that the grave has been visited and that the deceased has not been forgotten.

On the way out of the cemetery it is customary for those present to form two rows, and for the mourners to walk between the two rows. The lines should be formed at some distance from the graves.

As the mourners pass through the lines of comforters, they recite to him the accepted formula of consolation. The Ashkenazic custom is to declare:

הַמָּקוֹם יְנַחֵם אֶתְכֶם בְּתוֹךְ שְׁאָר אֲבֵלֵי   *HaMakom yenaḥem et'ḥem betokh*
צִיּוֹן וִירוּשָׁלָיִם וְיֵשׁ מוֹסִיפִים: וְלֹא תוֹסִיפוּ   *she'ar aveilei Tzion veyrushalayim.*
לְדַאֲבָה עוֹד.   Some add: *Velo tosifu leda'ava od.*

"May God console you among the other mourners of Zion and Jerusalem. Some add: And may you know no further sorrow."

Sephardim say:

תְּנוּחֲמוּ מִן הַשָּׁמַיִם אוֹ מִן הַשָּׁמַיִם תְּנוּחֲמוּ. *Tenuḥamu min hashamayim,* or: *Min hashamayim tenuḥamu.*

"May you be comforted from heaven."

The mourners then go to the house where they intend to sit shiva, which is the practice of sitting for seven days and receiving condolences from relatives and acquaintances. Some have the custom of accompanying the mourners to the house of mourning. When they come home, it is customary to serve the mourners a small meal called the *seudat havra'a* (see next section).

During the shiva, the mourners may not wear leather shoes. If they were not equipped in advance with appropriate non-leather footwear at the cemetery, they may wear their regular shoes until they arrive home. In such a case, some are stringent and put a small amount of dirt inside the shoes, to make them less comfortable.

Before leaving the cemetery, there is a custom to pluck a few weeds with a little dirt and throw them behind one's back. Some say while doing so: "He is mindful that we are but dust" (Psalms 103:14). One of the reasons given for this custom is that during the Temple period, individuals who had become ritually impure from contact with a corpse would be purified through the ashes of the Red Heifer mixed with water, which would be sprinkled on them with a bundle of hyssop (see Numbers 19). Nowadays, when ritual purification with the Red Heifer is impossible, the weeds and the dust are a symbolic reminder of that procedure.

Upon exiting the cemetery, one washes his hands, alternately pouring water on each hand three times. This washing ensures that negative spiritual forces present in the cemetery do not accompany us on our way. When finished washing the hands, one should put the cup back upside down, and instead of wiping his hands on a towel he should let them dry in the air.

Kohanim at Funerals
Kohanim are prohibited to become ritually impure through contact with the dead, as the verse states: "Speak to the priests, the sons of Aaron, and say to them: He shall not become impure from a dead person among his people" (Leviticus 21:1). The practical application of this prohibition is that a *kohen* may not touch a corpse, nor be under the same roof with a corpse. This last category also applies to an awning or a tree that extends over a dead body; a *kohen* may not stand anywhere under them. This law imposes various limitations on a *kohen* who wishes to attend a funeral.

Outer Row

Kohanim may not come within four cubits, approximately two meters, of a corpse or a grave. However, if a first-degree family member of a *kohen* passes away – a group that includes his father, mother, son, daughter, wife, brother, and unmarried sister from a common father – he is permitted to become ritually impure through proximity to the body at the funeral, and it is in fact a mitzva to do so. At the same time, he is prohibited – even during their funeral and burial – to become impure through contact with any other corpses or to approach their graves. For this reason, when the deceased is a *kohen* or if many of his family members are *kohanim*, the *hevra kadisha* will attempt to provide a burial plot in an outer row of graves, which can be accessed without passing in immediate proximity to other graves.

Other Limitations

There are other limitations that apply to *kohanim* as a result of the prohibition for them to have contact, be under the same roof, or in immediate proximity to a corpse:

Cemeteries

Kohanim should refrain as much as possible from visiting cemeteries. If they do visit one, they must be careful not to enter within four cubits (about two meters) of any grave, as stated above. They are also prohibited to enter a funeral home while a body is present there. Many funeral homes have a separate area for *kohanim*, which allows them to attend the funeral and hear the eulogies without being situated under the same roof as the deceased.

Medical centers

The entrance of *kohanim* into a hospital where there are likely to be corpses present at any given time also presents halakhic difficulties. There are medical centers in Israel which provide a warning to *kohanim* when there is a dead body on the premises. At such a time *kohanim* know for certain that they may not be there. When there is a special need for a *kohen* to enter a medical facility in order to visit a friend or relative, or if he himself requires medical attention, he should first consult with a rabbi. Of course, in life-threatening situations, these restrictions do not apply.

Medical studies

Medical studies present a halakhic problem for a *kohen*, as this field requires contact with cadavers and the examination of tissue taken from dead people, which also impart ritual impurity. A *kohen* who wishes to study medicine should consult a rabbi.

Burial of Children

The burial service of children up to the age of one year may differ from the usual arrangements. In such cases, the law and custom may depend on location and circumstances. It is recommended to consult a rabbi on a case-by-case basis.

Mourning Periods

Shiva, the First Thirty Days, and the First Twelve Months

The family of the deceased must observe the laws of mourning for three distinct periods of time: the first week after death [shiva, literally, "seven"]; the first thirty days after the relative's passing [*sheloshim*, meaning "thirty"]; and the first twelve months following the death of a parent. From each stage to the next, the level of mourning diminishes, and this is reflected in the *halakhot* that apply to the mourners.

The Torah records a precedent for a seven-day morning period. Upon the death of Jacob, it is stated of Joseph, viceroy of Egypt, that he "observed mourning for his father seven days" (Genesis 50:10). Later, the Sages added a series of specific rules and *halakhot* to observe during the days of mourning.

Mourning serves several purposes, one of which is to honor the memory of the deceased. Another purpose is to inspire family members and acquaintances to engage in soul-searching and to strive to improve their ways, as stated in the verse: "It is better to go to the house of mourning than to go to the house of feasting, as that is the end of every man, and the living will take it to his heart" (Ecclesiastes 7:7). In other words, the living must reflect on the sad event they have experienced and draw personal lessons from it.

This section details the laws and customs of mourning in each one of the aforementioned stages.

The Mourners

The laws of mourning apply to first-degree relatives: spouses, parents, siblings, and children. For the purposes of these *halakhot*, half-siblings (those who share only a common father or mother) are the same as full siblings.

Other Relatives

A divorced man or woman is not classified as a mourner for an ex-spouse. They do not tear their garments nor sit shiva. Likewise, more distant relatives do not tear their garments nor sit shiva.

With that said, there are certain restrictions that apply to some relatives from the more distant family circle: the grandchildren of the deceased, a son-in-law, and a daughter-in-law. They should not participate in celebrations such as weddings while their parents or spouses are sitting shiva.

📖 **Further reading:** For more on mourning, see *A Concise Guide to Mahshava*, p. 28.

The Shiva

The Sages established mourning practices for the shiva period. This period of mourning affords the family the opportunity to express their sorrow and to process their loss. It is also an opportunity for friends and admirers of the deceased to express their feelings and to join in the family's sorrow.

Place of Sitting

After the funeral, the mourners gather to sit together for seven days. It is worthwhile for all the mourners to sit in the same house, but sometimes this is not possible, such as when they are not all in the same country. In such a case, the mourners split up and sit shiva in different locations.

It is customary, and even desirable, to sit shiva in the house of the deceased, as his soul still lingers in his home. This practice, though preferred, is not mandatory.

Calculating the Days of the Shiva

The first day of the shiva begins immediately after the funeral. If the funeral ended shortly before nightfall, the remainder of that day is considered the first day of the shiva, and the second day begins at nightfall. If the funeral finishes after nightfall, the shiva will begin at that time, with the second day beginning only upon the following nightfall. If one is uncertain as to the exact time that the funeral ended or when exactly night started on that day, he should consult a rabbi.

The mourning practices are not observed for the full day on the seventh and final day of shiva. Rather, they are observed only for a short time immediately following the morning prayers. This is due to the halakhic concept that in certain cases part of a day is considered a complete day. For example, if the funeral took place on a Monday afternoon, ending before night, Monday is considered the first day of shiva, and the mourners will conclude their observance of shiva on Sunday morning. However, if the funeral ended on Monday night, Tuesday is the first day of shiva and the mourners will conclude their observance of shiva on the following Monday morning.

Even if the funeral was held on Friday close to sunset and the start of Shabbat, that Friday is considered the first day of the shiva and the mourners will finish on Thursday morning.

Shabbat during the days of the shiva is counted as one of the seven days, despite the fact that most mourning practices are not observed on that day.

When mourning begins on a Sunday, the shiva ends on Shabbat, and in effect the mourners conclude their week of mourning after the Shabbat morning prayers.

Festivals during the Shiva

If a person was buried before one of the major festivals – Rosh HaShana, Yom Kippur, *Sukkot*, Passover, or *Shavuot* – and the mourners began to sit shiva before the festival, the onset of the festival brings an immediate end to the shiva, and shiva is not resumed after the festival. This *halakha* applies even if they were able to observe the mourning practices for only a very short time before the festival.

If the burial takes place after the festival or during the intermediate days [*Hol HaMoed*] of the festival itself (in the cases of *Sukkot* and Passover), even if the death occurred before the festival, the shiva is postponed until after the festival, at which point it is observed for the full seven days. In such a situation, the family members should also observe some of the laws and customs of mourning during the intermediate festival days after the burial.

Other holidays, such as Hanukkah and Purim, do not affect the shiva. The laws of mourning on these days will be explained below.

If a wedding of one of the mourners had been scheduled to take place during the days of the shiva, a rabbi should be consulted.

Seudat Havra'a

When the mourners return from the funeral to the house where they intend to sit shiva, it is customary for friends and acquaintances to bring them food for their first meal. This is called a *seudat havra'a* (lit. a meal of healing), and it is meant to express the support of the community or of the mourners' friends, so that they do not sink into despondency and self-neglect in their grief.

In this meal it is customary to eat bread and eggs or lentils. Bread is served because it is considered the essential part of a meal, and eggs or lentils because a round food is considered a symbol of mourning. One should also serve the mourners something to drink.

If the departed was buried late on a Friday afternoon or the eve of a festival, it is advisable to avoid eating the *seudat havra'a*, or at least not to eat too much, so that the mourners are able to have an appetite for the Shabbat or festival meal. If a *seudat havra'a* is not eaten, it does not need to be made up for at a later stage.

Mourning Practices during the Shiva

These are some of the laws and customs of mourning observed during the shiva:

It is prohibited to work during the shiva period, regardless of whether one is an employee or self-employed. If there is a concern of heavy financial loss due to the avoidance of work (a factor that applies mainly to the self-employed), a rabbi should be consulted. If the mourner owns a store or business that can be run by others, he should consult a rabbi as to whether he must close it during the shiva, or whether it may continue running without his involvement.

It is prohibited for a mourner to bathe for pleasure throughout all the days of the shiva. Even when showering for the purpose of cleanliness, one should avoid using hot water as much as possible.

A mourner is not allowed to anoint himself, i.e., to use cosmetic products such as oils, creams, makeup, and so on. The use of medical ointments, or moisturizers to treat dryness of the skin, is permitted.

Mourners may not wear leather shoes during the shiva, but may wear shoes made of other materials such as rubber or plastic.

It is prohibited for mourners to wear laundered clothing during the shiva. It is customary for the mourner to wear the clothes that he tore at the funeral for the entire week of shiva. It is permitted for a mourner to change his undergarments. If his shirt can no longer be worn, he may put on a different shirt, but he must then tear that shirt as well.

Mourners are forbidden to engage in marital relations. They should even avoid sleeping in a shared bed with their spouse. A woman who is mourning does not immerse herself in a ritual bath during the shiva, but she is permitted to bathe herself lightly in order to perform a "separation of purity" [*hefsek tahara*] after menstruation and to begin counting her "seven clean days."

> **Further reading:** For more information dealing with these laws, see p. 81.

A mourner is prohibited to learn Torah, as Torah study gladdens the heart. Nevertheless, he may engage in the study of sad topics in the Bible, such as the book of Job, which deals mainly with the theme of sorrow and suffering in the world; the book of Lamentations, which mourns the destruction of the First Temple; as well as certain passages in the book of Jeremiah that describe the destruction of the First Temple. It is likewise permitted for mourners to study the laws of mourning.

In times past, mourners would sit shiva on the ground. In our days it is customary to sit on low chairs rather than on the floor.

A mourner may not cut his hair or shave during the seven-day mourning period (see below with regard to the first thirty days and the first year).

A mourner should refrain from cutting his nails during shiva, but he may do so without the use of implements, e.g., with his teeth or hands.

The mourner should not leave the house of mourning during the shiva, as every such outing distracts his mind from the mourning. If he feels it necessary for him to do so, he should consult a rabbi. If prayers are not held in the house of mourning, some hold that he may go to the synagogue in order to pray with a quorum of ten men [minyan] and to recite Kaddish for the soul of the deceased. If the synagogue is very far from his house, he should avoid going there.

It is customary for a candle to be lit in the house of shiva throughout the seven days. This custom is based on the verse: "The soul of man is the lamp of the Lord" (Proverbs 20:27). The candle symbolizes the survival of the soul after the person's death, and the aspiration of the soul to rise upward, just as the flame of a candle constantly strives to ascend.

It is also customary to cover the mirrors in the house of mourning. The origin of this custom is unknown, but two reasons have been suggested:

(1) The mourners should not see themselves in the mirrors and be led to improve their physical appearance by applying makeup and the like during the shiva.

(2) It is customary to hold prayer services in a house of mourning, and it is prohibited to pray while facing a mirror.

The mourning in the first three days of the shiva is more severe than that of the following four days. Therefore, during those last four days there may be room for certain leniencies regarding the mourning practices in situations of need, in consultation with a rabbi.

Comforting Mourners

During the shiva, when the mourners are sitting at home, it is a great mitzva for others to come and console them. Comforting the mourners provides a good opportunity to talk about the deceased and his life.

Rules of Conduct

Greetings are not offered in a house of mourning, neither from the consolers to the mourner nor vice-versa. Additionally, one should not initiate conversation with the mourner, but should wait for him to start the conversation. However, if one sees that it is difficult for a mourner to begin talking, one may ask a leading question pertaining to the deceased.

In some communities it is customary for visitors not to eat in a house of mourning. By contrast, Sephardim do the exact opposite: They hold large meals; anyone who comes to visit recites a blessing loudly before eating, and those present answer "amen" in response. They intend for the blessing and the amen to be a merit for the soul of the deceased.

When the comforters get up to leave, it is customary for them to say one of the following phrases of blessing to the mourners:

Ashkenazim say:

הַמָּקוֹם יְנַחֵם אֶתְכֶם בְּתוֹךְ שְׁאָר אֲבֵלֵי
צִיּוֹן וִירוּשָׁלַיִם.

HaMakom yenaḥem et'ḥem betokh she'ar aveilei Tzion veyrushalayim.

וְיֵשׁ מוֹסִיפִים: וְלֹא תוֹסִיפוּ לְדַאֲבָה עוֹד.

Some add: *velo tosifu leda'ava od.*

"May God console you among the other mourners of Zion and Jerusalem."
Some add: "And may you know no further sorrow."

Sephardim say:

תְּנוּחֲמוּ מִן הַשָּׁמַיִם אוֹ מִן הַשָּׁמַיִם תְּנוּחֲמוּ.

Min hashamayim tenuḥamu, or: *Tenuḥamu min hashamayim.*

"May you be comforted from heaven."

Learning *Mishnayot*

It is considered very praiseworthy to study passages of the Mishna as a merit for the soul of the deceased. The study of Mishna is preferred to other forms of Torah learning because the same Hebrew letters that spell Mishna also spell *neshama*, soul.

In a House of Mourning

It is very common to study Mishna as a group in a house of mourning. One of the comforters reads from the Mishna, while all the rest listen. It is possible, of course, for the comforters to take turns reading the *mishnayot*. This practice is acceptable and proper, even though the mourner himself is prohibited from learning Torah.

The study of Mishna in a house of mourning generally takes place during the interval between the afternoon and evening services. This is a period when people are relatively free, as those who come to the house of mourning for the afternoon service will often remain for the evening service as well. Thus, the waiting time is used for the communal study of Torah, and this learning is dedicated to the soul of the deceased.

It is recommended to learn *mishnayot* that begin with the letters of the deceased's name. If, for example, he was named Abraham, they should study a mishna that begins with the Hebrew letter *alef*, followed by others starting with the letters *bet, resh, heh*, and *mem*, thereby spelling his name. This can also be done with whole chapters of Mishna that start with the letters of the deceased's name. When they have finished the *mishnayot* that follow the order of the letters of the name, they should continue with the four *mishnayot* from tractate *Mikvaot* that begin with the letters spelling *neshama*, soul. These *mishnayot* appear in many prayer books.

Prayers in the House of Mourning

It is customary to hold all three daily prayers in the house of mourning, throughout the entire shiva (apart from Shabbat), in order to enable the mourners to pray with a *minyan* and recite Kaddish without having to leave the house.

Changes in the Prayer Service

Prayer in the house of mourning differs in certain aspects from the ordinary prayer in the synagogue. If the mourner can do so, he should serve as the prayer leader. The *Tahanun* prayer is omitted, and Psalm 20 [*Lamnatze'ah*], which is generally said in the morning service between *Ashrei* (Psalm 54) and *Uva LeTzion*, is not recited. Furthermore, in the *Uva LeTzion* prayer, the verse: "And as for Me, this is My covenant" (Isaiah 59:21) is omitted.

At the end of prayers, it is customary to add Psalm 49, which discusses death in general. On days when *Tahanun* is not said, Psalm 49 is omitted, and instead one recites Psalm 16, which speaks of God's providence and how He protects us from death.

The most common practice is for the prayer leader to omit the recitation of the priestly benediction during the repetition of the *Shemoneh Esrei*. Similarly, in Israel, where the priests pronounce this benediction on a daily basis, the most common practice is for them to omit this benediction in a house of mourning. However, there are some who do recite the priestly benediction even in a house of mourning.

It is customary to bring a Torah scroll to a house of mourning, so that the Torah reading can be conducted during the morning services of Mondays and Thursdays (as well as on other days of the year that the Torah is read) during the shiva. There are small, portable arks that are designed specifically for houses of mourning and similar situations. It is very important to be extra careful with the sanctity of the Torah scroll and bring it in and place it in the house of mourning in a dignified manner. If this is not possible, one should consider not bringing a Torah scroll to the house of mourning at all, and instead to pray in the synagogue on days when the Torah is read.

Some have a custom not to transfer a Torah scroll from one location to another unless it will be read in the new place at least three times. Therefore, in a house of mourning too, they should try to read from the scroll no less than three times. Typically, during a shiva, it is read twice during the week, on Monday and Thursday morning, and again in the afternoon prayer of Shabbat.

Shabbat

Private and Public Conduct

On the Shabbat that occurs during a shiva, all the laws of mourning that apply in private are observed, but not those which are noticeable to other people. Mourners wear Shabbat clothes, including their regular shoes (even if they are made of leather), and leave their house for the synagogue. A mourner should not be called up to the Torah, but if there is no one available to replace him it is permitted for him to be called up, as otherwise this would constitute a noticeable expression of mourning.

By contrast, all the laws of mourning that are observed privately apply even on Shabbat. Mourners during the shiva must abstain from marital relations and bathing for pleasure. Similarly, mourners are prohibited from studying Torah. Nevertheless, if one is accustomed to review the weekly Torah portion with the Aramaic translation [*shenayim mikra ve'ehad targum*] (see p. 379), he may do so even on the Shabbat during the shiva.

It is permitted to comfort mourners on Shabbat, but the opportunity to visit and comfort him should not purposely be postponed from a weekday to Shabbat. Rather, consolation visits should ideally take place on a weekday. On a practical level as well, mourners generally prefer to take advantage of Shabbat to rest, and they would rather not have to deal with visitors on this day.

It is generally accepted that a mourner enters the synagogue on Friday night only after the congregation has finished singing *Lekha Dodi*. In many communities the *gabbai* declares: "Comfort the mourner," at which point the mourner enters and the community recites to him the formula of consolation, thereby ending the public acknowledgement of his mourning on Shabbat.

Ending the Shiva

On the seventh day, on which the shiva concludes, the mourners rise to their feet after the morning service and thereby signal the end of the intense mourning of the first week.

Verses and a Meal

When the morning prayers have concluded, the mourners sit on their low chairs and those present instruct them to rise from their mourning, while adding: "May God mend the breaches of His people of Israel."

Some add verses of comfort from the prophecy of Isaiah: "Your sun will no longer set, and your moon will not be gathered in, as the Lord will be for you an eternal light; the days of your mourning will be completed" (Isaiah 60:20).

In Sephardic communities it is customary on the evening before the end of the shiva (i.e., the evening between the sixth and seventh days) to hold a memorial meal [*seudat azkara*] in honor of the departed and as a merit for his soul. There is a text that is recited at the meal which usually can be obtained from the local synagogue. The text includes verses, *mishnayot*, and passages from the Zohar that are recited in memory of the deceased.

With regard to visiting the grave of the deceased on the day that the mourner finishes the shiva, see below.

Sheloshim, the Thirty-Day Mourning Period

As stated at the beginning of the section, as time passes from the death and the burial, the intensity of mourning observances decreases, but some mourning customs must still be observed. These practices ensure that the mourner does not become completely distracted from thinking about the deceased and mourning for him, and they also constitute an expression of respect for the departed. The following are some of the unique laws and customs of this period between the shiva and the end of the first thirty days [the *sheloshim*].

Calculating the *Sheloshim* Period

Similar to the days of shiva, these thirty days are counted from the day of burial, not from the day of death. Consequently, if a person died and was buried on the same day, that day is the first in the thirty-day count. But if the person died on a Sunday and the burial was performed on Sunday night or Monday, the first day of the *sheloshim* will be Monday. The end of this mourning period will be on the morning of the thirtieth day, immediately after sunrise.

Festivals during the *Sheloshim*

When a major holiday, that is, Passover, *Shavuot*, Rosh HaShana, Yom Kippur, or *Sukkot*, occurs during the *sheloshim* period, the mourning period of the *sheloshim* ends at the onset of the holiday, and the mourners then move on to the less severe mourning observances that apply to the entire year of mourning (see below). The application of this *halakha* involves many details, and therefore each case will be discussed separately:

If a person is buried before Passover, the shiva will end when Passover begins, and the *sheloshim* will conclude fifteen days (or in Israel, sixteen days) after the end of Passover, on the morning of the seventh of Iyar. This is because when the arrival of the holiday terminates the shiva, it is considered as if seven days of mourning have been observed, and the first day of Passover is considered the eighth day of mourning, leaving just twenty-two more days.

If a burial takes place before *Shavuot*, the shiva will come to an end at the start of *Shavuot*, and the *sheloshim* will again continue until sixteen days after the end of the festival, finishing on the morning of the twenty-second of Sivan. This is because the shiva is considered to have been a full seven days regardless of how many days it was actually observed, and *Shavuot* itself is considered as though it were an additional seven days, leaving sixteen days left in the thirty days. The second day of the festival outside of Israel counts as one of those sixteen remaining days.

If a person is buried before Rosh HaShana, the shiva is stopped at the onset of Rosh HaShana (see above); after the holiday, the *sheloshim* period begins, but is then terminated by Yom Kippur.

For one who is buried between Rosh HaShana and Yom Kippur, the shiva will end on Yom Kippur, while the *sheloshim* period will be terminated by *Sukkot*.

In the case of one who is buried between Yom Kippur and *Sukkot*, the shiva concludes upon the start of *Sukkot*, and the *sheloshim* ends eight days (in Israel, nine days) after *Shemini Atzeret/Simhat Torah*, on the morning of the first of Marheshvan. This is because the first day of *Sukkot* is considered the eighth day of mourning, as explained above, and, moreover, the day of *Shemini Atzeret* is an independent festival and is therefore considered as if it were a full seven days. After *Simhat Torah*, then, only eight days (in Israel, nine days) of the *sheloshim* remain.

Mourning during *Sheloshim*

The following customs of mourning are observed during the *sheloshim* period:

Throughout the *sheloshim*, mourners may not shave or have their hair cut.

One should avoid cutting one's nails during the *sheloshim* (an exception is made for a woman before her ritual immersion).

Mourners may not wear new clothes during *sheloshim*, and the Ashkenazic custom is not to wear even a laundered garment. If another person has worn a new garment once, even if only for a short while, it is permitted for a mourner to wear it afterward. Some are more lenient and permit wearing a laundered garment if it has been placed on the floor for some time, thus reducing the freshly laundered feel of the garment. There are those who are lenient and allow wearing laundered undergarments.

It is prohibited to get married within the *sheloshim* period. But if the wedding date was already set beforehand, it is the accepted practice that the wedding may take place on time.

Mourners may not participate in parties and joyous events such as weddings. If the event is celebrating the marriage or another occasion of someone especially close to the mourner, a rabbi should be consulted.

Until the end of the *sheloshim* period, a mourner should not go on especially distant business trips.

Throughout the *sheloshim*, the custom is to avoid bathing for pleasure. Consequently, mourners should try not to bathe in warm water, and they should avoid pleasure swims.

With regard to visiting the grave at the end of the *sheloshim*, see below.

Erecting a Tombstone

It is customary to erect a tombstone on a grave. With regard to the timing, there are different customs. Many are careful to erect the tombstone by the end of the *sheloshim*.

The Monument

There are no special rules as to how the tombstone should be built, but it would be inappropriate to deviate significantly from what is customary in the cemetery where the deceased is buried. It is distasteful to put up a tombstone that attracts a great deal of attention, whether because it is significantly inferior to the others in the vicinity or because it displays excessive splendor.

Likewise, there are no definitive laws with regard to the inscription on the tombstone. However, there are some accepted norms in this regard: It is customary to write the name of the deceased and the names of his parents, as well as the Hebrew dates of his birth and death. Many people add a few lines that briefly describe the life and accomplishments of the deceased. Some include a biblical verse that expresses a central message of the deceased's personality. Here too, one should not use excessive praise, and should certainly not stray from the truth. It is proper for the inscription to be in Hebrew.

In the case of a *kohen*, it is often customary to engrave the image of a pair of hands spread out in the form used for the priestly benediction, a testimony to the status of the deceased.

It is a custom to add at the bottom of the tombstone the Hebrew letters *tav, nun, tzadi, bet, heh*, an acronym for: *Teheh nishmato/nishmata tzerura bitzror haḥayim*, meaning, "May his/her soul be bound in the bond of everlasting life" (see I Samuel 25:29).

When a Name Was Added

When someone is gravely ill, it is often customary to add on a name such as Hayim or Haya (meaning "life") or Rephael ("may God heal"), in order to change their fortune and increase their chances of recovery. Sometimes the patient indeed recovers, but on other occasions his death was already decreed by Heaven and he returns his soul to its Maker. The question then arises: In such a case, is it necessary or proper to include the added name on the tombstone? The answer is that if at least thirty days have passed from when the name was added until his death, the extra name should be included. But if he dies within thirty days of the addition of the name, the extra name is not considered an official addition to the original name and it is not engraved on the tombstone.

The Twelve-Month Mourning Period

Following the death of one's father or mother, mourning is observed for a period of twelve months. This mourning period is similar to the mourning of the *sheloshim*, but it is more lenient in certain respects. The mourning lasts for twelve months, not a full year, which means that in a leap year (which contains thirteen months), it will end one month before the conclusion of the year. Just as in the case of the shiva and the *sheloshim*, the twelve-month period starts from the day of burial, not from the day of death.

Laws of Mourning

After the passing of a father or mother, the following *halakhot* of mourning are observed during the twelve months: The mourner may not shave or have a haircut until his hair grows long and unkempt to the point where his friends admonish him for his appearance.

A mourner may not purchase or wear new garments during the twelve-month mourning period. However, if his existing clothing is in poor or neglected condition to the point that he would receive negative comments from his acquaintances, he may buy a new garment, provided that at least thirty days have elapsed since the death.

Mourners may not participate in joyous events or celebrations. With regard to an important event of a close relative, such as the wedding of one's child, a rabbi should be consulted.

In general, mourners should avoid gatherings and celebratory meals with many participants.

The prohibition of bathing and anointing oneself with oils does not apply at all after the first thirty days of mourning.

It is customary not to send *mishlo'ah manot* to a mourner on Purim, but the mourner himself does send *mishlo'ah manot* to others.

📖 **Further reading:** For more on the laws of *mishlo'ah manot* on Purim, see p. 265.

It is an Ashkenazic custom for the mourner to change his seat in the synagogue during the year of mourning. It is recommended to consult the *gabbai* of the synagogue in choosing a new seat. This change is maintained throughout the twelve months. Some have the custom that after the first month one returns to his original seat on Shabbatot.

It is customary for a mourner to serve as prayer leader in the synagogue during the weekday services of the first eleven months of mourning, but not on Shabbat, festivals, intermediate festival days, or *Rosh Hodesh*.

Visiting the Grave

And the Anniversary of the Death [Yahrzeit]

During the first year of mourning, there are several dates on which it is customary to visit the grave of the deceased: on the last day of the shiva, which is the seventh day after the burial; on the last day of the *sheloshim*; and on the yahrzeit, the anniversary of the day of death. At the grave, the attendees recite psalms, say Kaddish if there is a *minyan*, and recite the *El Malei Rahamim* or *Ashkava* prayer as a merit for the soul of the deceased. The mourner should not visit the grave at other times during the first year of mourning.

When to Visit the Grave

The dates of going to visit the grave may be adjusted slightly, forward or backward, if they would fall on a day when it is customary not to visit graves, as detailed below.

To Postpone or Move Forward?

In a case where the visit to the grave would fall on a Shabbat, a festival, including the intermediate days, or on Purim, the mourner does not visit the grave on that day. Some visit a day earlier whereas others delay the visit until the next day when it is possible to visit the grave.

This applies to the visit to the grave at the end of the *sheloshim* or on the yahrzeit. As for the end of the shiva, everyone agrees that when this day falls on a Shabbat or festival, the visit is postponed to Sunday or the day after the festival and is not moved forward.

Special Dates

With regard to visiting the grave during the month of Nisan, as well as on Hanukkah and *Rosh Hodesh*, there are different opinions, and each person should follow the ruling of his rabbi.

Calculating the Yahrzeit

If a person was not buried on the day of his passing, the first yahrzeit is observed, including the visit to the grave, on the anniversary of the burial, not of the death. In the following years the yahrzeit is observed on the date of the death. Some maintain that even the first yahrzeit is observed on the date of the death rather than the burial.

When the burial was delayed for more than three days after the death, all agree that even the first yahrzeit is held on the first anniversary of the burial.

The yahrzeit is the exact Hebrew date of the death or burial, not twelve months after the death. This means that if it was a leap year, which has thirteen months, the yahrzeit will be on the same day of the month as the death or burial of the previous year, despite the fact that, in actuality, thirteen months have passed.

In the case of one who died in the month of Adar of a regular year, in which there is only one month of Adar, the yahrzeit will always be observed in the first Adar, even in a leap year, which has two months of Adar. But if someone died in Adar of a leap year, in the subsequent leap years his yahrzeit will be observed on the date that he died: If he died in the first Adar, the yahrzeit will be in the first Adar, and if he passed away in the second Adar, it will be observed in the second Adar.

What Is Done at the Grave?

It is strongly recommended to have a *minyan* (ten men) at the graveside, so that one can recite Kaddish there. If it is not possible to bring a *minyan* to the grave, it is customary to recite all the usual prayers, but without Kaddish.

The Format of the Prayers

The following seven psalms are recited when visiting a grave: 33, 16, 17, 72, 91, 104, 130.

Psalm 119 is an alphabetical acrostic, with groups of eight verses that begin with each consecutive letter of the alphabet. It is customary at a cemetery visit to recite verses from Psalm 119 that spell out the letters of the name of the departed. Afterward one continues with the groups of verses that start with the letters *nun, shin, mem,* and *heh,* which spell out the word *neshama,* soul.

At the end of the recitation of the psalms, a prayer is recited for the soul of the departed:

אָנָּא ה' מָלֵא רַחֲמִים, אֲשֶׁר בְּיָדְךָ נֶפֶשׁ כָּל חַי וְרוּחַ כָּל בְּשַׂר אִישׁ, יְהִיֶה נָא לְרָצוֹן
לְפָנֶיךָ תּוֹרָתֵנוּ וּתְפִלָּתֵנוּ בַּעֲבוּר נִשְׁמַת (שם פרטי מלא של הנפטר) בֶּן/בַּת
(שם פרטי מלא של שני הוריו), וְגְמָל נָא עִמָּהּ בְּחַסְדְּךָ הַגָּדוֹל לִפְתֹּחַ לָהּ שַׁעֲרֵי
רַחֲמִים וָחֶסֶד וְשַׁעֲרֵי גַן עֵדֶן, וּתְקַבֵּל אוֹתָהּ בְּאַהֲבָה וּבְחִבָּה, וּשְׁלַח לָהּ מַלְאָכֶיךָ
הַקְּדוֹשִׁים וְהַטְּהוֹרִים לְהוֹלִיכָהּ וּלְהוֹשִׁיבָהּ תַּחַת עֵץ הַחַיִּים, אֵצֶל נִשְׁמוֹת
הַצַּדִּיקִים וְהַצִּדְקָנִיּוֹת, חֲסִידִים וַחֲסִידוֹת, לֵיהָנוֹת מִזִּיו שְׁכִינָתְךָ, לְהַשְׂבִּיעָהּ
מִטּוּבְךָ הַצָּפוּן לַצַּדִּיקִים. וְהַגּוּף יָנוּחַ בַּקֶּבֶר בִּמְנוּחָה נְכוֹנָה, בְּחֶדְוָה וּבְשִׂמְחָה
וְשָׁלוֹם, כְּדִכְתִיב: "יָבוֹא שָׁלוֹם יָנוּחוּ עַל מִשְׁכְּבוֹתָם הֹלֵךְ נְכֹחוֹ", וּכְתִיב: "יַעְלְזוּ
חֲסִידִים בְּכָבוֹד יְרַנְּנוּ עַל מִשְׁכְּבוֹתָם", וּכְתִיב: "אִם תִּשְׁכַּב לֹא תִפְחָד וְשָׁכַבְתָּ
וְעָרְבָה שְׁנָתֶךָ". וְתִשְׁמֹר אוֹתוֹ / אוֹתָהּ מֵחִבּוּט הַקֶּבֶר וּמֵרִמָּה וְתוֹלֵעָה, וְתִסְלַח
וְתִמְחַל לוֹ/לָהּ עַל כָּל פְּשָׁעָיו/פְּשָׁעֶיהָ, כִּי אָדָם אֵין צַדִּיק בָּאָרֶץ אֲשֶׁר יַעֲשֶׂה
טוֹב וְלֹא יֶחֱטָא, וְזְכֹר לוֹ/לָהּ זְכִיּוֹתָיו/זְכִיּוֹתֶיהָ וְצִדְקוֹתָיו/וְצִדְקוֹתֶיהָ אֲשֶׁר עָשָׂה/
עָשְׂתָה, וְתַשְׁפִּיעַ לוֹ/לָהּ מִנִּשְׁמָתוֹ/תָהּ לְדַשֵּׁן עַצְמוֹתָיו/עַצְמוֹתֶיהָ בַּקֶּבֶר מֵרֹב
טוּב הַצָּפוּן לַצַּדִּיקִים, דִּכְתִיב: "מָה רַב טוּבְךָ אֲשֶׁר צָפַנְתָּ לִּירֵאֶיךָ". וּכְתִיב:
"שֹׁמֵר כָּל עַצְמוֹתָיו אַחַת מֵהֵנָּה לֹא נִשְׁבָּרָה". וְתִשְׁכֹּן בֶּטַח בָּדָד, וְשַׁאֲנָן מִפַּחַד
רָעָה וְאַל תִּרְאֶה פְּנֵי גֵיהִנֹּם. וְנִשְׁמָתוֹ/וְנִשְׁמָתָהּ תְּהֵא צְרוּרָה בִּצְרוֹר הַחַיִּים
וּלְהַחֲיוֹתוֹ/תָהּ בִּתְחִיַּת הַמֵּתִים עִם כָּל מֵתֵי עַמְּךָ יִשְׂרָאֵל בְּרַחֲמִים. אָמֵן.

"Please, God full of mercy, in whose hands is the soul of all life and the spirit of all the flesh of man, may our Torah study and our prayers be accepted before You, on behalf of the soul of (full Hebrew name of the deceased), son/daughter of (full Hebrew name of both parents), and treat it with Your great mercy, opening the gates of compassion and kindness and the gates of the Garden of Eden for it, and receiving it with love and affection. Send Your holy and pure angels to lead it and place it under the tree of life, alongside the righteous men and women and the pious men and women, where it may joyfully experience the splendor of the Divine Presence [*Shekhinah*]. May the body be granted a proper rest in the grave, in delight and joy and tranquility, as it is written: 'May he depart in peace, may he who walks in his uprightness rest on their resting places' (Isaiah 57:2). And it is written: 'Let the devoted ones exult in honor; let them sing for joy in their beds' (Psalms 149:5), and it is written: 'When you lie down, you will not be afraid; you will lie down, and your sleep will be sweet' (Proverbs 3:24). Preserve him/her from the disturbance of the grave, and from maggots and worms. Forgive and pardon him/her for all his/her iniquities, 'for there is no righteous man upon the earth, who does good and does not sin' (Ecclesiastes 7:20).

Remember his/her merits and righteous deeds that he/she performed, and may influence flow from his/her soul to nourish his/her bones in the grave from the abundance of goodness hidden away for the righteous, as it is written: 'How great is the goodness You have in store for those who fear You' (Psalms 31:20), and it is written: 'He preserves all his bones; not one of them will be broken' (Psalms 34:21). Let [the soul] rest securely, alone (see Deuteronomy 33:28), at ease from the fear of evil, and may it not see Gehenna. May his/her soul be bound in the bond of everlasting life, and be revived at the resurrection of the dead with all the dead of Your people Israel in mercy, Amen."

The *El Malei Rahamim/Ashkava* Prayer

After the above prayer, the full Kaddish is recited, followed by the *El Malei Rahamim* or the *Ashkava* prayer.

Ashkenazim say:

For a male:

אֵל מָלֵא רַחֲמִים שׁוֹכֵן בַּמְּרוֹמִים, הַמְצֵא מְנוּחָה נְכוֹנָה עַל כַּנְפֵי הַשְּׁכִינָה, בְּמַעֲלוֹת קְדוֹשִׁים וּטְהוֹרִים כְּזֹהַר הָרָקִיעַ מַזְהִירִים, לְנִשְׁמַת (שם פרטי מלא של הנפטר) בֶּן (שם פרטי מלא של שני הוריו) שֶׁהָלַךְ לְעוֹלָמוֹ. בַּעֲבוּר שֶׁבְּלִי נֶדֶר אֶתֵּן צְדָקָה בְּעַד הַזְכָּרַת נִשְׁמָתוֹ (ויש אומרים במקום: בַּעֲבוּר שֶׁאָנוּ מִתְפַּלְלִים לְעִלּוּי נִשְׁמָתוֹ), בְּגַן עֵדֶן תְּהֵא מְנוּחָתוֹ. לָכֵן בַּעַל הָרַחֲמִים יַסְתִּירֵהוּ בְּסֵתֶר כְּנָפָיו לְעוֹלָמִים, וְיִצְרוֹר בִּצְרוֹר הַחַיִּים אֶת נִשְׁמָתוֹ, אֲדֹנָי הוּא נַחֲלָתוֹ וְיָנוּחַ בְּשָׁלוֹם עַל מִשְׁכָּבוֹ, וְנֹאמַר אָמֵן.

El maleh rahamim shokhen ba'meromim, hamtze menuha nekhona al kanfei hashekhina, bema'alot kedoshim ut'horim kezohar harakia mazhirim, lenishmat (full Hebrew name of the deceased) ben (full Hebrew name of both parents) shehalakh le'olamo. Ba'avur shebeli neder eten tzedaka be'ad hazkarat nishmato (some substitute: Ba'avur she'anu mitpalelim le'ilui nishmato). Be'gan eden tehe menuhato. Lakhen, ba'al harahamim yastirehu beseter kenafav le'olamim, veyitzror bitzror hahayim et nishmato, Adonai hu nahalato, veyanu'ah beshalom al mishkavo, venomar amen.

For a female:

אֵל מָלֵא רַחֲמִים שׁוֹכֵן בַּמְּרוֹמִים, הַמְצֵא מְנוּחָה נְכוֹנָה עַל כַּנְפֵי הַשְּׁכִינָה, בְּמַעֲלוֹת

El maleh rahamim shokhen ba'meromim, hamtze menuha

קְדוֹשִׁים וּטְהוֹרִים כְּזֹהַר הָרָקִיעַ מַזְהִירִים, לְנִשְׁמַת (שם פרטי מלא של הנפטרת) בַּת (שם פרטי מלא של שני הוריה) שֶׁהָלְכָה לְעוֹלָמָהּ. בַּעֲבוּר שֶׁבְּלִי נֶדֶר אֶתֵּן צְדָקָה בְּעַד הַזְכָּרַת נִשְׁמָתָהּ (ויש אומרים במקום: בַּעֲבוּר שֶׁאָנוּ מִתְפַּלְלִים לְעִלּוּי נִשְׁמָתָהּ), בְּגַן עֵדֶן תְּהֵא מְנוּחָתָהּ. לָכֵן בַּעַל הָרַחֲמִים יַסְתִּירֶהָ בְּסֵתֶר כְּנָפָיו לְעוֹלָמִים, וְיִצְרֹר בִּצְרוֹר הַחַיִּים אֶת נִשְׁמָתָהּ, אֲדֹנָי הוּא נַחֲלָתָהּ וְתָנוּחַ בְּשָׁלוֹם עַל מִשְׁכָּבָהּ, וְנֹאמַר אָמֵן.

nekhona al kanfei hashekhina, bema'alot kedoshim ut'horim kezohar harakia mazhirim, lenishmat (full Hebrew name of the deceased) bat (full Hebrew name of both parents) shehalekha le'olamah. Ba'avur shebeli neder eten tzedaka be'ad hazkarat nishmatah (some substitute: Ba'avur she'anu mitpalelim le'ilui nishmatah). Be'gan eden tehe menuhatah. Lakhen, ba'al harahamim yastirah beseter kenafav le'olamim, veyitzror bitzror hahayim et nishmatah, Adonai hu nahalatah, vetanu'ah beshalom al mishkavah, venomar amen.

"God full of mercy, who dwells on high, grant proper rest on the wings of the Divine Presence, in the heights of the holy and the pure who shine like the radiance of heaven, to the soul of (full name of the deceased), son/daughter of (full name of both parents) who has gone to his/her eternal rest. And for this I pledge, without making a formal vow, to give charity in his/her memory (some say instead: and for this we pray for the benefit of his/her soul). May his/her resting place be in the Garden of Eden. Therefore, Master of compassion, shelter him/her in the shadow of Your wings forever and bind his/her soul in the bond of everlasting life. The Lord is his/her heritage; may he/she rest in peace, and let us say: Amen."

Sephardim say:

For a male:

הַמְרַחֵם עַל כָּל בְּרִיּוֹתָיו, הוּא יָחֹס וְיַחְמֹל וִירַחֵם עַל נֶפֶשׁ, רוּחַ וּנְשָׁמָה שֶׁל (שם פרטי מלא של הנפטר) בֶּן (שם פרטי מלא של שני הוריו). רוּחַ אֲדֹנָי תְּנִיחֶנּוּ בְּגַן עֵדֶן. הוּא וְכָל יִשְׂרָאֵל הַשּׁוֹכְבִים עִמּוֹ בִּכְלַל הָרַחֲמִים וְהַסְּלִיחוֹת, וְכֵן יְהִי רָצוֹן, וְנֹאמַר אָמֵן.

Ha'merahem al kol beriyotav, hu yahus veyahmol virahem al nefesh, ru'ah, unshama shel (full Hebrew name of the deceased) ben (full Hebrew name of both parents), ru'ah Adonai tenihenu be'gan eden. Hu vekhol Yisrael hashokhevim imo bikhlal harahamim vehaselihot, vekhen yehi ratzon, venomar amen.

Life Cycle

For a female:

הַמְרַחֵם עַל כָּל בְּרִיּוֹתָיו, הוּא יָחֹס וְיַחְמֹל
וִירַחֵם עַל נֶפֶשׁ, רוּחַ וּנְשָׁמָה שֶׁל (שם פרטי
מלא שֶׁל הַנִּפְטֶרֶת) בַּת (שם פרטי מלא
שֶׁל שְׁנֵי הוֹרֶיהָ). רוּחַ אֲדֹנָי תְּנִיחֶנָּה בְּגַן
עֵדֶן. הִיא וְכָל יִשְׂרָאֵל הַשּׁוֹכְבוֹת עִמָּהּ
בִּכְלַל הָרַחֲמִים וְהַסְּלִיחוֹת, וְכֵן יְהִי רָצוֹן,
וְנֹאמַר אָמֵן.

Ha'merahem al kol beriyotav, hu yahus veyahmol virahem al nefesh, ru'ah, unshama shel (full Hebrew name of the deceased) bat (full Hebrew name of both parents), ru'ah Adonai tenihena be'gan eden. Hi vekhol Yisrael hashokhevot imah bikhlal harahamim vehaselihot, vekhen yehi ratzon, venomar amen.

"He who has mercy on all His creatures, may He pity and have compassion and mercy on the *nefesh, ru'ah,* and *neshama* [components of the soul] of (full Hebrew name of the deceased), son/daughter of (full Hebrew name of both parents). May the spirit of the Lord grant him/her a resting place in the Garden of Eden. May he/she and all Israel who rest with him/her be included in [Your] mercy and forgiveness. May this be [Your] will, and let us say: Amen."

Additional Laws and Customs

When leaving the grave, it is customary to place a small stone on the tombstone. This act serves as a kind of symbolic participation in the burial, and attests that people have come to visit the grave.

Upon leaving the cemetery, one washes his hands. There are some who wash their hands upon entering a cemetery as well.

One should not walk in a cemetery with his ritual fringes [*tzitzit*] visible; rather, they should be hidden under his clothing. The reason is that the dead are unable to perform mitzvot, and when one walks among graves with ritual fringes hanging out, it is considered a taunt, a fulfillment of the verse: "Whoever mocks the poor blasphemes his Maker" (Proverbs 17:5).

The Yahrzeit

According to Kabbala, on the anniversary of death (yahrzeit) the soul of the deceased rises to a higher spiritual level in heaven. This is the reason that on this day the descendants and acquaintances of the departed make a special effort to help their souls continue their ascent. Below are a some of the customs relating to the yahrzeit:

Providing Merit to the Soul

On the Shabbat before the yahrzeit of a parent, it is customary for the son to be called up to the Torah reading.

On the day of the yahrzeit itself, a 24-hour candle ("yahrzeit candle") is lit at home or in the synagogue, before sunset of the previous day. If the yahrzeit occurs on a Sunday, the candle is not lit until after *Havdala* is recited at the conclusion of Shabbat.

On this day, Kaddish is recited for the departed, and if possible, the son should serve as the prayer leader for the three daily prayer services in the synagogue. The custom to serve as a prayer leader and/or to recite Kaddish applies even when the yahrzeit falls on a Shabbat.

On the yahrzeit it is appropriate for the descendants of the deceased to give money to charity, as a merit for the soul of their loved one.

Some have the custom of holding a commemorative meal on this day, while others make do with bringing cake and drinks to the synagogue, so that those present can recite blessings and say "*lehayim*" ("for life") as a merit for the soul of the deceased.

It is appropriate on the yahrzeit to learn Mishna as a merit for the soul of the departed. It is customary to study the four *mishnayot* from Tractate *Mikvaot* that begin with the letters spelling *neshama*, meaning "soul": Chapter 7, *mishnayot* 4–7. In addition, some learn *mishnayot* whose initial letters spell the name or names of the deceased.

Some take this custom of Torah study in memory of the deceased one step further, and every year on the yahrzeit they conduct a *siyum*, a ceremony marking the completion of a unit of the Oral Torah, such as a tractate of the Talmud or one of the six orders of the Mishna.

Yearly Cycle

Rosh HaShana

Rosh HaShana is celebrated over the first two days of the Jewish calendar year, the first and second of the month of Tishrei. According to tradition, Adam was created on the first of Tishrei, and therefore his descendants, all of humankind, stand in judgment before the Creator on this day.

There are contrasting elements in the philosophical significance of Rosh HaShana: On the one hand, it is a festival. It is prohibited to engage in productive labor [*melakha*] on this day (except for certain tasks related to the preparation of food); *Kiddush* is recited over wine; the *Sheheheyanu* blessing, which is an expression of joy, is recited; and festive meals are served. On the other hand, Rosh HaShana is a day of judgment, on which the fate of humanity is determined for the entire new year. It is also a day on which we reaccept the kingship of God, and the shofar is sounded, filling the heart with fear and trepidation. Rosh HaShana is thus a time for internal reflection and self-examination. We may ask, then: What is the essence of Rosh HaShana? Is it a festive day or a day of awe and introspection?

In fact, Rosh HaShana combines joy and seriousness, celebration and solemnity, as in the phrase from the book of Psalms (2:11): "And rejoice with trembling."

This chapter details the laws and customs pertaining to the days immediately prior to Rosh HaShana and to Rosh HaShana itself, such as the Annulment of Vows on the morning before the festival, the sounding of the shofar, the custom of *Tashlikh*, and concluding with the *Havdala* rite at the end of the second day of the festival.

Rosh HaShana Eve

The lengthy preparations for the two Days of Judgment come to a climax on the evening of Rosh HaShana. In the early morning hours before Rosh HaShana, or during the preceding night, the Ashkenazic custom is to recite an exceptionally long service of penitential prayers [*Selihot*]. This night is sometimes called "the night of remember the covenant" [*leil zekhor habrit*], an allusion to the opening phrase of one of the liturgical poems that is recited: "Remember the covenant of Abraham and the binding of Isaac."

Prayer and the Annulment of Vows

As on every festival eve, *Tahanun* is not recited in the prayers of this day.

During the month of Elul, the shofar is sounded every morning after prayers. However, on the day before Rosh HaShana (the last day of Elul) the shofar is not blown, in order to create a separation between the custom-based shofar blasts of the month of Elul and the obligatory blasts of Rosh HaShana.

After the morning prayers, it is customary to perform the rite of the Annulment of Vows [*Hatarat Nedarim*]. This annulment serves to release a person from vows he may have uttered over the course of the past year but has forgotten to fulfill. Among these vows are included praiseworthy customs that one began to observe on a regular basis, which then automatically took on the status of a vow and became obligatory for him, even if he did not intend to undertake such a vow. The vows are annulled before Rosh HaShana begins so that one can start the new year without the burden of these vows and without concern over one's failure to fulfill them.

Among Sephardic communities it is customary to perform the Annulment of Vows on other occasions: on the nineteenth of Av (forty days before Rosh HaShana), and on *Rosh Hodesh* Elul (forty days before Yom Kippur). Some annul their vows on the day before Yom Kippur as well.

The Annulment of Vows is performed before three men (some do it in the presence of ten), who serve for this purpose as a "court." The wording of the Annulment of Vows, in the section below, can also be found in standard prayer books, the festival prayer book [*mahzor*], and in books of *Selihot*. In essence, it expresses the regret of the one seeking the annulment of the vows that he has accepted upon himself without explicitly stating that they were made without the force of a vow. The members of the "court" listen to the request and respond by annulling the past vows. In the second stage of the annulment, the one seeking the annulment issues a declaration that he wishes to cancel in advance the validity of all vows or virtuous customs that he may accept upon himself over the course of the following year, and in some versions the "court" approves the request and gives it halakhic validity.

Women fulfill the annulment of vows by reciting the *Kol Nidrei* prayer on the night of Yom Kippur. A married woman can also ask her husband to annul her vows together with his own vows.

Wording of the Annulment of Vows

This is the standard formula of the Annulment of Vows (there are minor textual variations for the different communities):

שִׁמְעוּ נָא רַבּוֹתַי דַּיָּנִים מֻמְחִים!

כָּל נֶדֶר אוֹ שְׁבוּעָה אוֹ אִסָּר אוֹ קוֹנָם אוֹ חֵרֶם, שֶׁנָּדַרְתִּי אוֹ נִשְׁבַּעְתִּי בְּהָקִי"ץ אוֹ בַּחֲלוֹם, אוֹ נִשְׁבַּעְתִּי בַּשֵּׁמוֹת הַקְּדוֹשִׁים שֶׁאֵינָם נִמְחָקִים וּבְשֵׁם הוי"ה בָּרוּךְ הוּא, וְכָל מִינֵי נְזִירוּת שֶׁקִּבַּלְתִּי עָלַי וַאֲפִלּוּ נְזִירוּת שִׁמְשׁוֹן, וְכָל שׁוּם אִסּוּר, וַאֲפִלּוּ אִסּוּר הֲנָאָה שֶׁאָסַרְתִּי עָלַי אוֹ עַל אֲחֵרִים, בְּכָל לָשׁוֹן שֶׁל אִסּוּר בֵּין בְּלָשׁוֹן אִסּוּר אוֹ חֵרֶם אוֹ קוֹנָם וְכָל שׁוּם קַבָּלָה אֲפִלּוּ שֶׁל מִצְוָה שֶׁקִּבַּלְתִּי עָלַי,

בֵּין בִּלְשׁוֹן נֶדֶר בֵּין בִּלְשׁוֹן נְדָבָה בֵּין בִּלְשׁוֹן שְׁבוּעָה בֵּין בִּלְשׁוֹן נְזִירוּת בֵּין בְּכָל
לָשׁוֹן, וְגַם הַנַּעֲשָׂה בִּתְקִיעַת כַּף. בֵּין כָּל נֶדֶר וּבֵין כָּל נְדָבָה, וּבֵין שׁוּם מִנְהַג שֶׁל
מִצְוָה שֶׁנָּהַגְתִּי אֶת עַצְמִי וְכָל מוֹצָא שְׂפָתַי שֶׁיָּצָא מִפִּי, אוֹ שֶׁנָּדַרְתִּי וְגָמַרְתִּי בְּלִבִּי
לַעֲשׂוֹת שׁוּם מִצְוָה מֵהַמִּצְוֹת, אוֹ אֵיזוֹ הַנְהָגָה טוֹבָה אוֹ אֵיזֶה דָּבָר טוֹב שֶׁנָּהַגְתִּי
שָׁלֹשׁ פְּעָמִים וְלֹא הִתְנֵיתִי שֶׁיְּהֵא בְּלִי נֶדֶר, הֵן דָּבָר שֶׁעָשִׂיתִי עַל עַצְמִי הֵן עַל
אֲחֵרִים, הֵן אוֹתָן הַיְדוּעִים לִי הֵן אוֹתָן שֶׁכְּבָר שָׁכַחְתִּי, בְּכֻלְּהוֹן אִתְחֲרַטְנָא בְּהוֹן
מֵעִקָּרָא (בְּכוּלָם אֲנִי מִתְחָרֵט בָּהֶם מֵעִיקָרָם), וְשׁוֹאֵל וּמְבַקֵּשׁ אֲנִי מִמַּעֲלַתְכֶם
הַתָּרָה עֲלֵיהֶם, כִּי יָרֵאתִי פֶּן אֶכָּשֵׁל וְנִלְכַּדְתִּי חַס וְשָׁלוֹם בַּעֲוֹן נְדָרִים, וּשְׁבוּעוֹת
וּנְזִירוּת, וַחֲרָמוֹת וְאִסּוּרִין, וְקוֹנָמוֹת וְהַסְכָּמוֹת.

וְאֵין אֲנִי תוֹהֵא חַס וְשָׁלוֹם עַל קִיּוּם הַמַּעֲשִׂים הַטּוֹבִים הָהֵם שֶׁעָשִׂיתִי, רַק אֲנִי
מִתְחָרֵט עַל קַבָּלַת הָעִנְיָנִים בִּלְשׁוֹן נֶדֶר אוֹ שְׁבוּעָה, אוֹ נְזִירוּת אוֹ אִסּוּר, אוֹ
חֵרֶם, אוֹ קוֹנָם, אוֹ הַסְכָּמָה, אוֹ קַבָּלָה בַּלֵּב. וּמִתְחָרֵט אֲנִי עַל זֶה שֶׁלֹּא אָמַרְתִּי
הִנְנִי עוֹשֶׂה דָּבָר זֶה בְּלִי נֶדֶר וּשְׁבוּעָה, וּנְזִירוּת וְחֵרֶם וְאִסּוּר, וְקוֹנָם וְקַבָּלָה בַּלֵּב.
לָכֵן אֲנִי שׁוֹאֵל הַתָּרָה בְּכֻלְּהוֹן, וַאֲנִי מִתְחָרֵט עַל כָּל הַנִּזְכָּר, בֵּין אִם הָיוּ הַמַּעֲשִׂים
מִדְּבָרִים הַנּוֹגְעִים בְּמָמוֹן, בֵּין מֵהַדְּבָרִים הַנּוֹגְעִים בַּגּוּף, בֵּין מֵהַדְּבָרִים הַנּוֹגְעִים
אֶל הַנְּשָׁמָה, בְּכֻלְּהוֹן אֲנִי מִתְחָרֵט, עַל לְשׁוֹן נֶדֶר וּשְׁבוּעָה וּנְזִירוּת וְאִסּוּר וְחֵרֶם
וְקוֹנָם וְקַבָּלָה בַּלֵּב.

וְהִנֵּה מִצַּד הַדִּין, הַמִּתְחָרֵט וְהַמְבַקֵּשׁ הַתָּרָה, צָרִיךְ לִפְרֹט לִפְרָט הַנֶּדֶר, אַךְ דְּעוּ נָא
רַבּוֹתַי, כִּי אִי אֶפְשָׁר לְפָרְטָם, כִּי רַבִּים הֵם. וְאֵין אֲנִי מְבַקֵּשׁ הַתָּרָה עַל אוֹתָם
הַנְּדָרִים שֶׁאֵין לְהַתִּיר אוֹתָם, עַל כֵּן יִהְיוּ נָא בְּעֵינֵיכֶם כְּאִלּוּ הָיִיתִי פּוֹרְטָם:

"Hear me now my masters, expert judges:

"Any vow or oath or prohibition or restriction or ban that I have vowed
or sworn, whether while awake or in a dream, or that I swore by one of the
holy names of God that may not be erased, or by the Tetragrammaton,
blessed be He, or any nazirite-vow that I have accepted upon myself, even
a nazirite-vow like that of Samson, or any proscription, even a proscription
against deriving benefit from something, whether I proscribed it for myself or for others, through any expression of prohibition, whether using the
language of prohibition or restriction or ban, or any commitment, even to
perform a mitzva, that I accepted upon myself, whether through the language of a vow or the language of a voluntary undertaking or the language
of an oath or the language of nazirite-vows, or any other such language, and
even those undertaken by handshake agreement, whether it was any vow or
voluntary undertaking, or virtuous custom for the fulfillment of a mitzva
that I have practiced, or any utterance that I have verbalized, or any vow
or acceptance of an obligation to perform a mitzva that I have undertaken

mentally in the heart, or some virtuous practice or conduct that I have performed three times without specifying that it should not have the force of a vow, whether it relates to myself or others, both those known to me and those I have already forgotten – with regard to all of them, I hereby express my retroactive regret at having undertaken these vows, and ask and seek their annulment from your eminences. For I am afraid lest I become entangled, Heaven forbid, in the transgressions of the violation of vows, oaths, nazirite-vows, bans, prohibitions, restrictions, and agreements.

"Now, I do not regret, Heaven forbid, the performance of the good deeds I have done. Rather, I regret having taken them upon myself in the language of a vow, oath, nazirite-vow, prohibition, ban, restriction, agreement, or acceptance in the heart, and I regret the fact that I did not say, 'I am doing this act without accepting it upon myself as a vow or oath or nazirite-vow or ban or prohibition or acceptance in the heart.' Therefore, I request release from all of them, and I express regret for all that has been mentioned, whether these actions were in matters pertaining to money, matters pertaining to the body, or matters pertaining to the soul. In all these matters I regret the use of the language of vow, oath, nazirite-vow, prohibition, ban, or acceptance in the heart.

"Now, according to the letter of the law, one who regrets and seeks annulment of a vow must specify the vow. But please be aware, my masters, that it is impossible for me to specify them, for they are numerous, and that I am not requesting annulment for vows that may not be annulled. Therefore, may it be considered by you as though I had specified them."

The "court" responds with the following declaration, which is recited three times:

הַכֹּל יִהְיוּ מֻתָּרִים לָךְ, הַכֹּל מְחוּלִים לָךְ, הַכֹּל שְׁרוּיִים לָךְ, אֵין כָּאן לֹא נֶדֶר, וְלֹא שְׁבוּעָה, וְלֹא נְזִירוּת, וְלֹא חֵרֶם, וְלֹא אִסּוּר וְלֹא קוֹנָם וְלֹא נִדּוּי, וְלֹא שַׁמְתָּא, וְלֹא אָרוּר. אֲבָל יֵשׁ כָּאן מְחִילָה סְלִיחָה וְכַפָּרָה. וּכְשֵׁם שֶׁמַּתִּירִים הַבֵּית דִּין שֶׁל מַטָּה כָּךְ יִהְיוּ מֻתָּרִים מִבֵּית דִּין שֶׁל מַעְלָה:

"All shall be permitted to you, all is forgiven you, all is released for you. There is no vow, oath, nazirite-vow, ban, prohibition, penalty, excommunication, or curse here. Rather, there is pardon, forgiveness, and atonement here. And just as the earthly court has permitted, so may these [vows] be permitted by the heavenly court."

The individual requesting annulment now adds the following disclaimer:

הֲרֵי אֲנִי מוֹסֵר מוֹדָעָה לִפְנֵיכֶם וַאֲנִי מְבַטֵּל מִכָּאן וּלְהַבָּא כָּל הַנְּדָרִים וְכָל
שְׁבוּעוֹת וּנְזִירוּת וְאִסּוּרִין וְקוֹנָמוֹת וַחֲרָמוֹת וְהַסְכָּמוֹת וְקַבָּלָה בַּלֵּב שֶׁאֲקַבֵּל
עָלַי בְּעַצְמִי. הֵן בְּהָקִיץ הֵן בַּחֲלוֹם חוּץ מִנִּדְרֵי תַעֲנִית בִּשְׁעַת מִנְחָה. וּבְאִם
שֶׁאֶשְׁכַּח לַתְּנַאי מוֹדָעָה הַזֹּאת וְאֶדֹּר מֵהַיּוֹם עוֹד, מֵעַתָּה אֲנִי מִתְחָרֵט עֲלֵיהֶם
וּמַתְנֶה עֲלֵיהֶם שֶׁיִּהְיוּ כֻּלָּן בְּטֵלִין וּמְבֻטָּלִין לָא שְׁרִירִין וְלָא קַיָּמִין וְלָא יְהוֹן חָלִין
כְּלָל וּכְלָל בְּכֻלָּן אִתְחֲרַטְנָא בְּהוֹן (וְלֹא יהיו חלים כלל וכלל, בכולם אני מתחרט
בהם) מֵעַתָּה וְעַד עוֹלָם:

"I hereby submit a disclaimer before you: I cancel from now onward all vows and all oaths, nazirite-vows, prohibitions, bans, agreements, and acceptances in the heart that I may accept upon myself, whether awake or in a dream, with the exception of vows to fast undertaken at the time of the afternoon prayer [of the previous day]. If I forget the conditions of this disclaimer and take any vows from this day onward, I regret them as of now, and stipulate that they should all be null and void, without effect or validity, and they shall have no force whatsoever. With regard to them all, I express regret over them from now and forever."

According to some customs, in response, the "court" recites the following three times:

כֻּלָּם מֻתָּרִים לָךְ, כֻּלָּם שְׁרוּיִם לָךְ, כֻּלָּם מְחוּלִים לָךְ, כְּשֵׁם שֶׁאֲנַחְנוּ מַתִּירִים לָךְ
בְּבֵית דִּין שֶׁל מַטָּה, כָּךְ יְהִיוּ מֻתָּרִים מִבֵּית דִּין שֶׁל מַעְלָה, וְכָל הַקְּלָלוֹת יִתְהַפְּכוּ
עָלֵינוּ לְטוֹבָה וְלִבְרָכָה כְּדִכְתִיב וַיַּהֲפֹךְ ה' אֱלֹהֶיךָ לְּךָ אֶת הַקְּלָלָה לִבְרָכָה כִּי
אֲהֵבְךָ ה' אֱלֹהֶיךָ (דברים כג, ו):

"All of these are permitted to you, all are released for you, all are forgiven you. And just as we have permitted [these vows] for you in the earthly court, so may these [vows] be permitted by the heavenly court. And may all curses be transformed for us into goodness and a blessing, as it is written: 'And the Lord your God transformed for you the curse into a blessing, because the Lord your God loved you'" (Deuteronomy 23:6).

Prozbol

The following *halakha* applies to the day before Rosh HaShana at the conclusion of a Sabbatical Year.

By Torah law (Deuteronomy 15:1-2), the Sabbatical Year effects the release from all interpersonal monetary debts. In order to ensure that people would not refrain from lending money to those in need for fear of losing their money in the Sabbatical Year, the Sages instituted the *prozbol*, a legal transfer of the responsibility for the collection of one's debts to the court, a step which prevents debts from becoming canceled.

Ideally, a lender should sign a *prozbol* document, which includes the signature of three men, who can function in this regard as a court. In various locales, the local rabbinate distributes *prozbol* documents. Nowadays one can also print a *prozbol* document from the internet. In case of need, one can make do with a verbal statement of the following formula, recited in the presence of three men:

הֲרֵינִי מוֹסֵר לָכֶם כָּל חוֹבוֹת שֶׁיֵּשׁ לִי, שֶׁאֶגְבֶּה אוֹתָם כָּל זְמַן שֶׁאֶרְצֶה.

"I hereby transfer to you all debts that I am owed, so that I may exact payment for them whenever I choose."

There is a disagreement with regard to the proper time to make out a *prozbol*. The common practice is to do so before Rosh HaShana at the conclusion of the Sabbatical Year. However, there is an opinion that the proper time is before Rosh HaShana at the beginning of the Sabbatical Year. Some people fill out a *prozbol* before Rosh HaShana at the beginning and end of the Sabbatical Year in order to fulfill this requirement according to all opinions. It is customary to do so immediately after the ceremony of the Annulment of Vows, when three men have already gathered into a makeshift court.

Customs for Rosh HaShana Eve

Some have the custom to visit a cemetery on the day before Rosh HaShana, in order to invoke the merit of the righteous individuals who are buried there, and thereby arouse divine mercy ahead of the day of judgment.

Many men immerse themselves in a ritual bath [*mikva*] on the eve of Rosh HaShana, in order to enter the new year in a state of ritual purity.

It is customary to get a haircut and to wear festive clothing for Rosh HaShana. Although these are somber days of judgment, we are confident that God will have mercy upon us and vindicate us in judgment. For the same reason, it is customary to eat festive meals on Rosh HaShana, just as on other festivals.

There are certain symbolic foods, called *simanim*, that are eaten on the night of the festival. These should be bought and prepared in advance of the holiday. Conversely, there are certain foods that it is customary to avoid eating on Rosh HaShana (see below, p. 141).

Before the holiday, one should light a candle from which he can transfer a flame during the festival for lighting the festival candles on the second night and for cooking if needed. It is best to use a candle that will remain burning for forty-eight hours. One who does not have such a candle should light one that lasts twenty-four hours, and if he will need a flame on the second day, he should light another twenty-four hour candle from that first candle before it expires.

When Rosh HaShana falls on Thursday and Friday, one must perform a procedure called *eruv tavshilin* before the festival. This procedure, which entails designating some bread and a cooked dish to be eaten on the Shabbat that immediately follows the festival, allows one to cook on the second day of the festival (through the transfer of fire from an existing flame) in honor of the approaching Shabbat. Likewise, the *eruv tavshilin* permits one to light Shabbat candles on the second day of Rosh HaShana before the start of Shabbat. One should make sure that the candle that is lit on the eve of the festival is large enough to remain burning until the time for lighting the Shabbat candles.

As mentioned above, Rosh HaShana is a festival, and therefore all the laws of the other festivals apply here as well. For more details on this topic, as well as how to perform an *eruv tavshilin*, see the chapters dealing with the *halakhot* of festivals (pp. 464, 474).

Lighting Candles

When the first day of Rosh HaShana is on a weekday, the candles may be lit before the festival begins, as is done for Shabbat. Alternatively, they can even be lit after the festival begins, as long as they are lit from an existing flame. However, when the festival occurs on Shabbat, the Shabbat/festival candles must be lit before sunset.

When lighting the candles on the first night of Rosh HaShana, two blessings are recited:

בָּרוּךְ אַתָּה אֲדֹנָי, אֱלֹהֵינוּ מֶלֶךְ הָעוֹלָם,
אֲשֶׁר קִדְּשָׁנוּ בְּמִצְוֹתָיו וְצִוָּנוּ לְהַדְלִיק נֵר
שֶׁל יוֹם טוֹב (וְאִם חָל בְּשַׁבָּת: שֶׁל שַׁבָּת
וְשֶׁל יוֹם טוֹב).

Barukh ata Adonai, Eloheinu, melekh ha'olam, asher kideshanu bemitzvotav, vetzivanu lehadlik ner shel yom tov (on Shabbat conclude instead: *lehadlik ner shel Shabbat veshel yom tov*).

"Blessed are You, Lord our God, King of the universe, who sanctified us through His commandments, and commanded us to light a candle for the festival (on Shabbat conclude instead: …for Shabbat and for the festival)."

Yearly Cycle

בָּרוּךְ אַתָּה אֲדֹנָי, אֱלֹהֵינוּ מֶלֶךְ הָעוֹלָם,
שֶׁהֶחֱיָנוּ וְקִיְּמָנוּ וְהִגִּיעָנוּ לַזְּמַן הַזֶּה.

Barukh ata Adonai, Eloheinu, melekh ha'olam, sheheheyanu vekiyemanu vehigi'anu la'zeman hazeh.

"Blessed are You, Lord our God, King of the universe, who has given us life, sustained us, and brought us to this time."

📖 **Further reading:** For more details on the *halakhot* of candle lighting, see p. 381.

Rosh HaShana Night

The night of Rosh HaShana is the night on which the new year begins, and this evening and its prayers are especially celebratory, although they also have a distinctive solemn tone. It is stated in the kabbalistic and hasidic literature that prayers on this night bear great weight for the continued existence of the entire world as well as for the life of the individual.

The structure and wording of the Rosh HaShana and Yom Kippur prayers differ from the prayers of the other festivals. Therefore, it is a good idea to review them in advance in order to understand the meaning of the prayers and to familiarize oneself with the order of the prayer service. There are also quite a few differences between the prayer texts of the various communities, and consequently it is recommended to have a *mahzor* that is suitable for the prayer service of the synagogue where one will be praying.

Communities and Customs

Some communities have the custom to sing before the Rosh HaShana evening prayer service the liturgical song "Little Sister" [*Ahot Ketana*], with its chorus of: "May the [old] year and its scourges end," and finishing with: "Let the [new] year and its blessings begin."

When Rosh HaShana occurs on Shabbat, the congregation recites before the evening prayer an abbreviated version of *Kabbalat Shabbat*, beginning with Psalms 92, "A psalm, a song for the Sabbath day" [*Mizmor shir leyom haShabbat*], or in some communities, with Psalms 29, "A song by David" [*Mizmor leDavid*]. At the end of the prayer service, the following sections are added: the passage beginning, "The heavens and the earth" [*Vaykhulu hashamayim veha'aretz*] (Genesis 2:1–3), the *Magen Avot* prayer, and in some communities Psalms 23, "A psalm by David [*Mizmor leDavid*].

After the service, it is customary to greet one another with the blessing: "May you be inscribed and sealed for a good year." Some add: "…immediately, for a good life and for peace," or "for a good, lengthy life and for peace." According to the Yemenite custom, the one issuing the greeting says: "May you be inscribed in the book of life and in the book of remembrance," and the one receiving the blessing responds: "And may you [too] be inscribed in the book of life and in the book of remembrance."

Kiddush at Night

As on every Friday and festival night, *Kiddush* is recited over a full cup of wine before the evening meal (for details of the laws of *Kiddush*, see p. 386). The wording of the *Kiddush* on Rosh HaShana differs from that of the other festivals.

If Rosh HaShana falls on Shabbat, one first says:

For Ashkenazim:

(בלחש: וַיְהִי עֶרֶב וַיְהִי בֹקֶר) יוֹם הַשִּׁשִּׁי
וַיְכֻלּוּ הַשָּׁמַיִם וְהָאָרֶץ וְכָל צְבָאָם. וַיְכַל
אֱלֹהִים בַּיּוֹם הַשְּׁבִיעִי מְלַאכְתּוֹ אֲשֶׁר
עָשָׂה, וַיִּשְׁבֹּת בַּיּוֹם הַשְּׁבִיעִי מִכָּל מְלַאכְתּוֹ
אֲשֶׁר עָשָׂה. וַיְבָרֶךְ אֱלֹהִים אֶת יוֹם הַשְּׁבִיעִי
וַיְקַדֵּשׁ אֹתוֹ, כִּי בוֹ שָׁבַת מִכָּל מְלַאכְתּוֹ
אֲשֶׁר בָּרָא אֱלֹהִים לַעֲשׂוֹת.

(Quietly: *Vayhi erev vayhi voker*) *yom hashishi. Vaykhulu hashamayim veha'aretz vekhol tzeva'am. Vaykhal Elohim bayom hashevi'i melakhto asher asa, vayishbot bayom hashevi'i mikol melakhto asher asa. Vayvarekh Elohim et yom hashevi'i vaykadesh oto, ki vo shavat mikol melakhto asher bara Elohim la'asot.*

When Rosh HaShana falls on a weekday, one begins here:

סַבְרִי מָרָנָן וְרַבָּנָן וְרַבּוֹתַי.

Savri meranan verabanan verabotai:

בָּרוּךְ אַתָּה אֲדֹנָי, אֱלֹהֵינוּ מֶלֶךְ הָעוֹלָם,
בּוֹרֵא פְּרִי הַגָּפֶן.

Barukh ata Adonai, Eloheinu, melekh ha'olam, boreh peri hagafen.

בָּרוּךְ אַתָּה אֲדֹנָי, אֱלֹהֵינוּ מֶלֶךְ הָעוֹלָם,
אֲשֶׁר בָּחַר בָּנוּ מִכָּל עָם, וְרוֹמְמָנוּ מִכָּל
לָשׁוֹן, וְקִדְּשָׁנוּ בְּמִצְוֹתָיו וַתִּתֶּן לָנוּ אֲדֹנָי
אֱלֹהֵינוּ בְּאַהֲבָה אֶת יוֹם (בשבת: הַשַּׁבָּת
הַזֶּה וְאֶת יוֹם) הַזִּכָּרוֹן הַזֶּה, יוֹם (בשבת:
זִכְרוֹן) תְּרוּעָה (בשבת: בְּאַהֲבָה) מִקְרָא
קֹדֶשׁ, זֵכֶר לִיצִיאַת מִצְרַיִם. כִּי בָנוּ בָחַרְתָּ
וְאוֹתָנוּ קִדַּשְׁתָּ מִכָּל הָעַמִּים, וּדְבָרְךָ אֱמֶת
וְקַיָּם לָעַד. בָּרוּךְ אַתָּה אֲדֹנָי, מֶלֶךְ עַל כָּל
הָאָרֶץ, מְקַדֵּשׁ (בשבת: הַשַּׁבָּת וְ)יִשְׂרָאֵל
וְיוֹם הַזִּכָּרוֹן.

Barukh ata Adonai, Eloheinu, melekh ha'olam, asher baḥar banu mikol am, veromemanu mikol lashon, vekideshanu bemitzvotav. Vatiten lanu Adonai Eloheinu be'ahava, et yom (on Shabbat: haShabbat hazeh ve'et yom) hazikaron hazeh, yom (on Shabbat: zikhron) teru'a (on Shabbat: be'ahava) mikra kodesh, zekher litziat Mitzrayim. Ki vanu vaḥarta ve'otanu kidashta mikol ha'amim, udvarekha emet vekayam la'ad. Barukh ata Adonai, melekh al kol ha'aretz, mekadesh (on Shabbat: ha-Shabbat ve) Yisrael veyom hazikaron.

(Quietly: "It was evening and it was morning,) the sixth day. The heavens and the earth and their entire host were completed. God completed on the seventh day His works that He had made; He rested on the seventh day from all His works that He had made. God blessed the seventh day, and sanctified it; because on it He rested from all His works that God created to make" (Genesis 1:31–2:3).

When Rosh HaShana falls on a weekday, one begins here:

"Attention, masters, rabbis, and my teachers:

"Blessed are You, Lord our God, King of the universe, who creates the fruit of the vine.

"Blessed are You, Lord our God, King of the universe, who has chosen us from all nations, and raised us above all tongues, and sanctified us through His commandments. And You have given us, Lord our God, in love, this (on Shabbat add: Shabbat day and this) Day of Remembrance, a day of (on Shabbat add: recalling) shofar-blasts, (on Shabbat add: with love,) a holy convocation, in memory of the exodus from Egypt. For You have chosen us and sanctified us above all nations, and Your word is true and endures forever. Blessed are You, Lord, King over all the earth, who sanctifies (on Shabbat add: the Shabbat,) Israel, and the Day of Remembrance."

For Sephardim:

וַיְהִי עֶרֶב וַיְהִי בֹקֶר יוֹם הַשִּׁשִּׁי. וַיְכֻלּוּ הַשָּׁמַיִם וְהָאָרֶץ וְכָל צְבָאָם. וַיְכַל אֱלֹהִים בַּיּוֹם הַשְּׁבִיעִי מְלַאכְתּוֹ אֲשֶׁר עָשָׂה, וַיִּשְׁבֹּת בַּיּוֹם הַשְּׁבִיעִי מִכָּל מְלַאכְתּוֹ אֲשֶׁר עָשָׂה. וַיְבָרֶךְ אֱלֹהִים אֶת יוֹם הַשְּׁבִיעִי וַיְקַדֵּשׁ אֹתוֹ, כִּי בוֹ שָׁבַת מִכָּל מְלַאכְתּוֹ אֲשֶׁר בָּרָא אֱלֹהִים לַעֲשׂוֹת.

Vayhi erev vayhi voker yom Hashishi. Vaykhulu hashamayim veha'aretz vekhol tzeva'am. Vaykhal Elohim bayom hashevi'i melakhto asher asa, vayishbot bayom hashevi'i mikol melakhto asher asa. Vayvarekh Elohim et yom hashevi'i vaykadesh oto, ki vo shavat mikol melakhto asher bara Elohim la'asot.

וּבְיוֹם שִׂמְחַתְכֶם וּבְמוֹעֲדֵיכֶם וּבְרָאשֵׁי חָדְשֵׁיכֶם וּתְקַעְתֶּם בַּחֲצֹצְרֹת עַל עֹלֹתֵיכֶם וְעַל זִבְחֵי שַׁלְמֵיכֶם וְהָיוּ לָכֶם לְזִכָּרוֹן לִפְנֵי אֱלֹהֵיכֶם אֲנִי אֲדֹנָי אֱלֹהֵיכֶם.

Uvyom simḥatkhem uvmo'a'deikhem uvrashei ḥodsheikhem, utka'tem baḥatzotzrot al oloteikhem ve'al zivḥei shalmeikhem, vehayu lakhem lezikaron lifnei Eloheikhem, ani Adonai Eloheikhem.

סַבְרִי מָרָנָן   *Savri meranan.*

הַשּׁוֹמְעִים עוֹנִים: לְחַיִּים!   Those listening respond: *Leḥayim.*

בָּרוּךְ אַתָּה אֲדֹנָי, אֱלֹהֵינוּ מֶלֶךְ הָעוֹלָם, בּוֹרֵא פְּרִי הַגָּפֶן.

Barukh ata Adonai, Eloheinu, melekh ha'olam, boreh peri hagefen.

בָּרוּךְ אַתָּה אֲדֹנָי, אֱלֹהֵינוּ מֶלֶךְ הָעוֹלָם, אֲשֶׁר בָּחַר בָּנוּ מִכָּל עָם, וְרוֹמְמָנוּ מִכָּל לָשׁוֹן, וְקִדְּשָׁנוּ בְּמִצְוֹתָיו וַתִּתֶּן לָנוּ אֲדֹנָי אֱלֹהֵינוּ בְּאַהֲבָה אֶת יוֹם (בשבת: הַשַּׁבָּת הַזֶּה וְאֶת יוֹם) הַזִּכָּרוֹן הַזֶּה, אֶת יוֹם טוֹב מִקְרָא קֹדֶשׁ הַזֶּה, יוֹם (בשבת: זִכְרוֹן) תְּרוּעָה (בשבת: בְּאַהֲבָה) מִקְרָא קֹדֶשׁ, זֵכֶר לִיצִיאַת מִצְרָיִם. וּדְבָרְךָ אֱמֶת וְקַיָּם לָעַד. בָּרוּךְ אַתָּה אֲדֹנָי, מֶלֶךְ עַל כָּל הָאָרֶץ, מְקַדֵּשׁ (בשבת: הַשַּׁבָּת וְ)יִשְׂרָאֵל וְיוֹם הַזִּכָּרוֹן.

Barukh ata Adonai, Eloheinu, melekh ha'olam, asher baḥar banu mikol am, veromemanu mikol lashon, vekidesha-nu bemitzvotav. Vatiten lanu Adonai Eloheinu be'ahava, et yom (on Shabbat: haShabbat hazeh ve'et yom) hazikaron hazeh, et yom tov mikra kodesh hazeh, yom (on Shabbat: zikhron) teru'a (on Shabbat: be'ahava) mikra kodesh, ze-kher litziat Mitzrayim. Udva'rekha emet vekayam la'ad. Barukh ata Ado-nai, melekh al kol ha'aretz, mekadesh (on Shabbat: HaShabbat ve) Yisrael veyom hazikaron.

"It was evening and it was morning, the sixth day. The heavens and the earth and their entire host were completed. God completed on the seventh day His works that He had made; He rested on the seventh day from all His works that He had made. God blessed the seventh day, and sanctified it; be-cause on it He rested from all His works that God created to make" (Genesis 1:31–2:3).

"And on the day of your rejoicing, and at your appointed times, and on your New Moons, you shall sound the trumpets over your burnt offerings, and over your peace offerings and they shall be a remembrance for you be-fore your God, I am the Lord your God" (Numbers 10:10).

"Attention, masters."

Those listening respond: "To life!"

"Blessed are You, Lord our God, King of the universe, who creates the fruit of the vine.

"Blessed are You, Lord our God, King of the universe, who has chosen us from all nations, and raised us above all tongues, and sanctified us through His commandments. And You have given us, Lord our God, in love, this (on Shabbat add: Shabbat day and this) Day of Remembrance, this festival day, a holy convocation, a day of (on Shabbat add: recalling) shofar-blasts, (on Shabbat add: with love,) a holy assembly, in memory of the exodus from Egypt. Your word is true and endures forever. Blessed are You, Lord, King of the universe, who sanctifies (on Shabbat add: the Shabbat), Israel, and the Day of Remembrance."

When the first day of Rosh HaShana falls on Shabbat, it is necessary to perform *Havdala* as part of the *Kiddush* of the second festival night, in order to distinguish between the sanctity of Shabbat and the lesser sanctity of the festival. Therefore, two additional blessings are added at this point in the *Kiddush*. First, one brings a candle that was lit before Shabbat, or one lights a candle from an existing flame. It is important to note that one may not extinguish any flame on the festival. The following blessings are then recited:

בָּרוּךְ אַתָּה אֲדֹנָי, אֱלֹהֵינוּ מֶלֶךְ הָעוֹלָם,
בּוֹרֵא מְאוֹרֵי הָאֵשׁ.

Barukh ata Adonai, Eloheinu, melekh ha'olam, boreh me'orei ha'esh.

בָּרוּךְ אַתָּה אֲדֹנָי, אֱלֹהֵינוּ מֶלֶךְ הָעוֹלָם,
הַמַּבְדִּיל בֵּין קֹדֶשׁ לְחוֹל בֵּין אוֹר לְחֹשֶׁךְ
בֵּין יִשְׂרָאֵל לָעַמִּים בֵּין יוֹם הַשְּׁבִיעִי לְשֵׁשֶׁת
יְמֵי הַמַּעֲשֶׂה. בֵּין קְדֻשַּׁת שַׁבָּת לִקְדֻשַּׁת
יוֹם טוֹב הִבְדַּלְתָּ וְאֶת יוֹם הַשְּׁבִיעִי מִשֵּׁשֶׁת
יְמֵי הַמַּעֲשֶׂה קִדַּשְׁתָּ הִבְדַּלְתָּ וְקִדַּשְׁתָּ אֶת
עַמְּךָ יִשְׂרָאֵל בִּקְדֻשָּׁתֶךָ. בָּרוּךְ אַתָּה אֲדֹנָי,
הַמַּבְדִּיל בֵּין קֹדֶשׁ לְקֹדֶשׁ.

Barukh ata Adonai, Eloheinu, melekh ha'olam, hamavdil bein kodesh lehol, bein or lehoshekh, bein Yisrael la'amim, bein yom hashevi'i lesheshet yemei hama'aseh. Bein kedushat Shabbat likdushat Yom Tov hivdalta, ve'et yom hashevi'i misheshet yemei hama'aseh kidashta. Hivdalta vekidashta et amekha Yisrael bikdushatekha. Barukh ata Adonai, hamavdil bein kodesh lekodesh.

"Blessed are You, Lord our God, King of the universe, who creates the lights of fire.

"Blessed are You, Lord our God, King of the universe, who distinguishes between sacred and mundane, between light and darkness, between Israel and the [other] nations, between the seventh day and the six days of work. You have distinguished between the sanctity of Shabbat and the sanctity of festivals, and You have sanctified the seventh day above the six days of activity. You have distinguished and sanctified Your people Israel with Your sanctity. Blessed are You, Lord, who distinguishes between sacred and sacred."

The additional section for the conclusion of Shabbat ends here.

As on the other festivals, at the end of *Kiddush* one adds the *Sheheheyanu* blessing on both nights (some place a new fruit on the table on the second night, so that one can look at it and have it in mind when the blessing is recited):

בָּרוּךְ אַתָּה אֲדֹנָי, אֱלֹהֵינוּ מֶלֶךְ הָעוֹלָם,   *Barukh ata Adonai, Eloheinu, melekh*
שֶׁהֶחֱיָנוּ וְקִיְּמָנוּ וְהִגִּיעָנוּ לַזְּמַן הַזֶּה.   *ha'olam, sheheheyanu vekiyemanu vehigi'anu la'zeman hazeh.*

"Blessed are You, Lord our God, King of the universe, who has given us life, sustained us, and brought us to this time."

The Festival Meals

Rosh HaShana is not only the first day of the year, but also the head [*rosh*] of the entire year. Just as the head of a person leads and directs all the limbs of the body, so too, Rosh HaShana can have an impact on the forthcoming year. Based on this idea, various customs have been introduced whose purpose is to augur good fortune for the new year.

Good Omens for a Good Year

It is customary to eat sweet foods on Rosh HaShana and to refrain from eating spicy or sour dishes, so that the coming year will be sweet. Likewise, there is a widespread custom to partake of foods whose taste or names allude to abundance and prosperity.

There is a custom not to eat nuts on Rosh HaShana, as the numerical value of *egoz*, the Hebrew word for "nut," is identical to that of the word for *het*, sin (not counting the silent letter *alef* at the end of *het*). There is also another, highly practical reason for this custom: Consuming nuts creates a lot of phlegm, which makes it more difficult to recite the many prayers of this day.

Additionally, in a practice unrelated to food, one should try as much as possible to avoid anger and quarrels on Rosh HaShana, so as not to arouse divine anger for the coming year. One should make an effort not to sleep during the daytime of Rosh HaShana, so that one's fortune [*mazal*] should not be dormant in the upcoming year.

Simanim for the Festival

The special foods eaten on Rosh HaShana, as a sign that the next year should be one of abundance and blessing, are appropriately called *simanim* (or in singular, *siman*), which means signs.

In many communities, it is customary before partaking of each *siman* to recite a prayer formula that begins with the following standard phrase:

יְהִי רָצוֹן מִלְּפָנֶיךָ (וְיֵשׁ מוֹסִיפִים: אֲדֹנָי | *Yehi ratzon milefanekha (some add:*
אֱלֹהֵינוּ וֵאלֹהֵי אֲבוֹתֵינוּ) | *Adonai Eloheinu velohei avoteinu)*

"May it be Your will (some add: Lord our God and God of our fathers)"

The formula continues with a prayer that suits the specific food being eaten. Some recite this formula before the blessing; they first say: "May it be Your will ...," and then recite the blessing for the food itself, whether it be "...who creates the fruit of the tree," or "...who creates fruit of the ground," or "... by whose word all things came to be," depending on the nature of the food being eaten. A single blessing is sufficient for all types of food covered by that blessing; see p. 514. Others recite the prayer formula after saying the blessing and taking a bite of the food. And there are also those, such as the Lubavitch Hasidim, who recite the formula between the blessing and the eating.

The following are the most common simanim used in most communities, some of which are mentioned in the Talmud:

Apple dipped in honey:

...שֶׁתְּחַדֵּשׁ עָלֵינוּ שָׁנָה טוֹבָה וּמְתוּקָה (וְיֵשׁ | *...shetehadesh aleinu shana tova um-*
מוֹסִיפִים: מֵרֵאשִׁית הַשָּׁנָה וְעַד אַחֲרִיתָהּ). | *tuka (some add: mereshit hashana ve'ad aharitah).*

"...that You initiate for us a good and sweet year (some add: from the beginning of the year until its conclusion)."

Gourd [*kara*]:

...שֶׁתִּקְרַע רוֹעַ גְּזַר דִּינֵנוּ וְיִקָּרְאוּ לְפָנֶיךָ | *... shetikra ro'a gezar dinenu veyikare'u*
זְכִיּוֹתֵינוּ. | *lefanekha zekhuyoteinu.*

"...that You tear up [*tikra*] the evil decree against us, and that our merit be read out [*yikaru*] before You."

Fenugreek [*rubya*] or cowpea [*luvya*]:

...שֶׁיִּרְבּוּ זְכִיּוֹתֵינוּ (וְהָאוֹכְלִים לוּבְיָה | *... sheyirbu zekhuyoteinu (those who*
מוֹסִיפִים: וּתְלַבְּבֵינוּ). | *eat luvya add: utlabeveinu).*

"…that our merits increase [*yirbu*] (those who eat *luvya* add: and You hearten us [*utlabeveinu*])."

Leek [*karti*]:

…שֶׁיִּכָּרְתוּ אוֹיְבֵינוּ (ויש מוסיפים: **שׂוֹנְאֵינוּ וְכָל מְבַקְשֵׁי רָעָתֵנוּ**). … *sheyikaretu oyeveinu* (some add: *sone'einu vekhol mevakeshai ra'atenu*).

"…that our enemies (some add: those who hate us and all those who seek our misfortune) be cut off [*yikartu*]."

Beet/spinach [*silka*]:

…שֶׁיִּסְתַּלְּקוּ אוֹיְבֵינוּ (ויש מוסיפים: **שׂוֹנְאֵינוּ וְכָל מְבַקְשֵׁי רָעָתֵנוּ**). … *sheyistalku oyeveinu* (some add: *sone'einu vekhol mevakeshai ra'atenu*).

"…that our enemies (some add: those who hate us and all those who seek our misfortune) be removed [*yistalku*]."

Date [*tamar*]:

…שֶׁיִּתַּמּוּ אוֹיְבֵינוּ (ויש מוסיפים: **שׂוֹנְאֵינוּ וְכָל מְבַקְשֵׁי רָעָתֵנוּ**). … *sheyitamu oyeveinu* (some add: *sone'einu vekhol mevakeshai ra'atenu*).

"…that our enemies (some add: those who hate us and all those who seek our misfortune) cease [*yitamu*]."

Pomegranate [*rimon*]:

…שֶׁיִּרְבּוּ זְכֻיּוֹתֵינוּ כָּרִמּוֹן. … *sheyirbu zekhuyoteinu karimon.*

"…that our merits increase like [the seeds of] a pomegranate [*rimon*]."

Head of a fish or lamb:

…שֶׁנִּהְיֶה לְרֹאשׁ וְלֹא לְזָנָב. … *sheniheye lerosh velo lezanav.*

"…that we be the head [*rosh*] and not the tail."

Those who are particular to eat the head of a lamb do so in order to invoke the merit of our forefather Abraham, who through supreme heroism withstood the trial of bringing his son Isaac for a sacrifice, and eventually offered a ram on the altar in his stead.

Fish [*dag*]:

שֶׁנִּפְרֶה וְנִרְבֶּה כַּדָּגִים. ...   ... *shenifreh venirbeh kedagim.*

"...that we be fruitful and multiply like fish [*dag*]."

The *simanim* are eaten at the nighttime meals of Rosh HaShana, although some have them only on the first night of the festival. There are also varying customs with regard to the exact timing. Some eat the *simanim* between *Kiddush* and the washing of the hands. Others have the custom to eat them after partaking of the bread. Yet others spread out the consumption of the *simanim* throughout the meal, with the sweet foods kept to the end and eaten as a dessert.

If the *simanim* are eaten between *Kiddush* and the start of the meal, one should recite the appropriate blessing before eating them, unless one has already recited that blessing over a different one of the *simanim*. In the event that one is about to eat several foods one after the other, it would be preferable to recite the blessing on fruit over a fruit from the seven species mentioned in Deuteronomy 8:8. In this case, one would recite the blessing over the dates, and if he does not have dates, than he would recite it over the pomegranate. If he does not have either one of those fruits, he would recite the blessing over whichever fruit he likes best. Some prefer to eat the apple first even if they have dates and pomegranates. In such a case, it would be preferable to bring those fruits to the table after he has recited the blessing over the apple. It should be noted that the blessings on fruit and on produce grown in the ground, such as vegetables, should precede the blessing: "...by whose word all things came to be," recited over the head of the fish or lamb.

If one eats the *simanim* after eating bread, one should recite a blessing only on foods that are not considered part of the meal, that is, only on the fruit, not the vegetables, fish, or meat.

Additional Laws

As with every Shabbat and festival, two whole loaves of bread [*lehem mishneh*] are placed on the table for each Rosh HaShana meal. But unlike other Shabbatot and festivals, when the first slice of bread of the meal is dipped in salt, on Rosh HaShana the first slice is eaten with honey, and some have the custom of dipping it in sugar. Some place a salt shaker on the table as well as a honey dish, and there are those who dip the slice in a little salt after applying the honey. In some communities it is the custom to eat the bread with honey on all the Shabbatot and festivals between Rosh HaShana and *Simhat Torah.*

In Grace after Meals, the *Ya'aleh VeYavo* prayer is added, mentioning therein "this Day of Remembrance." At the end of Grace after Meals, two additional lines beginning with the words "The Compassionate One" [*Haraḥaman*] are added: The standard one for every festival, "May the Compassionate One endow us with the day that is all good," and a special one for Rosh HaShana: "May the Compassionate One renew this year for us for goodness and for a blessing."

When Rosh HaShana occurs on a Shabbat, a passage is added to Grace after Meals in order to mention Shabbat. The passage of *Retzeh* is added before *Ya'aleh VeYavo*, and later in Grace after Meals one recites: "May the Compassionate One allow us to inherit the day [in the World to Come] that will be an eternal Shabbat and everlasting rest."

Some have the custom of learning one chapter of *mishnayot* from tractate *Rosh HaShana* after each of the four meals of the festival (two on each day), thereby finishing all four chapters of the tractate over the course of the festival.

Morning Prayers

On the morning of Rosh HaShana, one begins with the morning prayer service. This includes a variety of liturgical poems that are recited during the cantor's repetition of the *Amida* prayer. Unlike the rest of the festivals, on Rosh HaShana and Yom Kippur, *Hallel* is not recited. This is because the *Hallel* prayer expresses feelings of joy, whereas on Rosh HaShana and on Yom Kippur the experience is one of awe and and the dread of judgment. After the morning prayers, the Torah is read, after which the shofar blasts are sounded. This is followed by the additional prayer [*Musaf*].

Torah Reading

For the reading of the Torah, two Torah scrolls are removed from the ark (for more details on the procedure and *halakhot* of Torah reading, see pp. 392, 492). The reading from the first scroll is divided into five segments [*aliyot*]. If Rosh HaShana falls on a Shabbat, the same reading is divided into seven *aliyot*, the same number as on every Shabbat. An additional Torah segment, called the *maftir*, is read from a second Torah scroll, and consists of verses discussing the offerings sacrificed in the Temple on Rosh HaShana (Numbers 29:1–6).

On the first day of Rosh HaShana the reading is from the book of Genesis (chapter 21), relating the story of the birth of Isaac. The reason for this is that according to tradition Isaac was conceived on Rosh HaShana. On the second day of Rosh HaShana another passage from Genesis is read (chapter 22), which recounts the story of the binding [*akeida*] of Isaac. This is in order to arouse God's mercy upon us, in the merit of the righteous deeds of our forefathers.

The person called up for *maftir* reads the *haftara*, which consists of a passage from the Prophets. On the first day of Rosh HaShana the story of the birth of the prophet Samuel (I Samuel 1:1–2) is read, since according to rabbinic tradition he was also conceived on Rosh HaShana. The *haftara* for the second day of Rosh HaShana is from the book of Jeremiah (31:1–19), a selection that speaks of the merits of the children of Israel.

The Sounding of the Shofar

The sounding of the shofar is the central commandment on Rosh HaShana, and for this reason it is called by the Torah "the day of shofar blasts" [*yom terua*]. Rav Se'adya Gaon listed ten rationales for this mitzva. Among them are the following:

On this day we reaccept upon ourselves the kingship of God, and it is customary to blow trumpets to herald the arrival of a king.

The shofar awakens people's hearts to repentance, as the prophet Amos says: "Will the shofar be sounded in a city, and the people not tremble?" (Amos 3:6).

The ram's horn recalls before God the ram that Abraham sacrificed in place of his son Isaac.

The sound of the shofar evokes in our hearts the memory of the giving of the Torah at Mount Sinai, when the people heard "the blast of a shofar extremely powerful" (Exodus 19:16).

The commandment of the shofar is a time-bound positive mitzva, and as such, women are exempt from it. Nevertheless, many women have taken upon themselves to observe this mitzva, and therefore they too should hear the shofar; they may even recite the blessing over the shofar blowing when the shofar is being sounded for them alone. It is also recommended to bring one's children to the synagogue to hear the shofar as well, in order to educate them in the performance of mitzvot, provided that they will not disturb the congregation.

This mitzva can be fulfilled at any time throughout the day. Accordingly, if someone missed hearing the blasts in the synagogue, he should blow the shofar himself, or find someone who can do so for him, at any point before sunset.

The Shofar

After the reading of the Torah and the *haftara*, the congregation prepares itself for the sounding of the shofar, which is the climax of Rosh HaShana. The sounding of the shofar is performed on both days of the festival, except when the first day of Rosh HaShana falls on Shabbat, in which case the shofar is not sounded. Instead, the prayers continue directly with *Musaf*, and the shofar is sounded only on the second day of the festival.

The shofar can be made of the hollow horn of any kosher animal, as long as it is naturally hollow, as opposed to a unified mass that must be chiseled out. However, the horn of a cow may not be used. There is a halakhic preference for a shofar made from the horn of a ram, and it is a ram's horn that is used for the mitzva in almost all communities. In some Yemenite communities they use an elongated, twisted shofar, which is made from a horn of a kudu (an African antelope).

The Shofar Blasts

The mitzva of shofar on Rosh HaShana entails blowing or hearing a series of thirty blasts, consisting of three types of sound called *tekia*, *shevarim*, and *terua*. The *tekia* is one long blast; *shevarim* consists of three medium-length sounds; and *terua* is a series of at least nine short sounds.

By Torah law, one is obligated to hear only nine shofar blasts: three sets of *tekia-terua-tekia*. If so, how did we get to thirty? The requirement to blow thirty blasts evolved from a discussion among the Sages in the Talmud over the exact definition of the *terua* required by the Torah. Is it a sound that is reminiscent of moaning (that which we call *shevarim*), or whimpering (that which we call *terua*)? Or is it perhaps a combination of both (that which we call *shevarim-terua*)? Since the question was not decisively settled, the talmudic Sage Rabbi Abbahu instituted the series of blasts that is customarily performed today, which combines all the possibilities:

First a series is sounded that accounts for the possibility that the *terua* required by the Torah is a combination of the blasts currently known as *shevarim* and *terua*. Therefore, the series of *tekia-shevarim-terua-tekia* (sometimes referred to as "*tashrat*," which is an acronym of the words *tekia*, *shevarim*, *terua*, and *tekia*) is blown three times.

After this set, blasts are sounded that conform with the other two possibilities, that perhaps the *terua* referred to in the Torah is what is currently referred to as a *shevarim*, or what is currently referred to as a *terua*. Consequently, three sets of *tekia-shevarim-tekia* (sometimes called *"tashat"*) are sounded, followed by three sets of *tekia-terua-tekia* (sometimes called *"tarat"*).

This sequence of blasts, which includes all the possibilities, consists of a total of thirty sounds, and this is the basic obligation of the mitzva of shofar on Rosh HaShana.

Although one has certainly fulfilled the mitzva upon hearing thirty blasts, it is customary to blow one hundred blasts in the synagogue on the morning of Rosh HaShana. Thirty blasts are blown before the beginning of *Musaf*, the additional prayer service. During the cantor's repetition of the *Amida* of *Musaf*, an additional thirty blasts are blown, and then during Kaddish after the cantor's repetition an additional forty blasts are sounded, bringing the total to one hundred. In Sephardic and hasidic communities, besides the thirty blasts blown before *Musaf*, it is customary to sound thirty blasts during the silent *Amida* of *Musaf*, thirty more during the cantor's repetition, and only ten during Kaddish following the cantor's repetition.

The Procedure for Shofar Blowing

The person sounding the shofar, who is called the *ba'al toke'a*, should be a God-fearing man who is meticulous in his mitzva observance. It is preferable for him to be married, over the age of thirty, a father, and not involved in any conflict with any member of the congregation. Another man stands alongside the *ba'al toke'a* to call out the name of the upcoming sound, so as to avoid confusion in the sequence of the blasts.

Before the blasts it is customary to recite Psalms 47 seven times, and then to say a series of verses whose initial letters form the words *kera Satan*, meaning "hinder [literally, "tear"] Satan." This is an appeal to God to deter the accusations of the accusing angel against the Jewish people.

Before the blasts, the *ba'al toke'a* recites two blessings aloud:

בָּרוּךְ אַתָּה אֲדֹנָי, אֱלֹהֵינוּ מֶלֶךְ הָעוֹלָם, אֲשֶׁר קִדְּשָׁנוּ בְּמִצְוֹתָיו, וְצִוָּנוּ לִשְׁמֹעַ קוֹל שׁוֹפָר.	*Barukh ata Adonai, Eloheinu, melekh ha'olam, asher kideshanu bemitzvotav, vetzivanu lishmo'a kol shofar.*
בָּרוּךְ אַתָּה אֲדֹנָי, אֱלֹהֵינוּ מֶלֶךְ הָעוֹלָם, שֶׁהֶחֱיָנוּ וְקִיְּמָנוּ וְהִגִּיעָנוּ לַזְּמַן הַזֶּה.	*Barukh ata Adonai, Eloheinu, melekh ha'olam, sheheheyanu vekiyemanu vehigi'anu la'zeman hazeh.*

"Blessed are You, Lord our God, King of the universe, who sanctified us through His commandments, and commanded us to hear the sound of the shofar."

"Blessed are You, Lord our God, King of the universe, who has given us life, sustained us, and brought us to this time."

The congregation answers "amen" after each of the blessings, with the intention of fulfilling their obligation concerning both the recitation of the blessings and the blasts themselves. The *ba'al toke'a* should also have in mind that he is reciting the blessings and blowing the shofar on behalf of the entire congregation.

After the blessings, the *ba'al toke'a* sounds the first thirty blasts. They are called "the blasts heard while sitting," as in principle the congregation may listen to them when they are seated. Nevertheless, in most communities it is customary to stand for all the blasts. After these blasts, the congregation recites a few more verses and then the *Musaf* service begins.

The Additional [*Musaf*] Prayer

The *Amida* recited in the *Musaf* service of Rosh HaShana differs from that of Shabbat and the other festivals in that the *Amida* contains nine blessings instead of seven: the standard first three and the last three, as in all *Amida* prayers, and three unique blessings in the middle which each include ten specialized verses related to the blessings. These three blessings are called Kingship [*Malkhuyot*], Remembrance [*Zikhronot*], and Shofar [*Shofarot*]. The first blessing includes ten biblical verses that relate to God's kingship over all of creation. In the second blessing of Remembrance, ten verses are cited that attest to the fact that God remembers all deeds performed by every person throughout history. The third blessing about Shofar quotes ten verses describing the sound of the shofar in various historical settings, past and future, from the revelation at Sinai until the messianic redemption, about which it is stated: "It shall be on that day, that a great shofar will be sounded" (Isaiah 27:13).

Blasts Heard While Standing

The congregation first prays the *Musaf Amida* silently, each person to himself. In some communities, especially among Sephardim and Hasidim, the shofar is sounded during this silent prayer as well, at the end of each of the three aforementioned specialized blessings. These soundings are performed as follows: When reaching the end of the blessing of Kingship, each worshipper stops and waits for the sounding of the shofar. The *ba'al toke'a* waits until in his estimation most of the congregation has finished the blessing, and then he sounds ten blasts (*tashrat, tashat, tarat*). When he has concluded, each person returns to his personal prayer and recites the blessing of

Remembrance, at the end of which he waits for another series of blasts. The same process is repeated for the Shofar blessing. The total number of blasts sounded in the silent *Musaf* is thus thirty. These blasts are called "the blasts heard while standing" because the congregation listens to them during the *Amida* prayer, which must be recited while standing.

Even one who has not yet reached the end of the relevant blessing when the *ba'al toke'a* begins to sound the shofar must pause and listen to the blasts and only afterward continue with his silent prayer.

At the conclusion of the silent *Amida* prayer, the cantor begins his repetition of the *Amida*, which incorporates liturgical poems that he recites with the participation of the congregation. These poems were composed in ancient times, many of them rhyming and arranged in an alphabetical acrostic.

Thirty blasts are sounded during the cantor's repetition: Ten each at the end of the three blessings of Kingship, Remembrance, and Shofar.

After the cantor's repetition, in the middle of the Kaddish following the *Amida*, he pauses and ten more blasts are sounded, bringing the total number of blasts to one hundred.

Most Ashkenazic communities do not blow the shofar during the silent *Amida* prayer. Instead, they blow forty blasts during the Kaddish at the end of *Musaf*, bringing their total to one hundred as well.

The Sephardic custom is to sound one more blast at the end of the prayers, a "great *tekia*," containing the addition of many short blasts. The number of blasts they sound thus amounts to 101.

The Daytime Meal

In addition to the evening meals, a festive meal is held on both days of Rosh HaShana, at which fine foods are served.

Kiddush

After the completion of the morning and *Musaf* prayers in the synagogue, everyone goes home for the festival meal. At the beginning of the meal, *Kiddush* is recited over wine, in a formula unique for Rosh HaShana:

תִּקְעוּ בַחֹדֶשׁ שׁוֹפָר בַּכֶּסֶה לְיוֹם חַגֵּנוּ כִּי חֹק לְיִשְׂרָאֵל הוּא מִשְׁפָּט לֵאלֹהֵי יַעֲקֹב. וַיְדַבֵּר מֹשֶׁה אֶת מוֹעֲדֵי אֲדֹנָי אֶל בְּנֵי יִשְׂרָאֵל.

Tiku baḥodesh shofar, bakeseh leyom ḥagenu, ki ḥok leYisrael hu, mishpat lelohei Ya'akov. Vaydaber Moshe et mo'adei Adonai el benei Yisrael.

סַבְרִי מָרָנָן וְרַבָּנָן וְרַבּוֹתַי.

Savri meranan verabanan verabotai:

בָּרוּךְ אַתָּה אֲדֹנָי, אֱלֹהֵינוּ מֶלֶךְ הָעוֹלָם,   *Barukh ata Adonai, Eloheinu, melekh*
בּוֹרֵא פְּרִי הַגָּפֶן.   *ha'olam, boreh peri hagafen.*

"Blow the shofar at the showing of the New Moon, at the appointed time of our festival. For it is a statute for Israel, a law of the God of Jacob" (Psalms 81:4–5). "And Moses spoke to the children of Israel the appointed times of the Lord" (Leviticus 23:44). "Attention, masters, rabbis, and my teachers.

"Blessed are You, Lord our God, King of the universe, who creates the fruit of the vine."

As on the night of the festival, in the daytime meal too, the bread upon which the blessing is recited is eaten with honey or sugar, and a festive meal is eaten.

Utilizing One's Time

After the meal one should try not to sleep, as stated earler. One should devote every spare moment to reciting psalms or studying Torah. Some have the practice of rising for prayer early in the morning of Rosh HaShana, before sunrise, and as a result they take a midday nap. Some sources maintain that there is no reason to avoid sleeping in the afternoon.

The Custom of *Tashlikh*

Following the afternoon prayers of the first day of Rosh HaShana, many go to a place where there is a body of water to perform the custom of *Tashlikh* (literally, "cast away"). This practice symbolizes the discarding of one's sins.

Shaking Off Sin

The afternoon prayer service [*Minha*] is recited with a special formula for Rosh HaShana, as appears in the *mahzorim*.

Following the afternoon prayers, it is customary to recite *Tashlikh* near a body of water. The body of water can be a sea, river, pond or, if necessary, even a bowl of water. It is preferable to find water that contains live fish. Several verses and psalms are recited, and at the end of the rite some have the custom to shake the hem of their garments toward the water, as if to dust off their sins.

If the first day of Rosh HaShana falls on Shabbat, *Tashlikh* is postponed until the second day of the festival.

Some have the custom of performing *Tashlikh* during the Ten Days of Repentance rather than on Rosh HaShana. Likewise, one who did not perform *Tashlikh* on Rosh HaShana can do so until Yom Kippur.

The Second Day

Rosh HaShana is the only festival that is celebrated for two consecutive days in Israel. Outside Israel all festivals are observed for two days, with the exception of Yom Kippur. This practice, which was already established during the Temple period, stems from the extemporaneous manner by which the beginning of the months was determined, based on the testimony of witnesses who had sighted the new moon. The Sages discussed whether the two days of Rosh HaShana are considered like two separate, consecutive festivals or like one extended festival day that lasts for two days. This discussion has several halakhic ramifications.

Candle Lighting

The candles on the second day of Rosh HaShana should be lit only after the conclusion of the first day, following the appearance of three stars in the sky. The exact time is generally publicized in synagogue calendars. Some have the custom of lighting the candles just before the recitation of *Kiddush* at the evening meal. Since kindling a new fire is prohibited on a festival, the candles are lit by transferring fire from the existing flame of a long-burning candle, this being one of the main reasons it was lit. The match should not be extinguished after the lighting, but should be put down so that it can safely burn out on its own. On this night too, as on the first night of Rosh HaShana (see p. 135), two blessings are recited upon lighting the candles.

Similarities and Differences

Apart from a few minor changes, the second day of Rosh HaShana is observed essentially in the same manner as the first day. As on the first night, the *Sheheheyanu* blessing is recited:

"Blessed are You, Lord our God, King of the universe, who has given us life, sustained us, and brought us to this time."

Following *Kiddush*, before washing hands for the meal, many have the custom to eat a seasonal fruit that one has not yet eaten in this season. This is because there is an opinion that the two days of Rosh HaShana are to be considered like one long festival, in which case the *Sheheheyanu* blessing should not be recited since it was already recited the previous night. Although the accepted *halakha* is that one recites the *Sheheheyanu* blessing regardless, many have the custom to eat a new fruit (or to wear a new garment), which would require a *Sheheheyanu* blessing in any event, so as to remove any doubt as to whether the blessing should be recited.

📖 **Further reading:** In many communities, the eating of *simanim* that was performed on the first night (see p. 141) is repeated on the second night; in some it is not.

The *Tashlikh* ceremony is not performed on the second day unless the first day of the festival fell on Shabbat.

If the first day of the festival was Shabbat, one adds to the *Kiddush* of the second night a text of *Havdala*, ending with the words "…who distinguishes between sacred and sacred," as mentioned above in the section dealing with the wording of *Kiddush* (p. 140).

Havdala

At the conclusion of the second day of Rosh HaShana, after the evening prayers, *Havdala* is recited over a full cup of wine. The version of this *Havdala* is identical to the regular *Havdala* after Shabbat (for more on the procedure and *halakhot* of *Havdala*, see p. 398), except that one does not recite a blessing over a candle or spices, and many do not recite the opening sequence of verses: "Here is the God of my salvation…," that are said at the conclusion of Shabbat. One starts with the blessing over wine: "…who creates fruit of the vine [*hagafen*]," before proceeding to the blessing of: "…who separates [*hamavdil*] between the sacred and the secular." Some do recite the introductory verses of *Havdala* in the usual manner.

When Rosh HaShana falls on Thursday and Friday, one does not recite *Havdala* at all upon the conclusion of the festival, as it flows directly into Shabbat. Instead, one says only the regular *Kiddush* of Shabbat.

Yearly Cycle

The Ten Days of Repentance

The ten days from Rosh HaShana until Yom Kippur are called the Ten Days of Repentance [*Aseret Yemei Teshuva*]. The Talmud states regarding the verse, "Seek the Lord when He is found" (Isaiah 55:6), that it is an allusion to the ten days between Rosh HaShana and Yom Kippur (*Rosh HaShana* 18a). This means that during these days God is especially close and accessible to us, and it is therefore appropriate to seek Him out and to strive to approach Him.

These days are also designated as days of repentance because it is at this time that judgment is passed in heaven upon each indvidual. The verdict is written on Rosh HaShana but it is not signed until Yom Kippur. Consequently, it is a time to engage in repentence and good deeds in order to merit a good year. Additionally, Yom Kippur atones only for transgressions between a person and God, not for sins between people, unless the offender asks forgiveness from the individual he has harmed and makes amends. Therefore, one should take advantage of the days remaining until Yom Kippur in order to appease anyone he may have hurt or offended over the course of the past year, and request forgiveness from him. For all these reasons, these ten days are called the Ten Days of Repentance. This chapter presents the laws and customs of this special period, which includes the Fast of Gedaliah and *Shabbat Teshuva*, the Shabbat of Repentance.

Selihot and Prayers

During the Ten Days of Repentance the congregation recites penitential prayers [*Selihot*], and there are also some additions and changes to the formula of daily prayers. These changes express the atmosphere of these days, in which God renews His kingship over the world and we approach Him to seek His mercy.

Selihot

In the month of Elul, as well as during the Ten Days of Repentance, it is customary in most communities to recite *Selihot*. The *Selihot* should ideally be recited after the middle of the night or before dawn. Alternatively, many recite the *Selihot* right before the morning prayer service. The *Selihot* of the Ten Days of Repentance are slightly longer than those recited during the month of Elul.

The practice of the Lubavitch hasidic community is not to say *Selihot* during the Ten Days of Repentance.

Additions and Changes

In the morning prayers, it is customary in many communities to open the ark after the *Yishtabah* blessing and to recite Psalms 130: "A song of ascents. Out of the depths I call to You, Lord...."

In all the *Amida* prayers of the Ten Days of Repentance, the following supplications are inserted:

In the first blessing, after the words *lema'an shemo be'ahava*, "for the sake of His name, with love," one adds:

זָכְרֵנוּ לְחַיִּים, מֶלֶךְ חָפֵץ בַּחַיִּים, וְכָתְבֵנוּ   *Zochrenu lehayim, melekh hafetz*
בְּסֵפֶר הַחַיִּים, לְמַעַנְךָ אֱלֹהִים חַיִּים.   *bahayim, vekhotvenu besefer hahayim, lema'ankha Elohim hayim.*

"Remember us for life, King who desires life, and write us in the book of life, for Your sake, God of life."

In the second blessing, after the phrase *umatzmiah yeshua*, "And makes salvation grow," one says:

מִי כָמוֹךָ אָב הָרַחֲמִים (נוסח ספרד: *Mi khamokha Av harahamim (Nusah*
הָרַחֲמָן), זוֹכֵר יְצוּרָיו לְחַיִּים בְּרַחֲמִים.   *Sefarad: harahaman), zokher yetzurav lehayim berahamim.*

"Who is like You, compassionate Father, who remembers His creations for life, with compassion."

At the conclusion of the third blessing, instead of *Ha'El Hakadosh*, "the holy God," one says: *HaMelekh hakadosh*, "the holy King."

In the conclusion of the blessing about the restoration of justice, instead of *Melekh ohev tzedaka umishpat*, "the King who loves righteousness and justice," one says: *HaMelekh hamishpat* "the King of justice."

In the blessing of thanksgiving [*Modim*], before the words *vekhol hahayim*, "let all that lives," one adds:

וּכְתֹב לְחַיִּים טוֹבִים כָּל בְּנֵי בְרִיתֶךָ.   *Ukhtov lehayim tovim kol benei beritekha.*

"And inscribe for a good life all the children of Your covenant."

Lastly, just before concluding the final blessing one adds:

בְּסֵפֶר חַיִּים בְּרָכָה וְשָׁלוֹם וּפַרְנָסָה טוֹבָה,   *Besefer ḥayim, berakha, veshalom,*
(יְשׁוּעָה וְנֶחָמָה וּגְזֵרוֹת טוֹבוֹת,) נִזָּכֵר וְנִכָּתֵב   *ufarnasa tova, (yeshuva, unḥama,*
לְפָנֶיךָ, אֲנַחְנוּ וְכָל עַמְּךָ בֵּית יִשְׂרָאֵל לְחַיִּים   *ugzeirot tovot,) nizakher venikatev le-*
טוֹבִים וּלְשָׁלוֹם.   *fanekha, anaḥnu vekhol amkha beit*
   Yisrael, leḥayim tovim ulshalom.

"In the book of life, blessing, peace, and prosperity (some add: salvation, comfort, and good decrees), may we and all Your people of the house of Israel be remembered and inscribed before You for a good life, and for peace."

If one mistakenly concluded the third blessing with the usual formula, "the holy God," instead of "the holy King," he must repeat the *Amida* prayer from the beginning. If one concluded the blessing of the restoration of justice in the normal manner, instead of with "the King of justice," there are different halakhic opinions regarding how he should proceed, and each person should consult his rabbi.

If one forgot any of the other additions mentioned above (which are later additions historically), he does not need to recite the *Amida* prayer again.

After the *Amida* of the morning and afternoon prayers, the congregation recites "Our Father, our King" [*Avinu Malkeinu*], which can be found in prayer books.

The Fast of Gedalya

The day after Rosh HaShana, the third of Tishrei, is the Fast of Gedalya. This fast was instituted to commemorate the murder of Gedalya son of Ahikam, who was the representative of the royal family left by Nebuchadnezzar king of Babylon after he destroyed the First Temple. Gedalya was appointed to lead the remnant of the people of Judah who were left in the Land of Israel. He was murdered by Ishmael son of Netanya, who vehemently opposed the relationship between Gedalya and the king of Babylon. Following the murder, all the remaining people went down to Egypt, and thus the last embers of the rule of Judah in the Land of Israel were extinguished.

Times and Laws of the Fast

The fast begins at dawn, about an hour and a half before sunrise, and ends upon the emergence of the stars. The precise times can be found in Jewish calendars.

Every male over the age of thirteen and every female over the age of twelve are prohibited to eat or drink on this day. Pregnant and nursing women generally do not observe this fast. In a case of illness, weakness, or any other difficulty in fasting, one should consult a rabbi.

Morning prayers

Apart from the usual additions to all the prayers of the Ten Days of Repentance, there are special additions for the Fast of Gedalya.

The *Selihot* of the fast day are recited as on the rest of the Ten Days of Repentance, at night or at dawn. Some recite them during the morning prayers, before *Tahanun*.

After the repetition of the *Amida* by the prayer leader and the recitation of *Selihot*, the regular fast-day passages are read from the Torah (Exodus 32:11–14 and 34:1–10). These sections deal with Moses' request of God to have mercy upon the children of Israel and to forgive them after the sin of the Golden Calf. This is an appropriate reading for a fast day, on which we seek God's mercy.

Afternoon prayers [*Minha*]

Some, especially Sephardim and Hasidim, have the custom to don a prayer shawl [*tallit*] and *tefillin* for the afternoon prayer service on fast days.

After *Ashrei*, the Torah reading of the morning is repeated, but this time a *haftara* is read as well. The selection (Isaiah 55:6–56:8) opens with the phrase: "Seek the Lord when He is found," and discusses regret for one's sins, repentance, and requesting God's forgiveness.

In the blessing of *Shome'a Tefilla* in the *Amida* prayer, one adds the "Answer us" [*Aneinu*] passage. The prayer leader adds this in his repitition of the *Amida* after the blessing of "Who redeems Israel." In Israel only, during the prayer leader's repetition of the *Amida* prayer, the priests recite the priestly benediction (Numbers 6:24–26) in the afternoon prayer service, just as in the morning prayers, provided that the service takes place in the late afternoon.

When the third of Tishrei falls on a Shabbat, the fast is postponed to Sunday, the fourth of Tishrei.

Shabbat Teshuva

The Shabbat of the Ten Days of Repentance is called either *Shabbat Teshuva*, named for these days of repentance [*teshuva*], or *Shabbat Shuva*, after the opening of the *haftara* of that Shabbat: "Return (*Shuva*), Israel, to the Lord your God" (Hosea 14:2).

Laws and Customs

In the Shabbat prayers one includes the same additions as on the weekdays, except, of course, for "the King of justice," as this blessing is not part of the Shabbat *Amida*. The *Avinu Malkeinu* prayer is not recited on Shabbat. When taking out the Torah scroll from the ark one says the formula: "Holy and awesome is His name." It is customary on this Shabbat for the rabbi to deliver a special sermon that focuses on repentance.

Kaparot and Yom Kippur Eve

The day before Yom Kippur is an important and special day. It is even considered a festival of sorts, and a festive meal is eaten. The reason for this is as follows: A verse in the Torah (Leviticus 23:32) states: "And you shall afflict yourselves on the ninth of the month in the evening, from evening to evening." The Talmud wonders why the verse refers to the ninth of the month, when in fact the implication of fasting "from evening to evening" is that one must fast on the tenth of the month (Yom Kippur), which begins in the evening following the ninth, and concludes in the evening of the tenth. The Talmud explains: "Whoever eats and drinks on the ninth, the verse ascribes him credit as though he fasted on both the ninth and tenth." Hence, it is a mitzva to eat on the day before Yom Kippur. Eating well helps one fast more easily and in a better state of mind, and also demonstrates our joy over the atonement of our sins and that we trust that God will be compassionate.

Kaparot

During the period between Rosh HaShana and Yom Kippur, many people have the custom to perform the ritual of *Kaparot*. Many do so in the morning on the day before Yom Kippur, and some even wake up early to do it before dawn. This is an ancient custom, which dates back to the period of the *geonim* (between the end of the sixth century and the middle of the eleventh century) and even earlier, although it has changed slightly in form over time. The name of the ritual, *Kaparot*, has been interpreted in two ways: (1) The purpose of the action is to bring atonement [*kapara*] for our sins, similar to the offering of sacrifices in the Temple. (2) It serves as a "ransom" [*kofer*] and substitute for oneself, as one does to an animal what should have by right been done to himself.

Kapara and *Kofer*

The ancient custom is to take a chicken, a rooster for a male person and a hen for a female. A pregnant woman performs *kaparot* on two hens and one rooster, one hen for herself and a hen and rooster for her unborn child, whose sex is unknown.

Some first recite a few verses (primarily from Psalms 107 with an addition from Job), but others do not do so. Afterward, one rotates the animal over his head, while stating the following:

A man declares:

זֶה חֲלִיפָתִי, זֶה תְּמוּרָתִי, זֶה כַּפָּרָתִי. זֶה
הַתַּרְנְגוֹל יֵלֵךְ לְמִיתָה וַאֲנִי אֵלֵךְ לְחַיִּים
טוֹבִים אֲרֻכִּים וּלְשָׁלוֹם.

Zeh ḥalifati, zeh temurati, zeh kaparati. Zeh hatarnegol yelekh lemita, va'ani elekh leḥayim tovim arukim ulshalom.

"This is my exchange, this is my substitute, this is my atonement. This rooster shall go to death while I go to a good, long life and peace" (there are some slight variations of the wording in some prayer books).

A woman recites the same text, in the feminine form:

זֹאת חֲלִיפָתִי, זֹאת תְּמוּרָתִי, זֹאת כַּפָּרָתִי.
זֹאת הַתַּרְנְגֹלֶת תֵּלֵךְ לְמִיתָה וַאֲנִי אֵלֵךְ
לְחַיִּים טוֹבִים אֲרֻכִּים וּלְשָׁלוֹם.

Zot ḥalifati, zot temurati, zot kaparati. Zot hatarnegolet telekh lemita, va'ani elekh leḥayim tovim arukim ulshalom.

This formula is recited three times, after which the chicken is given to a ritual slaughterer. The slaughtered chicken or its value is then given to the poor.

In contemporary times, many people perform this ritual with money instead of a chicken. The process is the same except that the phrase: "This rooster shall go to death" is replaced with: "This money shall go to charity" [*zeh hakesef yelekh letzedaka*], and the money is subsequently given to the poor.

A Busy Day

The day before Yom Kippur is a busy day, as it includes prayers, meals, immersion in the ritual bath [*mikva*], and more. These are the details of the events in order:

Morning

The *Seliḥot* prayers on the eve of Yom Kippur are significantly shorter than those recited on other days. In the morning prayer service, some omit Psalms 100, *Mizmor LeToda* ("A psalm of thanksgiving") from *Pesukei DeZimra*.

From the day before Yom Kippur until after *Rosh Ḥodesh* of the month of Marḥeshvan, one does not recite *Taḥanun* in the daily prayers.

Some perform the ritual of the Annulment of Vows on the day before Yom Kippur, in addition to the day before Rosh HaShana. Likewise, there are those who visit the cemetery on the day before Yom Kippur, as on the day before Rosh HaShana.

📖 **Further reading:** With regard to these two customs, see the section dealing with the eve of Rosh HaShana, p. 129.

There is a custom on the day before Yom Kippur (especially among Hasidim) to seek from one another, and to give to one another, a slice of honey cake, called *lekakh* in Yiddish. The reason for this custom is that if on Rosh HaShana it was decreed upon a person that he should be dependent on the favors of others, he will fulfill this decree by asking for a slice of cake from a friend.

Noon

Some have the custom to eat several meals on this day. It is customary for men to immerse themselves in a *mikva* on the day before Yom Kippur, in order to cleanse themselves of any impurity.

Toward Evening

On this day, the congregation prays the afternoon prayer service relatively early. At the end of the *Amida* prayer one adds the long confession ("*Al ḥet* etc.") that is recited on Yom Kippur itself. This confession, which details all kinds of sins, can be found in the Yom Kippur prayer books.

Following the afternoon prayers, before the holiday begins, a festive meal is eaten. This is called the *seuda hamafseket*, the meal before the fast. One should avoid eating heavy foods, such as beef, at this meal so as not to burden the body and tire it out right before the fast and lengthy prayers.

Candle Lighting

One must be careful to light the holiday candles before Yom Kippur begins. Two blessings are recited over the lighting of the candles:

בָּרוּךְ אַתָּה אֲדֹנָי, אֱלֹהֵינוּ מֶלֶךְ הָעוֹלָם,
אֲשֶׁר קִדְּשָׁנוּ בְּמִצְוֹתָיו וְצִוָּנוּ לְהַדְלִיק נֵר
שֶׁל יוֹם הַכִּפּוּרִים (וְאִם יוֹם הַכִּיפּוּרִים חָל
בְּשַׁבָּת: שֶׁל שַׁבָּת וְשֶׁל יוֹם הַכִּפּוּרִים).

Barukh ata Adonai, Eloheinu, melekh ha'olam, asher kideshanu bemitzvotav, vetzivanu lehadlik ner shel Yom Hakipurim (on Shabbat conclude instead: *lehadlik ner shel Shabbat veshel Yom Hakipurim*).

"Blessed are You, Lord our God, King of the universe, who sanctified us through His commandments, and commanded us to light (on Shabbat add: the Shabbat candle and) the candle of the Day of Atonement."

בָּרוּךְ אַתָּה אֲדֹנָי, אֱלֹהֵינוּ מֶלֶךְ הָעוֹלָם, שֶׁהֶחֱיָנוּ וְקִיְּמָנוּ וְהִגִּיעָנוּ לַזְּמַן הַזֶּה. *Barukh ata Adonai, Eloheinu, melekh ha'olam, sheheheyanu vekiyemanu vehigi'anu la'zeman hazeh.*

"Blessed are You, Lord our God, King of the universe, who has given us life, sustained us, and brought us to this time."

For more details on the procedure of candle lighting, see p. 381.

In addition, it is customary to light a yahrzeit candle that will remaining burning until the end of Yom Kippur. Some have the custom of lighting another family candle, at home or in the synagogue. This candle is called the "candle of life," and it is lit by the father of the family.

Blessing for Sons and Daughters

It is customary that before going to the synagogue for the *Kol Nidrei* prayer service, each father blesses his sons and daughters. The text of the blessing appears in the Yom Kippur *mahzor*. Many have the custom of placing their hands on the head of each child while reciting that child's blessing.

The introduction to the blessing for sons is as follows:

יְשִׂימְךָ אֱלֹהִים כְּאֶפְרַיִם וְכִמְנַשֶּׁה. *Yesimekha Elohim ke'Efrayim vekhi-Menashe.*

"May God make you like Ephraim and like Manasseh" (Genesis 48:20).

For daughters:

יְשִׂימֵךְ אֱלֹהִים כְּשָׂרָה רִבְקָה רָחֵל וְלֵאָה. *Yesimekh Elohim keSara, Rivka, Rahel, veLe'ah.*

"May God make you like Sarah, Rebecca, Rachel, and Leah."

Then the father recites:

יְבָרֶכְךָ אֲדֹנָי וְיִשְׁמְרֶךָ, יָאֵר אֲדֹנָי פָּנָיו אֵלֶיךָ וִיחֻנֶּךָּ, יִשָּׂא אֲדֹנָי פָּנָיו אֵלֶיךָ וְיָשֵׂם לְךָ שָׁלוֹם. *Yevarekhekha Adonai veyishmerekha; ya'er Adonai panav elekha vihuneka; yisa Adonai panav elekha veyasem lekha shalom.*

"The Lord shall bless you, and keep you. The Lord shall shine His countenance toward you, and be gracious to you. The Lord shall lift His countenance to you, and grant you peace" (Numbers 6:24–26).

Some add the following prayer:

For a boy:

וִיהִי רָצוֹן מִלִּפְנֵי אָבִינוּ שֶׁבַּשָּׁמַיִם, שֶׁיִּתֵּן בְּלִבְּךָ אַהֲבָתוֹ וְיִרְאָתוֹ, וְתִהְיֶה יִרְאַת ה' עַל פָּנֶיךָ כָּל יָמֶיךָ שֶׁלֹּא תֶחֱטָא, וִיהִי חֶשְׁקְךָ בַּתּוֹרָה וּמִצְוֹת. עֵינֶיךָ לְנֹכַח יַבִּיטוּ, פִּיךָ יְדַבֵּר חָכְמוֹת, וְלִבְּךָ יֶהְגֶּה אֵימוֹת (=אֵימַת ה'), יָדֶיךָ יַעַסְקוּ בְמִצְוֹת, רַגְלֶיךָ יָרוּצוּ לַעֲשׂוֹת רְצוֹן אָבִיךָ שֶׁבַּשָּׁמַיִם. יִתֵּן לְךָ בָּנִים וּבָנוֹת צַדִּיקִים וְצִדְקָנִיּוֹת עוֹסְקִים בַּתּוֹרָה וּבַמִּצְוֹת כָּל יְמֵיהֶם, וִיהִי מְקוֹרְךָ בָּרוּךְ, וְיַזְמִין לְךָ פַּרְנָסָתְךָ בְּהֶתֵּר וּבְנַחַת וּבְרֶוַח מִתַּחַת יָדוֹ הָרְחָבָה וְלֹא עַל יְדֵי מַתְּנַת בָּשָׂר וָדָם, פַּרְנָסָה שֶׁתִּהְיֶה פָּנוּי לַעֲבוֹדַת הַשֵּׁם, וְתִכָּתֵב וְתֵחָתֵם לְחַיִּים טוֹבִים וַאֲרֻכִּים בְּתוֹךְ כָּל צַדִּיקֵי יִשְׂרָאֵל, אָמֵן.

Vihi ratzon milifnei Avinu shebashamayim sheyiten belibekha ahavato veyirato, vetihyeh yirat Adonai al panekha kol yamekha shelo teheta, vihi heshkekha beTorah uvmitzvot. Einekha lenokhah yabitu, pikha yedaber hokhmot, velibekha yehgeh eimot, yadekha ya'asku vemitzvot, raglekha yarutzu la'asot retzon Avikha shebashamayim. Yiten lekha banim uvanot tzadikim vetzidkaniyot osekim baTorah uvamitzvot kol yemeihem, vihi mekorkha barukh. Veyazmin lekha parnasatekha beheter uvnahat uvrevah metahat yado ha'rehava velo al yedei matnat basar vadam, parnasa shetihyeh panui la'avodat Hashem, vetikatev vetehatem lehayim tovim va'arukim betokh kol tzadikei Yisrael, amen.

For a girl:

וִיהִי רָצוֹן מִלִּפְנֵי אָבִינוּ שֶׁבַּשָּׁמַיִם, שֶׁיִּתֵּן בְּלִבֵּךְ אַהֲבָתוֹ וְיִרְאָתוֹ, וְתִהְיֶה יִרְאַת ה' עַל פָּנַיִךְ כָּל יָמַיִךְ שֶׁלֹּא תֶחֱטָאִי, וִיהִי חֶשְׁקֵךְ בַּתּוֹרָה וּמִצְוֹת. עֵינַיִךְ לְנֹכַח יַבִּיטוּ, פִּיךְ יְדַבֵּר חָכְמוֹת, וְלִבֵּךְ יֶהְגֶּה אֵימוֹת, יָדַיִךְ יַעַסְקוּ בְמִצְוֹת, רַגְלַיִךְ יָרוּצוּ לַעֲשׂוֹת רְצוֹן אָבִיךְ שֶׁבַּשָּׁמַיִם. יִתֵּן לָךְ בָּנִים וּבָנוֹת

Vihi ratzon milifnei Avinu shebashamayim sheyiten belibekh ahavato veyirato, vetihyeh yirat Adonai al panayikh kol yamayikh shelo teheti, vihi heshkekh beTorah uvmitzvot. Einayikh lenokhah yabitu, pikh yedaber hokhmot, velibekh yehgeh eimot, yadayikh ya'asku vemitzvot, raglayikh yarutzu la'asot retzon Avikh shebashamayim. Yiten lakh banim

צַדִּיקִים וְצִדְקָנִיּוֹת עוֹסְקִים בַּתּוֹרָה
וּבַמִּצְוֹת כָּל יְמֵיהֶם, וִיהִי מְקוֹרֶךָ בָּרוּךְ,
וְיַזְמִין לְךָ פַּרְנָסָתְךָ בְּהֶתֵּר וּבְנַחַת וּבְרֶוַח
מִתַּחַת יָדוֹ הָרְחָבָה וְלֹא עַל יְדֵי מַתְּנַת
בָּשָׂר וָדָם, פַּרְנָסָה שֶׁתִּהְיֶי פְּנוּיָה לַעֲבוֹדַת
הַשֵּׁם, וְתִכָּתְבִי וְתֵחָתְמִי לְחַיִּים טוֹבִים
וַאֲרֻכִּים בְּתוֹךְ כָּל צַדִּיקֵי יִשְׂרָאֵל, אָמֵן.

uvanot tzadikim vetzidkaniyot osekim baTorah uvamitzvot kol yemeihem, vihi mekorekh barukh. Veyazmin lakh parnasatekh beheter uvnahat uvrevah metahat yado ha'rehava velo al yedei matnat basar vadam, parnasa shetihyi penuya la'avodat Hashem, vetikatevi vetehatemi lehayim tovim va'arukim betokh kol tzadikei Yisrael, amen.

"May it be the will of our Father in heaven, that He place the love and awe of Him into your heart, and that the awe of the Lord be with you throughout your days, so that you do not sin. May your fervor be for the Torah and mitzvot. May your eyes look straight ahead (Proverbs 4:25), your mouth speak wisdom, and your heart ponder the awe [of God]. May your hands be occupied with mitzvot, may your legs run to perform the will of your Father in heaven. May He grant you righteous sons and righteous daughters, who will occupy themselves with Torah and mitzvot all their days. May your wellspring be blessed, and may God provide you your sustenance in a permitted manner, in comfort and abundance from His broad hand, and not through gifts of flesh and blood, a livelihood that will enable you to be free for the service of God. May you be inscribed and sealed for a good, long life, among all the righteous of Israel. Amen."

The Prohibitions of Yom Kippur

Yom Kippur is considered the holiest day of the year. All of the prohibitions of Shabbat apply on Yom Kippur as well. In addition, there are other prohibitions that stem from the Torah's requirement to afflict oneself on this day. The Torah states: "However, on the tenth day of this seventh month is the Day of Atonement; a holy convocation it shall be for you, and you shall afflict yourselves.... And you shall not perform any labor on that very day, as it is a day of atonement, to atone for you before the Lord your God" (Leviticus 23:27–28). In this section we shall explain the prohibitions stemming from the requirement of affliction.

The Five Types of Affliction

The laws of Yom Kippur take effect by sundown at the end of the ninth of Tishrei, and conclude with the emergence of three stars the following night. The exact times are publicized in synagogue calendars. The most well-known prohibition is that of eating and drinking, but there are four additional prohibitions included in the requirement of affliction: washing the body for pleasure, anointing, wearing leather shoes, and engaging in marital relations.

📖 **Further reading:** For more on the talmudic source for these five prohibitions, see *A Concise Guide to the Sages,* p. 286.

Eating and Drinking

The requirement to fast on Yom Kippur is quite strict, and in fact, this is the only fast day mandated by Torah law. Consequently, the rules governing this fast are more stringent than those governing other fasts. It is prohibited to put any food or drink into one's mouth even without swallowing it. The fast is so important that if it is impossible for one to fast and also to attend synagogue and participate in the prayers, it would be better to stay home and fast than to attend the synagogue. Nonetheless, there are exceptional circumstances when it is permitted for a person to eat and drink, as will be explained below.

Washing

Washing the body or any part of it for pleasure is prohibited on Yom Kippur. Washing for cleanliness is permitted but should be conducted in a limited fashion, only as necessary. Following are some examples of when it is permitted to wash parts of the body in a limited fashion:

Upon waking up in the morning one should wash his hands until the knuckles (where the fingers connect to the hands).

Upon using the restroom, one may wash his hands until the knuckles. If there is a need to wash more than that due to cleanliness, one may do so but only what is absolutely necessary.

One who is feeding children may, to the extent necessary, wash his hands or wash a dish even though his hands will get wet.

Those who are ill (even if there is no danger to life) may wash themselves if necessary. This allowance applies as well to women in the days following childbirth.

Anointing

It is prohibited to anoint any part of the body on Yom Kippur. This includes applying oil, cream, perfume, or any other product that soothes or nourishes the skin. One who is ill, or one who has a rash, may use a liquid (but not a cream) product to soothe his skin. However, if he is not sick, a medicated product may not be used due to the general prohibition against using non-essential medicinal products on any Shabbat or festival.

📖 **Further reading:** For more information, see the chapter dealing with medicine on Shabbat, p. 439.

Leather Shoes
It is prohibited to wear leather shoes on Yom Kippur. Even if only a part of the shoes is made from leather it is prohibited to wear them. However, it is permissible to wear shoes made from any other material.

Marital Relations
It is prohibited to engage in marital relations or any physical act that indicates closeness or intimacy. A couple should follow all the guidelines applicable when the wife is a *nidda* (see the chapter on the laws of family purity, p. 574).

Those Exempt from Fasting
The prohibitions of Yom Kippur apply to any male over the age of thirteen and any female over the age of twelve. Nonetheless, in situations where fasting can cause a life-threatening medical condition, there may be room for leniency, and in extreme cases it may be permissible to avoid fasting altogether. Before making any decision to eat or drink on Yom Kippur, it is advisable to consult with both a doctor and a rabbi.

📖 **Further reading:** For more on the significance of fasting on Yom Kippur, see *A Concise Guide to Mahshava*, p. 67.

Relevant Quantities
It is prohibited by Torah law to eat even a crumb or to drink even a drop on Yom Kippur. However, the severe punishment of *karet*[1] that applies to one who eats or drinks on Yom Kippur applies only if the amount of food he ate was the volume of a date (approximately 30 cc) or he drank the amount of liquid that can fit into a person's cheek. This latter measurement is subjective, and one can measure before Yom Kippur how much liquid fits into one of his cheeks. Consequently, in cases where it is medically warranted to eat or drink on Yom Kippur, one should eat or drink less than these quantities so as to minimize the violation. Even so, one must wait at least nine minutes

---

1. The punishment of *karet* means that one dies prematurely or that one's soul is excised from the World to Come.

between two acts of eating or two acts of drinking so that each act is judged individually, and the amounts do not combine. In more extreme circumstances, where there is possible danger to a person's life even if he eats in these quantities, he may eat or drink as necessary.

The requirement to fast on Yom Kippur applies even to pregnant and nursing women and to those who are ill. However, in any case in which there is a possibility that fasting could cause a danger to life, one should not fast. One should consult with a doctor and a rabbi to determine if his medical situation warrants eating or drinking on Yom Kippur, and if so, in what quantities.

Within the first three days after childbirth a woman is entirely exempt from fasting. From the third to seventh day after childbirth she is not entirely exempt but there are leniencies that apply, and a rabbi should be consulted.

Children

By Torah law, children under the age of bar and bat mitzva are not subject to any of the prohibitions of Yom Kippur. However, in order to communicate to them the importance of this day and in order to train them in the observance of its laws, it is customary to apply the following guidelines:

From the age when children are able to understand the nature of the day, even if only on a superficial level, it is customary to avoid washing them, anointing them, or having them wear leather shoes. Nonetheless, if it is particularly necessary to wash them, it is permissible.

From the age of nine, it is customary for them to wait to eat their meal later than usual.

From the age of eleven for girls and twelve for boys, it is customary for children to fast the entire day. However, if the child is weak and unable to fast the whole day, he can break his fast.

Once a girl turns twelve and a boy turns thirteen, they are considered adults in this regard and must fast the entire day and observe all the laws of Yom Kippur.

📖 **Further reading:** For more on the importance of introducing children to mitzva observance from a young age, see *A Concise Guide to the Sages*, p. 404; *A Concise Guide to Mahshava*, p. 186.

Yom Kippur
The Experience of the Day

As the afternoon draws to a close and Yom Kippur is about to begin, the serious atmosphere of this holy day becomes palpable. This is the time when the meals are finishing, and with them our physical preparations for the day, and we ready ourselves for the day about which the Torah states: "For on this day he shall atone for you, to purify you; from all your sins before the Lord you shall be purified" (Leviticus 16:30).

After the father has blessed his children (see p. 161) and the candles have been lit, it is time to go to the synagogue. It is customary for married men to wear a white garment known as a *kittel*, which they wear, together with their *tallit* (prayer shawl) for all of the prayer services of Yom Kippur. The *tallit* should be put on before sunset so that the appropriate blessing may be recited, as the blessing on *tzitzit* may not be recited at night. It is recommended to bring a prayer book for the festival [*mahzor*] that matches the version of the prayer service [*nusah*] used in that synagogue, as there are many differences between the different versions of the Yom Kippur prayer service. In this chapter we will introduce what to expect over the course of the day, including the five prayer services and other customs of the day.

The Beginning of the Holy Day

Before the *Kol Nidrei* service, there are those who read various psalms or prayers, the most common of which is known as *Tefilla Zaka*. This prayer includes a confession and expresses regret for the sins of the past year, as well as a request that God consider our thoughts of repentance and the suffering imposed by the fast. Additionally, there is a section in which one forgives others who may have wronged him over the course of the year. This prayer as well as *Kol Nidrei* should be completed before sunset. Following *Kol Nidrei* we accept upon ourselves the sanctity of the day, and thereby all the laws of Yom Kippur take effect.

 Further reading: For more on Yom Kippur, see *A Concise Guide to the Sages*, p. 285; *A Concise Guide to Mahshava*, p. 66.

Kol Nidrei

Before *Kol Nidrei*, two Torah scrolls are removed from the ark and given to two of the prominent members of the congregation. These individuals bring the Torah scrolls to the *bima*, where the *hazan*, the cantor or prayer leader, leads the prayer service. They stand on either side of the prayer leader, and the three of them comprise a sort of rabbinical court.

The prayer leader begins with the following declaration:

עַל דַּעַת הַמָּקוֹם וְעַל דַּעַת הַקָּהָל, בִּישִׁיבָה שֶׁל מַעְלָה וּבִישִׁיבָה שֶׁל מַטָּה, אָנוּ מַתִּירִין לְהִתְפַּלֵּל עִם הָעֲבַרְיָנִים.

"With the agreement of God, and the agreement of the community; in the heavenly assembly and the earthly assembly; we permit praying with the transgressors." (Some communities have slight variations in the terminology.)

The transgressors referred to here are individuals who have been excommunicated by the rabbinical court due to their sinful behavior, and it is therefore necessary to receive special permission for them to join the communal prayer service. Nowadays rabbinical courts do not excommunicate people, but we still say this line in order to express the fact that all participants stand jointly in prayer before God, regardless of their past.

Following this declaration, the prayer leader says the *Kol Nidrei* passage three times. It is customary for the congregation to recite it silently along with him.

כָּל נִדְרֵי וֶאֱסָרֵי וּשְׁבוּעֵי וַחֲרָמֵי וְקוֹנָמֵי וְקִנּוּסֵי וְכִנּוּיֵי, דְּאִנְדַּרְנָא וּדְאִשְׁתַּבַּעְנָא, וּדְאַחֲרִימְנָא וּדְאָסַרְנָא עַל נַפְשָׁתָנָא. מִיּוֹם כִּפּוּרִים [שֶׁעָבַר עַד יוֹם כִּפּוּרִים זֶה, וּמִיּוֹם כִּפּוּרִים] זֶה עַד יוֹם כִּפּוּרִים הַבָּא עָלֵינוּ לְטוֹבָה. בְּכֻלְּהוֹן אִיחֲרַטְנָא בְהוֹן, כֻּלְּהוֹן יְהוֹן שָׁרָן, שְׁבִיקִין שְׁבִיתִין בְּטֵלִין וּמְבֻטָּלִין, לָא שְׁרִירִין וְלָא קַיָּמִין. נִדְרָנָא לָא נִדְרֵי, וֶאֱסָרָנָא לָא אֱסָרֵי וּשְׁבוּעָתָנָא לָא שְׁבוּעוֹת.

Kol nidrei, ve'esarei, ushvu'ei, vaharamei, vekonamei, vekinusei, vekhinuyei de'indarna, ud'ishtabana, ud'aharimna, ud'asarna al nafshatana, miYom Kippurim zeh ad Yom Kippurim haba aleinu letova, bekhulhon iharatna behon, kulhon yehon sharan, shevikin, shevitin, betelin umvutalin, la sheririn vela kayamin. Nidrana la nidrei, ve'esarana la esarei, ushvuatana la shevuot.

"All vows, prohibitions, oaths, consecrations, restrictions, penalties, and vows accepted with substitute terms, that we have vowed, taken as an oath, consecrated, or prohibited upon ourselves, from [last Yom Kippur until this Yom Kippur, and from] this Yom Kippur until [next] Yom Kippur that will come upon us for the good; we regret all of them; they should all be permitted, absolved, released, utterly void, not confirmed, and not established.

Our vows should not be vows, our prohibitions should not be prohibitions, and our oaths should not be oaths." There are some textual variations to this passage and some congregations recite a version that is slightly different from the one cited above.

This formulation is like a communal annulment of vows. It is customary for each individual to perform an annulment of vows on the day before Rosh HaShana or Yom Kippur (see the chapter about Rosh HaShana, p. 129). Why then is it necessary to recite *Kol Nidrei*? This passage has great mystical significance pertaining to "releasing" the Divine Presence from being bound up, as it were, in exile, due to our sins. Similarly, in this passage we are praying that we should be released from the various negative habits that we have formed, and that we should be free to soar to great spiritual heights without being held back in any way.

Following *Kol Nidrei* and some additional verses, the prayer leader recites the *Sheheheyanu* blessing out loud, and the rest of the congregation recites it silently with him:

בָּרוּךְ אַתָּה אֲדֹנָי, אֱלֹהֵינוּ מֶלֶךְ הָעוֹלָם, שֶׁהֶחֱיָנוּ וְקִיְּמָנוּ וְהִגִּיעָנוּ לַזְּמַן הַזֶּה.

Barukh ata Adonai, Eloheinu, melekh ha'olam, sheheheyanu vekiyemanu vehigi'anu la'zeman hazeh.

"Blessed are You, Lord our God, King of the universe, who has given us life, sustained us, and brought us to this time."

This blessing is generally recited during the recitation of *Kiddush* on festivals. Since there is no *Kiddush* on Yom Kippur, it is recited during the prayer service. Those who have already recited this blessing when lighting the Yom Kippur candles should not recite it again with the prayer leader.

When Yom Kippur occurs on Shabbat, a condensed version of *Kabbalat Shabbat* is recited at this point, beginning with Psalms 92, "A psalm, a song for the Sabbath day" [*Mizmor shir leyom haShabbat*], or with Psalms 29, "A song by David" [*Mizmor leDavid*]. Some communities recite this before *Kol Nidrei*.

The recitation of *Shema* and the blessings surrounding it is the same on Yom Kippur as it is on Shabbat and other festivals, with one exception: Following the verse of *Shema Yisrael*, the phrase *Barukh shem kevod malkhuto le'olam va'ed* is recited aloud, unlike the rest of the year when it is recited in a whisper. This sentence is not part of the passage of *Shema* as it appears in the Torah, but is said by the angels in their prayers. For most of the year, it is not fitting for human beings to recite it aloud. However, on Yom Kippur, when God purifies us from our sins and we stand before Him like angels, we recite this phrase out loud.

📖 **Further reading:** For more on saying *Barukh shem* aloud on Yom Kippur, see *A Concise Guide to the Sages*, p. 231.

The *Amida* prayer on Yom Kippur is similar to that which is recited on Rosh HaShana, including an extended text of the third blessing. Additionally, on Yom Kippur, at the end of the *Amida*, a detailed confession is recited.

When Yom Kippur occurs on Shabbat, the *Amida* prayer includes several references to Shabbat, and the *Magen Avot* prayer is recited following the *Amida*.

Confession

A few words about the importance and structure of the confession recited at the end of each *Amida* on Yom Kippur: Confession is an essential stage in the process of repentance. In order for a person to repent, he must first acknowledge and express regret for his misdeeds. The confession recited at the conclusion of the *Amida* has two primary components: The short paragraph of "*Ashamnu*" lists various categories of sin organized by the Hebrew alphabet. Each category is represented by one or two words, and there is a word for each letter of the alphabet. Then there is an extensive and more detailed listing of sins. Each sentence begins with the phrase: "For the sin (*al het*) that we have sinned before you with…" A specific sin is then mentioned. This listing of sins also follows the order of the Hebrew alphabet, with two sentences devoted to each letter. After each cluster of sins, the following line is recited: "For all of them, God of forgiveness, forgive us, pardon us, grant us atonement."

The point of specifying so many sins and repeating this confession so many times over the course of Yom Kippur is so that one will remember any sins he has committed over the course of the year. The confession is formulated in the plural so that even if there is a particular sin that one knows he has not committed, he can still mention it in his confession on behalf of the Jewish people. When reciting the confession, one stands with a slightly lowered head, and strikes his chest with his right fist upon mentioning each sin.

Concluding the Nighttime Prayer Service

After the *Amida*, various *Selihot* prayers are recited, followed by another confession. When Yom Kippur occurs on a weekday, the *Avinu Malkeinu* prayer is recited. There are congregations that add some psalms as well.

Following the prayer service, there are some liturgical poems that are recited in many congregations, and many have the custom to study the *mishnayot* of tractate *Yoma*, which discusses the service of the High Priest in the Temple on Yom Kippur.

The Morning Prayer Service and Torah Reading

The general format of the morning prayer service is quite similar to that of Shabbat and festivals, except that many additional prayers are inserted into the cantor's repetition of the *Amida*. As in the evening service, the phrase *Barukh shem* is recited aloud during *Shema*, and the confession is recited at the conclusion of the private *Amida* prayer as well as during the cantor's repetition.

Torah Reading

Two Torah scrolls are removed from the ark. Six men are called to the Torah during the reading from the first scroll (if Yom Kippur occurs on Shabbat, seven men are called to the Torah). The reading is from the beginning of the Torah portion of *Aharei* (Leviticus 16), which includes the detailed instructions for the service in the Tabernacle or Temple on Yom Kippur. The *maftir* is read from the second scroll. This reading includes the additional offerings of Yom Kippur (Numbers 29:7–11). The *haftara* reading from Prophets (Isaiah 57) deals with the themes of fasting and repentance.

Yizkor

Following the *haftara*, it is customary in Ashkenazic congregations to recite *Yizkor*, a short prayer in which one who has lost a parent prays and pledges to give charity for the merit of his deceased parent or parents. This is followed by the prayer beginning "God who is full of compassion" (*El maleh raḥamim*). This practice is based on the assumption that Yom Kippur can be a time of atonement even for those who are no longer living; when their descendants pray for them and pledge to give charity on their behalf, divine compassion is aroused toward them. Before *Yizkor*, the *gabbai* of the synagogue announces: "*Yizkor!*" It is customary for those whose parents are both living to leave the room until the conclusion of the *Yizkor* service.

Even Sephardim, who do not recite *Yizkor*, have the custom to pledge donations to charity on Yom Kippur for the benefit of their deceased parents.

Many have the custom not to recite *Yizkor* within the first year of the passing of a parent.

The Additional [*Musaf*] Prayer Service

The *Musaf* service of Yom Kippur is similar in structure to the *Musaf* prayers of other holidays, except that it includes many additional liturgical compositions and *Selihot*, particularly in the prayer leader's repetition. The confession is recited once again at the conclusion of the individual *Amida* prayer and during the cantor's repetition.

Bowing

During the middle blessing of the prayer leader's repetition of the *Amida* prayer, the entire congregation recites, along with the prayer leader, the *Aleinu* prayer, which is a prayer recited every day at the conclusion of the three daily prayer services. It consists of praise to God and is followed in the Yom Kippur *Musaf* service by a liturgical composition describing the Temple service on Yom Kippur. This composition contains a historical account beginning with Adam and his sin, through the forefathers, and to Aaron the first High Priest. It then details the different stages of the Temple service performed by the High Priest in the Temple.

> Further reading: For a description of the High Priest's service in the Temple on Yom Kippur, see *A Concise Guide to the Torah*, p. 293.

During the *Aleinu* prayer, upon reaching the words "and we bow and prostrate ourselves" (ואנחנו כורעים ומשתחווים), and also during the description of how all assembled in the Temple would bow upon hearing the High Priest utter the name of God during the Temple service, it is customary for all those praying in the synagogue to bow down on the floor. Since it is prohibited to bow on a stone floor outside of the Temple, it is customary to spread a towel or cloth to separate between the floor and one's knees and forehead. It is recommended to prepare in advance by bringing something from home to use for this purpose.

In many congregations there is a break between the morning [*Shaharit*] and *Musaf* services and the afternoon [*Minha*] and concluding [*Ne'ila*] prayers. Many worshippers return to their homes during this time, which is meant to allow for people to rest a bit and to be able to return to the synagogue with renewed energy. However, in some congregations the prayers are conducted without any break, and worshippers remain in the synagogue for the entire day.

The Afternoon Prayer Service [Minha]

At the beginning of the afternoon prayer service, a Torah scroll is removed from the ark. Three men are called to read from the Torah, and the reading is about forbidden sexual relations (Leviticus 18). The reason this section is chosen for the reading at this time is because this area presents a significant challenge for people and requires a lot of reinforcement. Additionally, reading this section serves to remind those who have faltered in this area that they should take advantage of this auspicious time to fully repent.

Jonah and Another Confession

The third man called to the Torah also recites the *haftara*, which consists of the book of Jonah. This book describes the prophet Jonah's attempt to escape his mission from God, as well as the repentance of the inhabitants of the city of Nineveh.

The *Amida* prayer of the afternoon service includes added liturgical compositions as well as a confession upon the conclusion of the private *Amida* and during the cantor's repetition of the *Amida*. Some congregations also include *Selihot* in the afternoon prayer service as well.

The Concluding Service [Ne'ila]

At the conclusion of the day, but before sunset, the *Ne'ila* prayer service is conducted. This is the fifth prayer service of the day and it is unique to Yom Kippur. It expresses the most elevated moments, just before the gates of heaven close and the holy day comes to its conclusion. The term *ne'ila* means locking, and it is explained that this prayer is called *Ne'ila* because at this time God and the Jewish people are locked in a room together, as it were, and the relationship between them reaches its pinnacle. This is the final opportunity on Yom Kippur to repent, accept new resolutions, and begin a new, more pure and holy chapter in life. Due to the uniqueness of this prayer service, it is customary in many congregations to open the ark at the beginning of the prayer leader's repetition and to leave it open for the duration of the prayer service. The *Ne'ila* service should be timed such that it concludes at the end of Yom Kippur and can be immediately followed by the evening [Ma'ariv] prayer service.

Structure of the Prayer Service

The *Ne'ila* prayer service, particularly the cantor's repetition, includes various liturgical compositions and *Selihot*. A confession is recited at the conclusion of the private *Amida* and during the cantor's repetition.

There are several differences between this and the earlier prayer services of the day. Whenever we pray that God should "inscribe us" for a good new year, the terminology is altered so that in *Ne'ila* we pray that God should "seal us" in the book of life. Additionally, much of the version of the confession recited during the other prayer services (beginning "we have sinned") is omitted during *Ne'ila*, and replaced with a different prayer for atonement.

Following the cantor's repetition, the congregation recites *Avinu Malkeinu*, even if Yom Kippur is on Shabbat, when this prayer is not usually recited. Some congregations recite additional *Selihot* until nightfall. The climax of Yom Kippur occurs when the prayer leader, followed by the congregation, calls out *Shema Yisrael* ("Hear, Israel") once, *Barukh Shem* ("Blessed is the Name") three times, and *Hashem Hu HaElokim* ("The Lord is God!") seven times, or according to some Sephardim, twelve times. The recitation of these verses expresses our acceptance of God's authority for the duration of the upcoming year.

At the end of the prayer service (or just before the very end) a single, straight, long blast is sounded with the shofar. It is important to note that this blast does not signify the end of the fast. One should wait until the time publicized in local Jewish calendars before breaking the fast and performing other activities prohibited on Yom Kippur.

> Further reading: For a description of a particularly meaningful *Ne'ila* prayer in the study hall of the Ba'al Shem Tov, see *A Concise Guide to Mahshava*, p. 70.

The Conclusion of the Fast

The fast concludes upon the emergence of the stars. The exact time is generally publicized in synagogue calendars. One is obligated to extend the fast longer than necessary, in order to extend the sanctity of the day. However, there is no set amount of time that one needs to extend the fast. Some extend it only a very short time, while others extend it slightly longer.

From One Mitzva to the Next

Following the conclusion of the day, the congregation recites the evening prayer service, just like at the conclusion of Shabbat. Following the evening service, it is customary to recite the monthly blessing over the new moon (see p. 240), in order to engage in a mitzva immediately upon concluding Yom Kippur.

Following Yom Kippur, *Havdala* is recited over a cup of wine. If Yom Kippur was on a weekday, the blessing over spices, which is part of the *Havdala* after Shabbat, is not recited. Additionally, the blessing over the candle is recited only if there is a candle that was lit before Yom Kippur and remained burning until now. Some have the practice to recite the verses that precede *Havdala* after Shabbat, while others omit them.

It is customary to begin building the *sukka* following the conclusion of Yom Kippur so as to go directly from Yom Kippur to the fulfillment of mitzvot. If one finds it difficult to begin building the *sukka*, he should, alternatively, study some of the laws of *sukka* or at least talk about the *sukka*.

Sukkot

Preparations for the Festival

The festival of *Sukkot*, sometimes called in English "Tabernacles" or "Festival of Booths," is one of the three holidays called *regalim*, pilgrimage festivals, in the Torah (Exodus 23:14). It is celebrated for seven days, from the fifteenth of Tishrei through the twenty-first. The first day, or outside of Israel the first two days, are days of *yom tov*, on which many of the types of labor that are forbidden on Shabbat [*melakha*] may not be performed. At the conclusion of *Sukkot*, another festival is celebrated. It is known as *Shemini Atzeret* or *Simhat Torah*, and is also a *yom tov*. Outside of Israel this festival is celebrated for two days, the first of which is commonly referred to as *Shemini Atzeret* and the second of which is called *Simhat Torah*. In addition to its status as a festival, *Sukkot* has its own unique mitzvot: the mitzva to dwell in a *sukka* and the mitzva to pick up the four species, namely, a palm branch [*lulav*], a citron [*etrog*], and myrtle [*hadas*] and willow [*arava*] branches.

The festival of *Sukkot* is mentioned several times in the Torah: "On the fifteenth day of the seventh month it shall be a holy convocation for you, you shall not perform any toilsome labor, and you shall celebrate a festival to the Lord seven days" (Numbers 29:12). This is the basic command to observe the first day of *Sukkot* as a festival day [*yom tov*], similar to other festival days. Elsewhere the Torah introduces the mitzva to dwell in a *sukka*: "You shall live in booths seven days; every native in Israel shall live in booths. So that your generations will know that I had the children of Israel live in booths, when I took them out of the land of Egypt: I am the Lord your God" (Leviticus 23:42–43). The mitzva of taking the four species also appears in that passage: "You shall take for you on the first day the fruit of a pleasant tree, branches of date palms, and a bough of a leafy tree, and willows of the brook, and you shall rejoice before the Lord your God seven days" (Leviticus 23:40).

Sukkot is also characterized as a time of great joy, as the theme of rejoicing is mentioned three times by the Torah in connection to this festival (Leviticus 23:40; Deuteronomy 16:14–15). Indeed, the Sages refer to *Sukkot* as "the time of our joy."

This section, the first of three that deal with *Sukkot*, will discuss how to prepare properly for the festival by constructing a *sukka* and acquiring the four species. It will present the laws and customs pertaining to these mitzvot, as well as the rest of the mitzvot of the festival.

Building a *Sukka*

The *sukka* is used throughout the festival and it is the focal point of the holiday.

In constructing a *sukka*, one must pay attention to several factors: its location, its dimensions, the structure of the walls, and the correct form of its roofing [*sekhakh*]:

Location of a *Sukka*

A central principle in the *halakhot* of *sukka* construction is that the roofing of the *sukka* is meant to provide shade for those who dwell in it. Therefore, it is imperative that the *sukka* be built under the open sky, not beneath a house or tree or anything else. If this rule is not followed, the *sukka* is invalid.

It is preferable that the *sukka* be built on one's private property, not in the public domain. Nevertheless, a *sukka* that was erected in a public area is valid. It should be noted that one may not use another person's *sukka* without permission.

The Dimensions of a *Sukka*

The minimum dimensions of a valid *sukka* are seven by seven handbreadths, which is about 56 x 56 cm. On the other hand, there is no upper limit to the area of a *sukka*; it can be as large as one wants. The minimum height of a *sukka* is ten handbreadths, roughly eighty cm, while the maximum height is twenty cubits, approximately 9.6 meters.

Walls of the *Sukka*

The walls of a *sukka* may be built from any material, and one may even use the pre-existing walls of a building. One must be particular about several matters: the number of walls, their size, and their strength.

A *sukka* must have at least three walls; the fourth side may be left open. Two of the walls must be complete, extending along the entire side of the *sukka*, while the third wall may be a partial wall; that is, it does not have to cover the whole side of the *sukka*. Nevertheless, it is preferable to avoid having a shorter third wall, and to erect a *sukka* with at least three full walls.

When there is no other option, one may make do with the partial third wall mentioned above, but one must ensure that the following three conditions are fulfilled: (1) The partial wall must adjoin the end of one of the two whole walls; (2) the minimum width of the partial wall must be 8 cm; (3) an additional post should be placed opposite the end of the wall parallel to the short wall, and one should place a string or bar above it that will run from this post to the short wall (see diagram).

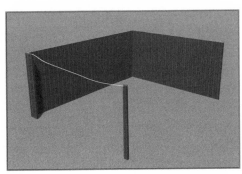

A *sukka* with three sides, with the two complete walls at right angles

If the two complete walls are parallel to each other, the short wall should be adjoined to the edge of one of them, and a string or bar should be placed above it, running from there to the top of the opposite complete wall (see diagram).

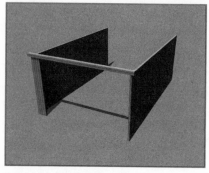

A *sukka* with three sides, with the two complete walls parallel to each other

The minimum height of the walls of a *sukka* is ten handbreadths (about 80 cm). A wall of this height is valid even if there is a gap between the top of the wall and the roofing, provided that the bottom of the wall is on the ground or within three handbreadths of the ground.

It is permitted to have open spaces or gaps in the walls of the *sukka* to serve as entrances and windows. When building a large *sukka,* one must make sure that the width of each of the spaces is no greater than ten cubits, 4.8 meters.

The walls should be strong enough to last for the entire festival. Therefore, they should not be made of materials that might get worn out or disintegrate over the course of the holiday. Additionally, the walls may not

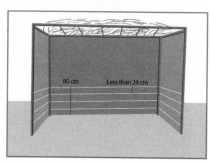

String surrounding the walls of the *sukka*

be so loose that they sway in the wind in normal weather. Accordingly, if one uses canvas or cloth *sukka* walls, he should tie them down firmly so that they will not move in the wind. To be on the safe side, it is advisable in such circumstances to tie a taut string along each of the walls of the *sukka,* from corner to corner. The strings should be tied no more than 24 cm apart from each other, and the highest one should reach a height of 80 cm (see diagram). Because of a halakhic concept known as *levud,* these strings can actually be considered walls due to the fact that the space between them is less than three handbreadths.

There are *sukkot* on the market that are very easy to assemble and that come with the necessary materials to address this issue.

Another relevant discussion pertains to a case where there is a horizontal gap between the *sekhakh* (*sukka* roofing) and the wall. If the *sekhakh* simply does not reach the wall and there is empty space between them, the *sukka* is still valid as long as the space is less than three handbreadths, approximately 24 cm.

However, if that part of the *sukka* is covered by materials invalid for *sekhakh* (see diagram), the wall of the *sukka* is viewed as a "bent wall" [*dofen akuma*] that includes this section of the roof. In such a case, as long as the invalid *sekhakh* extends no more than four cubits (approximately 1.9 m) beyond the wall, the *sukka* is valid. However, it should be noted that one may not eat underneath this section. This law applies even if the invalid materials are located above the roof of the *sukka*. Common applications of this law include situations where branches of a tree, a porch, or an air conditioning unit cover part of a *sukka*.

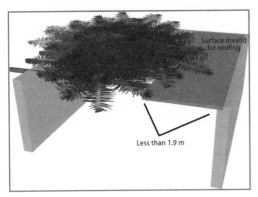

Bent wall

Sekhakh

Not all materials may be used for the *sukka* roofing, or *sekhakh*. In order for the *sekhakh* to be valid, the following requirements must be met:

The material from which the *sekhakh* is made must grow from the ground but no longer be attached to the ground.

However, wooden utensils, edible items such as fruit, and reed mats that are made to be used as carpets are all invalid for *sekhakh*. By contrast, mats that were produced specifically for roofing, such as those that are widely available at stores where *Sukkot* supplies are sold, are valid. A rabbi should be consulted about the halakhic status of mats whose intended purpose is unknown.

The *sekhakh*, like the walls, must be durable enough to last throughout the festival, so that it does not dry out and shrink, thereby creating gaps that will let in sunlight.

As for the validity of pergolas for *sekhakh*, one should consult with a rabbi concerning each specific case.

The density of the *sekhakh*

The *sekhakh* must be dense enough to ensure that there is more shade in the *sukka* than sunlight. A very dense thatch does not invalidate the *sukka*, provided that rain can penetrate, but it is proper to leave a few cracks.

For the sake of providing shade

The *sekhakh* must have been put in place for the purpose of providing shade. Consequently, if roofing was already there beforehand – for example, if branches fell on the *sukka* from a nearby tree, or a vine climbed up over the *sukka* and it was later detached from the soil – the roofing is invalid. It is possible to render such roofing valid by lifting it up from the *sukka* and placing it down again, this time for the purpose of serving as *sekhakh*.

Sukka Decorations

It is customary to decorate the *sukka* as an enhancement of the mitzva [*hiddur mitzva*]. When decorating it, two factors must be taken into account: First, the *sukka* decorations, like the structure of the *sukka* itself, are considered sanctified throughout the seven days of the festival, and therefore they may not be used for any other purpose during this time. Second, any decorations hanging from the *sekhakh* must be placed close to it, so that the distance between the *sekhakh* and the decorations does not exceed four handbreadths (32 cm).

The Four Species

The Torah (Leviticus 23:40) calls for taking in hand four plant species on *Sukkot*, which one must acquire before the festival. The four species consist of: one *etrog* (citron), one *lulav* (palm frond), three (at minimum; some add more than three) *hadas* (myrtle) branches (in plural, *hadasim*), and two *arava* (willow) branches (in plural, *aravot*). The identification of these four species as the ones mentioned in the Torah, and likewise the ways of determining their validity, have been passed down by oral tradition.

The Torah (Leviticus 23:40) refers to the *etrog* as "the fruit of a pleasant tree" [*pri etz hadar*], which can also be rendered "the pleasant fruit of a tree." The Sages learned from this expression that one must make an effort to ensure that all four species are of superior quality, in both beauty and in their fulfilling the halakhic qualifications for the mitzva. Therefore, one should not be overly economical when shopping for the four species, but rather should look to acquire species of superior quality and appearance.

General Guidelines

The following broad guidelines apply to all four species:

It is important that the species are fresh and not dried out.

Species obtained by theft are invalid for the mitzva. Therefore, one must be careful not to pick any of the species from private or public gardens without permission. Similarly, one should make every effort to purchase them from a trustworthy vendor.

One must be careful not to confuse the correct species with other, similar plants. In this regard too, the reliability of the seller is very important.

In addition, there are specific requirements that apply separately to each of the four species.

Citron [*Etrog*]

It is essential to make sure that the fruit is indeed an *etrog*, not a similar fruit, or the product of an *etrog* tree that was grafted onto a different tree. It must also not be an *etrog* of *orla*, i.e., from a tree that was planted less than three years before the *etrog* grew. The way to ensure all this is to buy the *etrog* from a vendor whose credibility is above reproach.

Since the Torah calls the *etrog* "the fruit of a pleasant tree," its general appearance must be beautiful, and this is the source of many of the halakhic requirements of the *etrog*.

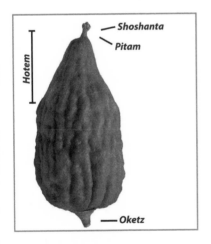

The parts of the *etrog* are as follows (see image):

(1) the edge of the branch on which the *etrog* grew and which remains attached to its underneath part, called the *oketz*, the stem or peduncle;

(2) the textured and rough body of the *etrog*;

(3) the upper part of the *etrog*, which narrows and becomes gradually pointed, called *hotem*, the upper slope.

(4) Some *etrogim* have a woody, elongated protrusion at their upper end, which is a remnant of the style that appeared during the flowering of the fruit; this is called the *pitam*.

(5) At the top of this protrusion there is a widened tip, which is a remnant of the stigma at the top of the style in the flowering stage. This is called the *shoshanta*.

Since the laws of *etrog* are numerous and complex, only the main ones will be detailed here, those which will assist one in choosing a quality *etrog*. If one finds it difficult to choose an *etrog* or if doubts arise about its validity, he should consult a rabbi.

These are the main considerations one should consider when choosing an *etrog*:

(1) The volume of the *etrog* must be larger than that of an average egg.

(2) It is highly desirable that the *etrog* be yellow in color (all shades of yellow are acceptable), or a light green tending toward yellow.

(3) If the *pitam* of an *etrog* fell off during its growth on the tree, it is valid, but if the *etrog* had a *pitam* when it was picked and the *pitam* subsequently fell off, it is invalid. By examining the top of an *etrog* that has no *pitam*, it is possible to discern whether it grew without a *pitam* or if it had a *pitam* that fell off.

(4) The body of the *etrog* should be as free of discoloration as possible. If there are more than two areas where its color differs from the regular appearance of an *etrog*, a rabbi should be consulted.

(5) No part of the body of the *etrog* may be missing. A hole or a scratch invalidates it. But if it is apparent that the scratches were caused to the *etrog* while it was still on the tree and then it formed a scab, it is valid.

Palm Branch [*Lulav*]

The *lulav* is a frond that grows in the center of the palm tree, before it begins to open up and branch out. The parts of the *lulav* are (see image):

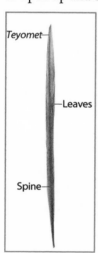

(1) the central branch, called the *shidra*, literally, the spine;

(2) the leaves that branch out from both sides of the spine;

(3) the top, central leaf that emerges from the upper edge of the spine, called *teyomet*, or twin-leaf.

Each of the leaves, including the *teyomet*, is folded over, and consists of two halves attached to each other along a fold for their entire length.

When selecting a *lulav*, one should look for the following:

(1) The length of the *lulav* should be at least four handbreadths (about 32 cm) from the point of the

connection of the lowest leaf to the spine, up to the end of the spine (the point from which the *teyomet* emerges). In practice, most of the *lulavim* on the market are considerably longer than this. In any event, the *lulav* should be longer than the *hadasim*.

(2) The spine should be covered with leaves on both sides. All the leaves should be adjacent to one another, all lying on the spine, so that the overall appearance of the *lulav* is similar to that of a single stick. Some people are particular that all the leaves should be stuck together, but this is not obligatory, and some actually prefer that the leaves should not be stuck together (see below, with regard to the laws of taking the *lulav*).

(3) One should make sure that in all the leaves, especially the *teyomet*, the two halves of the leaf are attached to each other along the fold for their entire length, and that the two halves are equal in width.

(4) The spine of the *lulav* should be straight, thereby ensuring that the overall appearance of the *lulav* is likewise straight.

(5) The *lulav* must be straight on the tip of the *teyomet* as well. It is also important that the *teyomet* be undamaged, meaning that the two halves of the leaf should not be separated and that it should not be dried out. For these reasons, some prefer to buy a *lulav* whose *teyomet* has a natural covering, called *koreh*, a thin brown membrane that encircles and protects the upper part of the *lulav* on the tree. In contrast, others prefer *lulavim* without *koreh*, so that one can see the *teyomet* and examine it to ensure its validity.

(6) If one cuts off a *lulav* from a tree by himself, he must make sure that the tree is a date-palm and not a different species of palm.

Myrtle [*Hadas*]

The Torah describes this species as "a bough of a leafy [*avot*] tree." The word *avot* literally means a rope, and indeed, the structure of the leaves on the branches of the *hadas*, which we use in accordance with a tradition passed down through the generations, resembles a braided rope. The parts of the *hadas* are (see image):

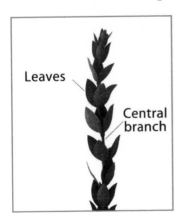

Leaves

Central branch

(1) the central branch;

(2) the leaves;

(3) the top of the branch.

Sometimes the *hadas* has berries growing on it.

In choosing a *hadas*, the following should be kept in mind:

(1) The leaves of a valid *hadas* grow in groups of three and cover the entire branch. It is important that every set of three leaves emerges from the same point in height on the branch, and that the tops of the leaves should at least reach the base of the three leaves above it.

(2) The minimum length of a *hadas* is three handbreadths (about 24 cm). This length is measured from the base of the three lowest leaves to the top of the central branch. One must make sure that along the entire length of the *hadas*, or at least most of it, the leaves are arranged in sets of three with the level sprouting point.

(3) It is proper to make sure that the upper edge of the branch is not cut or broken.

(4) If there are berries on the *hadas* and they are not green, they should be removed before the festival.

Willow [*Arava*]

The Torah states that one must take "*aravot* of the brook." Based on a tradition, the Sages explained that this is referring to what we call a willow tree,

Willow branch

which typically grows on river banks, and whose elongated leaves are reminiscent of a brook. The ends of its leaves are smooth and not serrated, and its branches are reddish in color (see image).

The following considerations should be taken into account when choosing an *arava*:

(1) The leaves of the *arava* should be long and relatively narrow.

(2) The edges of the leaves should be smooth or with small serrations that face a single direction, usually toward the tip of the leaf.

(3) Its branches should be red (this includes shades of dark brown). If the tree from which the *arava* was cut has some red branches, one may use the green branches of that tree as well. When buying the *arava* from a reliable vendor, there is no need to check for this.

(4) One must make sure that the top of the *arava* is not cut. Some prefer branches that have a young leaf sprouting from the top of the branch, known as the *lavluv*, as this is a clear indication that the branch is whole on top.

(5) The majority of the leaves of the *arava* must still be connected to the branch, and not have fallen off.

(6) Since the *arava* dries out quickly, it must be kept sufficiently moist in its package and one must take care that it remains fresh. If an *arava* has dried out, it should be replaced. To preserve the freshness of leaves of the *arava* and the *hadas*, many people keep the *lulav*, while bound with the *hadasim* and *aravot*, inside a plastic case or a damp towel. Many also keep the *aravot* in the refrigerator to maintain their freshness, especially before the festival.

Note: The laws regarding the validity of the four species on the first day of the festival are more stringent than on the other days of the festival. Therefore, if one of the species was damaged over the subsequent six days, it is recommended to ask a rabbi, as they might still be acceptable for use.

Practical Advice

Apart from the four species themselves, it is recommended to equip oneself with the materials necessary to protect them and to bind them. Most *etrogim* are sold with a padded wrapping of some kind. It is also recommended to obtain an *etrog* box, which will help protect it and will make it easier to carry it to the synagogue each day. In addition, it is advisable to have a plastic case (there are various types that are made especially for the *lulav*) to protect the *lulav* and to make it easier to transport.

Until the species are bound together, it is recommended to keep the *aravot* and *hadasim* in a plastic bag in the refrigerator.

Binding the *Lulav*

The proper way to perform the mitzva of taking the four species is to bind the *hadasim* and the *aravot* to the *lulav*. Since it is prohibited to tie a knot on the festival itself, this must be done before the holiday begins.

How Are They Bound?

When one recites the blessing over the four species, they should be held in the hand in the direction of their growth. Thus, when binding the three kinds of branches together, one must ensure that they are facing upward, while the ends from where they were detached from the tree are directed downward.

It is proper to ensure that the spine of the *lulav*, after the binding, is at least one handbreadth (about 8 cm) higher than the tops of the *hadasim* and *aravot*.

There are several customs regarding how to bind together the *lulav*, *hadasim*, and *aravot*. Most Ashkenazim place the three *hadasim* to the right of the *lulav* spine, with the *aravot* to its left. In contrast, most Sephardim, as well as many who follow the customs of the Arizal (the 16th century kabbalist Rabbi Yitzhak Luria), place one *hadas* on each side of the *lulav*, one *hadas* against the spine, slightly tilted to the right, and the two *aravot* between the two *hadasim* on the right and left of the spine (see image).

Binding of the *lulav* with the other species, in accordance with the opinion of the Arizal

📖 **Further reading:** For further information on the Arizal, see *A Concise Guide to Mahshava*, p. 330.

What to Use for the Binding

There are also several customs with regard to what to use to bind the species:

Many Sephardim bind the species with any type of thread. Ashkenazim, and some Sephardim as well, customarily use detached leaves of the *lulav* as bands; these can be removed from the bottom of one's *lulav* or from a spare or invalid *lulav*. Some people make special rings from leaves of the *lulav* that enable one to bind the species in an easy, convenient manner. One can make such rings oneself or buy them ready-made from vendors of the four species.

Many Ashkenazim use a holder made of *lulav* leaves woven together, commonly called a *koishikel*. This holder includes two sleeves designed for inserting the *hadasim* and *aravot*, and between these two sleeves there is a hole into which the *lulav* is inserted. Some argue that in this manner the three species are not firmly bound and connected to each other, and therefore they tie them together on top of the *koishikel*, or higher up along the *lulav* above the *koishikel*.

There is a long-standing custom among Sephardim and Hasidim to attach more than the three requisite *hadasim* to the *lulav*, in order to enhance the mitzva. These extra *hadasim* do not have to be halakhically valid, but they should be positioned so that their tops face upward, like the primary *hadas* branches.

Tying the *Lulav*

As for the *lulav* itself, some do not tie it at all, other than binding it together with the *hadasim* and *aravot*. Some add two more rings in the middle of the *lulav*, so that its leaves will be more tightly aligned with the spine. Yet others tie it in many places (some are careful to place precisely eighteen knots), to prevent it from opening when it is shaken. For this reason, there are those who wrap a thread around the *lulav* all the way up, almost to its edge, but even they keep the very top of the *lulav* loose so that it will produce a sound when shaken.

One Who Forgot to Bind the *Lulav*

If one forgot to bind the *lulav* before the onset of the festival, he may bind it on the festival itself with a string or with *lulav* leaves. In this case, he may not tie an ordinary knot, but should make a bow, or wrap thread around the species, wedging the edge of the thread into the binding. One may also use rubber bands. It is permissible to insert the species into a *koishikel* on the festival.

Sukkot
The Mitzvot of the Festival

The two central mitzvot of *Sukkot* are dwelling in the *sukka* and taking in hand the four species.

The mitzva of dwelling in the *sukka* means that the *sukka* becomes one's home for the seven days of the festival. The Torah states: "You shall live in booths seven days" (Leviticus 23:42), and the Sages expounded from the phrase "you shall live" that one must dwell in the *sukka* in the manner that one lives in his house (*Sukka* 28b). The practical significance of this instruction is that a person should spend as much time in the *sukka* as possible and use it for the all the activities he generally performs in his home. Additionally, one should strive to furnish and decorate the *sukka* so as to make it as pleasant and comfortable as possible.

The second mitzva, the taking in hand of the four species, is sometimes referred to as simply "taking the *lulav*," because the *lulav* is the most prominent and visible of the four species. The Sages derived from the verse: "You shall take for you on the first day the fruit of a pleasant tree…and you shall rejoice before the Lord your God seven days" (Leviticus 23:40), that this commandment applies outside of the Temple only on the first day of the festival, and in the Temple, where one stands most directly "before the Lord," it applies for all seven days of the festival. After the destruction of the Temple, the Sages instituted that the mitzva should be performed everywhere on all seven days of the festival (except for Shabbat).

This section, the second dealing with the festival of *Sukkot*, presents the *halakhot* and customs pertaining to the fulfillment of these two mitzvot.

Sitting in the *Sukka*

The reason given for the mitzva of dwelling in the *sukka* is "so that your generations will know that I had the children of Israel live in booths, when I took them out of the land of Egypt" (Leviticus 23:43).

According to a tradition recorded by the Sages, this verse is referring to supernatural "clouds of glory" that surrounded the Israelites from the moment they left Egypt until their arrival in the Land of Israel. These clouds shielded them from all the dangers of the perilous journey.

Who Is Obligated?

The mitzva of dwelling in the *sukka* is obligatory for every male aged thirteen and up. Furthermore, in the case of boys who have reached an age at which they can be trained to perform mitzvot, which is five or six years old (and in some cases even earlier), the father must accustom them to observing the mitzva of *sukka*.

People who are ill are exempt from the obligation of dwelling in the *sukka*, and the same applies to any person who suffers from a certain level of discomfort in the *sukka*, as will be explained below.

Women are exempt from the mitzva of *sukka*, in accordance with the general principle that women are exempt from time-bound, positive mitzvot.

Eating in the *Sukka*

The main activities one must perform in the *sukka* are eating and sleeping. Some are stringent not to eat or drink anything at all outside the *sukka* for the duration of the festival. This is a praiseworthy practice if one can adhere to it, but the halakhic requirement is that one is obligated to eat only fixed meals in the *sukka*. A "fixed meal" is defined as eating bread or a baked item on which one recites the blessing of *mezonot* ("…who creates various kinds of nourishment"; see the laws of blessings, p. 515). Even these foods are only considered a fixed meal if one eats at least the volume of an egg (about 86.4 cc). Even a smaller amount should be eaten in the *sukka* if one sits down to eat it in a fixed setting, e.g., with a cup of coffee or after reciting *Kiddush*.

In cases in which it is obligatory to eat in the *sukka*, one should recite the following blessing before eating:

בָּרוּךְ אַתָּה אֲדֹנָי, אֱלֹהֵינוּ מֶלֶךְ הָעוֹלָם, אֲשֶׁר קִדְּשָׁנוּ בְּמִצְוֹתָיו וְצִוָּנוּ לֵישֵׁב בַּסֻּכָּה.

Barukh ata Adonai, Eloheinu melekh ha'olam, asher kideshanu bemitzvotav, vetzivanu leisheiv basukka.

"Blessed are You, Lord our God, King of the universe, who sanctified us through His commandments, and commanded us to reside in the *sukka*."

After one has left the *sukka* for an extended period of time and then returns to it, he must recite this blessing again if he wants to eat something that must be eaten in the *sukka*.

If a person does not eat bread or other foods made of grains during *Sukkot*, as, for example, one who has celiac and may not eat grain products because of the gluten they contain, he must nevertheless recite the blessing when he enters the *sukka* for an extended period of time. Similarly, he should recite the blessing if he enters the *sukka* to eat a full meal, even if does not contain any grain products.

Sleeping in the *Sukka*

The obligation to sleep in the *sukka* is more stringent than the obligation to eat in the *sukka* in that it includes even a brief nap, and even if one is not lying down. This applies throughout the seven days of the festival. Nevertheless, in certain cases detailed below, one is exempt from sleeping in the *sukka* for reasons of discomfort. In addition, the custom of Lubavitch Hasidim and some other hasidic sects is not to sleep in the *sukka* at all, for various reasons.

📖 **Further reading:** For more information on the festival of *Sukkot*, see *A Concise Guide to the Torah*, pp. 318, 472; *A Concise Guide to the Sages*, p. 290; *A Concise Guide to Mahshava*, p. 72.

Discomfort in the *Sukka*

In situations in which being in the *sukka* would entail suffering or discomfort of some kind, e.g., due to a bad smell, rain, insects, or because it is too hot or too cold, there is no obligation to eat or sleep in the *sukka*. The reason for this is that the mitzva of *sukka* entails living in the *sukka* as one lives in his regular home. Consequently, if one would leave one's home under these circumstances in order to eat or sleep, one may leave the *sukka* as well. The *halakha* is different with regard to the first night of the festival, however, as detailed below.

One should avoid erecting a *sukka* in a manner that will cause discomfort to those using it. If necessary, one should bring fans into the *sukka* to aid with the heat, or a heater (taking care to follow safety precautions) to aid with the cold.

If one has to leave the *sukka* in the middle of a meal due to discomfort, or if he began a meal or went to sleep in the house because of discomfort in the *sukka*, even if the cause of the discomfort has passed, he need not return to the *sukka* to complete his meal or to continue the night's sleep. This permission to sleep outside the *sukka* extends until one wakes from his sleep or until daylight, whichever of the two is later.

Some halakhic authorities exempt a married man from sleeping in the *sukka*, if the conditions of the *sukka* do not allow him and his wife to sleep there in the privacy and comfort to which they are accustomed the rest of the year.

The First Night

On the first night of *Sukkot,* there is a special obligation to eat in the *sukka*. The minimum requirement on this night is to recite *Kiddush* and eat at least the minimal volume of an olive-bulk (about 27 cc) of bread in the *sukka*.

This is in contrast to the rest of the festival, during which one may avoid eating in the *sukka* completely by limiting himself to eating foods that do not have to be eaten in the *sukka*.

Likewise, on the first night of the festival, the obligation to eat in the *sukka* applies even if sitting there causes one suffering, e.g., if it is raining. In such a case, one should wait a while to see if the rain stops. If the rain shows no signs of letting up, one must begin the meal in the *sukka* anyway, by reciting *Kiddush* and eating an olive-bulk of bread. After this he may go back inside and continue the meal there.

In localities where there is frequent rainfall in the season of *Sukkot*, one may place thick *sukka* roofing [*sekhakh*] on the *sukka* so that it will take a longer time for the rain to penetrate. Additionally, one can cover the *sukka* with a sheet of plastic in advance and remove it just before entering the *sukka* to recite *Kiddush*. If one does use such a covering, he must be careful to remember to remove it every time he goes to eat in the *sukka*.

Traveling during the Intermediate Festival Days

Ideally, one should not undertake many trips during the intermediate festival days [*Hol HaMoed*] of *Sukkot*, so that one can maximize dwelling in the *sukka*. Nevertheless, since during the year it is customary from time to time to leave one's house and eat on the road, on *Sukkot* as well it is permitted to go on a trip even if one is not entirely sure that he will find a *sukka* on the way. If a person on the road is unable to find a *sukka*, he is permitted to eat without a *sukka*. At night he must make a special effort to find a *sukka* to sleep in, as even during the year one would try his utmost to find proper lodging for the night. If he could not find a *sukka*, he may sleep outside the *sukka*.

If one goes on a trip on *Hol HaMoed Sukkot* and intends to be away for several days in a row, he should make arrangements ahead of time to ensure that he will have a *sukka* in which he can eat and sleep. Nowadays it is relatively easy to obtain mobile *sukkot* that can be towed along, or which can be assembled in field conditions.

📖 **Further reading:** For more information on the idea that dwelling in the *sukka* is like a taste of the Garden of Eden, see *A Concise Guide to Mahshava*, p. 76.

Taking in Hand the Four Species

The Torah's mitzva of taking the four species has been expounded to allude to several deep concepts, and various reasons have been given for the choice of these particular species.

For example, the *lulav, etrog, hadas,* and *arava* are said to represent four general types among the Jewish people, and their being bound together expresses the unity of the people. With regard to the waving of the four species in all directions, the Talmud (*Sukka* 37b) explains that this is a symbolic act demonstrating God's mastery over everything in heaven and on earth and all over the world. Another suggestion given there is that it serves to protect against harmful winds and precipitation.

The First Day, and the Rest of the Festival

By Torah law, the obligation to pick up the four species applies in the Temple all seven days of *Sukkot*, and outside of the Temple only on the first day of *Sukkot*. Following the destruction of the second Temple, the Sages instituted that one must pick up the four species every day of the festival (except for Shabbat), in commemoration of the Temple. There are several halakhic ramifications of the fact that the mitzva on the first day is by Torah law and the mitzva on subsequent days is a rabbinic institution.

On the first day, the set of the four species must be owned by the one fulfilling the mitzva, whereas on the other days one may borrow a set from someone else. This *halakha* is derived from the wording of the verse: "You shall take for you on the first day" (Leviticus 23:40), which teaches that "on the first day" of the festival, the four species must be "for you," meaning that they must belong to you.

How, then, can an entire family recite a blessing over one set of four species that belongs to the head of the family? And how it is possible for someone who did not purchase a set before the festival to fulfill the mitzva?

The solution is to give over the set in the form of a gift. If one wishes, he can explicitly stipulate that it is a gift given on the condition that it be returned. The one who receives the gift with this condition may then take the four species and recite the blessing, returning it immediately afterward to its former owner, so as to fulfill the condition attached to the gift.

On the first day of the festival, the four species should not be given as a gift to minors (boys under the age of thirteen and girls under the age of twelve) before the adults have fulfilled the mitzva, as children have the legal ability to acquire items but not to transfer ownership over them to others. Consenquently, if a father gives his set of four species to his minor son as a gift, they will remain the child's property and will not revert back to the possession of the father, which means that the father will be unable to fulfill the mitzva after that. Accordingly, on the first day of *Sukkot* one should give the four species to the children for them to recite the blessing on them only after all the adults have already completed the mitzva.

On the rest of the festival days there is no problem with fulfilling the mitzva with a borrowed set of four species.

Another difference between the first day of the festival and the subsequent days is that on the first day, a higher level of halakhic specification is required for the four species than on the rest of the festival. If one's four species set was damaged on the first festival day, it is possible that it is nevertheless valid for the rest of the days. In such a case, it is worthwhile to consult a rabbi.

On the Shabbat of *Sukkot*, the mitzva of taking the four species is not observed, even if Shabbat is the first day of the festival.

📖 **Further reading:** To read about the great symbolic significance of the mitzva of the four species, see *A Concise Guide to the Sages*, p. 291; *A Concise Guide to Mahshava*, p. 74.

Who Is Obligated?

Every male, including a child who is old enough to be taught how to hold and wave the *lulav*, is obligated to perform the mitzva of the four species.

Women are exempt from taking the four species, as this is a time-bound positive mitzva. Nevertheless, many women have the custom of taking in hand the four species and reciting the blessing, while some do so without the blessing.

The Time of the Mitzva

The mitzva of taking the *lulav* may be fulfilled throughout the day, at any time from sunrise to sunset. It is proper to perform the mitzva as early as possible. Likewise, one should refrain from eating before fulfilling the mitzva. Therefore, many people have the custom to take the four species in hand upon awakening in the morning, in the *sukka* at home, even before reciting the morning prayers.

Others have the custom of taking the *lulav* in hand and reciting the blessing just before the recitation of the *Hallel* prayer in the synagogue. Some go out to the *sukka* at that point and recite the blessing over the *lulav* there, while others do so inside the synagogue.

In addition to the recitation of the blessing over the four species, there are several points during the morning prayer, during *Hallel* and *Hoshanot*, when the four species are held and waved (see the next section regarding the festival days, p. 204).

When fulfilling the mitzva, one must hold the four species as they grow, right side up. The *etrog* must also be held with its pointed side upward, since that is the position of the *etrog* as it begins to grow on the tree.

The blessing over a mitzva should generally be recited before performing the mitzva, but while holding the object used for the mitzva so that he can perform the mitzva immediately after reciting the blessing. In the case of the four species, performing the mitzva requires simply picking them up and holding them in the proper fashion. Therefore, the proper procedure is as follows: One should hold the *lulav* bound with the *hadasim* and the *aravot* in his right hand, and the *etrog* in his left hand, but the *etrog* should be upside down. After reciting the blessing, one should turn over the *etrog* so that he is holding it properly and fulfilling the mitzva. Alternatively, some have the custom to recite the blessing while holding the *lulav, hadasim*, and *aravot*, and to pick up the *etrog* after the blessing. One then holds the *etrog* directly adjacent to the *lulav* and waves them.

The Text of the Blessings

On each day of the festival, the following is recited before fulfilling the mitzva of taking the four species:

בָּרוּךְ אַתָּה אֲדֹנָי, אֱלֹהֵינוּ מֶלֶךְ הָעוֹלָם,
אֲשֶׁר קִדְּשָׁנוּ בְּמִצְוֹתָיו וְצִוָּנוּ עַל נְטִילַת
לוּלָב.

Barukh ata Adonai, Eloheinu, melekh ha'olam, asher kideshanu bemitzvotav, vetzivanu al netilat lulav.

"Blessed are You, Lord our God, King of the universe, who sanctified us through His commandments, and commanded us concerning the taking of the *lulav*."

On the first day of *Sukkot*, one adds the *Sheheheyanu* blessing:

בָּרוּךְ אַתָּה אֲדֹנָי, אֱלֹהֵינוּ מֶלֶךְ הָעוֹלָם,
שֶׁהֶחֱיָנוּ וְקִיְּמָנוּ וְהִגִּיעָנוּ לַזְּמַן הַזֶּה.

Barukh ata Adonai, Eloheinu, melekh ha'olam, sheheheyanu vekiyemanu vehigi'anu la'zeman hazeh.

"Blessed are You, Lord our God, King of the universe, who has given us life, sustained us, and brought us to this time."

One who did not take the four species on the first day of the festival should recite the *Sheheheyanu* blessing on the first occasion that he fulfills the mitzva that year, even if it is on one of the subsequent days of the festival.

Waving the Four Species

After the blessings, one waves the four species. The basic act of waving consists of slightly moving the four species while holding them together. There are several customs which expand upon this and provide an order to the wavings:

It is possible to wave the *lulav* forward, backward, up, and down. However, the more common practice is to wave the *lulav* toward all four directions (right, left, to the front, and behind), and also up and down. Among those who wave in these six directions, there are different customs regarding the order. Some start with the east side (forward, when facing east) and continue clockwise and then up and down. According to the kabbalistic teachings of the Arizal, the order is (when facing east): right, left, forward, up, down, and backward. There are other customs as well.

According to most customs, in each of the directions mentioned, one waves the *lulav* three times, in a to-and-fro movement.

Some are particular to place the four species next to their heart at the end of each waving.

There are those who make sure that in each of the movements the *lulav* is shaken to make a slight rustling sound.

Some turn their faces to each direction of the various wavings, while others face forward and move only their hands with the four species to the different sides.

One custom is to hold the *lulav* upright throughout the waving, whereas others direct its tip toward the side to which they are shaking.

Any manner of waving is acceptable, and one should follow the custom of his congregation and community. We have presented these various customs to illustrate some of the diverse traditions that have developed over the generations, as a way to express affection for the fulfillment of this mitzva.

Sukkot
The Festival

The previous sections dealt with building a valid *sukka*, selecting a choice set of four species, and some of the details of the laws and customs of the mitzvot of *Sukkot*. This third section about the festival of *Sukkot* is a guide to the practices followed in synagogue services, in the *sukka*, during mealtimes at home, and when traveling.

The Start of the Festival

As mentioned previously, the first day of *Sukkot* is a festival day [*yom tov*], which means that all the restrictions of Shabbat, in the manner in which they apply to any *yom tov* (see p. 466), are in effect. Before the holiday, one should perform all the necessary tasks of any festival eve, including preparing fire for use during the festival and for candle lighting.

Final Preparations and Candle Lighting

When a *yom tov* day occurs on any day of the week other than Shabbat, it is recommended to light a long-burning candle in advance, so that it can be used to transfer fire for cooking and other uses.

When the festival begins on a weekday, some are accustomed to light the candles just before the festival begins at sunset, whereas others light them after sunset, close to the beginning of the meal. Those who light after the festival has already begun should use only an existing flame; as it is prohibited to produce a new fire on *yom tov*, one lights the match from a fire that was burning from before the festival. It is also prohibited to extinguish a flame, and thefore the match should be left to burn out on its own. When the first day of *Sukkot* falls on a Shabbat, one must, of course, light the candles before the start of Shabbat (and the festival), at the times indicated in synagogue calendars.

When lighting the candles, one recites two blessings:

בָּרוּךְ אַתָּה אֲדֹנָי, אֱלֹהֵינוּ מֶלֶךְ הָעוֹלָם,
אֲשֶׁר קִדְּשָׁנוּ בְּמִצְוֹתָיו וְצִוָּנוּ לְהַדְלִיק נֵר
שֶׁל יוֹם טוֹב (וְאִם חל בשבת: שֶׁל שַׁבָּת
וְשֶׁל יוֹם טוֹב).

Barukh ata Adonai, Eloheinu, melekh ha'olam, asher kideshanu bemitzvotav, vetzivanu lehadlik ner shel yom tov (on Shabbat conclude instead: *shel Shabbat veshel yom tov*).

"Blessed are You, Lord our God, King of the universe, who sanctified us through His commandments, and commanded us to light a candle for the festival (on Shabbat: for the Shabbat and for the festival)."

בָּרוּךְ אַתָּה אֲדֹנָי, אֱלֹהֵינוּ מֶלֶךְ הָעוֹלָם, שֶׁהֶחֱיָנוּ וְקִיְּמָנוּ וְהִגִּיעָנוּ לַזְּמַן הַזֶּה.

Barukh ata Adonai, Eloheinu, melekh ha'olam, sheheḥeyanu vekiyemanu vehigi'anu la'zeman hazeh.

"Blessed are You, Lord our God, King of the universe, who has given us life, sustained us, and brought us to this time."

For more details regarding the *halakhot* of candle lighting, see p. 381.

Evening Prayer

The congregation recites the festival evening prayer, which can be found in most prayer books.

When the first day of *Sukkot* occurs on Shabbat, the congregation recites before the evening prayers an abbreviated version of *Kabbalat Shabbat*, beginning with Psalms 92, "A psalm, a song for the Sabbath day" [*Mizmor shir leyom haShabbat*], or in some communities, with Psalms 29, "A song by David" [*Mizmor leDavid*]. At the end of the prayer service, the following sections are added: the passage beginning: "The heavens and the earth" [*Vaykhulu hashamayim veha'aretz*] (Genesis 2:1–3), the *Magen Avot* prayer, and in some communities Psalms 23, "A psalm by David" [*Mizmor leDavid*]. References to Shabbat are also inserted in the *Amida* prayer, as indicated in the prayer books.

> **Further reading:** For more information on the festival of *Sukkot*, see *A Concise Guide to the Torah*, pp. 318, 472; *A Concise Guide to the Sages*, p. 290; *A Concise Guide to Mahshava*, p. 72.

Ushpizin

According to kabbalistic tradition, on each evening of the *Sukkot* festival the spirit of one of the illustrious forefathers of Israel, as detailed below, visits every *sukka*. In Aramaic, a visitor is called an *ushpiza*, or *ushpizin* in the plural. This is the meaning of the custom of *ushpizin* practiced in many communities, wherein the daily guest (*ushpiza*) is invited to the *sukka* each night before the meal.

According to the custom of the Arizal, one recites:

אֲזַמִּין לִסְעוּדָתִי אֻשְׁפִּיזִין עִלָּאִין אַבְרָהָם,
יִצְחָק, יַעֲקֹב, מֹשֶׁה אַהֲרֹן, יוֹסֵף וְדָוִד.

Azamin lesudati ushpizin ila'in: Avraham, Yitzḥak, Ya'akov, Moshe, Aharon, Yosef, veDavid.

"I invite to my meal the exalted guests Abraham, Isaac, Jacob, Moses, Aaron, Joseph, and David."

According to the custom of some Ashkenazim, one also recites the following:

עֻלוּ אֻשְׁפִּיזִין עִלָּאִין קַדִּישִׁין, עֻלוּ אֲבָהָן
עִלָּאִין קַדִּישִׁין לְמֵיתַב בְּצִלָּא דְּהֵימְנוּתָא
עִלָּאָה.

Ulu ushpizin ila'in kadishin, ulu avahan ila'in kadishin, lemetav betzila dehei'menuta ila'a.

"Enter exalted, holy guests, enter holy, exalted forefathers, to sit in the shadow of the exalted faith," which is a kabbalistic designation for the *sukka*.

Next, according to both versions one recites:

בְּמָטוּ מִנָּךְ (שם) אֻשְׁפִּיזִי עִלָּאִי, דְּיֵתְבֵי
עִמִּי וְעִמָּךְ כָּל אֻשְׁפִּיזֵי עִלָּאֵי (שמות שאר
הָאוּשְׁפִּיזִין).

Bematu minakh (name of that day's guest) ushpizi ila'i, deyatvei imi ve'imakh kol ushpizei ila'ei.

"Please, (here one adds the name of that day's guest) my exalted guest, may it be that all the exalted guests (here one lists all the other guests, apart from the guest for that day) will (come and) sit with me and you."

There are also two opinions regarding the order of the guests. According to the Arizal, the order is: Abraham, Isaac, Jacob, Moses, Aaron, Joseph, and David. This order is based on kabbalistic concepts. According to the accepted practice in the non-hasidic Ashkenazic community, the order corresponds with the historical chronology: Abraham, Isaac, Jacob, Joseph, Moses, Aaron, and David.

📖 **Further reading:** On *Sukkot*, as on all festivals, it is important to remember those who are less fortunate. See *A Concise Guide to the Sages*, p. 242.

Kiddush

As on the night of every festival and Shabbat, *Kiddush* is recited over a cup of wine at the beginning of the meal. The *Kiddush* must be performed in the *sukka*.

Text of the *Kiddush*

When the festival begins on a Friday night, the *Kiddush* starts with this paragraph:

For Ashkenazim:

(בלחש - וַיְהִי עֶרֶב וַיְהִי בֹקֶר)

(Quietly: *Vayhi erev vayhi voker*)

יוֹם הַשִּׁשִּׁי, וַיְכֻלּוּ הַשָּׁמַיִם וְהָאָרֶץ וְכָל צְבָאָם. וַיְכַל אֱלֹהִים בַּיּוֹם הַשְּׁבִיעִי מְלַאכְתּוֹ אֲשֶׁר עָשָׂה, וַיִּשְׁבֹּת בַּיּוֹם הַשְּׁבִיעִי מִכָּל מְלַאכְתּוֹ אֲשֶׁר עָשָׂה. וַיְבָרֶךְ אֱלֹהִים אֶת יוֹם הַשְּׁבִיעִי וַיְקַדֵּשׁ אֹתוֹ, כִּי בוֹ שָׁבַת מִכָּל מְלַאכְתּוֹ אֲשֶׁר בָּרָא אֱלֹהִים לַעֲשׂוֹת.

Yom hashishi. Vaykhulu hashamayim veha'aretz vekhol tzeva'am. Vaykhal Elohim bayom hashevi'i melakhto asher asa, vayishbot bayom hashevi'i mikol melakhto asher asa. Vayvarekh Elohim et yom hashevi'i vaykadesh oto, ki vo shavat mikol melakhto asher bara Elohim la'asot.

On a weekday one starts here:

סַבְרִי מָרָנָן וְרַבָּנָן וְרַבּוֹתַי:

Savri meranan verabanan verabotai:

בָּרוּךְ אַתָּה אֲדֹנָי, אֱלֹהֵינוּ מֶלֶךְ הָעוֹלָם, בּוֹרֵא פְּרִי הַגָּפֶן.

Barukh ata Adonai, Eloheinu, melekh ha'olam, boreh peri hagafen.

בָּרוּךְ אַתָּה אֲדֹנָי, אֱלֹהֵינוּ מֶלֶךְ הָעוֹלָם, אֲשֶׁר בָּחַר בָּנוּ מִכָּל עָם, וְרוֹמְמָנוּ מִכָּל לָשׁוֹן וְקִדְּשָׁנוּ בְּמִצְוֹתָיו, וַתִּתֶּן לָנוּ אֲדֹנָי אֱלֹהֵינוּ בְּאַהֲבָה (בשבת: שַׁבָּתוֹת לִמְנוּחָה וּ)מוֹעֲדִים לְשִׂמְחָה, חַגִּים וּזְמַנִּים לְשָׂשׂוֹן, אֶת יוֹם (בשבת: הַשַּׁבָּת הַזֶּה וְאֶת יוֹם) חַג הַסֻּכּוֹת הַזֶּה. זְמַן שִׂמְחָתֵנוּ (בשבת: בְּאַהֲבָה), מִקְרָא קֹדֶשׁ זֵכֶר לִיצִיאַת מִצְרָיִם. כִּי בָנוּ בָחַרְתָּ וְאוֹתָנוּ קִדַּשְׁתָּ מִכָּל הָעַמִּים, (בשבת: וְשַׁבָּת) וּמוֹעֲדֵי קָדְשֶׁךָ (בשבת: בְּאַהֲבָה וּבְרָצוֹן) בְּשִׂמְחָה וּבְשָׂשׂוֹן הִנְחַלְתָּנוּ, בָּרוּךְ אַתָּה אֲדֹנָי, מְקַדֵּשׁ (בשבת: הַשַּׁבָּת וְ) יִשְׂרָאֵל וְהַזְּמַנִּים.

Barukh ata Adonai, Eloheinu, melekh ha'olam, asher baḥar banu mikol am, veromemanu mikol lashon, vekidesha-nu bemitzvotav. Vatiten lanu Adonai Eloheinu be'ahava, (on Shabbat add: Shabbatot limnuḥa u)mo'adim lesim-ḥa, ḥagim uzmanim lesason, et yom (on Shabbat add: haShabbat hazeh ve'et yom) ḥag haSukkot hazeh, ze-man simḥateinu (on Shabbat add: be'ahava) mikra kodesh, zekher litziat Mitzrayim. Ki vanu vaḥarta ve'otanu kidashta mikol ha'amim, (on Shabbat add: veShabbat) umo'adei kodshekha (on Shabbat add: be'ahava uvratzon) besimḥa uvsason hinḥaltanu. Barukh ata Adonai, mekadesh (on Shabbat add: haShabbat ve)Yisrael vehaze-manim.

בָּרוּךְ אַתָּה אֲדֹנָי, אֱלֹהֵינוּ מֶלֶךְ הָעוֹלָם,
אֲשֶׁר קִדְּשָׁנוּ בְּמִצְוֹתָיו וְצִוָּנוּ לֵישֵׁב
בַּסֻּכָּה.

Barukh ata Adonai, Eloheinu, melekh ha'olam, asher kideshanu bemitzvotav, vetzivanu leishev basukka.

(כשמברכים 'שהחיינו', יש לחשוב
ולהתכוון שהברכה היא גם על מצוות
הישיבה בסוכה): בָּרוּךְ אַתָּה אֲדֹנָי, אֱלֹהֵינוּ
מֶלֶךְ הָעוֹלָם, שֶׁהֶחֱיָנוּ וְקִיְּמָנוּ וְהִגִּיעָנוּ
לַזְּמַן הַזֶּה.

When reciting the *Sheheheyanu* blessing, one should have in mind that it should apply to the mitzva of dwelling in the *sukka* as well: *Barukh ata Adonai, Eloheinu, melekh ha'olam, sheheheyanu vekiyemanu vehigi'anu la'zeman hazeh.*

(Quietly: "It was evening and it was morning,) the sixth day. The heavens and the earth and their entire host were completed. God completed on the seventh day His works that He had made; He rested on the seventh day from all His works that He had made. God blessed the seventh day, and sanctified it; because on it He rested from all His works that God created to make" (Genesis 1:31–2:3).

When *Sukkot* occurs on a weekday, one starts here:

"Attention, masters, rabbis, teachers:

"Blessed are You, Lord our God, King of the universe, who creates the fruit of the vine.

"Blessed are You, Lord our God, King of the universe, who has chosen us from all nations, and raised us above all tongues, and sanctified us through His commandments. And You have given us, Lord our God, in love, (on Shabbat add: Shabbatot for rest and) appointed times for joy, festivals and seasonal holidays for gladness, this day of (on Shabbat add: Shabbat and this day of) the festival of *Sukkot*, the time of our rejoicing (on Shabbat add: with love), a holy convocation, in commemoration of the exodus from Egypt. For You have chosen us and sanctified us above all nations, and (on Shabbat add: the Shabbat and) Your holy festivals (on Shabbat add: in love and favor,) in joy and in gladness You have given us for an inheritance. Blessed are You, Lord, who sanctifies (on Shabbat add: the Shabbat,) Israel and the seasonal holidays."

"Blessed are You, Lord our God, King of the universe, who sanctified us through His commandments, and commanded us to reside in the *sukka*."

When reciting the following blessing (called *Sheheheyanu*), one should have in mind that this blessing should apply to the mitzva of dwelling in the *sukka* as well:

"Blessed are You, Lord our God, King of the universe, who has given us life, sustained us, and brought us to this time."

For Sephardim:

וַיְהִי עֶרֶב וַיְהִי בֹקֶר יוֹם הַשִּׁשִּׁי. וַיְכֻלּוּ הַשָּׁמַיִם וְהָאָרֶץ וְכָל צְבָאָם. וַיְכַל אֱלֹהִים בַּיּוֹם הַשְּׁבִיעִי מְלַאכְתּוֹ אֲשֶׁר עָשָׂה, וַיִּשְׁבֹּת בַּיּוֹם הַשְּׁבִיעִי מִכָּל מְלַאכְתּוֹ אֲשֶׁר עָשָׂה. וַיְבָרֶךְ אֱלֹהִים אֶת יוֹם הַשְּׁבִיעִי וַיְקַדֵּשׁ אֹתוֹ, כִּי בוֹ שָׁבַת מִכָּל מְלַאכְתּוֹ אֲשֶׁר בָּרָא אֱלֹהִים לַעֲשׂוֹת.

Vayhi erev vayhi voker yom Hashishi. Vaykhulu hashamayim veha'aretz vekhol tzeva'am. Vaykhal Elohim bayom hashevi'i melakhto asher asa, vayishbot bayom hashevi'i mikol melakhto asher asa. Vayvarekh Elohim et yom hashevi'i vaykadesh oto, ki vo shavat mikol melakhto asher bara Elohim la'asot.

On a weekday one starts here:

אֵלֶּה מוֹעֲדֵי אֲדֹנָי מִקְרָאֵי קֹדֶשׁ, אֲשֶׁר תִּקְרְאוּ אֹתָם בְּמוֹעֲדָם. וַיְדַבֵּר מֹשֶׁה אֶת מֹעֲדֵי אֲדֹנָי, אֶל בְּנֵי יִשְׂרָאֵל.

Eleh mo'adei Adonai, mikra'ei kodesh, asher tikre'u otam bemo'adam. Vaydaber Moshe et mo'adei Adonai el benei Yisrael.

סָבְרִי מָרָנָן.

Savri meranan.

הַשּׁוֹמְעִים עוֹנִים: לְחַיִּים!

Those listening answer: *Leḥayim.*

בָּרוּךְ אַתָּה אֲדֹנָי, אֱלֹהֵינוּ מֶלֶךְ הָעוֹלָם, בּוֹרֵא פְּרִי הַגָּפֶן.

Barukh ata Adonai, Eloheinu, melekh ha'olam, boreh peri hagefen.

בָּרוּךְ אַתָּה אֲדֹנָי, אֱלֹהֵינוּ מֶלֶךְ הָעוֹלָם, אֲשֶׁר בָּחַר בָּנוּ מִכָּל עָם, וְרוֹמְמָנוּ מִכָּל לָשׁוֹן, וְקִדְּשָׁנוּ בְּמִצְוֹתָיו. וַתִּתֶּן לָנוּ אֲדֹנָי אֱלֹהֵינוּ בְּאַהֲבָה (בשבת: שַׁבָּתוֹת לִמְנוּחָה וּ)מוֹעֲדִים לְשִׂמְחָה, חַגִּים וּזְמַנִּים לְשָׂשׂוֹן, (בשבת: אֶת יוֹם הַשַּׁבָּת הַזֶּה וְ)אֶת יוֹם חַג הַסֻּכּוֹת הַזֶּה. אֶת יוֹם טוֹב מִקְרָא קֹדֶשׁ הַזֶּה, זְמַן שִׂמְחָתֵנוּ בְּאַהֲבָה מִקְרָא קֹדֶשׁ, זֵכֶר לִיצִיאַת מִצְרַיִם. כִּי בָנוּ בָחַרְתָּ, וְאוֹתָנוּ קִדַּשְׁתָּ מִכָּל הָעַמִּים (בשבת: וְשַׁבָּתוֹת וּ) מוֹעֲדֵי קָדְשֶׁךָ (בשבת: בְּאַהֲבָה וּבְרָצוֹן)

Barukh ata Adonai, Eloheinu, melekh ha'olam, asher baḥar banu mikol am, veromemanu mikol lashon, vekideshanu bemitzvotav. Vatiten lanu Adonai Eloheinu be'ahava, (on Shabbat add: Shabbatot limnuḥa u) mo'adim lesimḥa, ḥagim uzmanim lesason, et yom (on Shabbat add: haShabbat hazeh ve) ḥag haSukkot hazeh, et yom tov mikra kodesh hazeh, zeman simḥateinu be'ahava mikra kodesh, zekher litziat Mitzrayim. Ki vanu vaḥarta ve'otanu kidashta mikol ha'amim, (on Shabbat add: veShabbatot) umo'adei kodshekha

בְּשִׂמְחָה וּבְשָׂשׂוֹן הִנְחַלְתָּנוּ. בָּרוּךְ אַתָּה
אֲדֹנָי, מְקַדֵּשׁ (בשבת: הַשַּׁבָּת וְ) יִשְׂרָאֵל
וְהַזְּמַנִּים.

(on Shabbat add: be'ahava uvratzon) besimḥa uvsason hinḥaltanu. Barukh ata Adonai, mekadesh (on Shabbat add: HaShabbat ve) Yisrael vehazemanim.

בָּרוּךְ אַתָּה אֲדֹנָי, אֱלֹהֵינוּ מֶלֶךְ הָעוֹלָם,
אֲשֶׁר קִדְּשָׁנוּ בְּמִצְוֹתָיו וְצִוָּנוּ לֵישֵׁב
בַּסֻּכָּה.

Barukh ata Adonai, Eloheinu, melekh ha'olam, asher kideshanu bemitzvotav, vetzivanu leishev basukka.

(כשמברכים 'שהחיינו', יש לחשוב
ולהתכוון שהברכה היא גם על מצוות
הישיבה בסוכה): בָּרוּךְ אַתָּה אֲדֹנָי, אֱלֹהֵינוּ
מֶלֶךְ הָעוֹלָם, שֶׁהֶחֱיָנוּ וְקִיְּמָנוּ וְהִגִּיעָנוּ
לַזְּמַן הַזֶּה.

When reciting the Sheheḥeyanu blessing, one should have in mind that it should apply to the mitzva of dwelling in the sukka as well: Barukh ata Adonai, Eloheinu, melekh ha'olam, sheheḥeyanu vekiyemanu vehigi'anu la'zeman hazeh.

"It was evening and it was morning, the sixth day. The heavens and the earth and their entire host were completed. God completed on the seventh day His works that He had made; He rested on the seventh day from all His works that He had made. God blessed the seventh day, and sanctified it; because on it He rested from all His works that God created to make" (Genesis 1:31–2:3).

"These are the appointed times of the Lord, holy convocations, that you shall proclaim at their appointed time" (Leviticus 23:4). "And Moses spoke to the children of Israel the appointed times of the Lord" (Leviticus 23:44).

"Attention, masters."

The listeners respond: "To life!"

"Blessed are You, Lord our God, King of the universe, who creates the fruit of the vine.

"Blessed are You, Lord our God, King of the universe, who has chosen us from all nations, and raised us above all tongues, and sanctified us through His commandments. And You have given us, Lord our God, in love, (on Shabbat add: Shabbatot for rest and) appointed times for joy, festivals and seasonal holidays for gladness, this day of (on Shabbat add: Shabbat and this day of) the festival of Sukkot, this festival day of holy convocation, the time of our rejoicing, with love, in commemoration of the exodus from Egypt. For You have chosen us and sanctified us above all nations, and (on Shabbat add: the Shabbatot and) Your holy festivals (on Shabbat add: in love and favor,) in joy and in gladness You have given us for an inheritance. Blessed are You, Lord, who sanctifies (on Shabbat add: the Shabbat,) Israel and the seasonal holidays."

"Blessed are You, Lord our God, King of the universe, who sanctified us through His mitzvot, and commanded us to reside in the *sukka*."

When reciting the following *Sheheheyanu* blessing, one should have in mind that this blessing refers to the mitzva of dwelling in the *sukka* as well:

"Blessed are You, Lord our God, King of the universe, who has given us life, sustained us, and brought us to this time."

The Blessing over Bread [*HaMotzi*]

On the first night of *Sukkot* it is obligatory to eat a meal in the *sukka*. One must recite *Kiddush* and eat at least an olive-bulk of bread in the *sukka*.

(With regard to the procedure when it rains on the first night of the festival, or if other factors cause sitting in the *sukka* to be uncomfortable, see the section on the mitzvot of the festival, p. 190).

As on every Shabbat and festival, one recites the blessing of *HaMotzi*, "who brings forth bread from the earth," over two whole loaves of bread, and then slices one of them. Some have the custom to dip the slices of bread in honey, as on Rosh HaShana.

At the conclusion of the meal, Grace after Meals is recited, with the addition of the *Ya'aleh VeYavo* section (a special prayer for festivals and *Rosh Hodesh*). When the festival falls on Shabbat, before *Ya'aleh VeYavo* one adds the *Retzeh* prayer, which is recited as part of Grace after Meals every Shabbat.

It is important to remember that although the *sukka* is used as a dwelling on *Sukkot*, it has a sacred status. Therefore, it should be treated with reverence, and one should refrain from any activities or behaviors that display a lack of respect for the *sukka*.

The Festival Day

On the first morning of *Sukkot*, some people rise a bit early to fulfill the mitzva of the four species in their own *sukka* before leaving for the synagogue, as an expression of love for the mitzva. Others have the custom to recite the blessing on the four species in the synagogue, just before reciting the *Hallel*. If the first day of *Sukkot* falls on Shabbat, the mitzva of taking the four species is not observed until the following day.

Prayers and Waving

The congregation recites the festival morning *Amida* prayer, which can be found in most prayer books, even if the festival falls on Shabbat.

After the prayer leader has finished his repetition of the *Amida* prayer of the morning service, each member of the congregation picks up his set of the four species. One who did not recite the blessing over the four species at home should do so now. Afterward, everyone recites the full *Hallel* while holding the four species.

During the recitation of *Hallel*, there are several times that the four species are waved:

(1) After the prayer leader recites each of the four verses: "Give thanks to the Lord, for He is good, for His kindness is forever"; "Let Israel now say: His kindness is forever"; "Let the house of Aaron now say: His kindness is forever"; and "Let those who fear the Lord now say: His kindness is forever" (Psalms 118:1–4), the congregation responds to each verse with: "Give thanks to the Lord, for He is good, for His kindness is forever." While it is customary to wave the four species while reciting this verse, there are various customs concerning the details of this waving. Some perform the waving only upon the first recitation. Some do it during all four repetitions of the verse. There are also two customs with regard to the prayer leader. According to one custom, he waves his *lulav* only when he recites the first verse: Give thanks to the Lord, etc." whereas according to a different custom he also waves it at the second verse ("Let Israel now say ..."), but not for the third and fourth verses. One who is praying alone at home conducts the waving of the four species as though he were the prayer leader.

(2) The second occasion that one waves the four species is upon reciting: "Lord, save us, we beseech You!" (Psalms 118:25). Both the prayer leader and the congregation wave their *lulavim* during both recitations of this verse.

(3) The third instance is at the end of *Hallel*, when one recites the following verse twice: "Give thanks to the Lord, for He is good, for His kindness is forever" (Psalms 118:25). Upon each of these two recitations, both the prayer leader and the entire congregation wave the four species.

Further reading: With regard to the number of wavings and the manner of their performance, see p. 195.

Since one fulfills the mitzva through any manner of waving, everyone should do it in accordance with the custom of his family and/or congregation.

Hoshanot

Another prayer, which is accompanied by a special ceremony and is recited on every day of *Sukkot*, is *Hoshanot*. The text of this prayer includes a host of supplications and requests, all of which open with the word *Hoshana* ("Please save") and which deal, among other matters, with livelihood and well-being. This custom was established as a reminder of a similar ritual that was held in the Temple, during which the priests would circle the altar with *lulavim* and pray for salvation and success in the year that has just begun.

In most communities, especially those who follow the customs of the Arizal, the *Hoshanot* ceremony is conducted immediately after the recitation of *Hallel*. Some communities perform the *Hoshanot* after the additional prayer service [*Musaf*].

On each of the days of *Sukkot* (except for the seventh day, called *Hoshana Rabba*, on which there is a slightly different procedure that will be explained below), a Torah scroll is taken from the ark and placed on the reading desk [*bima*], or held by one of the worshippers next to the *bima*, while the congregation walks around the *bima* once, counterclockwise. During these circuits, one holds in his hand the four species and recites the text of a liturgical poem, which changes from day to day.

After circling the *bima*, another prayer is recited, which begins with the phrase: *Ani vahu* (according to some versions: *vaho*) *hoshia na*. This prayer mentions various episodes of redemption in Jewish history, as we request that just as our nation was redeemed in those times, so may God redeem us now.

The practice of Ashkenazim is that anyone who does not have a set of four species, and likewise someone who is in mourning, does not encircle the *bima* during the *Hoshanot*, but recites the prayer while standing in his place.

At the end of the prayer, the Torah scroll is returned to the ark, and then Kaddish is recited. In some congregations the psalm of the day is recited after Kaddish.

On Shabbat the congregation does not circle the *bima*, though a *Hoshana* prayer is recited. In some congregations no *Hoshana* prayer is recited on Shabbat.

Torah Reading

After *Hallel* and *Hoshanot*, two Torah scrolls are taken from the ark for the reading of the Torah. Five men are called up for the reading from the first

Yearly Cycle

scroll; if *Sukkot* falls on a Shabbat, seven are called up. The second scroll is used for the reading of the concluding section [*maftir*].

From the first scroll, a section of the book of Leviticus (22:26–23:44) is read, which details the commandments and laws of the three pilgrimage festivals, with special focus on *Sukkot* and its commandments of dwelling in the *sukka* and taking the four species. From the second scroll the *maftir* (Numbers 29:12–16) is read; it consists of a few verses detailing the sacrifices that were offered in the Temple on *Sukkot*.

Afterward, the *haftara* (reading from the Prophets) is read from the book of Zechariah (14:1–21), which describes the great war that will occur at the end of days, before the arrival of the redemption, after which all the nations will come on *Sukkot* to prostrate themselves before God in the Temple.

Following the reading of the Torah, the congregation recites the festival *Musaf* prayer service. When the festival falls on Shabbat, one mentions the Shabbat sacrifices in this additional prayer, as indicated in the prayer books.

Observances of the Day

After the prayer service, one goes home to eat the festival meal in the *sukka*. Before the meal, *Kiddush* is recited.

Text of *Kiddush*

For Ashkenazim:

There are different customs as to which verses to recite in the *Kiddush*. The following is the fullest text, which is recited according to some customs.

On Shabbat, one starts here:

אִם תָּשִׁיב מִשַּׁבָּת רַגְלֶךָ, עֲשׂוֹת חֲפָצֶךָ בְּיוֹם קָדְשִׁי. וְקָרָאתָ לַשַּׁבָּת עֹנֶג, לִקְדוֹשׁ אֲדֹנָי מְכֻבָּד. וְכִבַּדְתּוֹ מֵעֲשׂוֹת דְּרָכֶיךָ, מִמְּצוֹא חֶפְצְךָ וְדַבֵּר דָּבָר. אָז תִּתְעַנַּג עַל אֲדֹנָי, וְהִרְכַּבְתִּיךָ עַל בָּמֳתֵי אָרֶץ. וְהַאֲכַלְתִּיךָ נַחֲלַת יַעֲקֹב אָבִיךָ, כִּי פִּי אֲדֹנָי דִּבֵּר.

Im tashiv miShabbat raglekha asot ḥafatzekha beyom kodshi, vekarata laShabbat oneg likdosh Adonai mekhubad, vekhibadto me'asot derakhekha mimetzo ḥeftzekha vedaber davar, az titanag al Adonai, vehirkavtikha al bamotei aretz, veha'akhaltikha naḥalat Ya'akov avikha, ki pi Adonai diber.

וְשָׁמְרוּ בְנֵי יִשְׂרָאֵל אֶת הַשַּׁבָּת, לַעֲשׂוֹת אֶת הַשַּׁבָּת לְדֹרֹתָם בְּרִית עוֹלָם. בֵּינִי וּבֵין

Veshameru venei Yisrael et haShabbat, la'asot et haShabbat ledorotam berit

בְּנֵי יִשְׂרָאֵל, אוֹת הִיא לְעֹלָם, כִּי שֵׁשֶׁת יָמִים עָשָׂה אֲדֹנָי אֶת הַשָּׁמַיִם וְאֶת הָאָרֶץ, וּבַיּוֹם הַשְּׁבִיעִי שָׁבַת וַיִּנָּפַשׁ.

olam. Beini uvein benei Yisrael ot hi le'olam, ki sheshet yamim asa Adonai et hashamayim ve'et ha'aretz, uvayom hashevi'i shavat vayinafash.

זָכוֹר אֶת יוֹם הַשַּׁבָּת לְקַדְּשׁוֹ. שֵׁשֶׁת יָמִים תַּעֲבֹד וְעָשִׂיתָ כָּל מְלַאכְתֶּךָ. וְיוֹם הַשְּׁבִיעִי שַׁבָּת לַאֲדֹנָי אֱלֹהֶיךָ, לֹא תַעֲשֶׂה כָל מְלָאכָה אַתָּה וּבִנְךָ וּבִתֶּךָ, עַבְדְּךָ וַאֲמָתְךָ וּבְהֶמְתֶּךָ, וְגֵרְךָ אֲשֶׁר בִּשְׁעָרֶיךָ. כִּי שֵׁשֶׁת יָמִים עָשָׂה אֲדֹנָי אֶת הַשָּׁמַיִם וְאֶת הָאָרֶץ, אֶת הַיָּם וְאֶת כָּל אֲשֶׁר בָּם, וַיָּנַח בַּיּוֹם הַשְּׁבִיעִי.

Zakhor et yom haShabbat lekadesho. Sheshet yamim ta'avod ve'asita kol melakhtekha. Veyom hashevi'i Shabbat ladonai Elohekha. Lo ta'aseh khol melakha, ata uvinkha uvitekha, avdekha va'amtekha uvhemtekha, vegerekha asher bisharekha. Ki sheshet yamim asa Adonai et hashamayim ve'et ha'aretz, et hayam ve'et kol asher bam, vayanaḥ bayom hashevi'i.

עַל כֵּן בֵּרַךְ אֲדֹנָי אֶת יוֹם הַשַּׁבָּת וַיְקַדְּשֵׁהוּ.

Al ken berakh Adonai et yom haShabbat vaykadeshehu.

אִם חָל בְּיוֹם חוֹל מַתְחִילִים כָּאן:

On a weekday, one starts here:

אֵלֶּה מוֹעֲדֵי אֲדֹנָי, מִקְרָאֵי קֹדֶשׁ, אֲשֶׁר תִּקְרְאוּ אֹתָם בְּמוֹעֲדָם. וַיְדַבֵּר מֹשֶׁה אֶת מוֹעֲדֵי אֲדֹנָי אֶל בְּנֵי יִשְׂרָאֵל.

Eleh mo'adei Adonai, mikra'ei kodesh, asher tikre'u otam bemo'adam. Vaydaber Moshe et mo'adei Adonai el benei Yisrael.

סַבְרִי מָרָנָן וְרַבָּנָן וְרַבּוֹתַי.

Savri meranan verabanan verabotai:

בָּרוּךְ אַתָּה אֲדֹנָי, אֱלֹהֵינוּ מֶלֶךְ הָעוֹלָם, בּוֹרֵא פְּרִי הַגָּפֶן.

Barukh ata Adonai, Eloheinu, melekh ha'olam, boreh peri hagafen.

בָּרוּךְ אַתָּה אֲדֹנָי, אֱלֹהֵינוּ מֶלֶךְ הָעוֹלָם, אֲשֶׁר קִדְּשָׁנוּ בְּמִצְוֹתָיו וְצִוָּנוּ לֵישֵׁב בַּסֻּכָּה.

Barukh ata Adonai, Eloheinu, melekh ha'olam, asher kideshanu bemitzvotav, vetzivanu leishev basukka.

On Shabbat, one starts here:

"If you restrain your walking because of the Sabbath, pursuing your needs on the day of My holiness and you call the Sabbath a delight and the Lord's sacred, honored, and you honor it by refraining from doing your business, from seeking your needs and from speaking of matters, then you will delight in the Lord and I will mount you onto the heights of the earth and I will feed you the inheritance of Jacob your forefather, for the mouth of the

Lord has spoken" (Isaiah 58:13–14). "The children of Israel shall keep the Sabbath, to observe the Sabbath for their generations an eternal covenant. Between Me and the children of Israel, it is a sign forever. For in six days the Lord made the heaven and the earth and on the seventh day, He rested and was invigorated" (Exodus 31:16–17). "Remember the Sabbath day, to keep it holy. Six days you shall work and perform all your labor. The seventh day is Sabbath for the Lord your God; you shall not perform any labor, you, and your son, and your daughter, your slave, and your maidservant, and your animal, and your stranger who is within your gates, because in six days the Lord made the heavens and the earth, the sea and everything that is in them and He rested on the seventh day; therefore, the Lord blessed the Sabbath day and He sanctified it" (Exodus 20:8–11).

On a weekday, one starts here:

"These are the appointed times of the Lord, holy convocations, that you shall proclaim at their appointed time" (Leviticus 23:4). "And Moses spoke to the children of Israel the appointed times of the Lord" (Leviticus 23:44).

"Attention, masters, rabbis, teachers:

"Blessed are You, Lord our God, King of the universe, who creates the fruit of the vine.

"Blessed are You, Lord our God, King of the universe, who sanctified us through His commandments, and commanded us to reside in the *sukka*."

For Sephardim:

On Shabbat, one starts here:

מִזְמוֹר לְדָוִד, אֲדֹנָי רֹעִי לֹא אֶחְסָר. בִּנְאוֹת דֶּשֶׁא יַרְבִּיצֵנִי, עַל מֵי מְנֻחוֹת יְנַהֲלֵנִי. נַפְשִׁי יְשׁוֹבֵב, יַנְחֵנִי בְמַעְגְּלֵי צֶדֶק לְמַעַן שְׁמוֹ. גַּם כִּי אֵלֵךְ בְּגֵיא צַלְמָוֶת, לֹא אִירָא רָע כִּי אַתָּה עִמָּדִי, שִׁבְטְךָ וּמִשְׁעַנְתֶּךָ הֵמָּה יְנַחֲמֻנִי. תַּעֲרֹךְ לְפָנַי שֻׁלְחָן נֶגֶד צֹרְרָי, דִּשַּׁנְתָּ בַשֶּׁמֶן רֹאשִׁי כּוֹסִי רְוָיָה. אַךְ טוֹב וָחֶסֶד יִרְדְּפוּנִי כָּל יְמֵי חַיָּי, וְשַׁבְתִּי בְּבֵית אֲדֹנָי לְאֹרֶךְ יָמִים.

Mizmor LeDavid: Adonai ro'i lo ehsar. Binot deshe yarbitzeni, al mei menuhot yenahaleni. Nafshi yeshovev, yanheni vema'agelei tzedek lema'an shemo. Gam ki elekh begei tzalmavet lo ira ra, ki ata imadi, shivtekha umishantekha hema yenahamuni. Ta'arokh lefanai shulhan neged tzorerai. Dishanta vashemen roshi, kosi revaya. Akh tov vahesed yirdefuni kol yemei hayay, veshavti beveit Adonai le'orekh yamim.

אִם תָּשִׁיב מִשַּׁבָּת רַגְלֶךָ, עֲשׂוֹת חֲפָצֶךָ בְּיוֹם קָדְשִׁי, וְקָרָאתָ לַשַּׁבָּת עֹנֶג, לִקְדוֹשׁ אֲדֹנָי

Im tashiv miShabbat raglekha asot hafatzekha beyom kodshi, vekarata

מְכַבֵּד, וְכִבַּדְתּוֹ מֵעֲשׂוֹת דְּרָכֶיךָ,
מִמְּצוֹא חֶפְצְךָ וְדַבֵּר דָּבָר. אָז תִּתְעַנַּג
עַל אֲדֹנָי וְהִרְכַּבְתִּיךָ עַל בָּמֳתֵי אָרֶץ,
וְהַאֲכַלְתִּיךָ נַחֲלַת יַעֲקֹב אָבִיךָ כִּי פִּי אֲדֹנָי
דִּבֵּר.

laShabbat oneg likdosh Adonai mekhubad, vekhibadto me'asot derakhekha mimetzo ḥeftzekha vedaber davar, az titanag al Adonai, vehirkavtikha al bamotei aretz, veha'akhaltikha naḥalat Ya'akov avikha, ki pi Adonai diber.

וְשָׁמְרוּ בְנֵי יִשְׂרָאֵל אֶת הַשַּׁבָּת, לַעֲשׂוֹת
אֶת הַשַּׁבָּת לְדֹרֹתָם בְּרִית עוֹלָם. בֵּינִי וּבֵין
בְּנֵי יִשְׂרָאֵל אוֹת הִיא לְעֹלָם, כִּי שֵׁשֶׁת
יָמִים עָשָׂה אֲדֹנָי אֶת הַשָּׁמַיִם וְאֶת הָאָרֶץ,
וּבַיּוֹם הַשְּׁבִיעִי שָׁבַת וַיִּנָּפַשׁ.

Veshameru venei Yisrael et HaShabbat, la'asot et HaShabbat ledorotam berit olam. Beini uvein benei Yisrael ot hi le'olam, ki Sheshet yamim asa Adonai et hashamayim ve'et ha'aretz, uvayom hashevi'i shavat vayinafesh.

אם חל ביום חול מתחילים כאן:

On a weekday, one starts here:

אֵלֶּה מוֹעֲדֵי אֲדֹנָי, מִקְרָאֵי קֹדֶשׁ, אֲשֶׁר
תִּקְרְאוּ אֹתָם בְּמוֹעֲדָם. וַיְדַבֵּר מֹשֶׁה
אֶת מֹעֲדֵי אֲדֹנָי, אֶל בְּנֵי יִשְׂרָאֵל. שָׁלֹשׁ
פְּעָמִים בַּשָּׁנָה יֵרָאֶה כָּל זְכוּרְךָ אֶת פְּנֵי
אֲדֹנָי אֱלֹהֶיךָ בַּמָּקוֹם אֲשֶׁר יִבְחָר: בְּחַג
הַמַּצּוֹת וּבְחַג הַשָּׁבֻעוֹת וּבְחַג הַסֻּכּוֹת, וְלֹא
יֵרָאֶה אֶת פְּנֵי אֲדֹנָי רֵיקָם. אִישׁ כְּמַתְּנַת
יָדוֹ, כְּבִרְכַּת אֲדֹנָי אֱלֹהֶיךָ אֲשֶׁר נָתַן לָךְ.

Eleh mo'adei Adonai, mikra'ei kodesh, asher tikre'u otam bemo'adam. Vaydaber Moshe et mo'adei Adonai el benei Yisrael. Shalosh pe'amim bashana yera'e khol zekhurekha et penei Adonai Elohekha bamakom asher yivḥar: Beḥag hamatzot uvḥag hashavuot uvḥag hasukkot. Velo yera'e et penei Adonai reikam. Ish kematnat yado, kevirkat Adonai Elohekha asher natan lakh.

(בשבת: עַל כֵּן בֵּרַךְ אֲדֹנָי אֶת יוֹם הַשַּׁבָּת
וַיְקַדְּשֵׁהוּ)

On Shabbat, add: *Al ken berakh Adonai et yom haShabbat vaykadeshehu.*

סָבְרִי מָרָנָן.

Continue: *Savri meranan.*

השומעים עונים: לְחַיִּים!

Those listening answer: *Leḥayim.*

בָּרוּךְ אַתָּה אֲדֹנָי, אֱלֹהֵינוּ מֶלֶךְ הָעוֹלָם,
בּוֹרֵא פְּרִי הַגָּפֶן.

Continue: *Barukh ata Adonai, Eloheinu, melekh ha'olam, boreh peri hagefen.*

בָּרוּךְ אַתָּה אֲדֹנָי, אֱלֹהֵינוּ מֶלֶךְ הָעוֹלָם,
אֲשֶׁר קִדְּשָׁנוּ בְּמִצְוֹתָיו וְצִוָּנוּ לֵישֵׁב בַּסֻּכָּה.

Barukh ata Adonai, Eloheinu, melekh ha'olam, asher kideshanu bemitzvotav, vetzivanu leishev basukka.

On Shabbat, one starts here:

"A psalm by David. The Lord is my shepherd; I lack nothing. He has me lie down in green pastures; He leads me beside still waters. He restores my soul; He leads me in paths of righteousness for His name's sake. Even when I walk through the valley of the shadow of death, I fear no evil, for You are with me; Your rod and Your staff, they comfort me. You prepare a table before me in the presence of my enemies. You anoint my head with oil; my cup is full. May only goodness and kindness pursue me all the days of my life, and I will dwell in the House of the Lord forever" (Psalms 23).

"If you restrain your walking because of the Sabbath, pursuing your needs on the day of My holiness and you call the Sabbath a delight and the Lord's sacred, honored, and you honor it by refraining from doing your business, from seeking your needs and from speaking of matters, then you will delight in the Lord and I will mount you onto the heights of the earth and I will feed you the inheritance of Jacob your forefather, for the mouth of the Lord has spoken" (Isaiah 58:13–14).

"The children of Israel shall keep the Sabbath, to observe the Sabbath for their generations an eternal covenant. Between Me and the children of Israel, it is a sign forever. For in six days the Lord made the heaven and the earth and on the seventh day, He rested and was invigorated" (Exodus 31:16–17).

On a weekday, one starts here:

"These are the appointed times of the Lord, holy convocations, that you shall proclaim at their appointed time" (Leviticus 23:4). "And Moses spoke to the children of Israel the appointed times of the Lord" (Leviticus 23:44).

"Three times in the year all your males shall appear before the Lord your God in the place that He shall choose: On the Festival of Unleavened Bread, and on the Festival of Weeks, and on the Festival of Tabernacles, and they shall not appear before the Lord empty-handed. Each man according to the gift of his hand, in accordance with the blessing of the Lord your God that He gave you" (Deuteronomy 16:16–17).

(On Shabbat add: "Therefore, the Lord blessed the Sabbath day and He sanctified it" (Exodus 20:11).)

"Attention, masters."

The listeners respond: "To life!"

"Blessed are You, Lord our God, King of the universe, who creates the fruit of the vine."

"Blessed are You, Lord our God, King of the universe, who sanctified us through His commandments, and commanded us to reside in the *sukka*."

After *Kiddush*, everyone washes his hands and the meal begins with bread.

At this meal too, some have the custom to dip the bread in honey.

In the afternoon, the festival afternoon prayer service is recited. When the festival occurs on Shabbat, references to Shabbat are inserted in the prayers.

Havdala

In Israel, where only the first day of *Sukkot* is a festival day [*yom tov*], at the conclusion of the first day, one recites *Havdala* over a cup of wine in the *sukka*. The wording of this *Havdala* is similar to that of the *Havdala* of a Saturday night, but without the blessing over the candle and the spices. In many communities, the introductory verses before *Havdala* are also not recited.

One recites the blessing: "...who creates the fruit of the vine," over the wine, followed by the blessing of: "...who separates between the sacred and the secular," and finally: "...to reside in the *sukka*."

When the first day of *Sukkot* falls on Shabbat, the *Havdala* at the conclusion of the Shabbat and festival is the same as on every Saturday night, with the addition of the blessing: "...to reside in the *sukka*."

Second Festival Day Outside Israel

Outside of Israel all holidays [*yom tov*] ordained by the Torah (with the exception of Yom Kippur), are observed for two days. The additional day is called the "second festival day of the exiles." Originally, the calendar was determined by a central religious court in Israel on a month-by-month basis, based on the testimony of eyewitnesses who saw the new moon. Their decision determined when the new month would begin, and consequently, when the festivals would begin. After the court reached its decision, they would send out messengers to notify the Jews in all their communities of the day they had declared to be the first of the month (*Rosh Hodesh*). These messengers did not reach distant places in the Diaspora to inform them in time of the correct date for the festival. Therefore, the Jews living there would of necessity observe two days, due to the uncertainty of the dates of the month. Even at a later time, when the calendar dates became permanently fixed based on astronomical calculation, the Sages ordained that all communities outside of Israel should continue to observe each festival for two days, just as when there was a real doubt as to the date. This "second festival day of the exiles" is observed in the same manner, and treated with equal severity as the first day, and the prohibitions of the first day apply on the second day as well.

It should be noted that one may not prepare for the second festival day on the first day, even if the preparation does not involve the performance of a prohibited labor. For example, one may not set up the candles for the lighting of the second night in the afternoon of the first day, but rather one must wait for nightfall.

The prayers of the second festival day of *Sukkot* are basically the same as those of the first day. Likewise, the Torah reading is identical, except that a different *haftara* is read, from I Kings (8:2–21). This *haftara* recounts the inauguration of the Temple of Solomon, which took place during the festival of *Sukkot*.

If the first day of *Sukkot* was Shabbat, a *Havdala* blessing is inserted into the *Kiddush* recited on the second night, before the blessings of *Sheheheyanu* and "who... commanded us to reside in the *sukka*." The *Havdala* blessing is preceded by the blessing over a flame that is always recited in the *Havdala* ceremony after Shabbat. The text of these blessings is as follows:

Blessing over the flame:

בָּרוּךְ אַתָּה אֲדֹנָי, אֱלֹהֵינוּ מֶלֶךְ הָעוֹלָם,
בּוֹרֵא מְאוֹרֵי הָאֵשׁ.

Barukh ata Adonai, Eloheinu, melekh ha'olam, boreh me'orei ha'esh.

בָּרוּךְ אַתָּה אֲדֹנָי, אֱלֹהֵינוּ מֶלֶךְ הָעוֹלָם,
הַמַּבְדִּיל בֵּין קֹדֶשׁ לְחוֹל בֵּין אוֹר לְחֹשֶׁךְ
בֵּין יִשְׂרָאֵל לָעַמִּים בֵּין יוֹם הַשְּׁבִיעִי לְשֵׁשֶׁת
יְמֵי הַמַּעֲשֶׂה. בֵּין קְדֻשַּׁת שַׁבָּת לִקְדֻשַּׁת
יוֹם טוֹב הִבְדַּלְתָּ וְאֶת יוֹם הַשְּׁבִיעִי מִשֵּׁשֶׁת
יְמֵי הַמַּעֲשֶׂה קִדַּשְׁתָּ הִבְדַּלְתָּ וְקִדַּשְׁתָּ אֶת
עַמְּךָ יִשְׂרָאֵל בִּקְדֻשָּׁתֶךָ. בָּרוּךְ אַתָּה אֲדֹנָי,
הַמַּבְדִּיל בֵּין קֹדֶשׁ לְקֹדֶשׁ.

Barukh ata Adonai, Eloheinu, melekh ha'olam, hamavdil bein kodesh leḥol, bein or leḥoshekh, bein Yisrael la'amim, bein yom hashevi'i lesheshet yemei hama'aseh. Bein kedushat Shabbat likdushat Yom Tov hivdalta, ve'et yom hashevi'i misheshet yemei hama'aseh kidashta. Hivdalta vekidashta et amekha Yisrael bikdushatekha. Barukh ata Adonai, hamavdil bein kodesh lekodesh.

"Blessed are You, Lord our God, King of the universe, who creates the lights of fire.

"Blessed are You, Lord our God, King of the universe, who distinguishes between sacred and mundane, between light and darkness, between Israel and the [other] nations, between the seventh day and the six days of work. You have distinguished between the sanctity of Shabbat and the sanctity of festivals, and You have sanctified the seventh day above the six days of work. You have distinguished and sanctified Your people Israel with Your sanctity. Blessed are You, Lord, who distinguishes between sacred and sacred."

Travelers

What is the *halakha* for a resident of Israel who is abroad for the festival, and for one who lives outside of Israel and is in Israel for the festival?

A resident of Israel who is traveling abroad and plans to stay there during the festival, and similarly, a foreign resident who came to Israel to celebrate the festival, with the intent to return home afterward, should consult with a rabbi in advance on how to conduct himself on the second day of the festival.

"The Time of Our Rejoicing"

Sukkot is known as "the time of our rejoicing," as the theme of joy appears several times in the passages of the Torah which deal with this festival. One need only cite the central command in this regard: "You shall rejoice on your festival …and you shall be completely joyous" (Deuteronomy 16:14–15). Indeed, it is customary to accentuate the joy of the festival of *Sukkot* even more than on the other two pilgrimage festivals (Passover and *Shavuot*).

> 📖 **Further reading:** For more on the unique joy of the festival of *Sukkot*, see *A Concise Guide to the Sages*, p. 159; *A Concise Guide to Mahshava*, p. 76.

Simhat Beit HaSho'eva

One of the main manifestations of joy during the *Sukkot* festival is the *Simhat Beit HaSho'eva* (the "Celebration of the Place of the Water Drawing"), which is held on the nights of the intermediate days of the festival. These events constitute a reminder of the *Simhat Beit HaSho'eva* celebrations that were held in the Temple.

The historical background to this practice is as follows: The sacrifices were at the heart of the divine service in the Temple in Jerusalem. When sacrifices were offered, wine would be poured on a corner of the altar. This service, which was called the wine libation, was performed all year round. In addition, once a year, on *Sukkot*, they would pour water on the altar in addition to wine. This water was drawn from the Siloam pool near Jerusalem in a festive and joyous ceremony which the masses of pilgrims would gather to watch.

The festivities, accompanied by an orchestra, dancing, and torch-juggling stunts, were called *Simhat Beit HaSho'eva*. There was such great joy at these activities that the Sages said: "One who did not see the Celebration of the Place of the Water Drawing has never seen a celebration in his life" (Mishna *Sukka* 4:1).

📖 **Further reading:** For more information on a detailed description of the Celebration of the Place of the Water Drawing in the Temple, see *A Concise Guide to the Sages*, p. 292.

The Intermediate Festival Days [*Hol HaMoed*]

The period between the first festival day (or the first two days outside of Israel) and the last one, *Shemini Atzeret / Simhat Torah*, is referred to as the intermediate festival days [*Hol HaMoed*]. These days contain a partial degree of the sanctity of the festival. Some types of labor are permitted, but other tasks are prohibited (see the section dealing with the laws of *Hol HaMoed*, p. 471).

Prayers, *Sukka*, and Meals

The prayers on *Hol HaMoed* are similar to those of regular weekdays, with certain additions. In the *Amida* prayer and in Grace after Meals, one includes the *Ya'aleh VeYavo* section. Furthermore, *Hallel* and *Hoshanot* are recited as on the first day of the festival, while holding the four species.

For the Torah reading in Israel, on every one of the days of *Hol HaMoed*, four people are called up to the Torah, and the same three verses, describing the sacrifice for that day (from Numbers 29:17-34), are read for each of these four men. For instance, on the first day of *Hol HaMoed*, which is the second day of *Sukkot*, the reading describing the sacrifice of the second day (29:17-19) is read.

Outside Israel, the reading is different: On the first day of *Hol HaMoed*, which is the third day of *Sukkot*, the first section of the Torah reading, for which a priest is called up, describes the sacrifices of the second day of *Sukkot*; the second section, for a Levite, is about the sacrifices of the third day; the third section relates the sacrifices of the fourth day; the fourth section is comprised of the verses describing the sacrifices of both the second and the third days, reflecting the uncertainty of the exact date outside of Israel, as explained earlier. This pattern is followed on each day of *Hol HaMoed*: One starts the reading one day later than on the previous day (e.g., on the second day of *Hol HaMoed*, one starts with the section about the third day's sacrifice), reads the sacrifices of three consecutive days for the first three men who are called up, and for the fourth section one reads about the two festival days that reflect the uncertainty of that date.

At the end of the morning prayers, the *Musaf* service is recited, in which the sacrifices of the day are again mentioned. In Israel only the sacrifices pertaining to that day are recited. Outside Israel one mentions the two festival days to which the uncertainty of the date applies, as is done for the fourth portion of the Torah reading. For example, on the first day of *Hol HaMoed* (the third day of *Sukkot*), one recites the description of the sacrifices of the second and third days of the festival, while on the second day of *Hol Ha-Moed* (the fourth day of *Sukkot*), one mentions the sacrifices of the third and fourth days of the festival.

As stated previously, it is proper during *Hol HaMoed* as well to spend time in the *sukka* and to perform there all the routine activities that are usually carried out at home.

There are those who are particular to eat a meal with bread in the *sukka* every day and night of the festival, in order to complete fourteen meals over the course of the festival (in accordance with the opinion of Rabbi Eliezer in *Sukka* 27a). However, this is not a halakhic requirement.

Shabbat Hol HaMoed

The Shabbat that occurs during *Hol HaMoed* (when the first day of the festival is not a Shabbat) is naturally called "*Shabbat Hol HaMoed*." On this Shabbat, the order of prayers is basically the same as every Shabbat, except that one adds to the *Amida* prayer the *Ya'aleh VeYavo* passage, and *Hallel* is recited after the *Amida*. The mitzva of taking the four species is not observed and the congregation does not encircle the *bima*. With regard to the recitation of *Hoshanot* on Shabbat, there are several different customs, and everyone should follow the custom of his community.

In most Ashkenazic communities, it is customary to read aloud the book of Ecclesiastes before the reading of the Torah. The reason for this is that *Sukkot* is a time of joy and celebration, and Ecclesiastes includes verses warning about the emptiness of superficial merrymaking.

Two Torah scrolls are taken from the ark for the Torah reading. Seven men are called up for the reading from the first scroll, which is from Exodus 33:12–34:26, a passage that deals, among other things, with the three pilgrimage festivals. Next, the passage of the *maftir*, which deals with the sacrifices of the day, is read from the second scroll. In Israel, only the descriptions of the sacrifices for that day are read. Outside Israel, one reads for the *maftir* the sacrifices of that day as well as those of the previous day, reflecting the historical uncertainty as to which day of the festival it is. One person is called up for this reading, and afterward he reads the *haftara* (Ezekiel 38:18–39:16), which describes the war of Gog and Magog that will take place on the eve of the final redemption and which is connected in several ways to the festival of *Sukkot*.

After the Torah reading, the *Musaf* service is recited, with several extra insertions for Shabbat.

📖 **Further reading:** For more information about joy, see *A Concise Guide to the Sages*, p. 441; *A Concise Guide to Mahshava*, p. 263.

After the morning prayers, the daytime meal is eaten in the *sukka*, and of course one recites the blessing: "…to reside in the *sukka*." In Grace after Meals the *Retzeh* paragraph is added (as on every Shabbat), as well as *Ya'aleh VeYavo*.

The *Kiddush* and the *Havdala* of this day are identical to those of a regular Shabbat, except for the addition of the blessing: "…to reside in the *sukka*" at the end.

Hoshana Rabba

The seventh day of the festival of *Sukkot* is called *Hoshana Rabba*. The meaning of the name is "the great [day of] *Hoshana*," and it relates to an aspect of the service in the Temple. On each day of *Sukkot*, the priests in the Temple would encircle the altar once, whereas on this last day of *Sukkot* they would do so seven times. The Mishna relates: "How is the mitzva of the *arava* fulfilled? There was a place below Jerusalem called Motza. They would go down to Motza and gather boughs of willow trees to take to the Temple, and they would stand them upright at the sides of the altar… Each day they would circle the altar one time and say: 'Lord, please save us. Lord, please grant us success' (Psalms 118:25). Rabbi Yehuda says that they would say: *Ani vaho*, please save us. But on that day (*Hoshana Rabba*), they would circle the altar seven times" (Mishna *Sukka* 4:5). To commemorate that ritual, the custom was established to encircle the *bima* from which the Torah is read in the synagogue one time on the other days of *Sukkot*, while reciting *Hoshanot*, and seven times on *Hoshana Rabba*.

There are many other customs for *Hoshana Rabba*, some of which date all the way back to the days of the prophets. These are connected to the tradition of the Sages that on this day the world is "judged for water" (*Rosh HaShana* 16a), that is, it is the day on which it is determined how much rainfall there will be in the coming year. Since water is essential for life, combined with the fact that this is a day of judgment, *Hoshana Rabba* is considered to be the conclusion of the days of judgment that begin on Rosh HaShana. This day gives us one final chance to improve our verdict for the new year.

The following section presents the customs of this unique day, from the recitation of the *tikkun* at night, through the special prayers and the custom of "beating the *aravot*," and concluding with the farewell meal in the *sukka*.

The Customs of the Day
Hoshana Rabba includes special study and prayer arrangements, which express its unique status as a day on which justice can be mitigated and one can merit salvation.

Reciting the *Tikkun*
There are those who stay awake the whole night of *Hoshana Rabba*, either in the *sukka* or in the synagogue, and recite the special program for this night known as the *tikkun*. The *tikkun* includes the entire book of Deuteronomy, passages from the Zohar, and the entire book of Psalms. Some people immerse themselves in a ritual bath [*mikva*] before dawn, similar to the immersion done before Yom Kippur.

The Morning and Additional [*Musaf*] Prayer Services

The morning prayer and the *Musaf* prayer of *Hoshana Rabba* are similar to those of the other days of *Hol HaMoed*, with a few differences: In Ashkenazic communities, some men, especially the prayer leader, wear a white garment [*kittel*], as on Yom Kippur. Likewise, it is customary for the prayer leader to recite some of the prayers in the tune used on Rosh HaShana and Yom Kippur.

For other times when it is customary to wear a *kittel*, see pp. 53, 167, 294.

The first part of the morning prayers, which consists of chapters from the book of Psalms, is known as *Pesukei DeZimra*. On *Hoshana Rabba*, Ashkenazic communities include in *Pesukei DeZimra* the extra psalms that are added on Shabbat and holidays. In the later part of *Pesukei DeZimra*, one returns to the usual weekday liturgy.

For the *Hoshanot* after *Hallel*, it is customary to remove seven Torah scrolls, or even all the Torah scrolls that are in the ark, and place them on the *bima*. The congregation then encircles the *bima* seven times, and during each circuit [*hakafa*] they recite one *Hoshana* prayer, as appears in the prayer books. Then they add prayers and liturgical poems dealing with rainfall, the success of the harvest, and general requests for salvation in merit of our holy forebears. All this is performed while holding the four species in both hands.

In some communities it is customary to chant between the *hakafot* certain verses that are related to the seven kabbalistic *sefirot*.[1] The *hakafot* in Sephardic communities deal with this theme even more explicitly and at greater length.

The Beating of the *Aravot*

Toward the end of this session of prayers and supplications, one puts down the four species and picks up a bundle of five *aravot* tied together, in order to fulfill the custom of "the beating of the *aravot*." This custom dates back to the days of the later prophets.

The common practice is to beat the *aravot* on the ground, or on a chair and the like. In many communities it is accepted that women and children also perform this custom. For this purpose, every family head must acquire as many bundles of *aravot* as are needed for each member of his household.

---

1. In Kabbala, the *Sefirot* are the attributes or emanations through which the infinite God reveals Himself and continuously creates and supports all of existence.

In some synagogues, *aravot* are sold the night before, or even in the morning of *Hoshana Rabba*. It is advisable to check in advance where and when one can purchase *aravot*.

There are several customs with regard to the number and location of the beatings. Some strike the *aravot* two or three times on a chair or other furniture, so that most of their leaves will be torn off. Those who follow the customs of the Arizal are careful to beat them precisely five times on the ground and only on the bare ground. Some combine both customs and first beat the *aravot* on the ground and afterward on furniture.

After beating the *aravot*, some recite prayers, in accordance with the accepted texts in their communities. Among Sephardim, there are those who recite the prayer *Nishmat Kol Hai* ("The soul of all that lives") from the Shabbat and festival liturgy.

In many synagogues the battered *aravot* are thrown on top of the synagogue ark. Some have the custom to take them home and preserve them as a token for good fortune, until the day before Passover, at which point they burn them together with the *hametz*.

On the day of *Hoshana Rabba* itself, and likewise on *Shemini Atzeret* and *Simhat Torah*, the four species should not be used for any purpose other than the mitzva, but after the festival this restriction no longer applies. There are different customs in this regard: Some people pierce the *etrog* peel with cloves, and then use it for the smelling of spices during the *Havdala* service throughout the year. The *etrog* and cloves together provide a particularly good smell. Others make jam from the *etrog* after the festival. Some keep the *lulav*, together with the *hadasim* and the *aravot*, until Passover eve, and then burn them together with the *hametz*.

Halakhically, it is permitted to discard the four species after the festival, but this must be done respectfully, placing them inside two bags or wrapping them carefully, so as not to degrade these items with which a mitzva has been fulfilled.

Taking Leave of the *Sukka*

Some people hold a festive meal on the day of *Hoshana Rabba*. At this meal, many have the custom to eat *kreplakh*, which are dumplings stuffed with meat. Nevertheless, since *Hoshana Rabba* is also the day before *Shemini Atzeret*, one should refrain from eating a heavy meal at a late hour, so as not to spoil one's appetite for the festival meal to be served that night.

Toward the conclusion of *Sukkot* and the approach of *Shemini Atzeret*, some have the custom of entering the *sukka* and eating a small "farewell meal" there. This meal can consist of just cookies and cake and the like, so that one can recite the blessing of: "…to reside in the *sukka*" one final time.

At the end of this small meal, some recite a special prayer as they part from the *sukka*. The following is one example of such a prayer:

יְהִי רָצוֹן מִלְּפָנֶיךָ, אֲדֹנָי אֱלֹהֵינוּ וֵאלֹהֵי אֲבוֹתֵינוּ, כְּשֵׁם שֶׁקִּיַּמְתִּי וְיָשַׁבְתִּי בְּסֻכָּה זוֹ, כֵּן אֶזְכֶּה לְשָׁנָה הַבָּאָה לֵישֵׁב בְּסֻכַּת עוֹרוֹ שֶׁל לִוְיָתָן.

Yehi ratzon milefanekha, Adonai Eloheinu velohei avoteinu, keshem she-kiyamti veyashavti besukka zu, ken ezkeh leshana haba'a leishev besukkat oro shel livyatan.

"May it be your will, Lord our God and God of our forefathers, that just as I have fulfilled the mitzva and dwelt in this *sukka*, so may I merit next year to dwell in the *sukka* of the skin of Leviathan." (The expression "the *sukka* of the skin of Leviathan" alludes to an abode for the righteous in the messianic era.)

Because *Hoshana Rabba* is also the day before a holiday, it is necessary to prepare candles and other matters for the upcoming festival.

Shemini Atzeret and Simhat Torah

At the end of the seven days of *Sukkot*, another festival day is celebrated; it is known as *Shemini Atzeret*. Although it follows immediately after *Sukkot*, this final day is actually considered a separate festival. This festival is referred to in the Torah as *Shemini Atzeret*. Historically, it served as the conclusion of the series of festivals of the month of Tishrei, just before the pilgrims who had traveled to Jerusalem would return to their homes. Outside of Israel, this *yom tov*, like all other days of *yom tov*, is celebrated for two days. Over the generations, the second day of this festival has also marked the end of the yearly Torah-reading cycle. Due to this aspect of the holiday, it is commonly referred to as *Simhat Torah*, which means a celebration of the Torah. In Israel, this festival is celebrated for only one day and is popularly known as *Simhat Torah* rather than *Shemini Atzeret*.

This section will discuss the laws and customs pertaining to the festival services and meals, especially the *hakafot* and the unique Torah reading of *Simhat Torah*.

📖 **Further reading:** For more information on *Shemini Atzeret*, see *A Concise Guide to the Sages*, p. 294.

Final Preparations

It must be remembered that *Shemini Atzeret* is a festival day [*yom tov*], which means that performing certain kinds of labor [*melakha*] is prohibited, and in general, all the restrictions of Shabbat, with the modifications that apply to festivals, are applicable on this day (see p. 474). One should perform all the necessary preparations that are done on any festival eve, including setting up and lighting a 24-hour candle, for purposes of having a flame to transfer during the festival and for candle lighting.

Candle Lighting and *Eiruv Tavshilin*

On the day before the festival one should light a long-burning candle that will continue burning the whole day, so that it will be possible to transfer fire from it for cooking and other uses throughout the festival.

In Israel, *Simhat Torah* never occurs on a Friday. Outside of Israel, however, *Shemini Atzeret* and *Simhat Torah* can fall on Thursday and Friday, and when that happens one must make an *eiruv tavshilin* on Wednesday, before the start of the festival, so that it will be permissible to cook and prepare on Friday for Shabbat.

📖 **Further reading:** For the details of the laws of *eiruv tavshilin*, see p. 474.

When the festival falls on a weekday, some are accustomed to light the candles at the start of the festival, before sunset, while others light them after the onset of the festival, just before the meal. Those who do this should not create a new flame, but should take fire from a flame that was burning before the festival began. When *Shemini Atzeret* or *Simhat Torah* falls on a Shabbat, one must, of course, light the candles before sunset. For more details regarding the *halakhot* of candle lighting, see p. 381.

When lighting the candles, two blessings are recited:

בָּרוּךְ אַתָּה אֲדֹנָי, אֱלֹהֵינוּ מֶלֶךְ הָעוֹלָם, אֲשֶׁר קִדְּשָׁנוּ בְּמִצְוֹתָיו וְצִוָּנוּ לְהַדְלִיק נֵר שֶׁל יוֹם טוֹב (וְאִם חָל בשבת: שֶׁל שַׁבָּת וְשֶׁל יוֹם טוֹב).

Barukh ata Adonai, Eloheinu, melekh ha'olam, asher kideshanu bemitzvotav, vetzivanu lehadlik ner shel yom tov (on Shabbat conclude instead: *shel Shabbat veshel yom tov*).

"Blessed are You, Lord our God, King of the universe, who sanctified us through His commandments, and commanded us to light a candle for the festival (on Shabbat: for Shabbat and for the festival)."

בָּרוּךְ אַתָּה אֲדֹנָי, אֱלֹהֵינוּ מֶלֶךְ הָעוֹלָם, שֶׁהֶחֱיָנוּ וְקִיְּמָנוּ וְהִגִּיעָנוּ לַזְּמַן הַזֶּה.

Barukh ata Adonai, Eloheinu, melekh ha'olam, sheheheyanu vekiyemanu vehigi'anu la'zeman hazeh.

"Blessed are You, Lord our God, King of the universe, who has given us life, sustained us, and brought us to this time."

The Night of *Shemini Atzeret*

As mentioned above, in Israel *Shemini Atzeret* is observed for one day, which is also *Simhat Torah*. The special customs of *Simhat Torah* will be discussed below. Outside of Israel, the first day of *Shemini Atzeret* is a regular day of *yom tov*.

On the night of *Shemini Atzeret*, one recites the festival evening prayers, which can be found in prayer books. When *Shemini Atzeret* falls on a Shabbat, the congregation recites an abbreviated version of *Kabbalat Shabbat* before the evening prayer, and at the end of the prayer service they add the section of *Vayekhulu* (Genesis 2:1–3) and the *Magen Avot* passage. Some communities also recite Psalms 23.

Kiddush and the Night Meal

As explained earlier, the reason that days of *yom tov* are celebrated for two days outside of Israel is because in antiquity, communities outside of Israel did not know which day was declared to be the beginning of a given month by the central religious court in Israel. They thus could not be sure if a given day in Tishrei was the fifteenth day (the date when *Sukkot* begins) or the fourteenth; therefore, they celebrated two consecutive days in order to ensure that they observed the fifteenth as a *yom tov*. Later, when the calendar dates were fixed, the practice nevertheless continued.

The first day of *Shemini Atzeret* (twenty-second of Tishrei) is therefore regarded as possibly being the twenty-first of Tishrei. Since the twenty-first of Tishrei is actually the last day of *Sukkot*, there are many who eat their festival meals, or some of them, in the *sukka*.

> 📖 **Further reading:** As on every Friday night or festival night, *Kiddush* is recited over a cup of wine. For the details of the laws of *Kiddush*, see p. 386.

Text of Kiddush

For Ashkenazim:

When the festival falls on Friday night:

(בלחש - וַיְהִי עֶרֶב וַיְהִי בֹקֶר) יוֹם הַשִּׁשִּׁי,
וַיְכֻלּוּ הַשָּׁמַיִם וְהָאָרֶץ וְכָל צְבָאָם. וַיְכַל
אֱלֹהִים בַּיּוֹם הַשְּׁבִיעִי מְלַאכְתּוֹ אֲשֶׁר
עָשָׂה, וַיִּשְׁבֹּת בַּיּוֹם הַשְּׁבִיעִי מִכָּל מְלַאכְתּוֹ
אֲשֶׁר עָשָׂה. וַיְבָרֶךְ אֱלֹהִים אֶת יוֹם הַשְּׁבִיעִי
וַיְקַדֵּשׁ אֹתוֹ, כִּי בוֹ שָׁבַת מִכָּל מְלַאכְתּוֹ
אֲשֶׁר בָּרָא אֱלֹהִים לַעֲשׂוֹת.

(Quietly: *Vayhi erev vayhi voker*) *yom hashishi. Vaykhulu hashamayim veha'aretz vekhol tzeva'am. Vaykhal Elohim bayom hashevi'i melakhto asher asa, vayishbot bayom hashevi'i mikol melakhto asher asa. Vayvarekh Elohim et yom hashevi'i vaykadesh oto, ki vo shavat mikol melakhto asher bara Elohim la'asot.*

ביום חול מתחילים כאן:

On a weekday one starts here:

סַבְרִי מָרָנָן וְרַבָּנָן וְרַבּוֹתַי.

Savri meranan verabanan verabotai:

בָּרוּךְ אַתָּה אֲדֹנָי, אֱלֹהֵינוּ מֶלֶךְ הָעוֹלָם,
בּוֹרֵא פְּרִי הַגָּפֶן.

Barukh ata Adonai, Eloheinu, melekh ha'olam, boreh peri hagafen.

בָּרוּךְ אַתָּה אֲדֹנָי, אֱלֹהֵינוּ מֶלֶךְ הָעוֹלָם, אֲשֶׁר בָּחַר בָּנוּ מִכָּל עָם, וְרוֹמְמָנוּ מִכָּל לָשׁוֹן וְקִדְּשָׁנוּ בְּמִצְוֹתָיו, וַתִּתֶּן לָנוּ אֲדֹנָי אֱלֹהֵינוּ בְּאַהֲבָה (בשבת: שַׁבָּתוֹת לִמְנוּחָה וּ)מוֹעֲדִים לְשִׂמְחָה, חַגִּים וּזְמַנִּים לְשָׂשׂוֹן, אֶת יוֹם (בשבת: הַשַּׁבָּת הַזֶּה וְאֶת יוֹם) שְׁמִינִי עֲצֶרֶת הַחַג הַזֶּה (נוסח אשכנז: הַשְּׁמִינִי חַג הָעֲצֶרֶת הַזֶּה). זְמַן שִׂמְחָתֵנוּ (בשבת: בְּאַהֲבָה), מִקְרָא קֹדֶשׁ זֵכֶר לִיצִיאַת מִצְרָיִם. כִּי בָנוּ בָחַרְתָּ וְאוֹתָנוּ קִדַּשְׁתָּ מִכָּל הָעַמִּים, (בשבת: וְשַׁבָּת) וּמוֹעֲדֵי קָדְשֶׁךָ (בשבת: בְּאַהֲבָה וּבְרָצוֹן) בְּשִׂמְחָה וּבְשָׂשׂוֹן הִנְחַלְתָּנוּ, בָּרוּךְ אַתָּה אֲדֹנָי, מְקַדֵּשׁ (בשבת: הַשַּׁבָּת וְ) יִשְׂרָאֵל וְהַזְּמַנִּים.

Barukh ata Adonai, Eloheinu, melekh ha'olam, asher bahar banu mikol am, veromemanu mikol lashon, vekideshanu bemitzvotav. Vatiten lanu Adonai Eloheinu be'ahava, (on Shabbat add: Shabbatot limnuha u)mo'adim lesimha, hagim uzmanim lesason, et yom (on Shabbat add: haShabbat hazeh ve'et yom) Shemini Atzeret hahag hazeh (Nusah Ashkenaz: HaShemini, hag ha'atzeret hazeh), zeman simhateinu (on Shabbat add: be'ahava) mikra kodesh, zekher litziat Mitzrayim. Ki vanu vaharta ve'otanu kidashta mikol ha'amim, (on Shabbat add: veShabbat) umo'adei kodshekha (on Shabbat add: be'ahava uvratzon) besimha uvsason hinhaltanu. Barukh ata Adonai, mekadesh (on Shabbat add: haShabbat ve)Yisrael vehazemanim.

בָּרוּךְ אַתָּה אֲדֹנָי, אֱלֹהֵינוּ מֶלֶךְ הָעוֹלָם, שֶׁהֶחֱיָנוּ וְקִיְּמָנוּ וְהִגִּיעָנוּ לַזְּמַן הַזֶּה.

Barukh ata Adonai, Eloheinu, melekh ha'olam, sheheheyanu vekiyemanu vehigi'anu la'zeman hazeh.

When the festival falls on Friday night:

(Quietly: "It was evening and it was morning,) the sixth day. The heavens and the earth and their entire host were completed. God completed on the seventh day His works that He had made; He rested on the seventh day from all His works that He had made. God blessed the seventh day, and sanctified it; because on it He rested from all His works that God created to make" (Genesis 1:31–2:3).

On a weekday one starts here:

"Attention, my masters, gentlemen, teachers.

"Blessed are You, Lord our God, King of the universe, who creates the fruit of the vine.

"Blessed are You, Lord our God, King of the universe, who has chosen us from all nations, and raised us above all tongues, and sanctified us through His commandments. And You have given us, Lord our God, in love, (on Shabbat add: Shabbatot for rest and) appointed times for joy, festivals and seasonal holidays for gladness, this day of (on Shabbat add: Shabbat and this day of) the festival of *Shemini Atzeret*, the time of our rejoicing (on Shabbat add: with love), a holy assembly, in memory of the exodus from Egypt. For You have chosen us and sanctified us above all nations, and (on Shabbat add: the Shabbat and) Your holy festivals (on Shabbat add: in love and favor), in joy and in gladness you have given us for an inheritance. Blessed are You, Lord, who sanctifies (on Shabbat add: the Shabbat,) Israel and the seasonal holidays.

Blessed are You, Lord our God, King of the universe, who has given us life, sustained us, and brought us to this time."

For Sephardim:

When the festival falls on Friday night:

וַיְהִי עֶרֶב וַיְהִי בֹקֶר יוֹם הַשִּׁשִּׁי. וַיְכֻלּוּ הַשָּׁמַיִם וְהָאָרֶץ וְכָל צְבָאָם. וַיְכַל אֱלֹהִים בַּיּוֹם הַשְּׁבִיעִי מְלַאכְתּוֹ אֲשֶׁר עָשָׂה, וַיִּשְׁבֹּת בַּיּוֹם הַשְּׁבִיעִי מִכָּל מְלַאכְתּוֹ אֲשֶׁר עָשָׂה. וַיְבָרֶךְ אֱלֹהִים אֶת יוֹם הַשְּׁבִיעִי וַיְקַדֵּשׁ אֹתוֹ, כִּי בוֹ שָׁבַת מִכָּל מְלַאכְתּוֹ אֲשֶׁר בָּרָא אֱלֹהִים לַעֲשׂוֹת.

Vayhi erev vayhi voker yom Hashishi. Vaykhulu hashamayim veha'aretz vekhol tzeva'am. Vaykhal Elohim bayom hashevi'i melakhto asher asa, vayishbot bayom hashevi'i mikol melakhto asher asa. Vayvarekh Elohim et yom hashevi'i vaykadesh oto, ki vo shavat mikol melakhto asher bara Elohim la'asot.

On a weekday one starts here:

אֵלֶּה מוֹעֲדֵי אֲדֹנָי מִקְרָאֵי קֹדֶשׁ, אֲשֶׁר תִּקְרְאוּ אֹתָם בְּמוֹעֲדָם. וַיְדַבֵּר מֹשֶׁה אֶת מֹעֲדֵי אֲדֹנָי, אֶל בְּנֵי יִשְׂרָאֵל.

Eleh mo'adei Adonai, mikra'ei kodesh, asher tikre'u otam bemo'adam. Vaydaber Moshe et mo'adei Adonai el benei Yisrael.

סַבְרִי מָרָנָן.

Savri meranan.

הַשּׁוֹמְעִים עוֹנִים: לְחַיִּים!

Those listening respond: *Lehayim.*

בָּרוּךְ אַתָּה אֲדֹנָי, אֱלֹהֵינוּ מֶלֶךְ הָעוֹלָם, בּוֹרֵא פְּרִי הַגָּפֶן.

Barukh ata Adonai, Eloheinu, melekh ha'olam, boreh peri hagefen.

בָּרוּךְ אַתָּה אֲדֹנָי, אֱלֹהֵינוּ מֶלֶךְ הָעוֹלָם, אֲשֶׁר בָּחַר בָּנוּ מִכָּל עָם, וְרוֹמְמָנוּ מִכָּל לָשׁוֹן, וְקִדְּשָׁנוּ בְּמִצְוֹתָיו. וַתִּתֶּן לָנוּ אֲדֹנָי

Barukh ata Adonai, Eloheinu, melekh ha'olam, asher bahar banu mikol am, veromemanu mikol lashon,

אֱלֹהֵינוּ בְּאַהֲבָה (בשבת: שַׁבָּתוֹת לִמְנוּחָה
וּ)מוֹעֲדִים לְשִׂמְחָה, חַגִּים וּזְמַנִּים לְשָׂשׂוֹן,
(בשבת: אֶת יוֹם הַשַּׁבָּת הַזֶּה וְ)אֶת יוֹם
שְׁמִינִי עֲצֶרֶת הַחַג הַזֶּה. אֶת יוֹם טוֹב מִקְרָא
קֹדֶשׁ הַזֶּה, זְמַן שִׂמְחָתֵנוּ בְּאַהֲבָה מִקְרָא
קֹדֶשׁ, זֵכֶר לִיצִיאַת מִצְרָיִם. כִּי בָנוּ בָחַרְתָּ,
וְאוֹתָנוּ קִדַּשְׁתָּ מִכָּל הָעַמִּים (בשבת:
וְשַׁבָּתוֹת וּ)מוֹעֲדֵי קָדְשֶׁךָ (בשבת: בְּאַהֲבָה
וּבְרָצוֹן) בְּשִׂמְחָה וּבְשָׂשׂוֹן הִנְחַלְתָּנוּ. בָּרוּךְ
אַתָּה אֲדֹנָי, מְקַדֵּשׁ (בשבת: הַשַּׁבָּת וְ)
יִשְׂרָאֵל וְהַזְּמַנִּים.

vekideshanu bemitzvotav. Vatiten lanu Adonai Eloheinu be'ahava, (on Shabbat add: Shabbatot limnuha u) mo'adim lesimha, hagim uzmanim lesason, (on Shabbat add: et yom ha-Shabbat hazeh ve)et yom Shemini Atzeret hahag hazeh, et yom tov mikra kodesh hazeh, zeman simhateinu be'ahava mikra kodesh, zekher litziat Mitzrayim. Ki vanu vaharta ve'otanu kidashta mikol ha'amim, (on Shabbat add: veShabbatot) umo'adei kodshekha (on Shabbat add: be'ahava uvratzon) besimha uvsason hinhaltanu. Barukh ata Adonai, mekadesh (on Shabbat add: HaShabbat ve) Yisrael vehazemanim.

בָּרוּךְ אַתָּה אֲדֹנָי, אֱלֹהֵינוּ מֶלֶךְ הָעוֹלָם,
שֶׁהֶחֱיָנוּ וְקִיְּמָנוּ וְהִגִּיעָנוּ לַזְּמַן הַזֶּה.

Barukh ata Adonai, Eloheinu, melekh ha'olam, sheheheyanu vekiyemanu vehigi'anu la'zeman hazeh.

When the festival falls on Friday night:

"It was evening and it was morning, the sixth day. The heavens and the earth and their entire host were completed. God completed on the seventh day His works that He had made; He rested on the seventh day from all His works that He had made. God blessed the seventh day, and sanctified it; because on it He rested from all His works that God created to make" (Genesis 1:31–2:3).

On a weekday one starts here:

"These are the appointed times of the Lord, holy convocations, that you shall proclaim at their appointed time" (Leviticus 23:4). "And Moses spoke to the children of Israel the appointed times of the Lord" (Leviticus 23:44).

"Attention, my masters."

Those listening respond: "To life!"

"Blessed are You, Lord our God, King of the universe, who creates the fruit of the vine.

"Blessed are You, Lord our God, King of the universe, who has chosen us from all nations, and raised us above all tongues, and sanctified us through His commandments. And You have given us, Lord our God, in love, (on Shabbat add: Shabbatot for rest and) appointed times for joy, festivals and seasonal holidays for gladness, this day of (on Shabbat add: Shabbat and this day of) the festival of *Shemini Atzeret*, this festival day of holy convocation, the time of our rejoicing, with love, in memory of the exodus from Egypt. For You have chosen us and sanctified us above all nations, and (on Shabbat add: the Shabbatot and) Your holy festivals (on Shabbat add: in love and favor), in joy and in gladness you have given us for an inheritance. Blessed are You, Lord, who sanctifies (on Shabbat add: the Shabbat,) Israel and the seasonal holidays.

Blessed are You, Lord our God, King of the universe, who has given us life, sustained us, and brought us to this time."

> **Further reading:** If the night of *Simhat Torah* falls on a Saturday night, a *Havdala* blessing is inserted here. See section on *Sukkot,* p. 211.

Since *Shemini Atzeret* is a separate festival, independent of *Sukkot*, the *Sheheheyanu* blessing is added at the end of *Kiddush*, as is done on the first day of every festival.

As on every festival and Shabbat, the blessing for the bread should be recited over two whole loaves, after which one of them is sliced and given out to those around the table. Some dip the pieces of bread in honey, as on Rosh HaShana. In addition to honey, some customarily dip the slices in salt, as is done during the rest of the year.

After the meal, Grace after Meals is recited with the addition of the *Ya'aleh VeYavo* section (a special prayer for festivals and *Rosh Hodesh*). When the festival falls on a Shabbat, one adds the *Retzeh* paragraph as well.

The Morning Prayer and Torah Reading

In the morning, the festival morning prayer service is recited, as appears in the prayer books. After the *Amida* prayer, the congregation recites *Hallel*. In some congregations, the Psalm of the day is recited at this point. At this stage, as on every other festival and Shabbat, the Torah reading is begun. The Torah reading on this day, apart from the *maftir*, is from Deuteronomy (14:22–16:17) and it mentions the three pilgrimage festivals. The *haftara*, from I Kings (8:54–9:1), describes the lavish celebrations of King Solomon and the people for the inauguration of the Temple, which took place during *Sukkot* (I Kings 8:2), and climaxed "on the eighth day" (8:66).

A resident of Israel who is staying abroad for the festival should consult with a rabbi ahead of time on how to observe *Shemini Atzeret* and *Simhat Torah* there.

The Additional [*Musaf*] Prayer and the Prayer for Rain

According to Ashkenazic custom, the remembrance prayer for the departed [*Yizkor*] is recited before the *Musaf* service. For more on *Yizkor* and how it is performed, see p. 171.

Next the congregation recites the *Musaf* prayer service in which it is customary in most communities to recite the "prayer for rain," or the "*tikkun* for rain," which is a sequence of liturgical passages of praise to God for the rain that He brings, and a request for rains of blessing in the new year. Some congregations recite the prayer for rain before the silent *Amida* prayer of the *Musaf* service (that is, the prayer that each of the congregants recites himself), while others recite it in the course of the cantor's repetition of the *Amida*. From the time this prayer has been recited until the festival of Passover, one mentions in the second blessing of the *Amida* prayer the fact that God "causes the wind to blow and the rain to descend."

The Daytime Meal and the Afternoon Prayer [*Minha*]

After prayers, a festival meal is served. *Kiddush* is recited before the meal, as on every festival.

The Text of *Kiddush*

For Ashkenazim:

If it is Shabbat, one starts here:

אִם תָּשִׁיב מִשַּׁבָּת רַגְלֶךָ, עֲשׂוֹת חֲפָצֶךָ בְּיוֹם קָדְשִׁי. וְקָרָאתָ לַשַּׁבָּת עֹנֶג, לִקְדוֹשׁ אֲדֹנָי מְכֻבָּד. וְכִבַּדְתּוֹ מֵעֲשׂוֹת דְּרָכֶיךָ, מִמְּצוֹא חֶפְצְךָ וְדַבֵּר דָּבָר. אָז תִּתְעַנַּג עַל אֲדֹנָי, וְהִרְכַּבְתִּיךָ עַל בָּמֳתֵי אָרֶץ. וְהַאֲכַלְתִּיךָ נַחֲלַת יַעֲקֹב אָבִיךָ, כִּי פִּי אֲדֹנָי דִּבֵּר.

Im tashiv miShabbat raglekha asot hafatzekha beyom kodshi, vekarata laShabbat oneg likdosh Adonai mekhubad, vekhibadto me'asot derakhekha mimetzo heftzekha vedaber davar, az titanag al Adonai, vehirkavtikha al bamotei aretz, veha'akhaltikha nahalat Ya'akov avikha, ki pi Adonai diber.

וְשָׁמְרוּ בְנֵי יִשְׂרָאֵל אֶת הַשַּׁבָּת, לַעֲשׂוֹת אֶת הַשַּׁבָּת לְדֹרֹתָם בְּרִית עוֹלָם. בֵּינִי וּבֵין בְּנֵי יִשְׂרָאֵל, אוֹת הִיא לְעֹלָם, כִּי שֵׁשֶׁת יָמִים עָשָׂה אֲדֹנָי אֶת הַשָּׁמַיִם וְאֶת הָאָרֶץ, וּבַיּוֹם הַשְּׁבִיעִי שָׁבַת וַיִּנָּפַשׁ.

Vesha'meru venei Yisrael et haShabbat, la'asot et haShabbat ledorotam berit olam. Beini uvein benei Yisrael ot hi le'olam, ki sheshet yamim asa Adonai et hashamayim ve'et ha'aretz, uvayom hashevi'i shavat vayinafash.

זָכוֹר אֶת יוֹם הַשַּׁבָּת לְקַדְּשׁוֹ. שֵׁשֶׁת
יָמִים תַּעֲבֹד וְעָשִׂיתָ כָּל מְלַאכְתֶּךָ. וְיוֹם
הַשְּׁבִיעִי שַׁבָּת לַאדֹנָי אֱלֹהֶיךָ, לֹא תַעֲשֶׂה
כָל מְלָאכָה אַתָּה וּבִנְךָ וּבִתֶּךָ, עַבְדְּךָ
וַאֲמָתְךָ וּבְהֶמְתֶּךָ, וְגֵרְךָ אֲשֶׁר בִּשְׁעָרֶיךָ.
כִּי שֵׁשֶׁת יָמִים עָשָׂה אֲדֹנָי אֶת הַשָּׁמַיִם
וְאֶת הָאָרֶץ, אֶת הַיָּם וְאֶת כָּל אֲשֶׁר בָּם,
וַיָּנַח בַּיּוֹם הַשְּׁבִיעִי.

Zakhor et yom haShabbat leka'desho. Sheshet yamim ta'avod ve'asita kol melakhtekha. Veyom hashevi'i Shabbat ladonai Elohekha. Lo ta'aseh khol melakha, ata uvinkha uvitekha, avdekha va'amatekha uvhemtekha, vegerekha asher bisharekha. Ki sheshet yamim asa Adonai et hashamayim ve'et ha'aretz, et hayam ve'et kol asher bam, vayanaḥ bayom hashevi'i.

עַל כֵּן בֵּרַךְ אֲדֹנָי אֶת יוֹם הַשַּׁבָּת וַיְקַדְּשֵׁהוּ.

Al ken berakh Adonai et yom haShabbat vaykadeshehu.

אִם חָל בְּיוֹם חוֹל מַתְחִילִים כָּאן:

On a weekday, one starts here:

אֵלֶּה מוֹעֲדֵי אֲדֹנָי, מִקְרָאֵי קֹדֶשׁ, אֲשֶׁר
תִּקְרְאוּ אֹתָם בְּמוֹעֲדָם. וַיְדַבֵּר מֹשֶׁה אֶת
מוֹעֲדֵי אֲדֹנָי אֶל בְּנֵי יִשְׂרָאֵל.

Eleh mo'adei Adonai, mikra'ei kodesh, asher tikre'u otam bemo'adam. Vaydaber Moshe et mo'adei Adonai el benei Yisrael.

סַבְרִי מָרָנָן וְרַבָּנָן וְרַבּוֹתַי.

Savri meranan verabanan verabotai:

בָּרוּךְ אַתָּה אֲדֹנָי, אֱלֹהֵינוּ מֶלֶךְ הָעוֹלָם,
בּוֹרֵא פְּרִי הַגָּפֶן.

Barukh ata Adonai, Eloheinu, melekh ha'olam, boreh peri hagafen.

If it is Shabbat, one starts here:

"If you restrain your walking because of the Sabbath, pursuing your needs on the day of My holiness and you call the Sabbath a delight and the Lord's sacred, honored, and you honor it by refraining from doing your business, from seeking your needs and from speaking of matters, then you will delight in the Lord and I will mount you onto the heights of the earth and I will feed you the inheritance of Jacob your forefather, for the mouth of the Lord has spoken" (Isaiah 58:13–14). "The children of Israel shall keep the Sabbath, to observe the Sabbath for their generations an eternal covenant. Between Me and the children of Israel, it is a sign forever. For in six days the Lord made the heaven and the earth and on the seventh day, He rested and was invigorated" (Exodus 31:16–17). "Remember the Sabbath day, to keep it holy. Six days you shall work and perform all your labor. The seventh day is Sabbath for the Lord your God; you shall not perform any labor, you, and your son, and your daughter, your slave, and your maidservant, and your animal, and your stranger who is within your gates, because in six days the Lord made the heavens and the earth, the sea and everything that is in them and He rested on the seventh day; therefore, the Lord blessed the Sabbath day and He sanctified it" (Exodus 20:8–11).

On a weekday, one starts here:

"These are the appointed times of the Lord, holy convocations, that you shall proclaim at their appointed time" (Leviticus 23:4). "And Moses spoke to the children of Israel the appointed times of the Lord" (Leviticus 23:44).

"Attention, my masters, gentlemen, teachers.

"Blessed are You, Lord our God, King of the universe, who creates the fruit of the vine."

For Sephardim:

If it is Shabbat, one starts here:

מִזְמוֹר לְדָוִד, אֲדֹנָי רֹעִי לֹא אֶחְסָר. בִּנְאוֹת דֶּשֶׁא יַרְבִּיצֵנִי, עַל מֵי מְנֻחוֹת יְנַהֲלֵנִי. נַפְשִׁי יְשׁוֹבֵב, יַנְחֵנִי בְמַעְגְּלֵי צֶדֶק לְמַעַן שְׁמוֹ. גַּם כִּי אֵלֵךְ בְּגֵיא צַלְמָוֶת לֹא אִירָא רָע כִּי אַתָּה עִמָּדִי, שִׁבְטְךָ וּמִשְׁעַנְתֶּךָ הֵמָּה יְנַחֲמֻנִי. תַּעֲרֹךְ לְפָנַי שֻׁלְחָן נֶגֶד צֹרְרָי, דִּשַּׁנְתָּ בַשֶּׁמֶן רֹאשִׁי כּוֹסִי רְוָיָה. אַךְ טוֹב וָחֶסֶד יִרְדְּפוּנִי כָּל יְמֵי חַיָּי, וְשַׁבְתִּי בְּבֵית אֲדֹנָי לְאֹרֶךְ יָמִים.

Mizmor LeDavid: Adonai ro'i lo eḥsar. Binot deshe yarbitzeni, al mei menuḥot yenahaleni. Nafshi yeshovev, yanḥeni vema'agelei tzedek lema'an shemo. Gam ki elekh begei tzalmavet lo ira ra, ki ata imadi, shivtekha umishantekha hema yenaḥamuni. Ta'arokh lefanai shulḥan neged tzorerai. Dishanta vashemen roshi, kosi revaya. Akh tov vaḥesed yirdefuni kol yemei ḥayay, veshavti beveit Adonai le'orekh yamim.

אִם תָּשִׁיב מִשַּׁבָּת רַגְלֶךָ, עֲשׂוֹת חֲפָצֶךָ בְּיוֹם קָדְשִׁי, וְקָרָאתָ לַשַּׁבָּת עֹנֶג, לִקְדוֹשׁ אֲדֹנָי מְכֻבָּד, וְכִבַּדְתּוֹ מֵעֲשׂוֹת דְּרָכֶיךָ, מִמְּצוֹא חֶפְצְךָ וְדַבֵּר דָּבָר. אָז תִּתְעַנַּג עַל אֲדֹנָי וְהִרְכַּבְתִּיךָ עַל בָּמֳתֵי אָרֶץ, וְהַאֲכַלְתִּיךָ נַחֲלַת יַעֲקֹב אָבִיךָ כִּי פִּי אֲדֹנָי דִּבֵּר.

Im tashiv miShabbat raglekha asot ḥafatzekha beyom kodshi, vekarata laShabbat oneg likdosh Adonai mekhubad, vekhibadto me'asot derakhekha mimetzo heftzekha vedaber davar, az titanag al Adonai, vehirkavtikha al bamotei aretz, veha'akhaltikha naḥalat Ya'akov avikha, ki pi Adonai diber.

וְשָׁמְרוּ בְנֵי יִשְׂרָאֵל אֶת הַשַּׁבָּת, לַעֲשׂוֹת אֶת הַשַּׁבָּת לְדֹרֹתָם בְּרִית עוֹלָם. בֵּינִי וּבֵין בְּנֵי יִשְׂרָאֵל אוֹת הִיא לְעֹלָם, כִּי שֵׁשֶׁת יָמִים

Vesha'meru venei Yisrael et HaShabbat, la'asot et HaShabbat ledorotam berit olam. Beini uvein benei Yisrael ot

עָשָׂה אֲדֹנָי אֶת הַשָּׁמַיִם וְאֶת הָאָרֶץ, וּבַיּוֹם הַשְּׁבִיעִי שָׁבַת וַיִּנָּפַשׁ.

hi le'olam, ki sheshet yamim asa Adonai et hashamayim ve'et ha'aretz, uvayom hashevi'i shavat vayinafash.

אִם חָל בְּיוֹם חוֹל מַתְחִילִים כָּאן:

On a weekday, one starts here:

אֵלֶּה מוֹעֲדֵי אֲדֹנָי, מִקְרָאֵי קֹדֶשׁ, אֲשֶׁר תִּקְרְאוּ אֹתָם בְּמוֹעֲדָם. וַיְדַבֵּר מֹשֶׁה אֶת מֹעֲדֵי אֲדֹנָי, אֶל בְּנֵי יִשְׂרָאֵל. שָׁלֹשׁ פְּעָמִים בַּשָּׁנָה יֵרָאֶה כָל זְכוּרְךָ אֶת פְּנֵי אֲדֹנָי אֱלֹהֶיךָ בַּמָּקוֹם אֲשֶׁר יִבְחָר, בְּחַג הַמַּצּוֹת וּבְחַג הַשָּׁבֻעוֹת וּבְחַג הַסֻּכּוֹת, וְלֹא יֵרָאֶה אֶת פְּנֵי אֲדֹנָי רֵיקָם. אִישׁ כְּמַתְּנַת יָדוֹ, כְּבִרְכַּת אֲדֹנָי אֱלֹהֶיךָ אֲשֶׁר נָתַן לָךְ.

Eleh mo'adei Adonai, mikra'ei kodesh, asher tikre'u otam bemo'adam. Vaydaber Moshe et mo'adei Adonai el benei Yisrael. Shalosh pe'amim bashana yera'e khol zekhurekha et penei Adonai Elohekha bamakom asher yivhar: Behag hamatzot uvhag hashavuot uvhag hasukkot. Velo yera'e et penei Adonai reikam. Ish kematnat yado, kevirkat Adonai Elohekha asher natan lakh.

(בְּשַׁבָּת: עַל כֵּן בֵּרַךְ אֲדֹנָי אֶת יוֹם הַשַּׁבָּת וַיְקַדְּשֵׁהוּ).

On Shabbat, add: Al ken berakh Adonai et yom haShabbat vaykadeshehu.

סָבְרִי מָרָנָן.

Continue: Savri meranan.

הַשּׁוֹמְעִים עוֹנִים: לְחַיִּים!

Those listening answer: Lehayim.

בָּרוּךְ אַתָּה אֲדֹנָי, אֱלֹהֵינוּ מֶלֶךְ הָעוֹלָם, בּוֹרֵא פְּרִי הַגָּפֶן.

Continue: Barukh ata Adonai, Eloheinu, melekh ha'olam, boreh peri hagefen.

If it is Shabbat, one starts here:

"A psalm by David. The Lord is my shepherd; I lack nothing. He has me lie down in green pastures; He leads me beside still waters. He restores my soul; He leads me in paths of righteousness for His name's sake. Even when I walk through the valley of the shadow of death, I fear no evil, for You are with me; Your rod and Your staff, they comfort me. You prepare a table before me in the presence of my enemies. You anoint my head with oil; my cup is full. May only goodness and kindness pursue me all the days of my life, and I will dwell in the House of the Lord forever" (Psalms 23).

"If you restrain your walking because of the Sabbath, pursuing your needs on the day of My holiness and you call the Sabbath a delight and the Lord's sacred, honored, and you honor it by refraining from doing your business, from seeking your needs and from speaking of matters, then you will delight in the Lord and I will mount you onto the heights of the earth and I will feed you the inheritance of Jacob your forefather, for the mouth of the Lord has spoken" (Isaiah 58:13–14).

"The children of Israel shall keep the Sabbath, to observe the Sabbath for their generations an eternal covenant. Between Me and the children of Israel, it is a sign forever. For in six days the Lord made the heaven and the earth and on the seventh day, He rested and was invigorated" (Exodus 31:16–17).

On a weekday, one starts here:

"These are the appointed times of the Lord, holy convocations, that you shall proclaim at their appointed time" (Leviticus 23:4). "And Moses spoke to the children of Israel the appointed times of the Lord" (Leviticus 23:44).

"Three times in the year all your males shall appear before the Lord your God in the place that He shall choose: On the Festival of Unleavened Bread, and on the Festival of Weeks, and on the Festival of Tabernacles, and they shall not appear before the Lord empty-handed. Each man according to the gift of his hand, in accordance with the blessing of the Lord your God that He gave you" (Deuteronomy 16:16–17).

(On Shabbat: "Therefore, the Lord blessed the Sabbath day and He sanctified it" (Exodus 20:11).)

"Attention, my masters."

Those listening respond: "To life!"

"Blessed are You, Lord our God, King of the universe, who creates the fruit of the vine."

At this meal too, some dip the first piece of bread in honey.

One recites the afternoon prayer service for a festival, even if the festival falls on Shabbat.

Simhat Torah Night and the Hakafot

On the night of *Simhat Torah*, the evening prayer is recited, just as on the previous night. If it is Saturday night, a special paragraph is inserted into the *Amida* prayer. After the *Amida*, all the Torah scrolls are removed from the synagogue ark amid singing and rejoicing, accompanied by the recitation of certain verses that can vary depending on the community. Next, prayers and verses are recited while the *bima* is circled seven times. These circuits are known as *hakafot*.

Regarding the procedure of the *hakafot*, there are many different customs that vary from one community to another:

Some circle the *bima* while holding all the Torah scrolls, while others place the scrolls on the *bima* and circle it. Some communities honor certain individuals in the congregation with holding the Torah scrolls during the *hakafot*, while in other communities it is customary to sell the right to hold a Torah scroll in return for a donation to the synagogue or a personal resolution that is announced publicly. In some congregations, the *hakafot* are very lengthy, and for this reason they are sometimes accompanied by *Kiddush* and light refreshments. In certain synagogues children are given special flags to wave during the dancing, and in some places the children are allowed to hold the silver decorations of the Torah and dance with them.

At the end of the *hakafot*, the Torah scrolls are returned to the ark. In many communities, one Torah scroll is left out and three or five men are called up to the Torah reading, which is from the beginning of the final portion of the Torah (*VeZot HaBerakha*).

At home, *Kiddush* is recited and a festive meal is served, as on the previous night.

Simhat Torah Day

In the morning, the festival morning prayer service is recited, as appears in the prayer books. After the *Amida* prayer, the congregation recites *Hallel*. In some congregations, the psalm of the day is recited at this point. At this stage, on every other festival and Shabbat, the Torah reading is begun. On *Simhat Torah*, the *hakafot* are performed before the reading of the Torah. The procedure for these *hakafot* is identical to that of the *hakafot* at night. In many communities there is a *kiddush* with refreshments before or after the *hakafot*, so that the lengthy service will not be uncomfortable for the congregants.

Three Torah Scrolls

At the conclusion of the *hakafot*, all the Torah scrolls that had been taken out for the *hakafot* are returned to the ark, except for three scrolls that are left out for the Torah reading. The reason for requiring three Torah scrolls is that three different sections are read, from different places in the Torah. From the first scroll, the section of *VeZot HaBerakha*, the concluding portion of the Torah; from the second, the opening section of the Torah in the book of Genesis; and from the third, the passage dealing with the sacrifices of *Shemini Atzeret*.

Yearly Cycle

The procedure of reading and calling men up to the Torah on *Simhat Torah* differs from the rest of the festivals, and it also varies from community to community. The following are some common practices:

Five men are called up for the reading from the first Torah scroll, and a passage in *VeZot HaBerakha* is read for them, from Deuteronomy 33:1-26. If *Simhat Torah* falls on Shabbat (in Israel), a sixth man is called up, for whom the next three verses are read, until the end of the chapter.

In many communities it is customary to call up to the Torah reading every single man in the congregation. This expresses the idea that each and every one of the Jewish people has a portion in the Torah. In order to enable everyone to be called up, the passages intended for the first five men are repeated many times over. If the congregation is especially large, they may divide into several groups of at least ten men each, so that several Torah readings can be conducted simultaneously.

> 📖 **Further reading:** For more information on the connection of every Jew to Torah, see *A Concise Guide to the Sages*, p. 268.

In many communities, the last man to be called up in completion of the repeated reading from Deuteronomy 33:1-26 is accompanied by all the children in the synagogue who are not yet the age of bar mitzva, too young to be called up to the Torah themselves. This *aliya* is referred to as *kol hane'arim* ("all the boys"). The adult recites the blessings before and after the reading together with the children. In certain communities it is customary to spread a prayer shawl [*tallit*] above the heads of the children, like a canopy.

At the end of this reading, the custom is for the children to recite or sing together the verse:

הַמַּלְאָךְ הַגֹּאֵל אֹתִי מִכָּל רָע יְבָרֵךְ אֶת
הַנְּעָרִים וְיִקָּרֵא בָהֶם שְׁמִי וְשֵׁם אֲבֹתַי
אַבְרָהָם וְיִצְחָק וְיִדְגּוּ לָרֹב בְּקֶרֶב הָאָרֶץ.

Hamalakh hago'el oti mikol ra yevarekh et hane'arim, veyikareh vahem shemi veshem avotai Avraham veYitzḥak, veyidgu larov bekerev ha'aretz.

"May the angel who redeems me from all evil bless the lads and let my name and the name of my fathers, Abraham and Isaac, be called upon them and may they proliferate like fish in the midst of the earth" (Genesis 48:16).

In some Sephardic communities, a sixth section, consisting of Deuteronomy 33:27-29, is read separately after all the men of the congregation have been called up to the Torah. It is considered a special privilege to receive this *aliya,* and the one who is so honored is called "the bridegroom of *me'ona*" [*hatan me'ona*], after the first Hebrew word of this section.

Hatan Torah

The last man called to the reading of the first Torah scroll is called the "bridegroom of the Torah," the *hatan Torah,* as he concludes the reading of the entire Torah. Before he is called up, it is the custom in many communities to invite him to come forward as a special liturgical poem is recited in his honor, and a *tallit* is spread out above the *bima,* like a wedding canopy. The right to be called up to the Torah for this reading (as well the subsequent one) is generally granted to community dignitaries, or to benefactors who have pledged a substantial contribution to the synagogue. Some have the custom to read once again from the beginning of the final Torah portion *VeZot HaBerakha* until its conclusion, while others read only from verse 33:27 until the end of the Torah. At the end of the reading, the entire congregation, followed by the Torah reader, declares: *Hazak, hazak venit'hazek,* "Be strong, be strong, and let us [all] be strengthened!" During the year, this same phrase is chanted at the conclusion of each of the five books of the Torah.

Hatan Bereshit and Maftir

The man called up for the reading from the second Torah scroll is called the "bridegroom of *Bereshit*" [*hatan Bereshit*], as he begins the new reading cycle of the Torah, from the book of *Bereshit,* Genesis. Before this reading as well, it is customary in many communities to invite the honoree to come forward with a special liturgical poem in his honor, and to spread out a *tallit* above his head, in the form of a wedding canopy.

The reading from the second Torah scroll includes the story of the creation of the world, from the beginning of Genesis until the end of the seventh day (Genesis 1:1–2:3).

The *maftir* is read from the third scroll. This passage describes the sacrifices of the day (Numbers 29:35–30:1), followed by the *haftara* from the beginning of the book of Joshua (1:1–18, in accordance with the Ashkenazic custom, and up to verse 9 according to the custom of the Sephardim and the Yemenites). This section, which begins with the words, "It was after the death of Moses, servant of the Lord," is a direct continuation of the end of Deuteronomy.

In some Ashkenazic communities, the one who lifts up the Torah scroll on *Simhat Torah* at the end of the reading turns the scroll outward, so that the written side of the parchment faces the congregation.

It should be noted that in Israel, the *Yizkor* service and the prayer for rain are recited on *Simhat Torah*, as there is no separate day of *Shemini Atzeret*.

Following the prayer services, a festive meal is eaten and *Kiddush* is recited, as on the previous day. The afternoon prayer service is the same as on other festival days.

The Conclusion of the Festival

Upon the conclusion of *Simhat Torah*, *Havdala* is recited over a cup of wine. The wording of this *Havdala* is identical to that of the conclusion of Shabbat, but without the blessings over the candle and the spices, unless it is a Saturday night. The introductory verses before *Havdala* are also not recited if it is not Saturday night. The blessing over the wine: "…who creates the fruit of the vine," is directly followed by the blessing of: "…who distinguishes between the sacred and the mundane."

Second *Hakafot*

In many communities in Israel, it is customary to conduct an additional set of *hakafot* after the conclusion of *Simhat Torah*. The source of this custom is from the Arizal. These are called *hakafot sheniyot*, "second *hakafot*." Since these *hakafot* take place after the festival has ended, they are often performed with musical accompaniment. In certain places the *hakafot* are held outside the synagogue, in public squares and the like, in order to enable the participation of a large and diverse crowd. Another reason for this custom is to identify with Jewish communities outside Israel, which are celebrating *Simhat Torah* on this night.

Isru Hag

The day after a festival is called *Isru Hag*, based on the verse: "Bind the festival offering [*isru hag*] with cords, and from there to the horns of the altar" (Psalms 118:27). This is homiletically interpreted to mean: Tie (connect) the days of the festival to the weekdays that follow it. This day has a slightly festive nature, and it is customary to rejoice or to embellish one's meals slightly in its honor.

Rosh Hodesh

The Jewish calendar is based mainly on the lunar cycle. Before the beginning of a lunar month, the moon is not visible, as at that stage it is located between the earth and the sun, and it is therefore the dark side of the moon that faces the earth. It subsequently appears as a thin crescent. This is the moment of the renewal of the moon, which marks the beginning of the new month. Hence the Hebrew word for "month" [*hodesh*] is derived from the term for "new" [*hadash*]. Day by day the crescent thickens, and after a few days the moon looks like a semicircle, until it is fully illuminated at the midpoint of the lunar cycle. After this, the opposite process, the diminution of the visible part of the moon, begins, until it has completely disappeared. The entire lunar cycle lasts approximately twenty-nine and a half days. Since a new month cannot start in the middle of a day, some months will contain twenty-nine days and others thirty days. The first day of any given month is called *Rosh Hodesh* (the beginning of the month). When a month contains thirty days, the thirtieth day is also called *Rosh Hodesh*, which means that in these cases there are two consecutive days of *Rosh Hodesh*, the thirtieth day of the old month and the first day of the new month.

In Jewish tradition, *Rosh Hodesh* is looked upon as an auspicious and somewhat festive day. During the Temple period, additional sacrifices were brought on these days. Nowadays, *Rosh Hodesh* is marked by the recitation of *Hallel*, various modifications and additions to the prayers and Grace after Meals, as well as the recitation of an additional prayer [*Musaf*].

In the past, in accordance with the Torah's commandments, the precise date of *Rosh Hodesh* was determined by a central religious court, based on eyewitness testimony of trustworthy witnesses who had seen the month's new crescent. After the exile and dispersal of the Jewish people throughout the diaspora, the Sages decided to establish *Rosh Hodesh* by means of astronomical calculation, which enables an accurate prediction of the moment of the start of the lunar cycle.

This section will discuss the Blessing of the Month, the prayers and special customs of *Rosh Hodesh*, and the Blessing over the Moon, which is recited on one of the nights after *Rosh Hodesh*.

> **Further reading:** To read about the deeper significance of *Rosh Hodesh*, see *A Concise Guide to Mahshava*, p. 41.

Shabbat Mevarkhim

The Shabbat before *Rosh Hodesh* is called *Shabbat Mevarkhim*, the "Shabbat of Blessing of the Month," because of the prayer that is recited in the synagogue on that occasion. This "Blessing of the Month" consists of a proclamation of the day or days of the upcoming week upon which *Rosh Hodesh* will fall, together with a prayer that the new month will be one of material and spiritual blessing.

Blessing of the Month

The Blessing of the Month is recited after the reading of the Torah, before the *Musaf* prayer service. The congregation stands and recites the text of the blessing for the approaching month, and the exact day or days that will be *Rosh Hodesh* are announced. Before proclaiming the days of *Rosh Hodesh*, it is proper to be aware of the precise time of the "birth" [*molad*] of the moon, the moment when it becomes visible again after having disappeared from view. This represents the beginning of the new lunar cycle. In many communities it is customary to announce the time of the *molad* before announcing the days of *Rosh Hodesh*. The prayer leader [*hazan*] holds a Torah scroll during the Blessing of the Month.

Some observe special customs on this Shabbat that are not observed on a regular Shabbat. Lubavitch Hasidim have the custom to rise early in the morning so that the entire congregation can recite together the whole book of Psalms.

On a Shabbat when *Rosh Hodesh* will fall on the following day (Sunday), a special *haftara* (reading from the Prophets) is recited, from I Samuel 20:18–42, whose opening verse contains the phrase: "Tomorrow is the new moon."

Prayers on *Rosh Hodesh*

The *Rosh Hodesh* prayers are basically the same as the weekday prayers, with several additions, most notably *Hallel* and the *Ya'aleh VeYavo* paragraph. Likewise, on *Rosh Hodesh* the *Tahanun* prayer is not said, and a special *Amida* as an additional prayer [*Musaf*] is added.

Order of Prayers

Before the evening service, it is customary, mainly in Sephardic and Yemenite communities, to recite Psalms 104. This psalm includes the phrase: "He made the moon for appointed times" (Psalms 104:19), which alludes to *Rosh Hodesh*. In the *Amida* prayers of the evening, morning, and afternoon services one adds the *Ya'aleh VeYavo* paragraph, which mentions *Rosh Hodesh*. This passage appears in all daily prayer books.

One who forgot to say *Ya'aleh VeYavo* in the evening service is not required to repeat the *Amida*. But in the case of the morning and afternoon services, if one forgot *Ya'aleh VeYavo* and realizes his mistake only after he has already finished the *Amida* prayer, he must go back and recite the *Amida* once again, this time with *Ya'aleh VeYavo*. If he realized before he finished the *Amida* that he forgot to add *Ya'aleh VeYavo*, he should return to the blessing of the Temple Service ("*Retzeh*"), which is where *Ya'aleh VeYavo* is inserted, and continue from there until the end of the *Amida* prayer.

At the conclusion of the *Amida* in the morning service, following the repetition of the *Amida* by the prayer leader, everyone recites together the *Hallel* prayer, which is a sequence of chapters from the book of Psalms. The Ashkenazic custom is to recite a blessing before reciting *Hallel*: "Blessed are You, Lord our God, King of the universe, who sanctified us through His commandments, and commanded us to recite the *Hallel*," as well as a blessing at the end of *Hallel*. The Sephardim do not recite blessings on the recitation of *Hallel* on *Rosh Hodesh*.

The *Hallel* that is recited on *Rosh Hodesh* is in an abbreviated form, often referred to as "half *Hallel*," in which two passages are omitted, as noted in the prayer books. During *Hallel* there are several verses that the prayer leader reads aloud and the congregation responds after him.

After *Hallel*, some congregations recite the Song of the Day, which is the psalm that the Levites used to sing in the Temple on that particular day of the week. Many also add Psalms 104 (see above) at this point. In other congregations, both psalms are recited at the end of the entire prayer service. In some congregations, only Psalms 104 is recited.

Next, a Torah scroll is taken from the synagogue ark for the reading of the verses discussing the offerings that were brought in the Temple every day, on Shabbat, and on *Rosh Hodesh* (Numbers 28:1–15). Four men are called up for this reading: a priest, a Levite, and two ordinary Jews.

Afterward the congregation recites *Ashrei* (Psalms 145) and the *Uva LeTzion* passages, and then the *Amida* of the *Musaf* service. It is customary to remove the *tefillin* before reciting *Musaf*. There are two reasons for this:

The *Musaf* prayer service expresses the celebratory aspect of *Rosh Hodesh*, similar to that of festivals, and *tefillin* are not worn on festivals.

In the *Musaf* prayers, according to the *Edot HaMizrah* and *Nusah Sefarad* versions of the liturgy, the congregation recites: "A crown will be given to You, Lord our God," and it is not appropriate that when a crown is given to God we should be adorned with our own crown, the *tefillin*.

Shabbat Rosh Hodesh

When *Rosh Hodesh* occurs on Shabbat, there are several changes in the prayer services in the synagogue:

Instead of one Torah scroll, two scrolls are taken from the ark. From the first, one reads the regular Torah portion of that week, for which seven men are called up, as on every Shabbat. From the second Torah scroll the *maftir* is read, which consists of the verses that discuss the offerings brought in the Temple on Shabbat and *Rosh Hodesh* (Numbers 28:9–15).

Next, one reads the *haftara* (reading from the Prophets), that begins with the words: "So said the Lord: The heavens are My throne" (Isaiah 66:1–24), which includes the verse: "It shall be that on each and every New Moon and on each and every Sabbath all flesh will come to prostrate themselves before Me, said the Lord" (v. 23).

In the *Musaf* prayer service, the regular middle blessing for Shabbat is replaced with a blessing that begins *Ata yatzarta*, "You created," which combines the themes of the *Musaf* prayers of Shabbat and the *Musaf* prayers of *Rosh Hodesh*.

Special Customs

On *Rosh Hodesh* it is appropriate to enhance one's meals a bit. Some have the custom of serving a special meal to mark the day.

In Grace after Meals the *Ya'aleh VeYavo* section is added, with the mention of *Rosh Hodesh*. If one recited Grace after Meals and forgot to say *Ya'aleh VeYavo*, he is not required to repeat Grace after Meals.

Likewise, in the abridged Grace after Meals [*Me'ein Shalosh*] recited after eating foods made of grains or fruits from the Seven Species (Deuteronomy 8:8), or after drinking wine, one mentions *Rosh Hodesh*.

Some customarily honor *Rosh Hodesh* by wearing more formal attire than usual.

Many women reduce their performance of labor on *Rosh Hodesh*, especially household chores.

📖 **Further reading:** For a kabbalistic explanation of the special connection of women to *Rosh Hodesh*, see *A Concise Guide to Mahshava*, p. 43.

Blessing over the Moon

The Blessing over the Moon, also known as *Kiddush Levana*, "the Sanctification of the Moon," is a blessing recited in the first half of a lunar month, while the moon is still waxing. The blessing is said outdoors, under the open sky, while one can see the moon in the sky. In this blessing, one thanks God for the cycle of the moon and the renewal of its light every month.

An Important Blessing

The source of the Blessing over the Moon is from the Babylonian Talmud, which also explains the importance of this blessing:

"When one blesses the new month in its proper time, it is as though he is greeting the Divine Presence… The school of Rabbi Yishmael taught: If the Jewish people merited to greet their Father in Heaven only one time each month, it would suffice for them. Abaye said: Therefore, we will recite the blessing while standing [in honor of the Divine Presence]" (*Sanhedrin* 42a).

The blessing combines a text from the Talmud (*Sanhedrin* 42a) with the addition of various psalms and prayers. At the end of *Kiddush Levana,* the *Aleinu* prayer is recited, even though it was already recited at the end of the evening service.

When?

The blessing of the moon deals with the renewal of the moon, and therefore it is recited in the first half of each lunar month, while the moon is still growing fuller after its "birth." According to the Ashkenazic custom, the blessing is said after at least three days have elapsed since the time of the *molad.* Sephardim and Hasidim wait for seven days from the *molad* before reciting it. These dates are usually indicated in the calendars that list halakhic times.

The most recommended time for *Kiddush Levana* is on a Saturday night after the evening service. At this point there is a relatively large congregation in attendance, which lends honor to the occasion. Furthermore, on Saturday night everyone is still wearing their more formal Shabbat attire, which is also a mark of respect for the ritual.

If one did not perform *Kiddush Levana* on Saturday night, he may do so on any day of the week, within the dates specified above.

Good Visibility

Kiddush Levana is performed when it is dark outside, and when the moon is shining brightly and is not hidden by clouds. If clouds are covering the moon to the extent that it cannot be seen clearly, even if one can make out the halo of its light, one should not recite *Kiddush Levana.* If the clouds are not obscuring the moon entirely, and its form can be discerned, there are some (primarily Ashkenazim) who recite the blessing in such a situation, whereas others (especially Sephardim) do not do so.

The Request for Rain

During the winter, the phrase *Veten tal u'matar livrakha*, "and send dew and rain for a blessing," is inserted in the ninth blessing of the weekday *Amida* prayer (*Barekh Aleinu*). This request for adequate rainfall is recited from the fifth of December (or the sixth of December in years when the following February has 29 days), until Passover.

In Israel, whose rainy season starts earlier and which needs a lot of rain at this time of year, this insertion is recited from the evening prayer service of the seventh day of the month of Marheshvan. In actuality, the rainy season begins on *Sukkot*, but the request is delayed until the seventh of Marheshvan, and is not recited immediately after the festival of *Sukkot*. This guideline was established out of sensitivity for the needs of individuals. On *Sukkot*, residents of the Land of Israel and many Jews from abroad would make the pilgrimage to the Temple. After the holiday, everyone would return to their homes, near and far. In order that the rains would not catch the pilgrims on the road and make their journey difficult, the inhabitants of the Land of Israel would delay the request for rain until the seventh of Marheshvan, by which date the inhabitants of the most distant locations, on the banks of the Euphrates River in Babylonia, would have arrived home.

Various Laws

According to Sephardic custom, the text of the entire ninth blessing of the *Amida* changes from the winter to the summer. In the winter, starting in Israel from the seventh of Marheshvan, one recites the text of the blessing that begins with the words: "Bless this year for us," whereas in the summer (from Passover), one recites the version of the blessing that opens with the phrase: "Bless us, God."

One who forgot to recite the request for rain in the ninth blessing may instead say the formula "And bring dew and rain for a blessing" in the blessing of *Shema Koleinu* ("Hear our voice"). If he has already completed the *Amida* prayer without asking for rain, he must repeat the *Amida*.

One continues the request for rain until the festival of Passover.

In countries where rain is required during other periods of the year, e.g., Australia and South Africa, locals may ask for rain in the blessing of *Shema Koleinu*, as one is entitled to insert his own personal requests in that blessing.

📖 **Further reading:** For more on praying for rain, see *A Concise Guide to the Sages*, p. 352.

Songs of Supplication

On Shabbatot in the winter, when the nights are long, some Sephardic communities have the custom of waking up early in the morning and gathering together before the morning service to sing various songs that depict the greatness of the Creator, as well as songs of supplication. Some do this on Friday nights after the meal.

Yearly Cycle

Hanukka

The holiday of Hanukka lasts for eight days, and is celebrated by lighting candles. It begins on the twenty-fifth of the month of Kislev, and commemorates the victory of the Jews, led by Matityahu and his sons the priests from Modi'in, over the Greeks, during the Second Temple period, circa 170 BCE. The Greek king Antiochus IV had issued many decrees against the Jews, with the aim of uprooting the central mitzvot of the Torah and assimilating Jews into Greek culture. Matityahu and his sons, known as the Hasmoneans, overcame the more numerous and powerful Greeks. They then liberated Jerusalem and other parts of the Land of Israel. Afterward they purified the Temple and removed all the idolatrous images that the Greeks had placed there.

After the miraculous victory in battle, another miracle occurred, regarding the lighting of the candelabrum, the menorah, in the Temple. Since the Greeks had defiled the oil that was in the Temple, the Hasmoneans were able to find only a single cruse of ritually pure oil, which contained enough oil to light the menorah for only one day. A miracle occurred, and they were able to light the menorah with the oil from this cruse for eight days. To commemorate this miracle, we light candles for eight days. The two Hanukka miracles have a common aspect, namely, the triumph of quality over quantity and the spiritual over the material.

Another reason for the eight days of Hanukka is that the Hasmoneans held an inauguration for the renewed Temple and the altar for eight days, as was done in the First Temple, after its construction by King Solomon (I Kings 8:66).

This section will discuss the laws of Hanukka, its central mitzva of the lighting of the candles, its prayers and blessings, and other customs relevant to this holiday.

Candle Lighting

The mitzva of candle lighting on Hanukka is designed to memorialize and publicize the miracle of the cruse of oil. In order to fulfill the mitzva completely, several halakhic guidelines must be observed. These relate to the number of candles used, those who light them, the location of the menorah, or *hanukkiya* as it is called in Israel, the substance used for fuel, the wicks, the order of lighting, and the duration for which the candles must remain lit.

Number of Candles

The basic, minimal requirement of the mitzva as instituted by the Sages is to light one candle in each household on each of the eight nights of Hanukka, and one may indeed fulfill the mitzva in this manner if there are no available alternatives. Nevertheless, the universal custom is to observe the more enhanced version of the mitzva: On the first night of the holiday, one candle is lit, and on each subsequent night another candle is added, until on the eighth night, eight candles are lit.

It is prohibited to use Hanukka candles for one's own needs, as reflected in the declaration *HaNerot Halalu* ("These Candles"), recited after the lighting of the candles: "And we do not have permission to use them but only to see them." This is because their lighting should be solely for the sake of the mitzva and not for one's personal benefit. Candlelight is not generally used for lighting nowadays, when rooms are lit by electric lights, but in earlier generations, when candles were lit in order to see at night, there was a concern that people might use Hanukka candles for illumination. Therefore, it became customary to add an extra candle, which is called the *shamash*, or "attendant." This candle is used for lighting the other candles, after which it is placed next to them. If one subsequently does use the light of the menorah for personal purposes, it is considered that it is the *shamash*, and not the candles with which one fulfills the mitzva, that provides him with light.

This custom of placing a *shamash* candle remains to this day. It is positioned in such a manner that accentuates its status as an extraneous candle, that is, not directly alongside the actual Hanukka candles. In some menorahs the place for the *shamash* is in the center, while in others the *shamash* is at the end. Generally, it is placed on a higher stand than the other candles.

According to Sephardic custom, only the head of the household lights the Hanukka candles, and all the members of his household, including those who are not home at the time, fulfill their obligation through his lighting. By contrast, the Ashkenazic custom is for each member of the household to light candles in a separate menorah.

When a few menorahs are lit in one house, they should be kept apart from each other, so that an observer can identify the number of candles of that day.

Women are also obligated to fulfill the mitzva of Hanukka candles. Some have the custom to light the candles themselves, while others, in particular married women, fulfill their obligation through the lighting done by the head of the family. If a husband is absent from his home, his wife can light the candles at home and he can thereby fulfill his obligation.

Place of Lighting

The ideal location of the menorah is outside the house, next to the entrance from the street to the house, or from the street to a courtyard that leads

Yearly Cycle

to the house, in order to publicize the miracle in the public domain. The menorah is placed on the left side of the doorway, from the perspective of one entering the doorway, so that the *mezuza*[1] will be on the right and the Hanukka candles on the left. One who passes through the doorway will therefore be surrounded by mitzvot. The menorah should preferably be located at a height of 24–80 cm, as this makes it clear that it was lit for the mitzva and not for the purpose of illumination.

In order that the wind should not extinguish the candles, it is recommended to place the menorah inside a clear enclosure, which will protect it from the wind and at the same time allow the burning candles to be seen. Such items can be found in shops that sell religious objects. It is also permitted to place the menorah indoors next to a window that faces the street. In tall apartment buildings, when a menorah set in the window would not be seen from the street, the menorah should be placed at the entrance to the apartment or at the entrance to the stairwell.

If it is not feasible to place a lit menorah outside the doorway for any reason, such as opposition from neighbors, or fear of vandalism, theft, or anti-Semitic harassment, one may light the candles inside the house. If so, the menorah can be placed wherever one wants, but there are those who customarily position it at the entrance to the house on the inside. Others put the menorah on the table.

There are those who maintain that since Jews were unable for many generations to display the menorah in public, one should not deviate from this time-honored custom even nowadays, and the lighting should take place inside the house.

📖 **Further reading:** For more on how the Hanukka candles face the outside and light up the darkness, see *A Concise Guide to Mahshava*, p. 82.

One should light the Hanukka candles in the place where he will be sleeping that night. Consequently, if during Hanukka one spends the night away from home, he should light where he stays that night.

If one will not arrive at his home or at the location where he is staying overnight until later in the evening, he can have one of his household members, or even a neighbor, light at his home on his behalf. Alternatively, he should light when he arrives. However, since it is highly preferable to light at

---

1. A *mezuza* is attached to the right side of doorways of Jewish homes. For information about the mitzva of *mezuza*, see p. 539.

the correct time, one should make every effort to arrive where he is staying the night at the beginning of the evening.

Fuel and Wicks

All fuels and wicks are valid for the Hanukka candles if they can burn for the time necessary to fulfill the commandment, as detailed below. It is therefore permitted to use solid wax candles, which produce a beautiful and stable flame, but it is important to ensure that the candles are large enough to last for the required duration of the mitzva, especially on the eve of Shabbat; see below.

Notwithstanding the above, since the Hanukka miracle occurred with olive oil, it is preferable to use this oil. Additionally, olive oil produces a nice flame. In order to light with oil, one must procure receptacles into which the oil can be poured and a menorah that is suitable to hold such receptacles, as well as appropriate wicks and, of course, the oil itself.

Time of Lighting

Since the main aim of the candle lighting on Hanukka is to publicize the miracle, one should light the candles at an hour that their light is visible and many people will see them. Therefore, the Hanukka candles should be lit when it gets dark, about half an hour after sunset. The candles must remain lit for at least half an hour after they were lit.

One may light the candles until the time that the last passers-by still walk in the street. In talmudic times, this was assumed to be an hour after sunset. Nowadays, when people continue to walk in the streets far later than that, if one did not light at the ideal time, he may still light the candles as long as there are people outside. If one lights inside the house, he may light the candles as long as members of the household are awake.

In such cases, too, the candles should burn for at least half an hour after they were lit.

One who has to be out of the house at the time for lighting may light the candles even earlier, before he leaves, as long as it is within an hour and a quarter of the regular candle lighting time. In this case, he must use large candles that will burn long enough to last until a half hour after the regular candle lighting time.

Shabbat Eve

On the eve of Shabbat, one should light the candles just before the time for lighting the Shabbat candles. As above, it is important to make sure that the

Hanukka candles are large enough (or that the cups contain enough oil) to burn until about an hour after sunset. After lighting the Hanukka candles, one lights the Shabbat candles.

After Shabbat

On Saturday night, it is customary to light the Hanukka candles after *Havdala*. Some light them beforehand, immediately upon returning home after the evening prayer service, so that the lighting will be as close as possible to the time when many people are on the streets. One who lights before *Havdala* must be careful to recite the version of *Havdala* found in the fourth blessing of the evening *Amida*. If he failed to recite the *Havdala* in the evening prayer, he must say the following before lighting the Hanukka candles: "*Barukh hamavdil bein kodesh leḥol*," "Blessed be He who distinguishes between the sacred and the mundane." In the synagogue, the candles are lit after the evening prayers, before *Havdala*.

The absolute latest time for lighting Hanukka candles is at dawn, as from that point onward the light of the candles is not noticeable.

> **Further reading:** For more about Hanukka, see *A Concise Guide to the Sages*, p. 295; *A Concise Guide to Mahshava*, p. 79.

Procedure of Lighting

On the first night of the holiday, the candle should be placed on the right side of the menorah and the *shamash* in its designated place, separate from

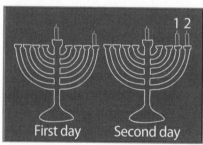

First day | Second day

Order of lighting Hanukka candles

the other candle. On the second night, two candles are placed on the right of the menorah; on the third night, three candles are placed, again on the right side of the menorah, and so on until the entire menorah is filled on the eighth night. The lighting itself is performed from left to right, that is, on each night the new, added candle is lit first, before one moves along to the right to light the rest of the candles in order.

First one lights the *shamash*, which is then used to light the Hanukka candles. If the *shamash* was extinguished, one may not relight it from the Hanukka candles that have already been lit. After lighting the *shamash* but before starting the lighting of the Hanukka candles, one recites the following two blessings:

בָּרוּךְ אַתָּה אֲדֹנָי, אֱלֹהֵינוּ מֶלֶךְ הָעוֹלָם, אֲשֶׁר קִדְּשָׁנוּ בְּמִצְוֹתָיו וְצִוָּנוּ לְהַדְלִיק נֵר (שֶׁל) חֲנֻכָּה.

Barukh ata Adonai, Eloheinu, melekh ha'olam, asher kideshanu bemitzvotav, vetzivanu lehadlik ner (shel) Ḥanukka.

"Blessed are You, Lord our God, King of the universe, who sanctified us through His commandments, and commanded us to light the Hanukka candle."

בָּרוּךְ אַתָּה אֲדֹנָי, אֱלֹהֵינוּ מֶלֶךְ הָעוֹלָם, שֶׁעָשָׂה נִסִּים לַאֲבוֹתֵינוּ בַּיָּמִים הָהֵם בַּזְּמַן הַזֶּה.

Barukh ata Adonai, Eloheinu, melekh ha'olam, she'asa nisim la'avoteinu, ba-yamim hahem, ba'zeman hazeh.

"Blessed are You, Lord our God, King of the universe, who performed miracles for our forefathers, in those days, in this season."

On the first night one adds the *Sheheheyanu* blessing:

בָּרוּךְ אַתָּה אֲדֹנָי, אֱלֹהֵינוּ מֶלֶךְ הָעוֹלָם, שֶׁהֶחֱיָנוּ וְקִיְּמָנוּ וְהִגִּיעָנוּ לַזְּמַן הַזֶּה.

Barukh ata Adonai, Eloheinu, melekh ha'olam, sheheheyanu vekiyemanu vehigi'anu la'zeman hazeh.

"Blessed are You, Lord our God, King of the universe, who has given us life, sustained us, and brought us to this time."

One who was unable to light Hanukka candles on the first night of the holiday recites the *Sheheheyanu* blessing on the first occasion on which he lights Hanukka candles that year.

After the lighting, it is customary to recite or sing the declaration *Ha-Nerot Halalu* ("These Candles"), which can be found in most prayer books. In many communities it is also customary to sing the song *Maoz Tzur* ("Refuge, Rock") which tells of God's salvation of the Jewish people over the generations.

If one is staying at a friend's house and he wishes to fulfill his obligation of lighting the candles through his friend's lighting, he must give him at least a token sum of money in order to share the cost of the candles. This allows the lighting to count for him as well.

What should a person do if he is not able to light Hanukka candles himself, and he has no one to light on his behalf? When he sees Hanukka candles burning, he may recite the blessing: "…who performed miracles," and the blessing of *Sheheheyanu* if it is the first night, but not the blessing: "...to light the Hanukka candle," as he himself is not lighting.

Many women have the custom not to do work, especially housework, while the Hanukka candles are burning. One of the reasons for this practice is the prominent role that women played in the miracle of Hanukka. This is demonstrated by the story of Judith, who gained access to the enemy camp and killed a Greek general.

📖 **Further reading:** For more about miracles, see *A Concise Guide to Mahshava*, p. 213.

Prayers and Blessings

The focus of Hanukka is on giving thanks for the miracle and publicizing it. Among other commemorations, the Sages instituted that this miracle should be noted in the holiday prayers and in the blessings recited on these days.

Al HaNisim and *Hallel*

In all the *Amida* prayers of Hanukka, including the Shabbat prayers and the *Musaf* prayer service of *Rosh Hodesh* Tevet, as well as in Grace after Meals, which is recited at the end of a meal that includes bread, one adds the *Al HaNisim* section. This passage consists of a concise description of the miracle of the military victory of the Jews against the Greeks as well as statements of thanksgiving to God.

One who forgot to say *Al HaNisim* in the prayers or in Grace after Meals does not need to repeat those prayers.

At the end of the morning *Amida* and the repetition of the *Amida* by the prayer leader, on each day of Hanukka, including *Rosh Hodesh*, the complete *Hallel* is recited, and it is preceded and followed by a blessing.

Torah Reading

On each of the days of Hanukka, the Torah is read following the recitation of *Hallel* in the synagogue. The passages selected for these readings describe the offerings of the tribal princes that were brought for the inauguration of the Tabernacle (Numbers 6:22–8:4). On the eighth day of Hanukka, the reading includes the offerings of the tribal princes that have not yet been read, as well as the subsequent section that sums up all those offerings, and the opening verses of the Torah portion of *Behaalotekha*, which discusses how the candelabrum was lit in the Tabernacle. The eighth day is sometimes called *Zot Hanuka*, after the first words of the summary of the offerings: "This was the dedication [*Zot hanukat*] of the altar" (Numbers 7:84).

On *Rosh Hodesh* Tevet, which occurs during Hanukka, two Torah scrolls are taken out of the ark. Three men are called up for the regular reading of *Rosh Hodesh* (Numbers 28:1-15) from the first scroll. A fourth person is called up for the reading from the second scroll, which is the passage that discusses the offerings of the tribal prince for that day.

Likewise, on the Shabbat of Hanukka, two Torah scrolls are taken out. The weekly portion is read from the first scroll, for which seven men are called up. For *maftir*, the passage describing the offering of the tribal prince of that day is read from the second scroll. This is followed by a special *haftara* for Shabbat Hanukka.

When *Rosh Hodesh* Tevet occurs on Shabbat, three Torah scrolls are taken from the ark. Six men are called up for the reading of the weekly Torah portion from the first scroll. The passage of the additional offerings for Shabbat and *Rosh Hodesh* is then read from the second scroll, for which one man is called up. Finally, for the third scroll, an eighth man is called up and the passage of the offerings of the prince of that day is read. Afterward, the special *haftara* for Shabbat Hanukka is read.

> **Further reading:** For more on *Rosh Hodesh* and its laws and customs, see p. 237; *A Concise Guide to Mahshava*, p. 41.

Additional Customs

Over the years, several Hanukka customs have become widely accepted in many Jewish communities. The following are some examples:

Milk and Oil

It is customary to eat certain foods on Hanukka. Dairy foods are eaten because, according to tradition, Judith served milk to the Greek general to make him drowsy before she killed him. It is also customary to eat foods fried in oil, such as potato pancakes (*latkes*) and jelly doughnuts. This is done to commemorate the miracle of the oil.

Hanukka *Gelt*

It is customary to give children money, called Hanukka *gelt*, on Hanukka. The source of this custom is apparently rooted in the practice of parents sending money with their children for their teachers during Hanukka. Over time, children asked to be given some money for themselves as well. Whatever its source, this custom has gained wide acceptance because it makes the children happy and thus makes Hanukka more exciting and memorable. It is also worthwhile to take advantage of this custom to educate children in the giving of charity by teaching them to give some of the money they have received to charity.

Dreidel

During the holiday, it is customary to play games, especially with a spinning top called a dreidel, or *sevivon* in Hebrew. Many explanations have been given for this custom. One of the most commonly cited ideas is that when Jewish children wanted to study Torah during the time that the ruling authorities decreed that it was forbidden, they would have dreidels in their possession, and when the Greeks came to see what they were doing, they would act as though they were merely playing games with the dreidels.

📖 **Further reading:** For the hidden significance of the letters on the dreidel, see *A Concise Guide to Mahshava*, p. 406.

The Tenth of Tevet

The tenth day of Tevet is a fast day because it was on this day in 588 BCE that Nebuchadnezzar king of Babylon began his siege of Jerusalem, as it is stated: "It was during the ninth year of his reign, during the tenth month, on the tenth of the month, and Nebuchadnezzar king of Babylon, he and his entire army came against Jerusalem, and encamped against it… The city remained under siege" (II Kings 25:1–2). The siege lasted for about a year and a half until the city walls fell, Jerusalem was conquered, the First Temple destroyed (on the ninth of Av, *Tisha BeAv* of 586 BCE), and the people were exiled to Babylon.

The Fast

On the fast of the Tenth of Tevet, it is prohibited to eat and drink. In general, the laws and customs of this day are very similar to those of the Fast of Gedaliah (see p. 156).

📖 **Further reading:** For more on the destruction of the Temple and the factors that precipitated it, see *A Concise Guide to the Sages*, p. 322.

When and Who

The fast begins at dawn (roughly an hour and a half before sunrise) and ends at the emergence of the stars. The exact times for the beginning and end of the fast can be found in calendars publicized by synagogues. Once a person goes to sleep for the night, if he did not have in mind that he was going to eat before dawn, it is considered as though he accepted the fast upon himself, and he should not eat. However, many hold that he can still drink. Nonetheless, it is recommended to have in mind when going to sleep that one is not accepting the fast yet.

Males over the age of thirteen and females over the age of twelve are obligated to fast.

Pregnant and nursing women are exempt from this fast. In cases of illness, weakness, or any other problem that makes it difficult for a person to fast, one should consult with a rabbi as to whether he must fast.

The Prayers

There are several additions to the prayers of the day:

In the repetition of the *Amida* of the morning prayer service, the prayer leader recites the paragraph beginning *Aneinu* ("Answer us, God, answer us, on the day of our fast"), after the blessing of Redemption.

At the end of the prayer leader's repetition of the *Amida*, the congregation recites penitential prayers known as *Selihot*. The ark is then opened for the *Avinu Malkeinu* prayer.

Afterward a Torah scroll is taken from the ark and is read for the congregation. The passages that are read (Exodus 32:11–14, 34:1–10) discuss Moses' pleading to God to have mercy on the children of Israel and to forgive them for the sin of the Golden Calf.

In the afternoon prayer service, after *Ashrei* (Psalm 145), the Torah reading of the morning is repeated, but this time, in Ashkenazic communities, a *haftara* is read as well. The *haftara* (Isaiah 55:6 –56:8), which opens with the words: "Seek the Lord when He is found," discusses abandoning one's sins and drawing close to God.

In the blessing of *Shema Koleinu* ("Hear our voice") in the *Amida* prayer, each individual adds the aforementioned *Aneinu* passage. In the final blessing of the *Amida*, the *Sim Shalom* formula is used rather than the *Shalom Rav* formula, even in communities that generally recite the *Shalom Rav* formula during the afternoon prayer.

During the prayer leader's repetition of the *Amida* prayer, he recites the paragraph beginning *Aneinu* after the blessing of Redemption. Prior to the blessing of *Sim Shalom*, he recites the passage commemorating the priestly benediction. In Israel it is customary that if the congregation is praying in the late afternoon, the priests recite the priestly benediction (Numbers 6:24–26).

After *Tahanun*, the congregation adds the *Avinu Malkeinu* prayer, which is recited with the ark open.

The Fast of Tevet is the only public fast that can occur on a Friday. In such a case, the prayers of *Kabbalat Shabbat* and the Friday evening service are recited more quickly than usual, in order to allow the congregants to get home and break the fast as soon as possible.

Tu BeShvat

The fifteenth day of the month of Shevat is known as the "New Year for Trees," and is called *Tu BeShvat* because in *gematriya*, the system whereby each Hebrew letter has a numerical value, fifteen is written as *tet-vav*, spelling "*Tu*." This is a date with halakhic significance that is connected to the mitzva to separate tithes from agricultural produce.

The Torah commands one to separate some of his produce, called *teruma*, to be given to the priests, as well as one-tenth of the remaining produce for the Levites, and one more tithe which varies year to year. For two years it is the "second tithe," which is to be brought to Jerusalem and eaten there; in the third year it is the "poor man's tithe," which is given to the poor.

The pattern of the years is as follows: Every Sabbatical-Year cycle consists of seven years. The seventh year is the Sabbatical Year, in which no agricultural work may be done, and whatever fruit grows naturally on the trees is ownerless and available for anyone to take. The laws of *teruma* and the tithes do not apply at all during that year. The six other years of the cycle are divided as follows: The first two years, and likewise the fourth and fifth years, are the years of the second tithe, while the third and sixth years of the cycle are the years of the poor man's tithe.

Tu BeShvat marks the end of one year and the beginning of the next year for fruits. The reason for this is that the rainy season begins on the festival of *Sukkot* (15 Tishrei), after which it takes another three months until the new rains saturate the ground and water the trees, and growth begins in earnest. Therefore, any fruit that grows before *Tu BeShvat* is considered to have been nourished by the previous year's rains, and it is treated as part of that year for the calculation of tithes. By contrast, fruits growing after that date belong to the current year from a halakhic perspective.

Aside from this halakhic aspect, *Tu BeShvat* is considered by many to be a day of spiritual and moral significance, in relation to the earth and its produce, in light of the similarities between man and "the tree of the field" (see Deuteronomy 20:19).

The Customs of *Tu BeShvat*

In the prayers of this day, *Tahanun* is not recited. Over the years, Jewish communities have developed various customs, all centered around the fruit of the tree. In the hasidic world it is customary to hold a special meal and discuss the spiritual meaning of the day.

Fruit, Blessings, and Prayers

In many communities, it is customary on this day to eat fruits, especially fruits that grow in the Land of Israel, and even more so the fruits listed among the Seven Species for which the land is praised (Deuteronomy 8:8): wheat, barley, grapes, figs, pomegranates, olives, and dates.

Since these fruits were not always available in this season, they were often eaten dried. This is the source of the custom to eat dried fruit on *Tu BeShvat*. Some eat carobs on *Tu BeShvat*. Before the dried fruit and carobs are eaten, they should be carefully examined for the presence of worms and other insects.

Before eating fruit, one recites the blessing:

בָּרוּךְ אַתָּה אֲדֹנָי, אֱלֹהֵינוּ מֶלֶךְ הָעוֹלָם,
בּוֹרֵא פְּרִי הָעֵץ.

Barukh ata Adonai, Eloheinu, melekh ha'olam, boreh peri ha'etz.

"Blessed are You, Lord our God, King of the universe, who creates fruit of the tree."

When a person eats a fruit for the very first time, or even if it is the first time in that particular season that he is eating the fruit, in addition to the blessing of "...who creates fruit of the tree," he also recites the *Sheheheyanu* blessing:

בָּרוּךְ אַתָּה אֲדֹנָי, אֱלֹהֵינוּ מֶלֶךְ הָעוֹלָם,
שֶׁהֶחֱיָנוּ וְקִיְּמָנוּ וְהִגִּיעָנוּ לַזְּמַן הַזֶּה.

Barukh ata Adonai, Eloheinu, melekh ha'olam, sheheheyanu vekiyemanu vehigi'anu la'zeman hazeh.

"Blessed are You, Lord our God, King of the universe, who has given us life, sustained us, and brought us to this time."

In some communities, children are given fruit packages on *Tu BeShvat*, or such packages are sent from one family to another.

Some have the practice, based on long-standing kabbalistic customs, to conduct a *Tu BeShvat* "Seder," in which all those gathered partake of a large selection of fruits, and drink red and white wine of different concentrations. Chapters of the Mishna are studied as well.

Since this date marks an important stage in the development of the fruits of the tree, some have the custom to recite a prayer that they will find a beautiful etrog for the next festival of *Sukkot*.

📖 **Further reading:** The source in the Torah where the Land of Israel is praised for the seven species of fruit can be found in *A Concise Guide to the Torah*, p. 456. For a deep spiritual message of *Tu BeShvat*, see *A Concise Guide to Mahshava*, p. 48.

The Month of Adar

Adar is considered to be a month of good fortune for the Jewish people. The Talmud states: "When the month of Adar begins, rejoicing increases" (*Ta'anit* 29a). In this month, the miracle of Purim occurred, regarding which it is stated: "The month that was transformed for them from sorrow to joy, and from mourning to holiday" (Esther 9:22). The verse refers to the entire month, indicating that all of it was turned into happy and auspicious days. Accordingly, there are sources that recommend scheduling, if possible, any risky procedure (e.g., medical treatment, legal proceedings, or significant business investments) for the month of Adar.

📖 **Further reading:** For more on the month of Adar and its unique happiness, see *A Concise Guide to the Sages*, p. 298; *A Concise Guide to Mahshava*, p. 48.

A Leap Year

While the Hebrew calendar is based mainly on the lunar cycle, it includes a mechanism designed to keep the calendar in tandem with the solar year, which is approximately eleven days longer than twelve lunar months. Therefore, every two or three years an extra month is inserted into the year, forming a "leap year," *shana me'uberet* in Hebrew. This extra month is added at the end of the year, after Adar, and is called "Second Adar." The periodic leap year ensures that the month of Nisan, containing Passover, will always fall during the spring, in accordance with the commandment of the Torah: "Observe the month of ripening" (Deuteronomy 16:1), a reference to spring.

Adar I and Adar II

As explained above, in a leap year there are two months of Adar. The second Adar is the main Adar, and most of the laws and customs of Adar apply then. Purim is celebrated in Adar II, and if a person was born in the month of Adar in a non-leap year, he will mark his birthday in Adar II in a leap year.

Adar I is also a special month, and the statement that rejoicing increases during the month of Adar applies to that month as well. In addition, the fourteenth and fifteenth of the first Adar are called *Purim Katan* ("Minor Purim") and *Shushan Purim Katan*, respectively. On these days, due to the joy associated with them, one does not recite *Tahanun*.

257

For information that is useful when determining the date of a bar mitzva, or a yahrzeit for a death that occurred in a leap year, see p. 37 and p. 120.

The Four Torah Portions

During the month of Adar, there are some additions to the weekly Torah reading. As well as the regular weekly Torah portion read on every Shabbat of the year, on almost every Shabbat of this month an additional portion is read, as detailed below. On these Shabbatot, two Torah scrolls are taken from the synagogue ark. Seven men are called up for the regular reading of the weekly Torah portion, while an eighth man is called up for the second scroll, from which the additional portion is read. This eighth passage is called the *maftir*, and the one called up for it subsequently reads the *haftara*. The content of the *haftara* on these Shabbatot is connected to the extra portion that is read.

Parashat Shekalim

The first of these special readings is *Shekalim* (Exodus 30:11–16), and it is read on the Shabbat before *Rosh Hodesh* Adar (in a leap year, before *Rosh Hodesh* of Adar II), or on *Rosh Hodesh* Adar itself if it occurs on Shabbat. This portion discusses the fixed annual tax that the Israelites would bring for the purchase of communal offerings that were sacrificed in the Tabernacle and the Temple. The portion is read at this particular time of year because the "tax year" for this purpose begins on *Rosh Hodesh* Nisan, and therefore the public would be given a reminder by means of this public reading thirty days in advance.

Parashat Zakhor

The second special reading is *Parashat Zakhor* (Deuteronomy 25:17–19), which is always read on the Shabbat before Purim. This passage discusses the obligation to always remember the war which the Amalekites instigated against the people of Israel when they had just left Egypt after more than two hundred years of suffering and hard labor.

This portion is read before Purim because the evil Haman was a descendant of Agag (Esther 3:1) the king of Amalek (I Samuel 15:8), and his war against the Jewish people is considered a continuation of the genocidal hatred of Jews that characterized the Amalekites.

In the opinion of many halakhic authorities, it is an obligation by Torah law to hear the reading of *Parashat Zakhor* from a Torah scroll. Therefore, it is customary to be very stringent regarding this reading. The one who reads from the Torah should make a special effort to read this portion in a loud voice and with especially clear enunciation, while the congregation for its part must listen carefully to every word.

One who was unable to hear the reading of *Parashat Zakhor* in the synagogue on the Shabbat before Purim should have in mind to fulfill the obligation on the morning of Purim itself, when the description of the war with Amalek (Exodus 17:8-16) is read from the Torah. It is also possible to fulfill this obligation in the summer, when the congregation reads the Torah portion of *Ki Tetze*, which contains the verses dealing with the duty to remember Amalek and blot out its memory. In such a case, it is best to ask the reader of the Torah to have intent to fulfill the listener's duty of this particular mitzva.

📖 **Further reading:** For more on the war with Amalek, see *A Concise Guide to the Torah,* pp. 176, 490; *A Concise Guide to the Sages,* pp. 100, 251.

Parashat Para

The third special reading is *Parashat Para* (Numbers 19:1–22), which is read on the Shabbat before the reading of *Parashat HaHodesh* (see next section). This portion discusses the preparation of the ashes of the Red Heifer, which was used for the purification of one who had contracted ritual impurity through proximity to a corpse (i.e., one who touched or carried a dead body or was together with a corpse under the same roof). This portion is read at this stage, several weeks before Passover, because during the Temple period it was necessary for everyone to undergo a purification process in order to partake of the Passover offering. According to some halakhic opinions, this reading too is required by Torah law, and therefore it is proper to make every effort to go and hear it in the synagogue. However, it is not customary to be as particular with regard to this reading as with the reading for *Parashat Zakhor.*

Parashat HaHodesh

The fourth and final special reading is *Parashat HaHodesh* (Exodus 12:1–20), which is read on the Shabbat before *Rosh Hodesh* Nisan, or on *Rosh Hodesh* Nisan itself if it occurs on a Shabbat. This portion discusses the month of Nisan, which is the "first for you of the months of the year" (Exodus 12:2), and the preparations for the festival of Passover and its *Pesach* sacrifice. This reading is a reminder of the many preparations required for Passover.

The Fast of Esther [*Ta'anit Esther*]

The thirteenth of Adar, the day before Purim, is a fast day, to commemorate the war that took place on this day against the enemies of the Jews in Persia and Medea (Esther 9:1-2). It also serves as a reminder of the fast of Queen Esther (4:16) before she entered the chamber of King Ahasuerus to plead for mercy for her people.

Laws of the Fast

In general, the laws and customs of this fast are very similar to those of the Fast of Gedaliah (see p. 156).

The fast begins at dawn (about an hour and a half before sunrise) and ends upon the emergence of the stars. The precise times can be found in synagogue calendars. The fast precludes only eating and drinking, unlike Yom Kippur and *Tisha BeAv*. All men over the age of thirteen and women over the age of twelve are obligated to fast. Pregnant and nursing women are exempt from this fast. Halakhically speaking, this is not considered a very strict fast, and therefore in cases of illness, weakness, or other difficulties, one might not need to fast. In such a situation, it is advisable to consult a rabbi.

Changes in the Prayers

In the morning prayers, after the *Amida*, the congregation recites *Selihot* and *Avinu Malkeinu*. Afterward, there is Torah reading, and the passages read (Exodus 32:11–14; 34:1–10) describe Moses' request of God to have mercy on the children of Israel and to forgive them for the sin of the Golden Calf.

> Further reading: For more on the sin of the Golden Calf and Moses' prayers in its aftermath, see *A Concise Guide to the Torah*, p. 218; *A Concise Guide to the Sages*, p. 120.

In the afternoon prayer service, after *Ashrei* (Psalms 145), the Torah reading of the morning is repeated. In Ashkenazic communities, the third man called to the Torah also reads a *haftara* (Isaiah 45:6–56:8), which discusses abandoning one's sins and returning to the upright path. In the blessing of *Shema Koleinu* in the *Amida* prayer, the *Aneinu* passage is added.

In the final blessing of the *Amida*, the *Sim Shalom* formula is used rather than the *Shalom Rav* formula, even in communities that generally recite the *Shalom Rav* formula during the afternoon prayer.

During the prayer leader's repetition of the *Amida* prayer, he recites the paragraph beginning *Aneinu* after the blessing of Redemption. Prior to the blessing of *Sim Shalom*, he recites the passage commemorating the priestly benediction. In Israel it is customary that if the congregation is praying in the late afternoon, the priests recite the priestly benediction (Numbers 6:24–26).

Since the fast occurs on the day before Purim, neither *Tahanun* nor *Avinu Malkeinu* is recited at the afternoon service. When Purim occurs on a Sunday, the Fast of Esther is advanced to the Thursday before Purim. In this case, one does say *Tahanun* and *Avinu Malkeinu* at the afternoon service of the fast day.

The Half-Shekel

Before the afternoon prayers of *Ta'anit Esther,* it is customary to give charity, to commemorate the "half-shekel" donation that was given in ancient times for the purpose of purchasing the Temple offerings. It is customary to give three "half-shekels." Some have the custom to give three coins that are half of the local currency, such as three silver half-dollars, or in Israel, three contemporary half-shekel coins. Others give the value of the original half-shekel, which was about twenty-one grams of silver.

📖 **Further reading:** For more on the half-shekel donation, see *A Concise Guide to the Torah,* p. 215; *A Concise Guide to the Sages,* p. 114.

End of the Fast

Since the end of the fast coincides with the beginning of the Purim holiday and the reading of the book of Esther [*Megillat Esther*], the fast is broken only after the reading of the megilla. However, one who finds it difficult to wait so long may have a drink or a snack, before the megilla is read.

Purim

Purim is celebrated on the fourteenth of Adar. This holiday was established following the miraculous salvation of the Jews in the Persian Empire, which ruled most of the world in those days. The evil Haman, who was viceroy to King Ahasuerus, incited the king against the Jews, and persuaded him to sign a sweeping order of extermination against all Jews in the kingdom. A wondrous sequence of events, that only the hand of Providence could have arranged, brought about the subsequent reversal: Haman and his sons were hanged, the enemies of Israel were defeated, and "for the Jews there was light, and joy, and gladness, and honor," as described in the book of Esther (8:16).

Purim is commonly observed as a jovial and light-hearted holiday, but kabbalistic sources state that the spiritual rank of Purim is very exalted, even higher, in a sense, than Yom Kippur. Homiletically, it has been said that *Yom Kippurim* (Yom Kippur) is *ke-Purim*, "like" Purim. The essence of this day is concealment and deception: The name of God does not appear explicitly in the book of Esther even once. The miracle of the annulment of Haman's decree and his hanging is also hidden behind a sequence of events that can be viewed as "coincidence." Likewise, to symbolize this theme of concealment, we hide behind costumes on Purim.

In cities that were surrounded by walls at the time of the conquest of Joshua son of Nun, Purim is celebrated on the fifteenth of Adar. This is also the date for Purim in Shushan, which is in present-day Iran. In these places, the Jews were granted respite from their enemies only on the fifteenth day of Adar (see Esther 9:18). For this reason, the second day of Purim is sometimes called "*Shushan Purim*."

This section presents the central mitzvot of Purim and their laws, together with various customs. Likewise, the nature of *Shushan Purim* will also be clarified, and we will discuss when and how Purim may be celebrated for three consecutive days.

📖 **Further reading:** For more on the holiday of Purim, see *A Concise Guide to the Sages*, p. 298; *A Concise Guide to Mahshava*, p. 86.

The Four Central Mitzvot

There are four primary mitzvot that apply on Purim, in addition to numerous customs. The four mitzvot are: the reading of the megilla (the book of Esther); *mishlo'ah manot*, sending portions of food to friends and neighbors; *matanot la'evyonim*, giving charity to the poor; and partaking of a celebratory meal.

Reading of the Megilla

The purpose of the mitzva of reading the megilla is to retell the story of how the Jews were saved from annihilation and to publicize this miracle. All Jews above the age of mitzvot are obligated to hear the reading of the megilla. This also includes women, "as they too were included in that miracle." It is proper to bring children to the reading as well, in order to educate them and accustom them to this ritual, but parents must ensure that their children do not make noise, so as not to disturb others who are trying to listen to the reading.

The megilla is read twice on Purim, once at night and again in the morning (as detailed below).

The reading of the megilla at night comes directly after the evening prayers and the conclusion of the previous day's fast, and one should not eat or drink anything before the megilla is read. As stated above, those who find the fast particularly difficult may drink and have a snack before the reading begins.

Before the reader starts the megilla, he recites three blessings. He should have in mind that he is saying these blessings on behalf of the congregation as well, and the congregation should intend to fulfill their obligation with his blessings. The blessings are as follows:

בָּרוּךְ אַתָּה אֲדֹנָי, אֱלֹהֵינוּ מֶלֶךְ הָעוֹלָם, אֲשֶׁר קִדְּשָׁנוּ בְּמִצְוֹתָיו וְצִוָּנוּ עַל מִקְרָא מְגִלָּה.

Barukh ata Adonai, Eloheinu, melekh ha'olam, asher kideshanu bemitzvotav, vetzivanu al mikra megila.

"Blessed are You, Lord our God, King of the universe, who sanctified us through His commandments, and commanded us concerning the reading of the megilla."

בָּרוּךְ אַתָּה אֲדֹנָי, אֱלֹהֵינוּ מֶלֶךְ הָעוֹלָם, שֶׁעָשָׂה נִסִּים לַאֲבוֹתֵינוּ בַּיָּמִים הָהֵם בַּזְּמַן הַזֶּה.

Barukh ata Adonai, Eloheinu, melekh ha'olam, she'asa nisim la'avoteinu, bayamim hahem, ba'zeman hazeh.

"Blessed are You, Lord our God, King of the universe, who performed miracles for our forefathers, in those days, in this season."

At night, all communities include the *Sheheheyanu* blessing:

בָּרוּךְ אַתָּה אֲדֹנָי, אֱלֹהֵינוּ מֶלֶךְ הָעוֹלָם, שֶׁהֶחֱיָנוּ וְקִיְּמָנוּ וְהִגִּיעָנוּ לַזְּמַן הַזֶּה.

Barukh ata Adonai, Eloheinu, melekh ha'olam, sheheheyanu vekiyemanu vehigi'anu la'zeman hazeh.

"Blessed are You, Lord our God, King of the universe, who has given us life, sustained us, and brought us to this time."

These same blessings are recited before the daytime reading as well. However, Sephardim do not say the *Sheheheyanu* blessing again before the daytime reading. Ashkenazim, who do recite the *Sheheheyanu* blessing, should have in mind that it applies to the other mitzvot of the day as well (see below). Some Sephardim have this intention during the recitation of the *Sheheheyanu* blessing before the nighttime reading.

One must read or hear the megilla read from a valid scroll, written by hand on parchment. The listeners must pay attention and hear every word. One may not talk or let oneself be distracted during the entire reading, from the blessings preceding the reading through the blessing upon the conclusion of the reading.

Whenever the name of Haman is mentioned during the megilla reading, it is customary to make noise and a commotion in order to "blot out his name." Some do this only when the name Haman is accompanied by some description, e.g., "Haman the Agagite," "this evil Haman," and the like. In some congregations, the noisemaking occurs only twice, upon the first and last mentions of Haman's name. It is important not to make too much noise and thereby prevent the congregation from hearing all the words of the megilla. One who missed a few words said by the reader may read them himself from the text in his hands, even if it is only a printed book.

📖 **Further reading:** For additional stories from the Sages that expand upon the events described in the megilla, see *A Concise Guide to the Sages*, p. 299.

At the conclusion of the reading of the megilla, the following blessing is recited:

בָּרוּךְ אַתָּה אַדֹנָי אֱלֹהֵינוּ מֶלֶךְ הָעוֹלָם, הָרָב אֶת רִיבֵנוּ, וְהַדָּן אֶת דִּינֵנוּ, וְהַנּוֹקֵם אֶת נִקְמָתֵנוּ, וְהַמְשַׁלֵּם גְּמוּל לְכָל אוֹיְבֵי נַפְשֵׁנוּ, וְהַנִּפְרָע לָנוּ מִצָּרֵינוּ. בָּרוּךְ אַתָּה אֲדֹנָי, הַנִּפְרָע לְעַמּוֹ יִשְׂרָאֵל מִכָּל צָרֵיהֶם, הָאֵל הַמּוֹשִׁיעַ.

Barukh ata Adonai, Eloheinu, melekh ha'olam, harav et rivenu, vehadan et dinenu, vehanokem et nikmatenu, vehamshalem gemul lekhol oyvei nafshenu, vehanifra lanu mitzareinu. Barukh ata Adonai, hanifra le'amo Yisrael mikol tzareihem, ha'El hamoshia.

"Blessed are You, Lord our God, King of the universe, the God who pleads our cause, and who judges our claim, and who avenges our vengeance, and who brings retribution to our enemies and who punishes our foes. Blessed are You, Lord, who, on behalf of His people Israel, exacts punishment from all of their foes; the God who brings salvation."

After the evening reading, according to Ashkenazic custom, the congregation recites the liturgical poem *Asher Heini* ("He who brought to naught the council of nations"), while after the daytime reading, they recite only the last part of it, from the words: *Shoshanat Ya'akov* ("The rose of Jacob was happy and joyous").

The custom of the Sephardim is to say after the blessing at night only the following passage: "Cursed be Haman, blessed be Mordechai, cursed be Zeresh, blessed be Esther, cursed be all the wicked, blessed be all Israel. And may Harvona also be remembered for good."

The megilla is read in the synagogue at night immediately after the evening prayer service, and in the morning following the reading of the Torah. However, one may fulfill the mitzva by hearing a megilla reading anytime at night, from the emergence of the stars until dawn. One may hear the daytime reading at any time during the day, from sunrise to sunset.

One who is unable to attend the megilla reading in the synagogue should find someone who knows how to read it with the proper cantillation notes from a valid megilla scroll. Megilla readings at various times are offered as a free service to the public in many cities, in synagogues, Chabad houses, etc. If one is unable to find such a reading or someone who can read for him, he should read it himself from a valid megilla scroll. In such a case, one might want to ask another person to follow the reading from a voweled and punctuated text, to make sure he is pronouncing all the words correctly.

Mishlo'ah Manot

During the day of Purim, from sunrise to sunset, every adult Jew is commanded to send at least two types of food or drink to one of his friends or acquaintances, as it is stated in the megilla: "And of sending portions [*mishlo'ah manot*] one to another" (Esther 9:19). The foods and drinks that one sends should be fit for immediate consumption, rather than requiring preparation.

With regard to this mitzva, it is important to emphasize:

Since the purpose of this mitzva is to increase friendship and goodwill between people, one must take care that it should not become a way of showing preference for one person over another, and that no one should be offended.

Sometimes it seems that the whole enterprise of sending food portions has been blown out of proportion. It must be remembered that this mitzva is not a competition to send the most expensive or creative food package. The Sages advised that it is preferable to invest most of one's available money in the mitzva of the gifts for the poor (see below) rather than for this mitzva.

Gifts for the Poor [*Matanot La'evyonim*]

During the day of Purim, at some point between sunrise and sunset, all adults must give money to at least two poor people. It is advisable to give each one an amount of money that covers the cost of a minimal meal.

In order to fulfill this mitzva properly, the money must be given to two poor people early enough so that they will have time to use the money to buy food for that day.

It goes without saying that although this is the minimum requirement of *halakha*, it is praiseworthy for whoever is able to give more money and to give to more than two poor people.

It is important to clarify that whereas throughout the rest of the year one should act judiciously when disbursing money to charity, doing due diligence in order to discern the genuine poor from various impostors, on Purim the rule is: "Whoever stretches out a hand, give to him." On this day one does not examine closely the person who asks for charity, and apart from the minimum two gifts to two poor people who really need it, one should give, even if only a small sum, to anyone who requests aid (in accordance with the giver's financial means, of course).

📖 **Further reading:** For more on the mitzva to give charity, see p. 615; *A Concise Guide to the Sages*, pp. 240, 245, 426, 458; *A Concise Guide to Mahshava*, p. 248.

Purim Celebration

The commandment of "feasting and joy" applies on the day of Purim, and that is when the celebratory meal should be held. Nevertheless, even on the night of Purim, after the reading of the megilla, it is proper to be joyful and to make the meal more festive than usual.

During the day of Purim, it is obligatory to eat at least one large meal that includes bread, and it is preferable to eat meat and other delicacies at this meal as well in order to enhance the celebration.

Some hold the Purim feast in the morning, after they have fulfilled the rest of the mitzvot of the day. But in most Jewish communities it is customary to eat the meal in the afternoon, after an early afternoon prayer service, and to extend the feast into the evening and night. Some eat two meals on Purim, a small but respectable meal in the morning, followed by a large feast in the afternoon.

When Purim falls on a Friday, many people advance the time of the meal to the morning, so that they will regain their appetites in time for the Friday night Shabbat meal. Others eat the Purim feast at the usual afternoon time, and when the time for Shabbat arrives, they stop the meal to allow the women to light the Shabbat candles, while the men declare, "I hereby accept upon myself the sanctity of Shabbat." Then all the bread on the table is covered and *Kiddush* is recited over a cup of wine. If one who follows this practice has already drunk wine during the Purim meal, he should recite *Kiddush* without saying the blessing over the wine. In such a case, in Grace after Meals, the *Al HaNisim* passage is inserted, because the meal began on Purim, but one also adds the Shabbat *Retzeh* section, since it is presently Shabbat. After the meal, the participants should recite *Kabbalat Shabbat,* followed by the Shabbat evening prayers.

> Further reading: For more on the mitzva of feasting and rejoicing on Purim, see *A Concise Guide to Mahshava*, p. 86.

As on every Jewish holiday, Purim also has customs involving specific types of food: In the daytime meal some eat foods that are seeds, such as beans, grits, or rice, as according to the tradition of the Sages, during the time Esther was in the king's palace she ate only these types of foods in order to maintain a kosher diet. Another custom is to eat meat-filled dumplings on Purim. The reason for this is that whereas it is a mitzva to eat meat on every festival, on this holiday, which is diminished or "hidden" in the sense that work is permitted, the meat is likewise wrapped and covered. These are merely representative examples, as there are many other customary foods that are eaten by the various communities.

Throughout Purim, and particularly during the meal, it is a mitzva to partake of alcoholic beverages, especially wine. The desired state one should reach is the blurring of the senses, to the point of drowsiness. Some halakhic authorities are lenient in this regard, and rule that it is enough to simply drink more wine than one is used to, and there is no need to become inebriated at all. If wine is harmful to someone's health, or if he knows in advance that drinking wine will lead him to act improperly or cause damage, he may rely on this lenient view. If someone nevertheless gets drunk on Purim and causes financial damage to another person, he should consult a rabbi concerning financial liability.

📖 **Further reading:** To read about the importance of limiting one's intake of alcohol, on Purim and all year long, see *A Concise Guide to Mahshava*, p. 89; *A Concise Guide to the Sages*, pp. 15, 141.

Purim Day

Purim is a busy day. In addition to the three daily prayer services, the Torah is read, as is the megilla, after which one must fulfill the other three mitzvot of Purim.

The Prayer Services

In all the *Amida* prayers of Purim, one includes in the *Modim* blessing, which consists of thanks to God, the passage of *Al HaNisim*, with the section: "In the days of Mordechai and Esther, etc." which appears in prayer books. In the evening prayers, at the end of the *Amida*, the megilla is read. Afterward, the congregation recites *Ve'ata Kadosh*, "And you are holy," which can also be found in prayer books. (On a Saturday night, this is preceded by the *Vihi Noam* passage, "May the graciousness of the Lord our God be upon us," Psalms 90:17). The service then concludes as usual.

In the morning service, after the *Amida* prayer, one Torah scroll is taken from the ark, and three men are called up for the Torah reading of Purim (Exodus 17:8-16), which tells of the first war of Amalek against Israel. This episode is read on Purim because the decree of Haman, who was a descendent of Agag king of Amalek, is viewed as a continuation of that evil Amalekite aspiration to harm and destroy the Jewish people. Afterward the Torah scroll is returned to the ark, the megilla is read, and the morning prayers are concluded as on a regular weekday.

Following the morning prayer service, it is appropriate to hurry to fulfill the mitzvot of sending portions of food and gifts to the poor, and to devote the remainder of the day to fulfilling the mitzva of "feasting and joy."

It is customary to recite the afternoon prayer service relatively early, so that the festive meal can be held in a relaxed, joyful atmosphere.

In Grace after Meals throughout the day, one includes the passage of *Al HaNisim*, with the section beginning: "In the days of Mordechai and Esther."

It is an accepted custom, especially among children, to dress up in costumes on Purim, in order to enhance the joy of the day. Many varied reasons have been suggested for this custom.

Shushan Purim and Purim Meshulash

In Jerusalem and other ancient cities, which were surrounded by a wall in the days of Joshua son of Nun, Purim is celebrated on the fifteenth of Adar, the day after it is celebrated in all other places. The reason for this is explained in the Book of Esther itself (9:15-19): The Jews fought their enemies on the thirteenth of Adar and rested from the war on the fourteenth, and therefore the fourteenth was established as a day of celebration and joy. By contrast, in Shushan the capital, the Jews were given permission to avenge themselves on their enemies on the fourteenth of Adar as well, and they rested from battle only on the fifteenth of the month. Consequently, when the holiday was established, it was set for everyone on the day that they rested from the war. The inhabitants of all other cities celebrated Purim on the fourteenth of Adar, whereas the residents of Shushan celebrated it on the fifteenth, and that day was called Shushan Purim. As the city of Shushan was surrounded by a wall, the Sages ruled that all cities surrounded by a wall in the days of the biblical Joshua have the status of Shushan in this regard, and they too celebrate Purim on the fifteenth of Adar (which is also called "Purim of the walled cities"). Anyone who has doubts about the date on which he should celebrate Purim should ask his local rabbi.

In principle, there is no difference between the laws and customs of Purim in other places, celebrated on the fourteenth of Adar, and the laws and customs of Purim in Jerusalem and other walled cities, on the fifteenth.

When the fifteenth of Adar occurs on a Shabbat, the mitzvot of Purim of the walled cities are spread out over three days, as detailed below. This Purim is called Purim Meshulash, "tripartite Purim." In such a case, one who is celebrating in Jerusalem or other walled cities proceeds as follows: The megilla is read as in all other places, on Thursday night and Friday morning. On Friday, one gives the gifts to the poor. The Al HaNisim prayer is inserted into the Amida and Grace after Meals only on Shabbat. In the morning service of Shabbat, two Torah scrolls are taken out of the ark; seven men are called up for the weekly Torah reading from the first scroll, while an eighth person is called up for the Purim reading (Exodus 17:8-16) that is read for maftir from the second scroll. This is followed by the haftara (I Samuel 15:2–34), which discusses the battle of Saul against Amalek. This is the same haftara that was read for Shabbat Zakhor. This Shabbat has a certain atmosphere of joy, and conversation centers around the megilla. On Sunday, one fulfills the mitzvot of sending portions of food and "feasting and joy" with a large meal, including the drinking of wine. Thus, all the mitzvot of Purim are performed over the course of three days.

The Month of Nisan

Nisan is the first month in the biblical calendar, as is stated in the Torah: "This month is for you the beginning of months, it is first for you of the months of the year" (Exodus 12:2). Several important events in the annals of our people occurred in Nisan, including the patriarch Jacob receiving the blessings from his father, and the inauguration of the Tabernacle where God rested His Presence amid the people of Israel. The most significant event of the month of Nisan is our ancestors' liberation from Egypt during this month. In commemoration of that momentous occasion, we celebrate the festival of Passover in the middle of Nisan.

According to the Sages, this month is more suitable and propitious than the rest of the year for the arrival of the messianic redemption for which we have been waiting for some two thousand years of exile, as the Talmud states: "The Jewish people were redeemed [from Egypt] in Nisan, and in the future the Jewish people will be redeemed [in the final redemption] in Nisan" (*Rosh HaShana*, 11a). All these factors give the days of Nisan their special celebratory character, which is expressed in several ways.

This section presents the laws and customs of the month of Nisan. (The *halakhot* of Passover and its preparations will be detailed in the subsequent sections.)

📖 **Further reading:** For more on the month of Nisan, see *A Concise Guide to Mahshava*, p. 48.

A Special Month

In the month of Nisan, *Tahanun* is not recited in the morning and afternoon prayers. The reason is that most days of the month are festive: During the first twelve days, the twelve tribal princes brought their offerings for the dedication of the Tabernacle in the wilderness (see below). On the day before Passover, as on the day before all festivals, there is no *Tahanun* in any case. This is followed by the days of Passover itself. Thus, as most days of Nisan are celebratory, it was decided that *Tahanun* should be omitted throughout the entire month.

The Offerings of the Princes

As described in the Torah (Exodus 40:17; Numbers 7:1), the building of the Tabernacle was completed on the first day of the month of Nisan. On the day that it was erected, the princes of the twelve tribes began bringing their inaugural offerings, one prince each day. Therefore, some have the custom to read on every day, from the first until the twelfth of Nisan, the verses describing the offerings of the prince of that day. These verses appear in Numbers, chapter 7. Some have the custom to continue on the thirteenth of Nisan with a passage from *Parashat Behaalotekha* (Numbers 8:1–4), which immediately follows the description of the princes' offerings.

In most of the communities that follow this practice, the verses about the princes' offerings are read from a printed *Humash* or prayer book, but there are some who take out a Torah scroll from the ark and read the verses from it, albeit without calling anyone up to the Torah and without reciting the blessings.

Some have the custom of reciting a special prayer every day after reading the portion of the princes: "May it be Your will...that if I am Your servant from the tribe of such and such that I have read in Your Torah, etc." This prayer can be found in some prayer books.

The Blessing over the Trees

Since the spring season begins in Nisan, with the renewal of nature and the flourishing of many trees, the Sages instituted a blessing over the beauty and pleasure of this flowering.

One who goes out during the month of Nisan and sees fruit trees that are blossoming recites:

בָּרוּךְ אַתָּה אֲדֹנָי, אֱלֹהֵינוּ מֶלֶךְ הָעוֹלָם, שֶׁלֹּא חִסֵּר בְּעוֹלָמוֹ כְּלוּם וּבָרָא בוֹ בְּרִיּוֹת טוֹבוֹת וְאִילָנוֹת טוֹבוֹת, לֵיהָנוֹת בָּהֶן בְּנֵי אָדָם.

Barukh ata Adonai, Eloheinu, melekh ha'olam, shelo hiser be'olamo kelum, uvara vo beriyot tovot ve'ilanot tovot, leihanot bahen benei adam.

"Blessed are You, Lord our God, King of the universe, who has withheld nothing from His world, and has created in it beautiful creatures and trees for human beings to enjoy." Some add other verses and prayers, which appear in many prayer books.

The obligation to recite this blessing applies only if and when one happens to see fruit trees blooming, but due to our fondness for the blessing, and because according to mystical sources this blessing is associated with a broader process of revival and renewal, one should make an active effort to seek out blossoming fruit trees in order to recite this blessing.

The custom is to recite the blessing only when one sees at least two blossoming fruit trees near one another. It is recited only on the first occasion that one sees the trees and the flowers. If one saw blossoming trees in the month of Nisan and for some reason (such as forgetfulness, lack of knowledge, etc.) neglected to recite the blessing, he may recite it the next time he sees them. One should try to say the blessing in the month of Nisan, as afterward the flowers fall off most trees. One who did not recite it during Nisan but sees fruit trees blooming in the following month (pomegranate trees, for example, bloom for a longer period), may still recite the blessing.

Kimha Depis'ha

Due to the extraordinary expenses associated with the festival of Passover, it is customary to give extra charity as the festival approaches. This charity is traditionally called *kimha depis'ha*, which is Aramaic for "Passover flour," or *ma'ot hittin*, "money for wheat." In the past, it was accepted in Jewish communities that the rabbi and the community leadership would impose a certain sum on each family to donate for this important cause. Nowadays there is no one who has the authority to force others to donate money, but there are many individuals and charitable organizations who ensure that every Jewish family can celebrate the festival of Passover with dignity, and it is proper to donate for this purpose as much money as one can afford.

> **Further reading:** For more on caring for the poor before festivals, see *A Concise Guide to the Sages*, p. 242.

Shabbat HaGadol

The Shabbat preceding Passover is referred to as *Shabbat HaGadol*, "the great Shabbat." The main reason given for this name is that it recalls a great miracle that took place on this Shabbat before the first Passover, a few days before the exodus of the Israelites from Egypt. As related by the sources, the children of Israel were commanded by Moses to prepare lambs in their homes, to be used for the Passover offering. Thus, in every Jewish home there was a lamb. At the time, sheep were considered sacred by the Egyptians, and naturally they would consider the Israelites' conduct as being blatantly contemptuous of their deity. A great miracle occurred, as not only did they not harm the Israelites, but when the Egyptians heard from them that in a few days God was going to strike the Egyptian firstborns and take Israel out of Egypt, the firstborns of Egypt rushed to Pharaoh and his ministers, demanding the immediate release of the Israelites, and when they refused, they waged a civil war against them that caused many deaths in Egypt.

Another reason for the name *Shabbat HaGadol* is that on this Shabbat the "great one" of the community, the rabbi of the city or the community,

HALAKHA _____ Yearly Cycle > The Month of Nisan

delivers a special public sermon. This address usually focuses on the many halakhic aspects of the approaching festival of Passover.

Many have the custom of reading a section of the Passover haggada on this Shabbat, from the passage beginning: "We were slaves" until the words "to atone for our souls."

Passover
Preparations for the Festival

The preparations for Passover begin weeks beforehand. These include cleaning the house, buying new clothes and dishes, and a significant amount of food preparation. The main mitzva of the days before the arrival of the holiday is to ensure that one's house is clean of every crumb of *hametz*, a term which is defined below. Likewise, the kitchen must be rendered kosher for Passover, in accordance with the Torah's command: "And neither leavened bread shall be seen with you, nor shall leaven be seen with you, within your entire border" (Exodus 13:7), and: "Seven days, leaven shall not be found in your houses" (Exodus 12:19). The laws of Passover are numerous and complex, and it is for this reason that the Sages state that one should start reviewing the *halakhot* of the holiday thirty days before Passover.

In addition, one must perform the requisite preparations for the Seder, which include buying matzot, wine, and the rest of the food that is needed for this night. Similarly, one should familiarize himself with the haggada, and one who is leading a Seder should prepare in advance so that he is ready to fulfill this important task as effectively as possible.

This section, the first that deals with Passover, provides a detailed list of all that one needs to do in order to prepare for celebrating Passover properly: cleaning, kashering the kitchen and dishes, selling *hametz*, and more.

The Prohibitions Against *Hametz*

There are three distinct prohibitions that apply to *hametz* on Passover: it is prohibited to eat it, it is forbidden to derive benefit from it (e.g., by selling it or feeding it to animals), and it is prohibited to have it in one's possession. Not only is actual *hametz* prohibited on Passover, but even a mixture that has *hametz* as one of its components is forbidden.

Definition of *Hametz*

Hametz is a product made from one of the five kinds of grain (see further) that has come into contact with water and reached a certain level of fermentation called *himutz*, "leavening." From a scientific perspective it is not easy to define this leavening, but there are clear and practical definitions of this category in *halakha*, some of which will be detailed below.

The five types of grain recognized by *halakha* are: wheat, barley, oats,[1] spelt, and rye. If any of these grains becomes leavened, it is strictly prohibited during Passover. In practice, this includes most regular baked goods and pastry products, pasta, etc. The same applies to many beverages, especially beer and some liquors, such as vodka or whiskey, which are made from fermented grains.

The Severity of the Prohibition

The prohibition of *hametz* is more severe than the prohibitions against most forbidden foods, such as non-kosher meat or mixtures of meat and milk.

This expresses itself in several ways:

(1) Eating *hametz* on Passover, like eating on Yom Kippur, is punishable by *karet*, meaning excision, being "excised from Israel" (Exodus 12:15).

(2) Generally, if a small amount of forbidden food becomes mixed with more than sixty times its volume of kosher food, the non-kosher component is halakhically "nullified" and it is permitted to eat the entire mixture. By contrast, if there is any admixture of *hametz* at all in a food on Passover, even a minute amount, all the food is prohibited.

(3) During Passover, it is prohibited not only to consume *hametz* but also to derive benefit from it. One may not feed it to an animal, sell it, or even use it as fuel for a fire from which one derives benefit. Therefore, those who raise animals or have pets must feed them food on Passover that does not contain *hametz*.

(4) *Hametz* may not even be found in the possession of a Jew on Passover.

Due to the severity of the prohibition of *hametz* on Passover, it is appropriate to exercise great caution to ensure that one does not violate this prohibition. Even rabbis who do not tend toward stringency in their rulings all year are stricter regarding any question that involves *hametz* on Passover. It is important to know that apart from basic, unprocessed animal and vegetable products, such as meat, fish, eggs, fruits, and vegetables, there is nothing that may be eaten on Passover without a reliable "kosher for Passover" certification.

The prohibition against having *hametz* in one's possession on Passover starts from the time of burning the *hametz* and lasts until the end of the last

---

1.   The Hebrew term used in halakhic literature is *shibolet shual*. Most identify this as oats, but there are some who claim it is a sub-species of barley.

day of the holiday. This accounts for the frenzy of house cleaning as Passover approaches that has taken hold of Jews for generations.

One should calculate one's shopping needs in the weeks before Passover, so that most of the *hametz* products that he buys will be consumed before the holiday and he will not have to dispose of them. If, nevertheless, some *hametz* remains in the house, it must be burned on the day before Passover or sold to a non-Jew, as detailed below in the *halakhot* of Passover eve.

📖 **Further reading:** For more on the severe prohibition of *hametz*, see *A Concise Guide to Mahshava*, p. 95.

Where Must One Clean?

According to the *halakha*, even a small amount of *hametz* is prohibited to be in one's possession on Passover. This is the basis for the requirement of thorough cleaning.

Even a cookie or a few pretzels that lie hidden between the upholstery and the backrest of an armchair in the living room causes one to violate the prohibition of "it may not be found" (Exodus 12:19). With that said, it is important to differentiate between the cleaning that is halakhically necessary, and activities undertaken by some, such as scrubbing walls and ceilings, which are entirely unnecessary from a halakhic perspective.

In general, the *halakha* requires one to inspect and clean only those places where there is a reasonable concern that *hametz* is located. This includes: all areas of the kitchen, pantry, and dining area, including chairs and cabinets; children's rooms, as children are likely to bring food there; and any other part of the house where it is possible that *hametz* was brought during the year. Children's toys should be checked, and if one wants them to be used on Passover they must be cleaned. It is recommended to put toys made of cloth or waterproof plastic inside a pillowcase and machine wash them gently. It is also necessary to thoroughly clean the family car.

By contrast, places such as clothing closets or bookcases, which do not generally contain food, do not have to be cleaned according to the *halakha*. Bear in mind that dust is not *hametz*.

📖 **Further reading:** To read about the inner spiritual cleansing that can be inspired by the process of cleaning for *hametz*, see *A Concise Guide to Mahshava*, p. 96.

Spices, Cosmetics, Medicines, etc.

Spices that have possibly become mixed with *hametz*, such as flour, should be burned or sold to a non-Jew.

The prohibition on Passover against deriving benefit from *hametz* or from a mixture of *hametz* leads many people to be very stringent, even regarding items that are not edible. There are those who are careful on Passover to use only those cosmetics and hygiene products, body lotions, shampoos, and the like, that are stamped as kosher for Passover.

One should consult lists of kosher-for-Passover products that are publicized by *kashrut* organizations. In Israel, lists of medicines that are certified kosher for Passover are readily available at pharmacies and on the internet. Anyone who needs to take medicine orally on Passover should consult a rabbi, as in some cases it is permitted to take medicine on Passover even if it contains *hametz* ingredients. Even if a medication is not kosher for Passover, this does not mean that it must be destroyed before the holiday, as long as it is unfit for consumption by a dog (this is the halakhic criterion for defining "food" when it comes to *hametz*).

There are products whose main ingredients are not *hametz*, but they nevertheless contain small amounts of *hametz*. Due to the miniscule percent of *hametz* overall in the product, the manufacturer is not required by law to list the *hametz* ingredient on the packaging. Therefore, one should look for specific kosher-for-Passover certification, confirming that there is no *hametz* in the product at all. It is not sufficient to merely read the list of ingredients on a product package.

Moreover, there are certain products that are sometimes made from *hametz* and on other occasions are not. For example, alcohol in its various forms can be produced from a variety of grains, in which case it is *hametz* and thus prohibited on Passover. Alcohol can also be made from sources that are not *hametz*. Therefore, one cannot assume that all products of the same general type have the same status.

Regarding kosher food in general, and the permissibility of products for Passover in particular, one should not rely on the statements of sellers in stores or even on the phrase "Kosher for Passover" that appears on the package. To ascertain that a product is indeed kosher for Passover, one must look for the seal of a known, reliable organization that certifies the product to be kosher for Passover.

Legumes [*Kitniyot*] and Other Stringencies

Another restriction regarding food on Passover stems from the custom that has been accepted by many communities to refrain from the consumption of plants that have kernels or seeds, due to the concern that grain kernels may be mixed in, or that grain products might be confused for these species. The plants included in this category are given the broad name of *kitniyot*. This is literally translated as "legumes," although that botanical term does not accurately describe all the species included in this custom. The category of *kitniyot* includes certain grain species that are not prohibited by Torah law, such as rice and corn, several types of legumes, and a few other plants whose edible seeds grow in pods.

"Kosher for Passover," for Whom?

The custom prohibiting the eating of *kitniyot* on Passover was fully accepted by all Ashkenazic communities. There are also several species of plants (that are not *hametz* by Torah law), which other, non-Ashkenazic, communities avoid on Passover.

The prohibition of eating *kitniyot* on Passover can cause some confusion, especially in Israel, where many products are labeled: "Kosher for Passover for those who eat *kitniyot*." Those who are stringent and avoid eating *kitniyot* should take care in inspecting the kosher for Passover seal to ensure that the product does not contain *kitniyot*.

Egg Matza [*Matza Ashira*]

Strictly speaking, flour that has been kneaded exclusively in a liquid other than water, such as eggs or fruit juice, does not become *hametz*. Therefore, it would be permitted to bake matza, or cakes and cookies in this manner for Passover. But if this liquid contains some water, the dough actually becomes more susceptible to fermentation than it does with water alone. Most Sephardim customarily eat baked goods that are prepared from dough with liquids other than water, which is classified as *matza ashira*, and generally referred to in English as egg matza. Nevertheless, because it is very hard to avoid some water being mixed in with the flour, if only from washing out the bowls, and due to the fact that some authorities disagree with the assumption that dough prepared with a liquid other than water does not become *hametz*, Ashkenazim and some Sephardim do not eat *matza ashira* on Passover.

Even those who do eat *matza ashira* on Passover must be strict to ensure that it is certified as strictly kosher. In any case of uncertainty, a rabbi should be consulted. It should also be noted that even those who eat *matza ashira* on Passover agree that it may not be used to fulfill the mitzva of eating matza on the Seder nights.

There are those who apply the term *matza ashira* to matza that has been baked in the usual manner and subsequently coated with other substances such as chocolate. Some Ashkenazim will eat this kind of matza.

Wetted Matza [*Gebrokts / Matza Sheruya*]

Another common stringency, which is observed mainly by Hasidim, is to refrain from eating *matza sheruya*, literally "soaked matza" (*gebrokts* in Yiddish). This refers to matza which may have been baked according to all the most exacting requirements of *halakha*, but which has then come into contact with water (or according to some, any liquid). The reason for this stringency is the concern that in the matza there may remain bits of flour that were not kneaded into the dough and baked, and therefore the contact with the water might cause them to leaven now. Those who are strict about *matza sheruya* do not use matza meal for cooking.

Halakha vs. Stringencies

The differences in customs among the various communities have led to a practice among some people to refrain from eating in the homes of others during Passover, even in the homes of friends and family. Sometimes people accept a certain stringency upon themselves that even their own siblings do not observe. As a result, a practice has developed in some circles that if one has guests on Passover, he will serve only assorted fruits and nuts, which are foods that anyone can eat.

At the same time, it is important to distinguish between laws that explicitly appear in the halakhic sources, and practices that are customs or stringencies. When it comes to basic halakhic matters, there is no room for compromise. By contrast, regarding stringencies that someone has accepted upon himself, it is important not to let matters get blown out of proportion and lead to quarrels and disputes. In complex situations or in any case of doubt, it is recommended to consult a rabbi.

Yearly Cycle

Kashering the Kitchen and Dishes

Due to the prohibition of *hametz*, one may not use on Passover the same utensils that are used throughout the rest of the year, because of the concern, or in many cases the certainty, that they have been used for *hametz*.

Preference for Another Set of Dishes

If one can afford it, he should buy special utensils and dishes to be used just for Passover. When the holiday ends, these dishes should be stored away until the next Passover. This practice is consistent with the custom accepted in most Jewish communities to enhance the Seder table with especially fine utensils. Nowadays there are also sets of quite elegant disposable plates and cutlery that one can buy before the holiday and use on Passover. In such a case, one must make sure the plates are indeed "kosher for Passover," as manufacturers sometimes use starch as coating for plates to keep them from sticking to each other, as well as various adhesives for cardboard cups, and these materials may contain *hametz* components.

Kashering Kitchen Utensils

One whose financial situation does not allow him to purchase a separate set of utensils for Passover, or who for any other reason wishes to use on Passover the same utensils he generally uses for *hametz*, must "kasher" the utensils, that is, make them kosher, in this case kosher for Passover. It should be noted that many utensils cannot be kashered. Whether a utensil can be kashered, as well as the specific form of kashering necessary, is determined by the material of the utensil and how it is used throughout the year. The *halakhot* on this subject are numerous and complex, and therefore it is recommended to consult a rabbi who is an expert in the field.

In the days leading up to the festival of Passover, many synagogues and private organizations perform kashering services available to the public, sometimes for a fee. Along with kashering items for Passover, it is recommended to take advantage of this opportunity to kasher any utensils that may have become non-kosher over the course of the year, so that one will be able to use these utensils again.

Those *hametz* utensils that are not kashered for Passover must be cleaned well, so that no edible *hametz* is left on them. One must be especially careful with regard to toasters and the like, which often have a significant amount of crumbs left in them. After cleaning, they should all be stored away in a closed cabinet or closet and marked as *"hametz,"* so that they will not be accidentally used.

Kashering the Kitchen

As mentioned above, the kashering of utensils is an option, and it can be avoided by keeping a separate set of dishes for Passover. With regard to the kitchen itself, there is no avoiding cleaning and kashering it for use on the holiday, as the vast majority of houses have only one kitchen, used all year round, including on Passover (though some families close their regular kitchen on the holiday and move to a separate, specially made Passover kitchen). The need for kashering applies mainly to the surfaces used in the preparation, cooking, and eating of food.

The kashering of these surfaces for Passover is basically the same as kashering from a non-kosher to kosher status. Since it is required for only a week, however, there are easier ways to ensure that the kitchen is kosher for Passover, as detailed below.

> Further reading: For the *halakhot* of kashering from non-kosher to kosher, see p. 560.

Countertops: Kitchen countertops must first be thoroughly cleaned. Then it is recommended to pour hot water directly over them from a boiling kettle. The counters should be covered with heavy silver foil, strong enough to last the entire holiday, or, alternatively, with oilcloth or another type of reusable covering that can be kept from year to year. Such coverings can be found in stores selling household items or hardware. Regarding some countertops, such as those made from granite, many hold that after pouring the boiling water over each part of the countertop, one may use it without covering it.

Sink: The kitchen sink must be cleaned thoroughly. Then hot water should be poured over the sink and faucet from a kettle that has just boiled. A special plastic insert that covers the entire sink should be purchased and used for the duration of the holiday. Such inserts are also sold in household goods stores. If the sink is made of stainless steel, many hold that after pouring boiling water on each part of it, the sink may be used as usual.

Stove: The surface of the stovetop should be thoroughly cleaned with a grease remover and covered with heavy aluminum foil. The grates of the stove (on which the pots sit) should be taken to a place where utensils are kashered, and one should ask them to perform *libbun* (intense heating by direct fire). Alternatively, they can be wrapped in silver foil. There is no need to kasher the burners, but at the end of the process of kashering and covering the surface and the grates, all the flames should be lit to the highest possible setting, and left burning for about half an hour.

Table: The dining table should be cleaned well and covered with plastic. One should take care during Passover not to eat directly on tables that are not covered with a tablecloth.

Miscellaneous: Tablecloths and towels should be washed. A baby's high chair and its tray require thorough cleaning, after which boiling water should be poured over them. Ovens should be thoroughly cleaned, including in all their crevices, with a grease remover, and then turned on, set to the highest temperature, for about an hour. Regarding other kitchen appliances, one should ask a rabbi whether and how they can be kashered for Passover.

Selling *Hametz*

It is proper to finish eating or disposing of all of one's *hametz* before Passover, but in practice this sometimes proves difficult. It is especially unfeasible for stores and factories that maintain a large inventory of *hametz*, as well as homes which have expensive *hametz* products, such as special whiskeys. Therefore, the Sages instituted the sale of *hametz*, whereby one's *hametz* can be sold to a non-Jew for the week of Passover.

Everyone Should Sell

Due to the concern over finding *hametz* on Passover, and given the severity of the prohibition, everyone, even someone who has cleaned his house well and removed all *hametz* of which he is aware, should sell his *hametz*, in case there is *hametz* in his possession of which he is unaware.

From a halakhic perspective, this sale is complicated, and the contract is highly complex, since the transaction must comply with all the criteria of *halakha* as well as the laws of the country in which the sale takes place. In practice, the seller signs a document which he can get from his local synagogue rabbi. This document empowers the rabbi or his representatives to sell to a non-Jew any *hametz* that is found at the address specified in the document. The transaction requires a halakhic act of acquisition. Usually this is done by the rabbi handing the seller a pen, which is a symbolic act of exchange.

One who does not live near a rabbi or does not know where he can make the sale in person can do so over the internet or by phone.

How Is the Sale Conducted?

At the time of the sale, the non-Jew pays a symbolic down payment for all the *hametz* in the transaction, while agreeing that after the holiday he will pay the actual value of the *hametz* being bought.

In practice, at the end of Passover the rabbi buys back the *hametz* and it returns to our possession. Thus, all sides benefit from the arrangement. In principle, if during the course of the holiday the non-Jew would want to actually pick up the *hametz* and take it home, he may do so, but then he would have to pay the full cost of those products.

All the products that are sold as *hametz* should be put in specific locations in the house, closed off, and marked as *hametz*.

The sale of *hametz* must be completed by the morning of the day before Passover, before the latest time allowed for the burning of *hametz*. Any *hametz* that was not sold to a non-Jew but remained in the possession of a Jew over the holiday is referred to as "*hametz* over which Passover has elapsed," and its consumption, as well as deriving any benefit from it, are prohibited, even after Passover.

One who leaves his home some time before Passover to spend the holiday elsewhere can leave instructions before his departure to carry out the sale, which will take effect at the usual time and be in force until the end of the festival.

Passover
The Day before the Seder

The fourteenth of Nisan, the day before Passover, is a special day. During the Temple period, on this day, all Jews would bring the paschal offering, which would be eaten in the evening at the Seder, as it is stated: "It shall be for you for safekeeping until the fourteenth day of this month and the entire assembly of the congregation of Israel shall slaughter it in the afternoon" (Exodus 12:6). Unfortunately, this very important mitzva cannot be fulfilled nowadays, until we merit the complete redemption and the rebuilding of the Temple. Nevertheless, even nowadays the eve of Passover is replete with preparations for the holiday in general and for Seder night in particular.

The prohibition against eating *hametz* begins in the morning of the fourteenth of Nisan. Likewise, the removal of any remains of *hametz* in our possession must be performed before a specific hour of this day, as detailed below.

This section clarifies what one must know in order to prepare properly for the Seder night. This includes searching for and burning *hametz*, making sure one has enough matzot, wine, and other necessities for the Seder, getting the table ready, and arranging the Seder plate.

The Search for *Hametz*

The series of special activities performed on the fourteenth of Nisan actually begins on the night before that day. On that evening, one must carry out the search for *hametz* and make sure that all the cleaning for Passover has been done properly and the house is indeed free of all *hametz* products. Although this search is seemingly a symbolic act, as the house has already been thoroughly cleansed of *hametz*, it should not be taken lightly, as it establishes halakhically that the house is kosher for Passover. It is also an opportunity to take a last look at places that might have been overlooked by those who helped clean the house and prepare it for the holiday.

Timing of the Search

The time for the search for *hametz* begins with the emergence of the stars; the exact time for any locale can be found in synagogue calendars and on the internet. The reason for performing the search after the stars emerge is that at this time it is dark and therefore the light of a candle can provide bright illumination, allowing one to search the cracks and crevices in one's home for any remaining *hametz*.

Because of its great importance, the search for *hametz* should be done immediately after dark. One should not begin any other activities that might distract him from carrying out his obligation to perform the search. One should not eat anything beforehand, no business may be carried out, and even learning Torah is prohibited from the moment the stars emerge until after the search is completed.

One who forgot or was unable to carry out the search at nightfall may perform it at any point during the night. If he neglected to do so all night, he should perform the inspection during the day. And if even that was not done, he should search for *hametz* during the holiday itself, as the very existence of *hametz* in the home is prohibited throughout the holiday. If he failed to search even then, he should do so after the holiday. The reason for this is that *hametz* that was in the possession of a Jew over the holiday is permanently prohibited for consumption and deriving benefit.

One who leaves his home several days before the holiday, and will not be home on the eve of Passover, must search his house for *hametz* on the last night before his departure, if he left within thirty days of the holiday (i.e., from Purim onward). He should perform the search by the light of a flame but without reciting a blessing (see below). One who can appoint an agent to search his home at the proper time, on the night of the fourteenth of Nisan, should do so.

One who is staying at a hotel when the time for the search for *hametz* arrives must search for *hametz* in his hotel room.

📖 **Further reading:** For more on the search of *hametz*, see *A Concise Guide to the Sages*, p. 306; *A Concise Guide to Mahshava*, p. 95.

Preparations for the Search

The Sages state that the best lighting to use for searching *hametz* is a flame. It is therefore the custom in most Jewish homes to use a candle, and it is appropriate to do so. Nevertheless, since the light of a flashlight is also suitable for searching, it can be used if no candle is available. In places where it is dangerous to hold a lit candle, e.g., in a car or when searching in the immediate proximity of flammable materials, a flashlight is preferable.

There are some who have the custom of using a feather and a wooden spoon to collect the *hametz* that they find during the search. This feather and spoon are then subsequently burned together with the *hametz*. In any case, it is recommended that the items used for the search be disposable so that they can be burned, to ensure that there are no utensils in the house that might have *hametz* attached to them.

The *halakha* is insistent that one should never recite a blessing "in vain." For example, if one recites the blessing "who creates the fruit of the tree" over an apple, but does not eat the apple, he has recited a blessing in vain.

In light of this law, since a blessing is recited over the search for *hametz*, there is a concern that if one searches the house and does not find any *hametz* at all, perhaps the blessing he recited before the search would be considered a blessing recited in vain.

Consequently, and for kabbalistic reasons as well, it is customary to place ten pieces of *hametz* around the house so that the head of the household will find *hametz* and his blessing will not be in vain.

When placing pieces of *hametz* throughout the house before the search, one must be careful to avoid two undesirable outcomes: crumbling of the *hametz* and losing it. In order to avoid such eventualities, it is advisable to wrap the *hametz* pieces well, so that crumbs should not spread around the area, and likewise to make a checklist of the places where the ten pieces were put, so that one can keep track of them and make sure that they are all found. The preparation of the pieces, their wrapping, their placement in the house, and recording their location, are often carried out by the wife and children of the head of the household.

The Blessing and the Nullification

The search is led by the head of the household. Before beginning the search, he recites the following blessing:

בָּרוּךְ אַתָּה אֲדֹנָי, אֱלֹהֵינוּ מֶלֶךְ הָעוֹלָם, *Barukh ata Adonai, Eloheinu, melekh*
אֲשֶׁר קִדְּשָׁנוּ בְּמִצְוֹתָיו וְצִוָּנוּ עַל בִּעוּר *ha'olam, asher kideshanu bemitzvotav,*
חָמֵץ. *vetzivanu al biur hametz.*

"Blessed are You, Lord our God, King of the universe, who sanctified us through His commandments, and commanded us concerning the elimination of hametz."

One says "the elimination" of hametz, even though the hametz is not actually destroyed until the next day, because the search is the beginning of the process of eliminating hametz from one's home.

The owner of the house may appoint his older children (above the age of bar/bat mitzva) to assist him, and once they have heard the blessing and answered "Amen," they too can conduct the search in various areas of the house.

After completing the search, one must make sure that all the hametz pieces that were hidden have been found, and then one makes the following declaration: "All hametz or leavened items that are in my possession, which I have not noticed and not seen and not removed, shall hereby be nullified and be ownerless like the dust of the earth." The declaration was formulated in ancient times in Aramaic, and it is this original formulation that is still commonly used today.

It is important to understand the meaning of this declaration and to say it with its proper intent. Through this statement one announces the removal of his ownership over all hametz that may still be in his possession without his knowledge, and he renders it ownerless. Therefore, those who do not understand the meaning of the formula in Aramaic should say it in Hebrew, English, or in any other language that he understands.

The pieces of hametz collected in the search should be kept together in a closed bag until the next morning, at which point they will be burned with the leftover hametz of dinner and breakfast.

The Fast of the Firstborn [Ta'anit Bekhorot]

On the day before Passover, it is customary that all firstborn males fast. The reason for this is that on the night of the first Passover, all the firstborn among the Egyptians died, whereas all the firstborn of Israel were spared. In commemoration of this miraculous deliverance, the firstborn males observe a fast. According to custom, the fast may be avoided if one participates in a *seudat mitzva*, a celebratory meal held in honor of the performance of a mitzva. Therefore, most synagogues, after the morning prayers of the fourteenth of Nisan, conduct a *siyum*, a ceremony marking the completion of a talmudic tractate, by learning the concluding section of a tractate that has been studied by one of the worshippers. The firstborn males who are present, and others as well, listen to the *siyum* and then partake of the refreshments served in honor of the occasion. Participating in this "meal" overrides the custom of the firstborn to fast on that day, and thereafter they may eat throughout the day.

> Further reading: For more on the plague of the firstborn, see *A Concise Guide to the Torah*, p. 162; *A Concise Guide to the Sages*, p. 94.

End of the Time for Eating *Hametz*, and Burning the *Hametz*

The prohibition of owning *hametz* begins on the morning of the fourteenth of Nisan. In order to allow for the removal of *hametz* before the prohibition takes effect, its consumption is forbidden some time earlier. The time when one must stop eating *hametz* is at one-third of the day, measured from sunrise to sunset. The exact time for a particular locale can be found in synagogue calendars.

After the time for eating *hametz* has ended, one has about an hour to finish destroying any remnants of *hametz*. One should remember to empty the vacuum cleaner bag before or during this time period.

Loaves of bread and other solid items of *hametz* might not burn well, so it may be a good idea to pour a small amount of a combustible substance on them after they have begun to burn.

Some have the custom to take the four species that had been used on the previous *Sukkot*, and the willow branches used on *Hoshana Rabba*, and burn them along with the *hametz*.

After the burning, one declares: "All *hametz* or leaven that is in my possession, whether I have noticed or not noticed it, whether I have seen it or not seen it, whether I have removed it or not removed it, shall be nullified and be ownerless like the dust of the earth."

This declaration, like the one made the previous night, is formulated in Aramaic, but since it is necessary to understand the meaning of the statement and to have the appropriate intent in order for the *hametz* to indeed be rendered ownerless and taken entirely out of one's possession, it may be said in any language.

One who, despite all the cleaning and inspections carried out before the holiday, nevertheless finds a piece of *hametz* in his house on the first day of Passover, may not touch the *hametz*, as it has the status of *muktze*, an item that may not be handled on Shabbat or a holy day. Instead, he must cover the *hametz* with something. After the festival day [*yom tov*], at the start of the intermediate festival days [*Hol HaMoed*], he must burn it or flush it down the toilet. If the *hametz* is found during *Hol HaMoed*, it must be destroyed immediately. If one *had* sold his hametz to a non-Jew, he should consult with a rabbi about what to do.

Midday

The fourteenth of Nisan, particularly after midday, is a festive time, similar to the intermediate festival days. Therefore, one who wishes to have a haircut should do so before midday (the precise time of midday, calculated as the middle of the time between sunrise and sunset, can be found in many synagogue calendars). One should bear in mind that according to *halakha*, one may not have a haircut during the entire ensuing period of *Sefirat Ha-Omer*, which means that whoever does not cut his hair before the festival will not be able to do so for several more weeks. After midday, one should avoid doing work that is not necessary for the preparations for the holiday.

Matza

For all seven days of Passover one may not eat *hametz* or food containing *hametz*. The only way it is permitted to eat any product made from the five species of grain (wheat, barley, oats, spelt, and rye) is when the entire baking process is performed in such a manner that the dough is prevented from rising and fermenting. Such food, which is produced under very specific and demanding conditions, is called "matza," and this is the only "bread" one may eat on Passover. Nowadays, matza is usually made from wheat flour, but it can also be produced from the other four types of grain (barley, oats, spelt, and rye).

📖 **Further reading:** For more on matza and its symbolism, see *A Concise Guide to Mahshava*, p. 94.

The Various Types of Matza

The obligation to eat matza applies only on the Seder night, when every adult man and woman must eat matza, in the amount detailed in the next section. Throughout the rest of Passover, although it is prohibited to eat *hametz*, there is no obligation to eat matza. On those days, if one wants to eat a full meal and recite the blessing of *HaMotzi* ("who brings forth bread from the earth") at the Passover meals, the only option is to eat matza. When purchasing matza, it is a good idea to calculate ahead of time the amount of matza that will be required for the entire family for the week of Passover.

One must take care that the matza does not contain any additional ingredients, apart from flour and water. It should be noted that the matza one eats on Passover should have a reliable kosher for Passover certification. There are companies that produce matza for consumption all year that is not kosher for Passover. The matza sold in most stores is baked by machines specially designed for matza baking. These machines work quickly, so that from the moment water is added to the flour until the dough is finished, there is not enough time for the dough to leaven.

Shemura Matza

Many people observe the stringency to eat only *shemura* matza throughout the holiday. This is matza baked from flour made from wheat that has been guarded [*shemura*] from the moment of its harvest to ensure that it does not come into any contact with water. Most halakhic authorities maintain that in order to fulfill the mitzva of eating matza on the first night of Passover, one must consume *shemura* matza. Therefore, even those who do not eat only *shemura* matza throughout the entire Passover holiday should make sure that the matza they eat on Seder night is *shemura*.

There are those who are particular to eat only handmade matza on Passover. These matzot are round and their size is not uniform. The reason for this stringency is the opinion of some of the great Torah scholars of recent generations that one should not deviate from the practice of our forefathers who ate only matza baked by hand. Moreover, there are halakhic authorities who maintain that even from a strictly halakhic point of view there is a preference for handmade matza, as it is only this type of matza that is acceptable for the mitzva to eat matza. Accordingly, even some of those who are not particular to eat only handmade matza throughout Passover try to make sure to eat handmade matza on the Seder night.

There are those who bake the matzot for the Seder night on the afternoon before the holiday begins, in commemoration of the Passover offering, which was slaughtered on the fourteenth of Nisan at this same time of day. Baking matza at this time, when the prohibition against possessing *hametz* is already in effect, requires great caution to ensure that pieces of dough do not fall onto the ground and leaven.

It is important to emphasize that since the *halakhot* involved in baking matzot are numerous and complex, one should not attempt to bake matza without the guidance and supervision of people with practical experience and expertise in this area of *halakha*. This is true of matza baking in general, and especially true regarding baking on the afternoon before Passover.

In order to help ensure that the experience of eating matza on the Seder night is fresh and exciting, it is customary to refrain from eating matza for a period of time prior to Passover. Some people stop eating matza from the beginning of the month of Nisan, while others refrain from eating matza for a whole month before Passover, i.e., from Purim. According to all opinions, at the very least, one should not eat matza on the day before Passover.

Preparing the Table and the Seder Plate

It is proper to set the table for the Seder, and to prepare the Seder plate, in advance, so that the Seder can begin as soon as possible once family members arrive home from the synagogue. In addition to the practical benefit of these advance preparations, namely, that one arrives home and finds the table ready for the Seder, they also contribute to a general atmosphere of freedom, comfort, and leisure. Following are the details of what is required to prepare the Seder table.

Advanced Planning

On Passover, which is also known as the Festival of Freedom, it is a mitzva to honor the evening with fine, elegant tableware. One should make sure that each of the diners has a cup or a glass for drinking the requisite four cups, and a comfortable, cushioned chair for the obligatory reclining (one may use pillows for this purpose).

One should purchase wine that is certified kosher for Passover, and use only bottles that were not opened before the holiday, making sure to have enough for four cups for each diner. All types of wine are halakhically acceptable for the four cups, but there is a preference for red wine.

While it is definitely preferred to drink actual wine for the four cups, those who find this difficult may use grape juice.

In the time of the Talmud, a small personal table would be set before each diner, on which they would place their food and drink. Nowadays, this practice no longer exists, but there are those who place a special Seder plate before each participant, with the matzot and the other symbolic foods of the Seder: a shank bone, egg, *haroset*, bitter herbs, etc. Others place the Seder plate only at the head of the table, before the leader of the Seder.

Following is a list of items that should be put on the Seder plate, with an explanation of each food. Except for the shank bone and roasted egg, which are not eaten, all the other items are consumed at some point during the Seder, and one must take care in advance that there is sufficient quantity of each type for everyone.

Maror: One of the mitzvot of the Seder that appears in the Torah is the eating of bitter herbs [*maror*], as will be detailed in the *halakhot* of the Seder, in the next section. There are several types of plants that can be used as *maror* on Passover, but the Talmud states that the optimum way of fulfilling the mitzva is with *hazeret*, which is identified as lettuce. Some people are particular to use specifically romaine lettuce. Initially the lettuce plant is not bitter, but after a while its leaves do become bitter, especially after the growth of its inflorescence stalks. There are several reasons given for why it is preferable to use this particular plant.

It should be noted that lettuce leaves often contain very small insects, which are similar in color to its leaves and are therefore not easily detected. These insects do not come off with a light rinse. It is necessary to soak the lettuce in water with dish soap, then to wash the leaves thoroughly, and finally to examine each leaf carefully under a bright light.

In Eastern Europe it was customary to eat horseradish (*ḥrain* in Yiddish) for *maror* instead of lettuce, which was not easily available there. In fact, the horseradish root has erroneously become known as *hazeret* in modern Hebrew. It is a tough root and quite sharp (pungent) and difficult to eat. If it is grated, it is easier to eat and its pungency is somewhat reduced as well. After grinding the horseradish in advance of the holiday, it should be kept in a closed container so that its pungency does not dissipate completely.

There are some people who combine these two practices on the Seder night and eat both lettuce leaves and horseradish. The Seder plate has separate places marked for *maror* and *hazeret*. Some eat lettuce for *maror* and horseradish for *korekh* (the *maror* sandwich; see below). Others eat both types together for both *maror* and *korekh*, after wrapping some of the ground horseradish in lettuce leaves.

📖 **Further reading:** For more on cleaning leafy vegetables from bugs, see p. 549.

Haroset: The source of the custom of dipping *maror* into a mixture known as *haroset* is found in the Mishna. The *haroset* mixture commemorates the mortar with which the children of Israel built the cities of Egypt, as it is stated: "They embittered their lives with hard work, with mortar and with bricks and with all work in the field, all their work with which they worked for them was with travail" (Exodus 1:14). *Haroset* is made from mashed fruit, such as apples, dates, and nuts, to which a little wine and cinnamon is added, so that it can serve as a dip.

There is another reason for the use of *haroset*: In the Song of Songs, the spiritual entity representative of the Jewish people is compared to various fruits, including apples, pomegranates, figs, dates, and nuts. The verse, "Who is that coming up from the wilderness, leaning upon her beloved? Under the apple tree I roused you" (Song of Songs 8:5), directly alludes to the special relationship that was maintained between the people of Israel and God even during the difficult years of bondage in Egypt.

Today one can buy prepared *haroset*, but one must add wine to it. When the Seder night falls on a Shabbat, the wine must be mixed with the *haroset* before Shabbat.

It is customary not to partake of the *haroset* before dipping the bitter herbs into it. After that, one may eat as much as one wishes.

Shank bone: The shank bone [*zeroa*] is placed on the Seder plate as a reminder of the paschal offering. In many Ashkenazic communities, a chicken wing, or sometimes a chicken neck, is used for the *zeroa*. In some communities, part of an animal's front leg is used. Whatever piece of meat is used, the *zeroa* should be roasted in fire; some are particular to cook it before roasting. As it is merely symbolic of the paschal offering, the *zeroa* should not be eaten. This restriction applies only on the Seder night, but after that it may be eaten.

The *zeroa* is also in commemoration of the Torah's statement that God took us out of Egypt "with a mighty hand and with an outstretched arm [*zeroa*]" (Deuteronomy 4:34).

Egg: A hard-boiled egg is placed on the Seder plate as a reminder of the festival peace offering that would be offered in the Temple together with the paschal offering on the fourteenth of Nisan. In many communities it is customary to begin the meal, after the matza and *maror* are eaten, with an egg dipped in salt water.

Karpas: One may use almost any vegetable for *karpas*, although it is highly preferable not to use a vegetable that can be eaten as *maror*. The word *karpas* actually refers to a type of celery, but in various communities other vegetables are used, including potatoes, onions, and radishes.

The *karpas* is dipped in salt water during the Seder. It is recommended to prepare the salt water ahead of time, especially in a year when the Seder takes place on Shabbat.

The Arrangement of the Seder Plate

According to the *halakha*, the order of placement of the items on the Seder plate does not matter, but over the generations, specific traditions have been established in this regard. The most common is that of the Arizal, the kabbalist Rabbi Yitzhak Luria, and it is based on kabbalistic concepts:

First one takes three matzot and places them on top of one another. Many people place a divider between each matza, such as a paper napkin or a cloth. In most of the cloth pouches and matza covers that are sold to be used with the Seder plates, there are cloth dividers sewn in for this purpose. The three matzot (with or without a cloth case) are placed on a plate.

One spreads a cover over the upper matza. If the matzot are in a pouch, there is of course no need for an additional cover. On top of that, one arranges, in small dishes or on napkins, the elements of the Seder plate: At the far right corner, the *zeroa*; at the far left corner, the egg; between these two, but a bit closer to the person, the lettuce; below the lettuce, at the closer right corner, the *haroset*; across from that, at the closer left corner, under the egg, the *karpas*; at a lower point under the lettuce, the *maror* to be used for *korekh*.

The Rema (Rabbi Moshe Isserles, the most authoritative Ashkenazic halakhic authority) had a slightly different arrangement, based on the order in which the Seder plate items are used.

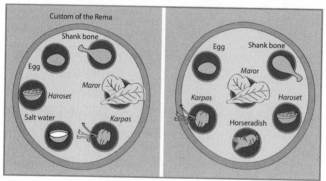

The arrangement of the Seder plate

Final Preparations for the Seder

When preparing for the Seder, it is important to make sure that one has enough *haggadot* for each of the participants. It is customary and appropriate, on Passover even more than on any other festival, to wear fine clothes in honor of the holiday, even finer than those worn on Shabbat. On Seder night in most Ashkenazic communities, it is customary for men who conduct the Seder to wear a *kittel*, the white cloak that is also worn on Yom Kippur.

Before the onset of the festival, one should light a long-burning candle, so that it will be possible to transfer fire from it for cooking and for other uses during the day.

The first day of Passover never comes out on a Friday. Outside of Israel, where every festival mentioned in the Torah is observed for two days, it can happen that the first two days of Passover fall on Thursday and Friday. In that case, one must perform on Wednesday (the day before the holiday) an *eiruv tavshilin*. This enables one to cook (by transferring fire from an existing flame) on Friday, though it is a holy day, in honor of the approaching Shabbat.

📖 **Further reading:** For an explanation of the *eiruv tavshilin* and instructions in how to perform it, see the chapter dealing with *eiruv tavshilin*, p. 474.

Lighting Candles

When the Seder falls on Friday night, one must light the candles before the start of Shabbat and the festival. When the holiday begins on a weekday, some light the candles after the festival has begun, just before the beginning of the Seder. Those who do so must remember that it is prohibited to create a new flame on a holy day, and therefore they must transfer fire from a flame that was lit before the festival began.

📖 **Further reading:** For more details on the *halakhot* of candle lighting, see p. 381.

When lighting the candles, one recites two blessings:

בָּרוּךְ אַתָּה אֲדֹנָי, אֱלֹהֵינוּ מֶלֶךְ הָעוֹלָם, אֲשֶׁר קִדְּשָׁנוּ בְּמִצְוֹתָיו וְצִוָּנוּ לְהַדְלִיק נֵר שֶׁל יוֹם טוֹב (וְאִם חָל בשבת: שֶׁל שַׁבָּת וְשֶׁל יוֹם טוֹב).

Barukh ata Adonai, Eloheinu, melekh ha'olam, asher kideshanu bemitzvotav, vetzivanu lehadlik ner shel yom tov (on Shabbat recite instead: *shel Shabbat veshel yom tov*).

"Blessed are You, Lord our God, King of the universe, who sanctified us through His commandments, and commanded us to light a candle for the festival (on Shabbat recite instead: for Shabbat and the festival)."

This blessing is immediately followed by:

בָּרוּךְ אַתָּה אֲדֹנָי, אֱלֹהֵינוּ מֶלֶךְ הָעוֹלָם, שֶׁהֶחֱיָנוּ וְקִיְּמָנוּ וְהִגִּיעָנוּ לַזְּמַן הַזֶּה.

Barukh ata Adonai, Eloheinu, melekh ha'olam, sheheḥeyanu vekiyemanu vehigi'anu la'zeman hazeh.

"Blessed are You, Lord our God, King of the universe, who has given us life, sustained us, and brought us to this time."

Passover Eve on Shabbat

When Passover falls on a Sunday, this creates a somewhat complicated situation, as one must have already finished most of the preparations for the festival before Shabbat (i.e., two days before the holiday). In addition, one must also observe Shabbat properly, which entails eating meals that include bread. Such timing requires slightly different preparation, as detailed below.

Guidelines and Suggestions

The search for *hametz* that is conducted by candlelight the night before Passover cannot be carried out on Friday night, so it is brought forward to Thursday night (the night between the twelfth and thirteenth of Nisan). Other than that, it is performed in the usual manner.

On Friday morning (the thirteenth of Nisan), the *hametz* should be burned as usual, but at this stage, the declaration of nullification of *hametz* ("All *hametz* or leavened items, etc.") is not yet recited. Some bread should be left over for eating at the Shabbat meals. It is recommended to leave only a minimum amount such that it can be entirely consumed. It is a good idea to use bread that does not crumble easily, such as pita bread.

On Friday before Shabbat, one lights a long-burning candle that will remain lit for more than twenty-four hours. From this candle, one can transfer a flame, after the conclusion of Shabbat, to light the festival candles and also, if one wishes, the fire of the stove for cooking and heating food for the festival.

For the Shabbat meals it is advisable to eat only foods that are kosher for Passover, except for the bread, of course. It is also recommended to use disposable utensils. If one is eating only kosher-for-Passover foods, he may use Passover dishes and utensils, but he must be careful that they do not come into contact with the bread on which he recites the *HaMotzi* blessing at the beginning of the meal. The bread should be eaten outside the house if possible, on a disposable tablecloth or the like, in order to ensure that no crumbs remain in the house. After one has eaten the requisite quantity of bread (see the laws of Shabbat, p. 391), one should remove all remaining bread, brush off one's clothes from any possible crumbs of *hametz*, and then go back to the dining table to continue the meal.

For the morning Shabbat meal, one must remember to finish eating the bread before the final time for eating *hametz*. Then one throws the remaining bread into a public garbage receptacle or flushes it down the toilet. This action replaces the traditional burning of *hametz*, which, of course, is forbidden on Shabbat. At this point, one recites the declaration of the nullification of *hametz* ("All *hametz* or leaven, etc.") which is said every year at the burning of *hametz*.

One should fulfill the mitzva to eat a third Shabbat meal [*seuda shelishit*] with kosher-for-Passover foods, but one may not eat bread or matza at that meal.

When the Seder falls on Saturday night, one should not set the Seder table or make other preparations for the Seder on Shabbat. The reason is that the sanctity of Shabbat is greater than that of the festival, and therefore any activity that involves preparing for the festival on Shabbat is prohibited.

The festival candles should be lit only after Shabbat has already ended. One may not light a new fire, but rather transfer fire from a flame that was already lit on Friday. Before lighting the candles or performing any other actions for the festival that are not permitted on Shabbat, one should recite the formula: "Blessed be He who distinguishes between the holy and the holy," i.e., between the sanctity of Shabbat and the lesser sanctity of the festival.

Passover
Seder Night

The Seder night is at the heart of Passover observance, and the focal point of this night is relating the story of the exodus from Egypt. This is the fulfillment of a biblical mitzva, expressed in the verse: "You shall tell your son on that day, saying: It is because of this that the Lord did this for me upon my exodus from Egypt" (Exodus 13:8). This story has been handed down through the generations for more than 3300 years.

The Seder night is a night of contrasts and balance. It incorporates commandments from the Torah alongside customs established by ancient tradition. Its rites are fixed and organized, and the Passover haggada has an established structure. At the same time, the essence of the night is to facilitate a deep bond and identification of all members of the family – with special emphasis on the children – to the ideas and messages of the Seder. Therefore, it is necessary to be flexible and to adapt the style of the evening to the personalities of those present so that everyone will find something interesting in its contents and feel part of this unique experience.

During the recitation of the haggada, as well as during the meal that follows, one can add in stories, riddles, songs, and so forth. One option is for one person to read the haggada and the others to listen, or it is possible for everyone to read together, or for each participant to recite a passage. It is also possible to sing passages from the haggada. The custom in the Yemenite community is to dramatize the story of slavery and liberty. Some of the participants go outside and then return as though they have arrived from a long journey. Those sitting around the table ask them where they have come from, and they relate the story of the trials and hardships they have "experienced."

The ultimate purpose of this night is for everyone to emerge with a sense of connection and belonging to the exodus narrative, as we ourselves say in the haggada: "Therefore we are obligated to thank, praise, glorify, extol, exalt, honor, bless, revere, and laud the One who performed for our forefathers and for us all these miracles: He took us out from slavery to freedom, from sorrow to joy, from a time of mourning to a festival day, from darkness to a great light, and from enslavement to redemption."

This section will review the main highlights of the Seder and present its varied customs, while noting those rites about which one must be especially careful.

Further discussion: For more on Passover and the exodus, see *A Concise Guide to the Torah*, pp. 135, 161, 315, 471; *A Concise Guide to the Sages*, pp. 84, 306; *A Concise Guide to Mahshava*, p. 93.

Preparing Ahead of Time

In preparing for the night of the Seder, it is important for the head of the family to review the haggada and to familiarize himself with its contents, so that he will be able to navigate the Seder in the best possible way. Prior study of the text of the haggada also enables one to see the coherent and logical progression in its various sections, which from a cursory glance might appear like a disorganized collection of verses and descriptions.

After the Evening Prayer

Immediately after the evening prayer service, one should hurry to get the Seder started, in order that the participants, especially the children, who are a central focus of the Seder, will remain awake and alert until the end of the evening.

The Main Mitzvot

The Seder consists of many details that come together to form a whole, and it is important to determine the significance of the various parts. There are the main points, namely, the mitzvot ordained by the Torah and the rabbinical requirements around which the Seder is constructed, whose fulfillment is the goal of this night. Then there are the customs and additions, which are indeed very important for the creation of the appropriate atmosphere and the overall experience, but whose significance is secondary and can even be dispensed with if necessary. The main mitzvot that must be fulfilled during the course of the Seder are: the story of the exodus from Egypt, eating matza, eating *maror*, drinking the four cups of wine, and reciting *Hallel*.

The Story of the Exodus

The mitzva to relate the story of the exodus from Egypt is the most important commandment of the Seder, and is in fact the main point and the essence of the night. A father has the obligation to fulfill the biblical command to "tell your son" (Exodus 13:8), and thereby to pass down to his children the story of the exodus and link them to the tradition of generations. The questions of *Ma Nishtana* ("How is this night different from all other nights?") that the children ask are meant to be an opening to a discussion of the story of the exodus from Egypt. Therefore, it is clearly not enough to applaud the children's successful chanting of the questions; rather one must provide them with answers that suit their level of understanding and knowledge.

This mitzva has no fixed measure or limit; one can continue learning about and discussing the exodus all night long, as the haggada itself relates concerning the talmudic Sages who expounded on the story of the exodus until sunrise. Those who have the strength to do so can carry on with telling the story of the exodus from Egypt even after the end of the meal and the reading of the entire haggada.

In order to make it easier for one to fulfill this central mitzva, the Sages formulated the *Maggid* section of the haggada, which describes the difficulty of enslavement in Egypt and the miracle of the redemption from slavery and exodus from Egypt.

Even within the section of *Maggid*, certain passages are more important than others, and therefore it is important to read them carefully and understand them fully. Some passages that are of central importance are the following:

(1) The aforementioned *Ma Nishtana* questions call attention to several unusual customs and observances of this night, and serve as an introduction to the story of the exodus from Egypt. Each child asks his father these questions, regardless of the ages of the child and the father. If there is no second-generation individual in the house, the Seder participants pose the questions to each other. Even if one conducts a Seder alone, he must ask these questions to himself aloud.

(2) Another important part of the haggada is the answer to the *Ma Nishtana* questions: "We were slaves to Pharaoh in Egypt, and the Lord our God took us out from there with a strong hand and with an outstretched arm. If the Holy One, blessed be He, had not taken our fathers out of Egypt, then we, our children, and our children's children would have remained enslaved to Pharaoh in Egypt." This answer summarizes the entire story, and it serves as a kind of headline for all that is said later in the haggada.

(3) It is also very important to recite the statement of Rabban Gamliel with regard to "the paschal offering, matza, and *maror*," which comes toward the end of the *Maggid* section. Rabban Gamliel explains the conceptual essence of the paschal offering, and the obligations to eat matza and *maror*. These are key aspects of the obligation to relate the exodus story.

Matza

The mitzva to eat matza is fulfilled three times over the course of the Seder, at the sections called *Motzi*, *Matza*, and *Tzafun* (see below for details of these three sections of the Seder). At *Motzi* and *Matza*, after washing one's hands and reciting the blessings, it is obligatory to eat a halakhically significant quantity of matza. Since one recites two blessings, for the breaking of bread and for the eating of the matza itself, one should consume a double portion.

The quantity that is considered halakhically significant is an olive-bulk [*kezayit*]; that is, the volume of a large olive. Since this measure is not precisely defined, many halakhic authorities accept a stringent measurement and determine that an olive-bulk is about 27 grams, though this amount may appear to be larger than an average olive. Some, however, maintain that the volume of an olive-bulk of matza is equivalent to 15 grams. The first measure equals roughly one-third of an average matza, while the second is approximately one-fifth of a matza.

In order to fulfill the mitzva, it is not enough to occasionally nibble on some matza over the course of the evening. Rather, one must be sure to eat the requisite amount immediately after the blessing. Also, this amount should be eaten without interruption, if possible.

Likewise, at the *Tzafun* section, which is at the end of the meal, one should eat an olive-bulk of matza from the *afikoman* (see below). This matza is eaten to commemorate the paschal offering, which was eaten before midnight and after which nothing else was consumed. Therefore, one should be as stringent as possible about eating the matza of the *afikoman* before the time of halakhic midnight, as publicized in synagogue calendars. After that, one should avoid eating anything else, so that the taste of the *afikoman* will remain in his mouth. It is, however, permitted to drink water after the *afikoman*, as well as the remaining two of the four cups of wine.

The matza must be eaten at the Seder while reclining on one's left side. According to many halakhic authorities, this is essential for the fulfillment of the mitzva. The reason for reclining is that at one time this was the manner of aristocratic diners, who had plenty of leisure time. They would eat in a half-reclining position on special couches made for this purpose, while leaning on their arm so that they could eat in comfort and converse as they ate.

Nowadays, people do not ordinarily recline while eating, but in order to emphasize our status as free people, or even as aristocrats, on the Seder night, we perform the central actions of the Seder, eating the matza and drinking the four cups of wine, while reclining. Each participant sits on his chair and leans on the table or a pillow. Among other reasons, one leans to the left side so that the right hand will be free for using while eating. However, it should be noted that even lefties should lean to their left side rather than to their right.

The obligation of reclining applies to every male over the age of bar mitzva. It is also appropriate for women to recline, although this is not customary in all communities. Each woman should follow the custom of her family and community.

Those people who are unable to eat wheat products, such as those who suffer from celiac disease, should consult a rabbi about how to fulfill the mitzva of eating matza.

Maror

For the mitzva of eating *maror*, which appears in the haggada in the sections of *Maror* and *Korekh*, one must likewise consume an olive-bulk of the bitter herbs immediately after reciting the blessing. This volume, for lettuce leaves, is equivalent to or slightly larger than one large leaf. If one eats horseradish for *maror*, there is no need to be overly stringent, and it is enough to make do with the volume of an actual olive. Those who want to add to this so that they can eat a larger quantity can do so by adding some lettuce to the horseradish.

The *maror* should be dipped in a little *haroset* before eating it. *Haroset* is a symbolic commemoration of the clay with which our forefathers performed backbreaking labor while building cities in Egypt. The *maror* dipped in *haroset* is not eaten while leaning, as it symbolizes bondage, not freedom.

For *Korekh* (literally, "wrap"), it is necessary to take an olive-bulk of *maror* together with an olive-bulk of matza and eat it, as described in the haggada. This *Korekh* is eaten while reclining, because it is also part of the mitzva of eating matza. One must be sure to prepare enough *maror* in advance for all the diners at the Seder.

Drinking the Four Cups

The drinking of the four cups of wine is performed in various stages over the course of the Seder, as follows: the first cup for *Kiddush*; the second cup after the first part of *Hallel*, at the end of *Maggid*, before the meal; the third cup immediately after Grace after Meals; and the fourth cup after concluding *Hallel*.

For the purpose of the mitzva of the four cups, as mentioned earlier, there is a preference for drinking wine, but those who cannot do so or find it difficult may drink natural grape juice.

One must use cups that contain a volume of a *revi'it*. This is about 86 cc, although some are more stringent and require a cup that contains approximately 150 cc. Most standard cups hold more than this amount. From each of the four cups one should drink at least a majority of a *revi'it*, but it is recommended to drink most of the contents of the cup. For purposes of comparison, a standard disposable cup holds 180 cc. (This is stated merely as an aid for estimating the quantity; one should not use a disposable cup for the Seder, but rather a nicer cup or glass.) The four cups should be drunk while reclining to the left.

> Further reading: For more on the symbolism of the four cups, see *A Concise Guide to the Sages*, p. 308.

Reciting *Hallel*

The first part of *Hallel* is recited at the end of *Maggid*, and is followed by the drinking of the second cup of wine. The remainder of the *Hallel* is recited following Grace after Meals and the opening of the door for Elijah the prophet, and is followed by the drinking of the fourth cup. It is important to read all of these passages.

These are the most important aspects of the Seder, and one must be more stringent about these than the other aspects. Old or sick people, young children, or those who for whatever reason cannot participate in the entire Seder, should at least recite the above passages and eat and drink as explained above. If they have any time left, they should add more passages from the haggada and extend the story of the exodus from Egypt as much as they can.

The Seder in Order

Many mitzvot and customs are performed at the Seder. In order to help one remember all of them, the rabbis through the ages provided mnemonics for the sequence of events of this night. The most famous and accepted of them is the one composed by Rabbi Samuel ben Solomon of Falaise (France, thirteenth century). It reads as follows: *Kadesh Urhatz/ Karpas Yahatz/ Maggid Rahtza/ Motzi Matza/ Maror Korekh/ Shulhan Orekh/ Tzafun Barekh/ Hallel Nirtza*. We will make use of this mnemonic to explain each part of the Seder.

Kiddush

Kadesh: *Kiddush* is recited over wine, as on all festivals, in accordance with the text that appears in the haggada. This is the first of the four cups that one will drink at the Seder, and one must remember to drink it while seated and reclining. Each of the participants must have a full cup.

When the Seder is held on Saturday night, the *Kiddush* is combined with *Havdala*, the ceremony separating between the sanctity of Shabbat and the lesser holiness of the festival. The exact formula for such an occasion can be found in the haggada. This *Kiddush-Havdala* ceremony also includes a blessing over a candle: "Who creates the lights of fire." One recites this blessing while looking at a candle that was lit before Shabbat or a candle lit by the transfer of a flame from such a candle. Under no circumstances may one produce a new flame on the festival, and at the end of the *Kiddush-Havdala* one should not extinguish the candle but rather leave it to burn out.

Washing the Hands

Urhatz: This is the washing of hands before eating the *karpas* dipped in salt water. The practice of hand washing before eating is an ancient enactment of the Sages, who ascribe it to King Solomon. This washing of hands was originally intended for the priests [*kohanim*] who eat consecrated foods, but it was later expanded to include anyone eating bread and, according to some opinions, any food dipped in liquid.

Washing one's hands before eating food is not merely for purposes of hygiene, but is performed primarily for ritual purification of the hands. Nowadays, most people wash their hands only before eating bread, but some are careful to wash before eating wet foods as well (i.e., foods that have been dipped in liquid). Many people are not particular about this on a regular basis, in line with the opinion of some authorities that this is not required nowadays. Nevertheless, the practice of washing hands before eating *karpas* dipped in salt water has been preserved over the generations. It is one of many actions that serve to heighten the wonder of the children about the various customs of this special night. This puzzlement is meant to arouse their curiosity about everything that goes on at the Seder table.

The blessing that is usually recited when washing the hands before eating bread or matza ("who commanded us concerning the washing of the hands") is not recited for this particular washing of the hands.

Some have the custom of bringing a cup of water and a bowl to the table, so that the hands can be washed near the table, in the manner of important people who do not get up from the table during dinner.

Eating *Karpas*

Karpas: The *karpas* vegetable is dipped in salt water or vinegar, in accordance with one's custom, and then it is eaten. In the past, it was customary to serve vegetables before a meal as appetizers. Eating vegetables before the meal at the Seder is an ancient custom, whose practice can be traced back to the Second Temple period, and it appears in the Mishna. The Talmud does not specify which vegetables should be eaten, but one should not eat the same vegetables that will later be used for the mitzva of eating *maror*. The early halakhic authorities recommended eating the vegetable called *karpas* (a kind of celery), as they found various allusions and connections between the word *karpas* and the exodus from Egypt. Different vegetables were customarily eaten in Jewish communities around the world, perhaps because the people did not have access to *karpas*, or because the identity of this vegetable was unclear. Today the most prevalent customs are to eat onions, potatoes, or celery.

The dipping of the *karpas* in salt water or vinegar is meant to arouse the wonder of the children. Before eating the *karpas*, the following blessing is recited:

בָּרוּךְ אַתָּה אֲדֹנָי, אֱלֹהֵינוּ מֶלֶךְ הָעוֹלָם, *Barukh ata Adonai, Eloheinu, melekh*
בּוֹרֵא פְּרִי הָאֲדָמָה. *ha'olam, boreh peri ha'adama.*

"Blessed are You, Lord our God, King of the universe, who creates the fruit of the ground."

When reciting the blessing one should also have in mind the vegetable that will be eaten in the meal for maror. One eats only a small amount of karpas, less than an olive-bulk.

Dividing the Matza

Yahatz: One breaks the middle matza of the three into two pieces. The larger portion is hidden away to be used as the *afikoman* (see below), while the smaller part is put back between the two remaining matzot. The main reason for this custom is the statement of the Sages that the Seder should be performed over a broken matza, as matza is called the "bread of poverty" (Deuteronomy 16:3, according to one interpretation), and it is typical of a poor man to eat only pieces of bread, not a whole loaf. With that said, in honor of the festival one should also have two whole matzot, the *lehem mishneh*, the customary two loaves used at every Shabbat and festival meal. Therefore, one places the split matza between the two whole matzot.

The larger piece of matza, which is put aside for the *afikoman*, is usually wrapped in a cloth. Some have the custom of slinging it for a while over the shoulder, like a man carrying a bundle, as described in the verse: "The people carried their dough before it became leavened, their kneading bowls bound in their garments on their shoulders" (Exodus 12:34). Afterward, one places the *afikoman* in a concealed place until the end of the Seder, when it is eaten

Yearly Cycle

in commemoration of the paschal offering, which was consumed at the conclusion of the meal.

In many Ashkenazic communities, it is customary for children to try to find the hiding place of the *afikoman*, from where they take it and conceal it in a hiding place of their own. Later, at the point when the *afikoman* is required for eating, the parents then redeem it from their children by means of a "ransom," a gift of the children's request. The aim of this custom is also to provoke the interest of the children during the Seder and to keep them alert throughout the evening.

Even though this hiding of the *afikoman* is done in good spirits, some communities reject this practice, in order not to teach the children that there is legitimacy in theft.

Reciting the Haggada

Maggid: The participants at the Seder recite the main text of the haggada. These passages include the mitzva of telling the story of the exodus from Egypt as well as the beginning of the *Hallel* prayer. At the end of *Maggid*, the second cup of wine is drunk. During the *Maggid* section, one may drink if he is thirsty.

Washing Hands and Eating Matza

Rahtza: One washes his hands before eating matza. The manner of this washing is identical to the washing before *karpas*, but on this occasion one recites a blessing before wiping the hands:

בָּרוּךְ אַתָּה אֲדֹנָי, אֱלֹהֵינוּ מֶלֶךְ הָעוֹלָם, אֲשֶׁר קִדְּשָׁנוּ בְּמִצְוֹתָיו וְצִוָּנוּ עַל נְטִילַת יָדָיִם.

Barukh ata Adonai, Eloheinu, melekh ha'olam, asher kideshanu bemitzvotav, vetzivanu al netilat yadayim.

"Blessed are You, Lord our God, King of the universe, who sanctified us through His commandments, and commanded us concerning the washing of the hands."

Motzi: The blessing of *HaMotzi* ("who brings forth bread from the earth") is recited on the matza, while holding the two whole matzot with the broken matza between them.

Matza: The Sages instituted a blessing for the mitzva of eating matza:

בָּרוּךְ אַתָּה אֲדֹנָי, אֱלֹהֵינוּ מֶלֶךְ הָעוֹלָם, *Barukh ata Adonai, Eloheinu, melekh*
אֲשֶׁר קִדְּשָׁנוּ בְּמִצְוֹתָיו וְצִוָּנוּ עַל אֲכִילַת *ha'olam, asher kideshanu bemitzvotav,*
מַצָּה. *vetzivanu al akhilat matza.*

"Blessed are You, Lord our God, King of the universe, who sanctified us through His commandments, and commanded us concerning the eating of matza."

While reciting this blessing, it is customary to let go of the lower whole matza, in order to emphasize the broken, "poor" status of the middle matza. Then one eats an olive-bulk from each of the two top matzot, consecutively.

Eating *Maror*
Maror: One recites the blessing:

בָּרוּךְ אַתָּה אֲדֹנָי, אֱלֹהֵינוּ מֶלֶךְ הָעוֹלָם, *Barukh ata Adonai, Eloheinu, melekh*
אֲשֶׁר קִדְּשָׁנוּ בְּמִצְוֹתָיו וְצִוָּנוּ עַל אֲכִילַת *ha'olam, asher kideshanu bemitzvotav,*
מָרוֹר. *vetzivanu al akhilat maror.*

"Blessed are You, Lord our God, King of the universe, who sanctified us through His commandments, and commanded us concerning the eating of *maror*," and then eats an olive-bulk of the *maror*, dipped in a little *haroset*, without reclining, as noted above.

Korekh: A sandwich is prepared from two pieces of matza, totaling an olive-bulk, between which there is an olive-bulk of *maror*. One recites the text that appears in the haggada, dips the *maror* in a bit of *haroset*, and eats the sandwich quickly and while reclining. It is recommended not to delay between eating the matza and the *maror* and the subsequent Korekh, but rather to eat them one after the other.

The Festive Meal
Shulhan Orekh: It is now time for the festive meal. Many Ashkenazic Jews have the custom of starting the meal with a hard-boiled egg dipped in salt water, commemorating the festival peace offering that was the main part of the meal during the Temple period. An egg was chosen for this purpose, as it is a customary food for mourners and reminds us that, sadly, we do not have a Temple today and we are not able to sacrifice offerings.

In most Jewish communities it is customary not to eat roasted meat at the Seder to avoid even the appearance that the food being served is the paschal offering, which had to be roasted. It is of course forbidden to sacrifice the paschal offering or any other offering outside the Temple, or to eat sacrificial meat outside the walls of Jerusalem.

One may eat and drink the festive meal with or without reclining, according to one's preference. During the meal it is permitted to drink additional wine that is not counted among the four cups. There is no limit to the amount of food one may eat at this meal, but it is wise to leave some room for the olive-bulk of the matza for the *afikoman* eaten at the end of the meal. Moreover, one should have a desire to eat the *afikoman* rather than forcing it down despite the fact that he is very full.

During the festive meal it is permitted and even desirable to sing festive songs, and to recount stories relating to the exodus and to redemption in general.

Afikoman

Tzafun: The *afikoman* is retrieved from the place where it was hidden (*tzafun*), and each of the participants eats an olive-bulk from it. Since this broken piece of matza is usually not large enough for an olive-bulk for each of the diners, they may also supplement their portion from other matzot. The *afikoman* is eaten while reclining.

If a child has hidden the *afikoman*, at this stage it is "redeemed" from him. If the child has fallen asleep or demands an excessive "ransom," or is simply unwilling to return it, one may use other matzot for the *afikoman*.

After eating the *afikoman*, one should not eat anything else until the morning, so that the flavor of the *afikoman* will remain in the mouth after the Seder. It is recommended to eat enough during the meal so that one will be full after the *afikoman*.

One should finish eating the *afikoman* matza before halakhic midnight. In the event that one missed this time, he is permitted to eat the *afikoman* even afterward.

Grace after Meals

Barekh: This refers to the blessing [*berakha*] of Grace after Meals. Beforehand, a cup of wine is poured for each of the participants. Then one recites Grace after Meals, remembering to say the *Ya'aleh VeYavo* section in its proper place, as appears in the haggada. When the Seder is held on Shabbat, one adds the *Retzeh* passage as well, before *Ya'aleh VeYavo*.

At the conclusion of Grace after Meals, the blessing is said over the third cup of wine, and it is drunk while reclining.

Before the resumption of *Hallel*, it is customary to pour a large glass of wine (called the cup of Elijah the prophet), which is placed at the center of the table, after which the door of the house should be opened. Some have the custom to announce to Elijah the prophet: "Welcome!"

While the door is open, the participants recite a passage that begins with the following verses: "Pour Your anger upon the nations that do not know You, and upon the kingdoms that do not call in Your name, as they have consumed Jacob; they have consumed him and annihilated him, and they have rendered his abode desolate" (see Jeremiah 10:25). We thereby remind God of the hardships of our people and ask Him to punish our enemies who persecute us. Since this hope will be realized at the final redemption of the Jewish people, it is customary at this stage to pour a cup for Elijah the prophet who, according to the sources (see Malachi 3:23), is the one who will arrive to herald the redemption. Opening the door of the house is also a demonstration of our absolute trust in God and in His protection of us, praying that we may witness the full redemption in merit of our faith in God.

> **Further reading:** Another event at which tradition has it that Elijah is present is a circumcision; see p. 12.

Conclusion of the Seder

Hallel: Now one completes the *Hallel*, which was begun before the meal and then interrupted. Before reciting the rest of the *Hallel*, the fourth cup of wine should be poured, and at the completion of *Hallel*, one drinks the wine while reclining. After drinking the fourth cup, one recites the abridged Grace over the wine, as printed in the haggada.

Nirtza: At the end of the Seder, we express our gratitude for having merited to fulfill it properly, and we offer the hope that it will be pleasing (*nirtza*) before God. We also pray that we will merit to perform the Seder for many more years, and that it will be held "next year, in the rebuilt Jerusalem!"

At the end of most *haggadot* there are liturgical poems and songs with which it is customary to end this special night. In this regard, there are differences among the various communities. Outside Israel there are different liturgical poems for the first Seder and the second Seder. Not everyone has the custom to recite these liturgical poems.

After the Seder has been concluded, some have the custom of reading the book of Song of Songs, as it is interpreted as a metaphorical description of the deep bond between God and the people of Israel, which was expressed at the time of the exodus. Those who have the energy to do so should continue to recount the story of the exodus from Egypt, as related in the haggada that the righteous talmudic scholars "were discussing the exodus from Egypt all that night, until their disciples came and told them: Our Masters! The time has come for reciting the morning *Shema.*"

The Seder night is referred to as a "night of vigilance," based on the verse: "It is a night of vigilance of the Lord to bring them out from the land of Egypt; it is this night for the Lord" (Exodus 12:42). Consequently, on this night we are protected from harmful spiritual forces. Therefore, the reading of *Shema* that is customarily performed every night before one goes to bed is abbreviated on this night. Sections that are recited for protection against those negative spiritual forces are omitted, and one says only the first paragraph of *Shema.*

Passover
The Festival Itself

The previous three sections presented the laws and details that one must know in order to prepare properly for the festival of Passover, various laws and customs of the Seder, and the sequence of events of the Seder. This fourth section on Passover deals with the day-to-day observance of the festival itself.

The First Festival Day

The structure of Passover is very similar to that of the festival of *Sukkot*, which also has a holy day [*yom tov*] at the beginning and at the end, with the intermediate festival days, *Hol HaMoed*, in between them. Outside of Israel, the first two days are *yom tov*, followed by four days of *Hol HaMoed*, and then two final days of *yom tov*.

Morning Prayer Service

The festival morning prayer service is basically the same as the morning service of Shabbat, until the *Amida*. The *Amida* prayer recited is the special one for the three pilgrimage festivals. If the festival falls on Shabbat, there are some changes and minor additions in the formula of the prayer.

After the *Amida* prayer, the congregation recites the complete *Hallel*, which is followed by Kaddish. In some congregations, the Song of the Day is recited at this point.

Torah Reading

Two Torah scrolls are now taken from the ark for the reading of the Torah. Five men are called up for the reading from the first scroll; if it is Shabbat, seven are called up. The reading is from Exodus 12:21–51. This passage includes the commandment for the first paschal offering in Egypt, and it also recounts the plague of the firstborn and the start of the exodus from Egypt. Furthermore, it contains the instruction to inform one's children about the exodus. The second scroll is for the shorter reading of the *maftir*, which deals with the festival offerings that were brought in the Temple on this day (Numbers 28:16–25).

📖 **Further reading:** The Torah reading can be found in *A Concise Guide to the Torah*, p. 162. The *maftir* can be found in *A Concise Guide to the Torah*, p. 412.

After this, the *haftara* is read from the book of Joshua (5:2–6:1). Some preface this reading with three verses from chapter 3 (verses 5–7). This passage describes the first Passover that was celebrated by the children of Israel after they entered the Land of Israel.

Musaf Prayer Service

Next, the congregation recites the festival *Musaf* prayer service, even if the festival falls on a Shabbat.

Starting from the *Musaf* service of this day, one stops saying in the second blessing of the *Amida* the phrase *mashiv haruaḥ umorid hageshem*, "He causes the wind to blow and the rain to descend." In Israel and in some congregations outside of Israel, the phrase *morid hatal*, "He causes the dew to fall," is recited instead from this day on. Therefore, most communities include in this *Musaf* service the "prayer for dew," or the "*tikkun* for dew," which is a sequence of liturgical prayers of praise for God for the descent of dew, together with a request for a dew of blessing in the approaching summer. Some Ashkenazic communities recite this section before the silent *Amida* prayer, in which case they make the change from "He causes the wind to blow and the rain to descend" to "He causes the dew to fall" already in the silent *Amida*. Others recite the prayer for dew in the cantor's repetition of the *Amida*, and therefore they make the switch from "He causes the wind to blow and the rain to descend" to "He causes the dew to fall" only in the repetition.

In those congregations where the change occurs already in the silent *Amida* prayer, the synagogue *gabbai* will announce beforehand in a loud voice: *Morid hatal* ("He causes the dew to fall").

📖 **Further discussion:** For more on the prayer for rain, see *A Concise Guide to the Sages*, p. 352.

The Festive Meal

After returning home from the morning prayer service, *Kiddush* is recited over a full cup of wine and everyone partakes of the festive meal.

The Text of *Kiddush*

For Ashkenazim:

If it is Shabbat, many recite some or all of the following verses:

אִם תָּשִׁיב מִשַּׁבָּת רַגְלֶךָ, עֲשׂוֹת חֲפָצֶךָ בְּיוֹם
קָדְשִׁי. וְקָרָאתָ לַשַּׁבָּת עֹנֶג, לִקְדוֹשׁ אֲדֹנָי
מְכֻבָּד. וְכִבַּדְתּוֹ מֵעֲשׂוֹת דְּרָכֶיךָ, מִמְּצוֹא
חֶפְצְךָ וְדַבֵּר דָּבָר. אָז תִּתְעַנַּג עַל אֲדֹנָי,
וְהִרְכַּבְתִּיךָ עַל בָּמֳתֵי אָרֶץ. וְהַאֲכַלְתִּיךָ
נַחֲלַת יַעֲקֹב אָבִיךָ, כִּי פִּי אֲדֹנָי דִּבֵּר.

Im tashiv miShabbat raglekha asot ḥafatzekha beyom kodshi, vekarata laShabbat oneg likdosh Adonai mekhubad, vekhibadto me'asot derakhekha mimetzo ḥeftzekha vedaber davar, az titanag al Adonai, vehirkavtikha al bamotei aretz, veha'akhaltikha naḥalat Ya'akov avikha, ki pi Adonai diber.

וְשָׁמְרוּ בְנֵי יִשְׂרָאֵל אֶת הַשַּׁבָּת, לַעֲשׂוֹת אֶת
הַשַּׁבָּת לְדֹרֹתָם בְּרִית עוֹלָם. בֵּינִי וּבֵין בְּנֵי
יִשְׂרָאֵל, אוֹת הִיא לְעֹלָם, כִּי שֵׁשֶׁת יָמִים
עָשָׂה אֲדֹנָי אֶת הַשָּׁמַיִם וְאֶת הָאָרֶץ, וּבַיּוֹם
הַשְּׁבִיעִי שָׁבַת וַיִּנָּפַשׁ.

Vesha'meru venei Yisrael et haShabbat, la'asot et haShabbat ledorotam berit olam. Beini uvein benei Yisrael ot hi le'olam, ki sheshet yamim asa Adonai et hashamayim ve'et ha'aretz, uvayom hashevi'i shavat vayinafash.

זָכוֹר אֶת יוֹם הַשַּׁבָּת לְקַדְּשׁוֹ. שֵׁשֶׁת יָמִים
תַּעֲבֹד וְעָשִׂיתָ כָּל מְלַאכְתֶּךָ. וְיוֹם הַשְּׁבִיעִי
שַׁבָּת לַאֲדֹנָי אֱלֹהֶיךָ, לֹא תַעֲשֶׂה כָל
מְלָאכָה אַתָּה וּבִנְךָ וּבִתֶּךָ, עַבְדְּךָ וַאֲמָתְךָ
וּבְהֶמְתֶּךָ, וְגֵרְךָ אֲשֶׁר בִּשְׁעָרֶיךָ. כִּי שֵׁשֶׁת
יָמִים עָשָׂה אֲדֹנָי אֶת הַשָּׁמַיִם וְאֶת הָאָרֶץ,
אֶת הַיָּם וְאֶת כָּל אֲשֶׁר בָּם, וַיָּנַח בַּיּוֹם
הַשְּׁבִיעִי.

Zakhor et yom haShabbat leka'desho. Sheshet yamim ta'avod ve'asita kol melakhtekha. Veyom hashevi'i Shabbat ladonai Elohekha. Lo ta'aseh khol melakha, ata uvinkha uvitekha, avdekha va'amtekha uvhemtekha, vegerekha asher bisharekha. Ki sheshet yamim asa Adonai et hashamayim ve'et ha'aretz, et hayam ve'et kol asher bam, vayanaḥ bayom hashevi'i.

עַל כֵּן בֵּרַךְ אֲדֹנָי אֶת יוֹם הַשַּׁבָּת וַיְקַדְּשֵׁהוּ.

Al ken berakh Adonai et yom haShabbat vayka'deshehu.

אִם חָל בְּיוֹם חוֹל מַתְחִילִים כָּאן:

On a weekday, one starts here:

אֵלֶּה מוֹעֲדֵי אֲדֹנָי, מִקְרָאֵי קֹדֶשׁ, אֲשֶׁר
תִּקְרְאוּ אֹתָם בְּמוֹעֲדָם. וַיְדַבֵּר מֹשֶׁה אֶת
מוֹעֲדֵי אֲדֹנָי אֶל בְּנֵי יִשְׂרָאֵל.

Eleh mo'adei Adonai, mikra'ei kodesh, asher tikre'u otam bemo'adam. Vaydaber Moshe et mo'adei Adonai el benei Yisrael.

סַבְרִי מָרָנָן וְרַבָּנָן וְרַבּוֹתַי. *Savri meranan verabanan verabotai:*

בָּרוּךְ אַתָּה אֲדֹנָי, אֱלֹהֵינוּ מֶלֶךְ הָעוֹלָם, *Barukh ata Adonai, Eloheinu, melekh*
בּוֹרֵא פְּרִי הַגָּפֶן. *ha'olam, boreh peri hagafen.*

"If you restrain your walking because of the Sabbath, pursuing your needs on the day of My holiness and you call the Sabbath a delight and the Lord's sacred, honored, and you honor it by refraining from doing your business, from seeking your needs and from speaking of matters, then you will delight in the Lord and I will mount you onto the heights of the earth and I will feed you the inheritance of Jacob your forefather, for the mouth of the Lord has spoken" (Isaiah 58:13–14).

"The children of Israel shall keep the Sabbath, to observe the Sabbath for their generations an eternal covenant. Between Me and the children of Israel, it is a sign forever. For in six days the Lord made the heaven and the earth and on the seventh day, He rested and was invigorated" (Exodus 31:16–17). "Remember the Sabbath day, to keep it holy. Six days you shall work and perform all your labor. The seventh day is Sabbath for the Lord your God; you shall not perform any labor, you, and your son, and your daughter, your slave, and your maidservant, and your animal, and your stranger who is within your gates, because in six days the Lord made the heavens and the earth, the sea and everything that is in them and He rested on the seventh day; therefore, the Lord blessed the Sabbath day and He sanctified it" (Exodus 20:8–11).

On a weekday, one starts here:

"These are the appointed times of the Lord, holy convocations, that you shall proclaim at their appointed time" (Leviticus 23:4). "And Moses spoke to the children of Israel the appointed times of the Lord" (Leviticus 23:44).

"Attention, masters, gentlemen, my teachers.

"Blessed are You, Lord our God, King of the universe, who creates the fruit of the vine."

For Sephardim:

If it is Shabbat, one starts here:

מִזְמוֹר לְדָוִד, אֲדֹנָי רֹעִי לֹא אֶחְסָר. בִּנְאוֹת *Mizmor LeDavid: Adonai ro'i lo ehsar.*
דֶּשֶׁא יַרְבִּיצֵנִי, עַל מֵי מְנֻחוֹת יְנַהֲלֵנִי. נַפְשִׁי *Binot deshe yarbitzeni, al mei menuhot*
יְשׁוֹבֵב, יַנְחֵנִי בְמַעְגְּלֵי צֶדֶק לְמַעַן שְׁמוֹ. *yenahaleni. Nafshi yeshovev, yanheni*
גַּם כִּי אֵלֵךְ בְּגֵיא צַלְמָוֶת לֹא אִירָא רָע *vema'agelei tzedek lema'an shemo. Gam*
כִּי אַתָּה עִמָּדִי, שִׁבְטְךָ וּמִשְׁעַנְתֶּךָ הֵמָּה *ki elekh begei tzalmavet lo ira ra, ki ata*

יְנַחֲמֻנִי. תַּעֲרֹךְ לְפָנַי שֻׁלְחָן נֶגֶד צֹרְרָי, דִּשַּׁנְתָּ
בַשֶּׁמֶן רֹאשִׁי כּוֹסִי רְוָיָה. אַךְ טוֹב וָחֶסֶד
יִרְדְּפוּנִי כָּל יְמֵי חַיָּי, וְשַׁבְתִּי בְּבֵית אֲדֹנָי
לְאֹרֶךְ יָמִים.

imadi, shivtekha umishantekha hema yenaḥamuni. Ta'arokh lefanai shulḥan neged tzorerai. Dishanta vashemen roshi, kosi revaya. Akh tov vaḥesed yird-efuni kol yemei ḥayay, veshavti beveit Adonai le'orekh yamim.

אִם תָּשִׁיב מִשַּׁבָּת רַגְלֶךָ, עֲשׂוֹת חֲפָצֶךָ בְּיוֹם
קָדְשִׁי, וְקָרָאתָ לַשַּׁבָּת עֹנֶג, לִקְדוֹשׁ אֲדֹנָי
מְכֻבָּד, וְכִבַּדְתּוֹ מֵעֲשׂוֹת דְּרָכֶיךָ, מִמְּצוֹא
חֶפְצְךָ וְדַבֵּר דָּבָר. אָז תִּתְעַנַּג עַל אֲדֹנָי
וְהִרְכַּבְתִּיךָ עַל בָּמֳתֵי אָרֶץ, וְהַאֲכַלְתִּיךָ
נַחֲלַת יַעֲקֹב אָבִיךָ כִּי פִּי אֲדֹנָי דִּבֵּר.

Im tashiv miShabbat raglekha asot ḥafatzekha beyom kodshi, vekarata laShabbat oneg likdosh Adonai mekhu-bad, vekhibadto me'asot derakhekha mimetzo ḥeftzekha vedaber davar, az titanag al Adonai, vehirkavtikha al bamotei aretz, veha'akhaltikha naḥalat Ya'akov avikha, ki pi Adonai diber.

וְשָׁמְרוּ בְנֵי יִשְׂרָאֵל אֶת הַשַּׁבָּת, לַעֲשׂוֹת
אֶת הַשַּׁבָּת לְדֹרֹתָם בְּרִית עוֹלָם. בֵּינִי וּבֵין
בְּנֵי יִשְׂרָאֵל אוֹת הִיא לְעֹלָם, כִּי שֵׁשֶׁת
יָמִים עָשָׂה אֲדֹנָי אֶת הַשָּׁמַיִם וְאֶת הָאָרֶץ,
וּבַיּוֹם הַשְּׁבִיעִי שָׁבַת וַיִּנָּפַשׁ.

Vesha'meru venei Yisrael et HaShabbat, la'asot et HaShabbat ledorotam berit olam. Beini uvein benei Yisrael ot hi le'olam, ki Sheshet yamim asa Adonai et hashamayim ve'et ha'aretz, uvayom hashevi'i shavat vayinafash.

On a weekday, one starts here:

אֵלֶּה מוֹעֲדֵי אֲדֹנָי, מִקְרָאֵי קֹדֶשׁ, אֲשֶׁר
תִּקְרְאוּ אֹתָם בְּמוֹעֲדָם. וַיְדַבֵּר מֹשֶׁה
אֶת מֹעֲדֵי אֲדֹנָי, אֶל בְּנֵי יִשְׂרָאֵל. שָׁלֹשׁ
פְּעָמִים בַּשָּׁנָה יֵרָאֶה כָל זְכוּרְךָ אֶת פְּנֵי
אֲדֹנָי אֱלֹהֶיךָ בַּמָּקוֹם אֲשֶׁר יִבְחָר, בְּחַג
הַמַּצּוֹת וּבְחַג הַשָּׁבֻעוֹת וּבְחַג הַסֻּכּוֹת, וְלֹא
יֵרָאֶה אֶת פְּנֵי אֲדֹנָי רֵיקָם. אִישׁ כְּמַתְּנַת
יָדוֹ, כְּבִרְכַּת אֲדֹנָי אֱלֹהֶיךָ אֲשֶׁר נָתַן לָךְ.

Eleh mo'adei Adonai, mikra'ei kodesh, asher tikre'u otam bemo'adam. Vayda-ber Moshe et mo'adei Adonai el benei Yisrael. Shalosh pe'amim bashana yera'e khol zekhurekha et penei Adonai Elo-hekha bamakom asher yivḥar: Beḥag hamatzot uvḥag hashavuot uvḥag hasukkot. Velo yera'e et penei Adonai reikam. Ish kematenat yado, kevirkat Adonai Elohekha asher natan lakh.

(בשבת: עַל כֵּן בֵּרַךְ אֲדֹנָי אֶת יוֹם הַשַּׁבָּת
וַיְקַדְּשֵׁהוּ).

On Shabbat, add: Al ken berakh Ado-nai et yom haShabbat vayka'deshehu.

סַבְרִי מָרָנָן.

Continue: Savri meranan.

הַשּׁוֹמְעִים עוֹנִים: לְחַיִּים!

Those listening answer: Leḥayim.

בָּרוּךְ אַתָּה אֲדֹנָי, אֱלֹהֵינוּ מֶלֶךְ הָעוֹלָם,   Continue: *Barukh ata Adonai, Elo-*
בּוֹרֵא פְּרִי הַגָּפֶן.   *heinu, melekh ha'olam, boreh peri*
hagefen.

"A psalm by David. The Lord is my Shepherd; I lack nothing. He has me lie down in green pastures; He leads me beside still waters. He restores my soul; He leads me in paths of righteousness for His name's sake. Even when I walk through the valley of the shadow of death, I fear no evil, for You are with me; Your rod and Your staff, they comfort me. You prepare a table before me in the presence of my enemies. You anoint my head with oil; my cup is full. May only goodness and kindness pursue me all the days of my life, and I will dwell in the House of the Lord forever" (Psalms 23).

"If you restrain your walking because of the Sabbath, pursuing your needs on the day of My holiness and you call the Sabbath a delight and the Lord's sacred, honored, and you honor it by refraining from doing your business, from seeking your needs and from speaking of matters, then you will delight in the Lord and I will mount you onto the heights of the earth and I will feed you the inheritance of Jacob your forefather, for the mouth of the Lord has spoken" (Isaiah 58:13–14).

"The children of Israel shall keep the Sabbath, to observe the Sabbath for their generations an eternal covenant. Between Me and the children of Israel, it is a sign forever. For in six days the Lord made the heaven and the earth and on the seventh day, He rested and was invigorated" (Exodus 31:16–17).

On a weekday, one starts here:

"These are the appointed times of the Lord, holy convocations, that you shall proclaim at their appointed time" (Leviticus 23:4). "And Moses spoke to the children of Israel the appointed times of the Lord" (Leviticus 23:44).

"Three times in the year all your males shall appear before the Lord your God in the place that He shall choose: On the Festival of Unleavened Bread, and on the Festival of Weeks, and on the Festival of Tabernacles, and they shall not appear before the Lord empty-handed. Each man according to the gift of his hand, in accordance with the blessing of the Lord your God that He gave you" (Deuteronomy 16:16–17).

(On Shabbat: "Therefore, the Lord blessed the Sabbath day and He sanctified it" (Exodus 20:11).)

"Attention, my masters."

The listeners respond: "To life!"

"Blessed are You, Lord our God, King of the universe, who creates the fruit of the vine."

The breaking of the bread and the blessing of *HaMotzi* ("who brings forth bread from the earth") are, of course, performed on matzot. In Grace after Meals, throughout the festival, the *Ya'aleh VeYavo* section is added.

Afternoon Prayer Service
The festival afternoon prayer service is recited, even if the festival falls on a Shabbat. In such a case, one must pay attention to the minor changes and additions that are made to the prayers.

Second Festival Day Outside Israel
In Israel, the second night of Passover is the beginning of the intermediate festival days [*Hol HaMoed*]. Outside of Israel, however, the second night and day are observed as festival days [*yom tov*] just like the first day, as with all other festivals other than Yom Kippur. This extra day of *yom tov* is called the "second festival day of the exiles." The origin of this second festival day was explained earlier regarding *Sukkot*, on p. 221.

It should be noted that one may not prepare for the second holy day on the first day, even if the preparations do not involve the performance of prohibited labor. For example, one may not set up the second day's candles in the afternoon of the first day, but must wait for nightfall. One may cook extra food on the first day which he will eat on the second day, provided that this does not involve additional effort, e.g., if extra stew ingredients are placed into the same pot.

A Seder is conducted again on the second night, identical to the first Seder, except for a slight difference in the liturgical songs that are recited toward the end of the Seder, as indicated in the haggada.

While the prayers of the second festival day of Passover are basically the same as those of the first day, the main Torah reading differs from that of the first day. It is the same as the Torah reading for the first day of *Sukkot*, which consists of a section of the book of Leviticus (22:26–23:44), which details the laws of the three pilgrimage festivals. The *haftara* is from II Kings (23:1–9, 21–25). This passage recounts the historical observance of Passover by King Josiah and his people. The prayer for dew, which was recited on the first day, is not repeated on this day.

A resident of Israel who is staying abroad for the festival, or one visiting Israel from abroad, should consult with a rabbi ahead of time on how to conduct himself on the second day of the festival.

Counting the *Omer* [*Sefirat HaOmer*]

In the evening prayer service at the conclusion of the first day of Passover, one begins the counting of the *omer*, as explained on p. 331, in fulfillment of the Torah's command: "And you shall count for yourselves... seven weeks; they shall be complete" (Leviticus 23:15).

> **Further reading:** For more on the mitzva of counting of the *omer*, see *A Concise Guide to the Torah*, p. 316.

Havdala

At the end of the second day of *yom tov* (or in Israel, after the first day), *Havdala* is recited on a full cup of wine. The wording of this *Havdala* is identical to the *Havdala* of Shabbat, but without the blessing over the flame and the spices. Likewise, it is customary not to recite the introductory verses before *Havdala*. One recites the blessing over the wine: "who creates the fruit of the vine," followed by the blessing of: "who separates between the sacred and the mundane." If it is a Saturday night, the regular weekly *Havdala* of Shabbat is recited.

Hol HaMoed

On Passover, as on *Sukkot*, the days between the first and last holy days of the festival are called the intermediate festival days [*Hol HaMoed*]. As their name indicates, these are weekdays [*hol*] rather than festival days [*yom tov*], but they maintain certain characteristics of the festival [*moed*]. Certain forms of labor are prohibited, as detailed in the section on the laws of *Hol HaMoed*, p. 471.

Prayers and Customs

The morning and afternoon prayers on *Hol HaMoed* are similar to those of regular weekdays, except that in the *Amida* prayer the *Ya'aleh VeYavo* section is added, with the phrase: "On this day of the Festival of Matzot." *Ya'aleh VeYavo* is also added to Grace after Meals each time it is recited throughout Passover, in the third blessing, the Blessing for Jerusalem (*Rahem*). Likewise, in the abridged Grace recited after drinking wine and after eating foods made of matza meal or fruits of the Seven Species, the festival of Passover is mentioned. After the *Amida* of the morning prayers, the abridged *Hallel* (sometimes called "half *Hallel*") is recited.

It should be noted that beginning with *Hol HaMoed* on Passover, one recites the appropriate summertime formula in the blessing for prosperity (*Barekh Aleinu*) in the weekday *Amida* prayer on a daily basis.

On each day of *Hol HaMoed,* two Torah scrolls are used for the Torah reading. Three men are called up for the reading from the first scroll, and the Torah portion on each day is from a different section of the Torah that discusses Passover. For the second scroll, one man is called up for the reading about the offerings that were sacrificed on Passover in the Temple.

The congregation then prays the *Musaf* service, in which the offerings of Passover are mentioned.

During *Hol HaMoed*, it is worthwhile to take advantage of free time to learn Torah. There is no obligation to eat matza on these days, but according to some halakhic opinions, one who does eat matza during these days fulfills a mitzva.

Shabbat Hol HaMoed

The Shabbat that occurs during the intermediate days is appropriately called *Shabbat Hol HaMoed*. On this Shabbat, the order of prayers is basically the same as on every Shabbat, except that the *Ya'aleh VeYavo* passage is added to the *Amida* prayer, and after the *Amida* the abridged *Hallel* is recited.

In some communities it is customary before the reading of the Torah to read the book of Song of Songs, which is interpreted as a metaphor for, among other ideas, the special connection between God and the people of Israel that was formed at the exodus.

Two Torah scrolls are then taken from the ark for the Torah reading.

Seven men are called up for the reading from the first scroll. The passage is from Exodus (33:12–34:26) and it presents Moses' discussion with God after the sin of the Golden Calf, at which time he was informed of the thirteen attributes of God's mercy. This chapter is read because at its conclusion God commands Moses regarding the three pilgrimage festivals and Shabbat.

Next, one man is called up for the reading of the *maftir* from the second scroll, which discusses the additional offerings sacrificed on Passover in the Temple. This is followed by the *haftara* (Ezekiel 37:1–14) that relates the "vision of the dry bones," which alludes to the future redemption.

After that, the festival *Musaf* service is recited, even if the festival falls on Shabbat.

For the meal of the day, one recites the blessing of *HaMotzi* ("Who brings forth bread from the earth") on two matzot, in place of the two loaves of bread used on a regular festival or Shabbat. In Grace after Meals, the *Retzeh* section is recited in honor of Shabbat, as well as *Ya'aleh VeYavo*, for the festival.

Hametz on Passover

It has already been mentioned that if, after all the cleaning for Passover, one nevertheless finds *hametz* in his home during *Hol HaMoed*, he must flush the *hametz* down the toilet or remove it from the house and burn it. If one finds *hametz* in his house on one of the festival days [*yom tov*] of Passover (the first and last days), or on *Shabbat Hol HaMoed*, he may not move the *hametz* from its place, as it is considered *muktze*, an item that may not be handled on Shabbat or on festival days. In such a case, he must cover the *hametz* with a vessel and after the conclusion of the holy day or Shabbat destroy it by flushing it down the toilet or burning it. If one had sold his hametz to a non-Jew, he should consult with a rabbi about what to do.

The Seventh Day of Passover

The seventh day of Passover is a holy day. It was on this night that the splitting of the Red Sea occurred; the sea was split by God into two, and the Israelites marched through while the pursuing Egyptians entered and drowned. This anniversary has ramifications for the laws and customs of the day, as detailed below. On the day before the holy day, i.e., on the sixth day of Passover, one should get ready as on every festival eve and prepare the table and everything else needed for the festival.

Just before the festival day begins, one should light a long-burning candle, so that it will be possible to transfer fire from it for cooking and for other uses throughout the day.

When the seventh day of Passover falls on Friday, one must make an *eiruv tavshilin* before the start of the festival day, so that it will be permitted to cook and make other preparations on the festival day for Shabbat.

📖 **Further reading:** For the details of the laws of *eiruv tavshilin*, see p. 474.

Candle Lighting

If the seventh day of Passover falls on Shabbat, one must light the festival and Shabbat candles before the entry of Shabbat and the festival. Under no circumstances may one light them on Shabbat.

When the seventh day of Passover falls on a weekday, some are accustomed to light the candles after the festival day has begun, near the start of the evening meal. Those who do so should not create a new flame, but rather they should light the candles from a fire that was burning before the holy day began. When lighting the candles, one recites only one blessing:

בָּרוּךְ אַתָּה אֲדֹנָי, אֱלֹהֵינוּ מֶלֶךְ הָעוֹלָם, אֲשֶׁר קִדְּשָׁנוּ בְּמִצְוֹתָיו וְצִוָּנוּ לְהַדְלִיק נֵר שֶׁל יוֹם טוֹב (וְאִם חָל בְּשַׁבָּת: שֶׁל שַׁבָּת וְשֶׁל יוֹם טוֹב).

Barukh ata Adonai, Eloheinu, melekh ha'olam, asher kideshanu bemitzvotav, vetzivanu lehadlik ner shel yom tov (on Shabbat, say instead: *lehadlik ner shel Shabbat veshel yom tov*).

"Blessed are You, Lord our God, King of the universe, who sanctified us through His commandments, and commanded us to light a candle for the festival (on Shabbat, say instead: for Shabbat and the festival)."

📖 **Further reading:** For more details on the *halakhot* of candle lighting, see p. 381.

The Festival Night

The festival evening prayer service can be found in most prayer books. When the festival falls on Shabbat, the congregation recites before the evening prayers an abbreviated version of *Kabbalat Shabbat*, and at the end of the prayer service they add the passages *Vaykhulu* (Genesis 2:1–3), *Magen Avot* (a condensed form of the *Amida* service), and in some communities Psalms 23.

Kiddush

As on every Friday night or festival night, *Kiddush* is recited over a cup of wine. The formula of this *Kiddush* is identical to the *Kiddush* recited on every festival, except that unlike the other festivals, on this occasion one does not add the *Sheheheyanu* blessing at the end of the *Kiddush*. The reason is that this festival day is a continuation of Passover, not a new festival in its own right, and the *Sheheheyanu* blessing was already recited for Passover, on the first festival night.

Text of Kiddush

For Ashkenazim:

When the festival falls on a Friday night:

(בְּלַחַשׁ: וַיְהִי עֶרֶב וַיְהִי בֹקֶר)   (Quietly: *Vayhi erev vayhi voker*)

יוֹם הַשִּׁשִּׁי, וַיְכֻלּוּ הַשָּׁמַיִם וְהָאָרֶץ וְכָל צְבָאָם. וַיְכַל אֱלֹהִים בַּיּוֹם הַשְּׁבִיעִי   *Yom hashishi. Vaykhulu hashamayim veha'aretz vekhol tzeva'am. Vaykhal*

Yearly Cycle

מְלַאכְתּוֹ אֲשֶׁר עָשָׂה, וַיִּשְׁבֹּת בַּיּוֹם
הַשְּׁבִיעִי מִכָּל מְלַאכְתּוֹ אֲשֶׁר עָשָׂה. וַיְבָרֶךְ
אֱלֹהִים אֶת יוֹם הַשְּׁבִיעִי וַיְקַדֵּשׁ אֹתוֹ,
כִּי בוֹ שָׁבַת מִכָּל מְלַאכְתּוֹ אֲשֶׁר בָּרָא
אֱלֹהִים לַעֲשׂוֹת.

Elohim bayom hashevi'i melakhto ash-
er asa, vayishbot bayom hashevi'i mikol
melakhto asher asa. Vayvarekh Elohim
et yom hashevi'i vaykadesh oto, ki vo
shavat mikol melakhto asher bara Elo-
him la'asot.

אם חל ביום חול מתחילים כאן:

On a weekday one starts here:

סַבְרִי מָרָנָן וְרַבָּנָן וְרַבּוֹתַי:

Savri meranan verabanan verabotai:

בָּרוּךְ אַתָּה אֲדֹנָי, אֱלֹהֵינוּ מֶלֶךְ הָעוֹלָם,
בּוֹרֵא פְּרִי הַגָּפֶן.

Barukh ata Adonai, Eloheinu, melekh
ha'olam, boreh peri hagafen.

בָּרוּךְ אַתָּה אֲדֹנָי, אֱלֹהֵינוּ מֶלֶךְ הָעוֹלָם,
אֲשֶׁר בָּחַר בָּנוּ מִכָּל עָם, וְרוֹמְמָנוּ מִכָּל
לָשׁוֹן וְקִדְּשָׁנוּ בְּמִצְוֹתָיו, וַתִּתֶּן לָנוּ אֲדֹנָי
אֱלֹהֵינוּ בְּאַהֲבָה (בשבת: שַׁבָּתוֹת לִמְנוּחָה
וּ)מוֹעֲדִים לְשִׂמְחָה, חַגִּים וּזְמַנִּים לְשָׂשׂוֹן,
אֶת יוֹם (בשבת: הַשַּׁבָּת הַזֶּה וְאֶת יוֹם)
חַג הַמַּצּוֹת הַזֶּה, זְמַן חֵרוּתֵנוּ (בשבת:
בְּאַהֲבָה), מִקְרָא קֹדֶשׁ זֵכֶר לִיצִיאַת
מִצְרָיִם. כִּי בָנוּ בָחַרְתָּ וְאוֹתָנוּ קִדַּשְׁתָּ
מִכָּל הָעַמִּים, (בשבת: וְשַׁבָּת) וּמוֹעֲדֵי
קָדְשְׁךָ (בשבת: בְּאַהֲבָה וּבְרָצוֹן) בְּשִׂמְחָה
וּבְשָׂשׂוֹן הִנְחַלְתָּנוּ, בָּרוּךְ אַתָּה אֲדֹנָי,
מְקַדֵּשׁ (בשבת: הַשַּׁבָּת וְ) יִשְׂרָאֵל וְהַזְּמַנִּים.

Barukh ata Adonai, Eloheinu, me-
lekh ha'olam, asher bahar banu mikol
am, veromemanu mikol lashon, ve-
kideshanu bemitzvotav. Vatiten lanu
Adonai Eloheinu be'ahava, (on Shab-
bat: Shabbatot limnuha u)mo'adim
lesimha, hagim uzmanim lesason, et
yom (on Shabbat: haShabbat hazeh
ve'et yom) hag hamatzot hazeh, zeman
heruteinu (on Shabbat: be'ahava) mi-
kra kodesh, zekher litziat Mitzrayim.
Ki vanu vaharta ve'otanu kidashta
mikol ha'amim, (on Shabbat: veShab-
bat) umo'adei kodshekha (on Shabbat:
be'ahava uvratzon) besimha uvsason
hinhaltanu. Barukh ata Adonai, me-
kadesh (on Shabbat: haShabbat ve)
Yisrael veha'zemanim.

("It was evening and it was morning,) the sixth day. The heavens and the earth and their entire host were completed. God completed on the seventh day His works that He had made; He rested on the seventh day from all His works that He had made. God blessed the seventh day, and sanctified it; because on it He rested from all His works that God created to make" (Genesis 1:31–2:3).

On a weekday one starts here:

"Attention, masters, gentlemen, my teachers.

"Blessed are You, Lord our God, King of the universe, who creates the fruit of the vine.

"Blessed are You, Lord our God, King of the universe, who has chosen us from all nations, and raised us above all tongues, and sanctified us through His commandments. And You have given us, Lord our God, in love, (on Shabbat add: Shabbatot for rest and) appointed times for joy, festivals and seasonal holidays for gladness, this day of (on Shabbat add: Shabbat and this day of) the Festival of Matzot, the time of our freedom, (on Shabbat add: with love), a holy convocation, in commemoration of the exodus from Egypt. For You have chosen us and sanctified us above all nations, and (on Shabbat add: the Shabbat and) Your holy festivals (on Shabbat add: in love and favor), in joy and in gladness You have given us for an inheritance. Blessed are You, Lord, who sanctifies (on Shabbat add: the Shabbat,) Israel, and the seasonal holidays."

If it is Saturday night, a *Havdala* blessing is recited at the end of *Kiddush*. The *Havdala* blessing is preceded by the blessing over a flame that is always recited in the *Havdala* ceremony after Shabbat. The text of these blessings is as follows:

בָּרוּךְ אַתָּה אֲדֹנָי, אֱלֹהֵינוּ מֶלֶךְ הָעוֹלָם, בּוֹרֵא מְאוֹרֵי הָאֵשׁ.

Blessing over the flame: *Barukh ata Adonai, Eloheinu, melekh ha'olam, boreh me'orei ha'esh.*

בָּרוּךְ אַתָּה אֲדֹנָי, אֱלֹהֵינוּ מֶלֶךְ הָעוֹלָם, הַמַּבְדִּיל בֵּין קֹדֶשׁ לְחוֹל בֵּין אוֹר לְחֹשֶׁךְ בֵּין יִשְׂרָאֵל לָעַמִּים בֵּין יוֹם הַשְּׁבִיעִי לְשֵׁשֶׁת יְמֵי הַמַּעֲשֶׂה. בֵּין קְדֻשַּׁת שַׁבָּת לִקְדֻשַּׁת יוֹם טוֹב הִבְדַּלְתָּ וְאֶת יוֹם הַשְּׁבִיעִי מִשֵּׁשֶׁת יְמֵי הַמַּעֲשֶׂה קִדַּשְׁתָּ הִבְדַּלְתָּ וְקִדַּשְׁתָּ אֶת עַמְּךָ יִשְׂרָאֵל בִּקְדֻשָּׁתֶךָ. בָּרוּךְ אַתָּה אֲדֹנָי, הַמַּבְדִּיל בֵּין קֹדֶשׁ לְקֹדֶשׁ.

Barukh ata Adonai, Eloheinu, melekh ha'olam, hamavdil bein kodesh leḥol, bein or leḥoshekh, bein Yisrael la'amim, bein yom hashevi'i lesheshet yemei hama'aseh. Bein kedushat Shabbat likdushat Yom Tov hivdalta, ve'et yom hashevi'i misheshet yemei hama'aseh kidashta. Hivdalta vekidashta et amekha Yisrael bikdushatekha. Barukh ata Adonai, hamavdil bein kodesh lekodesh.

"Blessed are You, Lord our God, King of the universe, who creates the lights of fire.

"Blessed are You, Lord our God, King of the universe, who distinguishes between sacred and mundane, between light and darkness, between Israel and the [other] nations, between the seventh day and the six days of work. You have distinguished between the sanctity of Shabbat and the sanctity of festivals, and You have sanctified the seventh day above the six days of work. You have distinguished and sanctified Your people Israel with Your sanctity. Blessed are You, Lord, who distinguishes between sacred and sacred."

For Sephardim:

When the festival falls on a Friday night:

וַיְהִי עֶרֶב וַיְהִי בֹקֶר יוֹם הַשִּׁשִּׁי. וַיְכֻלּוּ הַשָּׁמַיִם וְהָאָרֶץ וְכָל צְבָאָם. וַיְכַל אֱלֹהִים בַּיּוֹם הַשְּׁבִיעִי מְלַאכְתּוֹ אֲשֶׁר עָשָׂה, וַיִּשְׁבֹּת בַּיּוֹם הַשְּׁבִיעִי מִכָּל מְלַאכְתּוֹ אֲשֶׁר עָשָׂה. וַיְבָרֶךְ אֱלֹהִים אֶת יוֹם הַשְּׁבִיעִי וַיְקַדֵּשׁ אֹתוֹ, כִּי בוֹ שָׁבַת מִכָּל מְלַאכְתּוֹ אֲשֶׁר בָּרָא אֱלֹהִים לַעֲשׂוֹת.

Vayhi erev vayhi voker yom Hashishi. Vaykhulu hashamayim veha'aretz ve-khol tzeva'am. Vaykhal Elohim bayom hashevi'i melakhto asher asa, vayishbot bayom hashevi'i mikol melakhto asher asa. Vayvarekh Elohim et yom hashevi'i vaykadesh oto, ki vo shavat mikol melakhto asher bara Elohim la'asot.

On a weekday one starts here:

אֵלֶּה מוֹעֲדֵי אֲדֹנָי מִקְרָאֵי קֹדֶשׁ, אֲשֶׁר תִּקְרְאוּ אֹתָם בְּמוֹעֲדָם. וַיְדַבֵּר מֹשֶׁה אֶת מֹעֲדֵי אֲדֹנָי, אֶל בְּנֵי יִשְׂרָאֵל.

Eleh mo'adei Adonai, mikra'ei kodesh, asher tikre'u otam bemo'adam. Vayda-ber Moshe et mo'adei Adonai el benei Yisrael.

סַבְרִי מָרָנָן.

Savri meranan.

הַשּׁוֹמְעִים עוֹנִים: לְחַיִּים!

Those listening answer: *Leḥayim.*

בָּרוּךְ אַתָּה אֲדֹנָי, אֱלֹהֵינוּ מֶלֶךְ הָעוֹלָם, בּוֹרֵא פְּרִי הַגָּפֶן.

Barukh ata Adonai, Eloheinu, melekh ha'olam, boreh peri hagefen.

בָּרוּךְ אַתָּה אֲדֹנָי, אֱלֹהֵינוּ מֶלֶךְ הָעוֹלָם, אֲשֶׁר בָּחַר בָּנוּ מִכָּל עָם, וְרוֹמְמָנוּ מִכָּל לָשׁוֹן, וְקִדְּשָׁנוּ בְּמִצְוֹתָיו. וַתִּתֶּן לָנוּ אֲדֹנָי אֱלֹהֵינוּ בְּאַהֲבָה (בשבת: שַׁבָּתוֹת לִמְנוּחָה וּ)מוֹעֲדִים לְשִׂמְחָה, חַגִּים וּזְמַנִּים לְשָׂשׂוֹן, (בשבת: אֶת יוֹם הַשַּׁבָּת הַזֶּה וְ) חַג הַמַּצּוֹת

Barukh ata Adonai, Eloheinu, me-lekh ha'olam, asher baḥar banu mikol am, veromemanu mikol lashon, ve-kideshanu bemitzvotav. Vatiten lanu Adonai Eloheinu be'ahava, (on Shab-bat: Shabbatot limnuḥa u) mo'adim lesimḥa, ḥagim uzmanim lesason, et yom (on Shabbat: haShabbat hazeh

הַזֶּה. אֶת יוֹם טוֹב מִקְרָא קֹדֶשׁ הַזֶּה,
זְמַן חֵרוּתֵנוּ בְּאַהֲבָה מִקְרָא קֹדֶשׁ, זֵכֶר
לִיצִיאַת מִצְרָיִם. כִּי בָנוּ בָחַרְתָּ, וְאוֹתָנוּ
קִדַּשְׁתָּ מִכָּל הָעַמִּים (בשבת: וְשַׁבָּתוֹת וּ)
מוֹעֲדֵי קָדְשֶׁךָ (בשבת: בְּאַהֲבָה וּבְרָצוֹן)
בְּשִׂמְחָה וּבְשָׂשׂוֹן הִנְחַלְתָּנוּ. בָּרוּךְ אַתָּה
אֲדֹנָי, מְקַדֵּשׁ (בשבת: הַשַּׁבָּת וְ) יִשְׂרָאֵל
וְהַזְּמַנִּים.

*ve) ḥag hamatzot hazeh, et yom tov
mikra kodesh hazeh, zeman ḥeruteinu
be'ahava mikra kodesh, zekher litziat
Mitzrayim. Ki vanu vaḥarta ve'otanu
kidashta mikol ha'amim, (on Shabbat:
veShabbatot) umo'adei kodshekha (on
Shabbat: be'ahava uvratzon) besimḥa
uvsason hinḥaltanu. Barukh ata
Adonai, mekadesh (on Shabbat: Ha-
Shabbat ve) Yisrael veha'zemanim.*

("It was evening and it was morning,) the sixth day. The heavens and the
earth and their entire host were completed. God completed on the seventh
day His works that He had made; He rested on the seventh day from all His
works that He had made. God blessed the seventh day, and sanctified it; because on it He rested from all His works that God created to make" (Genesis
1:31–2:3).

On a weekday one starts here:

"These are the appointed times of the Lord, holy convocations, that you
shall proclaim at their appointed time" (Leviticus 23:4). "And Moses spoke
to the children of Israel the appointed times of the Lord" (Leviticus 23:44).

"Attention, my masters."

The listeners respond: "To life!"

"Blessed are You, Lord our God, King of the universe, who creates the
fruit of the vine.

"Blessed are You, Lord tour God, King of the universe, who has chosen us from all nations, and raised us above all tongues, and sanctified us
through His commandments. And You have given us, Lord our God, in love,
(on Shabbat add: Shabbatot for rest and) appointed times for joy, festivals
and seasonal holidays for gladness, this day of (on Shabbat add: Shabbat
and this day of) the Festival of Matzot, this festival day of holy convocation,
the time of our freedom, with love, in commemoration of the exodus from
Egypt. For You have chosen us and sanctified us above all nations, and (on
Shabbat add: the Shabbatot and) Your holy festivals (on Shabbat add: in
love and favor), in joy and in gladness, You have given us for an inheritance.
Blessed are You, Lord, who sanctifies (on Shabbat add: the Shabbat,) Israel,
and the seasonal holidays."

If it is Saturday night, a *Havdala* blessing is recited at the end of *Kiddush*. The *Havdala* blessing is preceded by the blessing over a flame that is always recited in the *Havdala* ceremony after Shabbat. The text of these blessings is as follows:

בָּרוּךְ אַתָּה אֲדֹנָי, אֱלֹהֵינוּ מֶלֶךְ הָעוֹלָם,
בּוֹרֵא מְאוֹרֵי הָאֵשׁ.

Blessing over the flame: *Barukh ata Adonai, Eloheinu, melekh ha'olam, boreh me'orei ha'esh.*

בָּרוּךְ אַתָּה אֲדֹנָי, אֱלֹהֵינוּ מֶלֶךְ הָעוֹלָם,
הַמַּבְדִּיל בֵּין קֹדֶשׁ לְחוֹל בֵּין אוֹר לְחֹשֶׁךְ
בֵּין יִשְׂרָאֵל לָעַמִּים בֵּין יוֹם הַשְּׁבִיעִי לְשֵׁשֶׁת
יְמֵי הַמַּעֲשֶׂה. בֵּין קְדֻשַּׁת שַׁבָּת לִקְדֻשַּׁת
יוֹם טוֹב הִבְדַּלְתָּ וְאֶת יוֹם הַשְּׁבִיעִי מִשֵּׁשֶׁת
יְמֵי הַמַּעֲשֶׂה קִדַּשְׁתָּ הִבְדַּלְתָּ וְקִדַּשְׁתָּ אֶת
עַמְּךָ יִשְׂרָאֵל בִּקְדֻשָּׁתֶךָ. בָּרוּךְ אַתָּה אֲדֹנָי,
הַמַּבְדִּיל בֵּין קֹדֶשׁ לְקֹדֶשׁ.

Barukh ata Adonai, Eloheinu, melekh ha'olam, hamavdil bein kodesh leḥol, bein or leḥoshekh, bein Yisrael la'amim, bein yom hashevi'i lesheshet yemei hama'aseh. Bein kedushat Shabbat likdushat Yom Tov hivdalta, ve'et yom hashevi'i misheshet yemei hama'aseh kidashta. Hivdalta vekidashta et amekha Yisrael bikdushatekha. Barukh ata Adonai, hamavdil bein kodesh lekodesh.

"Blessed are You, Lord our God, King of the universe, who creates the lights of fire.

"Blessed are You, Lord our God, King of the universe, who distinguishes between sacred and mundane, between light and darkness, between Israel and the [other] nations, between the seventh day and the six days of work. You have distinguished between the sanctity of Shabbat and the sanctity of festivals, and You have sanctified the seventh day above the six days of work. You have distinguished and sanctified Your people Israel with Your sanctity. Blessed are You, Lord, who distinguishes between sacred and sacred."

The blessing of *HaMotzi* ("who brings forth bread from the earth") is then recited on two whole matzot. In Grace after Meals, the *Ya'aleh VeYavo* section is added, and if it is Shabbat, the *Retzeh* passage as well.

Some have the custom of reading on the night of the seventh of Passover the "Song at the Sea" near midnight, which is the time when the splitting of the Red Sea occurred. There are those who do this on the seashore.

Another custom is to learn Torah all night long on the seventh night of Passover. In hasidic communities it is customary to pour some water on the floor of the synagogue at around midnight and dance in the water until it dries, in memory of the splitting of the Red Sea and the transformation of the sea to dry land.

In the morning, the festival morning prayer service is recited, as appears in the prayer books, even when the festival falls on Shabbat. Some have the custom for the prayer leader and the congregation to sing the "Song at the Sea" (Exodus 15:1–18) with a special melody, verse by verse.

After the repetition of the Amida by the prayer leader, the congregation recites the abridged *Hallel*, which is followed by Kaddish and, in some congregations, the Song of the Day. If the seventh day of Passover falls on a Shabbat, some congregations have the custom of reading Song of Songs at this point.

After this, two Torah scrolls are taken out of the ark for the Torah reading.

Torah Reading

Five men are called up for the reading from the first scroll; seven men if it is a Shabbat. The reading is from Exodus (13:17–15:26), a passage which relates the story of the departure of the children of Israel from Egypt, the splitting of the Red Sea, and the "Song at the Sea."

The *maftir* is read from the second scroll and it discusses the Passover additional offerings (Numbers 28:16–25). Afterward, the *haftara* is read (II Samuel 22). It is called the "Song of David," and is reminiscent of the "Song at the Sea" in its general content and manner of composition.

After the *haftara*, the congregation prays the festival *Musaf* service, even if the festival falls on a Shabbat. In Israel, Ashkenazim recite *Yizkor*, a prayer in memory of the departed, before *Musaf*, on this day. Outside of Israel, *Yizkor* is recited on the eighth day of Passover.

After the prayers, *Kiddush* is recited and the festive meal is eaten. The *Kiddush* is identical to that of the first festival day. The breaking of bread and the blessing of *HaMotzi* ("who brings forth bread from the earth") are, of course, performed on matzot. In Grace after Meals the *Ya'aleh VeYavo* section is added.

In the afternoon, one prays the festival afternoon prayer service, even if the festival falls on Shabbat.

The Eighth Day of Passover

Outside of Israel, the eighth day is observed as a festival day [*yom tov*] as well. The observance of this day is the same as the previous day, other than any customs pertaining to the splitting of the sea. There are many who allow various leniencies on this extra day. For example, those who are careful not to eat wetted matza on Passover (*matza sheruya*, or *gebrokts*, matza that has come into contact with water or another liquid) will eat such matza on the eighth day of the festival.

The main Torah reading for the eighth day is a section from Deuteronomy (15:19–16:17), which mentions the three pilgrimage festivals and the counting of the *omer*. Five men are called up for this reading. The *maftir* is the same as the one for the seventh day. If the eighth day of Passover falls on a Shabbat, the main Torah reading is expanded to include Deuteronomy 14:22–16:17, and seven men are called up for the reading. The *haftara* is a passage from Isaiah (10:32–12:6), which includes a famous description of the messianic era, thereby linking the original redemption from Egypt with the final redemption.

Ashkenazic communities recite the *Yizkor* prayer for the deceased before the *Musaf* prayer service.

The Festive "Meal of *Mashiah*"

In various hasidic communities, and especially among Lubavitch Hasidim, it is customary following the afternoon prayer service of the last day of Passover to partake of a third meal, which is called the "the festive meal of *mashiah* [the messiah]." This meal was instituted by the founder of the Hasidic movement, Rabbi Israel Ba'al Shem Tov, with the explanation that "on this day the light of the messiah shines." This meal, which is accompanied by Torah discourses or thoughts, is meant to inculcate and sharpen the belief and longing for the complete redemption. Some have the custom to wash their hands, eat matza, and drink four cups of wine, similar to the Seder. According to mystic sources, the Seder relates to the redemption of the Israelites from Egypt, while the conclusion of Passover is linked to the future redemption.

It is interesting to note that even the Vilna Gaon, who generally did not partake of a third meal on festivals, was particular to do so on the last day of Passover. The accepted reason for his observance of this custom is that this was a special expression of fondness for the mitzva of eating matza by continuing to eat it until the end of Passover.

In Israel, Passover is observed for seven days rather than eight. When the seventh day of Passover falls on Friday, the prohibition against eating and possessing *hametz* lapses at the end of the day in Israel, which means that on Shabbat it is theoretically permitted to eat *hametz* and to keep it in one's house. Nevertheless, for technical reasons there is no way to prepare *hametz*, because as soon as the festival ends, Shabbat has already begun, and therefore, practically speaking, it is as though Passover continues for another day. The implication of this is that one must continue to eat only food that is kosher for Passover, and use only Passover dishes. With that said, even those who are strict not to eat wetted matza throughout Passover may dip their matza in other foods on this Shabbat, even with their Passover utensils. Many Ashkenazim in Israel eat *kitniyot* on this Shabbat.

Havdala

Upon the conclusion of the holiday, *Havdala* is recited over a full cup of wine. The text of this *Havdala* is identical to the *Havdala* of Shabbat, but without the blessings over the candle and the spices. Likewise, the introductory verses before *Havdala* are not recited. One recites the blessing over the wine: "who creates the fruit of the vine," followed by the blessing of: "who separates between the sacred and the secular." If the last day of Passover falls on Shabbat, the *Havdala* will be like that of a regular Saturday night.

📖 **Further reading:** For the laws of *Havdala*, see p. 398.

At the conclusion of Passover, one should put away the Passover utensils and dishes before bringing *hametz* into the house, so that the dishes will not come into contact with *hametz*.

If one wishes to purchase *hametz* from a Jewish owned establishment following the conclusion of Passover, one must be sure to buy it only in a store with a certificate from a reliable organization or rabbi that attests that the owner of the business had sold all his *hametz* before Passover. This is because, as noted in the previous chapter, *hametz* that was in the possession of a Jew during Passover is permanently prohibited to eat or to derive benefit from. One must be careful in this regard during the weeks after Passover as well. If a Jewish store owner did not sell its *hametz*, or if it is uncertain if he did so, one should buy *hametz* products in that store only if the products were produced after Passover.

Isru Hag

The day after any festival is called *Isru Hag*, based on the verse: "Bind the festival offering [*isru hag*] with cords, and thence to the horns of the altar" (Psalms 118:27). This is homiletically interpreted to mean: Attach the days of the festival to the secular weekdays that follow it.

This day has a slightly festive nature, and some enhance the meals eaten on this day in its honor.

The Mimouna

On the night of the conclusion of Passover and on *Isru Hag*, Jews from North Africa hold a celebration called "Mimouna."

Several possible explanations have been offered for this custom. One is that throughout the festival many people were hesitant to eat in the homes of others, due to the severity of the Passover laws. Now they wish to demonstrate that this was certainly not done out of miserliness or lack of consideration, and so immediately after the festival they invite each other to come and eat in their homes. Another explanation is that "Mimouna" is derived from *emuna*, "faith," as according to the Talmud (*Rosh HaShana* 10b), the month of Nisan is a time especially suitable for the messianic redemption. The Mimouna event thus expresses this belief that the redemption will soon arrive.

The Counting of the Omer
And the Second Passover
[Pesah Sheni]

From the start of the second night of Passover, we begin counting the *omer*. This mitzva appears in the Torah: "And you shall count for yourselves from the day after the sabbath, from the day of your bringing of the sheaf [*omer*] of the waving; seven weeks; they shall be complete. Until the day after the seventh week, you shall count fifty days" (Leviticus 23:15–16). The counting of the *omer*, *Sefirat HaOmer* in Hebrew, is performed over the forty-nine days between the first day of Passover and *Shavuot*.

The mitzva of counting the *omer* is incumbent on every Jewish male who is over the age of bar mitzva. Women are not required to fulfill this mitzva because it is performed at a particular time, and women are generally exempt from positive, time-bound mitzvot. Nevertheless, any woman who wishes to count the *omer* may do so, and this is considered praiseworthy.

This section deals with the laws of counting the *omer*, the customs of mourning during the time period of the *omer*, and the reason for these practices. It then goes on to discuss the "second Passover," known as *Pesah Sheni*.

Seven Weeks
The verse from Leviticus cited above states: "Seven weeks; they shall be complete," which is understood to mean that each day should be entirely included in the count. In order for this to be accomplished, it is preferable for the counting to take place at the beginning of the night, which is about half an hour after sunset. For those who pray the evening service in the synagogue, the counting is done immediately after the evening prayers. Nevertheless, one who forgot to count at the beginning of the night may do so all night, with the blessing, and he may even count throughout the following day until sunset, albeit without reciting the blessing (see below).

Before Counting

Before counting the *omer* at night, one recites the following blessing:

בָּרוּךְ אַתָּה אֲדֹנָי, אֱלֹהֵינוּ מֶלֶךְ הָעוֹלָם,
אֲשֶׁר קִדְּשָׁנוּ בְּמִצְוֹתָיו וְצִוָּנוּ עַל סְפִירַת
הָעֹמֶר.

*Barukh ata Adonai, Eloheinu, melekh
ha'olam, asher kideshanu bemitzvotav,
vetzivanu al sefirat ha'omer.*

"Blessed are You, Lord our God, King of the universe, who sanctified us
through His commandments, and commanded us concerning the counting
of the *omer*."

Before the blessing and the counting, some have the custom to recite the
formula of *Leshem yihud* ("For the sake of the unification"), in preparation
for the fulfillment of the mitzva. This passage can be found in prayer books.

How Does One Count?

As cited above, the Torah states: "You shall count fifty days." In another
verse, the Torah states: "You shall count seven weeks for you" (Deuteronomy 16:9). Taken together, these verses indicate that one must count both
the days and the weeks. Therefore, the counting is performed in a manner
that combines the two requirements. On the first day one says: "Today is
one day of the *omer*," and on the next day: "Today is two days of the *omer*,"
and so on. When one reaches the seventh day, he begins to add the number of weeks: "Today is seven days, which are one week, of the *omer*." From
the eighth day onward, one first counts the number of days and then the
number of weeks that have passed plus the days that have been added to the
present week: "Today is eight days, which are one week and one day, of the
omer." The same pattern continues for each of the subsequent days. Following is an example of how to count the thirty-first day:

הַיּוֹם אֶחָד וּשְׁלֹשִׁים יוֹם, שֶׁהֵם אַרְבָּעָה
שָׁבוּעוֹת וּשְׁלֹשָׁה יָמִים לָעֹמֶר (נוסח אשכנז:
בָּעֹמֶר).

*Hayom eḥad ushloshim yom, shehem
arba'a shavuot ushlosha yamim la'omer
(Nusaḥ Ashkenaz: ba'omer).*

"Today is thirty-one days, which are four weeks and three days, in the *omer*."

Sephardim use a slightly different formula:

הַיּוֹם אֶחָד וּשְׁלֹשִׁים יוֹם לָעֹמֶר, שֶׁהֵם
אַרְבָּעָה שָׁבוּעוֹת וּשְׁלֹשָׁה יָמִים.

Hayom ehad ushloshim yom la'omer, shehem arba'ah shavuot ushlosha ya-mim.

"Today is thirty-one days of the *omer*, which are four weeks and three days."

This is the correct way to count the *omer*. Nevertheless, if one specified the right number of days, even if he did not mention the number of weeks, he has still fulfilled the mitzva. If one counts in any language, he has fulfilled the mitzva, provided that he understands that language. One who counts in a language that he does not understand, even if he says the full formula in the exact manner, has not fulfilled the mitzva.

After the counting, there are those who have the custom to recite various additional prayers, some of which are based on the Kabbala. These can be found in prayer books.

📖 **Further reading:** For more on counting the weeks, see *A Concise Guide to Mahshava*, p. 100.

One Who Forgot to Count

One who forgot or did not have a chance to count the *omer* at night should count during the ensuing day, but without reciting the blessing. If he neglected to count one of the days completely, not having counted at night or during the ensuing day, there are halakhic authorities who maintain that from that point onward he may no longer continue counting. Their reasoning is that the forty-nine days of counting the *omer* are a single mitzva, which means that if one day is missing from the count, the entire mitzva is unfulfilled.

According to a different opinion in *halakha*, each day of counting the *omer* is a separate, independent mitzva, and therefore, even if an entire day is missed, one can and should continue to count the following days with the blessing. Since this is subject to dispute, one should continue counting, but without reciting the blessing. It is best for a person in this situation to listen to the blessing of the prayer leader in the synagogue, or to someone else who is reciting the blessing, to intend to fulfill his own obligation with this blessing, and respond: Amen, before counting for himself.

If one is uncertain as to whether or not he counted on a given day, he should continue to count on the following days with a blessing.

The Prohibition of *Hadash*

During the Temple period, the *omer* offering was brought on the first day of the counting, the sixteenth of Nisan, which is the first day of the intermediate days of Passover in Israel. The first harvested barley sheaf was brought to the Temple as a sacrifice together with an accompanying animal offering. This act served to permit the consumption of that year's new produce, which could not be eaten before the *omer* offering was brought (Leviticus 23:14). The term "new produce," or, in Hebrew, *hadash*, refers to grain that took root after the *omer* offering of the previous year.

Even today, when there is no *omer* offering, it is prohibited to eat grain from the new produce of the year until the end of the second day of Passover. In Israel, the Chief Rabbinate does not give kosher certification to any product that contains grain that is *hadash*. Outside of Israel, most organizations that certify products as kosher do not concern themselves with the possible presence of *hadash* grain, relying on the fact that most of the grain in the market is not *hadash*, and that according to some authorities this prohibition does not apply to grain grown outside of Israel. However, some are careful to eat only products that are known not to contain any *hadash* grain; such products are called *yashan* (literally, "old").

📖 **Further reading:** For more on the *omer* offering, see *A Concise Guide to the Torah*, p. 316; *A Concise Guide to the Sages*, p. 158.

Mourning Customs

During some of the days of the period of the counting of the *omer*, several mourning customs are practiced: Weddings are not held and one may not have a haircut. According to some, one should try to avoid reciting the *Sheheheyanu* blessing, which is normally said when buying significant new items of clothing or major household goods, or when tasting a fruit for the first time in its season. Some are strict about not listening to instrumental music. The reason for this observance of mourning is that according to a tradition of the Sages, 24,000 students of Rabbi Akiva (who was from the third generation of the tannaitic period and one of the greatest and most influential scholars of that period) died in a plague during these days, because they did not treat one another with respect.

Calculating the Days

The period during which Rabbi Akiva's students died was thirty-three or thirty-four days. Accordingly, some observe the customs of mourning only until *Lag BaOmer*, the thirty-third day of the *omer* counting, which, according to one tradition, was the day that the students of Rabbi Akiva stopped dying. Ashkenazim are lenient with regard to the observance of mourning on *Lag BaOmer* itself (the eighteenth of Iyar), whereas Sephardim continue with some of the mourning practices until the following day, the thirty-fourth of the *omer* (the nineteenth of Iyar).

In contrast, some begin the mourning period only from the first of Iyar, because Nisan is a month during which mourning should not be observed. They then continue until the day before the festival of *Shavuot*, with the exception of *Lag BaOmer*, on which, according to all opinions, no students died. Here too, the number of days of mourning amounts to thirty-three.

Some observe the customs of mourning throughout the period of the counting of the *omer*, except for the days of Passover, *Rosh Hodesh* Iyar, *Rosh Hodesh* Sivan, Shabbatot, and *Lag BaOmer*, which together add up to sixteen days. Taking into account these days of exception, the days of mourning are once again thirty-three.

In light of the different customs, it is appropriate for each person to ask his rabbi how to conduct himself regarding the *omer* and its observances. This is particularly relevant in determining possible wedding dates during the period of the *omer*.

The Second Passover

The fourteenth day of Iyar is known as *Pesah Sheni*, or the Second Passover. On this day during the Temple period, there was an additional opportunity to bring the paschal offering, for those who were unable to bring the offering on the proper date (the fourteenth of Nisan) because they were ritually impure on that day or situated too far from the Temple. Such individuals would bring their offering on the fourteenth of Iyar instead, and eat matza with it. It was not necessary for them to remove all *hametz* from their homes even though they were bringing the paschal offering.

Customs of the Day

Today, although offerings are no longer sacrificed, there are still some customs that are observed in recognition of the special status of the Second Passover:

In the prayers of this day, *Tahanun* (a prayer of supplication omitted on festive occasions) is not recited. Some have the custom of not saying *Tahanun* already in the afternoon prayer preceding the Second Passover (the thirteenth of Iyar), as on every other eve of a festival.

Some people eat matza on the Second Passover, to commemorate the paschal offering that was eaten with matza. Some eat it on the night before the fourteenth, while others do so during the day, but the most correct custom would seem to be to eat the matza at the end of the day, i.e., on the night following the fourteenth of Iyar, as that is the time when they would eat the paschal offering in the Temple.

In some hasidic circles, it is customary for the Rebbe to hold a special meal, including words of Torah that focus on the nature of the day and its unique qualities. Some even conduct a kind of Seder on this night.

📖 **Further reading:** For more on the Second Passover, see *A Concise Guide to the Torah*, p. 364; *A Concise Guide to the Sages*, p. 182; *A Concise Guide to Mahshava*, p. 314.

Lag BaOmer

Between Passover and *Shavuot,* there is a special day of celebration called *Lag BaOmer,* which falls on the eighteenth of Iyar, the thirty-third day of the *omer.* (For more on the *omer* counting, see the previous section.)

There are two main reasons for *Lag BaOmer* celebrations: First, this date marks the end of the plague that broke out in the days of the renowned *tanna* Rabbi Akiva, which killed 24,000 of his students. According to the Talmud (*Yevamot* 62b), the spiritual cause of the plague was "because they did not treat one another with respect." On *Lag BaOmer,* the students of Rabbi Akiva stopped dying, and therefore we rejoice on this date. Second, this is believed to be the anniversary of the death of the *tanna* Rabbi Shimon bar Yohai, whose kabbalistic teachings are collected in the Zohar. In the hours leading up to his death, his students gathered around him and he revealed before them the most hidden secrets of the Torah and requested that they adopt the practice of annually marking the date of his death with joy and celebration.

> **Further reading:** For more on the Zohar, see *A Concise Guide to Mahshava,* p. 328. For more about Rabbi Akiva, his life and death, see *A Concise Guide to the Sages,* pp. 335, 364.

The Customs of the Day

The celebratory nature of *Lag BaOmer* is observed through the omission of *Tahanun* in the day's prayers, and through other customs that have developed over the generations.

Lighting Bonfires

On the night of *Lag BaOmer,* it is customary to light candles or bonfires in memory of Rabbi Shimon Bar Yohai, and to sing liturgical poems composed in his honor. The most well-known lighting is the one performed at the tomb of Rabbi Shimon in Meron, in the Galilee, with the participation of hasidic rabbis and tens of thousands of celebrants. This custom is based on the comparison of the Torah to light, as it is stated: "For the commandment is a lamp, and the Torah is light" (Proverbs 6:23), and likewise, the Torah is likened to fire, as it is written: "So is My word like fire, the utterance of the Lord" (Jeremiah 23:29). Since Rabbi Shimon bar Yohai was one of the greatest Torah scholars of his generation, who also revealed the secrets of the Torah, it became customary to light bonfires on the anniversary of the day of his passing. Moreover, it is related in the Zohar that when Rabbi Shimon revealed the secrets of Kabbala to his students, the house was filled with light and fire to such an extent that the students could not approach and look at their rabbi.

In a year when *Lag BaOmer* falls on a Sunday, in which case the bonfires are lit after the conclusion of Shabbat, it is very important not to light them nor even to start the preparations (by collecting firewood and the like) before the end of Shabbat. There is no value in acting "in honor of Rabbi Shimon" if it is done through the desecration of Shabbat, which is prohibited by Torah law.

Pilgrimage to Meron

In Israel it is popular to travel to the tomb of Rabbi Shimon Bar Yohai in Meron and participate in the lighting of bonfires and reciting of prayers in an atmosphere of great joy that prevails at the site throughout the day of *Lag BaOmer*. On this day, some recite the passage from the Zohar called *Idra Zuta*, which tells the story of the day of Rabbi Shimon Bar Yohai's passing and the secrets of the Torah that he uttered to his disciples on the day of his death.

The Custom of the First Haircut [*Upsherin* or *Halaka*]

Some have the custom not to cut the hair of young boys until they turn three years old. Among those with such a practice, many give the first haircut, often called an *upsherin* or *halaka*, on *Lag BaOmer*. This is because it is the first opportunity to cut the hair of boys who turned three between Passover and *Lag BaOmer* due to the mourning customs that are practiced during this time period. The child's first haircut is of special educational importance, as one leaves the boy with sidelocks or *pe'ot* (the hair that grows parallel to and slightly above the ears) on both sides of his head.

In Israel, some have the custom of taking their sons to the grave of the *tanna* Rabbi Shimon bar Yohai in Meron, in order to combine the haircutting with the celebrations that are conducted there. According to tradition, this was the practice of the renowned kabbalist Rabbi Yitzhak Luria, as he took his three-year-old son to the grave of Rabbi Shimon and cut his hair there.

Going Out to Nature

In many communities, *Lag BaOmer* is a kind of holiday celebrated by educators who teach Torah to children, and also by the children themselves. On this day, the teachers and pupils venture out together to the fields to take in the fresh air and talk about the greatness of Rabbi Shimon bar Yohai.

In the past, it was customary, and some even continue the practice to this day, to play with bows and arrows. Two reasons have been suggested for this custom: First, because in the days of Rabbi Shimon no rainbow was seen in the sky. This expresses the greatness of his merit, as he protected his generation to such an extent that they did not need the sign that God gave after the flood of His oath not to destroy the world again (see Genesis 9:13).

Second, there is a tradition that teachers in the days of the Romans (during the period of Rabbi Akiva and Rabbi Shimon) went to teach Torah to Jewish children, which was an activity that was strictly forbidden by the government. So as not to be seen studying Torah, they would move away from inhabited areas and do it secretly, out in nature. The children would come equipped with bows and arrows, and if a Roman soldier happened upon the place, they would take them out and pretend to be practicing shooting.

Sivan and Shavuot

The third of the three pilgrimage festivals is *Shavuot*, which falls on the sixth of Sivan. It is called *Shavuot* ("weeks") because it is celebrated exactly seven weeks after Passover, as it is stated: "You shall count seven weeks for you... You shall hold the Festival of Weeks to the Lord your God" (Deuteronomy 16:9–10). Other names of the festival that are mentioned in the Torah are "the festival of the harvest" (Exodus 23:16) and "the day of the first fruits" (Numbers 28:26), as the crops are harvested at this time of year, and when the Temple was standing they would bring a special offering of loaves from the new flour of the year (Leviticus 23:17). *Shavuot* is also referred to as "the time of the giving of our Torah" in the prayer service, because on this day, the sixth of Sivan, the children of Israel received the Torah at Mount Sinai. Therefore, most of the customs of this festival are connected to the giving of the Torah and its acceptance by the Israelites.

In ancient times, the Jewish calendar was determined on a month-by-month basis by a central religious court in accordance with the testimony of witnesses who would come before them and testify that they had seen the new moon. Since the Torah does not specify a date for *Shavuot*, stating only that it occurs on the fiftieth day after the first day of Passover, the festival could have fallen on the fifth or the seventh of Sivan as well, as the preceding months of Nisan and Iyar could each consist of twenty-nine or thirty days. Nowadays, when there is a fixed yearly calendar, the first day of *Shavuot* always occurs on the sixth of Sivan.

On *Shavuot* (as on Passover and *Sukkot*), all the people of Israel were commanded to undertake a pilgrimage to the Temple and to bring their offerings there. Like the months of Nisan and Tishrei, when Passover and *Sukkot* are observed, there is also a celebratory element to the month of Sivan, due to the festival. This festive quality is reflected mainly in the fact that *Tahanun* (a prayer of supplication, which is omitted on festive occasions) is not recited for almost the entire first half of the month, as detailed below.

Shavuot is a holiday [*yom tov*], a festival day on which the laws of Shabbat apply, according to their unique application to festival days. This section presents the laws and customs of the days before *Shavuot*, the festival itself, and the days that follow.

The Start of the Month

Tahanun Is Not Recited

During the first part of the month of Sivan, *Tahanun* is not recited, for several reasons.

The first day of Sivan is *Rosh Hodesh*, and *Tahanun* is never recited on *Rosh Hodesh*.

The second day of Sivan is called *Yom HaMeyuhas*, the "Day of Distinction," and this is also a reason not to say *Tahanun*. Two explanations have been offered for the name "Day of Distinction."

(1) It is on this day that God said to the children of Israel: "You shall be for Me a kingdom of priests and a holy nation" (Exodus 19:6), and the people of Israel thereby received a special "distinction."

(2) This day has a particular distinction because it occurs between *Rosh Hodesh* and the three days before *Shavuot*, which are called the "three days of demarcation," during which the Israelites surrounded Mount Sinai and prepared themselves for the receiving of the Torah (Exodus 19:15). Accordingly, it was determined that *Tahanun* should not be recited on this day either.

As mentioned, the third, fourth, and fifth days of Sivan are known as the "three days of demarcation." God commanded the children of Israel to demarcate Mount Sinai so no one would ascend, and to encamp around it. They were to use these days to prepare themselves physically and spiritually in a variety of ways to receive the Torah. Even today these are considered festive days, on which *Tahanun* is not recited.

The sixth and seventh days of Sivan are *Shavuot* itself. The following day (or in Israel, the seventh of Sivan) is called *Isru Hag*, and it is considered a festive day.

For the next several days (through the twelfth of Sivan), many communities do not recite *Tahanun*, because these are "days of compensation" for the festival (see explanation at the end of the section, p. 357).

> **Further reading:** For a description of the days leading up to the receiving of the Torah, see *A Concise Guide to the Torah*, p. 180.

Preparations for the Festival

In addition to preparing the festival meals, there are other important preparations that are carried out before the onset of the festival, including ones that are unique to *Shavuot*.

Decorating the Home

On the eve of the festival, many people decorate their homes and synagogues with green vegetation. The reason for this custom is twofold: First, the Midrash derives from the verse: "The flocks and the cattle shall not graze before that mountain" (Exodus 34:3), that Mount Sinai was covered with greenery in anticipation of the giving of the Torah there. Another reason, based on a mishna (*Rosh HaShana* 1:2), is that on *Shavuot* we are judged concerning the fruits that will grow on our trees during the upcoming year, and the decorative vegetation reminds us to request from God that the trees should yield a substantial and quality harvest.

Final Preparations

There are other things that one should do on the eve of *Shavuot*:

One should leave a twenty-four-hour candle burning before the holiday, so that it will be possible to transfer fire from it for cooking and other uses during the holiday.

When the holiday occurs on a Friday, one must make an *eiruv tavshilin* before the start of *Shavuot*, so that it will be permitted to cook food on the holiday for the adjacent Shabbat, and also to light the Shabbat candles toward the end of the holiday.

📖 **Further reading:** For the laws of *eiruv tavshilin*, see p. 474.

Candle Lighting

If *Shavuot* is on a Sunday, one must be careful to light the festival candles only after Shabbat has ended. This time is generally listed in synagogue calendars. The candles must be lit from an existing flame that was lit before Shabbat. Before lighting the candles, one should recite the formula: "Blessed be He who separates between the sacred and the sacred," that is, between the more intense holiness of Shabbat and the lesser holiness of the holiday. Under no circumstances may one light the candles any earlier, as this would be a desecration of Shabbat.

When *Shavuot* falls on a weekday, some are accustomed to light the candles at the start of the festival, before sundown, while others light them after the holiday has already begun, just before the beginning of the meal. Those who light after the festival has started should use only an existing flame; that is, they should light a match from a fire that was burning before the festival began. One may not produce a new fire on the holiday itself.

When lighting the candles, one recites two blessings:

בָּרוּךְ אַתָּה אֲדֹנָי, אֱלֹהֵינוּ מֶלֶךְ הָעוֹלָם,
אֲשֶׁר קִדְּשָׁנוּ בְּמִצְוֹתָיו וְצִוָּנוּ לְהַדְלִיק נֵר
שֶׁל יוֹם טוֹב.

Barukh ata Adonai, Eloheinu, melekh ha'olam, asher kideshanu bemitzvotav, vetzivanu lehadlik ner shel yom tov.

"Blessed are You, Lord our God, King of the universe, who sanctified us through His commandments, and commanded us to light a candle for the festival."

בָּרוּךְ אַתָּה אֲדֹנָי, אֱלֹהֵינוּ מֶלֶךְ הָעוֹלָם,
שֶׁהֶחֱיָנוּ וְקִיְּמָנוּ וְהִגִּיעָנוּ לַזְּמַן הַזֶּה.

Barukh ata Adonai, Eloheinu, melekh ha'olam, sheheheyanu vekiyemanu vehigi'anu la'zeman hazeh.

"Blessed are You, Lord our God, King of the universe, who has given us life, sustained us, and brought us to this time."

📖 **Further reading:** For more details regarding the *halakhot* of candle lighting, see p. 381. For more on the festival of *Shavuot*, see *A Concise Guide to the Sages*, p. 309; *A Concise Guide to Mahshava*, p. 99.

The Night of the Festival

In addition to the standard festival prayers, as well as *Kiddush* and the festive meal, the night of *Shavuot* has the special status of a "night of guarding," on which it is customary to stay awake and devote time to Torah study and to reciting the *Tikkun Leil Shavuot*.

Evening Prayer

The festival evening prayer can be found in most prayer books. This prayer service is generally started relatively late on *Shavuot* night, so that the period of the counting of the *omer* will be complete, in accordance with the commandment of the Torah: "Seven weeks; they shall be complete" (Leviticus 23:15), as explained in the previous section.

The Meal

Kiddush: As is done on the eve of every Shabbat and festival, *Kiddush* is recited over a full cup of wine.

📖 **Further reading:** For details of the laws of *Kiddush*, see p. 386.

The Wording of *Kiddush*

For Ashkenazim:

When *Shavuot* is on Friday night, begin here:

(בלחש - וַיְהִי עֶרֶב וַיְהִי בֹקֶר) יוֹם הַשִּׁשִּׁי,
וַיְכֻלּוּ הַשָּׁמַיִם וְהָאָרֶץ וְכָל צְבָאָם. וַיְכַל
אֱלֹהִים בַּיּוֹם הַשְּׁבִיעִי מְלַאכְתּוֹ אֲשֶׁר
עָשָׂה, וַיִּשְׁבֹּת בַּיּוֹם הַשְּׁבִיעִי מִכָּל מְלַאכְתּוֹ
אֲשֶׁר עָשָׂה. וַיְבָרֶךְ אֱלֹהִים אֶת יוֹם הַשְּׁבִיעִי
וַיְקַדֵּשׁ אֹתוֹ, כִּי בוֹ שָׁבַת מִכָּל מְלַאכְתּוֹ
אֲשֶׁר בָּרָא אֱלֹהִים לַעֲשׂוֹת.

(Quietly: *Vayhi erev vayhi voker*) *yom hashishi. Vaykhulu hashamayim veha'aretz vekhol tzeva'am. Vaykhal Elohim bayom hashevi'i melakhto asher asa, vayishbot bayom hashevi'i mikol melakhto asher asa. Vayvarekh Elohim et yom hashevi'i vaykadesh oto, ki vo shavat mikol melakhto asher bara Elohim la'asot.*

On weekdays begin here:

סַבְרִי מָרָנָן וְרַבָּנָן וְרַבּוֹתַי.

Savri meranan verabanan verabotai:

בָּרוּךְ אַתָּה אֲדֹנָי, אֱלֹהֵינוּ מֶלֶךְ הָעוֹלָם,
בּוֹרֵא פְּרִי הַגָּפֶן.

Barukh ata Adonai, Eloheinu, melekh ha'olam, boreh peri hagafen.

בָּרוּךְ אַתָּה אֲדֹנָי, אֱלֹהֵינוּ מֶלֶךְ הָעוֹלָם,
אֲשֶׁר בָּחַר בָּנוּ מִכָּל עָם, וְרוֹמְמָנוּ מִכָּל
לָשׁוֹן וְקִדְּשָׁנוּ בְּמִצְוֹתָיו, וַתִּתֶּן לָנוּ אֲדֹנָי
אֱלֹהֵינוּ בְּאַהֲבָה (בשבת: שַׁבָּתוֹת לִמְנוּחָה
וּ)מוֹעֲדִים לְשִׂמְחָה, חַגִּים וּזְמַנִּים לְשָׂשׂוֹן,
אֶת יוֹם (בשבת: הַשַּׁבָּת הַזֶּה וְאֶת יוֹם)
חַג הַשָּׁבוּעוֹת הַזֶּה, זְמַן מַתַּן תּוֹרָתֵנוּ
(בשבת: בְּאַהֲבָה), מִקְרָא קֹדֶשׁ זֵכֶר
לִיצִיאַת מִצְרָיִם. כִּי בָנוּ בָחַרְתָּ וְאוֹתָנוּ
קִדַּשְׁתָּ מִכָּל הָעַמִּים, (בשבת: וְשַׁבָּת)
וּמוֹעֲדֵי קָדְשֶׁךָ (בשבת: בְּאַהֲבָה וּבְרָצוֹן)
בְּשִׂמְחָה וּבְשָׂשׂוֹן הִנְחַלְתָּנוּ, בָּרוּךְ אַתָּה
אֲדֹנָי, מְקַדֵּשׁ (בשבת: הַשַּׁבָּת וְ) יִשְׂרָאֵל
וְהַזְּמַנִּים.

Barukh ata Adonai, Eloheinu, melekh ha'olam, asher bahar banu mikol am, veromemanu mikol lashon, vekideshanu bemitzvotav. Vatiten lanu Adonai Eloheinu be'ahava, (on Shabbat: Shabbatot limnuha u)mo'adim lesimha, hagim uzmanim lesason, et yom (on Shabbat: hashabbat hazeh ve'et yom) hag haShavuot hazeh, zeman matan toratenu (on Shabbat: be'ahava) mikra kodesh, zekher litziat Mitzrayim. Ki vanu vaharta ve'otanu kidashta mikol ha'amim, (on Shabbat: veShabbat) umo'adei kodshekha (on Shabbat: be'ahava uvratzon) besimha uvsason hinhaltanu. Barukh ata Adonai, mekadesh (on Shabbat: haShabbat ve)Yisrael veha'zemanim.

When *Shavuot* is on Shabbat, begin here:

(Quietly: "It was evening and it was morning,) the sixth day. The heavens and the earth and their entire host were completed. God completed on the seventh day His works that He had made; He rested on the seventh day from all His works that He had made. God blessed the seventh day, and sanctified it; because on it He rested from all His works that God created to make" (Genesis 1:31–2:3).

On weekdays begin here:

"Attention, my masters, gentlemen, teachers.

"Blessed are You, Lord our God, King of the universe, who creates the fruit of the vine.

"Blessed are You, Lord our God, King of the universe, who has chosen us from all nations, and raised us above all tongues, and sanctified us through His commandments. And You have given us, Lord our God, in love, appointed times for joy, festivals and seasonal holidays for gladness, this day of the festival of *Shavuot*, the time of the giving of our Torah, a holy convocation, in commemoration of the exodus from Egypt. For You have chosen us and sanctified us above all nations, and Your holy festivals, in joy and in gladness You have given us for an inheritance. Blessed are You, Lord, who sanctifies Israel and the seasonal holidays."

When *Shavuot* begins on Saturday night, it is necessary to incorporate *Havdala* into the *Kiddush* in order to distinguish between the sanctity of Shabbat and the lesser sanctity of the festival. Therefore, two additional blessings are added at this point in the *Kiddush*. First one brings a candle that was lit before Shabbat, or one lights a candle from an existing flame. It is important to note that one may not extinguish any flame on the festival. The following blessings are then recited:

בָּרוּךְ אַתָּה אֲדֹנָי, אֱלֹהֵינוּ מֶלֶךְ הָעוֹלָם, בּוֹרֵא מְאוֹרֵי הָאֵשׁ.

Barukh ata Adonai, Eloheinu, melekh ha'olam, boreh me'orei ha'esh.

בָּרוּךְ אַתָּה אֲדֹנָי, אֱלֹהֵינוּ מֶלֶךְ הָעוֹלָם, הַמַּבְדִּיל בֵּין קֹדֶשׁ לְחוֹל בֵּין אוֹר לְחֹשֶׁךְ בֵּין יִשְׂרָאֵל לָעַמִּים בֵּין יוֹם הַשְּׁבִיעִי לְשֵׁשֶׁת יְמֵי הַמַּעֲשֶׂה. בֵּין קְדֻשַּׁת שַׁבָּת לִקְדֻשַּׁת יוֹם טוֹב הִבְדַּלְתָּ וְאֶת יוֹם הַשְּׁבִיעִי מִשֵּׁשֶׁת יְמֵי הַמַּעֲשֶׂה קִדַּשְׁתָּ הִבְדַּלְתָּ וְקִדַּשְׁתָּ אֶת

Barukh ata Adonai, Eloheinu, melekh ha'olam, hamavdil bein kodesh leḥol, bein or leḥoshekh, bein Yisrael la'amim, bein yom hashevi'i lesheshet yemei hama'aseh. Bein kedushat Shabbat likdushat Yom Tov hivdalta, ve'et yom hashevi'i misheshet yemei hama'aseh kidashta. Hivdalta vekidashta et

עַמְּךָ יִשְׂרָאֵל בִּקְדֻשָּׁתֶךָ. בָּרוּךְ אַתָּה אֲדֹנָי,
הַמַּבְדִּיל בֵּין קֹדֶשׁ לְקֹדֶשׁ.

amekha Yisrael bikdushatekha. Barukh ata Adonai, hamavdil bein kodesh lekodesh.

"Blessed are You, Lord our God, King of the universe, who creates the lights of fire.

"Blessed are You, Lord our God, King of the universe, who distinguishes between sacred and mundane, between light and darkness, between Israel and the [other] nations, between the seventh day and the six days of work. You have distinguished between the sanctity of Shabbat and the sanctity of festivals, and You have sanctified the seventh day above the six days of activity. You have distinguished and sanctified Your people Israel with Your sanctity. Blessed are You, Lord, who distinguishes between sacred and sacred."

The additional section for the conclusion of Shabbat ends here.

As on the other festivals, at the end of *Kiddush* one adds the *Sheheheyanu* blessing on both nights (some place a new fruit on the table on the second night, so that one can look at it and have it in mind when the blessing is recited):

בָּרוּךְ אַתָּה אֲדֹנָי, אֱלֹהֵינוּ מֶלֶךְ הָעוֹלָם,
שֶׁהֶחֱיָנוּ וְקִיְּמָנוּ וְהִגִּיעָנוּ לַזְּמַן הַזֶּה.

Barukh ata Adonai, Eloheinu, melekh ha'olam, sheheheyanu vekiyemanu vehigi'anu la'zeman hazeh.

"Blessed are You, Lord our God, King of the universe, who has given us life, sustained us, and brought us to this time."

For Sephardim:

When *Shavuot* is on Friday night, begin here:

(בלחש - וַיְהִי עֶרֶב וַיְהִי בֹקֶר) יוֹם הַשִּׁשִּׁי,
וַיְכֻלּוּ הַשָּׁמַיִם וְהָאָרֶץ וְכָל צְבָאָם. וַיְכַל
אֱלֹהִים בַּיּוֹם הַשְּׁבִיעִי מְלַאכְתּוֹ אֲשֶׁר
עָשָׂה, וַיִּשְׁבֹּת בַּיּוֹם הַשְּׁבִיעִי מִכָּל מְלַאכְתּוֹ
אֲשֶׁר עָשָׂה. וַיְבָרֶךְ אֱלֹהִים אֶת יוֹם הַשְּׁבִיעִי
וַיְקַדֵּשׁ אֹתוֹ, כִּי בוֹ שָׁבַת מִכָּל מְלַאכְתּוֹ
אֲשֶׁר בָּרָא אֱלֹהִים לַעֲשׂוֹת.

(Quietly: *Vayhi erev vayhi voker*) *yom hashishi. Vaykhulu hashamayim veha'aretz vekhol tzeva'am. Vaykhal Elohim bayom hashevi'i melakhto asher asa, vayishbot bayom hashevi'i mikol melakhto asher asa. Vayvarekh Elohim et yom hashevi'i vaykadesh oto, ki vo shavat mikol melakhto asher bara Elohim la'asot.*

346

On weekdays begin here:

אֵלֶּה מוֹעֲדֵי אֲדֹנָי מִקְרָאֵי קֹדֶשׁ, אֲשֶׁר תִּקְרְאוּ אֹתָם בְּמוֹעֲדָם. וַיְדַבֵּר מֹשֶׁה אֶת מֹעֲדֵי אֲדֹנָי אֶל בְּנֵי יִשְׂרָאֵל.

Eleh moʿadei Adonai, mikraʾei kodesh, asher tikreʾu otam bemoʿadam. Vaydaber Moshe et moʿadei Adonai el benei Yisrael.

סַבְרִי מָרָנָן.

Savri meranan.

הַשּׁוֹמְעִים עוֹנִים: לְחַיִּים!

Those listening answer: *Lehayim.*

בָּרוּךְ אַתָּה אֲדֹנָי, אֱלֹהֵינוּ מֶלֶךְ הָעוֹלָם, בּוֹרֵא פְּרִי הַגָּפֶן.

Barukh ata Adonai, Eloheinu, melekh haʿolam, boreh peri hagefen.

בָּרוּךְ אַתָּה אֲדֹנָי, אֱלֹהֵינוּ מֶלֶךְ הָעוֹלָם, אֲשֶׁר בָּחַר בָּנוּ מִכָּל עָם, וְרוֹמְמָנוּ מִכָּל לָשׁוֹן, וְקִדְּשָׁנוּ בְּמִצְוֹתָיו. וַתִּתֶּן לָנוּ אֲדֹנָי אֱלֹהֵינוּ בְּאַהֲבָה (בשבת: שַׁבָּתוֹת לִמְנוּחָה וּ)מוֹעֲדִים לְשִׂמְחָה, חַגִּים וּזְמַנִּים לְשָׂשׂוֹן, (בשבת: אֶת יוֹם הַשַּׁבָּת הַזֶּה וְ)אֶת יוֹם חַג הַשָּׁבוּעוֹת הַזֶּה. אֶת יוֹם טוֹב מִקְרָא קֹדֶשׁ הַזֶּה, זְמַן מַתַּן תּוֹרָתֵנוּ בְּאַהֲבָה מִקְרָא קֹדֶשׁ, זֵכֶר לִיצִיאַת מִצְרָיִם. כִּי בָנוּ בָחַרְתָּ, וְאוֹתָנוּ קִדַּשְׁתָּ מִכָּל הָעַמִּים (בשבת: וְשַׁבָּתוֹת וּ)מוֹעֲדֵי קָדְשְׁךָ (בשבת: בְּאַהֲבָה וּבְרָצוֹן) בְּשִׂמְחָה וּבְשָׂשׂוֹן הִנְחַלְתָּנוּ. בָּרוּךְ אַתָּה אֲדֹנָי, מְקַדֵּשׁ (בשבת: הַשַּׁבָּת וְ) יִשְׂרָאֵל וְהַזְּמַנִּים.

Barukh ata Adonai, Eloheinu, melekh haʿolam, asher bahar banu mikol am, veromemanu mikol lashon, vekideshanu bemitzvotav. Vatiten lanu Adonai Eloheinu beʾahava, (on Shabbat: Shabbatot limnuha u)moʿadim lesimha, hagim uzmanim lesason, (on Shabbat: et yom haShabbat hazeh ve) et yom hag haShavuot hazeh, et yom tov mikra kodesh hazeh, zeman matan toratenu beʾahava mikra kodesh, zekher litziat Mitzrayim. Ki vanu vaharta veʾotanu kidashta mikol haʾamim, (on Shabbat: veShabbatot) umoʿadei kodshekha (on Shabbat: beʾahava uvratzon) besimha uvsason hinhaltanu. Barukh ata Adonai, mekadesh (on Shabbat: HaShabbat ve) Yisrael vehaʾzemanim.

When *Shavuot* is on Shabbat, begin here:

(Quietly: "It was evening and it was morning,) the sixth day. The heavens and the earth and their entire host were completed. God completed on the seventh day His works that He had made; He rested on the seventh day from all His works that He had made. God blessed the seventh day, and sanctified it; because on it He rested from all His works that God created to make" (Genesis 1:31–2:3).

On weekdays begin here:

"These are the appointed times of the Lord, holy convocations, that you shall proclaim at their appointed time" (Leviticus 23:4). "And Moses spoke to the children of Israel the appointed times of the Lord" (Leviticus 23:44).

"Attention, my masters."

The listeners respond: "To life!"

"Blessed are You, Lord our God, King of the universe, who creates the fruit of the vine.

"Blessed are You, Lord our God, King of the universe, who has chosen us from all nations, and raised us above all tongues, and sanctified us through His commandments. And You have given us, Lord our God, in love, appointed times for joy, festivals and seasonal holidays for gladness, this day of the festival of *Shavuot*, this festival day of holy convocation, the time of the giving of our Torah, with love, in commemoration of the exodus from Egypt. For You have chosen us and sanctified us above all nations, and Your holy festivals, in joy and in gladness You have given us for an inheritance. Blessed are You, Lord, who sanctifies Israel and the seasonal holidays."

When *Shavuot* begins on Saturday night, it is necessary to incorporate *Havdala* into the *Kiddush* in order to distinguish between the sanctity of Shabbat and the lesser sanctity of the festival. Therefore, two additional blessings are added at this point in the *Kiddush*. First one brings a candle that was lit before Shabbat, or one lights a candle from an existing flame. It is important to note that one may not extinguish any flame on the festival. The following blessings are then recited:

בָּרוּךְ אַתָּה אֲדֹנָי, אֱלֹהֵינוּ מֶלֶךְ הָעוֹלָם, בּוֹרֵא מְאוֹרֵי הָאֵשׁ.

Barukh ata Adonai, Eloheinu, melekh ha'olam, boreh me'orei ha'esh.

בָּרוּךְ אַתָּה אֲדֹנָי, אֱלֹהֵינוּ מֶלֶךְ הָעוֹלָם, הַמַּבְדִּיל בֵּין קֹדֶשׁ לְחוֹל בֵּין אוֹר לְחֹשֶׁךְ בֵּין יִשְׂרָאֵל לָעַמִּים בֵּין יוֹם הַשְּׁבִיעִי לְשֵׁשֶׁת יְמֵי הַמַּעֲשֶׂה. בֵּין קְדֻשַּׁת שַׁבָּת לִקְדֻשַּׁת יוֹם טוֹב הִבְדַּלְתָּ וְאֶת יוֹם הַשְּׁבִיעִי מִשֵּׁשֶׁת יְמֵי הַמַּעֲשֶׂה קִדַּשְׁתָּ הִבְדַּלְתָּ וְקִדַּשְׁתָּ אֶת עַמְּךָ יִשְׂרָאֵל בִּקְדֻשָּׁתֶךָ. בָּרוּךְ אַתָּה אֲדֹנָי, הַמַּבְדִּיל בֵּין קֹדֶשׁ לְקֹדֶשׁ.

Barukh ata Adonai, Eloheinu, melekh ha'olam, hamavdil bein kodesh lehol, bein or lehoshekh, bein Yisrael la'amim, bein yom hashevi'i lesheshet yemei hama'aseh. Bein kedushat Shabbat likdushat Yom Tov hivdalta, ve'et yom hashevi'i misheshet yemei hama'aseh kidashta. Hivdalta vekidashta et amekha Yisrael bikdushatekha. Barukh ata Adonai, hamavdil bein kodesh lekodesh.

"Blessed are You, Lord our God, King of the universe, who creates the lights of fire.

"Blessed are You, Lord our God, King of the universe, who distinguishes between sacred and mundane, between light and darkness, between Israel and the [other] nations, between the seventh day and the six days of work. You have distinguished between the sanctity of Shabbat and the sanctity of festivals, and You have sanctified the seventh day above the six days of activity. You have distinguished and sanctified Your people Israel with Your sanctity. Blessed are You, Lord, who distinguishes between sacred and sacred."

The additional section for the conclusion of Shabbat ends here.

As on the other festivals, at the end of *Kiddush* one adds the *Sheheheyanu* blessing on both nights (some place a new fruit on the table on the second night, so that one can look at it and have it in mind when the blessing is recited):

בָּרוּךְ אַתָּה אֲדֹנָי, אֱלֹהֵינוּ מֶלֶךְ הָעוֹלָם, שֶׁהֶחֱיָנוּ וְקִיְּמָנוּ וְהִגִּיעָנוּ לַזְּמַן הַזֶּה.

Barukh ata Adonai, Eloheinu, melekh ha'olam, sheheheyanu vekiyemanu vehigi'anu la'zeman hazeh.

"Blessed are You, Lord our God, King of the universe, who has given us life, sustained us, and brought us to this time."

The blessing of *HaMotzi*: The blessing is recited over two whole loaves of bread. After the meal, Grace after Meals is recited with the addition of the *Ya'aleh VeYavo* section.

Tikkun Leil Shavuot

On the night of *Shavuot*, it is customary to conduct an all-night study vigil. Many concentrate on a prescribed set of selections from various Torah sources, called *Tikkun Leil Shavuot*. It consists mainly of the first and last verses of each weekly portion in the Torah, and also the first and last verses from the books of the Prophets and the Writings. Some have the custom to also read the first and last mishna of each of the sixty-three tractates of the Talmud, a list of the 613 commandments, and certain passages from the Zohar.

This custom of *Tikkun Leil Shavuot* was originally instituted by the kabbalists of Safed, based on a statement of the Zohar. The meaning of the word *tikkun* in Aramaic is "decoration"; just as one decorates a bride on the eve of her marriage, likewise, through reciting the *tikkun* one adorns the Torah before accepting it anew.

Another explanation for this custom is that it is based on the statement of the Midrash that on the night of the sixth of Sivan, the children of Israel sank into a deep sleep, so that in the morning, Moses had to wake them and hurry them to gather around Mount Sinai to receive the Torah. In order to make up for this behavior, we remain awake all night long, waiting eagerly for the Ten Commandments, which are read from the Torah in the morning.

Just before dawn, some people immerse themselves in a *mikva*, as part of their spiritual preparation for receiving the Torah.

Over the course of the generations, many communities developed the practice of conducting different types of study sessions all night on *Shavuot*, including independent Torah study as well as a variety of lectures. Some maintain that these are less preferable alternatives to the saying of the formulated *tikkun*, which is the main custom of this night.

At the end of the recitation of the *tikkun*, some have the custom of praying the morning prayer service in a manner called *vatikin*, which means that *Shema* is recited just before sunrise, and exactly at the moment of sunrise, the *Amida* prayer is recited. Others first go home to rest and then reconvene for the morning prayers after a few hours of sleep, so that they will be able to concentrate properly on their prayers.

📖 **Further reading:** For more on *Tikkun Leil Shavuot*, see *A Concise Guide to Mahshava*, p. 99.

The Festival Day
After the preparations that last the whole night, the great moment arrives when the Ten Commandments are read from the Torah. This reading is considered a kind of reenactment of the giving of the Torah at Sinai.

Morning Prayers
In the morning, the congregation prays the festival morning prayer service, as appears in prayer books. After the *Amida* prayer, the full *Hallel* is recited. Afterward, *Kaddish* is said and, in some congregations, the Song of the Day is recited at this point. Two Torah scrolls are removed from the synagogue ark.

Torah Reading and the Additional Prayer [*Musaf*]
Five men are called up for the reading from the first scroll, a passage from Exodus (19:1–20:22) that recounts the giving of the Torah. By reading this

passage from the Torah on *Shavuot*, it is considered as though we ourselves are standing at the foot of Mount Sinai and receiving the Torah. According to Chabad custom, it is appropriate to bring children of all ages, and even babies, to hear the Ten Commandments being read as, according to the Midrash, the young children of Israel played an important role in God's decision to give us the Torah.

The second scroll is for the shorter reading of the *maftir*, which discusses the additional festival offerings (Numbers 28:26–31) for *Shavuot*. The man called up for the *maftir* then reads the *haftara*, which is from the book of Ezekiel (1:1–28; 3:12). This *haftara* describes the Divine Chariot, the divine revelation experienced by the prophet Ezekiel. This vision is reminiscent of God's revelation to the people of Israel at Mount Sinai.

There is a custom to recite certain liturgical poems before the reading of the Torah. Ashkenazim recite the liturgical rhyme *Akdamut*, a poem in Aramaic that describes the praise of the Torah and the reward of those who study it.

Sephardim chant the poem *Ketuba*, by Rabbi Yisrael Najara, which is written as a kind of marriage contract [*ketuba*] between God and Israel, who are compared to a groom and bride.

Afterward, the congregation recites the festival *Musaf* prayer.

The Festive Meal
After the prayer service, *Kiddush* is recited, followed by the festival meal.

The Text of *Kiddush*

For Ashkenazim:

On Shabbat, many begin with all or some of the following verses:

אִם תָּשִׁיב מִשַּׁבָּת רַגְלֶךָ, עֲשׂוֹת חֲפָצֶךָ בְּיוֹם קָדְשִׁי. וְקָרָאתָ לַשַּׁבָּת עֹנֶג, לִקְדוֹשׁ אֲדֹנָי מְכֻבָּד. וְכִבַּדְתּוֹ מֵעֲשׂוֹת דְּרָכֶיךָ, מִמְּצוֹא חֶפְצְךָ וְדַבֵּר דָּבָר. אָז תִּתְעַנַּג עַל אֲדֹנָי, וְהִרְכַּבְתִּיךָ עַל בָּמֳתֵי אָרֶץ. וְהַאֲכַלְתִּיךָ נַחֲלַת יַעֲקֹב אָבִיךָ, כִּי פִי אֲדֹנָי דִּבֵּר.

Im tashiv miShabbat raglekha asot ḥafatzekha beyom kodshi, vekarata laShabbat oneg likdosh Adonai mekhubad, vekhibadeto me'asot derakheikha mimetzo ḥeftzekha vedaber davar, az titanag al Adonai, vehirkavtikha al bamotei aretz, veha'akhaltikha naḥalat Ya'akov avikha, ki pi Adonai diber.

וְשָׁמְרוּ בְנֵי יִשְׂרָאֵל אֶת הַשַּׁבָּת, לַעֲשׂוֹת אֶת הַשַּׁבָּת לְדֹרֹתָם בְּרִית עוֹלָם. בֵּינִי וּבֵין בְּנֵי יִשְׂרָאֵל, אוֹת הִיא לְעֹלָם, כִּי שֵׁשֶׁת יָמִים עָשָׂה אֲדֹנָי אֶת הַשָּׁמַיִם וְאֶת הָאָרֶץ, וּבַיּוֹם הַשְּׁבִיעִי שָׁבַת וַיִּנָּפַשׁ.

Vesha'meru venei Yisrael et haShabbat, la'asot et haShabbat ledorotam berit olam. Beini uvein benei Yisrael ot hi le'olam, ki sheshet yamim asa Adonai et hashamayim ve'et ha'aretz, uvayom hashevi'i shavat vayinafash.

זָכוֹר אֶת יוֹם הַשַּׁבָּת לְקַדְּשׁוֹ. שֵׁשֶׁת יָמִים תַּעֲבֹד וְעָשִׂיתָ כָּל מְלַאכְתֶּךָ. וְיוֹם הַשְּׁבִיעִי שַׁבָּת לַאדֹנָי אֱלֹהֶיךָ, לֹא תַעֲשֶׂה כָל מְלָאכָה אַתָּה וּבִנְךָ וּבִתֶּךָ, עַבְדְּךָ וַאֲמָתְךָ וּבְהֶמְתֶּךָ, וְגֵרְךָ אֲשֶׁר בִּשְׁעָרֶיךָ. כִּי שֵׁשֶׁת יָמִים עָשָׂה אֲדֹנָי אֶת הַשָּׁמַיִם וְאֶת הָאָרֶץ, אֶת הַיָּם וְאֶת כָּל אֲשֶׁר בָּם, וַיָּנַח בַּיּוֹם הַשְּׁבִיעִי.

Zakhor et yom haShabbat lekadesho. Sheshet yamim ta'avod ve'asita kol melakhtekha. Veyom hashevi'i Shabbat ladonai Elohekha. Lo ta'aseh khol melakha, ata uvinkha uvitekha, avdekha va'amtekha uvhemtekha, vegerekha asher bisharekha. Ki sheshet yamim asa Adonai et hashamayim ve'et ha'aretz, et hayam ve'et kol asher bam, vayanaḥ bayom hashevi'i.

עַל כֵּן בֵּרַךְ אֲדֹנָי אֶת יוֹם הַשַּׁבָּת וַיְקַדְּשֵׁהוּ.

Al ken berakh Adonai et yom haShabbat vayka'deshehu.

אִם חָל בְּיוֹם חוֹל מַתְחִילִים כָּאן:

On weekdays, start here:

אֵלֶּה מוֹעֲדֵי אֲדֹנָי, מִקְרָאֵי קֹדֶשׁ, אֲשֶׁר תִּקְרְאוּ אֹתָם בְּמוֹעֲדָם. וַיְדַבֵּר מֹשֶׁה אֶת מוֹעֲדֵי אֲדֹנָי אֶל בְּנֵי יִשְׂרָאֵל.

Eleh mo'adei Adonai, mikra'ei kodesh, asher tikre'u otam bemo'adam. Vaydaber Moshe et mo'adei Adonai el benei Yisrael.

סַבְרִי מָרָנָן וְרַבָּנָן וְרַבּוֹתַי.

Savri meranan verabanan verabotai:

בָּרוּךְ אַתָּה אֲדֹנָי, אֱלֹהֵינוּ מֶלֶךְ הָעוֹלָם, בּוֹרֵא פְּרִי הַגָּפֶן.

Barukh ata Adonai, Eloheinu, melekh ha'olam, boreh peri hagafen.

On Shabbat, many begin with all or some of the following verses:

"If you restrain your walking because of the Sabbath, pursuing your needs on the day of My holiness and you call the Sabbath a delight and the Lord's sacred, honored, and you honor it by refraining from doing your business, from seeking your needs and from speaking of matters, then you will delight in the Lord and I will mount you onto the heights of the earth and I will feed you the inheritance of Jacob your forefather, for the mouth of the Lord has spoken" (Isaiah 58:13–14).

"The children of Israel shall keep the Sabbath, to observe the Sabbath for their generations an eternal covenant. Between Me and the children of Israel, it is a sign forever. For in six days the Lord made the heaven and the earth and on the seventh day, He rested and was invigorated" (Exodus 31:16–17). "Remember the Sabbath day, to keep it holy. Six days you shall work and perform all your labor. The seventh day is Sabbath for the Lord your God; you shall not perform any labor, you, and your son, and your daughter, your slave, and your maidservant, and your animal, and your stranger who is within your gates, because in six days the Lord made the heavens and the earth, the sea and everything that is in them and He rested on the seventh day; therefore, the Lord blessed the Sabbath day and He sanctified it" (Exodus 20:8–11).

On weekdays, begin here:

"These are the appointed times of the Lord, holy convocations, that you shall proclaim at their appointed time" (Leviticus 23:4). "And Moses spoke to the children of Israel the appointed times of the Lord" (Leviticus 23:44).

"Attention, my masters, gentlemen, teachers.

"Blessed are You, Lord our God, King of the universe, who creates the fruit of the vine."

For Sephardim:

On Shabbat, begin here:

מִזְמוֹר לְדָוִד, אֲדֹנָי רֹעִי לֹא אֶחְסָר. בִּנְאוֹת דֶּשֶׁא יַרְבִּיצֵנִי, עַל מֵי מְנֻחוֹת יְנַהֲלֵנִי. נַפְשִׁי יְשׁוֹבֵב, יַנְחֵנִי בְמַעְגְּלֵי צֶדֶק לְמַעַן שְׁמוֹ. גַּם כִּי אֵלֵךְ בְּגֵיא צַלְמָוֶת, לֹא אִירָא רָע כִּי אַתָּה עִמָּדִי, שִׁבְטְךָ וּמִשְׁעַנְתֶּךָ הֵמָּה יְנַחֲמֻנִי. תַּעֲרֹךְ לְפָנַי שֻׁלְחָן נֶגֶד צֹרְרָי, דִּשַּׁנְתָּ בַשֶּׁמֶן רֹאשִׁי כּוֹסִי רְוָיָה. אַךְ טוֹב וָחֶסֶד יִרְדְּפוּנִי כָּל יְמֵי חַיָּי, וְשַׁבְתִּי בְּבֵית אֲדֹנָי לְאֹרֶךְ יָמִים.

Mizmor LeDavid: Adonai ro'i lo ehsar. Binot deshe yarbitzeni, al mei menuhot yenahaleni. Nafshi yeshovev, yanheni vema'agelei tzedek lema'an shemo. Gam ki elekh begei tzalmavet lo ira ra, ki ata imadi, shivtekha umishantekha hema yenahamuni. Ta'arokh lefanai shulhan neged tzorerai. Dishanta vashemen roshi, kosi revaya. Akh tov vahesed yirdefuni kol yemei hayay, veshavti beveit Adonai le'orekh yamim.

אִם תָּשִׁיב מִשַּׁבָּת רַגְלֶךָ, עֲשׂוֹת חֲפָצֶךָ בְּיוֹם קָדְשִׁי, וְקָרָאתָ לַשַּׁבָּת עֹנֶג, לִקְדוֹשׁ אֲדֹנָי מְכֻבָּד, וְכִבַּדְתּוֹ מֵעֲשׂוֹת דְּרָכֶיךָ, מִמְּצוֹא

Im tashiv miShabbat raglekha asot hafatzekha beyom kodshi, vekarata laShabbat oneg likdosh Adonai mekhubad, vekhibadeto me'asot derakhekha

353

Yearly Cycle

חֶפְצְךָ וְדַבֵּר דָּבָר. אָז תִּתְעַנַּג עַל אֲדֹנָי
וְהִרְכַּבְתִּיךָ עַל בָּמֳתֵי אָרֶץ, וְהַאֲכַלְתִּיךָ
נַחֲלַת יַעֲקֹב אָבִיךָ כִּי פִּי אֲדֹנָי דִּבֵּר.

וְשָׁמְרוּ בְנֵי יִשְׂרָאֵל אֶת הַשַּׁבָּת, לַעֲשׂוֹת אֶת
הַשַּׁבָּת לְדֹרֹתָם בְּרִית עוֹלָם. בֵּינִי וּבֵין בְּנֵי
יִשְׂרָאֵל אוֹת הִיא לְעֹלָם, כִּי שֵׁשֶׁת יָמִים
עָשָׂה אֲדֹנָי אֶת הַשָּׁמַיִם וְאֶת הָאָרֶץ, וּבַיּוֹם
הַשְּׁבִיעִי שָׁבַת וַיִּנָּפַשׁ.

אם חל ביום חול מתחילים כאן:

אֵלֶּה מוֹעֲדֵי אֲדֹנָי, מִקְרָאֵי קֹדֶשׁ, אֲשֶׁר
תִּקְרְאוּ אֹתָם בְּמוֹעֲדָם. וַיְדַבֵּר מֹשֶׁה
אֶת מֹעֲדֵי אֲדֹנָי, אֶל בְּנֵי יִשְׂרָאֵל. שָׁלֹשׁ
פְּעָמִים בַּשָּׁנָה יֵרָאֶה כָל זְכוּרְךָ אֶת פְּנֵי
אֲדֹנָי אֱלֹהֶיךָ בַּמָּקוֹם אֲשֶׁר יִבְחָר, בְּחַג
הַמַּצּוֹת וּבְחַג הַשָּׁבֻעוֹת וּבְחַג הַסֻּכּוֹת, וְלֹא
יֵרָאֶה אֶת פְּנֵי אֲדֹנָי רֵיקָם. אִישׁ כְּמַתְּנַת
יָדוֹ, כְּבִרְכַּת אֲדֹנָי אֱלֹהֶיךָ אֲשֶׁר נָתַן לָךְ:

סַבְרִי מָרָנָן.

השומעים עונים: לְחַיִּים!

בָּרוּךְ אַתָּה אֲדֹנָי, אֱלֹהֵינוּ מֶלֶךְ הָעוֹלָם,
בּוֹרֵא פְּרִי הַגָּפֶן.

mimetzo ḥeftzekha vedaber davar, az titanag al Adonai, vehirkavtikha al bamotei aretz, veha'akhaltikha naḥalat Ya'akov avikha, ki pi Adonai diber.

Vesha'meru venei Yisrael et HaShabbat, la'asot et HaShabbat ledorotam berit olam. Beini uvein benei Yisrael ot hi le'olam, ki Sheshet yamim asa Adonai et hashamayim ve'et ha'aretz, uvayom hashevi'i shavat vayinafash.

On a weekday, begin here:

Eleh mo'adei Adonai, mikra'ei kodesh, asher tikre'u otam bemo'adam. Vaydaber Moshe et mo'adei Adonai el benei Yisrael. Shalosh pe'amim bashana yera'e khol zekhurekha et penei Adonai Elohekha bamakom asher yivḥar: Beḥag hamatzot uvḥag hashavuot uvḥag hasukkot. Velo yera'e et penei Adonai reikam. Ish kematnat yado, kevirkat Adonai Elohekha asher natan lakh.

Savri meranan.

Those listening answer: Leḥayim.

Continue: Barukh ata Adonai, Eloheinu, melekh ha'olam, boreh peri hagefen.

On Shabbat, begin here:

"A psalm by David. The Lord is my Shepherd; I lack nothing. He has me lie down in green pastures; He leads me beside still waters. He restores my soul; He leads me in paths of righteousness for His name's sake. Even when I walk through the valley of the shadow of death, I fear no evil, for You are with me; Your rod and Your staff, they comfort me. You prepare a table before me in the presence of my enemies. You anoint my head with oil; my cup is full. May only goodness and kindness pursue me all the days of my life, and I will dwell in the House of the Lord forever" (Psalms 23).

"If you restrain your walking because of the Sabbath, pursuing your needs on the day of My holiness and you call the Sabbath a delight and the Lord's sacred, honored, and you honor it by refraining from doing your business, from seeking your needs and from speaking of matters, then you will delight in the Lord and I will mount you onto the heights of the earth and I will feed you the inheritance of Jacob your forefather, for the mouth of the Lord has spoken" (Isaiah 58:13–14).

"The children of Israel shall keep the Sabbath, to observe the Sabbath for their generations an eternal covenant. Between Me and the children of Israel, it is a sign forever. For in six days the Lord made the heaven and the earth and on the seventh day, He rested and was invigorated" (Exodus 31:16–17).

On a weekday, begin here:

"These are the appointed times of the Lord, holy convocations, that you shall proclaim at their appointed time" (Leviticus 23:4). "And Moses spoke to the children of Israel the appointed times of the Lord" (Leviticus 23:44).

"Three times in the year all your males shall appear before the Lord your God in the place that He shall choose: On the Festival of Unleavened Bread, and on the Festival of Weeks, and on the Festival of Tabernacles, and they shall not appear before the Lord empty-handed. Each man according to the gift of his hand, in accordance with the blessing of the Lord your God that He gave you" (Deuteronomy 16:16–17).

"Attention, my masters."

The listeners respond: "To life!"

"Blessed are You, Lord our God, King of the universe, who creates the fruit of the vine."

The *HaMotzi* blessing is recited over two whole loaves of bread, and in Grace after Meals the *Ya'aleh VeYavo* section is added.

> Further reading: To read about the choice of Mount Sinai for the giving of the Torah, see *A Concise Guide to the Sages*, p. 310.

Dairy Foods

On *Shavuot*, it is customary to eat dairy foods. Several reasons have been suggested for this:

(1) When the Torah was given to the children of Israel and the laws concerning what one may eat came into effect, they had no kosher meat, as preparing kosher meat requires the use of special slaughtering knives, and likewise it is necessary to soak the meat in water and to salt it, all of which takes time. Therefore, they ate dairy foods on that day.

(2) The Torah is compared to milk, as it is stated: "Honey and milk are under your tongue" (Song of Songs 4:11). Just as milk has many nutritional qualities, so too, the Torah provides spiritual nourishment to the soul of a Jew. As the Torah is also likened to honey in the above verse, some likewise eat foods with honey on *Shavuot*.

(3) Mount Sinai is called "a mountain of ridges [*gavnunim*]" (Psalms 16:16). Thus, the Hebrew word for cheese, *gevina*, is seen as a verbal allusion to Mount Sinai.

That said, it is a mitzva to eat meat on festivals. This requires special attention and planning, so that the consumption of dairy and meat is done in a permissible manner.

📖 **Further reading:** See the chapter dealing with the laws of kosher food, p. 545.

There are various customs regarding the manner of eating the dairy foods. Some serve them immediately after *Kiddush*, as a separate meal, and only later serve a meat meal. Others partake of the dairy foods as an afternoon meal. Yet others start the daytime meal as a dairy meal, and when they have finished eating the dairy foods, they clear the table, change the tablecloth and the bread, rinse out their mouths, and then eat the rest of the meal with meat.

In the afternoon, the festival afternoon prayer service is recited.

📖 **Further reading:** Why doesn't the Torah explicitly identify *Shavuot* as the festival of the giving of the Torah? See *A Concise Guide to Mahshava*, p. 102. What else is the Torah compared to? See *A Concise Guide to the Sages*, p. 449.

Second Day of *Shavuot*

As with all the Torah's holy days except Yom Kippur, *Shavuot* is celebrated outside of Israel for two days.

It is customary to read the book of Ruth on the second day of *Shavuot*, as its story occurred during the wheat and barley harvests, which are connected to the period of the counting of the *omer*. Furthermore, the book of Ruth also mentions the birth and lineage of King David who, according to tradition, passed away on *Shavuot*. In Israel, where only one day of *Shavuot* is observed, the book of Ruth is read on that day.

The main Torah reading for the second day is a section from Deuteronomy (15:19–16:17), which mentions the three pilgrimage festivals and the counting of the *omer*. Five men are called up for this reading. If it is a Shabbat, seven men are called up and the reading is expanded by beginning from Deuteronomy 14:22. The *maftir* is the same as on the first day, and the

Yearly Cycle

haftara is from Habakkuk (2:20–3:19), a prayer by Habakkuk that includes a depiction of the Divine Chariot, linking this *haftara* to that of the previous day, which describes the revelation of Ezekiel. After the first verse of the *haftara*, the reading is interrupted for the recitation of the Aramaic liturgical poem *Yetziv Pitgam*, which praises God, who gave us the Torah and created the universe.

According to the Ashkenazic custom, the *Yizkor* prayer, in memory of the deceased, is recited before *Musaf*. In Israel, this is recited on the previous day.

One who travels to Israel for *Shavuot*, or a resident of Israel who is abroad, should consult a rabbi regarding how to conduct himself on this second day.

Havdala

Upon the conclusion of the festival, *Havdala* is recited over a full cup of wine. The wording of this *Havdala* is identical to the *Havdala* of Shabbat, but without the blessings over the candle and the spices. Likewise, the introductory verses before *Havdala* are not recited. One recites the blessing over the wine: "who creates the fruit of the vine," followed by the blessing of: "who separates between the sacred and the mundane."

The Days After the Festival

Unlike *Sukkot* and Passover, *Shavuot* consists of only one day, not seven. However, there are special customs that pertain to the days following the festival.

Isru Hag

The day after a festival is called *Isru Hag*, based on the verse: "Bind the festival offering [*isru hag*] with cords, and thence to the horns of the altar" (Psalms 118:27). This is homiletically interpreted to mean: Tie the days of the festival to the following mundane weekdays. Therefore, this day has a slightly festive nature, and some have the custom to add something special to their meal in its honor.

Days of Compensation

The six days, from the seventh to the twelfth of Sivan, are "days of compensation" for the festival offerings. By Torah law, Passover and *Sukkot* are celebrated for seven days, during which all Jews were required to make pilgrimages to the Temple and bring the festival offerings. In contrast, the

Yearly Cycle

festival of *Shavuot* lasts only one day, which made it difficult for everyone to ascend to Jerusalem and bring their offerings in that single day. Therefore, six days were added after the festival during which one could bring his individual *Shavuot* offerings, to make a total of seven days during which the festival offerings of *Shavuot* may be brought.

Consequently, it is customary in many Jewish communities not to recite *Tahanun* during all these days of compensation.

"Between the Straits"

From the Seventeenth of Tamuz to Tisha BeAv

The period of time between the fast of the seventeenth of Tamuz and the fast of the ninth of Av is known as "Between the Straits," or simply the "Three Weeks." On the seventeenth of Tamuz in 70 CE, the walls of Jerusalem were breached and the Roman army burst into the city. Three weeks later, on the ninth of Av, the Temple was burned and destroyed. Both the First and Second Temples were destroyed on the same date, the ninth of Av [*Tisha BeAv*]. The First Temple was destroyed in the year 422 BCE by Nebuzaradan, the captain of the guard of Nebuchadnezzar king of Babylon, while the Second Temple was burned in 70 CE by the army of the Roman Empire, under the command of Titus, the son of the Roman Emperor Vespasian. The expression "between the straits" comes from a verse in the book of Lamentations (1:3), which eulogizes the destruction of the Temple: "Judah was exiled in affliction and in great enslavement. She has settled among the nations, finding no rest; all her pursuers have overtaken her between the straits" (Lamentations 1:3).

This period of the Three Weeks is a time of mourning, which gradually increases in intensity as *Tisha BeAv* nears. The Three Weeks may be divided into four stages: the days between the seventeenth of Tamuz and *Rosh Hodesh* Av; from the beginning of the month of Av until the ninth of Av, which is called the "Nine Days"; the week during which *Tisha BeAv* falls; and of course, *Tisha BeAv* itself, when the mourning reaches its climax.

This chapter will focus on the laws and customs of this time of year, in which we are instructed to avoid obvious expressions of joy, and to increase our study of the parts of the Torah that deal with the Temple and the details of its service and the events that led to its destruction, all while anticipating its rebuilding, at the coming of the messiah.

A separate section will be devoted to *Tisha BeAv* itself.

Further reading: For more on the destruction of the Temple and the events that precipitated it, see *A Concise Guide to the Sages*, p. 322.

Five Events

The seventeenth of Tamuz is a fast day. The main reason for the fast is that on that date, the walls of Jerusalem were breached by the Romans, a significant step in the process of the destruction of the Temple. Several other dramatic events also occurred on that date that left their mark on Jewish history: Moses broke the tablets of the Ten Commandments when he descended from Mount Sinai and found the Israelites worshipping the Golden Calf. The daily offering, which was sacrificed in the Temple twice each day, in the morning and in the afternoon, was forced to come to a halt. Furthermore, on the seventeenth of Tamuz, a Roman general named Apostomus publicly burned a Torah scroll. In addition, an idol was placed inside the Temple.

📖 **Further reading:** For more on the breaking of the tablets, see *A Concise Guide to the Torah*, p. 218; *A Concise Guide to the Sages*, p. 120.

Laws of the Fast

In general, the laws and customs of the day are similar to those of the fast of Gedaliah (see p. 156). The fast of the seventeenth of Tamuz begins at dawn (about an hour and a half before sunrise) and ends at the emergence of the stars. The precise times can be found in synagogue calendars.

The fast includes only a prohibition against eating and drinking, and it applies to every male over the age of thirteen and female over the age of twelve. Pregnant and nursing women need not observe this fast. In a case of illness, weakness, or any other difficulty in fasting, one should consult a rabbi.

There are several additions to the prayers of the day:

In the morning service, the prayer leader inserts the prayer *Aneinu* ("Answer us, God, answer us, on the day of our fast") in the *Amida*, after the seventh blessing, the blessing of redemption. At the end of the prayer leader's repetition of the *Amida*, the congregation recites *Selihot*. Next, the ark is opened for the *Avinu Malkeinu* prayer, followed by *Tahanun*. Then a Torah scroll is taken out of the ark and read. The reading is from Exodus (32:11–14; 34:1–10), and discusses Moses' request from God to have mercy on the children of Israel and forgive them for their sins.

In the afternoon prayer service, after *Ashrei* (Psalms 145), the same Torah passage that was read in the morning is repeated, but in the afternoon a *haftara* is read as well, in Ashkenazic congregations. This *haftara* (Isaiah 55:6–56:8), which opens with the words: "Seek the Lord when He is found," deals with leaving behind one's sins and drawing closer to God. In the *Amida*, in the blessing of *Shome'a Tefilla* (acceptance of prayer), each individual adds the aforementioned *Aneinu* passage. As with the morning prayer, the prayer leader inserts the prayer *Aneinu* in the *Amida*, after the seventh blessing. In Israel, it is customary for the priests to recite the priestly benediction (Numbers 6:24–26) if the prayer is taking place toward the end of the day. After the *Amida*, the congregation adds the *Avinu Malkeinu* prayer, which is recited with the ark open, followed by *Tahanun*.

When the seventeenth of Tamuz falls on a Shabbat, the fast is postponed to Sunday, the eighteenth of Tamuz, and all the laws of the day mentioned above apply.

The Three Weeks

During the period of the seventeenth of Tamuz until after *Tisha BeAv*, it is customary to avoid reciting the *Sheheheyanu* blessing, which one would recite upon eating a new fruit or when first wearing a new garment. If someone comes across a new fruit during this time, he should preserve it until after *Tisha BeAv* if possible. Likewise, one should postpone purchasing new clothes and other items whose acquisition brings joy, until after *Tisha BeAv*. In addition, during the Three Weeks, one should be extra careful about activities and situations that involve a degree of danger (e.g., surgery, challenging hikes).

Below are the laws of mourning, which increase in intensity as *Tisha BeAv* approaches.

First Stage of Mourning

In addition to refraining from reciting the *Sheheheyanu* blessing, Ashkenazim observe several other practices of mourning beginning on the seventeenth of Tamuz: no weddings are held; one does not shave or have a haircut; there are no joyous events involving dancing, and one does not listen to instrumental music. In Sephardic communities, all these laws of mourning come into effect only at the beginning of the month of Av.

Second Stage of Mourning

The mishna states: "When Av begins, one decreases rejoicing" (*Ta'anit* 4:6). Accordingly, the main mourning period starts from *Rosh Hodesh* Av. The Sages also state that in the month of Av, the fortune of the Jewish people is at its lowest ebb, and therefore on the days between *Rosh Hodesh* Av and *Tisha BeAv*, it is recommended to avoid negotiations and legal proceedings with non-Jews.

In this period, called the Nine Days, Ashkenazic communities observe more stringent customs of mourning: One does not eat animal or poultry meat; one does not drink wine; one does not bathe (as described below); and one does not launder clothes or wear clothes that have been laundered

Yearly Cycle

(see below). In contrast, Sephardic Jews observe these latter two stringencies only during the week in which *Tisha BeAv* falls. In a year when *Tisha BeAv* occurs on a Sunday, or even if the date of the ninth of Av is on Shabbat and the fast is therefore postponed to Sunday, some Sephardim do not observe at all the stringencies of the week in which *Tisha BeAv* falls, while others observe them throughout the previous week.

Strictly speaking, the *halakha* is that during the Nine Days, or the week in which *Tisha BeAv* falls, one may not bathe in hot water or even in cold water with soap. Nevertheless, since in our times bathing is a daily activity that is not an indulgence or a special pleasure, many halakhic authorities permit it, although even they say that it is best to bathe quickly and with lukewarm water that does not cause discomfort but is also not pleasurable. Swimming, bathing for pleasure, and using a Jacuzzi or sauna, are prohibited.

During this time period, it is prohibited to launder clothing and to wear freshly laundered clothes, but if one has small children, who often get their clothes dirty, one may be lenient and wash their clothing. If adults wash their own clothes and wear them just before *Rosh Hodesh* Av, even if only for a short time, they may wear them during the Nine Days as well. In this regard too, some are lenient and permit wearing freshly laundered clothes even though they have not been worn beforehand. The reason, once again, is that in our time, the frequent changing of clothing is part of the reality of daily life and does not cause one special pleasure. There is no restriction on wearing laundered undergarments.

> **Further reading:** For more on the reduction of joy in the month of Av, see *A Concise Guide to the Sages*, p. 298; *A Concise Guide to Mahshava*, p. 50.

Third Stage of Mourning

On the day before *Tisha BeAv*, and especially at the *seuda hamafseket*, the meal before the fast (for more on this meal, see next chapter), it is absolutely prohibited to eat meat or drink wine. Likewise, at noon of this day, a few of the halakhic restrictions that are customary on *Tisha BeAv* itself come into effect, as detailed in the next chapter.

Leniencies at a Mitzva Celebration

There are some leniencies in the customs of mourning for a meal held in celebration of a mitzva that occurs during the Nine Days:

At a circumcision or redemption of a firstborn, the main celebrants, namely, the parents of the baby, the *sandak*, and the *mohel*, are all permitted to wear new and festive clothes. Meat and wine may be served at the celebratory meal, and all participants may partake of them, provided they would have participated in this celebration even had it occurred during the rest of the year, and they did not come especially so that they could eat meat.

📖 **Further reading:** For more on the *sandak* and *mohel*, see the section on circumcision, p. 5.

A meal that is held on the occasion of the completion of the study of a tractate of the Mishna or the Talmud is considered a *seudat mitzva*, a mitzva celebration, and it is permitted to eat meat and drink wine at this meal. Some go out of their way to hold many such meals, in order to increase this permitted type of joy, even if they abstain from meat and wine.

Shabbat in the Nine Days

In the past, it was customary to observe a certain measure of mourning, albeit in a muted fashion, even on the Shabbatot that occur during the Nine Days. In recent generations, this custom has ceased to be widespread. In practice, it is permitted, and even preferable, not to observe any form of mourning on Shabbat, and to eat meat and drink wine, as is done on all Shabbatot of the year. The preparations for the Shabbatot of the Nine Days are similar to those of every Shabbat eve, except for the prohibition to have a haircut and shave, which remains in force. Some are also stringent not to bathe or shower in hot water.

For *Havdala* on Saturday night during the Nine Days, or, for Sephardim, the week during which *Tisha BeAv* falls, some have the custom of using beer or other alcoholic beverages, rather than wine, in order to avoid drinking the wine. Some use grape juice, which they give to a child to drink instead of drinking it themselves. By contrast, others perform *Havdala* on wine in the usual manner, and drink it themselves, in accordance with the *halakha* of a mitzva celebration. Even the *melaveh malka* meal, which is held after Shabbat, is considered by some to be a mitzva celebration and they therefore maintain that one may eat meat and drink wine then as well.

Three *Haftarot* of Retribution and *Shabbat Hazon*

On the three Shabbatot during the Three Weeks, the *haftarot* that are read are called the "three (*haftarot*) of retribution." These readings discuss the prophecies that foretold of the destruction of the Temple and the need to repent completely of the sins that would eventually cause this national tragedy.

Prophecy of Isaiah

The Shabbat before *Tisha BeAv* is called *Shabbat Hazon* because of the opening words of the *haftara* that is read on this Shabbat: "The vision [*hazon*] of Isaiah son of Amotz, that he envisioned concerning Judah and Jerusalem" (Isaiah 1:1). This passage speaks of the sins of the children of Israel and of the future troubles that will befall them as a result of these transgressions. The renowned hasidic Rebbe, Rabbi Levi Yitzhak of Berdichev, interpreted the name *Shabbat Hazon* as referring to a different kind of vision. He said that on this Shabbat, the soul of every Jew has a vision of the Third Temple, and this vision gives rise to a deep inner yearning for the redemption of the people of Israel and the rebuilding of the Temple.

📖 **Further reading:** For more on anticipating the future redemption and the arrival of the messiah, see *A Concise Guide to the Sages*, p. 391; *A Concise Guide to Mahshava*, p. 145.

Yearly Cycle

Tisha BeAv

Tisha BeAv is the great day of mourning for the Jewish people over the many tragedies they have experienced through the generations. The main reason for the mourning is that on this day the two Temples were destroyed. This date was already marked as a day of retribution earlier in history: On this day, the children of Israel were punished for the sin of the spies who were sent to scout out the Land of Israel and returned with a negative report, sending the people into a rebellious panic. It was thereupon decreed, on the ninth of Av, that the entire nation would have to wander in the wilderness for forty years, until all the adults of that generation would die there without entering the Land of Israel. In addition, at the time of the Bar Kokhba revolt, the city of Betar, the last stronghold of Jewish national independence, was conquered by the Romans on this date and its inhabitants were massacred. Another event that occurred in that time was the command of the Roman general in Judea that the area of the Temple should be plowed over, as a symbol of its complete destruction. Generations later, the edict to expel the Jews of England was signed in 1290, and the Jews of Spain were expelled in 1492, on or in the days near Tisha BeAv.

The fast of Tisha BeAv is mentioned in the book of Zechariah (8:19), as a day of mourning for the destruction of the Temple. It is referred to there as "the fast of the fifth" because it occurs in the fifth month counting from Nisan, which is considered the first of the Jewish months. It was subsequently also considered to be a general day of mourning for all the other disasters that have befallen our people throughout history. Halakhically, the fast of Tisha BeAv is more severe than all the other fast days established by the Sages to commemorate the destruction of the Temple, namely, the fast of Gedaliah on the third of Tishrei, the fast of the tenth of Tevet, and the fast of the seventeenth of Tamuz.

📖 **Further reading:** To read about the talmudic description of the events leading to the destruction of the Temple, see *A Concise Guide to the Sages*, p. 322.

While Tisha BeAv is closest in its severity to the fast of Yom Kippur, there is a stark difference between the nature of these two fasts: Yom Kippur is a day of joy because it is a time when our sins are forgiven; the fast serves to enable atonement and purification. Tisha BeAv, by contrast, is a day of mourning, whose fast and other halakhot and customs of mourning are meant to arouse in us sorrow over the exile and an internal cry for the complete redemption. Whereas Yom Kippur will remain a holy and lofty day in the future, it is stated with regard to Tisha BeAv and the other fasts of mourning: "So said the Lord of hosts: The fast of the fourth [month, Tamuz], and the fast of the fifth [month, Av], and the fast of the seventh [month, Tishrei], and the fast of the tenth [month, Tevet], will be for gladness and for joy, and for happy festivals for the house of Judah" (Zechariah 8:19). This change will occur when the messiah arrives and the Third Temple is built.

This section details the *halakhot* of *Tisha BeAv*, from the afternoon of the day before (the eighth of Av) until noon of the day following the fast (the tenth of Av), as some of the observances of mourning remain in effect until then.

The Prohibitions of the Day

Although the prohibitions of *Tisha BeAv* are similar to those that apply on Yom Kippur, the restrictions of *Tisha BeAv* apply only by rabbinic law while Yom Kippur is decreed by the Torah. For this reason, *Tisha BeAv* is considered to be less severe a fast than Yom Kippur. Consequently, in some cases there is greater room for leniency regarding a sick person, a woman after childbirth, and a nursing woman. In any case, before adopting a leniency, one must consult a rabbi regarding each particular case.

All five prohibitions that apply on Yom Kippur also apply on *Tisha BeAv*: eating and drinking, bathing the body, anointing the body, wearing leather shoes, and engaging in marital relations.

Further reading: For more on the laws of Yom Kippur, see p. 163.

Other Restrictions

In order to increase the feeling of mourning on *Tisha BeAv*, several other prohibitions were added to the five basic restrictions of the day.

No Torah study: Studying Torah brings one joy and may cause a person to forget the sad, mournful mood of the day. Therefore, learning most sections of the Torah is prohibited on this day. According to some Ashkenazic halakhic authorities, the prohibition against studying Torah begins at midday on the eve of *Tisha BeAv* (the eighth of Av). Despite this restriction, it is permitted to study Torah topics that have a sad aspect, such as the book of Lamentations with its commentaries and midrashim, the book of Job, the parts of the book of Jeremiah that deal with the destruction of the Temple, as well as other midrashim and talmudic passages that focus on the destruction.

One may recite verses from the Torah that are included in the prayer liturgy. There are communities in which it is customary to postpone the recitation of several of these passages until the afternoon service, which is held after midday when mourning is not as severe. Likewise, some permit reading excerpts from the book of Psalms and the weekly Torah portion with its Aramaic translation after midday.

No sitting on chairs: From the start of the fast until midday on *Tisha BeAv*, one may not sit on a regular chair, but rather only on the ground or on a low stool, in the manner of a person who is mourning the passing of a family member.

No greetings: On *Tisha BeAv* one does not extend greetings to others. If one is walking in the street and a neighbor or acquaintance greets him absent-mindedly or due to a lack of knowledge, one may respond. He should do so in a soft voice and in a manner that emphasizes his state of sorrow and that he is uncomfortable with the exchange.

No distractions: As a general rule, the day of *Tisha BeAv* should be dedicated to reciting lamentations [*kinnot*] and thinking about the tragedy of the destruction of the Temple. It is inappropriate to deal with anything that might distract one from the solemn nature of the day. This means that one should not work or engage in various tasks, even if postponing certain activities might cause him a moderate financial loss.

The Eighth of Av

The *halakhot* of mourning begin on the day before *Tisha BeAv*, the eighth of Av, and they are expressed mainly in the laws of the last meal before the fast [*seuda hamafseket*].

Seuda Hamafseket

The last meal before the fast begins, called the *seuda hamafseket*, is subject to certain customs of mourning. It is customary to eat this meal while sitting on the ground or on a low stool, and to partake only of bread and a single cooked food. Even this single food should be something very simple, and some even maintain that this single course should consist of those items considered to be "mourners' food," such as a dish of lentils. Some Ashkenazim eat an egg dipped in ashes. According to one custom, the bread eaten at this meal is also dipped in ashes. It is preferable to eat the *seuda hamafseket* alone, not as a group. Even if several diners eat together, at its conclusion they do not perform the *zimmun*. These *halakhot* do not apply when the eighth or ninth of Av is Shabbat.

Further reading: For more on the *halakhot* of mourning, see p. 82. For more on *zimmun*, (the reciting of: "Gentlemen, let us bless…") before Grace after Meals, see p. 528.

In the time that is left between the end of the *seuda hamafseket* and the beginning of the fast, one may drink and even eat a little, but one should not eat a new meal.

No *Tahanun*

Although *Tisha BeAv* is the most severe day of mourning, one does not recite *Tahanun* in the afternoon service before *Tisha BeAv* nor in all the prayers of *Tisha BeAv* itself. The source for the reason is a verse in the Book of Lamentations: "The Lord...proclaimed a festival against me to break my young men" (Lamentations 1:15). The Sages understood from here that *Tisha BeAv* is called a "festival," and just as *Tahanun* is not said on all happy festival days, so too, on this painful "festival" no *Tahanun* is recited.

The Night of *Tisha BeAv*

As the sun sets on the eighth of Av, all the laws of mourning take effect. In the synagogue, the curtain is removed from the ark. For the evening service, the brighter lights are turned off, and only a dim light is left, just enough to allow one to read from the prayer book. The congregation sits on the floor or on low stools.

Kinnot and the Book of Lamentations

Before the evening prayer is recited, it is the custom in some Sephardic communities to read the song of *Ha'azinu* (Deuteronomy 32:1–43) and the psalm "By the rivers of Babylon" (Psalms 137).

Some Sephardim have the custom to insert in the *Amida* prayer of all three daily services the *Nahem* paragraph ("May God comfort the mourners of Zion"), in the blessing of rebuilding Jerusalem. They also recite the paragraph of *Aneinu* ("Answer us, God, answer us, on the day of our fast") in the blessing of *Shome'a Tefilla*, as appears in the prayer books. Others recite *Aneinu* in all the prayers, but add the paragraph of *Nahem* only in the afternoon service and, according to some customs, also in the prayer leader's repetition of the *Amida* prayer of the morning service. By contrast, according to the custom of the Ashkenazim, both *Aneinu* and *Nahem* are recited by the congregation in the afternoon service only, while in the morning and afternoon prayer service the prayer leader inserts the *Aneinu* prayer in the *Amida*, after the seventh blessing.

After the *Amida* prayer of the evening service, the congregation sits on the ground or on low stools and the book of Lamentations is read. This is followed by the recitation of a few *kinnot* (lamentational poems), which appear in special *Tisha BeAv* books of *kinnot*. Next the congregation recites the *Ve'ata Kadosh* ("You are holy") prayer, with minor alterations, which can be found in prayer books.

In some communities it is customary to proclaim after the recitation of *kinnot*: "Our brethren, children of Israel, know that today is the year such-and-such (specifying the number of years) since the destruction of our holy and glorious Temple!"

Tisha BeAv Day

The prayers on *Tisha BeAv* differ from those of the rest of the year, both in the morning service and the afternoon service. The changes are reflected in the structure of the prayer as well as with regard to wearing a *tallit* or *tefillin*.

Tallit and Tefillin

Ashkenazim have the custom of praying the morning service without wearing a *tallit* or *tefillin*. Among the Sephardim, some wear a *tallit* and *tefillin* at home, read the *Shema*, and then remove them and go to the synagogue. Others wear the *tallit* and *tefillin* in the synagogue, as on every morning. For those who follow this custom, the order of the morning service will differ from that of other communities, as detailed below.

Morning Service

On *Tisha BeAv* morning, some have the custom of reciting *Pesukei DeZimra* (the series of psalms between the blessings of *Barukh She'amar* and *Yishtabah*) silently.

Some recite the song of *Ha'azinu* (Deuteronomy 32:1–43) instead of the Song at the Sea (Exodus 15:1–18); others recite it after the morning prayer service.

📖 **Further reading:** *Ha'azinu* can be found in *A Concise Guide to the Torah*, p. 508.

At the end of the *Amida* prayer, the Torah reading is from Deuteronomy (4:25–40). This passage relates that if the children of Israel sin, they will be exiled from their land, but when they repent, they will be redeemed and return to Israel. Afterward, a *haftara* is read from the book of Jeremiah (8:13–9:23), which also deals with the sins of the Israelites and the ensuing destruction and exile. The Ashkenazic custom is to read the verses of the *haftara* in the melancholy tune of the book of Lamentations.

Yearly Cycle

At this stage, the congregation recites *kinnot* that deal with the destruction of the Temple and the other troubles that have plagued our people over the years. Paying attention to the meaning and tone of the poetic words will increase one's identification with the theme of *Tisha BeAv*. It is proper to draw out the recitation of *kinnot* until midday.

At the end of the *kinnot*, the congregation recites *Ashrei* (Psalms 145) and the *Uva LeTzion* passage, followed by *Aleinu*. According to the Ashkenazic custom, the morning prayer service ends here, and the recitation of the Song of the Day and the description of the daily incense offering are postposed until later, when they are said at the beginning of the afternoon service. Sephardim complete the prayer service as usual. For those Sephardim who wear *tefillin* for the entire morning service, they finish the whole morning prayer in its usual order, including *Aleinu*, and then remove the *tefillin*. Only then do they proceed to recite *kinnot* and the other additions of mourning.

After the prayer service, some have the custom to go to a cemetery. There are several reasons for this custom: The dead also share in the sorrow of the living; the dead can help us by beseeching God for the complete redemption; it shows that in our present state we are comparable to the dead.

Those who follow the customs of the Arizal do not go to the cemetery on *Tisha BeAv*.

After Midday

After midday, the intensity of mourning of *Tisha BeAv* diminishes, and several leniencies come into effect: It is permitted to sit on a proper chair, at the normal height, and one may start preparing and cooking the meal for the end of the fast. Some even have the custom to clean the house in order to express their anticipation and preparation for the coming of the messiah.

Afternoon Service

The common practice is that *tallit* and *tefillin* are worn at the afternoon prayer service. Those who already prayed in the morning while wearing *tallit* and *tefillin* do not wear them again for the afternoon service.

Before the afternoon service, some Ashkenazim complete those portions of prayer that they had omitted in the morning, namely, the Song of the Day and the description of the incense offering.

After *Ashrei*, the Torah is removed from the ark and the passages generally read on a fast day are read aloud (Exodus 32:11–14; 34:1–10). These passages deal with Moses' request of God to have mercy on the children of

Israel and to forgive them after the sin of the Golden Calf. Furthermore, the reading includes the list of God's Thirteen Attributes of Mercy, which are mentioned as a plea to God to be merciful toward us. The Torah reading is followed by the *haftara* generally read on fast days (Isaiah 45:6–56:8), which also deals with abandoning sin and returning to God.

> **Further reading:** For more on Moses' prayers for atonement on behalf of the children of Israel, see *A Concise Guide to the Torah*, p. 219; *A Concise Guide to the Sages*, p. 123.

In the *Amida* prayer, the *Nahem* paragraph, beseeching God to have mercy and rebuild Jerusalem, is added in the regular blessing about rebuilding Jerusalem, and the paragraph of *Aneinu* ("Answer us, God, answer us, on the day of our fast") is inserted into the blessing of acceptance of prayer (*Shome'a Tefilla*). As with the morning prayer, the prayer leader inserts the prayer *Aneinu* in the *Amida* after the seventh blessing. In Israel, it is customary for the priests to bless the congregation with the priestly benediction (Numbers 6:24–26) if the prayer is taking place close to the end of the day.

The fast ends upon the emergence of the stars; the precise time is publicized in synagogue calendars.

Tenth of Av

Since the Temple was set on fire at the end of the ninth of Av and continued to burn throughout the next day, the tenth of Av, the mourning customs observed from *Rosh Hodesh* Av are still observed until midday of the day following *Tisha BeAv*. Among other things, one may not have a haircut, recite the *Sheheheyanu* blessing over a new garment or a new fruit, eat meat or drink wine, nor listen to music during that morning.

Tisha BeAv on Sunday

When *Tisha BeAv* falls on a Sunday, or if the ninth of Av is a Shabbat and therefore the fast is postponed to Sunday, there are some changes in the manner in which the day is observed.

Seuda Hamafseket

When the eve of the fast is Shabbat, the customs of mourning are not observed, and all food and drink is permitted at all the Shabbat meals, including the third meal in the afternoon. In such a case, one must be very careful not to continue eating and drinking beyond sunset.

Laws of Mourning

One should not remove his leather shoes, nor display any kind of mourning until the conclusion of Shabbat. In many congregations, the evening service is delayed somewhat, so that the congregants can, at the end of Shabbat, say *barukh hamavdil bein kodesh leḥol*, "blessed is He who distinguishes between the sacred and the mundane," and then remove their leather shoes. Some have the practice to also change out of their Shabbat clothes before going to the synagogue.

As on every other Saturday night, the passage of *Ata ḥonantanu* ("You have graced us, etc.") is added in the fourth blessing of the *Amida* prayer. Since it is prohibited to drink, *Havdala* is not performed over a cup of wine on Saturday night, but rather is postponed to the end of the fast on Sunday night. At the conclusion of the evening service, however, the blessing of "who creates the lights of fire" should be recited over a candle. Alternatively, it may be recited at home anytime on Saturday night following the conclusion of Shabbat and the recitation of the phrase: "Blessed is He who distinguishes between the sacred and the mundane."

The next evening, upon the conclusion of the fast but before eating and drinking, *Havdala* should be recited over a cup of wine, and only the blessing over the wine: "who creates the fruit of the vine," and the blessing: "who distinguishes between the sacred and the mundane," are recited, without the introductory verses.

When the ninth of Av is a Shabbat and the fast is postponed to Sunday, its severity is somewhat reduced, and certain leniencies are possible when needed. Nevertheless, one should not rule leniently for oneself, but rather consult with a rabbi who will examine each case on its own merits.

Shabbat Nahamu and *Sheva De'nehemta*

The seven Shabbatot following *Tisha BeAv* are called the Shabbatot of consolation, and the first of them is called *Shabbat Nahamu*.

The name *Shabbat Nahamu* comes from the opening words of the *haftara* that is read on the first Shabbat after *Tisha BeAv*: "Comfort [*nahamu*], comfort My people, will say your God" (Isaiah 40:1). The verses of the *haftara* deal with the consolation of the people of Israel after their redemption from exile. This *haftara* is the first of a series of seven *haftarot*, known as *sheva de'nehemta*, the seven [*haftarot*] of consolation," which are read on the seven Shabbatot between *Tisha BeAv* and the end of the year. All of these *haftarot* are from the book of Isaiah, and they each deal with the consolation of the people of Israel after the exile.

The Month of Elul

Elul is the last month of the year, and is considered to be a month of preparation for the New Year. This is a period of soul-searching, repentance, and prayers for mercy. There are several unique customs in this month, as well as some changes in the prayers.

Historically, the forty days between *Rosh Hodesh* Elul and Yom Kippur (the tenth of Tishrei) was the period when Moses stood on Mount Sinai when he went to receive the two Tablets of the Covenant for the second time. He broke the first tablets when he came down from the mountain and saw the Israelites worshipping the Golden Calf. Afterward, Moses ascended the mountain again to plead with God to forgive the people of Israel. This forgiveness was granted on *Rosh Hodesh* Elul, at which point Moses went up the mountain for another forty days, at the end of which he descended with the second tablets. Since then, Elul has been considered a month of mercy and forgiveness.

In addition, the fact that Rosh HaShana is the Day of Judgment for all of creation naturally dictates that the preceding period should be a time of soul-searching and improving one's behavior. During this month, one should evaluate his spiritual "balance sheet," in which the goals he has set are weighed against his actual achievements, and successes are examined against failures. This is the time to take a deep look inside oneself, into one's soul, and to contemplate matters of substance and the purpose of life, in the hope that next year will be better from this perspective.

In hasidic thought, the month of Elul is compared to days when "the king is in the field." In other words, in this month God is not hidden in His palace, with the resultant necessity to go through "governmental bureaucracy" in order to reach Him. Rather, the King Himself ventures out to the people and meets each individual in the "field," where he lives his daily life, and each and every one can lay out needs and requests before Him. In the month of Elul, one's access to God is easy and direct, and, in the words of Rabbi Shneur Zalman of Liadi, "He welcomes all with a friendly countenance and shows favor to everyone."

📖 **Further reading:** For more on the month of Elul, see *A Concise Guide to Mahshava*, p. 50.

The Customs of Elul

There are several customs that are observed during the month of Elul, and their purpose is to inspire each person to amend his actions and sincerely repent.

Shofar and *Selihot*

Sephardic communities begin to recite *Selihot* (penitential prayers) as early as the day after *Rosh Hodesh* Elul, as detailed below. Ashkenazic communities start to sound the shofar every morning after prayers, from the first of

Elul until the twenty-eighth of the month. On the day before Rosh HaShana, the shofar is not sounded.

Psalms 27

At the end of the prayer service, Psalms 27 is added, which begins with the words: "By David. The Lord is my light and my salvation." This psalm deals with various aspects of approaching God while expressing complete trust in Him, as well as a longing to be in His shadow. It also contains an allusion to the upcoming festivals of Tishrei, including *Sukkot*, and therefore one continues to recite the psalm daily until the last day of *Sukkot*, which is *Hoshana Rabba*. Among Sephardic and hasidic communities, the psalm is recited following the morning and afternoon services, whereas Ashkenazic communities say it after the morning and evening services.

Chapters of Psalms

According to the Lubavitch custom, which dates back to the time of Rabbi Israel Ba'al Shem Tov, three chapters from the book of Psalms are added after every morning service in the month of Elul, starting from the second day of *Rosh Hodesh*, which is the first of Elul. On the first day, one says Psalms 1–3, on the second day Psalms 4–6, and so on. One continues to recite the psalms in order throughout the Ten Days of Repentance as well, and on the Day of Atonement one says nine psalms before *Kol Nidrei*, nine before going to bed, nine after the *Musaf* prayer, and nine after *Ne'ila*. One thereby completes the entire book of Psalms.

Selihot

During the month of Elul, it is customary to recite penitential prayers called *Selihot*. These are liturgical poems and verses that focus on one's remorse for the wrongdoings that he has performed in the past year, while asking forgiveness from God. There are two main sections recited between the liturgical poems:

(1) God's Thirteen Attributes of Mercy, from Exodus 34:6-7 ("The Lord, the Lord, God, merciful and gracious, slow to anger and abounding in kindness and truth, etc."), which Moses invoked when he prayed for the children of Israel after the sin of the Golden Calf, and which evoke God's forgiveness when they are recited with a full heart.

(2) The "confession," a list of various sins that helps us recall and regret our misdeeds.

On Which Days?

There are different customs among the various communities with regard to *Selihot*: Among the Sephardim, it is customary to start saying them from the second day of Elul. The formula of *Selihot* throughout the month is fixed, but a few liturgical poems are added during the Ten Days of Repentance, from Rosh HaShana until Yom Kippur. The *Selihot* are commonly recited in song and verse. In some communities it is customary to sound the shofar when saying the Thirteen Attributes of Mercy.

Ashkenazim begin saying *Selihot* on a Saturday night toward the end of the month of Elul. When Rosh HaShana falls on a Thursday or Saturday, they start to say *Selihot* on the last Saturday night of the year. But if Rosh HaShana falls on a Monday or Tuesday, the *Selihot* are begun a week earlier, on the previous Saturday night, which means that the period of *Selihot* before Rosh HaShana lasts for a week and a half. The structure of the *Selihot* and their main sections remains the same throughout the period, but the individual liturgical poems change daily. Some recite the formula of the "confession" three times each day, while others recite it once. On the eve of Rosh HaShana, the *Selihot* are lengthier than on the other days.

At What Time?

The preferred time to recite *Selihot* is between the middle of the night and dawn. If one cannot say *Selihot* during that time frame, or if he failed to do so, one may recite *Selihot* before the morning prayer service, or at any point throughout the day. If there is no other choice, one may say *Selihot* even at night before midnight. One should keep in mind that according to Jewish chronology, a day starts from the preceding night, which means that the *Selihot* that are recited at night belong to the following day.

Shabbat and Festivals

Structure of Shabbat

Shabbat observance is one of the most fundamental commandments of Judaism. At first glance, it might seem that Shabbat exists to provide an opportunity for physical rest from the week's toil. But far beyond this simple purpose, Shabbat has many profound spiritual and transcendent layers. In the Torah, Shabbat is defined both as a covenant between us and the Creator, and as a sign of our deep bond with Him.

Shabbat is of great value in God's eyes, as the Talmud relates: "The Holy One, Blessed be He, said to Moses: I have a great gift in My treasure house, known as Shabbat. I seek to give it to Israel – go and tell them" (*Shabbat* 10b). Proper observance of Shabbat leads to many rewards. One of them is to hasten the redemption of the Jewish people, as the Midrash states, "If you observe the [commandment to light the] Shabbat candles, I [God] will show you the candles of Zion" (*Yalkut Shimoni, Behaalotekha*).

The observance of Shabbat incorporates both positive mitzvot, meaning actions that we are commanded to perform in honor of Shabbat, and prohibitions, activities from which one must abstain on Shabbat. This chapter presents the laws of Shabbat, from the necessary preparations for the holy day, to the *Havdala* ceremony and *melaveh malka* meal that take place when it concludes.

> **Further reading:** For more on Shabbat, see *A Concise Guide to the Torah*, pp. 6, 174, 192, 226; *A Concise Guide to the Sages*, p. 275; *A Concise Guide to Mahshava*, p. 33.

Preparations for Shabbat

The Sages compare Shabbat to a queen, in that one must prepare for its arrival both practically and spiritually. The Talmud relates that many Sages personally participated in cooking and other household chores to prepare for Shabbat. Rabbi Hanina would don his Shabbat clothes on Friday afternoon a bit early, saying, "Come, let us go out to greet Shabbat, the queen" (*Shabbat* 119a).

Torah and *Targum*

On each Shabbat, the Torah portion for that week is read in the synagogue. In order to be prepared for this reading and to be properly familiar with the text of the Torah, the Sages mandated that prior to Shabbat, everyone should read that week's Torah portion twice, and in addition read *Targum*

Onkelos, the authorized Aramaic translation of the Torah, once. This process is called *shenayim mikra ve'ehad targum,* meaning "Scripture twice and translation once." Since Jews no longer speak Aramaic, it is recommended to also read a thorough commentary, such as that of Rashi, in addition to or in place of the Aramaic translation.

Honor and Delight

We are commanded by the prophets to honor Shabbat and make it a pleasurable day, as the verse states: "And you call the Sabbath a delight and the Lord's sacred, honored" (Isaiah 58:13). The Sages instructed us how to fulfill this command.

Shabbat Food

One should begin cooking for Shabbat in advance, and it is considered meritorious to expend special effort to prepare the Shabbat food. In order to fulfill the commandment to experience pleasure at the Shabbat meals, each person should eat foods that he enjoys.

Since for most people a significant meal includes meat, it is customary to serve meat at the Shabbat meals, provided that the diners enjoy it. It is also customary to eat fish on Shabbat, provided that the diners enjoy it. Some people bake their own homemade loaves (*hallot*) for the Shabbat meals. This is a beautiful custom, but is not obligatory.

> Further reading: Those who bake bread of any kind, including *hallot,* must ensure they fulfill the commandment to separate a piece of dough before baking, as detailed on p. 547.

Cleanliness

One also demonstrates honor for Shabbat through straightening and cleaning one's home. One should lay a clean, fine tablecloth reserved for Shabbat on the dining table. It is advisable to set the table in advance, so that one can enter Shabbat in a calm and peaceful atmosphere.

The honor of Shabbat also requires one to welcome it in a state of personal cleanliness. One should shower in hot water and cut his nails before Shabbat. If this is not possible, he should at least wash his face, hands, and feet. It is also proper for everyone to own and wear a special set of clean, nice clothes for Shabbat.

Immersion

Some men have the custom to immerse themselves in a ritual bath [*mikva*] on Friday to increase their level of purity in honor of Shabbat.

Candle Lighting

The Sages instituted the practice of lighting candles before Shabbat. Three reasons have been given for this commandment: (1) The extra light in the home honors the Shabbat; (2) light from the candles adds to the enjoyment of Shabbat; and (3) the light of the candles enhances the atmosphere of peace in the home and prevents friction among members of the family. Lighting Shabbat candles is considered so important that one who does not have enough money to buy candles for Shabbat must seek help from others so that he can fulfill the mitzva.

Time of Lighting

Shabbat begins at sunset. From this moment onward it is prohibited to perform labor, which includes kindling a fire. Since it is a mitzva to impart the sanctity of the Shabbat onto some time of the weekday, one "brings in" Shabbat a bit early. The time for candle lighting that appears on calendars is approximately eighteen minutes before sunset.

One must be careful to light candles on time, and not to do so later than the permissible time. One can begin Shabbat early by lighting candles earlier than the published candle lighting time, and may then recite the *Kabbalat Shabbat* service before the standard time for the start of Shabbat. In the winter one may light candles as early as an hour before sunset, and in the summer from about an hour and twenty minutes before sunset. (These times are valid in Israel. In other parts of the world, one should consult the calendars prepared by local halakhic authorities).

Who Lights the Candles?

The mitzva of lighting Shabbat candles is primarily the woman's responsibility. There are two reasons for this: First, in practice it is generally the woman who manages the affairs of the home; second, lighting Shabbat candles is a remedy for the sin of eating from the Tree of Knowledge (which was brought about by the first woman, Eve), as this transgression "extinguished the light of the world" (*Tanḥuma, Noah* 1).

The obligation to light Shabbat candles applies to married women. Some have the custom that all girls above the age of bat mitzva light candles and recite the blessing. In some homes it is customary for girls from the age of three and above to light as well, and to recite the blessing. If there is no woman available to light the Shabbat candles, a man must do so.

Candles

The Shabbat candles that are sold in stores are well-suited for this purpose, as they burn brightly. Some people have the custom to light specifically with olive oil. In any event, the candles should be substantial enough to burn into the night, and should be positioned where they can be seen from the dining table.

How Many Candles?

While one candle suffices to fulfill the obligation to light Shabbat candles, over the generations the Sages instituted a common practice to light two candles, one corresponding to the verse, "Remember the Shabbat day" (Exodus 20:8), and the other corresponding to the verse, "Observe the Shabbat day" (Deuteronomy 5:12).

One may add as many candles as she wishes to these two lights. Many women add candles according to the number of children in the family. For example, a mother of four adds four candles to the two that every woman lights, for a total of six. Girls who light in addition to their mother light only one candle.

Forgetting

A woman who usually lights Shabbat candles but as a result of negligence failed to do so (even on one occasion) rectifies her error by lighting an additional candle every week from that point forward. For example, if until then she would generally light six candles, afterward she lights seven every week.

Procedure

It is a worthy custom to give money to charity before lighting the candles.

There are differences in custom with regard to when the blessing is recited. In the Ashkenazic tradition, the woman lights the candles first, then covers her eyes, and only then recites the blessing. After removing her hands from her eyes, she looks at the candles for a moment. Many Sephardic women first recite the blessing and then light the candles.

Text of Blessing

בָּרוּךְ אַתָּה אֲדֹנָי, אֱלֹהֵינוּ מֶלֶךְ הָעוֹלָם,
אֲשֶׁר קִדְּשָׁנוּ בְּמִצְוֹתָיו, וְצִוָּנוּ לְהַדְלִיק נֵר

*Barukh ata Adonai, Eloheinu, melekh
ha'olam, asher ki'deshanu bemitzvotav,*

שֶׁל שַׁבָּת (וְיֵשׁ הָאוֹמְרִים: ...שֶׁל שַׁבָּת קֹדֶשׁ).

vetzivanu lehadlik ner shel Shabbat (some say: *shel Shabbat kodesh*).

"Blessed are You, Lord our God, King of the universe, who sanctified us through His mitzvot, and commanded us to light the candle of Shabbat" (some say, "of holy Shabbat").

A woman who is a guest in a house where candles are already being lit also lights candles. In Ashkenazic communities and in some Sephardic communities it is customary for her to light and recite a blessing. In other Sephardic communities, the practice in this situation is to light without reciting a blessing.

Personal Prayer

Some add a personal prayer after lighting the candles, such as the prayer that follows:

יְהִי רָצוֹן מִלְּפָנֶיךָ אֲדֹנָי אֱלֹהַי וֵאלֹהֵי אֲבוֹתַי. שֶׁתְּחוֹנֵן אוֹתִי (וְאֶת אִישִׁי / וְאֶת בָּנַי / וְאֶת אָבִי / וְאֶת אִמִּי) וְאֶת כָּל קְרוֹבַי. וְתִתֵּן לָנוּ וּלְכָל יִשְׂרָאֵל חַיִּים טוֹבִים וַאֲרֻכִּים, וְתִזְכְּרֵנוּ בְּזִכְרוֹן טוֹבָה וּבְרָכָה. וְתִפְקְדֵנוּ בִּפְקֻדַּת יְשׁוּעָה וְרַחֲמִים וּתְבָרְכֵנוּ בְּרָכוֹת גְּדוֹלוֹת, וְתַשְׁלִים בָּתֵּינוּ, וְתַשְׁכֵּן שְׁכִינָתְךָ בֵּינֵינוּ. וְזַכֵּנִי לְגַדֵּל בָּנִים וּבְנֵי בָנִים חֲכָמִים וּנְבוֹנִים. אוֹהֲבֵי אֲדֹנָי, יִרְאֵי אֱלֹהִים, אַנְשֵׁי אֱמֶת, זֶרַע קֹדֶשׁ, בַּאדֹנָי דְּבֵקִים, וּמְאִירִים אֶת הָעוֹלָם בַּתּוֹרָה וּבְמַעֲשִׂים טוֹבִים וּבְכָל מְלֶאכֶת עֲבוֹדַת הַבּוֹרֵא. אָנָּא שְׁמַע אֶת תְּחִנָּתִי בָּעֵת הַזֹּאת, בִּזְכוּת שָׂרָה וְרִבְקָה וְרָחֵל וְלֵאָה אִמּוֹתֵינוּ. וְהָאֵר נֵרֵנוּ שֶׁלֹּא יִכְבֶּה לְעוֹלָם וָעֶד וְהָאֵר פָּנֶיךָ וְנִוָּשֵׁעָה, אָמֵן.

Yehi ratzon milefanekha, Adonai Elohai velohai avotai, shetehonen oti (ve'et ishi / ve'et banai / ve'et avi / ve'et imi) ve'et kol kerovai. Vetiten lanu ulkhol Yisrael hayim tovim va'arukim, vetizkerenu bezikhron tova uvrakha. Vetifkedenu befkudat yeshua verahamim utvarekhenu berakhot gedolot, vetashlim bateinu, vetashken shekhinatekha beineinu. Vezakeni legadel banim uvnei vanim hakhamim unvonim, ohavei Adonei, yirei Elohim, anshei emet, zera kodesh, badonai devekim, ume'irim et ha'olam baTorah uvma'asim tovim uvkhol melekhet avodat haboreh. Ana, shema et tehinati ba'et hazot, bizkhut Sarah veRivka veRahel veLeah imoteinu. Veha'er nerenu shelo yikhbe le'olam va'ed, veha'er panekha venivashe'a, amen.

"May it be Your will, Lord my God and God of my forefathers, that You give grace to me (and my husband / and my children / and my father / and my mother) and all those close to me, and give us and all Israel good and long lives. And remember us with a legacy of goodness and blessing; come to us with compassion and bless us with great blessings. Build our homes until they are complete, and allow Your Presence to live among us.

"And may I merit to raise children and grandchildren, each one wise and understanding, loving the Lord and in awe of God, people of truth, holy children, who will cling to the Lord, and light up the world with Torah and with good deeds, and with all the service that serves the Creator. Please, hear my pleading at this time, in the merit of Sarah, Rebecca, Rachel, and Leah our mothers, and light our candle so that it will never be extinguished, and light up Your face so that we shall be saved. Amen."

> Further reading: To learn about a miracle that occurred with the Shabbat candles, see *A Concise Guide to the Sages*, p. 349.

Kabbalat Shabbat

As on every evening, the congregation recites the prayers of the evening service, but on Friday night they first recite a supplement called *Kabbalat Shabbat*, which means receiving Shabbat. It is a formal and celebratory welcome for Shabbat, which is compared to a queen. *Kabbalat Shabbat*, which consists of several psalms and one liturgical poem, praises the greatness of the Creator and the special nature of Shabbat.

Lekha Dodi

At the heart of *Kabbalat Shabbat* is the liturgical poem *Lekha Dodi*, "Let us go, my beloved," with the refrain "Let us go, my beloved, to meet the bride; we will welcome the presence of Shabbat." Composed in the sixteenth century by the kabbalist Rabbi Shlomo HaLevi Alkabetz, the poem alludes to the author in an acrostic formed by the first letter of each verse. In most synagogues it is customary for the entire congregation to sing the poem together.

Before the last verse ("Come in peace"), everyone turns around and chants or sings that verse while facing westward, since according to the Talmud the Divine Presence is revealed from the west (*Menaḥot* 98b).

Evening Service

After *Kabbalat Shabbat* the congregation recites the evening service. The *Amida* prayer for Shabbat is shorter than that of the rest of the week, as it contains only seven blessings instead of the usual nineteen. One who erroneously proceeded from the third blessing, the blessing of Holiness, to the first words of the formula of the weekday evening service should finish the blessing he started, and then return to the text of the Shabbat *Amida* prayer.

After the *Amida*, the entire congregation stands up and loudly recites the passage beginning "The heavens and the earth and their entire host were completed [*vaykhulu*]" (Genesis 2:1–3). These verses describe the completion of the process of creation, on the first Shabbat in history.

Immediately following this passage, the prayer leader [*hazan*] continues with a highly condensed version of the seven blessings of the *Amida* that the congregation just recited. In the middle of the passage, the rest of the congregation joins him. This section is recited only when praying in a congregation; an individual praying alone does not say it.

Blessing Children

In many communities it is customary for each father to bless his children on Friday night. In some homes the mother gives these blessings as well. This can be done in the synagogue at the conclusion of the evening service, or after returning home. Some fathers lay their hands on the head of the child receiving the blessing.

Before the blessing one first recites:

לְבֵן: יְשִׂימְךָ אֱלֹהִים כְּאֶפְרַיִם וְכִמְנַשֶּׁה.

For a son: *Yesi'mekha Elohim ke'Efrayim vekhiMenashe.*

לְבַת: יְשִׂימֵךְ אֱלֹהִים כְּשָׂרָה רִבְקָה רָחֵל וְלֵאָה.

For a daughter: *Yesimekh Elohim ke-Sara, Rivka, Raḥel, veLeah.*

For a son: "May God make you like Ephraim and like Manasseh" (Genesis 48:2).

For a daughter: "May God make you like Sarah, Rebecca, Rachel, and Leah."

The text of the blessing itself is the Priestly Benediction:

יְבָרֶכְךָ אֲדֹנָי וְיִשְׁמְרֶךָ. יָאֵר אֲדֹנָי פָּנָיו אֵלֶיךָ וִיחֻנֶּךָ. יִשָּׂא אֲדֹנָי פָּנָיו אֵלֶיךָ וְיָשֵׂם לְךָ שָׁלוֹם.

Yevarekhekha Adonai veyishmerekha; ya'er Adonai panav elekha viḥuneka; yisa Adonai panav elekha veyasem lekha shalom.

"The Lord shall bless you, and keep you. The Lord shall shine His countenance to you, and be gracious to you. The Lord shall lift His countenance to you, and grant you peace" (Numbers 6:24–26).

Before the Meal

Shalom Aleikhem

When a person comes home from the synagogue on Friday night, he is said to be accompanied by two ministering angels, one good and the other bad. If the house is tidy and the table is set and ready for the meal, the good angel blesses the family that the same situation should prevail next week too, and the evil angel is forced to respond Amen. If the situation at home is otherwise, the evil angel "blesses" the family that the same situation should prevail the following week, and the good angel is forced to respond Amen. This idea is the basis for the liturgical poem *Shalom Aleikhem*, "Welcome to you, ministering angels," which is sung upon one's return from the synagogue, before *Kiddush* and the meal.

Eshet Hayil

After *Shalom Aleikhem*, the family recites or sings the verses of Woman of Valor [*Eshet Hayil*], an alphabetical acrostic from the book of Proverbs (31:10–31). The basic reason for this recitation is that it constitutes a good opportunity to thank the woman of the house, a true woman of valor, who works hard to prepare Shabbat. According to another explanation, the Divine Presence is also called "a woman of valor," and the passage is chanted in its honor. A third reason is that according to kabbalistic tradition, the twenty-two verses of *Eshet Hayil* correspond to the twenty-two "channels" of spiritual abundance that are given to us on Shabbat.

Evening *Kiddush*

The Torah states, "Remember the Sabbath day, to keep it holy [*lekadesho*]" (Exodus 20:8). Remembering Shabbat means that we sanctify it through a verbal declaration. Consequently, one performs the ritual of sanctification [*Kiddush*] at the beginning of Shabbat, before eating. In *Kiddush* one mentions the commandments of rest and of cessation from labor on this day, in addition to having mentioned them in the evening service. While reciting *Kiddush*, one holds a cup filled with wine in order to bestow importance upon the rite. One should not eat or drink anything from the beginning of Shabbat until after reciting *Kiddush*.

Preparations for *Kiddush*

One prepares for *Kiddush* as follows:

Hallot

Two or more *hallot* are placed on the table. These are termed double loaves [*lehem mishneh*]. The reason for this is that the obligation of Shabbat meals is derived from the story of the manna provided to the Israelites in the wilderness. On Friday, a double portion of manna was given, so that they would not have to gather it on Shabbat and thereby profane the day's rest. The two *hallot* serve as a reminder of this event.

The *hallot* are placed on a tray or cloth and are covered with a cloth, as the manna was "wrapped" from above and below in two layers of dew.

The *hallot* must be covered during *Kiddush*. The reason stems from the fact that the bread and its blessing are of greater prominence than the wine and its blessing, which means that theoretically one should recite the blessing over the *hallot* before *Kiddush* over the wine. Since in practice one first recites *Kiddush* over the wine, the *hallot* are covered throughout *Kiddush*, so that they will not be snubbed and their blessing will not be overlooked.

Cup

The *Kiddush* cup must be whole, not broken, cracked, or damaged. It is proper to use an attractive cup that honors the blessing. Many use a silver goblet for *Kiddush*. One must rinse the cup thoroughly before pouring the wine.

Wine

One recites *Kiddush* on wine. Those who cannot drink wine should recite *Kiddush* on grape juice. Only grape juice made from actual grapes is suitable for *Kiddush*; a grape-flavored soft drink is not.

Procedure

Some are accustomed to stand for *Kiddush*. Others sit, while yet others stand for the first section and then sit before the blessing "Who creates fruit of the vine." Each person should follow the custom of his community or family. *Kiddush* is recited out loud, even if one is dining alone. One must be able to at least hear his own voice.

From the start of *Kiddush* until after drinking the wine, no one should talk. This applies equally to the one reciting the *Kiddush* and to those listening to him.

Before starting, the one reciting the *Kiddush* should hold the cup of wine in his right hand and raise it. He should glance briefly at the lit candles.

During *Kiddush* itself, and especially during the blessing "Who creates fruit of the vine," he should look at the wine in the cup.

Women are obligated in the mitzva of *Kiddush*, and they may recite *Kiddush* themselves.

Text

Kiddush comprises three sections: verses describing the first Shabbat after the creation of the world, the blessing "Who creates fruit of the vine" over the wine, and the sanctification [*kiddush*] blessing itself.

For Ashkenazim:

(בלחש: וַיְהִי עֶרֶב וַיְהִי בֹקֶר) יוֹם הַשִּׁשִּׁי. וַיְכֻלּוּ הַשָּׁמַיִם וְהָאָרֶץ וְכָל צְבָאָם. וַיְכַל אֱלֹהִים בַּיּוֹם הַשְּׁבִיעִי מְלַאכְתּוֹ אֲשֶׁר עָשָׂה, וַיִּשְׁבֹּת בַּיּוֹם הַשְּׁבִיעִי מִכָּל מְלַאכְתּוֹ אֲשֶׁר עָשָׂה. וַיְבָרֶךְ אֱלֹהִים אֶת יוֹם הַשְּׁבִיעִי וַיְקַדֵּשׁ אֹתוֹ, כִּי בוֹ שָׁבַת מִכָּל מְלַאכְתּוֹ אֲשֶׁר בָּרָא אֱלֹהִים לַעֲשׂוֹת.

(Quietly: *Vayhi erev vayhi voker*) *Yom hashishi. Vaykhulu hashamayim veha'aretz vekhol tzeva'am. Vaykhal Elohim bayom hashevi'i melakhto asher asa, vayishbot bayom hashevi'i mikol melakhto asher asa. Vayvarekh Elohim et yom hashevi'i vaykadesh oto, ki vo shavat mikol melakhto asher bara Elohim la'asot.*

סַבְרִי מָרָנָן וְרַבָּנָן וְרַבּוֹתַי.

Savri (maranan verabanan verabotai):

בָּרוּךְ אַתָּה אֲדֹנָי, אֱלֹהֵינוּ מֶלֶךְ הָעוֹלָם, בּוֹרֵא פְּרִי הַגָּפֶן.

Barukh ata Adonai, Eloheinu melekh ha'olam, boreh peri hagafen.

בָּרוּךְ אַתָּה אֲדֹנָי, אֱלֹהֵינוּ מֶלֶךְ הָעוֹלָם, אֲשֶׁר קִדְּשָׁנוּ בְּמִצְוֹתָיו וְרָצָה בָנוּ, וְשַׁבַּת קָדְשׁוֹ בְּאַהֲבָה וּבְרָצוֹן הִנְחִילָנוּ, זִכָּרוֹן לְמַעֲשֵׂה בְרֵאשִׁית. (כִּי הוּא יוֹם) תְּחִלָּה לְמִקְרָאֵי קֹדֶשׁ זֵכֶר לִיצִיאַת מִצְרָיִם. (כִּי בָנוּ בָחַרְתָּ וְאוֹתָנוּ קִדַּשְׁתָּ מִכָּל הָעַמִּים) וְשַׁבַּת קָדְשְׁךָ בְּאַהֲבָה וּבְרָצוֹן הִנְחַלְתָּנוּ. בָּרוּךְ אַתָּה אֲדֹנָי, מְקַדֵּשׁ הַשַּׁבָּת.

Barukh ata Adonai, Eloheinu, melekh ha'olam, asher ki'deshanu bemitzvotav veratza vanu, veShabbat kodsho be'ahava uvratzon hinhilanu, zikaron lema'aseh vereshit. (Ki hu yom) tehila lemikra'ei kodesh, zekher litziat Mitzrayim. (Ki vanu vaharta ve'otanu kidashta mikol ha'amim), veShabbat kodshekha be'ahava uvratzon hinhaltanu. Barukh ata Adonai, mekadesh haShabbat.

(Quietly: "It was evening and it was morning,) the sixth day. The heavens and the earth and their entire host were completed. God completed on the seventh day His works that He had made; He rested on the seventh day from all His works that He had made. God blessed the seventh day, and sanctified it; because on it He rested from all His works that God created to make" (Genesis 1:31–2:3).

"Attention, (masters, gentlemen, my teachers):

"Blessed are You, Lord our God, King of the universe, who creates fruit of the vine.

"Blessed are You, Lord our God, King of the universe, who sanctified us through His commandments and desired us; and He has given us, with love and with desire, His holy Shabbat, in remembrance of the work of creation. (For it is the) first (day) of the holy festivals, in memory of the exodus from Egypt. (For You chose us and it is us You have sanctified above all the nations,) and You have given us Your holy Shabbat with love and with desire. Blessed are You, Lord our God, King of the universe, who sanctifies the Shabbat."

For Sephardim:

מְקַדֵּשׁ: וַיְהִי עֶרֶב וַיְהִי בֹקֶר יוֹם הַשִּׁשִּׁי. וַיְכֻלּוּ הַשָּׁמַיִם וְהָאָרֶץ וְכָל צְבָאָם. וַיְכַל אֱלֹהִים בַּיּוֹם הַשְּׁבִיעִי מְלַאכְתּוֹ אֲשֶׁר עָשָׂה, וַיִּשְׁבֹּת בַּיּוֹם הַשְּׁבִיעִי מִכָּל מְלַאכְתּוֹ אֲשֶׁר עָשָׂה. וַיְבָרֶךְ אֱלֹהִים אֶת יוֹם הַשְּׁבִיעִי וַיְקַדֵּשׁ אֹתוֹ, כִּי בוֹ שָׁבַת מִכָּל מְלַאכְתּוֹ אֲשֶׁר בָּרָא אֱלֹהִים לַעֲשׂוֹת.

Leader: *Vayhi erev vayhi voker yom hashishi. Vaykhulu hashamayim veha'aretz vekhol tzeva'am. Vaykhal Elohim bayom hashevi'i melakhto asher asa, vayishbot bayom hashevi'i mikol melakhto asher asa. Vayvarekh Elohim et yom hashevi'i vaykadesh oto, ki vo shavat mikol melakhto asher bara Elohim la'asot.*

סָבְרִי מָרָנָן.

Savri maranan.

נוכחים: לְחַיִּים!

Others: Leḥayim.

מְקַדֵּשׁ: בָּרוּךְ אַתָּה אֲדֹנָי, אֱלֹהֵינוּ מֶלֶךְ הָעוֹלָם, בּוֹרֵא פְּרִי הַגָּפֶן.

Leader: Barukh ata Adonai, Eloheinu, melekh ha'olam, boreh peri hagefen.

בָּרוּךְ אַתָּה אֲדֹנָי, אֱלֹהֵינוּ מֶלֶךְ הָעוֹלָם, אֲשֶׁר קִדְּשָׁנוּ בְּמִצְוֹתָיו וְרָצָה בָנוּ, וְשַׁבָּת קָדְשׁוֹ בְּאַהֲבָה וּבְרָצוֹן הִנְחִילָנוּ, זִכָּרוֹן לְמַעֲשֵׂה בְרֵאשִׁית, תְּחִלָּה לְמִקְרָאֵי קֹדֶשׁ, זֵכֶר לִיצִיאַת מִצְרַיִם. וְשַׁבַּת קָדְשְׁךָ בְּאַהֲבָה

Barukh ata Adonai, Eloheinu, melekh ha'olam, asher ki'deshanu bemitzvotav veratza vanu, veShabbat kodsho be'ahava uvratzon hinḥilanu, zikaron lema'aseh vereshit. Teḥila lemikra'ei kodesh, zekher litziat Mitzrayim,

וּבְרָצוֹן הִנְחַלְתָּנוּ, בָּרוּךְ אַתָּה אֲדֹנָי, מְקַדֵּשׁ הַשַּׁבָּת.

veShabbat kodshekha be'ahava uvratzon hinhaltanu. Barukh ata Adonai, mekadesh HaShabbat.

Leader: "It was evening and it was morning, the sixth day. The heavens and the earth and their entire host were completed. God completed on the seventh day His works that He had made; He rested on the seventh day from all His works that He had made. God blessed the seventh day, and sanctified it; because on it He rested from all His works that God created to make" (Genesis 1:31–2:3).

"Attention, masters."

Others: "To life!"

Leader: "Blessed are You, Lord our God, King of the universe, who creates fruit of the vine.

"Blessed are You, Lord our God, King of the universe, who sanctified us through His commandments and desired us, and He has given us, with love and with desire, His holy Shabbat, in remembrance of the work of creation. [It is] first among the holy festivals, in memory of the exodus from Egypt. And You have given us Your holy Shabbat with love and with desire. Blessed are You, Lord our God, King of the universe, who sanctifies the Shabbat."

Drinking the Wine

The one reciting *Kiddush* should drink from the wine, at least a quantity that fills one side of his mouth. After he has drunk from the wine, it is proper for each of the listeners to also taste some of it.

Location

Kiddush should be recited in the location where one intends to eat his meal. This is derived from the verse "And you call the Sabbath a delight" (Isaiah 58:13), which is interpreted to mean that the place where one recites the "calling," i.e., *Kiddush*, should be the place where one enjoys the "delight" of the Shabbat meal. One who recites *Kiddush* over wine but does not sit down straightaway to eat his meal in that place has not fulfilled the obligation of *Kiddush*.

One who returns from the synagogue and needs to postpone the meal must wait to recite *Kiddush* until the time of the meal, at which point he should recite *Kiddush* and immediately afterward sit down to eat. Alternatively, one may recite *Kiddush* and immediately eat a food whose blessing is "Who creates various kinds of nourishment [*mezonot*]," in a quantity that renders him liable to recite the blessing after food (see p. 518). The reason is that such eating is itself considered a "meal." Then, when the time comes for the actual meal, he merely washes his hands, recites the blessing over the *hallot*, and partakes of the meal.

It is important to know that with regard to *Kiddush* in the evening and in the day, if one merely tastes the wine or eats only refreshments whose blessing is not "Who creates various kinds of nourishment," he does not fulfill the requirement that *Kiddush* be recited in the place of the meal. Therefore, those who were present at a "*kiddush*" in the synagogue but did not eat bread or those types of baked goods must later recite *Kiddush* in the place that they will be eating their meal.

Kiddush over Hallot

When there is no wine available, or when the one reciting *Kiddush* is forbidden or unable to drink wine, he may perform the evening *Kiddush* over the *hallot* intended for the blessing of *HaMotzi*, "Who brings forth bread from the earth." In such a case, the procedure is as follows: He washes his hands for the meal (as detailed on p. 525, in the section dealing with the ritual washing of the hands for a meal), places his hands on the two *hallot* that are covered with a cloth, recites the first part of *Kiddush* (the *Vaykhulu* passage), then removes the cloth, holds the *hallot* themselves, and recites the blessing of *HaMotzi*. He subsequently recites the sanctification blessing ("Who sanctified us through His commandments and desired us"), cuts the bread, takes a bite, and distributes slices of bread among the rest of the diners.

The Evening Meal

Both men and women are obligated to eat three meals over the course of Shabbat: on Friday night, Shabbat day, and Shabbat afternoon. The third meal is referred to as *seuda shelishit*, meaning "the third meal." This *halakha* is also derived from the manna provided to the children of Israel in the wilderness, as the verse that describes Moses' instruction to the Israelites to gather the manna mentions the word "today" three times (Exodus 16:25).

Bread

The Shabbat meal should include bread, and therefore it starts with ritually washing one's hands and reciting the blessing of *HaMotzi* over the *hallot*. One should eat at least an olive-bulk of the bread, roughly equivalent to one slice the thickness of ordinary sliced bread. Ideally, one should eat bread at each of the three meals, including the third, as the Torah refers to the manna as "bread."

Singing

During the Shabbat meal it is customary to sing Shabbat songs, which are called *zemirot*. Some of these songs are customarily sung in all communities, while others are unique to a particular community. Some of the *zemirot* are specific to particular Shabbat meals.

Grace after Meals

At the end of the meal, one recites Grace after Meals, as one does after every meal at which bread was eaten (see p. 527).

The Sages instituted that on special days like Shabbat or festival days, the events of that day should be mentioned in the prayers. Accordingly, in Grace after Meals of Shabbat one adds a special paragraph for Shabbat, called *Retzeh*, which begins, "Favor [*retzeh*] and strengthen us…through the commandment of the seventh day, this great and holy Shabbat, etc."

Likewise, in the final blessing, *Al hamihya*, which is recited after eating food products from the five species of grain, eating a fruit of the seven species, or drinking wine, one mentions and commemorates Shabbat.

Prayers on Shabbat Morning

Morning Service

In the Shabbat morning service, certain selected psalms are added which are not recited on weekdays. The *Amida* prayer on Shabbat is shorter than on the other days of the week, and contains only seven blessings.

At the end of the morning service, the Torah is read. On every Shabbat a different weekly Torah portion [*parashat hashavua*] is read, in sequence, so that the congregation completes the entire Torah each year.

Reading the Torah

The public reading of the Torah on Monday, Thursday, and Shabbat mornings was instituted by Moses himself, so that the people would not go for three days without Torah study.

Subsections of the Torah Portion

The weekly Torah portion, which is read on Shabbat morning, is divided into seven sections, known as *aliyot*. A different person ascends [*oleh*] for the reading of each section and recites blessings before and after the reading. An individual section is called an *aliya*, and the person called up for the reading is called the *oleh*.

The first person called up to the reading of the Torah is a *kohen* (if there is a *kohen* among the congregants), followed by a Levite (if one is present). The rest of the *aliyot* are for Israelites, i.e., those who are not *kohanim* or Levites. The seventh *aliya* completes the weekly Torah portion, after which the last verses of the Torah portion are repeated. This repetition of the final verses is called the *maftir*. A *kohen*, Levite, or Israelite may be called up for *maftir*.

Raising the Torah [*Hagbaha*]
The custom of Sephardim is to lift up the Torah scroll before the reading. By contrast, Ashkenazim raise the scroll after the reading. This ceremonial lifting is performed so that the congregation can see the writing of the Torah scroll.

At the end of the reading in Ashkenazic communities, the scroll is rolled up, tied with a belt, and wrapped in its special cover. Sephardim close up and protect their Torah scrolls in a hard, decorative case.

Haftara
At this stage the person called for *maftir* reads the *haftara*, a passage from one of the books of the Prophets. Every week a different *haftara* is read. The verses of the *haftara* are generally connected to the content of the weekly portion.

Whereas the Torah portion must be read from a Torah scroll that was written by a scribe on parchment, with no vocalization or cantillation marks, in many congregations the *haftara* is read from a printed book, which contains both of these aids to accurate reading.

If the one who is called up for the reading of the *maftir* finds it difficult to read the *haftara* or to chant its melody, he may recite the blessing before and after the *haftara*, while leaving the reading of the *haftara* itself for another person who is well versed in the reading.

Additional [*Musaf*] Service
After the Torah reading, the congregation recites the additional [*Musaf*] prayer service. This festive prayer is unique to Shabbatot, festivals, and *Rosh Hodesh*. It was instituted by the Sages as a substitute for the additional [*musaf*] offering that was brought in the Temple on these holy days. This prayer also contains seven blessings. At the conclusion of the *Musaf* service, some have the custom to recite or even sing together certain liturgical poems, such as *Anim Zemirot*.

The Daytime Meal

Daytime *Kiddush*

One must recite *Kiddush* over a full cup of wine before the Shabbat daytime meal as well. All the laws of *Kiddush* mentioned with regard to the *Kiddush* of Friday night also apply to this *Kiddush*, including that both men and women are obligated in its recitation. One does not have the option to recite *Kiddush* over *hallot* in the day.

The main part of the daytime *Kiddush* is the blessing over the wine, "Who creates fruit of the vine." Some add verses that deal with Shabbat before the blessing.

For Ashkenazim:

אִם תָּשִׁיב מִשַּׁבָּת רַגְלֶךָ עֲשׂוֹת חֲפָצֶךָ בְּיוֹם קָדְשִׁי, וְקָרָאתָ לַשַּׁבָּת עֹנֶג לִקְדוֹשׁ אֲדֹנָי מְכֻבָּד, וְכִבַּדְתּוֹ מֵעֲשׂוֹת דְּרָכֶיךָ מִמְּצוֹא חֶפְצְךָ וְדַבֵּר דָּבָר. אָז תִּתְעַנַּג עַל אֲדֹנָי וְהִרְכַּבְתִּיךָ עַל בָּמֳתֵי אָרֶץ, וְהַאֲכַלְתִּיךָ נַחֲלַת יַעֲקֹב אָבִיךָ, כִּי פִּי אֲדֹנָי דִּבֵּר.

Im tashiv miShabbat raglekha asot hafatzekha beyom kodshi, vekarata laShabbat oneg likdosh Adonai mekhubad, vekhibadto me'asot derakhekha mimetzo heftzekha vedaber davar, az titanag al Adonai, vehirkavtikha al bamotei aretz, veha'akhaltikha nahalat Ya'akov avikha, ki pi Adonai diber.

וְשָׁמְרוּ בְנֵי יִשְׂרָאֵל אֶת הַשַּׁבָּת, לַעֲשׂוֹת אֶת הַשַּׁבָּת לְדֹרֹתָם בְּרִית עוֹלָם. בֵּינִי וּבֵין בְּנֵי יִשְׂרָאֵל, אוֹת הִיא לְעוֹלָם כִּי שֵׁשֶׁת יָמִים עָשָׂה אֲדֹנָי אֶת הַשָּׁמַיִם וְאֶת הָאָרֶץ, וּבַיּוֹם הַשְּׁבִיעִי שָׁבַת וַיִּנָּפַשׁ.

Vesha'meru venei Yisrael et haShabbat, la'asot et haShabbat ledorotam berit olam. Beini uvein benei Yisrael ot hi le'olam, ki sheshet yamim asa Adonai et hashamayim ve'et ha'aretz, uvayom hashevi'i shavat vayinafash.

זָכוֹר אֶת יוֹם הַשַּׁבָּת לְקַדְּשׁוֹ. שֵׁשֶׁת יָמִים תַּעֲבֹד וְעָשִׂיתָ כָּל מְלַאכְתֶּךָ, וְיוֹם הַשְּׁבִיעִי שַׁבָּת לַאֲדֹנָי אֱלֹהֶיךָ לֹא תַעֲשֶׂה כָל מְלָאכָה, אַתָּה וּבִנְךָ וּבִתֶּךָ עַבְדְּךָ וַאֲמָתְךָ וּבְהֶמְתֶּךָ וְגֵרְךָ אֲשֶׁר בִּשְׁעָרֶיךָ, כִּי שֵׁשֶׁת יָמִים עָשָׂה אֲדֹנָי אֶת הַשָּׁמַיִם וְאֶת הָאָרֶץ, אֶת הַיָּם וְאֶת כָּל אֲשֶׁר בָּם, וַיָּנַח בַּיּוֹם הַשְּׁבִיעִי.

Zakhor et yom haShabbat lekadesho. Sheshet yamim ta'avod ve'asita kol melakhtekha. Veyom hashevi'i Shabbat ladonai Elohekha. Lo ta'aseh khol melakha, ata uvinkha uvitekha, avdekha va'amtekha uvhemtekha, vegerekha asher bisharekha. Ki sheshet yamim asa Adonai et hashamayim ve'et ha'aretz, et hayam ve'et kol asher bam, vayanah bayom hashevi'i.

עַל כֵּן בֵּרַךְ אֲדֹנָי אֶת יוֹם הַשַּׁבָּת וַיְקַדְּשֵׁהוּ.

Al ken berakh Adonai et yom haShabbat vayka'deshehu.

סָבְרִי מָרָנָן וְרַבָּנָן וְרַבּוֹתַי.

Savri (maranan verabanan verabotai):

בָּרוּךְ אַתָּה אֲדֹנָי, אֱלֹהֵינוּ מֶלֶךְ הָעוֹלָם, בּוֹרֵא פְּרִי הַגָּפֶן.

Barukh ata Adonai, Eloheinu, melekh ha'olam, boreh peri hagafen.

"If you restrain your walking because of the Sabbath, pursuing your needs on the day of My holiness, and you call the Sabbath a delight and the Lord's sacred, honored, and you honor it by refraining from doing your business, from seeking your needs, and from speaking of matters, then you will delight in the Lord, and I will mount you onto the heights of the earth and I will feed you the inheritance of Jacob your forefather, for the mouth of the Lord has spoken" (Isaiah 58:13–14).

"The children of Israel shall keep the Sabbath, to observe the Sabbath for their generations, an eternal covenant. Between Me and the children of Israel, it is a sign forever. For in six days the Lord made the heaven and the earth, and on the seventh day He rested and was invigorated" (Exodus 31:16–17).

"Remember the Sabbath day, to keep it holy. Six days you shall work and perform all your labor. The seventh day is Sabbath for the Lord your God; you shall not perform any labor, you, and your son, and your daughter, your slave, and your maidservant, and your animal, and your stranger who is within your gates, because in six days the Lord made the heavens and the earth, the sea and everything that is in them and He rested on the seventh day; therefore, the Lord blessed the Sabbath day and He sanctified it" (Exodus 20:8–11).

"Attention, (masters, rabbis, my teachers).

"Blessed are You, Lord our God, King of the universe, who creates fruit of the vine."

For Sephardim:

מִקְדָּשׁ: מִזְמוֹר לְדָוִד, אֲדֹנָי רֹעִי לֹא אֶחְסָר. בִּנְאוֹת דֶּשֶׁא יַרְבִּיצֵנִי, עַל מֵי מְנֻחוֹת יְנַהֲלֵנִי. נַפְשִׁי יְשׁוֹבֵב, יַנְחֵנִי בְמַעְגְּלֵי צֶדֶק לְמַעַן שְׁמוֹ. גַּם כִּי אֵלֵךְ בְּגֵיא צַלְמָוֶת, לֹא אִירָא רָע כִּי אַתָּה עִמָּדִי, שִׁבְטְךָ

Leader: *Mizmor LeDavid: Adonai ro'i lo ehsar. Binot deshe yarbitzeni, al mei menuhot yenahaleni. Nafshi yeshovev, yanheni vema'agelei tzedek lema'an shemo. Gam ki elekh begei tzalmavet lo ira ra, ki ata imadi, shivtekha*

וּמִשְׁעַנְתֶּךָ הֵמָּה יְנַחֲמֻנִי. תַּעֲרֹךְ לְפָנַי שֻׁלְחָן נֶגֶד צֹרְרָי, דִּשַּׁנְתָּ בַשֶּׁמֶן רֹאשִׁי כּוֹסִי רְוָיָה. אַךְ טוֹב וָחֶסֶד יִרְדְּפוּנִי כָּל יְמֵי חַיָּי, וְשַׁבְתִּי בְּבֵית אֲדֹנָי לְאֹרֶךְ יָמִים.

umishantekha hema yenaḥamuni. Ta'arokh lefanai shulḥan neged tzorerai. Dishanta vashemen roshi, kosi revaya. Akh tov vaḥesed yirdefuni kol yemei ḥayay, veshavti beveit Adonai le'orekh yamim.

אִם תָּשִׁיב מִשַּׁבָּת רַגְלֶךָ, עֲשׂוֹת חֲפָצֶךָ בְּיוֹם קָדְשִׁי, וְקָרָאתָ לַשַּׁבָּת עֹנֶג לִקְדוֹשׁ אֲדֹנָי מְכֻבָּד, וְכִבַּדְתּוֹ מֵעֲשׂוֹת דְּרָכֶיךָ, מִמְּצוֹא חֶפְצְךָ וְדַבֵּר דָּבָר. אָז תִּתְעַנַּג עַל אֲדֹנָי וְהִרְכַּבְתִּיךָ עַל בָּמֳתֵי אָרֶץ, וְהַאֲכַלְתִּיךָ נַחֲלַת יַעֲקֹב אָבִיךָ כִּי פִּי אֲדֹנָי דִּבֵּר.

Im tashiv miShabbat raglekha asot hafatzekha beyom kodshi, vekarata laShabbat oneg likdosh Adonai mekhubad, vekhibadto me'asot derakhekha mimetzo ḥeftzekha vedaber davar, az titanag al Adonai, vehirkavtikha al bamotei aretz, veha'akhaltikha naḥalat Ya'akov avikha, ki pi Adonai diber.

וְשָׁמְרוּ בְנֵי יִשְׂרָאֵל אֶת הַשַּׁבָּת, לַעֲשׂוֹת אֶת הַשַּׁבָּת לְדֹרֹתָם בְּרִית עוֹלָם. בֵּינִי וּבֵין בְּנֵי יִשְׂרָאֵל אוֹת הִיא לְעֹלָם. כִּי שֵׁשֶׁת יָמִים עָשָׂה אֲדֹנָי אֶת הַשָּׁמַיִם וְאֶת הָאָרֶץ, וּבַיּוֹם הַשְּׁבִיעִי שָׁבַת וַיִּנָּפַשׁ.

Vesha'meru venei Yisrael et haShabbat, la'asot et haShabbat ledorotam berit olam. Beini uvein benei Yisrael ot hi le'olam, ki Sheshet yamim asa Adonai et hashamayim ve'et ha'aretz, uvayom hashevi'i shavat vayinafash.

עַל כֵּן בֵּרַךְ אֲדֹנָי אֶת יוֹם הַשַּׁבָּת וַיְקַדְּשֵׁהוּ.

Al ken berakh Adonai et yom haShabbat vayka'deshehu.

סַבְרִי מָרָנָן.

Savri maranan.

נוכחים: לְחַיִּים!

Others: Leḥayim.

מקדש: בָּרוּךְ אַתָּה אֲדֹנָי, אֱלֹהֵינוּ מֶלֶךְ הָעוֹלָם, בּוֹרֵא פְּרִי הַגָּפֶן.

Leader: Barukh ata Adonai, Eloheinu, melekh ha'olam, boreh peri hagefen.

Leader: "A psalm by David. The Lord is my shepherd; I lack nothing. He has me lie down in green pastures; He leads me beside still waters. He restores my soul; He leads me in paths of righteousness for His name's sake. Even when I walk through the valley of the shadow of death, I fear no evil, for You are with me; Your rod and Your staff, they comfort me. You prepare a table before me in the presence of my enemies. You anoint my head with oil; my cup is full. May only goodness and kindness pursue me all the days of my life, and I will dwell in the House of the Lord forever" (Psalms 23).

"If you restrain your walking because of the Sabbath, pursuing your needs on the day of My holiness, and you call the Sabbath a delight and the Lord's sacred, honored, and you honor it by refraining from doing your business, from seeking your needs, and from speaking of matters, then you will delight in the Lord and I will mount you onto the heights of the earth and I will feed you the inheritance of Jacob your forefather, for the mouth of the Lord has spoken" (Isaiah 58:13–14).

"The children of Israel shall keep the Sabbath, to observe the Sabbath for their generations, an eternal covenant. Between Me and the children of Israel, it is a sign forever. For in six days the Lord made the heaven and the earth, and on the seventh day He rested and was invigorated" (Exodus 31:16–17).

"Therefore, the Lord blessed the Sabbath day and He sanctified it" (Exodus 20:11).

"Attention, masters."

Others: "To life!"

Leader: "Blessed are You, Lord our God, King of the universe, who creates fruit of the vine."

Two *Hallot*

For the daytime meal as well, one should recite the blessing "Who brings forth bread from the earth" over *lehem mishneh*, double loaves.

Shabbat Customs

Sleep

As it is a mitzva to enjoy the Shabbat, and it has been said that "sleep on Shabbat is a delight," one who is accustomed to taking a nap on a weekday should do so on Shabbat as well.

Torah on Shabbat

At the same time, the Sages stated in the Talmud, "Shabbat and festivals were given to Israel only to occupy themselves with Torah" (Jerusalem Talmud, *Shabbat* 16:3). It is therefore appropriate to make use of the leisure hours of Shabbat to study Torah, whether independently or by attending public lectures.

Further reading: For more on using Shabbat for Torah study, see *A Concise Guide to the Sages*, p. 125; *A Concise Guide to Mahshava*, p. 35.

Afternoon Service

In the Shabbat afternoon service, the Torah is read again. Generally, the reading, like the readings during the morning service on Mondays and Thursdays, consists of the first *aliya* of the upcoming week's Torah portion. This reading was instituted by Ezra the Scribe as an extra reading for the benefit of laborers who were unable to come to the synagogue during the week to listen to the Torah reading that is conducted on Mondays and Thursdays.

Torah Reading

This reading, unlike the one on Shabbat morning, is divided among only three people: A *kohen*, a Levite, and an Israelite. When there are no *kohanim* or Levites, three Israelites are called up.

Seuda Shelishit

After the afternoon service one eats the third meal of Shabbat, *seuda shelishit*. As noted above, both men and women are obligated to partake in this meal.

There is no *Kiddush* at this meal. It is fitting to recite the *HaMotzi* blessing on *lehem mishneh*, as at the previous two meals. If one does not have two *hallot*, he may also recite the blessing on a single *halla*. On this occasion there is no need to cover the *hallot* before the blessing, as no *Kiddush* is recited over wine.

What to Eat

If one is still full from the previous meal, to the extent that eating a third meal will cause him significant discomfort, he is not obligated to eat another meal. It is therefore advisable to consider this possibility in advance and not to eat too much at the daytime meal, in order to leave room for the third meal. Although it is preferable to eat bread at this meal, one who finds it difficult to eat bread may eat other foods.

Conclusion of Shabbat

Shabbat concludes when one can discern three small stars in the sky, close to one another. To avoid error in identifying the stars, and also to extend the sanctity of Shabbat, it is proper not to bring Shabbat to an end before the time printed in synagogue calendars.

> **Further reading:** For the source of the principle that one is supposed to extend the sanctity of Shabbat, see *A Concise Guide to the Sages*, p. 277.

Havdala

Just as it is a mitzva to acknowledge the Shabbat verbally at its beginning, through *Kiddush*, it is likewise a mitzva to commemorate it and speak highly of it at its conclusion. This is done in the ceremony of *Havdala*, "separation," which is performed on Saturday night. As its name indicates, *Havdala* separates between the sanctity of the Shabbat, which has just ended, and the mundane quality of the weekdays that lie ahead.

Much of *Havdala* is actually recited twice: in a passage in the *Amida* prayer of the evening service, which begins with the words "You have graced us" [*Ata honantanu*], and afterward during the *Havdala* ceremony over a cup of wine. One who forgot to add the paragraph "You have graced us" in the *Amida* prayer of the evening service does not repeat the prayer, as he will later perform *Havdala* at home over the cup of wine.

Performing Labor and Eating

The recitation of "You have graced us" in the *Amida* prayer allows one to perform labor immediately after the service, and there is no need to wait until *Havdala* is performed on the cup of wine at home. Such labor includes, among other things, lighting the candle before *Havdala*.

If one forgot to say "You have graced us" in the *Amida* prayer, after the service he can say the formula, "Blessed is He who distinguishes between the sacred and the mundane" [*Barukh hamavdil ben kodesh leḥol*]; this too permits him to perform labors prohibited on Shabbat. This method can also be used by women who do not recite the evening service.

Although one may perform labor after saying "You have graced us" in the *Amida*, or after saying the formula "Blessed is He who distinguishes between the sacred and the mundane," he may not yet eat or drink anything other than water. For that, he must first recite *Havdala* over a cup of wine.

Preparations for *Havdala*

Before *Havdala*, one must prepare a few items:

Wine

Wine, and according to many authorities, grape juice, is the main and preferred beverage for *Havdala*. If there is no wine available, or if it is difficult for the one reciting *Havdala* to drink wine, he can recite *Havdala* on a drink that is considered an important beverage in that time and place. There are differences of opinion among the halakhic authorities as to exactly which beverages are included in this category today, and one should consult his rabbi. Unlike *Kiddush* of Friday night, *Havdala* may not be recited over bread.

Spices

One must prepare spices for smelling during *Havdala*. The reason for this practice is that when Shabbat starts, every Jew receives an additional soul, which leaves him at the end of Shabbat. Smelling the spices helps the soul that remains in the body overcome the sadness of separation from that additional soul.

Ideally, it is proper to smell spices that come from plants. One may not use perfume for this part of *Havdala*. According to Sephardic custom, the wording of the blessing over the spices varies in accordance with its particular type (see p. 529). But according to the Ashkenazic custom, one recites the blessing "Who creates various spices" over all types of spices at *Havdala*, even if they are herbs or leaves of trees.

📖 **Further reading:** For more on the additional soul, see *A Concise Guide to Mahshava*, p. 37.

Candle

One should also prepare a candle, preferably from wax, for *Havdala*. It is proper to light a candle with at least two wicks in order to increase the amount of light. If one does not have a specially prepared braided *Havdala* candle, he can bring together the flames of two candles, or even two matches.

The candle is lit before *Havdala*, and during *Havdala* one recites the blessing "Who creates the lights of fire." The reason for this blessing is that upon the conclusion of the first Shabbat after the creation of the world, Adam discovered how to generate fire. The lighting of the candle and the blessing "Who creates the lights of fire" remind us of that seminal moment.

After the blessing, one brings his hands close to the candle and gazes at his fingernails. The reason is that in order to recite a blessing over the candle, one should benefit from its light by distinguishing between items that look somewhat similar, such as the fingers and the fingernails.

One extinguishes the candle at the end of *Havdala*, after drinking the wine. It is customary to extinguish it by means of the overflow of the wine from the cup, in order to emphasize that the candle was lit solely for the purpose of the mitzva. Some have the custom to dip their fingers in the wine and wet the corners of the eyes with it, for good luck.

The spices and the candle are not indispensable for the performance of the *Havdala* ritual; in their absence one can recite *Havdala* on a cup of wine alone.

Order of *Havdala*

First one pours wine into a cup. It is customary to pour the wine until it overflows, as this is a sign of a blessing for a good week. One also lights the candle.

One holds the full cup in his right hand and raises it, as for *Kiddush*.

The recitation begins with a collection of verses (each community according to its custom). One then recites the blessing over the wine. Next, one recites the blessing over the spices and smells them. Afterward one recites the blessing over the candle, brings his fingers close to the candle, and looks at his fingernails.

Havdala ends with the blessing "Who distinguishes between sacred and mundane." The one performing *Havdala* then drinks the majority of the wine in the cup and extinguishes the candle.

For Ashkenazim:

הִנֵּה אֵל יְשׁוּעָתִי אֶבְטַח וְלֹא אֶפְחָד. כִּי עָזִּי וְזִמְרָת יָהּ אֲדֹנָי, וַיְהִי לִי לִישׁוּעָה. וּשְׁאַבְתֶּם מַיִם בְּשָׂשׂוֹן מִמַּעַיְנֵי הַיְשׁוּעָה. לַאֲדֹנָי הַיְשׁוּעָה עַל עַמְּךָ בִרְכָתֶךָ סֶּלָה. אֲדֹנָי צְבָאוֹת עִמָּנוּ, מִשְׂגָּב לָנוּ אֱלֹהֵי יַעֲקֹב סֶּלָה. אֲדֹנָי צְבָאוֹת, אַשְׁרֵי אָדָם בֹּטֵחַ בָּךְ. אֲדֹנָי הוֹשִׁיעָה, הַמֶּלֶךְ יַעֲנֵנוּ בְיוֹם קָרְאֵנוּ. לַיְהוּדִים הָיְתָה אוֹרָה וְשִׂמְחָה וְשָׂשֹׂן וִיקָר, כֵּן תִּהְיֶה לָנוּ. כּוֹס יְשׁוּעוֹת אֶשָּׂא, וּבְשֵׁם אֲדֹנָי אֶקְרָא.

Hinei El yeshuati evtaḥ velo efḥad. Ki ozi vezimrat Yah Adonai, vayhi li lishua. Ush'avtem mayim besason mima'aynei hayshua, ladonai hayshua al amekha virkhatekha, sela. Adonai tzeva'ot imanu, misgav lanu, Elohei Ya'akov, sela. Adonai tzeva'ot, ashrei adam bote'aḥ bakh. Adonai hoshia, hamelekh ya'anenu veyom korenu. Layhudim ha'yeta ora vesimḥa vesason vikar, ken tihye lanu. Kos yeshuot esa, uvshem Adonai ekra.

סַבְרִי מָרָנָן וְרַבָּנָן וְרַבּוֹתַי.

Savri (maranan verabanan verabotai):

בָּרוּךְ אַתָּה אֲדֹנָי, אֱלֹהֵינוּ מֶלֶךְ הָעוֹלָם, בּוֹרֵא פְּרִי הַגָּפֶן.

Blessing over the wine: *Barukh ata Adonai, Eloheinu, melekh ha'olam, boreh peri hagafen.*

Blessing over the spices:

בָּרוּךְ אַתָּה אֲדֹנָי, אֱלֹהֵינוּ מֶלֶךְ הָעוֹלָם, בּוֹרֵא מִינֵי בְשָׂמִים.

Barukh ata Adonai, Eloheinu, melekh ha'olam, boreh minei vesamim.

Shabbat and Festivals

מברך על הנר: בָּרוּךְ אַתָּה אֲדֹנָי, אֱלֹהֵינוּ מֶלֶךְ הָעוֹלָם, בּוֹרֵא מְאוֹרֵי הָאֵשׁ.

Blessing over the candle: *Barukh ata Adonai, Eloheinu, melekh ha'olam, boreh me'orei ha'esh.*

בָּרוּךְ אַתָּה אֲדֹנָי, אֱלֹהֵינוּ מֶלֶךְ הָעוֹלָם, הַמַּבְדִּיל בֵּין קֹדֶשׁ לְחֹל, בֵּין אוֹר לְחֹשֶׁךְ, בֵּין יִשְׂרָאֵל לָעַמִּים, בֵּין יוֹם הַשְּׁבִיעִי לְשֵׁשֶׁת יְמֵי הַמַּעֲשֶׂה. בָּרוּךְ אַתָּה אֲדֹנָי, הַמַּבְדִּיל בֵּין קֹדֶשׁ לְחֹל.

Havdala blessing: *Barukh ata Adonai, Eloheinu, melekh ha'olam, hamavdil bein kodesh leḥol, bein or leḥoshekh, bein Yisrael la'amim, bein yom hashevi'i lesheshet yemei hama'aseh. Barukh ata Adonai, hamavdil bein kodesh leḥol.*

"Here is the God of my salvation; I trust and will not fear, as my strength and song is God the Lord and He is my salvation. You will draw water with gladness from the springs of salvation" (Isaiah 12:2–3). "Salvation belongs to the Lord. Your blessing is on Your people, Selah" (Psalms 3:9). "The Lord of hosts is with us; the God of Jacob is our stronghold, Selah" (Psalms 46:8). "Lord of hosts, happy is the man who trusts in You" (Psalms 84:13). "Deliver us, Lord. The King will answer us on the day we call" (Psalms 20:10). "For the Jews there was light, and joy, and gladness, and honor" (Esther 8:16), so may it be for us. "I will lift a cup of salvation, and I will call in the name of the Lord" (Psalms 116:130).

"Attention, (masters, rabbis, my teachers):"

Blessing over the wine: "Blessed are You, Lord our God, King of the universe, who creates fruit of the vine."

Blessing over the spices: "Blessed are You, Lord our God, King of the universe, who creates various spices."

Blessing over the candle: "Blessed are You, Lord our God, King of the universe, who creates the lights of fire."

Havdala blessing: "Blessed are You, Lord our God, King of the universe, who distinguishes between sacred and mundane, between light and darkness, between Israel and the nations, between the seventh day and the six days of work. Blessed are You, Lord, who distinguishes between sacred and mundane."

For Sephardim:

רִאשׁוֹן לְצִיּוֹן הִנֵּה הִנָּם, וְלִירוּשָׁלַיִם מְבַשֵּׂר אֶתֵּן. אַל תִּשְׂמְחִי אוֹיַבְתִּי לִי כִּי נָפַלְתִּי, קַמְתִּי, כִּי אֵשֵׁב בַּחֹשֶׁךְ אֲדֹנָי אוֹר לִי.

Leader: *Rishon letziyon hinei hinam, velirushalayim mevaser eten. At tismeḥi oyavti li; ki nafalti, kamti; ki eshev baḥoshekh, Adonai or li.*

לַיְּהוּדִים הָיְתָה אוֹרָה, וְשִׂמְחָה, וְשָׂשֹׂן וִיקָר. וַיְהִי דָוִד לְכָל דְּרָכָיו מַשְׂכִּיל, וַאדֹנָי עִמּוֹ. וְנֹחַ מָצָא חֵן בְּעֵינֵי אֲדֹנָי. כֵּן נִמְצָא חֵן (וְתִמְצְאוּ חֵן) וְשֵׂכֶל טוֹב בְּעֵינֵי אֱלֹהִים וְאָדָם. קוּמִי אוֹרִי כִּי בָא אוֹרֵךְ, וּכְבוֹד אֲדֹנָי עָלַיִךְ זָרָח. כִּי הִנֵּה הַחֹשֶׁךְ יְכַסֶּה אֶרֶץ וַעֲרָפֶל לְאֻמִּים, וְעָלַיִךְ יִזְרַח אֲדֹנָי וּכְבוֹדוֹ עָלַיִךְ יֵרָאֶה.

Layhudim ha'yeta ora vesimḥa vesason vikar. Vayhi David lekhol derakhav maskil, vadonai imo. VeNoaḥ matza ḥen be'eini Adonai, ken nimtza ḥen (vetimtze'u ḥen) vesekhel tov be'einei Elohim ve'adam. Kumi ori ki va orekh, ukhvod Adonai alayikh zaraḥ. Ki hinei haḥoshekh yekhaseh eretz, va'arafel le'umim, ve'alayikh yizraḥ Adonai, ukhvodo alayikh yera'e.

Take the cup and recite:

כּוֹס יְשׁוּעוֹת אֶשָּׂא, וּבְשֵׁם אֲדֹנָי אֶקְרָא. אָנָּא אֲדֹנָי הוֹשִׁיעָה נָּא. אָנָּא אֲדֹנָי הַצְלִיחָה נָּא. הַצְלִיחֵנוּ, הַצְלִיחַ דְּרָכֵינוּ, הַצְלִיחַ לִמּוּדֵינוּ. וּשְׁלַח בְּרָכָה רְוָחָה וְהַצְלָחָה בְּכָל מַעֲשֵׂה יָדֵינוּ. כְּדִכְתִיב: יִשָּׂא בְרָכָה מֵאֵת אֲדֹנָי וּצְדָקָה מֵאֱלֹהֵי יִשְׁעוֹ. לַיְּהוּדִים הָיְתָה אוֹרָה וְשִׂמְחָה, וְשָׂשֹׂן וִיקָר. וּכְתִיב וַיְהִי דָוִד לְכָל דְּרָכָיו מַשְׂכִּיל, וַאדֹנָי עִמּוֹ. כֵּן יִהְיֶה עִמָּנוּ.

Kos yeshhuot esa, uvshem Adonai ekra. Ana Adonai, hoshia na. Ana Adonai, hatzliḥa na. Hatzliḥeinu, hatzliaḥ derakheinu, hatzliaḥ limudeinu. Ushlaḥ berakha revaḥa vehatzlaḥa bekhol ma'aseh yadeinu, kedikhtiv: Yisa verakha me'et Adonai, utzdaka me'Elohei yisho. Layhudim ha'yeta ora vesimḥa vesason vikar. Ukhtiv: Vayhi David lekhol derakhav maskil, vadonai imo. Ken yehyeh imanu.

סָבְרִי מָרָנָן.

Savri maranan.

הַנּוֹכְחִים עוֹנִים: לְחַיִּים!

Others: *Leḥayim.*

בָּרוּךְ אַתָּה אֲדֹנָי, אֱלֹהֵינוּ מֶלֶךְ הָעוֹלָם, בּוֹרֵא פְּרִי הַגָּפֶן.

Leader (blessing over the wine): *Barukh ata Adonai, Eloheinu, melekh ha'olam, boreh peri hagefen.*

מברך על הבשמים: בָּרוּךְ אַתָּה אֲדֹנָי, אֱלֹהֵינוּ מֶלֶךְ הָעוֹלָם, בּוֹרֵא מִינֵי בְשָׂמִים.

Blessing over the spices: *Barukh ata Adonai, Eloheinu, melekh ha'olam, boreh minei vesamim.*

מברך על הנר: בָּרוּךְ אַתָּה אֲדֹנָי, אֱלֹהֵינוּ מֶלֶךְ הָעוֹלָם, בּוֹרֵא מְאוֹרֵי הָאֵשׁ.

Blessing over the candle: *Barukh ata Adonai, Eloheinu, melekh ha'olam, boreh me'orei ha'esh.*

בָּרוּךְ אַתָּה אֲדֹנָי, אֱלֹהֵינוּ מֶלֶךְ הָעוֹלָם, הַמַּבְדִּיל בֵּין קֹדֶשׁ לְחוֹל וּבֵין אוֹר לְחֹשֶׁךְ

Havdala blessing: *Barukh ata Adonai, Eloheinu, melekh ha'olam, hamavdil*

Shabbat and Festivals

403

וּבֵין יִשְׂרָאֵל לָעַמִּים וּבֵין יוֹם הַשְּׁבִיעִי
לְשֵׁשֶׁת יְמֵי הַמַּעֲשֶׂה. בָּרוּךְ אַתָּה אֲדֹנָי,
הַמַּבְדִּיל בֵּין קֹדֶשׁ לְחוֹל.

bein kodesh leḥol, uvein or leḥoshekh, uvein Yisrael la'amim, uvein yom hashevi'i lesheshet yemei hama'aseh. Barukh ata Adonai, hamavdil bein kodesh leḥol.

Leader: "The first to Zion, behold, here it is and to Jerusalem I will provide a herald" (Isaiah 41:27). "Do not rejoice, my enemy, on me; though I fell, I will rise; though I sit in darkness, the Lord is a light for me" (Micah 7:8). "For the Jews there was light, and joy, and gladness, and honor" (Esther 8:16). "David was successful in all his ways, and the Lord was with him" (I Samuel 18:14). "But Noah found grace in the eyes of the Lord" (Genesis 6:8), so may we find grace and high favor in the eyes of God and man (see Proverbs 3:4). "Arise, shine, for your light has come and the glory of the Lord has shone upon you. For, behold, the darkness will cover the earth and peoples, a fog; but upon you the Lord will shine, and His glory will be seen upon you" (Isaiah 60:1–2).

Take the cup and recite: "I will lift a cup of salvation, and I will call in the name of the Lord" (Psalms 116:130). "Lord, save us, we beseech You! Lord, grant us success, we beseech You!" (Psalms 118:25). Make us successful; make our ways successful; make our studies successful, and send a blessing, relief and success in all the work of our hands, as it is written, "He will receive the blessing of the Lord, righteousness from the God of his deliverance" (Psalms 24:5); "for the Jews there was light, and joy, and gladness, and honor" (Esther 8:16), and it is written, "David was successful in all his ways, and the Lord was with him" (I Samuel 18:14), so may He be with us.

"Attention, masters."

Others: "To life!"

Leader (blessing over the wine): "Blessed are You, Lord our God, King of the universe, who creates fruit of the vine."

Blessing over the spices: "Blessed are You, Lord our God, King of the universe, who creates various spices."

Blessing over the candle: "Blessed are You, Lord our God, King of the universe, who creates the lights of fire."

Havdala blessing: "Blessed are You, Lord our God, King of the universe, who distinguishes between sacred and mundane, and between light and darkness, and between Israel and the nations, and between the seventh day and the six days of work, Blessed are You, Lord, who distinguishes between sacred and mundane."

Al HaGefen

After drinking the *Havdala* wine, one recites the appropriate blessing, which is *Al HaGefen* (see p. 518).

Melaveh Malka

On the conclusion of Shabbat, it is customary to eat a meal for *melaveh malka*, "escorting the queen." The purpose of this meal is to honor the queen, Shabbat, upon her departure, just as she is honored at her arrival.

Ideally, it is proper to eat bread at this meal, even if one can eat only a small amount. If it is difficult for one to eat a meal, because he is still full from the meals of the day or for any other reason, he should at least eat pastries or fruit.

Elijah the Prophet

Since this meal is eaten in honor of Shabbat upon its conclusion, there are various customs meant to ensure that it is conducted in a dignified manner, for example spreading a tablecloth on the table, lighting candles, and reciting or singing liturgical poems that revolve around the figure of Elijah the Prophet.

According to the Talmud, Elijah the Prophet, who is the harbinger of redemption, is not expected to appear on Shabbat, so as not to disturb the observance of Shabbat. Therefore, immediately after Shabbat has ended, as soon as Elijah's arrival becomes possible, we await him and his tidings, and express this yearning through songs and liturgical poems.

> **Further reading:** For more on yearning for redemption and the messiah, see *A Concise Guide to the Sages*, p. 391; *A Concise Guide to Mahshava*, p. 145.

Forbidden Labor on Shabbat: Basic Principles

The Torah instructs us to work during the week for our livelihoods, but prohibits the performance of labor on Shabbat, as it is stated, "Six days you shall work and perform all your labor. The seventh day is the Sabbath for the Lord your God; you shall not perform any labor" (Exodus 20:8–9; Deuteronomy 5:12–13). The definition of labor that is prohibited on Shabbat cannot be open to personal interpretation, as one person might define labor as toiling in the field, while another will also include slicing vegetables for salad. It is thus necessary to establish fixed and clear definitions of the activities prohibited on Shabbat.

Although the Torah explicitly mentions a few of these prohibited labors, including kindling a fire, plowing, and harvesting, most of them are merely alluded to by the Torah's mentioning the prohibition of labor on Shabbat alongside the commandment for the Israelites to construct the Tabernacle in the wilderness. The Torah provides detailed instructions for the construction of the Tabernacle, and in that context also warns against performing labor on

Shabbat. From this juxtaposition, it is derived that those tasks which were required for the construction of the Tabernacle are the same labors that are prohibited on Shabbat.

Based on this, the Sages of the Mishna and Talmud detailed the prohibited labors, on the basis of two fundamental principles:

(1) It must be a planned, thoughtful act, performed intentionally.

(2) The labor must have been required for making the Tabernacle.

This chapter lists the labors prohibited on Shabbat, as well as the principles behind the prohibitions.

Primary Categories [*Avot*] and Subcategories [*Toladot*]

The total number of categories of labor performed in the construction of the Tabernacle is thirty-nine. In halakhic literature these are commonly referred to as the thirty-nine primary categories [*avot*] of labor. They are called *avot*, literally fathers, because they also have *toladot*, "descendants" or subcategories, which are actions that are similar to the *avot*. These too are prohibited by Torah law, just like the primary categories.

The Thirty-Nine Prohibited Labors

These are the thirty-nine primary categories of labor:

1. Plowing: All actions performed on the earth to improve, straighten, or soften it, or in order to benefit the growth of crops, are included in the labor of plowing. This includes deliberately making a groove in the ground.

2. Sowing: Laying seeds in the ground so that they will grow. This prohibition also includes all actions that lead to the cultivation and strengthening of existing plants, such as irrigation.

3. Reaping: Detaching a plant from the source of its growth. Plucking leaves from trees, cutting grass, and the like are all included in this labor.

4. Gathering: Collecting and accumulating crops into piles within their area of growth.

5. Threshing: Detaching and separating crops from their shell or from the waste that grows together with them, such as separating grain from sheaves and chaff. This labor also includes squeezing out certain liquids from solids, most prominently squeezing fruit that is generally squeezed in order to make juice.

6. Winnowing: Separating waste from food by the aid of the wind.

7. Selecting: Separating food and waste that are mixed together. For the purposes of this labor, "waste" is not necessarily an absolutely unwanted substance; the prohibition also applies to the separation of two types of food from one another, if one of them is unwanted by the person at that time.

8. Grinding: Reducing a crop into small parts, e.g., grinding grains or spices.

9. Sifting: Separating waste from food by means of a perforated vessel, such as sifting flour with a sieve.

10. Kneading: Causing small items to adhere to each other by means of liquid, thus forming a uniform solid. The most prominent example of this is kneading dough. Even the preparation of porridge or oatmeal in the usual manner is prohibited due to the labor of kneading.

11. Baking: Preparing substances for eating, through the heat of a fire. This prohibition includes baking, cooking, and frying.

12. Shearing: Disconnecting an item from the place of its natural growth on the human body or the body of animals. This labor includes cutting one's hair or nails.

13. Whitening: An action that cleans or even merely adds a shine to objects that are typically laundered.

14. Combing: Preparing raw materials that will be made into yarn or thread.

15. Dyeing: An action aimed at permanently changing the color of an object.

16. Spinning: Making threads from raw material, in any manner.

17. Stretching: Stretching the threads of the warp in the loom as a prelude to the act of weaving.

18. Constructing two meshes: Inserting two threads of the warp through the heddle rings. This refers to sticks with holes through which one inserts the threads of the warp before weaving, each thread into a different mesh.

19. Weaving: Passing threads of the woof through the threads of the warp.

20. Severing: Completing the work of weaving a garment by removing the remaining threads.

21. Tying: Tying a permanent knot.

22. Untying: Untying a permanent knot.

23. Sewing: Attaching two items to each other. Even gluing together two pieces of paper is included in this labor.

24. Tearing: Tearing something for a particular purpose, such as to repair or sew it.

25. Trapping: Capturing animals that are typically hunted, whether to eat them or to use them for any other purpose. It should be noted that

potentially harmful animals, such as snakes, may be trapped and even killed on Shabbat.

26. Slaughtering: Killing an animal in order to use it. This labor also includes the prohibition against bruising another person.

27. Flaying: Stripping the hide from the flesh of animals.

28. Tanning: Processing raw materials to prepare them for use. An example of this labor is pickling cucumbers.

29. Smoothing: Smoothing animal skins as part of their preparation for use. This labor includes polishing shoes with a thick shoe polish.

30. Etching: Etching or drawing a line on an object in order to cut it evenly.

31. Cutting: Cutting something in a precise manner and according to a particular measure.

32. Writing: Writing letters, or other shapes that have meaning.

33. Erasing: Erasing an enduring writing in order to write at least two other letters in their place.

34. Building: An action that assists in the construction of buildings or parts of them. While this labor refers mainly to building items that are connected to the ground, construction of furniture or utensils in a professional manner is also included in this prohibition.

35. Demolishing: Dismantling all or part of an item in order to repair it, or in preparation for alternative construction.

36. Kindling: Lighting a fire, as well as increasing or extending the duration of a fire.

37. Extinguishing: Putting out or reducing a fire, e.g., extinguishing coals in order to make charcoal.

38. Striking a blow with a hammer: Applying the finishing touches to an item.

39. Carrying from one domain to another: Transferring an object from a private domain to a public domain or vice versa.

📖 Further reading: The directive to observe Shabbat appears in many places in the Torah, see *A Concise Guide to the Torah*: pp. 174, 183, 192, 217, 224, 302, 315, 449.

Rabbinic Prohibitions

Besides the thirty-nine primary categories of labor and their subcategories, which are all prohibited by Torah law, the Sages added additional prohibitions. These rabbinic decrees form a category known as *shevut*, a term derived from the verse, "And on the seventh day you shall rest [*tishbot*]" (Exodus 34:21).

The *shevut* prohibitions include actions prohibited by the Sages for one of the following reasons: It is similar to one of the thirty-nine labors, e.g., collecting honey from a beehive, which is like the labor of reaping; it may lead to the performance of a labor that is prohibited by the Torah, e.g., smelling fruit that is attached to the tree, as one might detach the fruit; and actions that spoil the atmosphere of rest and the sanctity of Shabbat, such as talking about matters of work and business.

The category of *shevut* also includes the prohibition against instructing or asking a gentile to perform a labor on behalf of a Jew that the Jew is not allowed to do himself. Nevertheless, this is permitted under certain circumstances, subject to several halakhic qualifications (see p. 456).

📖 **Further reading:** Why must we refrain from labor on Shabbat? See *A Concise Guide to Mahshava*, p. 35ff.

Intentional Labor

As noted above, the prohibited labors of Shabbat are derived from the work for the Tabernacle, and on this basis, it was determined that only planned, intentional labor is prohibited on Shabbat. This requirement includes several details and stipulations, as enumerated in the following sections. All of these conditions must be fulfilled in order for the labor to be prohibited by Torah law on Shabbat.

Prior Intent

A prohibited labor constitutes a desecration of Shabbat only if the person performing the act intended to do it on Shabbat. If he did it unintentionally, he has not violated a prohibition.

For example, it is prohibited on Shabbat to make grooves in the ground, as this is a form of plowing. Nevertheless, if one drags a chair from place to place on Shabbat, and as an inadvertent result of his action the legs of the chair create grooves in the ground, he has not transgressed the prohibition of plowing. The reason is that he intended merely to move the chair and not to create a groove.

Notwithstanding the above, in the case of a permitted action whose prohibited result is inevitable, one is not exempt despite his lack of intent. For example, one who cuts off the head of a chicken on Shabbat cannot claim that his sole interest was the head and he had no intention of killing the chicken. This person has violated the prohibition of slaughtering, because

Shabbat and Festivals

one cannot sever a creature's head without killing it. The Sages expressed this idea with the phrase, "Can one sever its head [*pesik reisha*] and it will not die?"

The words *pesik reisha* have become a halakhic term that is used in many situations. For example, if at the opening of a bottle there is a cotton plug in which wine is absorbed, and one removes that plug, he has performed the labor of squeezing out; he cannot claim that all he wanted was the wine inside the bottle. Since squeezing out the wine from the cotton is an inevitable result of removing the cotton plug, this action is a *pesik reisha*.

The category of *pesik reisha* may be divided into two different situations. The first occurs when the person did not intend the inevitable result, but ultimately, he was pleased with the outcome. To return to the above example, although his intent was to access the wine inside the bottle, when the cotton wool was squeezed, he was pleased with that result as well, since it meant that he could also benefit from the wine that was squeezed out. In such a case, he has violated a Torah prohibition.

The second situation occurs when the person is not interested in the prohibited, unintended result of his action. If so, his action is defined as "a *pesik reisha* that does not please him," and by Torah law he has not performed a prohibited labor. Nevertheless, the Sages prohibited labors of that kind as well, due to the concern that people might take advantage of this claim even when they are actually pleased about the result, even if only subconsciously.

Purpose of the Labor

In order for a labor to be prohibited by Torah law, it must be done for the purpose of its prohibited end result. For example, it is prohibited to dig a hole in the ground, as this is a violation of the labor of plowing. But this prohibition applies by Torah law only when the goal of the person's action is to create a hole. However, if a person removes dirt from the ground because he wants to use the dirt, and he thereby creates a hole, then by Torah law he has not violated the prohibition of plowing. Nevertheless, the Sages prohibited labor of this type as well.

From Start to Finish

A labor is prohibited by the Torah only when a single person performs the entire labor from start to finish. For example, if one carries an object from a private domain to a public domain, he has violated a prohibited labor by Torah law. However, if two people together carry an object that can be carried by a single individual, they have violated only a rabbinic prohibition but not a Torah prohibition. If the object could not be carried by a single person, then they would both have violated a Torah prohibition.

The Typical Manner

The prohibition against performing labor on Shabbat applies only when it was performed in the ordinary manner. If the labor was performed in an unusual manner, it is not prohibited by Torah law.

For example, if a person leaves his home (a private domain) on Shabbat to the street (the public domain) with a toothpick in his mouth, he has violated the prohibition of carrying an object from the private domain to the public domain. The reason is that holding a toothpick in one's mouth is a usual and acceptable manner of carrying it. By contrast, if one left his house on Shabbat with a needle in his mouth, he has not violated a Torah prohibition, because people do not normally hold needles in their mouths. But here too, the Sages prohibited the performance of labor in an atypical manner.

Direct Action

When the Torah prohibits performing labor on Shabbat, it states, "You shall not perform any labor." The Talmud infers from the wording of the verse that "performance [of the act] is what is prohibited, but indirect causation is permitted" (*Shabbat* 120b). In other words, only a direct action is prohibited, not a labor caused indirectly through a different action performed by the person. In this case as well, though, the Sages prohibited the performance of forbidden labors through indirect action.

For example, if a light in one's house is controlled on Shabbat by an automatic timer, and right now the light is off, is it permitted to move the pins of the clock and to thereby cause the lights to go on sooner than they otherwise would? This is a classic case of an indirect action, as the person would not be turning on the light directly but rather indirectly causing it to go on earlier than planned prior to Shabbat. Such an act is permitted by Torah law, but prohibited by rabbinic law.

It is important to emphasize that the rabbinic prohibition of indirectly causing a prohibited labor to take place does not apply in cases of special need, such as in cases of illness or for security needs. In cases such as these, the Sages did not apply their decree. On this basis, technological devices have been developed in recent years using indirect actions to power certain electric devices to help the sick, the elderly, the handicapped, etc.

Appearance of Transgression [*Marit Ayin*]

Some actions are permitted on Shabbat by Torah law but prohibited by the Sages due to their having the appearance of a transgression of Torah law. The purpose of these prohibitions is to prevent error, lest one see people performing such an action, and be led to believe that a similar, prohibited act is also permissible. Furthermore, these prohibitions also serve to prevent false suspicions, as onlookers might think that the person is guilty of performing a prohibited labor.

📖 **Further reading:** For more on prohibitions due to the appearance of transgression, see p. 454.

Preventing Mistakes

Prohibitions that stem from a concern for the appearance of transgression are not exclusive to Shabbat; they exist in a variety of halakhic areas. There is nevertheless a particularly long list of actions that are prohibited on Shabbat for this reason. Two examples which express the aforementioned reasons for the prohibition are as follows:

If a garment became wet during the course of Shabbat, it is prohibited to hang it out to dry on a clothesline on Shabbat, so that people will not mistakenly think that these clothes were washed on Shabbat and that laundering is permitted on Shabbat.

It is prohibited for a Jew to rent out his place of business that bears his name, to a gentile who would operate it on Shabbat. In this case, the reason for the prohibition is that people might suspect the Jew of desecrating Shabbat.

Prohibition against Deriving Benefit from Prohibited Labor

If one sinned and willfully committed a prohibited labor on Shabbat, he is prohibited from deriving benefit from the results of his transgression. This applies to food cooked on Shabbat, as well as any other product that was produced through the desecration of Shabbat.

Intentional versus Unwitting Acts

The prohibition against deriving benefit from a prohibited labor applies permanently only to the person who performed the labor. Others may use and benefit from the results of his labor immediately upon the conclusion of Shabbat.

But when the prohibition is performed unwittingly, i.e., due to lack of knowledge or forgetfulness, it is permitted even for the one who performed the labor to benefit from its results, after Shabbat has ended.

Saving a Life

Despite the great severity of the prohibition against desecrating Shabbat, an action defined as lifesaving [pikuah nefesh] overrides Shabbat. In other words, if in order to save a life one must desecrate Shabbat, it is permitted and even a mitzva to do so.

Two explanations are given for this principle (Yoma 85b). The first is fundamentally logical: "Desecrate one Shabbat for him so that he can observe many Shabbatot." It is worth having the holiness of one Shabbat desecrated in order for a sick person, for example, to recover and observe more Shabbatot. Another explanation is based on the verse, "You shall observe My statutes and My ordinances, which a man shall perform and live by them" (Leviticus 18:5). The Sages interpret the term "live by them" to mean "and not die by them." This means that almost all commandments in the Torah are overridden in life-threatening situations. The exceptions are the three most serious offenses: idolatry, severe sexual violations such as adultery or incest, and murder.

Even in Cases of Uncertainty

The category of *pikuah nefesh* includes possibly life-threatening situations. That is, even when there is only a concern for the person's life, and there is no certainty that his life is indeed in danger, this is also considered *pikuah nefesh*. It is also permitted to desecrate Shabbat even if it is not clear that the actions performed for the endangered person will in fact save his life.

 **Further reading:** For more on the sanctity of life and saving lives, see *A Concise Guide to the Sages*, pp. 6, 150.

Muktze

Shabbat is intended not only for physical rest; it is also a holy day on which one must rise above the secular world. Accordingly, the prophet defines Shabbat in the following terms: "If you restrain your walking because of the Sabbath, pursuing your needs on the day of My holiness, and you call the Sabbath a delight and the Lord's sacred, honored, and you honor it by refraining from doing your business, from seeking your needs, and from speaking of matters, then you will delight in the Lord" (Isaiah 58:13–14). On this basis, the Sages prohibited several actions, despite the fact that these are not prohibited labors by Torah law.

One of the acts the Sages prohibited was carrying or moving certain items on Shabbat. This prohibition is referred to as *muktze*, meaning "set-aside," as it applies to items that a person removes [*maktze*] from his mind, since he does not intend to use them on Shabbat. It is important to note that the prohibition relates to moving or handling those items, not to merely touching them.

While there are several reasons for the prohibition of handling *muktze* items on Shabbat, the main idea is the preservation of the Shabbat atmosphere and the concern that as a result of carrying these items one might come to perform prohibited tasks on Shabbat.

This chapter will present the different types of *muktze*. It should be noted that *muktze* involves many complex laws, and therefore we will present only the basic principles.

Further reading: For more on the elevated status of a person and the entire world on Shabbat, see *A Concise Guide to Mahshava*, p. 36ff.

Different Categories

All objects can be divided into three categories: Some items are not considered *muktze* and they may be handled on Shabbat; others may not be handled at all; and yet others may be handled, but only for specific purposes.

Items That May Be Handled

It is permitted to handle all utensils used for serving food and for eating on Shabbat, and one may handle the food itself. It is also permitted to handle items that are to be used on Shabbat, including books, clothing, bedding, and furniture such as chairs, tables, and beds.

Items One May Not Handle at All

The list of items that one may not handle on Shabbat at all is divided into several groups:

Raw materials that have not been prepared for use: This includes stones, soil, planks, branches, thorns, food scraps that are not edible at all, even for animal consumption, such as nutshells (see below on how to remove them from the table), and fragments of vessels that can no longer be used.

Items that may not be moved due to a Shabbat prohibition: For example, since a candle that is burning at the start of Shabbat may not be moved due to a concern that doing so will extinguish the flame, it may not be moved for the duration of Shabbat, even if the flame has already been extinguished. Likewise, since a rag that is soaking-wet at the beginning of Shabbat may not be handled lest one perform the prohibited labor of squeezing, it may not be moved later on, even after it has dried.

Implements intended for labors that are prohibited on Shabbat, and due to their value or fragility one is particular not to use them for other purposes: For example, a drill, electric saw, slaughtering knife, or laptop computer. This category also includes items that are not prohibited for use on Shabbat, but which are of great worth, such as valuable works of art. These items are termed "set aside due to fear of monetary loss," and may not be moved on Shabbat.

It is also prohibited to carry the item or surface on which one of the above items was placed at the start of Shabbat. For example, if a laptop computer was on a chair at the start of Shabbat, it is prohibited to move the chair for the duration of Shabbat, even if, for whatever reason, the computer is no longer on it. In such a case, the chair is classified as a base for a *muktze* item, which itself becomes *muktze*. This *halakha* applies only if the *muktze* item was deliberately placed on its base (e.g. the chair) by the owner of the chair before Shabbat, with the intent that it remain in that place for all of Shabbat. But if the *muktze* item (e.g., the laptop) was forgotten on the chair at the start of Shabbat, it is permissible to move the chair after the computer is no longer on it.

If two different items were placed on the chair, one of which is *muktze* and the other is not, the determining factor for the status of the chair is which of them is more important. For example, if alongside the laptop a spoon was placed on the chair, the presence of the spoon does not mean that the chair may be carried. But if the item that was placed next to the laptop was valuable, e.g., a piece of jewelry, and yet it is one that is permitted to be carried on Shabbat, and it is more important than the laptop, the chair itself does not become *muktze*.

If someone dies on Shabbat, it is prohibited to move the body throughout the entire duration of Shabbat.

Items That May Be Carried Only for Specific Purposes

Some items may be carried on Shabbat for specific purposes only: Implements that are intended for prohibited labors on Shabbat, but which can also be used for tasks that are permitted on Shabbat (for example, a hammer that can be used for cracking nuts, or an eraser that can serve as a doorstop), may be carried on Shabbat to perform those permitted tasks. This permission is called *letzorekh gufo*, "for the purpose of utilizing the item itself" for a permitted action.

A utensil whose primary purpose is for performing forbidden labors may also be carried for the purpose of utilizing its place [*letzorekh mekomo*]. If the *muktze* item is taking up space that is needed, it is permitted to move the item. For example, if a screwdriver was left on the dining room table and one needs to set the table for the Shabbat meal, it is permitted to remove the screwdriver.

Exceptions to the Prohibition of *Muktze*

Even with regard to those items which are *muktze* and thus generally may not be carried, in case of need, one may move them in specific ways.

Indirect Carrying

It is permitted to move a *muktze* item in an indirect manner, if this is done for the purpose of a permitted item or activity. It is therefore permitted to remove nutshells from the table by means of a fork or a knife, in order to enable people to sit around the table more comfortably. This is permitted because one is moving the shells indirectly, by means of a fork or knife rather than picking them up by hand, and the end goal, which is the comfort of the diners, is permitted.

One may not do so for the sake of a prohibited item. Thus, it is prohibited to use a fork to move a laptop that was accidentally left on an open porch, if the goal is to prevent possible damage to the computer. In this case, the handling of the *muktze* item is indeed indirect, but its purpose is to save the computer, which is a prohibited item.

Moving with One's Body

Another way to permit the moving of a *muktze* item on Shabbat is when this is done with the person's body rather than his hands. For example, if someone discovers money that fell from his pocket before Shabbat outside the door of his house, he is allowed to use his foot to move the bill into the house (assuming that the area is surrounded by an *eiruv* – see p. 460).

A *Muktze* Item That Causes Revulsion

As noted above, shells and non-edible residues are *muktze* and generally may not be moved in the ordinary manner. Nevertheless, if these remains are scattered on the table and are a source of disgust to those present, the Sages permitted them to be carried, even directly with one's hands, to the trash can. This *halakha* also applies to carrying a soiled diaper or anything dirty that bothers a person, in order to throw it into the garbage.

To Prevent Damage

Likewise, objects that might cause physical injury or damage may be carried on Shabbat, despite their *muktze* status. For example, it is permitted to collect and remove broken glass or nails that are scattered across the floor of a house, in order to prevent danger and possible harm to the members of the household.

Food Preparation on Shabbat

Shabbat is meant for enjoyment and rest, and therefore the vast majority of the actions necessary for the preparation of the Shabbat meals must be completed before the holy day begins. The Talmud states, "One who exerts himself [with preparations] on Friday will eat on Shabbat; but one who did not exert himself on Friday, from where will he eat on Shabbat?" (*Avoda Zara* 3a). Therefore, one must prepare all the food in advance, and leave for Shabbat only the final steps that are permitted on Shabbat, and even these must be performed in accordance with the conditions and restrictions set by *halakha*.

This chapter deals with a range of issues affecting the kitchen and food preparation on Shabbat. It presents the halakhic foundations of these issues, including which actions are prohibited and which are permitted, and under what conditions.

Labor of Cooking

One of the thirty-nine prohibited labors on Shabbat is cooking. This prohibition is derived from the baking that was performed for the Tabernacle, and it includes all kinds of preparation of food for consumption by means of heat: cooking, frying, roasting, and the like.

Definition of Cooking

The labor that is prohibited on Shabbat is not only cooking in its classical sense, meaning the initial placement of a pot containing raw materials on a fire. Rather, any heating of foods that are not cooked and that contain liquid, to a certain temperature is considered cooking. The *halakha* defines the degree of heat that is considered cooking by means of the point at which one's hand spontaneously recoils from the item's heat [*yad soledet bo*]. In modern terminology, this is a temperature of roughly 45° C (113° F) and above.

Even if the person intends to remove the food from the source of heat before it gets cooked, it is prohibited on Shabbat to place it on top or inside a source of heat that could eventually bring it to the prohibited temperature.

Three Vessels

With regard to the prohibition of cooking on Shabbat, the *halakha* distinguishes among three basic types of vessels, with a different law applying to each: a primary vessel [*keli rishon*], a secondary vessel [*keli sheni*], and a tertiary vessel [*keli shelishi*]. The primary vessel is one that is placed on the heat source itself. Thus, a vessel that is positioned on a flame is a primary vessel. Likewise, a vessel that is placed on a Shabbat hot plate is also a primary vessel, as is an electric water heater. A primary vessel retains this status even after it has been removed from the heat source, until it has cooled off. Adding food to a primary vessel is prohibited on Shabbat as a form of cooking. Later, we will explain this in greater depth, and show how there are cases and situations in which one can nevertheless derive benefit from the heat of a primary vessel.

A "secondary vessel," as its name implies, is one to which food was transferred after it was cooked in a primary vessel. The sides of the second vessel begin as cold, and although the hot food that was placed into it warms them, the *halakhot* regarding this vessel are more lenient than those of a primary vessel, as will be explained below.

A tertiary vessel is one to which the food was transferred from a secondary vessel. One can usually assume that the heat of this vessel and its contents have cooled to such an extent that they will no longer cook. Nevertheless, there are some foods that maintain a particularly high temperature even when they are in a tertiary vessel, and therefore it is prohibited to place ingredients inside them that have not yet been cooked. This too will be detailed below.

Preparations for the Meal

Although it is prohibited to cook on Shabbat, this should not be considered a recommendation to eat cold food on Shabbat. On the contrary, one should eat hot foods on Shabbat, in order to honor Shabbat and enjoy the holy day. The Sages criticized one who refrains from eating hot food on Shabbat, saying that such a practice is overly stringent. It is therefore necessary to know the relevant *halakhot*, in order to ensure that the food will be heated in permitted ways.

Heating Food before Shabbat

The simplest way to eat hot food on Shabbat is to cook the food before Shabbat and place it before Shabbat begins on a source of heat, which will keep it warm until the meal. The Sages prohibited leaving food on a regular fire that is used for cooking, lest one forget that it is Shabbat and, out of habit, increase or lower the intensity of the flame under the pot. They therefore instituted that food should be placed on a source of heat in a manner that does not enable a change in the intensity of the fire.

For this purpose, one may use an electric hot plate that does not have an open burner, and on which it is impossible to intensify or moderate the heat. One can also place cooked dishes on top of a stove, provided that the fire is covered and is not visible. This can be accomplished by means of a metal sheet (often called a *blekh* in Yiddish) that is placed over the flames and bent in such a way that it also covers the control knobs of the stove. This serves to avert the possibility of adjusting the flame on Shabbat.

Ovens and Warming Trays

There is a problem with leaving food in a preheated oven at a low temperature, because opening the door lets in cold air, and as a result, in an ordinary oven the heating mechanism is activated, which means that the one who opened the door is in effect the indirect cause of this heating. Some ovens have a special switch enabling a "Shabbat mode." This switch ensures that the activity of the heating system will remain constant, and will not be affected at all by the penetration of cold air. One may place food in an oven of this type on Friday and remove it from the oven before or during meals on Shabbat. However, some are stringent and do not use an oven even in such a manner.

Putting food before Shabbat into a slow-cooking pot, such as a crock pot, so that it will cook during Shabbat, entails halakhic complications, and one should ask a rabbi if and how it is permitted to do so.

Many people use electric warming trays to keep their food warm on Shabbat. Before Shabbat, many people place a covering over the pots that are on the warming tray, to better preserve the heat. This is permitted only if the covering is not wrapped around the pots on all sides.

It is permitted to move a pot from one place to another on a warming tray on Shabbat.

When the pot is on a heat source (warming tray or a covered stove) one may not mix the contents with a spoon, a ladle, or the like, or even use these utensils to remove food from it. This action is prohibited because it speeds and improves the cooking process. One should remove the pot from the heat source and then take out the food.

Salt and Spices

Soup or any other food that is on a heat source such as an electric warming tray, is classified as being in a primary vessel, and it is therefore prohibited to add salt or other spices to it. If one accidentally did salt or spice the dish, it is permitted to eat the food.

In the event that the food has been transferred to a secondary vessel that is not on the heat source, spices may be added to the food. However, some are stringent even with regard to the secondary vessel while it is still hot, if the spices have never been cooked before.

Hot Water

When preparing hot water for use on Shabbat, one must be careful not to violate the prohibition against cooking. One option is to boil the water on Friday and place it before Shabbat on a hot plate (or a covered stove, as explained above). It is also permitted to use an electric urn that is appropriate for Shabbat use. Nowadays, there are electric urns with regulated temperatures that have halakhic certification for use on Shabbat.

On Shabbat, one may not use ordinary electric water dispensers that provide hot and cold water for drinking, as pushing the button immediately activates the heating or cooling system. There are devices today whose operating system is specially adapted for Shabbat use. These devices are marked with appropriate halakhic certification.

Returning Food to a Heat Source

Sometimes one might want to remove food from a pot and then return the pot to the heat source, e.g., if not everyone is eating at the same time. This is permitted if the following conditions are met: (1) At the time one removes the pot from the heat source he intends to return it there; (2) by the time one returns the pot, it has not cooled below 45° C (113° F); (3) one holds the pot while it is off the heat source, or at least does not place it down in a manner indicating that he has decided not to put it back on the heat source; (4) the heat source is covered rather than an open fire or an oven. This includes a metal sheet over a flame. Similarly, an electric warming tray is acceptable.

Refrigerator

Opening and closing a refrigerator door may activate various electronic systems. Therefore, it is important to use a refrigerator that is adapted for Shabbat use.

Shabbat Mode

The opening and closing of a refrigerator door activate certain electronic systems, which involve prohibited labors. In older models of refrigerators there were only two problems: turning on or off the light, and the stopping or activating of the cooling fan in the refrigerator. The solution was relatively simple: Disconnecting the light before Shabbat and likewise disconnecting the switch that informs the internal fan that the door has opened or closed. Some refrigerators had one switch that performed both operations, and it was easy to disable it before Shabbat with adhesive tape.

In newer models of refrigerators, the operating systems are digital, and the opening or closing of the door activates systems that are difficult for a non-expert to neutralize. The best way to use such a refrigerator on Shabbat is to buy one that has a Shabbat mode that is certified by a qualified rabbinical authority, or to have a Shabbat mode installed after purchasing the refrigerator. The Shabbat mode prevents the opening or closing of the door from activating any electrical systems. One who has a refrigerator that lacks a Shabbat mode, or who has forgotten to transfer the refrigerator to Shabbat mode before Shabbat, should ask a rabbi how to proceed.

Freezing and Defrosting Food

It is permitted to place any food or drink in a freezer in order to maintain its quality and freshness over time.

Freezing Liquids

With regard to freezing water to make ice cubes or inserting an ice cream solution into the freezer to make ice cream, this should preferably be done before Shabbat. If it was not done before Shabbat, it is permitted to do it on Shabbat itself, provided that one intends to consume the item on Shabbat.

Thawing all types of foods, solid or liquid, for use on Shabbat is allowed, but liquids may not be placed on a heat source to speed up the thawing.

Heating Food on Shabbat on a Warming Tray

In situations where one is not returning food to a heat source in keeping with the conditions outlined above (see: Returning Food to a Heat Source, p. 421), it is still permitted to heat food on Shabbat itself under certain conditions, which ensure that one does not violate the prohibited labor of cooking and one does not heat the food in a manner reminiscent to cooking.

First, an important note: Every time it is stated below that it is permitted to place a certain food on a warming tray on Shabbat itself, there is a difference between the practice of

Ashkenazim and Sephardim: In the opinion of many Ashkenazic authorities, even when it is permitted to place a food item on a warming tray on Shabbat, it must be placed on top of an object that separates the food from the warming tray, for example, an inverted pot or roasting pan that is on the warming tray, with the food that one wishes to heat placed only on top of it. By contrast, many Sephardic authorities maintain that one may place the dish directly on the warming tray.

Dry and Liquid Foods

A dry food that has already been fully cooked: Dry foods, such as frozen *halla* (that does not have small pieces of ice on it) or roasted nuts, may be placed on a warming tray on Shabbat in order to defrost and get warm, even if they will get warmer than the temperature known as *yad soledet bo* (45° C, 113° F). As stated above, according to the ruling accepted by Ashkenazim, one must place them on something such as an inverted tin pan that will interpose between them and the warming tray, whereas according to Sephardim, one may place them directly on the warming tray.

Likewise, any food that is dry and cooked, such as a breaded cutlet or a casserole, even if it is entirely cold, may be placed on a warming tray on Shabbat. Some are stringent not to do so even when the food is fully cooked.

Liquids: Liquid foods that have cooled may not be heated on Shabbat. One also may not put them in a place where they can warm up above the temperature of *yad soledet bo*. However, according to Ashkenazim, even if they have cooled below the temperature of *yad soledet bo*, if they are still noticeably warm and would be eaten even though they are not generally eaten cold, then one may heat them up.

According to Sephardim, there is a distinction between a dish that is entirely liquid, such as soup, and a solid dish that contains a small amount of liquid, such as fish cooked in a sauce. In the case of fish, it is permitted to place it on a source of heat and warm it even more than *yad soledet bo*. The reason is that the dish is considered to be a dry food because the majority of the food is dry, notwithstanding the small amount of liquid.

Preparing Salads on Shabbat, and Other Preparations for the Meal

Food preparation that does not involve cooking, such as preparing salads, is permitted on Shabbat. However, care must still be taken to avoid other Shabbat prohibitions. Some actions are permitted only when performed near the beginning of the meal. Furthermore, on Shabbat it is preferable not to use specialized implements intended for peeling, chopping, or crushing (peeling should be done with a knife, crushing with a fork, etc.).

Preparing Vegetables or Fruit for a Salad

It is permitted to prepare a salad on Shabbat for the Shabbat meal, but one should avoid using specialized tools such as a slicer or grater, and instead use a regular knife. One may peel and cut fruits and vegetables only for the upcoming meal.

Seasoning Cold Food

It is permitted to add oil, vinegar, or mayonnaise onto a vegetable salad or a potato salad. It is also permitted to sprinkle salt and other spices on the salad.

It is permitted to squeeze lemon on the salad, but this should be done by hand, not with a juice extractor. The lemon must be squeezed directly onto the salad, not into an empty vessel from which it will be placed on the salad.

Tahini

There are different opinions as to the permissibility of preparing a tahini dip from unprocessed sesame-seed paste by adding water, lemon juice or vinegar, and other spices. It is recommended to consult a rabbi on this matter.

Instant Foods

Instant powdered foods (such as mashed potatoes) and instant noodles, which require only the addition of boiling water for them to be ready to eat, may not be prepared on Shabbat.

Squeezing Out Juice

One may not squeeze fruit on Shabbat in order to produce juice (but see above with regard to squeezing directly into a salad).

Folding Napkins or Paper

It is prohibited on Shabbat to fold napkins or any other paper in a precise manner, as in origami folding, even if this is done for the purpose of setting the table. Simple rolling or folding, such as a single fold for placement in a napkin holder, is permitted.

During the Meal

During the meal itself as well, there are several actions that could entail a Shabbat prohibition.

Seasoning a Hot Dish

After food has been transferred from the vessel in which it was cooked to another vessel, the new one is classified as a secondary vessel. For example, the pot in which the soup is cooked is a primary vessel, and when it is transferred to a bowl, that bowl becomes a secondary vessel.

With regard to sprinkling salt on soup in a bowl (the secondary vessel), Sephardim are permitted to do so. For Ashkenazim, if the soup is still as hot as the temperature of *yad soledet bo*, then one should add salt only if it has already undergone a preliminary process of cooking, which is the case for most types of table salt. This is based on the halakhic principle that "there is no cooking after cooking." By contrast, if the salt has not undergone a preliminary process of cooking, it is prohibited.

If the soup has been transferred from the pot to a soup tureen, and from there it was ladled into bowls, those soup bowls are defined as tertiary vessels. In such a case, it is certainly permitted to add salt, even if the soup is very hot.

One may add croutons, cooked noodles, and the like to soup in a secondary vessel.

For Sephardim, it is permitted to pour cold water into soup that is in a secondary vessel in order to cool it, if it is still too hot to eat. Some Ashkenazim are stringent not to do this if the soup is burning hot, even though it is in a secondary vessel.

Solid foods, such as potatoes, chicken, etc., have a special status in *halakha*, and the law is more stringent with regard to seasoning them, because they preserve their warmth for a long time. It is proper to refrain from sprinkling spices or pouring cold, uncooked sauce directly onto such items, even after they have been transferred to a secondary vessel. It is permitted to pour ketchup on solid dishes, as ketchup is cooked during the process of production.

Ice in Drinks

If one wants to put ice in a drink, first one should pour a drink into a glass and only then put ice cubes in the drink. If one mistakenly put the ice in first and then poured the drink over it, it is permitted to drink the beverage.

Labor of Selecting (*Borer*)

One of the prohibited labors on Shabbat is *borer*, the separation of waste materials from items that one wants. Even during a meal, one must be careful not to pick out waste or unusable materials from food. For example, if there is meat on a bone, it is prohibited to remove the bone from the meat. Instead, the diner has two options: he may remove the meat from the bones, or he may put a piece of meat into his mouth with the bones and then remove the bones from his mouth.

In other words: On Shabbat, it is permitted to separate food from waste, but not waste from food. It is therefore permitted to pick the meat from the bones, but not the bones from the meat. The same rules apply when eating fish and other foods that contain inedible components.

Food and Waste

The prohibition of *borer* applies not only to actual waste, but also to subjective waste, such as in a situation where there are two types of food and one wishes to eat only one type and does not want the other. For example, if one has a vegetable salad with onion and he does not want the onion, the onion is considered waste as far as he is concerned, and he is not permitted to remove it from the salad. He may still enjoy the salad by selecting the vegetables he wants from the salad and leaving the onions on the plate.

If an insect or dirt falls into a beverage, some authorities permit one to spoon it out with a little of the drink, while others prohibit it to be removed in this way. According to this stricter opinion, one must pour out some of the drink from the cup until the insect or dirt comes out.

Fruit with Seeds

When eating a fruit that contains seeds or pits, such as watermelon, it is prohibited to remove the seeds from the fruit on Shabbat, as this constitutes a violation of the labor of selecting. Instead, one should insert a slice of watermelon into his mouth together with the seeds, and remove the seeds from his mouth in the course of eating. One who is uncomfortable with this method may shake the watermelon over a plate so that all or most of the seeds fall off, and remove the few remaining seeds by hand. It should be noted that the allowance to shake a piece of watermelon and remove its seeds applies only when this is done right before eating the watermelon, not at an earlier stage.

If one eats fruit with a pit that cannot be shaken off from the fruit, e.g., a peach, and he wants to remove it before eating the fruit, he may remove the pit together with a little bit of the fruit itself.

📖 **Further reading:** For information on the concept of selecting, see *A Concise Guide to Mahshava*, p. 170.

Preparing a Hot Drink

The preparation of a hot drink on Shabbat should be done with due attention to ensure that it is done in a permitted manner, without violating the prohibited labor of cooking. Here too, there are disagreements between Sephardic and Ashkenazic authorities, and there are different opinions among Ashkenazic authorities themselves.

With regard to instant coffee or hot chocolate prepared from powdered chocolate mix on Shabbat, Sephardim permit one to prepare these drinks in the usual manner. In other words, one may put coffee and sugar or powdered chocolate mix in a cup and pour hot water on them from the urn, despite the fact that this water comes from a primary vessel.

Ashkenazim require that the water come from a secondary vessel. According to this opinion, the order of inserting the coffee or powdered chocolate mix must be done as follows: First one fills the cup with water from the urn, which means that the water in that cup has the status of a secondary vessel. Only then may one put the coffee and sugar or powdered chocolate mix into the water. Alternatively, one may pour the water from the secondary vessel onto coffee and sugar or powdered chocolate mix that are in another cup.

In contrast to the items mentioned above, which have already been cooked in their processing, ground coffee, Turkish coffee, and cocoa powder have been roasted during processing but they have not been cooked, which therefore gives them a different status than instant coffee. Many Sephardic authorities nonetheless permit one to pour water directly from the urn onto the coffee or cocoa, but it is best not to do so. Rather, one should first fill the cup with hot water and only then add the coffee or cocoa powder. Ashkenazim should first fill an empty cup with hot water (a secondary vessel), and then pour it from there onto the coffee or cocoa powder.

Tea

One may prepare tea on Shabbat in two ways: by means of tea essence (strong, concentrated tea that one prepares before Shabbat) or with a tea bag. When using tea essence, the best method is to leave it over Shabbat on a heat source, such as on top of the urn, so that when preparing the tea, the essence will already be hot.

When preparing tea from tea essence, it is recommended to do so in the following manner: One should place a little essence into an empty cup, take another cup and fill it with water from the urn, and then pour the hot water from this cup into the cup with the essence. One should follow a similar procedure when using a tea bag: Place the bag and the sugar in a separate cup and pour water over it from a cup that was filled from the urn, so that the tea and the sugar will be mixed with the hot water only in a tertiary vessel.

If one wants to place a slice of lemon in the cup of tea, he must be careful not to cook the lemon. Accordingly, one must put the lemon slice into a tertiary vessel and pour hot water over it from a secondary vessel. Some rule stringently, that one may not place a slice of lemon in a hot cup of tea on Shabbat at all.

After the Meal

When the meal is over and it is time to clear the table and clean up, one must still take care to perform the necessary activities in a way that avoids Shabbat prohibitions.

Leftover Food

One may put any leftover food into the refrigerator so that it will not spoil, even if it will not be eaten on that Shabbat. It is permitted to return food to the warming tray or another heat source only under the conditions outlined above (see p. 421).

It is permitted to remove any leftover food from the table in order to throw it away. The garbage bag should not be tied with a double knot, as this constitutes the prohibited labor of tying. With regard to giving food remains to animals, see the section dealing with caring for animals on Shabbat.

Clearing and Cleaning the Table

With regard to clearing the table at the end of the meal, there is a distinction between the middle of Shabbat, when there is still significant time left until the end of the day, and just before the end of Shabbat. When Shabbat will end shortly, it is prohibited to clear the table, as this is considered preparing on Shabbat for a weekday. In other words, if it is evident that in the short time remaining on Shabbat the table will not be used, then clearing the table is therefore not in honor of Shabbat, and it is prohibited.

If a few hours remain until the end of Shabbat, it is permitted to clear and clean the table, for two reasons: (1) There is a likelihood that the members of the household or guests will want to sit at the table during Shabbat; and (2) order and cleanliness themselves are considered a mark of respect for Shabbat and add to the pleasant atmosphere.

Nevertheless, even at a time when it is permitted to clear and clean the table, one must be careful about the following:

If one wants to wipe down a table, it should be done with a dry cloth. If one uses a wet cloth there is the problem that it may entail squeezing, which is a prohibited labor on Shabbat. Therefore, if liquid is spilled on the table, one should gently place a dry, absorbent cloth on it, and avoid pressing the cloth onto the liquid. According to some halakhic authorities, it is permitted to clean the table with wet wipes, but others are stringent and prohibit this.

Washing Dishes

Washing dishes on Shabbat is permitted if one intends to use them over the course of Shabbat. Even if there is no clear intention to use them on Shabbat, it is permitted to wash them, provided that a long time still remains until the end of the day and there is a possibility that they will indeed be used.

Even when it is known for certain that one will not use these dishes before the end of Shabbat, it is permitted to soak them in water with soap, in a container or in a sink, in order to prevent an unpleasant smell or so that the dirty dishes do not attract insects.

Using hot water from an electric boiler for washing dishes or any other purpose is prohibited, as this causes water to enter the boiler and become heated, which is considered a violation of the prohibited labor of cooking.

If one wishes to warm up cold water, so that it will be more comfortable to wash the dishes, one may fill a container with cold water and pour boiling water into it from the Shabbat urn, provided that the water in the container will not reach the temperature of *yad soledet bo* (45° C or 113° F). One may also act in the opposite manner: Fill a container with boiling water and pour into it a larger amount of cold water, to yield warm water. Here too, it is necessary to be careful to add a considerable amount of cold water at once, so that the temperature of the mixture will be below the temperature of *yad soledet bo*.

Washing dishes should not be done with a regular sponge, due to the fact that sponges absorb liquid, which one then squeezes out in the course of their use. Rather, one must use a special non-absorbent pad or "Shabbat sponge."

With regard to operating a dishwasher on Shabbat by means of a timer that is set before Shabbat, some authorities permit this under certain conditions, and it is advisable to consult a rabbi about the details. In any event, it is permitted to place dirty dishes in a dishwasher in order to operate it after Shabbat, provided that one does not separate a jumble of dishes or cutlery into separate compartments in the dishwasher, as this kind of sorting is a sub-category of the prohibited labor of selecting.

One may wipe washed dishes dry with a towel.

Housework on Shabbat

Shabbat is a time for rest, for both the body and the soul. On Shabbat one spends much of his time at home, but even within the walls of the house there are activities that are prohibited on Shabbat due to their similarity to labors that were performed for the Tabernacle. It is important to know these *halakhot* well, so that one will not mistakenly permit himself to do prohibited acts, and also so as not to unnecessarily avoid permitted conduct.

This section presents the laws involving various forms of housework, including cleaning, repairing household items and clothes, and caring for plants or a garden.

Home Maintenance

Many home maintenance activities could entail Shabbat prohibitions. Some of these are related to cleaning, while others involve the repair of damaged objects.

Cleaning

Sweeping a tiled or other finished floor surface on Shabbat is permitted, but it is prohibited to sweep an uncovered earthen floor. One should not wash the floor on Shabbat. However, if the floor becomes exceptionally dirty one may pour a small quantity of water on the dirt and wipe it away with a rubber squeegee, but not a mop.

It is permitted to wipe up liquids that spilled on any surface such as a table or the floor, on the condition that the action does not involve squeezing. One may place a cloth on the liquid to absorb it, without pressing or squeezing it.

It is permitted to remove dust from furniture with a dry cloth, but one may not use polishing products.

Cleaning a carpet or shaking it out on Shabbat is prohibited, but one may sweep it a little, in order to remove dirt or waste from it.

Fixing and Dismantling

Any action that is similar to building a structure, whether outdoors or indoors, is prohibited on Shabbat. Adding to an existing structure is also prohibited. Therefore, it is prohibited to plug a small hole in the wall or to add cement or plaster to the wall.

It is also prohibited to dismantle anything one is forbidden to build. This prohibition applies by Torah law only when the destruction is of some benefit, for example, digging a hole in the ground in order to establish the foundations for future building, or drilling a hole in the wall to place a screw there.

Sticking a nail or a thumbtack to the wall, and likewise attaching a hook or rack, are prohibited on Shabbat. Nor should they be removed from their places on Shabbat.

The prohibition against building or dismantling applies to tools as well. For example, one may not fix a handle onto a hammer or attach a stick to a broom brush.

It is prohibited to disassemble objects, such as the door of a closet, and likewise one may not return them to their places if they fell off by themselves. Similarly, if a window or shutter has become detached from its place it is prohibited to return it to its normal location. One may not reaffix a door handle that has been dislodged, if the handle was connected to the door in a permanent manner. The handle itself, which has been detached from the door, is defined as *muktze* and may not be moved on Shabbat. Likewise, one may not oil a creaking door hinge on Shabbat.

It is permitted on Shabbat to use an item that is generally operated by screwing a piece onto another piece, such as the lid of a jar, the top of a salt shaker, and so on. One may also look through binoculars that are focused by turning dials. The common denominator of all of these actions is that this is the typical way they are used, and therefore the act of screwing or unscrewing, or tightening or loosening, does not constitute the performance of labor.

Clothing

Laundering is prohibited on Shabbat as it is the labor of whitening, one of the activities that was performed in the construction of the Tabernacle. It is therefore prohibited to wash clothes on Shabbat, either in a machine or by hand. Even laundering a specific spot on one's clothing is prohibited. Therefore, if there is a stain of any kind on a garment one may not clean it with water or any type of cleansing agent, and likewise one may not rub or scratch the stain from the garment. In addition, one may not soak the garment in water. Aside from laundering, there are several other actions related to clothing that are prohibited on Shabbat.

Laundering, Ironing, and Folding

The *halakha* regarding the removal of dust from a garment depends on several factors: If it is a new garment, or one which the owner is very particular about keeping clean, then it is prohibited to remove dust from it. By contrast, if it is an item of clothing that one is not as particular about, one may remove the dust by brushing lightly with his hand, but may not rub the garment or shake it with force.

Squeezing a garment that has absorbed water is prohibited on Shabbat. Likewise, one may not place wet clothes near a heat source to dry, or hang them on clotheslines. It is permitted to hang them in a place that is not designated for drying clothes and which is not near a source of heat. This should be done discreetly.

It is permitted to remove laundry from a clothesline on Shabbat only if the clothes were dry at the start of Shabbat. If not, they may not be taken off the line. The exception is babies' clothes that are urgently needed; they may be removed from the line even if they were not completely dry at the beginning of Shabbat.

Sorting, folding, and ironing clothes are all prohibited on Shabbat.

Mending Clothes

Sewing garments or parts of clothing on Shabbat is prohibited. Not only is actual sewing prohibited, but even tightening an existing thread on a garment is prohibited on Shabbat.

This prohibition notwithstanding, it is permitted to use a safety pin to tighten a garment or connect two torn parts of an item of clothing. But even here, some rule that the pin may be inserted through each garment or each part of the garment only once.

If an elastic band was threaded into a garment and it came out, one may not return it to its place on Shabbat. This is in contrast with a belt that is not attached to the garment, which one may remove and reinsert on Shabbat.

It is permitted to remove the pins that are typically inserted in new garments at the factory to preserve their folds.

It is prohibited to remove temporary sewing threads from new clothes; to open pockets in suits and coats that were sewn in advance to be opened later; to remove labels that have been sewn into a garment or glued onto it; to separate a pair of socks or other types of clothing that are attached by a thread; and similarly to pluck off remains of wool that are left hanging and attached to the edges of a garment.

With regard to an item of clothing that is packaged in plastic, one may tear off the plastic on Shabbat in order to remove the garment and put it on, if one tears it in such a way that it cannot be reused.

Plant Care

Any kind of plant care is prohibited on Shabbat. This includes planting, irrigation, spraying, fertilization, pruning, removing thorns, breaking branches, and clearing stones.

Gardening

It is prohibited to water plants on Shabbat. Even washing one's hands over the ground in such a way that the water will fall directly onto grass, vegetation, seeds, and the like, is prohibited on Shabbat. When washing hands does not directly irrigate the soil, but rather the water flows through a pipe or a drainage channel to another area where it waters the plants, it is permitted as long as one's intention is not to water the vegetation.

It is permitted to activate an automatic irrigation system in advance so that it will operate on Shabbat (but see the section on "the appearance of transgression," p. 454).

Picking fruit from a tree, or uprooting vegetables or grass from the ground, is prohibited on Shabbat. Collecting fruits that have fallen from a tree and are lying under it is also prohibited on Shabbat.

It is even prohibited to pass through one's garden with the intention of seeing what requires fixing or what task needs to be done after Shabbat.

A flowerpot is classified as *muktze* and may not be moved on Shabbat from one place to another. If the pot fell and some soil spilled from it, one may not return the soil to the pot.

Flowers in a Vase

It is permitted to move a vase with flowers from one spot to another on Shabbat.

One may not put flowers in a vase of water on Shabbat. Likewise, one may not add water to a vase that has flowers in it.

Bathing and Hygiene on Shabbat

It is a mitzva to clean one's body in honor of Shabbat, before Shabbat starts. But on Shabbat itself, certain actions related to bathing and hygiene are prohibited. This chapter will review the *halakhot* concerning various activities in this area, such as bathing, brushing teeth, applying perfumes and other cosmetics, and various grooming activities, as well as cleaning the bathroom and improving its fragrance.

Showering on Shabbat

The Sages prohibited bathing one's entire body in hot water on Shabbat. There are also certain limitations with regard to bathing in cold water on Shabbat.

Washing One's Body

Even if water is heated before Shabbat, washing one's entire body on Shabbat in hot water is prohibited, so that it will not lead to people heating water on Shabbat for the purpose of bathing.

Water that is heated on Shabbat in a prohibited manner may not be put to any use. Even if the water was heated in a permitted manner, e.g., for a sick person, a healthy individual may not use it. If the water warmed up without someone performing any action in order to heat it, such as water in a solar heater, it is permitted to wash individual parts of the body with it, as long as one does not wash the majority of one's body.

With regard to showering in cold water, there is a difference between Ashkenazic and Sephardic practice: Sephardim permit one to take a cold shower on Shabbat and even wash his entire body. By contrast, although Ashkenazim permit the washing of all parts of one's body on Shabbat in cold water sequentially, they do not allow one to wash his entire body at one time.

On Shabbat it is permitted to use only liquid soap, not solid soap.

Tooth Brushing

Tooth brushing raises various halakhic concerns: spreading an ointment, which is prohibited on Shabbat; squeezing water from the bristles of the toothbrush; pulling bristles out of the toothbrush; and causing bleeding in the gums. For this reason, it is recommended to use mouthwash rather than toothbrush and toothpaste. Those who wish to use a toothbrush should find a high-quality brush with soft bristles that do not absorb water.

Some halakhic authorities do permit brushing teeth on Shabbat even with a regular toothbrush and toothpaste, if neglecting to brush the teeth causes discomfort, and even if the discomfort is only due to unpleasant breath. But even according to this lenient opinion, if it is known for certain that the brushing will cause the gums to bleed, it is prohibited. By contrast, there are authorities who completely prohibit using a toothbrush and permit only the use of mouthwash.

Bodily Perfume

The use of stick deodorant is prohibited on Shabbat, but spray or liquid roll-on deodorant is permitted.

One may also spray perfume directly on one's body on Shabbat. It is prohibited to spray it on clothing, as this would violate the prohibition against creating a scented object on Shabbat. Furthermore, some authorities are more stringent and permit the use of a deodorant or perfume spray only in order to disperse an unpleasant odor, but not in order to create a pleasant aroma. This is because they maintain that the prohibition of creating a scented object on Shabbat applies to the human body as well.

Hair Care

Haircuts and hair removal are prohibited on Shabbat, in every manner and form. Additionally, one may not comb one's hair on Shabbat with a regular comb or brush, as there is a reasonable concern that one might detach hairs from his head, which is prohibited on Shabbat. One may use a soft-bristled brush if it does not necessarily remove hair from one's head.

It is permitted to insert a pin or clip into one's hair, but it is prohibited to braid the hair. Gathering one's hair in order to tie it together with a ribbon or hair band is permitted.

Cosmetics and Skin Care

As a rule, it is prohibited to apply makeup on Shabbat. In recent years, various types of cosmetics have been developed that purport to be permissible for use on Shabbat. One should consult a rabbi before using any particular product.

One may not apply lipstick or nail polish (colored or transparent) on Shabbat. One should not remove nail polish on Shabbat with a piece of cotton or the like to which one has applied a liquid. It is prohibited to trim nails on Shabbat, whether by hand, with scissors, with another implement, or even with one's teeth. Therefore, manicures are prohibited on Shabbat.

Applying ointment of any kind, whether hand cream, body cream, or face cream, is generally prohibited. Nevertheless, a person suffering from a skin condition should consult a rabbi regarding the possibility of using cream or ointment in such circumstances.

Bathroom Cleanliness

It is prohibited to cut toilet paper on Shabbat, and therefore it is necessary to prepare sufficient quantities of cut toilet paper for Shabbat, or to buy tissues or precut toilet paper. If one forgot to ensure that he has tissues or cut paper, or it all ran out and he cannot obtain any more or any substitute, he may cut toilet paper from an ordinary roll for immediate use, but should cut it not along the perforated lines. This dispensation is due to concern for human dignity.

It is permitted to clean a toilet with a rubber or plastic brush, as these do not absorb liquids, and therefore there is no concern regarding the labor of squeezing. Furthermore, one may use cleaning fluid in the toilet during Shabbat. There is no problem with placing an air freshener in the bathroom on Shabbat, or with using an air freshener spray to dispel a foul odor.

On Shabbat, it is prohibited to use a toilet with an electronic eye that causes the toilet to flush automatically. Those who have no other solution should consult a rabbi.

Miscellaneous

It is permitted to apply liquid insect repellant to one's body on Shabbat.

If one wishes to use cotton wool on Shabbat, he should prepare pieces of the desired size in advance. If one neglected to do so and he needs it on Shabbat in order to attend to an injury, it is permitted to separate a piece of cotton from a larger wad.

Fire and Electricity on Shabbat

Lighting a fire on Shabbat is prohibited by Torah law, as it is stated, "You shall not kindle fire in all your dwellings on the Sabbath day" (Exodus 35:3). This prohibition extends to the enhancement or enlargement of an existing fire. It is also prohibited to turn electric lights on or to operate electrical appliances on Shabbat.

This chapter presents the *halakhot* regarding the use of electricity and electrical appliances on Shabbat.

Turning On and Off

Turning anything electric on or off is prohibited. This includes lights, hot-water urns, air conditioners, stoves, computers, and telephones. It is similarly prohibited to adjust their intensity or power settings.

Permitted Uses

It is permitted to set a timer before Shabbat to turn lights and certain other devices, such as air conditioners, on and off during the course of Shabbat (see below for an important limitation). The reason for this permission is that when a device is operated by an electric timer, the labor is performed as a result of an action the person performed before Shabbat, not on Shabbat itself.

It is permitted to use an electric blanket or pillow that was activated before Shabbat, but one must be careful not to remove the plug from the socket.

Silent or Noisy

The use of a timer is permitted for only some electric appliances but not for all appliances. Quiet devices, such as a hot plate, may be activated by a timer. By contrast, noisy devices like washing machines may not be activated by means of a timer, as the noise draws attention, and people might suspect that the device was activated on Shabbat itself. This type of reason, called *marit ayin*, "the appearance of transgression," is discussed at length in a separate chapter (p. 454).

Nonetheless, a loud electric appliance which is commonly set on a timer, such as an air conditioner, may be activated by a timer.

Shabbat Elevator

It is prohibited to use an elevator on Shabbat. In recent years, a special "Shabbat elevator" has been developed, which stops for predefined periods of time on each floor, without any human action necessary on Shabbat. Some halakhic authorities allow the use of such an elevator. Opinions are divided; each person should follow the instructions of his rabbi.

Hotels

Staying in a hotel on Shabbat often raises halakhic problems, so one must take great care to avoid violating prohibitions. Some of the common challenges are lights that turn on automatically when a person walks in a corridor, electronic locks for rooms, automatic systems for turning on lights and appliances such as air conditioning upon entering or exiting rooms, and toilets that flush automatically.

The best solution, when possible, is to avoid all these problems by disabling the relevant systems before Shabbat and requesting a manual key to one's room. If this cannot be done, one should obtain guidance from a rabbi who is knowledgeable about these matters.

Lifesaving Activities

In situations where electricity is required for lifesaving activities [*pikuah nefesh*], such as in hospitals or on military bases, one may use electric devices on Shabbat as necessary for these lifesaving functions.

Extinguishing a Fire

It is prohibited to extinguish a fire on Shabbat. Nevertheless, if a fire breaks out and there is a concern that it might be life-threatening, one is permitted – and indeed obligated – to put it out. It is generally assumed that a fire does pose a danger to human life. If the fire poses absolutely no danger to anyone's life but will cause only monetary damage, one may not extinguish it on Shabbat.

Medical Treatment on Shabbat

"Saving a life [*pikuah nefesh*] overrides the entire Torah," including Shabbat. In fact, in a situation where human life is in danger, it is a mitzva to desecrate Shabbat. The halakhic principle about this is as follows: "When these actions are done, they should not be performed by gentiles, nor by minors, nor by slaves, nor by women, so that [the desecration of] Shabbat should not become light in their eyes, but rather [it should be done] by the great Sages and wise men of Israel. And it is prohibited to delay the desecration of Shabbat for an ill person whose life is in danger, as it is stated: '[You shall observe My laws and My statutes,] which a person shall do and live by them' (Leviticus 18:5) – and not to die by them" (Rambam, *Sefer Moed, Hilkhot Shabbat* 2:3).

When it comes to medical treatment that is not in order to save a life, the laws are more complex. The Sages prohibited taking medications or performing actions that are defined as medical treatment on Shabbat. Nevertheless, the *halakha* recognizes several degrees of medical need, and there are different laws that apply depending on the level of need.

Saving a Life

While it is permitted to perform any labor necessary to save lives, it is important to remember, when deciding how to act, that on the other side of the scale is the sanctity of Shabbat. Therefore, permission to desecrate Shabbat applies only to actions that are necessary to save lives; it is not a blanket permission to perform any action. It is also imperative to refrain from knowingly putting oneself in any life-threatening situation on Shabbat.

Uncertain *Pikuah Nefesh*

The permission to desecrate Shabbat in a case of *pikuah nefesh* includes situations where it is uncertain whether human life is actually in danger or if a particular treatment will indeed save the person's life; even possible *pikuah nefesh* overrides Shabbat. Furthermore, even if it is clear that the person's life will not be spared in the long run, but there is reason to assume or hope that the action will extend his life, even for a very brief period of time, it is permitted to desecrate Shabbat for his sake.

If the person whose life is in danger refuses to allow others to desecrate Shabbat for him, he should be persuaded that this is permitted and even a mitzva.

📖 **Further reading:** For more on the sanctity of life and *pikuaḥ nefesh*, see *A Concise Guide to the Sages*, pp. 6, 150.

Life-Threatening Illness

The following are examples of patients defined as someone whose life is in danger and for whom it is permitted to desecrate Shabbat: one whose doctor has determined that his life is in danger; a sick person who believes that his own life is in danger, even if the doctor thinks otherwise; and one who has a high fever for an unknown reason and generally feels unwell. It is permitted to desecrate Shabbat even for the sake of one who is currently feeling well but whose condition might deteriorate into a life-threatening state if he does not receive treatment on Shabbat.

A woman in childbirth is defined as being in a life-threatening situation from the beginning of the birth process until the conclusion of the seventh day after the baby is born. If a complication develops during or after birth, she may be considered in danger even longer.

Permitted Actions

When one needs to speak on the phone to call for help or to receive medical guidance, it is not necessary to limit the scope of the discussion of the medical situation in order to minimize the Shabbat violation; rather, one may conduct the conversation about the medical matter unhurriedly, for as long as the situation requires.

At a time of need, it is permitted to transport a person in a car for emergency treatment, and likewise one may drive to bring him medicines or lifesaving equipment. Ideally, it is advisable to travel to the nearest medical center. Nevertheless, if a medical center that is farther away can give better treatment, or even if the patient believes that to be the case and therefore wants to travel to a more distant medical center, it is permitted to drive there. If one does not know the way there, he may turn on a navigation device.

Advance Preparation

If there is certainty or high probability that during Shabbat one will have to drive a car, e.g., in the case of a woman in the final stages of her pregnancy, one should perform certain actions before Shabbat in order to minimize the desecration of Shabbat:

(1) Disable the car alarm.

(2) Disable the automatic light that turns on upon opening the doors. If for some reason this was not done, then it is best when entering the car, before closing the doors, to switch the light to the permanently on state, so that future closing and opening of the doors will not cause the light to turn on and off again.

(3) Before Shabbat, one should remove from the vehicle any items that will not be needed on Shabbat. If this was not done before Shabbat, one should remove any heavy items on Shabbat itself before departing, even if those items are classified as *muktze*.

When traveling on Shabbat to save a life, one must ensure that the trip and all other prohibited actions be performed solely for the sake of the person whose life is in danger. Nevertheless, the drive itself must be conducted carefully while avoiding speeding and in accordance with all the traffic laws, just like on a weekday, to make sure not to endanger additional human lives.

Taking Medications

The discussion so far has focused on a person in life-threatening danger; such a person may take any necessary medication or undergo any treatment, and it is also permitted for others to desecrate Shabbat on his behalf. By contrast, in most conditions of illness, the individual is not in life-threatening danger. In these situations, it is prohibited to desecrate Shabbat for him, and there are also limitations on when the patient himself may take medications. The following section describes the various levels of illness, and the actions that are permitted and prohibited in each situation.

Advanced Planning

The Sages instituted a prohibition to take medicine on Shabbat. This even includes consuming substances that are not actual medications but which are not normally used by healthy people. For example, one may not use throat lozenges on Shabbat to relieve a sore throat. Similarly, any action that is clearly done for medical purposes, even if it does not constitute a Shabbat violation itself, is prohibited on Shabbat. See the next section for an example.

The reason for the prohibition against taking medicines on Shabbat is the concern that it may lead to the crushing of herbs for medicinal purposes on Shabbat (see *Shabbat* 5b). Accordingly, the fact that nowadays people usually do not produce their own medicines, but rather purchase them from a pharmacy, eases the severity of the prohibition slightly, as detailed below, although the basic prohibition remains in effect.

It is important to consider in advance whether one's condition allows one to take medicine on Shabbat, and to ask a rabbi in a case of doubt. If one is not permitted to take medicine on Shabbat but feels that the medicine would help him, he should take it just before Shabbat.

The following is an explanation of different types of medical conditions, from the lightest to the most severe, with explanations as to what is permitted and prohibited in each situation:

Minor Aches

This category describes a basically healthy person who can function normally but suffers from a minor ailment such as a mild cold or cough, or a mild skin condition. In such cases it is prohibited to take medications or perform any acts that constitute prohibited labor in order to ease his pain. In addition, he may not perform any action which is clearly done for medicinal purposes, such as gargling saltwater. Nevertheless, it is permitted to rest, drink large quantities of cold or hot beverages, or perform other potentially helpful actions that healthy people also engage in.

Ill Person Whose Life Is Not in Danger

When a person is suffering not just minor aches and pains but is actually ill, even if his condition is not life-threatening, he is permitted to take medicine and perform other actions that provide medical benefit, as long as they do not involve a prohibited labor. In severe situations he may even perform prohibited labors in certain ways (see below).

The following cases are ones in which the individual is defined as "ill" according to *halakha*:

A person who is in bed due to pain or illness.

A person who is in such pain that it emanates from the source of the pain and affects his entire body, e.g., someone suffering from a migraine.

A person who currently appears healthy but his condition will deteriorate if he does not receive treatment. Examples include people suffering from asthma, diabetes, and arthritis.

A person who suffered an internal wound or one of whose body parts is in danger, even if his state is not life-threatening in the present moment or in the future. An example of this is a broken bone.

A woman after childbirth, from the eighth day through the thirtieth day of birth. (Until the eighth day she is considered to be in life-threatening danger.)

In the case of young children, any medical need is treated like that of an actual illness for an adult, and therefore it is permitted to give them medicine (as noted in the next section, which addresses the laws regarding children on Shabbat).

When a person is injured and there is a concern about possible infection, the injury must be treated and dressed as required. In milder cases, the wound should at least be cleaned and disinfected.

Miscellaneous

There is a halakhic principle that "all are [deemed] ill with regard to cold." This means that when it is especially cold, even a person who is halakhically defined as "healthy" is treated as a sick person. Consequently, if one forgot to turn on the heater before Shabbat on a particularly cold day, and the members of the family are suffering from the cold, and certainly if there is a sick person or small children in the house, it is permitted to ask a gentile to turn on the heater on Shabbat.

There are cases in which a person is not defined as currently ill but is nevertheless allowed to take medication on Shabbat, because he began the prescription before Shabbat and he must take the medication regularly over a period of time. Examples of this include one who began a treatment of antibiotics or fertility drugs.

It is prohibited to exercise on Shabbat.

A person who requires a hearing aid may use it on Shabbat, provided that the device was activated before Shabbat. It is permitted to adjust the volume.

Children on Shabbat

By Torah law, minors are exempt from the observance of mitzvot. Nevertheless, the Sages declared that children must begin fulfilling various commandments of the Torah in a gradual manner, for educational purposes [ḥinukh]. The aim of this obligation is to accustom them to the performance of mitzvot.

This obligation applies not only to the children themselves, but primarily to their parents, who are commanded to instruct their offspring in the observance of mitzvot. Therefore, children may not perform actions that violate Shabbat, and adults must prevent them from doing so, at least from the age when they become subject to ḥinukh.

With regard to adults performing prohibited acts on Shabbat on behalf of their children, as a general rule, it is prohibited to do anything on behalf of a child that one may not do for himself. There are some exceptions to this rule, and at certain ages and in particular cases, adults are permitted to perform vital tasks for their children.

This chapter details the acts that are permitted and prohibited to be performed on behalf of children and toddlers, from issues related to nutrition and medicine to toys and games and matters of cleanliness.

Feeding Babies and Children

The preparation of food on Shabbat can entail the performance of prohibited labor. For children in general and infants in particular, the Sages were lenient and permitted the performance of certain essential activities.

Nursing and Pumping

It is prohibited to pump breast milk into a container on Shabbat if there is no special need. If the baby will not nurse and therefore the mother needs to pump milk to feed him, she should consult with a rabbi about how to do this on Shabbat. A woman suffering from engorgement at a time when the baby does not want to eat may express the milk but only if it becomes immediately unusable. Thus, she may express the milk directly into a sink or into a bottle that has soap in it.

Heating Food

Any food that can be prepared before Shabbat must be prepared in advance. Food that one cannot prepare before Shabbat, such as baby cereal and baby formula, may be prepared on Shabbat, but this should be done as follows:

To prepare formula from powder, one should pour the hot water from a secondary vessel (as defined in the chapter dealing with the kitchen and food on Shabbat, p. 419) onto the powder.

Baby cereal should be prepared by putting the powder into water that is in a secondary vessel. It is also preferable to make the cereal with a liquid consistency, rather than thick. If necessary, it is permitted to make thick cereal, but one should not stir the cereal in the normal way. Rather, one may mix the contents with distinct vertical and horizontal movements.

If it is necessary to warm cold milk or any other cold food which has already been fully cooked for a baby, one may place it in warm water in a secondary vessel. Alternatively, it may be placed near, but not on, a source of heat such as an electric hot plate, such that it will get warm but not reach the temperature of *yad soledet bo* (45° C, or 113° F).

Medication for Infants and Children

As a rule, it is prohibited to take medicine on Shabbat if one is not defined as sick (see above, p. 442, with regard to one suffering from minor aches), but with regard to young children the Sages were lenient and did not apply this prohibition. Thus, medicine may be given to a young child, even if he has a minor pain or other medical condition, as though he was actually sick.

The following include some common treatments for babies that are permitted on Shabbat:

Treatments

It is permitted to apply oil to a baby's skin, including to treat skin irritations such as diaper rash, or for dry skin on the scalp. The oil should be as thin a liquid as possible, and it must be applied by hand, not with cotton wool. With regard to ointment or cream, some permit one only to dab it on the baby's body but not to rub it in, while others even permit spreading it, if it becomes fully absorbed into the skin. It is permitted to sprinkle powder, such as talc, onto a baby's skin, despite the fact that the express purpose of the powder is medicinal.

A baby or a young child may be given any medicine he needs, including pills and syrups as well as drops for the nose, eyes, or ears. If necessary, it is permitted to crush a pill for a baby or child (although a regular pill crusher should not be used) and dissolve it in water.

If a child requires a humidifier, one should consult a rabbi.

If a baby or a child is suffering from rectal worms, it is permitted to remove them on Shabbat. One may also administer oral medication to treat this condition.

Washing Babies

In general, bathing on Shabbat is subject to various restrictions, especially with regard to the use of hot water (see the section dealing with hygiene on Shabbat), but in the case of infants, the Sages were lenient and permitted one to wash them under certain conditions.

Time of Need

If necessary, a baby may be bathed in hot water that was heated before Shabbat, or in water heated by a solar water heater. Likewise, at a time of need, bath salts may be added to a baby bath.

If a baby's body temperature has risen and he must be cooled in a lukewarm bath, one may pour boiling water into the cold water, so that the water will not be too cold.

The use of wet wipes on Shabbat is permitted according to most opinions.

Games for Children

Shabbat was given to us so that we can rest from the toil of the week and turn our attention from mundane pursuits to sacred and spiritual matters. It is therefore fitting for adults to devote Shabbat to prayer and Torah study to the extent possible. By contrast, it is difficult to expect children to spend Shabbat focused entirely on spiritual matters, and therefore they are allowed to play games. Obviously, this does not include games which involve the desecration of Shabbat, such as those that involve the use of electricity. Such games and toys are prohibited on Shabbat, and parents must prevent their children from playing with them.

Permitted and Prohibited Games

The following is a list of various types of games and toys, and the *halakha* regarding each of them.

Chutes and Ladders, and other games played with dice, spinners, or the like: Permitted.

Lego: Permitted.

Jacks: Permitted.

Tag, jumping games, hide and seek, games with a rope: Permitted.

Binoculars: Permitted. One may look through binoculars and even focus them.

Sandbox: It is permitted to play in a designated sandbox, but one may not mix water with the sand. It is prohibited to play with sand on the seashore, or any sand that was not set aside for playing with, such as sand that is designated as construction material. Children should also be prevented from writing words or drawing pictures in the sand.

Games with sticks, stones, or fruit pits: These can be played with on condition that the materials were designated as toys before the start of Shabbat. It is prohibited to collect stones and sticks on Shabbat and play with them. It is also prohibited to play with apricot pits that were extracted from the fruit on Shabbat.

Toys with springs: Permitted, provided that they do not produce sounds or sparks.

Necklaces: Stringing beads on a string is prohibited, if the product is meant to last. But if the stringing is done as part of a game and the necklace produced is meant to be temporary, it is permitted.

Chess, dominoes, cards: Permitted.

Puzzles: Permitted, provided that one does not intend to leave the puzzle assembled for an extended period of time.

Games involving cutting and pasting: Prohibited.

Rattles, bells, whistles, horns: It is prohibited to use these on Shabbat. Furthermore, they are classified as *muktze* and should not be moved on Shabbat.

Modeling clay, modeling compound such as Play-Doh, wax, clay, plaster: Prohibited, and they are *muktze*.

Electric toys, including battery-powered toys: Prohibited and they are *muktze*.

Paper folding (origami): Prohibited.

Swimming in the sea or a pool: Prohibited.

Rungs connected to a tree trunk or a treehouse: One may not climb a tree, whether it is alive or dead, whole or partially cut, if its trunk is connected to the ground.

Marbles: In the house or on a paved area, it is permitted to play with marbles. On an unpaved surface, it is prohibited.

Riding on bicycles: There is a difference between a tricycle, which has hard, plastic wheels and is designed for small children, and ordinary, two-wheeled bicycles. Tricycles are permitted, whereas riding a bicycle is prohibited on Shabbat.

Ball games: The *halakha* depends on the specific type of game: Ping-pong (table tennis) is permitted; soccer and basketball are permitted inside the house but should be avoided outside the house.

📖 **Further reading:** For more on educating young children on mitzvot, see *A Concise Guide to the Sages,* p. 404; *A Concise Guide to Mahshava,* p. 186.

Miscellaneous

There are various other halakhic questions that can arise with regard to child care. Here are guidelines for a few common situations:

A folding highchair, playpen, and a baby carriage may be opened on Shabbat. It is also permitted to attach a food tray to a highchair, if the tray is normally detached and reattached. With regard to opening a canopy that is connected to a baby carriage to protect the child from sun or rain, opinions are divided, and therefore it is recommended to consult with a rabbi on this matter.

If a rubber mat or sheet became wet from urine and the like, it is permitted to pour water on it in order to clean it. This dispensation does not apply to clothing. Even so, one may not rub its sides together, nor rub it with a wet cloth.

If a small child gets lost and no one knows who his relatives are, and the child himself is frightened and panicky, one should call the police and desecrate Shabbat in order to return the child to his family.

Animals on Shabbat

Not only people are commanded to refrain from work on Shabbat; we must also allow the animals in our possession to rest. The Torah states, "Six days you shall perform your activities, and on the seventh day you shall rest so that your ox and your donkey will rest" (Exodus 23:12). It is also stated, "The seventh day is Sabbath for the Lord your God; you shall not perform any labor, you, and your son, and your daughter, your slave, and your maidservant, and your animal, and your stranger who is within your gates" (Exodus 20:10). Although the verses mention explicitly only an ox and a donkey, the command applies to all animals in one's possession.

Working and Using Animals

The prohibition against causing animals to work on Shabbat includes not only actively drawing the animal along as it performs a prohibited labor, but also merely causing it to perform the prohibited action; for example, if the animal has a load on its back and one calls to it, thereby causing it to carry outside a permitted area.

Details of the Prohibition

One may not cause an animal to perform work on Shabbat, but one may whistle or signal to an animal to come to him.

It is prohibited to ride an animal on Shabbat, regardless of whether it belongs to the rider or not, and regardless of whether there is an *eiruv*.

A blind person who requires a guide dog may walk outdoors with it.

📖 **Further reading:** For the story of a cow that kept Shabbat, see *A Concise Guide to the Sages*, p. 280.

Feeding and Moving

Not only is it prohibited to put animals to work on Shabbat, but one may generally not even move an animal, as they are classified as *muktze*. It is also prohibited on Shabbat to feed animals that are not one's direct responsibility.

Feeding and Moving Animals

One must provide food and water to animals that are in his possession and which depend on him, such as cows and chickens. It is prohibited to give food and water to animals that can find food on their own, such as doves from a dovecote, or bees. Although feeding them is not a prohibited labor by Torah law, it is nevertheless rabbinically forbidden.

A hungry animal which has not found food on its own may be fed on Shabbat, even if it is not one's responsibility to feed it, in order to avoid causing suffering to animals.

One who is accustomed to throwing leftover food into a specific area may do so on Shabbat as well, even if the food attracts animals that are not owned by him or are not his responsibility.

It is prohibited to move animals on Shabbat, as they are defined as *muktze*. With regard to pets that one usually plays with, there are differences of opinion among halakhic authorities as to whether or not it is permitted to pick them up and play with them on Shabbat.

In a situation that involves the suffering of living beings, such as animals that are stuck in a cage or in the burning sun, one may carry them in order to spare them pain. If a fish died in a fish tank and there is a concern that the other fish might die if the dead one is left in the water, it is permitted to remove it from the fish tank on Shabbat and to dispose of it.

📖 **Further reading:** For more on the prohibition of causing animals to suffer, see p. 613; *A Concise Guide to the Sages*, p. 435; *A Concise Guide to Mahshava*, p. 122.

Trapping

The trapping of animals is one of the labors that was performed in the Tabernacle, as the children of Israel were required to catch an animal called a *tahash* in order to make the curtains for the Tabernacle from its skin, and to catch snails to use their blood to produce the light-blue dye that was required for the threads of the curtains.

Trapping and Spraying

Trapping animals in any way is prohibited on Shabbat, except for animals that are already in one's possession and will not run away. Therefore, if a bird flies into one's house on Shabbat, he may not close the door or the window to prevent it from escaping. If one has a bird cage in his home, he should consult a rabbi about when it may be permitted to open and close the door of the bird cage on Shabbat.

It is permitted to set a mousetrap on Friday, as the actual act of trapping occurs on Shabbat without human involvement. Furthermore, one may release an animal from a trap, as the prohibition applies solely to trapping.

One may use a spray on Shabbat to get rid of flies or mosquitoes on two conditions: (1) One must spray into the air, not directly onto the bugs themselves; and (2) the room must have an open window or door, as this demonstrates that one does not want to kill the insects but merely to chase them away.

It is permitted to trap a snake, scorpion, or other harmful creature in order to prevent it from attacking a person or causing damage.

Restrictions on Speech on Shabbat

Shabbat is a day of rest and sanctity whose purpose is to elevate us to a higher spiritual plane. Therefore, the Sages imposed restrictions on certain activities which, although not themselves defined as prohibited labor, in effect serve as preparations for future actions that are prohibited on Shabbat. For example, one may not walk on Shabbat to a bus station so that he can start his journey immediately after Shabbat. Likewise, speech and conversations that might impair the atmosphere of holiness and rest of Shabbat, such as discussing business matters, are prohibited.

These prohibitions are derived from the verse, "If you restrain your walking because of the Sabbath, pursuing your needs on the day of My holiness and you call the Sabbath a delight and the Lord's sacred, honored, and you honor it by refraining from doing your business, from seeking your needs and from speaking of matters" (Isaiah 58:13). This verse teaches that one must refrain from actions that are defined as "your needs," that is to say, one's mundane interests. It also teaches that one must avoid speech that is incompatible with the sanctity of Shabbat, which the prophet calls, "speaking of matters." The aim of these restrictions is to ensure that Shabbat is set aside for its true purpose: "And you call the Shabbat a delight and the Lord's sacred, honored." Shabbat should be spent engaged in Torah study, prayer, family meals accompanied by the singing of *zemirot*, and an overall atmosphere of transcendence.

This chapter provides examples of actions and speech that are prohibited on Shabbat based on this verse.

Weekday Activities

Some actions are prohibited because they spoil the atmosphere of sanctity and relaxation of Shabbat, while others are prohibited because they are considered preparation on Shabbat for a weekday.

Spoiling the Shabbat Atmosphere

Any kind of commerce is prohibited on Shabbat. It is prohibited even to read financial reports or documents or anything related to business.

One may not take measurements of a space or object on Shabbat. Likewise, it is prohibited to weigh people or objects on Shabbat, even with a non-electronic scale.

One should not give gifts on Shabbat, apart from food and drink or items that are to be used on that Shabbat, provided that it is actually permitted to use them on Shabbat.

The sanctity of Shabbat should also be evident in one's manner of walking. On Shabbat one should walk with restraint; he should not run or even walk fast. If one wants to run because of the rain or for the purpose of a mitzva, e.g., to get to the synagogue in time for prayers, it is permitted. Running in order to provide urgent medical assistance or to save someone from danger is obviously permitted.

📖 **Further reading:** For more on the sanctity of Shabbat, see *A Concise Guide to the Sages,* p. 275; *A Concise Guide to Mahshava,* p. 33.

Preparing on Shabbat for a Weekday

One may not prepare on Shabbat for a weekday or even for a future Shabbat. This prohibition applies even in the case of preparing for a mitzva, such as washing dishes in order to serve the *melaveh malka* meal after the conclusion of Shabbat.

It is prohibited to walk on Shabbat to one's workplace in order to start work immediately after Shabbat. It is also prohibited to go to see an apartment with the thought of buying or renting it after Shabbat. By the same token, it is prohibited to tour a marketplace or a fair to examine goods that one is thinking of purchasing.

The above prohibition applies only if the action itself clearly discloses one's intention. For example, if a contractor visits a construction site and examines the progress of the work, the purpose of the tour is obvious to all, and therefore it is prohibited. But if one is strolling along and happens to approach a certain place where he must do some work after Shabbat, he has not violated the prohibition of "seeking your needs," as an onlooker would assume that he is simply enjoying a walk.

Notwithstanding the above, it is permitted to stop in the street in front of a shop window to view the display, if one does not intend to buy the items displayed. In this context it is important to emphasize that the permission applies only to looking at the display itself; one may not examine the price labels.

It is permitted to learn Torah on Shabbat in order to prepare for a lesson or test later in the week. Some permit students to study even for tests in secular subjects on Shabbat, such as science. The reason for this lenient ruling is that the learning itself provides immediate benefit by enriching the student.

Mundane Speech

The types of speech included in the prohibition of mundane speech are prohibited not because they indirectly cause the performance of prohibited acts on Shabbat, but because the very act of speaking about mundane matters impinges upon the sanctity of Shabbat; as such talk does not suit the holy atmosphere of Shabbat, it is appropriate to avoid meaningless chatter as well.

Permitted and Prohibited

Any conversation about commerce and business is prohibited on Shabbat. It is also prohibited to talk about plans for future transactions, for example to say, "I will buy a new car soon." Nevertheless, it is permitted to think about business on Shabbat. Even so, it is advisable to avoid thinking about such matters as well, in order to enjoy true mental rest, which can be achieved only by total detachment from all mundane matters.

Not only is discussion of business matters prohibited on Shabbat, but one may also not talk about other prohibited labors, for example, to say, "On Tuesday, people will be coming to paint the house." Furthermore, during Shabbat one may not ask a person to perform work after Shabbat that is prohibited on Shabbat. For example, one may not arrange with a taxi driver to take him somewhere after the conclusion of Shabbat.

Although one may not say on Shabbat, "I am going to sleep so that I will have the strength to work after Shabbat," in practice one may sleep for that same purpose, as the act of sleeping itself does not indicate one's intention.

Appearance of Transgression
And Producing a Sound on Shabbat

These categories consist of actions that are rabbinically prohibited because onlookers might confuse these actions with similar actions that are prohibited. They might then infer from the permitted acts that similar actions are also permitted, when in fact they are prohibited. The Sages also wished to prevent those who perform such activities from being suspected of violating Shabbat. Even if one claims that he is not troubled by this possibility, the Torah warns, "And you shall be absolved before the Lord, and before Israel" (Numbers 32:22). In other words, one is required to avoid actions and situations that would lead him to be suspected of committing a transgression, even if in fact there is nothing wrong with his behavior. Such actions that might be seen as a desecration of Shabbat are thus prohibited because they give the appearance of transgression. This chapter will explain and illustrate those activities that are included in this category of prohibited acts.

Even in Private

It is important to emphasize that when the Sages prohibit an action because of the appearance of transgression, the prohibition is absolute, and applies even if the act is performed in private. As it is stated in the Talmud, "Wherever the Sages prohibited an action due to the appearance of prohibition, it is prohibited even in the innermost chambers" (*Shabbat* 64b).

An example of an action that is prohibited due to "the appearance of transgression" is having a television turn on by means of a timer, even if the television is muted. The reason is that an onlooker might see the television on and think that it was turned on in a prohibited manner on Shabbat.

Noise That Arouses Suspicion

In addition to the prohibition against performing certain actions on Shabbat due to "the appearance of transgression," the Sages also prohibited certain acts whose performance is not seen by anyone, but which produce noise and may therefore mislead people and arouse suspicion.

An example of this is a washing machine that is operated automatically by a timer. Despite the fact that activating the machine with a timer is not a desecration of Shabbat, it is prohibited because one who hears the noise of the washing machine does not know when and how it was turned on, and he might suspect that the device was activated by its owner on Shabbat. This is also one of the reasons it is prohibited to operate a radio by means of a timer.

Exception

That said, anything that people are used to seeing turned on automatically may be used in that manner. For example, lighting, sprinkler systems, and the like may be operated by means of a timer. Similarly, noisy appliances such as air conditioners, which generally turn on and off automatically after being set ahead of time, may be operated by means of a timer.

Instructing Others

The Torah's command to rest on Shabbat included one's gentile servants: "And the seventh day is a Sabbath for the Lord your God; you shall not perform any labor, you, and your son, and your daughter, and your slave, and your maidservant...so that your slave and your maidservant may rest like you" (Deuteronomy 5:14). This means that anyone who is part of a Jew's household must abstain from prohibited labor on Shabbat, even if he is not Jewish.

In our time the concept of a slave, as it existed in the distant past, is no longer relevant. Some people have maids or household employees, but these are not slaves. The relationship between them and the owner of the house is not that of a slave and a master but of an employee and employer. Therefore, a Jew is not commanded to ensure that his gentile workers rest on Shabbat, and they themselves are not obligated to rest either. Nevertheless, utilizing the services of gentiles to perform forbidden labors on Shabbat is far from simple, as this is subject to various halakhic restrictions.

This chapter presents the halakhic principles involved in the performance of labor on Shabbat on behalf of a Jew by those who are not commanded to observe Shabbat.

Shabbat Gentile

There is a widespread misconception that one can have a non-Jew perform any forbidden labor on Shabbat on one's behalf, and some even have a non-Jew who regularly performs forbidden labors for them (a "Shabbos goy"). In fact, this it is not simple at all, as issuing a direct instruction to a gentile can be entirely prohibited, depending on the circumstances.

A Jew may not instruct a gentile to perform labor for him on Shabbat, and it is also forbidden to derive benefit from labor that a gentile performed on the Jew's behalf. This is derived from the verse, "No labor shall be performed on them" (Exodus 12:16), i.e., no labor may be performed for a Jew on Shabbat.

Reasons for the Prohibition

Three reasons are given for prohibiting one to instruct a gentile to perform labor for a Jew, and to derive benefit from the labor that a gentile performed on a Jew's behalf:

(1) The gentile is effectively acting as the Jew's agent to perform the labor, and there is a general halakhic principle that the legal status of a person's agent is like that of himself.

(2) Performance of prohibited labor on Shabbat, even if through the agency of a gentile, impairs the atmosphere of sanctity and rest on Shabbat.

(3) There is a concern that the performance of labor by means of a gentile will lead to the general belittlement of Shabbat, and the eventual outcome will be that Jews themselves would do the labor.

When Is It Permitted?

Nevertheless, there are instances in which it is permitted to ask a gentile to perform labor on Shabbat. The *halakhot* of instructing gentiles on Shabbat are highly complex, and therefore, before any situation when the need to take advantage of this possibility might arise, it is recommended to ask a rabbi about the details of that particular case.

Here we will present some examples of situations in which one may ask a gentile to perform a task on Shabbat that is prohibited to a Jew:

When the labor will enable the performance of a mitzva, e.g., if the light in the house has gone out and the family cannot enjoy the Shabbat meal (this ruling is subject to halakhic dispute).

When a person has an illness that prevents him from functioning on his own, and he requires warm food.

When one faces a large financial loss.

When the task in question, if not done, will cause a Jew great sorrow, e.g., if one's journey has taken longer than expected, and he is stuck with his belongings outside of an inhabited area. Such a person is allowed to ask a gentile to move his belongings to a safe place.

When the act will prevent the suffering of animals, e.g., milking cows on Shabbat.

Hinting to a Gentile

The above *halakhot* refer to an explicit directive to a gentile. If one does not issue a direct instruction but only alludes to what he needs done, the law is more lenient, and this is permitted in case of need.

Here are two examples: If one forgot to turn off a light before Shabbat or to activate the timer, which would turn off the light, it is permitted to hint to a gentile by telling him, "the light is on," and he will understand on his own what to do. It is also permitted to ask a gentile on a weekday, "Why didn't you do such and such last Shabbat," from which he will realize what is expected of him on the following Shabbatot.

If there is no real need, it is prohibited to hint to a gentile to perform prohibited labor on Shabbat.

Noisy Labors

One may not allow a gentile to perform prohibited work on Shabbat in the domain of a Jew if the labor produces noise that can be heard by others in the vicinity. This prohibition applies even if the gentile acts of his own accord. The reason for the prohibition is "the appearance of transgression" (for more on this, see the chapter dealing with this issue, p. 454).

Instructing a Shabbat Desecrator

A Jew who inadvertently engaged in prohibited labor on Shabbat may not use the product of the labor during that Shabbat. If he acted deliberately, it is prohibited for him to derive benefit from the product of the labor even after Shabbat.

It is certainly prohibited to tell another Jew, even one who identifies as nonreligious, to perform prohibited labor on Shabbat. One may not even hint at this possibility.

📖 **Further reading:** For more on the *halakhot* of benefiting from labors performed on Shabbat, see p. 412.

Before the Start of Shabbat

If one accepted Shabbat earlier than the time specified in the calendar, he may ask others who have not yet accepted Shabbat to perform actions that he himself is no longer allowed to do. Similarly, if a woman has lit the candles, and there are men or women in the house who have not yet accepted Shabbat, she may instruct them to perform chores that she personally may no longer carry out.

Instructing Children

From the stage when a child understands the meaning of performing mitzvot, his parents must educate him with regard to Shabbat observance, and certainly may not encourage him to perform acts involving desecration of Shabbat on their behalf. This generally refers to children from age six or seven, and applies not only to explicit prohibitions of the Torah, but also to actions that were later prohibited by the Sages. At this age, it is proper to prevent the children from performing prohibited labor on Shabbat, even if they would do it of their own accord.

With younger children, although one is not necessarily obligated to stop them from doing things on their own, he should not ask or hint that they should perform actions that are prohibited on Shabbat.

Further reading: For more on the importance of educating children from a young age, see *A Concise Guide to the Sages*, p. 404; *A Concise Guide to Mahshava*, p. 186.

Eiruv

What is commonly referred to as an *eiruv* is a halakhic solution instituted by the Sages with regard to rabbinic prohibitions against transferring objects from one domain to another. There is another type of *eiruv*, called *eiruv tehumin*, which extends the distance that one may walk outside one's city or town on Shabbat. (A third type, the *eiruv tavshilin*, is discussed below in the section regarding festivals.)

The prohibition against carrying objects from a private domain to a public domain is one of the thirty-nine primary labors that are prohibited on Shabbat (see the chapter dealing with these labors, p. 406). The Sages added a series of other restrictions and proscriptions to this prohibition, in order to emphasize the importance of Shabbat as a day of rest that must be dedicated to Torah study, prayer, and spiritual improvement.

The main prohibitions instituted by the Sages are: (1) carrying objects that are not required on Shabbat, even inside one's personal domain (see the chapter that presents the laws of *muktze*, p. 414); (2) carrying objects for a distance greater than four cubits (about 2 m) in many areas that do not qualify as private domains but also are not considered public domains by Torah law, or within a private domain that is shared by multiple residents; and (3) walking more than two thousand cubits (roughly 1 km) beyond the limits of a settlement. The last two prohibitions are based, or are at least supported, by the verse, "See that the Lord has given you the Sabbath...no man shall leave his place on the seventh day" (Exodus 16:29).

The basic principle of the *eiruv* is to generate a situation where the whole area is considered a single private domain. This is accomplished in two ways. First, the entire area is enclosed, either by actual fences or by a symbolic barrier consisting of poles with wires stretched between them. This creates a single enclosed area, but since it is divided into different privately owned areas, all of these must be joined together (hence *eiruv*, meaning joining or combining). This joining is accomplished by someone, usually the rabbi, taking a certain amount of food and ensuring that it is the common property of every Jew who lives within the *eiruv*. Since this food is common property and everyone, at least theoretically, has access to it, the entire area enclosed in the area is considered common property for the purposes of carrying on Shabbat. One may transfer objects from a private domain into this area, and may also carry items within that area itself. This type of *eiruv* is known as an *eiruv hatzerot*.

The prohibition against traveling more than two thousand cubits from his home base or home town on Shabbat can be mitigated by establishing an *eiruv tehumin*: Prior to Shabbat, one places food items at a point within two thousand cubits (approximately 1 km) from the edge of the town, thereby symbolically defining that spot as the place where he is based for that Shabbat. This causes the two thousand cubit radius in which he can travel to begin from that point.

This chapter will present the prohibitions against carrying and transferring objects from one domain to another on Shabbat, the additional permissions granted by these two types of *eiruv*, and also a series of laws relating to this area of the *halakhot* of Shabbat.

Shabbat Domains

In addition to a private domain and a public domain, there are two other domains to which unique laws apply. The first, which is an area that is exempt from the prohibitions of carrying on Shabbat, is called an exempt domain. The other, a *karmelit*, is defined by the Sages as a domain whose halakhic status is in between the private and public domains.

Below are brief descriptions and definitions of these four domains:

Four Domains of Shabbat

Private domain: This term refers to a zone with a minimum area of about 32 cm (four handbreadths) by 32 cm, and which is separated from its surroundings by a partition of about 80 cm (ten handbreadths) or more. This partition could be a wall, a fence, or a deep ditch, or created by the topography of the domain itself, if is at least 80 cm higher than the ground around it. This zone, as well as the airspace above it, is halakhically defined as a private domain.

Public domain: A zone at least 8 m (sixteen cubits) wide, which is used by many people. Some authorities maintain that only an open area through which at least six hundred thousand people pass every day is considered a public domain by Torah law. The laws of the public domain apply to the airspace above this area only up to a height of about 80 cm, but not to the airspace above that height.

Exempt domain: This term refers to a zone that is separated from its surroundings by a partition, but which has an area that is smaller than 32 cm by 32 cm. The airspace higher than 80 cm above a public domain or a *karmelit* (see below) is also included in this category. One is allowed to transfer objects between an exempt domain and a public or private domain on Shabbat.

These are the three domains of Shabbat according to Torah law, but the Sages added a fourth one, known as a *karmelit*.

Karmelit: This term refers to a zone with an area greater than 32 cm by 32 cm, which is not surrounded by a partition, but which is not heavily used by the public. (A partition would isolate the area and render it a private domain, whereas regular use by the public could make it a public domain.) Classic examples of a *karmelit* include an open field or the ocean, although

Shabbat and Festivals

in contemporary times the streets of many towns and cities do not fit the definition of a public domain and are considered to be a *karmelit*. By rabbinic law, the status of a *karmelit* is similar to that of a public domain.

Actions Permitted by Use of an *Eiruv*

Some rabbinic prohibitions can be alleviated by establishing an *eiruv hatzerot* or by placing an *eiruv tehumin* to extend the Shabbat limit.

How an *Eiruv* Is Made

The prohibition against carrying objects from one private domain to another, and likewise the prohibition against carrying in a *karmelit*, can be effectively negated by establishing a joining of courtyards, an *eiruv hatzerot*. The Sages enacted this possibility, and it has been put into practice in most towns and cities in Israel as well as many communities in other countries. The function of the *eiruv* is to create a symbolic fence around an inhabited area, by means of a system of posts with stable wires stretched over them. Some natural topographical features may also be incorporated into the *eiruv*. In the absence of an *eiruv*, it is prohibited to transfer objects from one domain to another, or to carry them a distance of four cubits (about 2 m) within a public domain or *karmelit*.

One may walk an additional two thousand cubits (1 km) beyond the Shabbat limit by placing a quantity of food sufficient for two minimal meals just before the limit. The idea is that the person is intentionally establishing his place of Shabbat rest on the place where he put the food. Since this is now his official base for Shabbat, he is permitted to walk from there another two thousand cubits in any direction, and to any inhabited area contiguous to an area inside that radius.

Important note: The "Shabbat limit" applies not only on Shabbat, but also on Yom Kippur and the festivals. By contrast, the prohibition against transferring objects from one domain to another and the prohibition against carrying in the public domain are in effect only on Shabbat and Yom Kippur, not on the festivals, provided that one is carrying an item needed on the festival. The third prohibition that was mentioned at the beginning of the chapter, the carrying of objects that are classified as *muktze*, also applies on festivals.

Definition of Carrying

The prohibitions of transferring an object from one domain to another or carrying an object for a distance of four cubits (2 m) within a public domain apply to all types of objects, including keys, bags, handkerchiefs, or even a rubber band wrapped around one's wrist.

If one is in an area where there is no *eiruv*, he is obligated to empty the pockets of his clothes before the start of Shabbat, so that he does not violate these prohibitions. Some items may be transferred from one domain to another or carried within the public domain in certain ways, as explained below.

Asking a Rabbi

Carrying a key is prohibited. Nevertheless, there are ways to make a key part of one's garment, e.g., by integrating it into a belt buckle, which would enable it to be carried. One who wishes to use this system should consult a rabbi.

Carrying a child in one's arms is also prohibited in a place where there is no *eiruv*. Likewise, pushing a child's stroller is prohibited. If the child is sick and cannot walk on his own, or if there is a concern that he will not be able to walk the whole way, one should consult with a rabbi to find a solution.

Clothing, Jewelry, and Medical Accessories

A garment that a person wears on his body is not included in the category of objects that may not be carried from one domain to another. This rule applies even to an outer garment, such as a hat, scarf, coat, and so on.

It is permitted to wear a coat positioned on both shoulders, even if one's arms are not inside the sleeves. But if a garment such as a coat or sweater is thrown over one shoulder, this is not considered wearing the garment. Transferring it from one domain to another and carrying it in the public domain in this manner is thus prohibited.

A person wearing jewelry may walk with it from one domain to another, or through a public domain.

If a person requires a walker or cane and cannot walk without it, he may use it even outdoors in a place where there is no *eiruv*. One may also wear prescription eyeglasses without an *eiruv*. Similarly, one who needs a hearing aid may leave the home with the device attached to his ear. The same applies to an artificial limb (prosthesis).

In life-threatening situations, prohibitions against carrying do not apply. It is therefore permitted to carry a child whose condition requires urgent examination or medical treatment. It is also permitted to carry any object required to help someone whose life is in danger (as detailed in the chapter dealing with the laws of medical treatments on Shabbat, p. 439).

The Unique Aspects of Festivals

The cycle of the year includes six days that are each defined as festival days [*yom tov*] by Torah law: the first day of Passover; the seventh day of Passover, *Shavuot*, Rosh HaShana, the first day of *Sukkot*, and the day that follows the festival of *Sukkot*, called *Shemini Atzeret*. Although by Torah law each of these festivals is one day long, by rabbinic law they are each observed for two days outside of the Land of Israel. Rosh HaShana is observed as two days both inside and outside of the Land of Israel.

On these days one may not perform any of the labors prohibited on Shabbat, with certain exceptions that will be detailed below. In practice, most of the *halakhot* of these festivals are identical to the laws of Shabbat.

Just as it is a mitzva to honor and enjoy Shabbat, so too, it is a mitzva to honor and enjoy the festivals. This is derived from the verse, "And you call the Sabbath a delight and the Lord's sacred, honored" (Isaiah 58:13). This verse teaches us that it is necessary to honor and take delight not only in Shabbat but also in all "sacred" days, including the festivals.

This chapter will describe the character of the festivals and their laws. It will start with the preparations for a festival, continue with its meals, and then proceed to the *halakhot* regarding cooking, carrying, bathing, and more. It will explain which labors are permitted on a festival and which are prohibited, as on Shabbat.

Preparations for a Festival

Preparations for a festival should start thirty days beforehand. At that stage the Sages would start delivering sermons on the laws of the forthcoming festival. Nowadays, when halakhic works are available and accessible to all, each person should review the laws of the festival and refresh his knowledge thirty days before the festival.

How to Prepare

As the festival approaches, the husband and father should bring joy to his family. He should buy his wife a new piece of jewelry or clothing, the children can be given a new toy, and the entire family should enjoy festive meals.

Part of honoring the festival is to prepare for it ahead of time, by, e.g., getting a haircut, cutting one's fingernails, and taking a hot shower (as also noted with regard to the preparations for Shabbat). In addition, due to the honor of the festival, one should not eat a significant meal a few hours before its start, so that he will eat the festival meal with a hearty appetite.

During the Temple period, every adult male was obligated to ritually purify himself for the festival so that he could enter the Temple. Although there is no longer a Temple and therefore there is no longer an obligation to become ritually pure, many have the practice nonetheless to immerse themselves in a ritual bath before each festival.

When the festival falls on a Friday, one must make an *eiruv tavshilin* (see below, p. 474) prior to the commencement of the festival. Without this *eiruv*, it is not permitted to prepare food for Shabbat on the festival day or even to light candles for Shabbat.

Festival Meals

There is a mitzva to rejoice on a festival. In this regard, the talmudic Sages said that the recommended way to treat a festival is to "divide it: Half for God, and half for yourselves" (*Beitza* 15b). In other words, there must be a balance between activities "for God," such as prayer and Torah study, and activities "for yourselves," such as enjoying festive meals.

Joy and Sanctity

One expresses delight in the festival, among other ways, by eating the obligatory two meals, one in the evening and the other during the day. One is obligated to eat bread at these meals, as in the Shabbat meals. But for the festival meals it is a mitzva to increase one's consumption of meat and other fine dishes, and to drink wine, even more than on Shabbat. All this is done in order to increase the joy of the festival.

On a festival, unlike on Shabbat, there is no obligation to eat a third meal in the afternoon.

Despite the emphasis on joy on festivals, one must not forget that it is a holy day. It is therefore appropriate to dedicate a large part of one's time to prayer and Torah study, more than on weekdays.

In Grace after Meals, as well as in the blessing known as "*Me'ein Shalosh*" (which is recited after eating grain-based foods or fruits that are included in the seven species of produce mentioned in connection with the Land of Israel), one adds a reference to the festival. In Grace after Meals this is done by reciting a passage known as *Ya'aleh VeYavo*, which includes a reference to the specific festival being observed.

📖 **Further reading:** For more on festivals, see *A Concise Guide to Mahshava*, p. 53.

Food Preparation

The talmudic Sages derived from the verses of the Torah that on festivals, even more than on Shabbat, it is particularly important for people to enjoy the festival even in the simple physical sense of eating and drinking. This idea has halakhic implications, as explained below.

Difference between Festivals and Shabbat

With regard to performance of labor on a festival, the Sages determined that "the difference between a festival and Shabbat is only with regard to the preparation of food" (Mishna *Beitza* 5:2). This means that in general the prohibitions against performing labor apply equally on Shabbat and the festivals, except for some of the labors involved in food preparation. Such labor is prohibited on Shabbat but permitted on festivals. This law is explicitly stated in the Torah: "Except for that which shall be eaten for each person, it alone may be performed for you" (Exodus 12:16).

In addition, the prohibition against transferring objects from one domain to another, which exists on Shabbat (see the chapter that deals with the laws of *eiruv*, p. 460), does not apply in the same manner on festivals, when one is permitted to transfer objects that will be used on the festival. Apart from these differences, *halakhot* of festivals are the same as Shabbat, and all the other labors that are prohibited on Shabbat are likewise prohibited on a festival.

Important note: When a festival falls on Shabbat, the leniencies with regard to cooking food and transferring objects on a festival are not in effect, as all the *halakhot* of Shabbat are applicable.

Cooking on a Festival

It is permitted to cook on a festival that falls on a weekday, if two conditions are met: (1) The food must be intended for use on the festival itself; and (2) the fire used for cooking must not be kindled on the festival itself, but rather kindled before the festival or transferred from another fire that was kindled before the festival.

In practice, if one wishes to cook on a festival on a gas stove it is permitted to turn on the gas and then to light the desired fire from a candle or another existing source of fire. In order to enable one to cook on the festival, it is a common practice to light a large candle such as a yahrzeit candle before the festival and to leave it burning for twenty-four hours, thereby ensuring that there will be fire available throughout the festival.

The Torah permits lighting a fire from an existing flame on a festival, but under no circumstances does it permit extinguishing fire. Therefore, when a fire is transferred to the stove, for example with a match, one may not put out the match; rather, it should be placed carefully in a non-flammable spot until it goes out by itself. Similarly, when the flame of a stove is no longer needed, it is prohibited to extinguish the fire. Furthermore, just as one may not extinguish the fire on the stove, it is likewise prohibited to reduce its flame; partially extinguishing a flame is equally prohibited as fully extinguishing it.

If one nevertheless wants to put out the flame on his stove, one solution is to allow water to boil over the sides of a pot and to extinguish the fire. Another option is to attach a special timer to the gas line leading to the stove. Such a timer predetermines when gas will flow to the stove. After setting the timer, the burner should be lit, and then at the set time, the gas flow will stop and the flame will go out of its own accord. In any event, after the fire has been extinguished, whether due to the overflow of liquids from the pot or due to the operation of the gas timer, one may turn off the burner knob in order to prevent the leakage of gas.

Fire and Electricity

Some permit smoking on a festival, by lighting a cigarette from an existing fire, while others prohibit this.

Important note: Although one may use a fire on a festival, it is not permitted to turn electrical appliances on or off.

Labor in the Kitchen

Peeling fruits and vegetables is permitted on festivals, even by means of a peeler designed for this purpose.

It is permitted to whip an egg, and to make whipped cream or mayonnaise, even with a manual device designed for this purpose. One may not do so with an electrical appliance.

It is permitted to crush or grind spices and the like that will lose some of their taste if they are ground up before the festival. For items that grow from the ground and can be ground up before the festival, such as nuts, one should grind them before the festival. However, if one did not do so, he may grind them on the festival, even with a nut grater. The sole restriction is that one may not crush or grind into a vessel, as is customary on weekdays, but only onto the table itself or on a tablecloth that is spread over it.

It is permitted to grate hard cheese or hard-boiled eggs on a festival. Some are particular to do so in a slightly different manner than on a weekday, for example, by not using the standard implement designed for this purpose (a grater).

It is permitted to strain noodles in a pasta strainer after cooking them.

In conclusion, it is permitted to cook on a festival, and this is even praiseworthy if it will enhance the festival. However, if the food preparation can be done before the festival without compromising the quality of the food, one may not leave the work to be done on the festival.

At the Meal

Unlike on Shabbat, on a festival it is permitted to remove waste from food, if the food will thereby improve or preserve its freshness, cleanliness, or quality. It is therefore permitted to remove bones from fish or meat during a meal, to remove seeds from slices of watermelon, and the like. On a Shabbat and on a festival that falls on a Shabbat, such actions are prohibited due to the labor of selecting.

Festival Needs

As indicated above, the Torah states that various labors are permissible on festivals for food preparation. The Sages explained that this allowance is not limited only to food preparation. Rather, since these labors are permitted for food preparation, they are also permitted for any festival need.

Here are some examples:

Since it is permitted to light a fire from an existing flame for the purpose of cooking, it is similarly permissible to do so for illumination or in order to light the festival or Shabbat candles. Additionally, just as cooking itself is permissible, it is similarly permissible to heat up water on a festival for one's other needs. Consequently, it is permissible to open the hot water tap in a home that has an electric or gas boiler, despite the fact that cold water will then enter the boiler and become hot. However, it is prohibited to heat water by activating an electrical appliance.

Showering or Bathing

With regard to washing one's entire body in hot water, Sephardic and Ashkenazic halakhic authorities disagree. Sephardim permit bathing the entire body in warm water that has been heated in a permitted manner, whereas most Ashkenazic authorities prohibit bathing the whole body in hot water all at once, and permit bathing only parts of the body, one after the other.

Carrying

Similarly, with regard to objects that are not defined as *muktze*, the above rule applies to carrying from the private to the public domain and vice versa: Since it is permitted to carry food products and accessories that are required for the preparation of food on a festival, it is also permitted to carry other objects, which are not needed for food preparation, from one domain to another, even when there is no *eiruv*.

It is important to qualify this *halakha*: This permission applies only to carrying items that fulfill some need for the festival. For example, it is permitted to walk on a festival with a baby in a carriage even in a place where there is no *eiruv*. It is also permitted to carry a *lulav* or a Torah scroll from one place to another. In contrast, it is prohibited to carry an object from one domain to another on behalf of a gentile, as, since the gentile can do it himself, the Jew's action is defined as not for the purpose of the festival.

Rabbinic Decrees on Festivals

In order to ensure that the festival day will be used for physical and mental rest and for spiritual improvement, and to help people avoid violating explicit Torah prohibitions, the Sages enacted a series of prohibitions and restrictions. In this respect, the *halakhot* of festivals are similar to those of Shabbat, and actions prohibited on Shabbat are also generally prohibited on a festival.

In this context, there are three categories: The first category includes most of the decrees of the Sages for Shabbat, which likewise apply on festivals. A second category consists of labors prohibited on Shabbat that may be performed for the requirements of the festival (labors for the purpose of preparing food). The third category includes unique actions that are permitted on Shabbat but prohibited on festivals, as detailed below.

Labors Prohibited by the Sages

The following is a list of actions that were banned by the Sages on Shabbat and festivals, in addition to those prohibited by the Torah: climbing trees, riding animals, swimming in water (the sea, a pool, etc.), playing musical instruments, dancing in a manner that might lead the dancers to fashion or repair musical instruments, holding court hearings, and performing a wedding or divorce ceremony.

Likewise, separation of *teruma* or tithes may not be performed even on a festival, and one may also not immerse utensils in a ritual bath for the purpose of permitting their use.

The prohibition against a Jew asking a gentile to perform a prohibited labor on his behalf on Shabbat also applies on festivals.

An Item That Came into Being [*Nolad*]

Any object that did not exist prior to the start of the festival is considered *nolad* (literally, "born"), an item that has just come into being. Such an item is *muktze* and may not be used or even moved on a festival. The classic example, which appears in the Talmud, is that of an egg that was laid on a festival (see *Beitza* 2a). This category can apply to a wide range of objects.

Although in many ways the laws of festivals are more lenient than the laws of Shabbat, the category of *nolad* is more stringent on festivals than on Shabbat. Even an object that existed before the festival but whose intended use has changed on the festival is considered *nolad* and is *muktze*, which is not the case on Shabbat. Consequently, if there are chicken or beef bones left on one's plate after dinner, and one wants to take them to give them to his dog, this is permitted on Shabbat, whereas on a festival the bones are *muktze*. This is because at the beginning of the festival the piece of chicken or beef was considered food for people, and now the bones are viewed on their own as animal food, which is a new purpose. Nevertheless, even on a festival it is permitted to remove bones, seeds, and peels from the table in order to throw them into the garbage.

Intermediate Days of the Festival
[Hol HaMoed]

The festivals of *Sukkot* and Passover include a period called *Hol HaMoed*, the intermediate days of the festival. These two festivals begin and end with days of greater sanctity [*yom tov*], while the intermediate days have a certain limited measure of sanctity. As indicated by its Hebrew name, the intermediate days of the festival are a mixture of festival [*moed*] and mundane [*hol*]. Consequently, there are instances when it is permitted to perform acts that are prohibited labors on Shabbat or *yom tov*, but in many instances it is prohibited to perform these labors.

The main reason that some labors are prohibited on *Hol HaMoed* is to leave one with time for Torah study on these days. As stated in *Sefer Haḥinnukh*, which provides reasons for the mitzvot, "the days of *Hol HaMoed* were not given in order for one to engage in his work, but to rejoice before God, that is, to gather in study halls and listen to the pleasant words of the book" (*Sefer Haḥinnukh* 323).

This chapter details the labors that are prohibited and permitted on *Hol HaMoed*.

Prohibited and Permitted Labors
In general, performing unnecessary labor is prohibited during *Hol HaMoed*, but under certain conditions various tasks are permitted.

Preventing Monetary Loss [*Davar Ha'aved*]
It is permitted to perform labor on *Hol HaMoed* in order to prevent one's property from being ruined or in order to prevent monetary loss. This category of cases is known as *davar ha'aved*. An example of this is a merchant who has merchandise in his possession before the festival that will be ruined if he does not sell it during *Hol HaMoed*. In such cases, it is permitted to engage in labor.

For the Festival
It is permissible to perform labors that are necessary for one's observance of the festival. This includes food preparation or the attainment of anything

one needs for the festival. Similarly, it is permitted to shop on *Hol HaMoed* for things that one needs for the festival.

If one is in a difficult financial state, such that if he does not work during *Hol HaMoed* he will be unable to provide the basic festival needs for his family and guests, he may work during the intermediate festival days on condition that he does so as discreetly as possible.

Public Need

The category of a labor that is performed for the needs of the public includes anything that must be done to satisfy the needs of many people. For example, in an Israeli town where the government is run by Jews, if it becomes necessary to repair torn electrical wires, or simply to remove the garbage, this is considered "for public need" and it is permitted on *Hol HaMoed*.

Without Great Effort

Any action that does not involve much effort, i.e., which does not take long and does not require any special exertion or concentration, is permitted on *Hol HaMoed*, even if it is defined as a labor according to the *halakhot* of Shabbat and festivals. This category includes lighting a fire, driving a car, using the telephone, turning on an electrical appliance, or carrying objects from one domain to another. By contrast, actions that are not defined as prohibited labor on Shabbat and festival days but which involve great effort, e.g., carrying heavy objects from one corner of a room to another, are prohibited on *Hol HaMoed* if they are not necessary.

In addition to all of the above, one must be careful with regard to the appearance of transgression in the case of work on *Hol HaMoed*. For an explanation of this concept, see the chapter "The Appearance of Transgression" in the *halakhot* of Shabbat (p. 454).

It is permitted to talk about business matters during *Hol HaMoed*.

Additional Laws of *Hol HaMoed*

The festive nature of *Hol HaMoed* is expressed in several ways in addition to the restrictions on the performance of certain labors.

Tefillin

On the intermediate days of the festival, many do not don *tefillin*. This is the universal custom in Israel. However, among Ashkenazim outside of Israel there are those who have the custom to don *tefillin* even on *Hol HaMoed*.

Ya'aleh VeYavo

In Grace after Meals, as well as in the blessing known as *"Me'ein Shalosh"* (which is recited after eating grain-based foods or fruits that are included in the seven species of produce mentioned in connection with the Land of Israel), and likewise in the *Amida* prayers during *Hol HaMoed*, one adds a reference to the festival. In Grace after Meals and the *Amida*, this is done by reciting a passage known as *Ya'aleh VeYavo*, which includes a reference to the specific festival being observed. On *Hol HaMoed* of *Sukkot* one inserts the line "On this day of the festival of *Sukkot*," and on *Hol HaMoed* of Passover one says, "On this day of the festival of matzot."

Isru Hag

The day after Passover, *Shavuot*, and *Sukkot* is called *Isru Hag*, based on the verse, "Bind the festival offering [*isru hag*] with cords, and from there to the horns of the altar" (Psalms 118:27). This is homiletically interpreted to mean: Bind the days of the festival to the rest of the calendar. Accordingly, one extra day "accompanies" the festival, although it is almost completely a normal weekday. The slightly festive nature of the day is expressed in the fact that the supplicatory *Tahanun* prayer is not recited. Some add special dishes to their meals in honor of *Isru Hag*.

Shabbat and Festivals

473

Eiruv Tavshilin

Purpose

On a festival it is permitted to cook and to perform certain labors for the sake of the festival itself, provided that one uses an existing fire rather than igniting a new flame. What is the *halakha* when the festival falls on a Friday and one wishes to cook on the festival for the sake of Shabbat?

It is permitted by Torah law to cook on the festival for Shabbat, but it is prohibited by rabbinic law unless one prepares an *eiruv tavshilin* before the festival. There are two reasons for this decree of the Sages: (1) To prevent people from mistakenly thinking that just as it is permitted to cook on the festival in honor of Shabbat, so too, it is permitted to cook on a festival for the weekdays that follow Shabbat; and (2) due to the concern that the great deal of cooking done for the festival might cause one to forget to set aside good-quality food for the next day, Shabbat.

Therefore, the Sages instituted the *eiruv tavshilin*, which has a dual purpose: (1) To serve as a reminder that it is prohibited to cook on a festival for the weekdays, as even in honor of Shabbat one may not cook on the festival without preparing an *eiruv tavshilin*; and (2) the *eiruv tavshilin*, which is preserved for Shabbat, reminds the members of the household to prepare fine food for Shabbat.

This section explains what an *eiruv tavshilin* is and how it is prepared.

Significance

An *eiruv tavshilin* is a symbolic preparation of food from the eve of the festival for Shabbat. It is called an *eiruv*, meaning mixture, because it serves to combine the food for the festival and Shabbat; the result is that just as it is permitted on the festival to cook and bake for the festival itself, so too, it is permitted to cook and bake on the festival for Shabbat.

Even one who is not planning to cook during the festival should prepare an *eiruv tavshilin*, as otherwise it is prohibited to perform any action on the festival for Shabbat, including lighting Shabbat candles toward the end of the festival.

Method

The *eiruv tavshilin* must be prepared before the festival begins. One holds a baked food such as bread together with a cooked dish, such as fish, meat, or even a boiled egg, and recites the blessing:

בָּרוּךְ אַתָּה אֲדֹנָי, אֱלֹהֵינוּ מֶלֶךְ הָעוֹלָם, אֲשֶׁר קִדְּשָׁנוּ בְּמִצְוֹתָיו וְצִוָּנוּ עַל מִצְוַת עֵרוּב.

Barukh ata Adonai, Eloheinu, melekh ha'olam, asher kideshanu bemitzvotav, vetzivanu al mitzvat eiruv.

"Blessed are You, Lord our God, King of the universe, who sanctified us through His mitzvot, and commanded us concerning the mitzva of *eiruv*."

Then one recites the following paragraph, which can be said in any language one understands:

בְּעֵרוּב זֶה, יִהְיֶה מֻתָּר לָנוּ לֶאֱפוֹת וּלְבַשֵּׁל וּלְהַטְמִין וּלְהַדְלִיק נֵר וְלַעֲשׂוֹת כָּל צָרְכֵינוּ מִיּוֹם טוֹב לְשַׁבָּת, לָנוּ וּלְכָל יִשְׂרָאֵל הַדָּרִים בָּעִיר הַזֹּאת.

"By this *eiruv* we shall be permitted to bake, cook, insulate food, light a flame, and do all that we require on the festival for the sake of Shabbat, for us and for all Jews living in this city."

One sets aside the baked item and the cooked food to be eaten at one of the Shabbat meals. They should be put in a safe place to ensure that they will not be eaten before Shabbat.

Important clarification: When a festival falls on Saturday night there is no way to cook on Shabbat in honor of the festival, not even by means of an *eiruv tavshilin*. Not only may one not cook on Shabbat, but all preparation from Shabbat to the festival is prohibited, as the sanctity of Shabbat is greater than that of the festival. It is permitted to cook the festival food on the festival itself.

Daily Routine

Beginning the Day

The Torah's instructions accompany a person from the moment he wakes up in the morning until he goes to bed at night. Thus, each new day has special meaning, as it is another day on which one arises to serve God. Fittingly, the canonic work of *halakha*, the *Shulḥan Arukh* (written by Rabbi Yosef Karo of Safed, fifteenth century CE), begins with the sentence, "One should strengthen himself in the morning like a lion, to arise for the service of his Creator." Waking up early constitutes a positive start to a new day, since if one manages his time properly, he will have innumerable opportunities to perform mitzvot and thereby imbue his everyday routine with an element of holiness.

This chapter details the laws and customs of the first part of the day, waking up in the morning.

Waking Up

When one opens his eyes in the morning, he should immediately thank the Creator for returning his soul to him for another day of life and activity. He should then wash his hands with water.

Modeh Ani

The first words a Jew says when he wakes up in the morning is the *Modeh ani* formula:

מוֹדֶה אֲנִי לְפָנֶיךָ, מֶלֶךְ חַי וְקַיָּם, שֶׁהֶחֱזַרְתָּ בִּי נִשְׁמָתִי בְּחֶמְלָה, רַבָּה אֱמוּנָתֶךָ.

Modeh (Women say: *Moda*) *ani lefanekha, melekh ḥai vekayam, sheheḥezarta bi nishmati beḥemla, raba emunatekha.*

"I thank You [*modeh ani*], living and eternal King, for restoring my soul to me with compassion; great is Your faithfulness."

Washing the Hands

After reciting *Modeh ani*, one should purify his hands. One reason for this practice is that one's hands may touch unclean parts of the body during sleep. In addition, while one sleeps at night, a spirit of impurity rests upon him, and one purifies himself from it by washing his hands. Consequently, before washing hands in the morning one should avoid touching his eyes, mouth, nose, or ears. Washing one's hands is also reminiscent of the handwashing of the priests at the start of every day of service in the Temple. One washes his hands by pouring water from a cup three times on each hand, alternately.

📖 **Further reading:** This rite differs somewhat from the washing of hands that is performed before eating bread; see p. 525.

The washing is performed as follows: One fills the cup, transfers it to the left hand and pours enough water onto the right hand to rinse the entire hand, up to the wrist. Next, one transfers the cup to the right hand and pours water in the same manner on the left hand. This sequence is repeated two more times, so that in total, he washes each hand three times.

After washing his hands, one recites the blessing:

בָּרוּךְ אַתָּה אֲדֹנָי, אֱלֹהֵינוּ מֶלֶךְ הָעוֹלָם,
אֲשֶׁר קִדְּשָׁנוּ בְּמִצְוֹתָיו וְצִוָּנוּ עַל נְטִילַת
יָדָיִם.

Barukh ata Adonai, Eloheinu, melekh ha'olam, asher kideshanu bemitzvotav, vetzivanu al netilat yadayim.

"Blessed are You, Lord our God, King of the universe, who sanctified us through His commandments and commanded us concerning the washing of the hands."

This is the first blessing one recites every morning.

It is proper to avoid walking four cubits (about 2 m) before washing one's hands in the morning. For this reason, some people prepare a small bowl in the evening with a cup full of water and leave it beside their beds so that they can wash their hands next to the bed in the morning. One who did not place water near his bed in this manner should go to the nearest sink and wash his hands.

Blessing after Using the Bathroom, *Asher Yatzar*

After relieving oneself, one again washes his hands and recites the *Asher yatzar* blessing:

בָּרוּךְ אַתָּה אֲדֹנָי, אֱלֹהֵינוּ מֶלֶךְ הָעוֹלָם,
אֲשֶׁר יָצַר אֶת הָאָדָם בְּחָכְמָה וּבָרָא בוֹ
נְקָבִים נְקָבִים חֲלוּלִים חֲלוּלִים. גָּלוּי וְיָדוּעַ
לִפְנֵי כִסֵּא כְבוֹדֶךָ,

Barukh ata Adonai, Eloheinu, melekh ha'olam, asher yatzar et ha'adam behokhma, uvara vo nekvaim nekavim, halulim halulim. Galuy veyadu'a lifnei khiseh khevodekha,

"Blessed are You, Lord our God, King of the universe, who formed [*asher yatzar*] man in wisdom, and created in him many orifices and cavities. It is revealed and known before the throne of Your glory,"

Ashkenazim conclude:

שֶׁאִם יִפָּתֵחַ אֶחָד מֵהֶם אוֹ יִסָּתֵם אֶחָד מֵהֶם, אִי אֶפְשָׁר לְהִתְקַיֵּם וְלַעֲמֹד לְפָנֶיךָ (אֲפִלּוּ שָׁעָה אֶחָת). בָּרוּךְ אַתָּה אֲדֹנָי, רוֹפֵא כָל בָּשָׂר וּמַפְלִיא לַעֲשׂוֹת.

she'im yipate'aḥ eḥad mehem, oh yisatem eḥad mehem, ee efshar lehitkayem vela'amod lefanekha (afilu sha'a eḥat). Barukh ata Adonai, rofeh khol basar umafli la'asot.

"that if one of them were to be ruptured or one of them were to be blocked, it would be impossible to survive and to stand before You (for even one moment). Blessed are You, Lord, Healer of all flesh, who does wondrous deeds."

Sephardim conclude:

שֶׁאִם יִסָּתֵם אֶחָד מֵהֶם, אוֹ אִם יִפָּתֵחַ אֶחָד מֵהֶם, אִי אֶפְשָׁר לְהִתְקַיֵּם אֲפִלּוּ שָׁעָה אֶחָת. בָּרוּךְ אַתָּה אֲדֹנָי, רוֹפֵא כָל בָּשָׂר וּמַפְלִיא לַעֲשׂוֹת.

she'im yisatem eḥad mehem, oh im yipate'aḥ eḥad mehem, ee efshar le-hitkayem afilu sha'a eḥat. Barukh ata Adonai, rofeh khol basar umafli la'asot.

"that if one of them were to be blocked or if one of them were to be ruptured, it would be impossible to survive for even one moment. Blessed are You, Lord, Healer of all flesh, who does wondrous deeds."

📖 **Further reading:** The concluding phrase "Who does wondrous deeds" refers to the wondrous connection between body and soul; see *A Concise Guide to Mahshava*, p. 223.

This blessing can be found in a standard prayer book, immediately after the blessing over the washing of hands. In the blessing of *Asher yatzar*, we thank the Creator for the wondrous body He gave us. This blessing is recited not only in the morning, but also throughout the day, each time one leaves the bathroom after attending to his bodily functions.

After *Asher yatzar* (in the morning), one recites the passage beginning "My God, the soul you placed within me is pure," [*Elokai neshama*] as it appears in prayer books. This is a blessing of thanksgiving for the pure soul that God has given us, and it is the third of the "Morning Blessings."

481

Morning Blessings

At this point, one recites the rest of the Morning Blessings [*Birkot HaShahar*], which are a series of blessings recited every day upon arising from bed. There are two sequences of blessings to be recited. The first sequence is the Blessings over the Torah, in which we thank God for the Torah He gave us and request that we, and all our descendants, merit to cleave to it with all our hearts. A second sequence (from "who gives the heart understanding" to "who bestows loving-kindness on His people Israel") consists of blessings of thanksgiving for the ordinary functions and pleasures of daily life, such as our ability to wake up refreshed, to open our eyes and see, stand erect, walk and move around, provide ourselves with clothing to wear, and more.

Order of the Blessings

The Blessings over the Torah, which are recited once in the morning, apply to all Torah study throughout the day. One should not study Torah before he has recited the Blessings over the Torah in the morning.

There are various customs with regard to the specific order of the Morning Blessings. Each person should recite them in the order in which they appear in his or her prayer book. One should recite the Morning Blessings one after the other, without skipping any of them, even if he is not benefiting from the particular function mentioned in the blessing at the time that he recites it.

Women recite all the Morning Blessings. In place of the blessing which ends, "who has not made me a woman," they say, "who made me according to His will." Some have the custom to recite simply, "Blessed be He who made me according to His will," without the name of God, while others do not recite this blessing at all. Each woman should follow her custom, in accordance with the prayer book she uses.

The Daily Prayers

The mitzva of prayer appears in the Torah, in the verse, "And to serve Him with all your heart" (Deuteronomy 11:13). The Sages commented on this verse: "What is the service of the heart? It is prayer" (*Ta'anit* 2a), because prayer must be recited in a heartfelt manner and it is the heart, more so than the words, that is most essential for prayer. During prayer one should be thinking about two matters: the fact that one is standing before the King of Kings, and the meaning of the words he is uttering.

The mitzva of prayer, at its core, consists of beseeching God when one needs something, or praising God when one feels obliged to thank Him. It is essentially a personal experience, and was initially offered by each person in his own words. Over the generations, as the Sages saw that people were finding it difficult to implement this mitzva, they instituted a uniform formulation of the prayers. Once the standard text of the prayers was established, it became binding.

The Sages also said that nowadays, when there is no Temple and one cannot offer sacrifices, the prayers serve as a substitute for sacrifices, as indicated by the verse, "And we will pay bulls with our lips" (Hosea 14:3). In other words, we pay, or fulfill, the obligation of the sacrifices ("bulls") by means of prayer ("with our lips"). Accordingly, the morning service corresponds to the daily morning sacrifice and the afternoon service to the daily afternoon sacrifice, while the evening service corresponds to the burning of the fats and internal organs of the sacrifices, which was done at night (see *Berakhot* 26b). The times of the three prayers are derived from the time of the offering of each particular sacrifice.

This chapter presents the order and *halakhot* of the prayers, over the course of the day.

Morning Service [*Shaharit*]

The morning service starts the day and is the longest of the three daily services. Its central prayer, like the central prayer of the other two services of the day, is the *Shemoneh Esrei*, also known as the *Amida*. *Shemoneh Esrei* means eighteen, and the prayer is so called because it originally had eighteen blessings. Although another blessing was added later, its name remained unchanged. The term *Amida* means standing, and this prayer must be recited silently while standing.

> Further reading: For more on prayer and its meaning, see *A Concise Guide to the Sages*, p. 457; *A Concise Guide to Mahshava*, p. 300.

Another fundamental component of the morning service, as well as of the evening service, is the recitation of *Shema*, which consists of three passages from the Torah that deal with the obligation to love God and fulfill His commandments. The opening verse is, "Hear [*Shema*], Israel: The Lord is our God, the Lord is one" (Deuteronomy 6:4), hence the name *Shema*.

Time of the Prayer

The *Amida* of the morning service is to be recited during the period from sunrise until the end of the fourth hour of the day (calculated using "halakhic hours," which are each one-twelfth of the period of daylight). One who missed this time is permitted, after the fact, to pray until midday. The exact times for sunrise, the fourth hour, midday, and other halakhically significant times of day appear in special timetables produced for this purpose, which are sold in book form and can also be accessed online.

The Time for the Recitation of *Shema*

One may recite *Shema* from about an hour before sunrise until the conclusion of the third hour of the day, calculated using halakhic hours. Here too, these times are listed in daily halakhic timetables. In this regard, there are two methods of calculating the time, with a discrepancy of about forty-five minutes between them. Each person should follow the custom of his community.

Recitation of *Shema* is an important part of the morning prayer service, but sometimes the service is scheduled such that *Shema* will be recited by the congregation after the appropriate time. In such a case one must remember that reciting *Shema* is a mitzva in its own right, with its own schedule, and therefore, in order to fulfill this mitzva one must recite it before the morning service.

Public Prayer

The preferred form of prayer is in the synagogue with a quorum [*minyan*] of ten adult male Jews praying together. Public prayer is preferable to solitary prayer and is heard and accepted with more grace in heaven. In addition, only when praying with a *minyan* may one recite Kaddish, *Kedusha, Barekhu, Selihot*, or read the Torah. Nevertheless, one who cannot come to the synagogue and pray with the congregation should pray alone.

> **Further reading:** For more on the significance of praying in a *minyan*, see *A Concise Guide to Mahshava*, p. 309.

It is desirable for every person to choose a regular spot where he recites *Shemoneh Esrei*. This applies both to prayer in the synagogue and to prayer at home.

Women and Prayer

The Torah exempts women from almost all positive, time-bound mitzvot. This refers to mitzvot which are to be performed at a certain time (e.g., *tefillin*, *Shema*, *sukka*, and *lulav*), in contrast to mitzvot that are not dependent on a particular time (e.g., *mezuza*, giving charity, and returning lost property). Therefore, women are exempt from reciting *Shema*, which must be recited at certain hours of the day and night. Nevertheless, it is proper for every woman to accept the yoke of Heaven every day, by reciting the first verse, "Hear, Israel: The Lord is our God, the Lord is one."

Women are obligated to recite the *Amida* prayer of the morning and afternoon services. In certain Sephardic communities, the custom is for women to pray only one *Amida* prayer every day. If a woman finds it particularly difficult to recite the *Amida* every day, then reciting the Morning Blessings each morning suffices, as these blessings include the basic components of the entire prayer service.

Preparations for Prayer

The verse states, "Prepare to meet your God, Israel" (Amos 4:12). The Sages derive from this verse that one must prepare for prayer both physically and mentally.

Physical Preparation

Bodily preparation involves relieving oneself as necessary, clearing phlegm from one's throat, and removing any other physical disturbance that might interfere with his concentration during prayer. One who feels a need to relieve himself is prohibited to pray until he does so. Also, since one must ensure that his hands are clean during prayer, he should wash his hands before beginning. This law applies primarily before the afternoon and evening services; as for the morning service, one may rely on the washing of hands performed after waking in the morning.

Mental Preparation

Preparing mentally and spiritually means commencing the prayer in a calm, deliberate state of mind. Before praying, it is desirable to give charity. Some recite the following sentence every day before the morning service:

הֲרֵינִי מְקַבֵּל עָלַי מִצְוַת עֲשֵׂה שֶׁל וְאָהַבְתָּ
לְרֵעֲךָ כָּמוֹךָ.

Hareini mekabel alai mitzvat aseh shel ve'ahavta lere'akha kamokha.

"I hereby accept upon myself the positive commandment, 'You shall love your neighbor as yourself.'"

It is highly recommended, even for one who is completely fluent in the words of the prayer and knows them by heart, to pray from a prayer book. This will help him to concentrate better on the words.

📖 **Further reading:** For more on the preparations for prayer, see *A Concise Guide to the Sages*, p. 457; *A Concise Guide to Mahshava*, p. 308.

The Structure and *Halakhot* of the Morning Service

The structure of the morning service recalls a gradual climb up a mountain, with the *Amida* prayer at its summit. The passages that come before the *Amida* prayer are like the stops along the climb, while the sections of prayer that follow the *Amida* are comparable to the descent from the summit to the plains of everyday life.

After reciting the Morning Blessings, it is customary to recite a compilation of verses and *mishnayot* that describe the bringing of the sacrifices in the Temple. One who finds it hard to recite the entire order of the Sacrifices should at least read the verses dealing with the daily sacrifice, to which the morning service corresponds.

Following this, one says *Pesukei DeZimra*, a sequence of hymns of praise to God. These psalms are preceded by the blessing of *Barukh She'amar*, and followed by the blessing of *Yishtabah*.

Yishtabah is followed by the recitation of *Shema* and its accompanying blessings. In the morning service two blessings are recited before *Shema* and one blessing after it. The *Amida* prayer comes immediately after that last blessing. The laws concerning the recitation of *Shema* and the *Amida*, as well as the sections of the service that follow the *Amida*, are clarified below.

One who has very limited time may shorten *Pesukei DeZimra* and say only the following passages: *Barukh She'amar*, *Ashrei* (Psalms 145), and *Yishtabah*. He should then recite *Shema* and its blessings, followed by the *Amida* prayer.

Shema

Reciting *Shema* is of great importance, because one thereby accepts upon himself the rule of Heaven. While reciting the verse "Hear, Israel: The Lord is our God, the Lord is one," the worshipper must concentrate on the words and have in mind that he is accepting the yoke of Heaven.

Text

The *Shema* consists of three passages from the Torah: the passages beginning "Hear, Israel [*Shema Yisrael*]" (Deuteronomy 6:4–9) and "It shall be if you will heed [*Vehaya im shamo'a*]" (Deuteronomy 11:13–21), and the passage dealing with *tzitzit*, ritual fringes (Numbers 15:37–41). The text is as follows:

שְׁמַע יִשְׂרָאֵל אֲדֹנָי אֱלֹהֵינוּ אֲדֹנָי אֶחָד:

Shema Yisrael: Adonai Eloheinu, Adonei eḥad.

בָּרוּךְ שֵׁם כְּבוֹד מַלְכוּתוֹ לְעוֹלָם וָעֶד.

Barukh shem kevod malkhuto le'olam va'ed.

וְאָהַבְתָּ אֵת אֲדֹנָי אֱלֹהֶיךָ בְּכָל לְבָבְךָ וּבְכָל נַפְשְׁךָ וּבְכָל מְאֹדֶךָ: וְהָיוּ הַדְּבָרִים הָאֵלֶּה אֲשֶׁר אָנֹכִי מְצַוְּךָ הַיּוֹם עַל לְבָבֶךָ: וְשִׁנַּנְתָּם לְבָנֶיךָ וְדִבַּרְתָּ בָּם בְּשִׁבְתְּךָ בְּבֵיתֶךָ וּבְלֶכְתְּךָ בַדֶּרֶךְ וּבְשָׁכְבְּךָ וּבְקוּמֶךָ: וּקְשַׁרְתָּם לְאוֹת עַל יָדֶךָ וְהָיוּ לְטֹטָפֹת בֵּין עֵינֶיךָ: וּכְתַבְתָּם עַל מְזֻזוֹת בֵּיתֶךָ וּבִשְׁעָרֶיךָ:

Ve'ahavta et Adonai Elohekha bekhol levavekha, uvkhol nafshekha, uvkhol meodekha. Vehayu ha'devarim ha'eleh asher anokhi metzavekha hayom al levavekha. Veshinantam levanekha, vedibarta bam beshivtekha beveitekha uvlekhtekha vaderekh uvshokhbekha uvkumekha. Ukshartam le'ot al yadekha vehayu letotafot bein einekha. Ukhtavtam al mezuzot beitekha uvisharekha.

וְהָיָה אִם שָׁמֹעַ תִּשְׁמְעוּ אֶל מִצְוֹתַי אֲשֶׁר אָנֹכִי מְצַוֶּה אֶתְכֶם הַיּוֹם לְאַהֲבָה אֶת אֲדֹנָי אֱלֹהֵיכֶם וּלְעָבְדוֹ בְּכָל לְבַבְכֶם וּבְכָל נַפְשְׁכֶם: וְנָתַתִּי מְטַר אַרְצְכֶם בְּעִתּוֹ יוֹרֶה וּמַלְקוֹשׁ וְאָסַפְתָּ דְגָנֶךָ וְתִירֹשְׁךָ וְיִצְהָרֶךָ: וְנָתַתִּי עֵשֶׂב בְּשָׂדְךָ לִבְהֶמְתֶּךָ וְאָכַלְתָּ וְשָׂבָעְתָּ: הִשָּׁמְרוּ לָכֶם פֶּן יִפְתֶּה לְבַבְכֶם וְסַרְתֶּם וַעֲבַדְתֶּם אֱלֹהִים אֲחֵרִים וְהִשְׁתַּחֲוִיתֶם לָהֶם: וְחָרָה אַף אֲדֹנָי בָּכֶם וְעָצַר אֶת הַשָּׁמַיִם וְלֹא יִהְיֶה מָטָר וְהָאֲדָמָה לֹא תִתֵּן אֶת יְבוּלָהּ וַאֲבַדְתֶּם מְהֵרָה מֵעַל

Vehaya im shamo'a tishme'u el mitzvotai asher anokhi metzaveh etkhem hayom, le'ahava et Adonei Eloheikhem ulovdo bekhol levavkhem uvkhol nafshekhem. Venatati metar artzekhem be'ito, yoreh umalkosh, ve'asafta deganekha vetiroshekha veyitzharekha. Venatati esev besadekha livhemtekha ve'akhalta vesavata. Hishameru lakhem pen yifteh levavkhem, vesartem va'avadtem elohim aḥerim vehishtaḥavitem lahem. Veḥara af Adonai bakhem, ve'atzar et hashamayim velo yihyeh matar, veha'adama lo titen et yevulah, va'avadtem mehera me'al ha'aretz

הָאָרֶץ הַטֹּבָה אֲשֶׁר אֲדֹנָי נֹתֵן לָכֶם: וְשַׂמְתֶּם אֶת דְּבָרַי אֵלֶּה עַל לְבַבְכֶם וְעַל נַפְשְׁכֶם וּקְשַׁרְתֶּם אֹתָם לְאוֹת עַל יֶדְכֶם וְהָיוּ לְטוֹטָפֹת בֵּין עֵינֵיכֶם: וְלִמַּדְתֶּם אֹתָם אֶת בְּנֵיכֶם לְדַבֵּר בָּם בְּשִׁבְתְּךָ בְּבֵיתֶךָ וּבְלֶכְתְּךָ בַדֶּרֶךְ וּבְשָׁכְבְּךָ וּבְקוּמֶךָ: וּכְתַבְתָּם עַל מְזוּזוֹת בֵּיתֶךָ וּבִשְׁעָרֶיךָ: לְמַעַן יִרְבּוּ יְמֵיכֶם וִימֵי בְנֵיכֶם עַל הָאֲדָמָה אֲשֶׁר נִשְׁבַּע אֲדֹנָי לַאֲבֹתֵיכֶם לָתֵת לָהֶם כִּימֵי הַשָּׁמַיִם עַל הָאָרֶץ:

וַיֹּאמֶר אֲדֹנָי אֶל מֹשֶׁה לֵּאמֹר: דַּבֵּר אֶל בְּנֵי יִשְׂרָאֵל וְאָמַרְתָּ אֲלֵהֶם וְעָשׂוּ לָהֶם צִיצִת עַל כַּנְפֵי בִגְדֵיהֶם לְדֹרֹתָם וְנָתְנוּ עַל צִיצִת הַכָּנָף פְּתִיל תְּכֵלֶת: וְהָיָה לָכֶם לְצִיצִת וּרְאִיתֶם אֹתוֹ וּזְכַרְתֶּם אֶת כָּל מִצְוֹת אֲדֹנָי וַעֲשִׂיתֶם אֹתָם וְלֹא תָתוּרוּ אַחֲרֵי לְבַבְכֶם וְאַחֲרֵי עֵינֵיכֶם אֲשֶׁר אַתֶּם זֹנִים אַחֲרֵיהֶם: לְמַעַן תִּזְכְּרוּ וַעֲשִׂיתֶם אֶת כָּל מִצְוֹתָי וִהְיִיתֶם קְדֹשִׁים לֵאלֹהֵיכֶם: אֲנִי אֲדֹנָי אֱלֹהֵיכֶם אֲשֶׁר הוֹצֵאתִי אֶתְכֶם מֵאֶרֶץ מִצְרַיִם לִהְיוֹת לָכֶם לֵאלֹהִים אֲנִי אֲדֹנָי אֱלֹהֵיכֶם: אֱמֶת.

hatova asher Adonai noten lakhem. Vesamtem et devarai eleh al levavkhem ve'al nafshekhem, ukshartem otam le'ot al yedkhem vehayu letotafot bein eineikhem. Velimadtem otam et beneikhem ledaber bam beshivtekha beveitekha uvlekhtekha vaderekh uvshokhbekha uvkumekha. Ukhtavtam al mezuzot beitekha uvisharekha. Lema'an yirbu yemeikhem vimei veneikhem al ha'adama asher nishba Adonai la'avoteikhem latet lehem, kimei hashamayim al ha'aretz.

Vayomer Adonai el Moshe lemor. Daber el benei Yisrael ve'amarta alehem ve'asu lahem tzitzit al kanfei vigdeihem ledorotam. Vena'tenu al tzitzit hakanaf petil tekhelet, vehaya lakhem letzitzit. Uritem oto uzkhartem et kol mitzvot Adonai va'asitem otam, velo taturu aharei levavkhem ve'aharei eineikhem asher atem zonim ahareihem. Lema'an tizkeru, va'asitem et kol mitzvotai vihyitem kedoshim leloheikhem. Ani Adonai Eloheikhem asher hotzeti etkhem me'eretz Mitzrayim lihyot lakhem lelohim, ani Adonai Eloheikhem – emet.

"Hear, Israel: The Lord is our God, the Lord is one.

"Blessed be the name of His glorious kingdom for ever and ever.

"You shall love the Lord your God with all your heart, and with all your soul, and with all your might. These matters that I command you today shall be upon your heart. You shall inculcate them in your children, and you shall speak of them while you are sitting in your house, and while you are walking on the way, and while you are lying down, and while you are rising. You shall bind them as a sign on your hand, and they shall be for ornaments between your eyes.

Daily Routine

"It shall be if you will heed My commandments that I command you today, to love the Lord your God, and to serve Him with all your heart and with all your soul, I will provide the rain of your land at its appointed time, the early rain and the late rain, and you will gather your grain, and your wine, and your oil. I will provide grass in your field for your animals, and you will eat and you will be satisfied. Beware, lest your heart be seduced, and you stray and serve other gods, and prostrate yourself to them. The wrath of the Lord will be enflamed against you, and He will curb the heavens and there will be no rain, and the ground will not yield its produce and you will be quickly eradicated from upon the good land that the Lord is giving you. You shall place these words of Mine upon your heart and upon your soul and you shall bind them as a sign upon your arm, and they shall be as ornaments between your eyes. You shall teach them to your children to speak of them, while you are sitting in your house, and while you are walking on the way, and while you are lying, and while you are arising. You shall write them on the doorposts of your house, and on your gates; so that your days will be increased, and the days of your children, on the land with regard to which the Lord took an oath to your forefathers to give them, like the days of the heavens above the earth.

"The Lord spoke to Moses, saying: Speak to the children of Israel, and say to them, and they shall make for themselves a fringe on the corners of their garments for their generations, and they shall put on the fringe of the corner a sky-blue thread. It shall be for you a fringe, and you shall see it, and remember all the commandments of the Lord and perform them; and you shall not rove after your heart and after your eyes, after which you stray; so that you shall remember, and perform all My commandments, and be holy to your God. I am the Lord your God, who took you out of the land of Egypt, to be your God: I am the Lord your God; true."

Covering One's Eyes

To ensure that nothing will distract his attention while reciting the first verse of *Shema*, one should cover his eyes with his hand and say the words out loud. Then, while his hand is still covering his eyes, he should whisper the second line, beginning *Barukh shem*, "Blessed be the name." This sentence is also part of one's acceptance of the yoke of Heaven, and its recitation likewise requires one's full concentration on the words and their significance.

📖 Further reading: *Shema* is linked to devotion to God, see *A Concise Guide to Mahshava*, p. 199.

Likewise, in all the subsequent verses of *Shema* (from "You shall love the Lord your God" until "the Lord your God; true"), one must strive to think carefully about what he is saying. These verses should be said slowly and measuredly, with particular attention to the proper pronunciation of words and to not slurring words together or "swallowing" letters.

During the recitation of *Shema*, one may not perform any action that is unrelated to the recitation itself. It is prohibited not only to speak, but even to signal, whether with the movement of a hand or head, or by winking.

The blessing recited after *Shema* concludes with the words *Ga'al Yisrael*, "Blessed are You, who redeemed Israel." The *Amida* prayer immediately follows this blessing, and one must continue with the *Amida* without interruption after reciting *Ga'al Yisrael*.

The *Amida* Prayer

The *Amida* prayer is the climax of the service. When reciting the *Amida* one is likened to a person who was brought into a royal palace and is standing, with awe, in the presence of the king. It is prohibited to interrupt the *Amida* prayer; one may not talk, move from his spot, signal with his hands, or the like.

The Laws of the *Amida*

One recites the *Amida* prayer while standing, with his feet together and facing the Land of Israel. One who is in Israel should face Jerusalem, and one who is in Jerusalem should face the Temple Mount.

The *Amida* is also called the Silent Prayer, because it is recited in a whisper, so that one's voice will not be heard by those standing nearby.

A verbal interruption unconnected to the *Amida* is permitted only in a life-threatening situation. One may not signal through body movement or walk from one place to another, except in a case of great need, e.g., if a baby begins to cry and this interferes with one's concentration, or if a person praying without a prayer book forgets how to continue the *Amida* and thus needs a prayer book.

Order of the *Amida*

The *Amida* prayer begins with three blessings of praise to the Creator, continues with thirteen blessings that contain various requests, and concludes with three blessings of thanksgiving.

During the *Amida* prayer, one bows down four times: (1) when saying *Barukh Ata Hashem*, "Blessed are You, Lord" at the beginning of the *Amida*; (2) when saying "Blessed are You, Lord" at the end of the first blessing,

Daily Routine

which concludes *Magen Avraham*, "Shield of Abraham"; (3) at the blessing of Thanksgiving [*Modim*], "We give thanks to You, for You are the Lord"; and (4) when saying "Blessed are You, Lord" at the end of the blessing of Thanksgiving. It is prohibited to bow down at the start or close of any of the other blessings of the *Amida*.

The bowing for "Blessed are You, Lord" is performed as follows: When saying the word *Barukh* ("Blessed are"), one bends the knees slightly; when saying *Ata*, "You," one bends the entire upper body quickly and in one movement at the waist, until one's entire back is bent; and while pronouncing God's name, one rises again. The prostration of "We give thanks to You" [*Modim*] is performed similarly, but without the first step, of bending one's knees. Here too, when one says the name of God in the phrase "for You are the Lord," he straightens up.

In the second blessing of the *Amida* prayer, and also in the ninth blessing (which ends with the words *Mevarekh hashanim*, "Who blesses the years"), there are differences between the text that is recited during the winter and during the summer. Both versions appear in prayer books.

End of the *Amida*

At the end of the *Amida* prayer, one acts like someone taking leave of a king: Before saying *Oseh shalom*, "May He who makes peace," one bends his upper body and takes three small steps backward, with his body still bent. At the end of the three steps he stops, turns his head to the left and says, *Oseh shalom bimromav*, "May He who makes peace in His high places," then turns his bent head to the right and says, *Hu ya'aseh shalom aleinu*, "make peace for us," before ending with his bent head turned forward while saying *ve'al kol Yisrael ve'imru amen*, "and all Israel, and say Amen."

At the conclusion of the *Amida* prayer, one remains standing in the spot where his three backward steps ended. He waits there until the prayer leader reaches *Kedusha*, or at least until he begins his repetition of the *Amida*, and then takes three steps forward again. One who is praying without a *minyan* should wait a few seconds in the spot where the three steps ended, before returning to his place.

Repetition of the *Amida*

After the congregation has finished the silent *Amida* prayer, the prayer leader [*shaliaḥ tzibbur*, abbreviated in Hebrew as *shatz*] repeats this prayer out loud. This is called *Hazarat Hashatz*, "the prayer leader's repetition," and it is done only when praying with a *minyan*. During the prayer leader's repetition, those present must listen carefully. Every time he mentions the name of God toward the end of a blessing, those who are listening respond *Barukh Hu uvarukh shemo*, "Blessed be He and blessed be His name," and when he finishes the blessing, they answer "Amen."

The response of "Amen" expresses one's belief that the blessing that was recited is true and I believe in its content. When a blessing includes praise and supplication, which is the case for the blessings in the prayer leader's repetition of the *Amida*, there is another meaning to the response of Amen. One who says Amen participates in the praise and the request, reinforcing and strengthening them. In this regard, the Sages said, "One who answers Amen is even greater than the one who recites the blessing."

Following the second blessing in the prayer leader's repetition, everyone stands straight with their feet together to recite *Kedusha*. At the end of *Kedusha* the congregation may sit down, although many have the practice to stand for the duration of the repetition.

Tahanun

After the *Amida* prayer, the congregation recites *Tahanun*, a set of passages of supplication [*tehina*], as well as various hymns and verses. On Mondays and Thursdays, one recites an extended form of *Tahanun*.

Torah Reading

The Torah is read after *Tahanun* during the morning service on Mondays and Thursdays. This practice was instituted by none other than Moses himself, in what was possibly the very first rabbinic enactment in history. The idea behind this enactment is that there should not be three consecutive days without a public reading of the Torah. The Torah is also read on Shabbat, *Rosh Hodesh*, and festivals.

Further reading: For more on the Shabbat Torah reading, see p. 392.

Those Called Up to the Torah

A Torah scroll is taken out of the ark, and someone reads out of it aloud from the beginning of that week's Torah portion. The reading of the Torah may be conducted only in the presence of at least ten men.

Three men are called up to the Torah, i.e., honored by approaching the Torah and saying blessings before and after a section of the reading: a *kohen*, a Levite, and an Israelite. When there is no *kohen* present, a Levite is called up first, followed by two Israelites; alternatively, if there is no *kohen*, three

Israelites may be called up. If no Levite is there, the *kohen* is called up again, instead of a Levite. If there are no *kohanim* or Levites, three Israelites are called up to the Torah.

The Blessings

The *oleh*, the one who is called up to the Torah, opens the Torah scroll and looks at the place where the reading will start. It is customary to touch the first word of the reading with the edge of one's *tallit* or with the girdle of the scroll and then kiss the *tallit* or girdle. He then recites the following:

עוֹלֶה: בָּרְכוּ אֶת אֲדֹנָי הַמְבֹרָךְ.   Oleh: *Barekhu et Adonai hamvorakh.*

קהל: בָּרוּךְ אֲדֹנָי הַמְבֹרָךְ לְעוֹלָם וָעֶד.   Congregation: *Barukh Adonai hamvorakh le'olam va'ed.*

Oleh: "Bless the Lord, the blessed One."
     Congregation: "Bless the Lord, the blessed One, for ever and all time."

Many Sephardic Jews say instead:

עוֹלֶה: הַשֵּׁם עִמָּכֶם.   Oleh: *Hashem imakhem.*

קהל: יְבָרֶכְךָ הַשֵּׁם.   Congregation: *Yevarekhekha Hashem.*

עוֹלֶה: רַבָּנָן, בָּרְכוּ אֶת אֲדֹנָי הַמְבֹרָךְ.   Oleh: *Rabanan: Barekhu et Adonai hamvorakh.*

קהל: בָּרוּךְ אֲדֹנָי הַמְבֹרָךְ לְעוֹלָם וָעֶד.   Congregation: *Barukh Adonai hamvorakh le'olam va'ed.*

Oleh: "May God be with you."
     Congregation: "May God bless you."
   Oleh: "Masters, bless the Lord, the blessed One."
     Congregation: "Bless the Lord, the blessed One, for ever and all time."

The *oleh* then recites the blessing itself:

בָּרוּךְ אַתָּה אֲדֹנָי, אֱלֹהֵינוּ מֶלֶךְ הָעוֹלָם, אֲשֶׁר בָּחַר בָּנוּ מִכָּל הָעַמִּים וְנָתַן לָנוּ אֶת תּוֹרָתוֹ, בָּרוּךְ אַתָּה אֲדֹנָי, נוֹתֵן הַתּוֹרָה.   *Barukh ata Adonai, Eloheinu, melekh ha'olam, asher baḥar banu mikol ha'amim, venatan lanu et torato. Barukh ata Adonai, noten haTorah.*

"Blessed are You, Lord our God, King of the universe, who has chosen us from all peoples and given us His Torah. Blessed are You, Lord, Giver of the Torah."

The congregation answers "Amen," and then the reader chants the passage from the Torah aloud, according to the traditional cantillation notes. The one called up to the Torah also joins in the reading, in an undertone. At the conclusion of the reading, the one who was called up recites the following blessing:

בָּרוּךְ אַתָּה אֲדֹנָי, אֱלֹהֵינוּ מֶלֶךְ הָעוֹלָם,
אֲשֶׁר נָתַן לָנוּ (עֵדוּת הַמִּזְרָח מוֹסִיפִים:
אֶת תּוֹרָתוֹ) תּוֹרַת אֱמֶת וְחַיֵּי עוֹלָם נָטַע
בְּתוֹכֵנוּ, בָּרוּךְ אַתָּה אֲדֹנָי, נוֹתֵן הַתּוֹרָה.

Barukh ata Adonai, Eloheinu, melekh ha'olam, asher natan lanu (Sephardim add: *et torato*) *torat emet, vehayey olam nata betokhenu. Barukh ata Adonai, noten haTorah.*

"Blessed are You, Lord our God, King of the universe, who has given us (Sephardic Jews add: 'His Torah,') the Torah of truth, and planted everlasting life in our midst. Blessed are You, Lord, Giver of the Torah."

End of the Service

After the Torah reading on Mondays and Thursdays, or after the recitation of *Tahanun* on other weekdays, one continues the prayer as detailed in the prayer book: *Ashrei* (Psalms 145); *Lamnatzeah* (Psalms 20); *Uva LeTzion*, a compilation of prayers and verses from various passages in the Prophets and Writings; the Song of the Day, a different psalm for each day of the week corresponding to the psalm that the Levites would sing in the Temple on that day; in some congregations, the passage *Ein Keloheinu*, "There is none like our God," which mainly details the incense service in the Temple; and *Aleinu*, "It is our duty," an ancient prayer that focuses on belief in God and the expectation that the entire universe will one day acknowledge His reign. In congregations that recite the prayers in the *nusah Ashkenaz* format, *Aleinu* is recited before the Song of the Day.

The Blessing of *HaGomel*

One who is saved from a dangerous situation must thank God by reciting the *HaGomel* blessing in the presence of ten men.

Procedure

It is customary for a man who is obligated to recite the *HaGomel* blessing to be called up to the Torah. After the reading is completed and he recites the concluding blessing, he recites the *HaGomel* blessing.

Text

Ashkenazim:

עוֹלֶה: בָּרוּךְ אַתָּה אֲדֹנָי, אֱלֹהֵינוּ מֶלֶךְ הָעוֹלָם, הַגּוֹמֵל לְחַיָּבִים טוֹבוֹת שֶׁגְּמָלַנִי כָּל טוֹב.

Oleh: Barukh ata Adonai, Eloheinu, melekh ha'olam, hagomel lahayavim tovot, shegemalani kol tov.

קהל: מִי שֶׁגְּמָלְךָ כָּל טוֹב, הוּא יִגְמָלְךָ כָּל טוֹב סֶלָה.

Congregation: Amen. Mi shegemalkha kol tov, Hu yigmalkha kol tov, sela.

Oleh: "Blessed are You, Lord our God, King of the universe, who bestows good upon the culpable, who has bestowed all goodness upon me."

Congregation: "Amen. May He who bestowed all goodness upon you, always bestow all goodness upon you, Selah."

Sephardim:

עוֹלֶה: אוֹדֶה ה׳ בְּכָל לֵבָב, בְּסוֹד יְשָׁרִים וְעֵדָה.

Oleh: Odeh Adonai bekhol levav, besod yesharim ve'eda.

עוֹלֶה: בָּרוּךְ אַתָּה אֲדֹנָי, אֱלֹהֵינוּ מֶלֶךְ הָעוֹלָם, הַגּוֹמֵל לְחַיָּבִים טוֹבוֹת שֶׁגְּמָלַנִי כָּל טוֹב.

Oleh: Barukh ata Adonai, Eloheinu, melekh ha'olam, hagomel lahayavim tovot, shegemalani kol tov.

קהל: אָמֵן. הָאֵל שֶׁגְּמָלְךָ כָּל טוֹב, הוּא יִגְמָלְךָ כָּל טוֹב סֶלָה.

Congregation: Amen. Ha'El shegemalkha kol tov, Hu yigmalkha kol tov, sela.

Oleh: "I will thank the Lord with all my heart in the assembly and council of the upright" (Psalms 111:1).

Oleh: "Blessed are You, Lord our God, King of the universe, who bestows good upon the culpable, who has bestowed all goodness upon me."

Congregation: "Amen. May the God who bestowed all goodness upon you, always bestow all goodness upon you, Selah."

If one is obligated to recite the *HaGomel* blessing but was not called up to the Torah, he should wait until the reading is over, and then approach the Torah scroll and recite the blessing.

Those Obligated to Recite the Blessing

The Talmud (*Berakhot* 14b) lists four situations in which one is obligated to recite the *HaGomel* blessing: if he sailed in the sea and arrived safely at the shore; if he passed through the desert and arrived safely at an inhabited area; if he recovered from illness; and if he was released from prison.

Nowadays, the case of crossing a desert is exceedingly rare, whereas air travel over the sea is commonplace. The most prevalent custom is to recite *HaGomel* after an overseas flight. It is not customary to recite *HaGomel* after road trips, although in some Sephardic communities the custom is to recite *HaGomel* after a journey between urban areas that takes more than 72 minutes.

With regard to one who has recovered from illness, the common practice among Sephardic Jews is for every person who was bedridden due to illness to recite the *HaGomel* blessing upon his recovery. The Ashkenazic custom is to recite *HaGomel* only after recovering from a life-threatening illness. According to another custom, one also recites *HaGomel* after he recovers from an illness that was not life-threatening but which caused him to be confined to his bed for at least three days.

With regard to one who survived a danger that is not one of the four situations listed above, such as a car accident, there is a difference of practice between different communities. Ashkenazim recite *HaGomel*, whereas Sephardim recite the blessing without mentioning God's name: "Blessed is He who bestows good upon the culpable, who has bestowed all goodness upon me."

A woman who is obligated to recite the *HaGomel* blessing should do so in the presence of ten men. Many have the custom that a woman after childbirth recites *HaGomel* in the same manner as an ill person does upon recovery. If she gave birth to a son, she can recite *HaGomel* at the circumcision, in the presence of ten men. If she gave birth to a girl, she can recite the blessing in the synagogue, from her place in the women's section. She should arrange this in advance with the rabbi and *gabbai* of the synagogue.

Afternoon Service [*Minha*]

The afternoon prayer service was instituted to correspond to the daily afternoon sacrifice that was brought in the Temple. It is called *Minha* due to the fact that immediately after the daily sacrifice was offered every day, a meal offering [*minha*] of flour and oil was also brought. The hour of the *minha* offering is a time of special closeness between God and the Jewish people. Even nowadays, after the destruction of the Temple, the afternoon service is a favorable time, during which prayers are accepted more readily. The Talmud states, "One must always be vigilant with regard to the afternoon prayer, as Elijah's prayer [during his confrontation with the prophets of Baal on Mount Carmel] was answered only at the afternoon service, as it is stated (I Kings 18:36–37): 'And it was at the time of the afternoon offering that Elijah the prophet came near, and he said…Answer me, Lord, answer me'" (*Berakhot* 6b).

> 📖 **Further reading:** For more on the destruction of the Temple and the historical processes that led to this tragedy, see *A Concise Guide to the Sages*, p. 322ff.

Time of the Prayer

The time for the afternoon service begins half an hour after midday and ends at sunset. It is preferable to pray the afternoon service within the final two and a half hours before sunset. This timeframe is called *minha ketana*, "the small *minha*," whereas the earliest time to recite the afternoon prayer is known as *minha gedola*, "the large *minha*." Note that as in the case of the morning service, the hours referred to here are not the standard hours in general use, but "halakhic hours," calculated as one-twelfth of the daylight period. This means that during the summer, when the day is long, these "hours" will be longer than sixty regular minutes, whereas in the winter, when the day is shorter, each "hour" will be less than sixty minutes. Similarly, halakhic midday is not 12:00 but rather the midpoint between sunrise and sunset. These times for any particular day can be found in special calendars or online.

Order of the Service

The main part of the afternoon service is the silent *Amida* prayer. Before the *Amida* it is customary to recite *Ashrei*, which consists primarily of Psalms 145. Some recite beforehand the passages detailing the daily sacrifice and the incense offering in the Temple (some also add the *Patah Eliyahu* passage from the introduction to *Tikkunei Zohar*).

When praying in a *minyan*, the prayer leader repeats the *Amida* [*Hazarat Hashatz*] after the silent *Amida* prayer. At the end of the prayer, *Tahanun* and *Aleinu* are recited (see above with regard to the morning service).

The Evening Service [*Ma'ariv*]

At night, the evening service is recited. This prayer corresponds to the burning of the limbs and fats of the sacrifices upon the altar in the Temple, which continued throughout the night. At the center of this prayer is the nighttime recitation of *Shema*, which is a commandment from the Torah, and the *Amida*.

Structure of the Prayer

The Sages instituted two blessings to be recited before the nighttime recitation of *Shema* and two blessings to be recited afterward. These are followed by the silent *Amida* prayer. Unlike in the morning and afternoon services, in the evening service the prayer leader does not repeat the *Amida* aloud. The service concludes with the recitation of *Aleinu*.

Time of the Service

The time for the nighttime recitation of *Shema* begins when at least three stars appear in the sky. In Israel, this takes place approximately twenty minutes after sunset; in other parts of the world this may vary greatly. The proper time for reciting *Shema* continues until halakhic midnight. One who missed this deadline and did not recite *Shema* before the middle of the night may do so until the morning.

While the time frame for the evening service is similar to that for *Shema*, there is a difference between them: When necessary, one may pray the evening service earlier, before the emergence of the stars. If one does so, he must recite *Shema* again later, after the emergence of the stars. It is common to schedule the evening service a bit early in many communities, especially among Sephardim, because it is difficult for people to assemble for the afternoon service, go their separate ways, and then reconvene a short while later for the evening service. For this and other reasons, these communities hold the afternoon service shortly before sunset and immediately afterward pray the evening service. However, since at that point it is still too early to fulfill the commandment of reciting *Shema*, they recite these three paragraphs again after the emergence of the stars. This additional *Shema* is recited individually by each person, without the blessings before or after.

Bedtime *Shema*

Before going to sleep for the night, one recites *Shema* again, and thereby symbolically deposits his soul in God's hands. These moments before sleep should also be used for a brief period of reflection about the day that has just passed, including one's achievements, successes, and mistakes, while resolving to make the next day even better.

Just before Bed

It is customary to add verses that incorporate repentance for one's sins and a request for mercy from God. Some have the custom to recite all three passages of *Shema*. Each person should follow his community's custom, as listed in his prayer book. At the end of the recitation of *Shema* one recites the *HaMapil* blessing, beginning "Blessed are You, Lord our God, King of the universe, who makes the bands of sleep fall [*hamapil*] upon my eyes and slumber upon my eyelids," as it appears in prayer books. One should try to recite *Shema* as close as possible to sleep, as indicated by the name "bedtime *Shema*."

Tikkun Hatzot

We engage in practices of mourning for the destruction of the Temple at many moments in our lives. According to kabbalistic sources, the middle of the night is an especially fitting time to arouse heavenly mercy to end the exile and rebuild the Temple. Accordingly, kabbalists instituted a sequence of hymns and supplications to be said at midnight. This is called *Tikkun Hatzot*, "Midnight Rectification," and it can be found in prayer books.

Contemporary Practice

Previous generations customarily went to sleep in the early hours of the evening. Pious individuals would then rise at midnight, recite *Tikkun Hatzot*, and study Torah until the morning service. Nowadays as well, some people get up before dawn to say *Tikkun Hatzot*, or stay awake until midnight and recite *Tikkun Hatzot* before going to sleep. The vast majority of the public does not recite *Tikkun Hatzot* today; it remains a practice followed only by exceptional individuals.

Daily Routine

Kaddish

The primary subject of the Kaddish is the proclamation of God's glory to the world. Kaddish, which has a prominent place in public prayer, is also recited after studying Torah, and it plays an important role in funeral and burial services. Most of Kaddish is written in Aramaic, with parts in Hebrew. In order to recite Kaddish, there must be at least ten males present who are over the age of bar mitzva, age thirteen. These men form a *minyan*, and all present answer "Amen" in the appropriate places.

There are several types of Kaddish: Half Kaddish, Full Kaddish, Rabbis' Kaddish [*Kaddish DeRabbanan*], Mourner's Kaddish [*Kaddish Yatom*], and others. The primary difference between Mourner's Kaddish and other versions of Kaddish is that the others are recited by the prayer leader, whereas the Mourner's Kaddish is recited by one who is mourning the loss of a close family member. One may also accept upon himself a commitment to recite Kaddish for the elevation of the soul of another person who has passed away. With regard to the Rabbis' Kaddish, recited after Torah study, there are different customs; in some communities it is also recited only by mourners.

This chapter presents the various types of Kaddish and details when and by whom each one is recited.

Half Kaddish

The main body of Kaddish is called Half Kaddish. This passage is present in all of the varieties of Kaddish. At certain points during the service, this part alone is recited by the prayer leader.

The text of Half Kaddish is as follows:

חזן: יִתְגַּדַּל וְיִתְקַדַּשׁ שְׁמֵהּ רַבָּא.	Prayer leader: *Yitgadal veyitkadash shemeh raba.*
הציבור: אָמֵן.	Congregation: *Amen.*
חזן: בְּעָלְמָא דִּי בְרָא כִרְעוּתֵהּ וְיַמְלִיךְ מַלְכוּתֵהּ	Prayer leader: *Be'alma di vera khiruteh, veyamlikh malkhuteh*
(ספרדים ונוסח ספרד: וְיַצְמַח פֻּרְקָנֵהּ וִיקָרֵב מְשִׁיחֵהּ. ציבור: אָמֵן.)	(Sephardim and nusah Sefarad: *veyatzmaḥ purkaneih vikarev meshiḥeh.* Congregation: *Amen.*)

חזן: בְּחַיֵּיכוֹן וּבְיוֹמֵיכוֹן וּבְחַיֵּי דְכָל בֵּית יִשְׂרָאֵל בַּעֲגָלָא וּבִזְמַן קָרִיב וְאִמְרוּ אָמֵן.	Prayer leader: *Behayekhon uvyomeikhon, uvhayei dekhol beit Yisrael, ba'agala uvizman kariv, ve'imru amen.*
צִיבּוּר: אָמֵן.	Congregation: *Amen.*
כּוּלָם: יְהֵא שְׁמֵהּ רַבָּא מְבָרַךְ לְעָלַם וּלְעָלְמֵי עָלְמַיָּא.	All: *Yehe shemeh raba mevarakh le'alam ul'almei almaya.*
חזן: יִתְבָּרַךְ וְיִשְׁתַּבַּח וְיִתְפָּאַר וְיִתְרוֹמַם וְיִתְנַשֵּׂא וְיִתְהַדָּר וְיִתְעַלֶּה וְיִתְהַלָּל שְׁמֵהּ דְּקֻדְשָׁא בְּרִיךְ הוּא.	Prayer leader: *Yitbarakh veyishtabah veyitpa'ar veyitromam veyitnaseh veyit'hadar veyitaleh veyit'hallal shemeh dekudsha berikh hu.*
צִיבּוּר: אָמֵן (אשכנזים: בְּרִיךְ הוּא).	Congregation: *Berikh hu* or: *Amen.*
חזן: לְעֵלָּא מִן כָּל בִּרְכָתָא וְשִׁירָתָא תֻּשְׁבְּחָתָא וְנֶחֱמָתָא דַּאֲמִירָן בְּעָלְמָא וְאִמְרוּ אָמֵן.	Prayer leader: *Le'ela min kol birkhata veshirata tushbehata venehemata, da'amiran be'alma ve'imru amen.*
צִיבּוּר: אָמֵן.	Congregation: *Amen.*

Prayer leader: "May His great Name be magnified and sanctified."

Congregation: "Amen."

Prayer leader: "In the world He created by His will, may He establish His kingdom

(Sephardim and *nusah Sefarad*: and bring forth His redemption and hasten the coming of His messiah." Congregation: "Amen.")

Prayer leader: "In your lifetime and in your days, and in the lifetime of the entire house of Israel, swiftly and soon, and say: Amen."

Congregation: "Amen."

All: "May His great name be blessed forever and for all time."

Prayer leader: "Blessed and praised, glorified and exalted, raised and honored, uplifted and lauded, be the name of the Holy One, blessed be He."

Congregation: "Blessed be He" or: "Amen."

Prayer leader: "Above any blessing, song, praise, and consolation uttered in the world, and say: Amen."

Congregation: "Amen."

Full Kaddish

At other points in the service, Kaddish continues, and it is called Full Kaddish. The additional section of Full Kaddish that is inserted after the Half Kaddish is as follows:

Daily Routine

חזן: תִּתְקַבַּל צְלוֹתְהוֹן וּבָעוּתְהוֹן דְּכָל בֵּית יִשְׂרָאֵל קֳדָם אֲבוּהוֹן דִּי בִשְׁמַיָּא (וְאַרְעָא) וְאִמְרוּ אָמֵן.

Prayer leader: *Titkabal tzelotehon uva'utehon dekhol beit Yisrael kadam avuhon di vishmaya (ve'ara) ve'imru amen.*

הַצִּבּוּר עוֹנֶה: אָמֵן.

Congregation: *Amen.*

יְהֵא שְׁלָמָא רַבָּא מִן שְׁמַיָּא וְחַיִּים (נוסח ספרד מוסיפים: טוֹבִים) עָלֵינוּ וְעַל כָּל יִשְׂרָאֵל וְאִמְרוּ אָמֵן.

Prayer leader: (Ashkenazim say:) *Yehe shelama raba min shemaya vehayim [nusah Sefarad add: tovim] aleinu ve'al kol Yisrael, ve'imru amen.*

(הַסְּפָרַדִים אוֹמְרִים כָּאן: יְהֵא שְׁלָמָא רַבָּא מִן שְׁמַיָּא וְחַיִּים טוֹבִים וְשָׂבָע וִישׁוּעָה וְנֶחָמָה וְשֵׁיזָבָא וּרְפוּאָה וּגְאֻלָּה וּסְלִיחָה וְכַפָּרָה וְרֶוַח וְהַצָּלָה לָנוּ וּלְכָל עַמּוֹ יִשְׂרָאֵל וְאִמְרוּ אָמֵן.)

(Sephardim say:) *Yehe shelama raba min shemaya vehayim tovim vesava vishu'a venehama veshezava urfu'a ugula u'seliha vekhapara verevah vehatzala, lanu ulkhol amo Yisrael, ve'imru amen.*

הַצִּבּוּר עוֹנֶה: אָמֵן.

Congregation: *Amen.*

(פּוֹסְעִים שָׁלוֹשׁ פְּסִיעוֹת אֲחוֹרָה וְאוֹמְרִים:) עֹשֶׂה שָׁלוֹם בִּמְרוֹמָיו הוּא (וְיֵשׁ הַמּוֹסִיפִים: בְּרַחֲמָיו) יַעֲשֶׂה שָׁלוֹם עָלֵינוּ וְעַל כָּל יִשְׂרָאֵל וְאִמְרוּ אָמֵן.

Prayer leader takes three steps backward and says: *Oseh shalom bimromav, hu* (some add: *verahamav*) *ya'aseh shalom aleinu, ve'al kol Yisrael, ve'imru amen.*

הַצִּבּוּר עוֹנֶה: אָמֵן.

Congregation: *Amen.*

Prayer leader: "May the prayers and supplications of all Israel be accepted by their Father in heaven (and on earth), and say: Amen."

Congregation: "Amen."

Prayer leader: (Ashkenazim say: "May there be great peace from heaven and life for us and for all Israel, and say: Amen.")

(Sephardim say: "May there be great peace from heaven and good life and contentment, salvation and consolation, and escape and healing, and redemption and forgiveness and atonement, and relief and deliverance, for us and for all His nation Israel, and say: Amen.")

Congregation: "Amen."

Prayer leader takes three steps backward and says: "May He who makes peace in His high place make peace (some add: in His mercy) for us and all Israel, and say: Amen."

Congregation: "Amen."

Rabbis' Kaddish [*Kaddish DeRabbanan*]

The Rabbis' Kaddish is recited after public Torah study (when there are at least ten men present), or after the recitation of certain passages in prayer that are likewise composed of quotes from the Sages. It is called the Rabbis' Kaddish because it contains a blessing for Torah scholars and their disciples. The additional section of the Rabbis' Kaddish that is inserted after the Half Kaddish is as follows:

עַל יִשְׂרָאֵל וְעַל רַבָּנָן וְעַל תַּלְמִידֵיהוֹן וְעַל כָּל תַּלְמִידֵי תַלְמִידֵיהוֹן וְעַל כָּל מָאן דְּעָסְקִין בְּאוֹרַיְתָא (קַדִּישְׁתָּא) דִּי בְאַתְרָא (בארץ יש המוסיפים: קַדִּישָׁא) הָדֵין וְדִי בְכָל אֲתַר וַאֲתַר יְהֵא (יש מוסיפים: לָנָא וּ) לְהוֹן וּלְכוֹן שְׁלָמָא רַבָּא חִנָּא וְחִסְדָּא וְרַחֲמֵי וְחַיֵּי אֲרִיכֵי וּמְזוֹנֵי רְוִיחֵי וּפֻרְקָנָא מִן קֳדָם אֲבוּהוֹן דִּי בִשְׁמַיָּא (ויש מוסיפים: וְאַרְעָא) וְאִמְרוּ אָמֵן.

Prayer leader: *Al Yisrael, ve'al raban-an, ve'al talmideihon, ve'al kol talmidei talmideihon, ve'al kol man de'askin be'oraita (kadishta) di ve'atra (in Israel, some add: kadisha) hadein vedi vekhol atar ve'atar, yehe (some add: lana ve) lehon ulkhon shelama raba, hina vehisda, verahamei, vehayei arikhei, umzonei revihei, ufurkana min kodam avuhon di vishmaya (some add: ve'ara), ve'imru amen.*

הַצִּבּוּר עוֹנֶה: אָמֵן.

Congregation: *Amen.*

יְהֵא שְׁלָמָא רַבָּא מִן שְׁמַיָּא וְחַיִּים (לפי 'נוסח ספרד' מוסיפים: טוֹבִים) עָלֵינוּ וְעַל כָּל יִשְׂרָאֵל וְאִמְרוּ אָמֵן.

Prayer leader: (Ashkenazim say: *Yehe shelama raba min shemaya vehayim aleinu ve'al kol Yisrael, ve'imru amen.*)

(הספרדים אומרים כאן: יְהֵא שְׁלָמָא רַבָּא מִן שְׁמַיָּא וְחַיִּים וְשָׂבָע וִישׁוּעָה וְנֶחָמָה וְשֵׁיזָבָא וּרְפוּאָה וּגְאֻלָּה וּסְלִיחָה וְכַפָּרָה וְרֶוַח וְהַצָּלָה לָנוּ וּלְכָל עַמּוֹ יִשְׂרָאֵל וְאִמְרוּ אָמֵן.)

(Sephardim say:) *Yehe shelama raba min shemaya vehayim tovim vesava yeshu'a venehama veshezava urfu'a ugula u'seliha vekhapara verevah vehatzala, lanu ulkhol amo Yisrael, ve'imru amen.*

הַצִּבּוּר עוֹנֶה: אָמֵן.

Congregation: *Amen.*

(פוסעים שלוש פסיעות אחורה ואומרים:) עֹשֶׂה שָׁלוֹם בִּמְרוֹמָיו הוּא (ויש המוסיפים: בְּרַחֲמָיו) יַעֲשֶׂה שָׁלוֹם עָלֵינוּ וְעַל כָּל יִשְׂרָאֵל וְאִמְרוּ אָמֵן.

Prayer leader takes three steps backward and says: *Oseh shalom bimromav, hu (some add: berahamav) ya'aseh shalom aleinu, ve'al kol Yisrael, ve'imru amen.*

הַצִּבּוּר עוֹנֶה: אָמֵן.

Congregation: *Amen.*

Prayer leader: "To Israel, to the teachers, their disciples and their disciples' disciples, and to all who engage in the study of (the holy) Torah, in this (in Israel, some add: holy) place or in any other place, may there come to them and you great peace, grace, kindness and compassion, long life, ample sustenance and deliverance, from their Father in Heaven (some add: and on earth), and say: Amen."

Congregation: "Amen."

Prayer leader: (Ashkenazim say: "May there be great peace from heaven and life for us and for all Israel, and say: Amen.")

(Sephardim say: "May there be great peace from heaven and good life and contentment, salvation and consolation, and escape and healing, and redemption and forgiveness and atonement, and relief and deliverance, for us and for all His nation Israel, and say: Amen.")

Congregation: "Amen."

Prayer leader takes three steps backward and says: "May He who makes peace in His high place make peace (some add: in His mercy) for us and all Israel, and say: Amen."

Congregation: "Amen."

Mourner's Kaddish

During the mourning period, the mourner recites Kaddish on behalf of the soul of the deceased. This recitation is very important for the deceased, as it can assist him in his judgment before the Heavenly Court and tip the scales in his favor.

The Mourner's Kaddish is recited at the funeral, as well as at designated points during prayers in the synagogue throughout the mourning period and on the anniversary of the death (known in Yiddish as the yahrzeit). During the year of mourning it is customary for the mourners to say the Rabbis' Kaddish at the end of public Torah study and at fixed points during prayers in the synagogue.

Further reading: For more on the significance of Kaddish for the soul of the departed, see *A Concise Guide to Mahshava*, p. 29. The full text of the Mourner's Kaddish appears in the chapter that deals with the laws and customs of funerals and burial; see p. 504.

Who Recites Kaddish

The Mourner's Kaddish is recited by the sons of the deceased for eleven months. In the event that the deceased did not have sons, it is customarily recited by another descendant or relative, but if necessary, one can ask or even hire someone else to recite Kaddish for the deceased. Boys who have not reached the age of bar mitzva (thirteen) may nonetheless recite Kaddish for their parents.

If a person must recite Kaddish for another relative while his parents are alive, e.g., his wife or one of his children died, he should ask his parents for permission to say the Mourner's Kaddish during their lifetimes.

In most communities, the custom is that women do not say Kaddish. In other communities women may recite Kaddish if they so desire (according to some opinions, only if the deceased had no sons), and in this regard there are different customs: Some maintain that she should recite Kaddish only if a man there is also saying Kaddish, while others permit Kaddish to be recited by a woman without any such conditions. In any case, a *minyan* of ten men is required for the recitation of Kaddish, including Kaddish said by a woman, and they must all respond with "Amen" in the appropriate places.

Period of Reciting Kaddish

Although the period of mourning for a parent lasts twelve months, one recites Kaddish for only eleven months. The reason for this is that the Mishna states that "the punishment of the wicked in Gehenna is for twelve months" (*Eduyyot* 2:10). Consequently, if a son were to say Kaddish for his father or mother for twelve months, it might appear that he suspects them of having been wicked, which is disrespectful. Therefore, if the parent died, for example, on the fifth of Av, the period of saying Kaddish will end eleven months later, on the fourth of Tamuz. In a leap year, it will conclude on the fourth of Sivan.

The above practice is the most widespread, but there are other customs as well. Some stop saying Kaddish at the end of the eleventh month for a week and then resume it until the end of the twelfth month. Others do not stop at the end of eleven months, but say Kaddish continually until a week before the conclusion of twelve months. Each person should follow the custom of his family and community.

It follows that one who says Kaddish for someone other than his parents may do so throughout the twelve months following the death, since the reason for avoiding this ordinarily is the parent's honor, which does not apply in this case. Nevertheless, as there are several opinions on this matter, it is recommended to consult a rabbi.

Kaddish in the Synagogue

In most communities, all mourners in the synagogue recite Kaddish together. It is advisable for them to maintain a uniform pace, so that the congregation can answer "Amen" to all of them at the same time. For this reason, in some communities all those saying Kaddish gather together in a particular area of the synagogue. In some Ashkenazic communities it is customary for only one person to recite Kaddish, and the sexton of the synagogue establishes a rotation for who will recite which Kaddish and when, based on priorities established by *halakha*.

One recites Kaddish while standing. As for the rest of the congregation, the Sephardic practice is for them to listen and respond while sitting, while the general Ashkenazic custom is to stand.

Kaddish in the Morning Service

Some instances of Kaddish during prayer are recited by the prayer leader and not specifically by a mourner, although a mourner often serves as prayer leader. Kaddish is recited at the following times during the prayer service: The Rabbis' Kaddish is recited by the mourners in the synagogue between the passage beginning *Rabbi Yishmael omer* and the beginning of *Pesukei DeZimra*. If there are no mourners present, the prayer leader should say it. According to the *nusah Ashkenaz* tradition, between the first passage of *Pesukei DeZimra* (Psalms 30) and *Barukh She'amer* ("Blessed is He who spoke"), the mourners recite the Mourner's Kaddish. If there are no mourners, this Kaddish is not recited.

At the end of *Pesukei DeZimra*, the prayer leader says Half Kaddish. After *Tahanun* the prayer leader again says Half Kaddish. Following the Torah reading, Half Kaddish is recited, generally by the Torah reader. At the end of *Uva LeTzion* the prayer leader says Full Kaddish. Then, according to the *nusah Sepharad* tradition, after the Song of the Day the mourners recite the Mourner's Kaddish. If there are no mourners present, a member of the congregation who has no parents should say Kaddish. If there is no one in the congregation who can say Kaddish, it is not recited.

At the end of *Pitum haKetoret* ("the incense mixture"), the mourners say the Rabbis' Kaddish. If there are no mourners, it is recited by the prayer leader. After this Kaddish, someone, generally one of the mourners, says *Barekhu*. After the *Aleinu* prayer the mourners recite the Mourner's Kaddish. The order of the passages and recitation of Kaddish in the Sephardic tradition is similar to that of *nusah Sefarad*.

📖 Further reading: For more on the structure of the daily prayers, see the chapter on prayers, p. 483.

In the *nusah Ashkenaz* tradition, the order is somewhat different, but Kaddish is recited the same number of times. After *Aleinu* the mourners say the Mourner's Kaddish; then the congregation says the Song of the Day; then the mourners recite the Mourner's Kaddish. In Israel, it is customary for congregations that use the *nusah Ashkenaz* format to then recite *Pitum haKetoret*, following which the mourners or the prayer leader recite the Rabbis' Kaddish; and then *Barekhu* is said on days when there is no Torah reading.

There are synagogues in which it is customary to hold a short Torah study session (of Mishna or *halakha*) or to recite chapters of Psalms after the prayer service, to give the mourners the opportunity to recite an additional Rabbis' Kaddish.

Kaddish in the Afternoon and Evening Services

In the afternoon service, the prayer leader recites the Half Kaddish after *Ashrei* and mourners recite the Mourner's Kaddish after *Aleinu*. According to the Sephardic tradition, the Kaddish is recited before *Aleinu*, after the recitation of Psalms 67.

In the evening service according to the *nusah Sefarad* prayer format, the mourners recite the Mourner's Kaddish after the *Shir HaMa'alot* that precedes *Aleinu*, and at the end of Kaddish one of the mourners says *Barekhu*. According to the *nusah Ashkenaz* prayer format, mourners say the Mourner's Kaddish after *Aleinu*. In Israel it is customary to say *Barekhu* following the Kaddish.

This is a general review of the recitations of Kaddish in the daily prayers. On Shabbat, festivals, and holidays there are changes to the order of the prayers and the recitation of Kaddish.

After Communal Study

In many synagogues it is customary that at the completion of public Torah study attended by at least ten men, one of those present recites the Rabbis' Kaddish. In order to ensure that the conditions for reciting the Rabbis' Kaddish are properly fulfilled, one of the men first reads aloud the following mishna:

רַבִּי חֲנַנְיָה בֶּן עֲקַשְׁיָא אוֹמֵר: רָצָה הַקָּדוֹשׁ בָּרוּךְ הוּא לְזַכּוֹת אֶת יִשְׂרָאֵל, לְפִיכָךְ הִרְבָּה לָהֶם תּוֹרָה וּמִצְוֹת שֶׁנֶּאֱמַר, אֲדֹנָי חָפֵץ לְמַעַן צִדְקוֹ יַגְדִּיל תּוֹרָה וְיַאְדִּיר.

Rabi Ḥananya ben Akashya omer: Ratza Hakadosh Barukh Hu lezakot et Yisrael, lefikhakh hirba lahem Torah umitzvot, shene'emar: Adonai ḥafetz lema'an tzidko, yagdil Torah veyadir.

"Rabbi Hananya ben Akashya says: The Holy One, blessed be He, sought to confer merit upon the Jewish people; therefore, He increased for them Torah and mitzvot, as it is stated (Isaiah 42:21): 'It pleased the Lord for the sake of His righteousness to make the Torah great and glorious'" (*Makkot* 3:16).

One reason for reciting this mishna is that it consists of aggada (a rabbinic statement that does not deal with matters of *halakha*), and the Rabbis' Kaddish is recited after matters of aggada but not *halakha*. Another reason is that while the study session is ongoing, people often come in and out, and therefore it is not always clear that ten men actually heard and participated in the class. Consequently, this mishna is read aloud to ensure that all those present are paying attention. This particular mishna was chosen from the many passages of aggada, as its content, praise of the Torah and its commandments, is particularly relevant.

Torah Study

Torah study is a fundamental mitzva. The more one studies the Torah, the more layers and depths he will discover. Four of these levels are known as the *Pardes* ("orchard"), an acronym for *Peshat* (plain meaning), *Remez* (allusion), *Derash* (exegesis), and *Sod* (esoterica). Each one of these four realms of Torah study is infinite, and for this reason it is stated about the Torah, "Its measure is longer than the earth and broader than the sea" (Job 11:9).

The importance of Torah study is highlighted in the first mishna in tractate *Pe'a*. This mishna lists a series of important mitzvot and details their unique qualities, before concluding with the phrase, "And Torah study is equal to them all." In other words, occupying oneself with Torah study is equal in importance to fulfillment of all the other mitzvot.

Torah study is also the gateway to the fulfillment of the other commandments, for if one does not learn Torah, he will not know what mitzvot to do and how to perform them. This is underscored in the verse, "Hear, Israel, the statutes and the ordinances that I am speaking in your ears today, and you shall learn them, and you shall take care to perform them" (Deuteronomy 5:1).

This chapter discusses who is obligated to study Torah, as well as the parameters of this obligation.

The Obligation

The obligation to study Torah is all-encompassing. Every man must study Torah, whether he is preoccupied due to poverty and must even solicit alms, or whether he is absorbed with managing great wealth; whether he is healthy or he is ill and suffering; whether he is a young man or a venerable elder. Each man, whoever he is, must set aside times for Torah study every day and night, as it is stated, "This book of the Torah shall not depart from your mouth, and you shall ponder it day and night" (Joshua 1:8).

How Much Should One Study

The mitzva of learning Torah can be divided into two parts: the obligation to *study* Torah, and the obligation to *know* it.

Torah Study: In addition to the objective obligation to engage in Torah study for at least a brief amount of time every day and night, one should devote whatever other time one has available to Torah study. The amount of time one will actually be able to dedicate depends on the occupation and other personal obligations of each individual.

One who does not work at all or who works part-time must use his free time for learning Torah. Obviously, he may pause during his studies to eat, rest, and gather strength for further study, but he may not waste his time in worthless pursuits.

One who works for a living from morning to evening must establish a specific time for Torah study or complete a certain defined amount of material in the morning and in the evening. A person whose circumstances allow him to devote only a short time to studying Torah fulfills his duty even by studying a very small amount in the morning and a very small amount in the evening.

Torah knowledge: Every person must make an effort to know and remember as much of the Torah as possible. In order to meet this challenge, one must constantly review his studies.

Written Torah and Oral Torah

The recommended order of study is as follows: One must learn the Five Books of the Torah and the nineteen other books of the Prophets and Writings, which are together called the Written Torah. Concurrently, one must become fluent in the entire Oral Law, with a focus on the *halakhot* that pertain to one's practical life. It is highly recommended to study Maimonides' *Yad HaHaḥazaka*, also called the *Mishneh Torah*, as it is the only work that includes all the laws of the Torah, and in fact it incorporates the entire Oral Law.

Practical *Halakha*

As the rulings of Maimonides are not always followed in practice, one must also study the halakhic works of later authorities, the most famous of which are the *Shulḥan Arukh* of Rabbi Yosef Karo, *Shulḥan Arukh HaRav*, *Mishna Berura*, *Kitzur Shulḥan Arukh*, as well as the *Ben Ish Ḥai* and *Yalkut Yosef* for Sephardim. Together with studying the practical laws themselves, one should also learn the reasons for them, at least in brief.

Foundations of the Faith

At the same time, one must also familiarize himself with the foundations of Jewish thought and faith, from the midrashim of the Sages of the Mishna and the Talmud to the works of the other great scholars over the generations.

In-Depth Study

One who has already accumulated a comprehensive knowledge of the basic areas mentioned above should invest the bulk of his time in gaining a deeper understanding of halakhic principles and their applications, including analysis of the underpinnings of different opinions that exist on any given topic. Through this type of study one can develop innovative Torah ideas, as there is no end to the Torah.

Mystical Sources

One should also study the so-called deeper aspects of Torah. This includes hasidic works, which render parts of the esoteric teachings of the Torah more accessible to the masses. They thereby bring one closer to an understanding of God's greatness and the profundity of Torah and mitzvot, and provide the inner strength necessary to overcome the trials and tribulations of life.

Priorities in Study

Priorities in Torah study depend on one's age. Ideally, children should be educated such that they become proficient in the Written Torah at a relatively young age, and then as they get older, they should be taught the parts of the Oral Torah systematically until they become proficient in that as well. An adult who did not merit to study Torah in this manner in his youth must fill in the gaps and divide his free time between the various areas of Torah. It is advisable for him to consult with a rabbi who knows him well, in order to devise a program for doing so in the optimal manner.

Women

There is no independent obligation for women and girls to study Torah. Nevertheless, they must know all the laws pertaining to daily life, as well as the parts of the Torah that relate to the foundations of faith in God and establishing a well-rounded Jewish worldview.

With regard to the study of other areas of the Torah, such as the Talmud, there have been significant changes over the past several decades. In previous generations, when women were focused solely on managing the household, they were generally discouraged from this type of study. However, in contemporary times, when women are no less educated than men in secular subjects, they should also broaden their knowledge in a range of Torah subjects that in the past were reserved for men.

Daily Routine

📖 **Further reading:** For more on the topic of women studying Torah, see *A Concise Guide to Mahshava*, p. 280.

Children

A boy under the age of thirteen is not personally obligated to observe the mitzvot, although his father must educate him to do so, in accordance with the child's age and abilities. Furthermore, the Torah commands each father to teach his son Torah, or to arrange for someone else to teach him, as it is stated, "You shall teach them to your children to speak of them" (Deuteronomy 11:19).

Blessings and Meals

The Sages instituted many blessings, which can be divided into three broad types: blessings over mitzvot, which are recited prior to the performance of many mitzvot (e.g., the blessing recited before donning phylacteries [*tefillin*]); blessings recited before eating, drinking, and smelling certain pleasant aromas; and blessings of thanksgiving for certain special events.

This chapter presents various blessings that are recited during meals and at other times.

Blessing with Care

It is prohibited to recite a "blessing for naught," i.e., a blessing that is not obligatory and that is unnecessary in the circumstances. Almost all the blessings that one recites were instituted by the Sages, and are not a requirement by Torah law. A principle was established, that in cases of uncertainty involving blessings, the *halakha* is to be lenient. This means that when there is doubt as to whether or not a particular blessing should be recited, one does not recite the blessing.

Exceptions to this rule are the blessing of *Asher baḥar banu* ("Who has chosen us"), which is recited as part of the Morning Blessings, and Grace after Meals after eating bread, if one has eaten to satiation. These blessings are required by Torah law, and therefore one who is uncertain as to whether or not he said them is obligated to recite them.

A man should not recite a blessing with his head uncovered. Merely placing one's hand on his head is not considered a head covering, because the body cannot cover itself. However, if necessary, if another person puts his hand on the head of the one reciting the blessing, that is considered a covering for his head.

When reciting a blessing, it is proper to hold the item over which one is reciting the blessing in his right hand, and to have that item in mind. For example, when reciting a blessing before eating an apple, one should hold the apple in his right hand and intend for the blessing to refer to this particular apple.

One may not talk between the end of the blessing and starting to eat.

One who hears another person reciting a blessing should answer "Amen" at the end of the blessing, meaning, "The blessing that he recited is true and I believe in its content." One who recites a blessing does not answer "Amen" to his own blessing.

One Hundred Blessings

One should recite at least one hundred blessings every day. A person who is careful to say all the blessings that the Sages instituted for the three daily prayer services and eats two meals with bread will recite more than a hundred blessings during the course of a day. On Shabbat and festivals, when the *Amida* prayer is shorter, one should try to complete the one hundred daily blessings by eating and drinking between meals.

Blessings before Eating

The Sages instituted blessings to be recited before eating and drinking. In this context, it is stated in the Talmud, "One is prohibited to derive benefit from this world without a blessing, and anyone who derives benefit from this world without a blessing is guilty of misuse of a consecrated object" (*Berakhot* 35). This is because the entire world belongs to God, and the recitation of a blessing is akin to asking His permission to enjoy His world. Therefore, one who does not recite a blessing before deriving benefit from the world is guilty of misuse of divine property.

Even over a Crumb

There is no minimum quantity of food for the blessing before eating. Consequently, even if one takes just a small bite of food or a tiny sip of a drink, he must first recite the appropriate blessing.

Specific Blessings

There are several different blessings that are recited before eating food. There is a specific blessing for fruit grown on trees (*Ha'etz*), a different blessing for other produce that grows from the ground (*Ha'adama*), and a general blessing for water and other foods that are not included in the first two categories (*Shehakol*).

Additionally, the Sages instituted specific blessings for bread (*HaMotzi*) and wine (*Hagafen*), due to their special importance, as the verse states, "And wine, which gladdens man's heart ... and bread, to sustain man's heart" (Psalms 104:15). Other grain-based foods are also considered important, and therefore they too have a special blessing (*Mezonot*).

Bread: *HaMotzi*

Before eating all kinds of bread, including rolls, pita, baguettes, and the like, one recites the following blessing:

בָּרוּךְ אַתָּה אֲדֹנָי, אֱלֹהֵינוּ מֶלֶךְ הָעוֹלָם,
הַמּוֹצִיא לֶחֶם מִן הָאָרֶץ.

Barukh ata Adonai, Eloheinu, melekh ha'olam, hamotzi leḥem min ha'aretz.

"Blessed are You, Lord our God, King of the universe, who brings forth [*hamotzi*] bread from the earth."

There are special *halakhot* that apply when one eats bread, and they are detailed below in the section "A Meal with Bread."

Wine: *Hagafen/Hagefen*

For wine and grape juice, one recites the blessing,

בָּרוּךְ אַתָּה אֲדֹנָי, אֱלֹהֵינוּ מֶלֶךְ הָעוֹלָם,
בּוֹרֵא פְּרִי הַגָּפֶן/ (לספרדים): הַגֶּפֶן.

Barukh ata Adonai, Eloheinu, melekh ha'olam, boreh peri hagafen (Sephardim: hagefen).

"Blessed are You, Lord our God, King of the universe, who creates fruit of the vine [*hagafen / hagefen*]."

Grain Based Foods: *Mezonot*

There are five types of grain recognized by *halakha*: wheat, barley, spelt, rye, and oats. Before eating a cooked or baked item which is made from one of these types of grain and which is not defined as bread, one recites the following blessing:

בָּרוּךְ אַתָּה אֲדֹנָי, אֱלֹהֵינוּ מֶלֶךְ הָעוֹלָם,
בּוֹרֵא מִינֵי מְזוֹנוֹת.

Barukh ata Adonai, Eloheinu, melekh ha'olam, boreh minei mezonot.

"Blessed are You, Lord our God, King of the universe, who creates various kinds of nourishment [*mezonot*]."

Bread is produced from a dough that is baked in an oven. However, there are instances where a dough is baked in an oven and does not attain the full-fledged status of bread. This occurs if the dough is prepared in one of the following three ways: (1) The dough is filled with some kind of filling, e.g., turnovers. (2) The final product is brittle and crunchy, such as pretzels or crackers. (3) It is made from dough that was kneaded in a natural juice or with sugar, oil, eggs, and the like, e.g., cake (as opposed to bread, whose dough is kneaded in water). In these instances, the blessing recited over the baked good is *Mezonot*. However, if one intends to eat a quantity that would comprise a full meal for most people, the *HaMotzi* blessing is recited. This is because the baked good is similar to bread and is also being used in the same manner as bread, which is generally eaten as a meal rather than as a snack.

With regard to a pastry made from a dough that contains additives such as sugar, juice, or the like, but the amount of water in the dough is greater than the other additional substances, the Ashkenazic community regards it as bread. By contrast, some Sephardic authorities rule that if one can taste the additional substance, one recites *Mezonot* (unless eating it as a full meal). For example, in the case of a *halla* or roll with a sweet taste, if it was baked from a dough that in addition to its flour contained sixty percent water and forty percent fruit juice, oil, and sugar, Ashkenazim recite the blessing of *HaMotzi*, whereas (some) Sephardim recite the blessing of *Mezonot*.

The blessing of *Mezonot* is recited over foods such as pasta and couscous, which are grain based and are cooked. It should be noted that the blessing of *Mezonot* is also recited over cooked rice, despite the fact that rice is not one of the five grains. For other foods that many consider to be similar to a grain, such as corn or quinoa, the appropriate blessing is *Ha'adama*.

Fruit: *Ha'etz*

Before eating fruit of the tree, including tree nuts and grapes, one recites the blessing,

בָּרוּךְ אַתָּה אֲדֹנָי, אֱלֹהֵינוּ מֶלֶךְ הָעוֹלָם, *Barukh ata Adonai, Eloheinu, melekh*
בּוֹרֵא פְּרִי הָעֵץ. *ha'olam, boreh peri ha'etz.*

"Blessed are You, Lord our God, King of the universe, who creates fruit of the tree [*ha'etz*]."

Vegetables: *Ha'adama*

Before eating vegetables or legumes, including fruits that grow from a non-perennial trunk or stem, such as bananas, strawberries, and pineapples, one recites the blessing,

בָּרוּךְ אַתָּה אֲדֹנָי, אֱלֹהֵינוּ מֶלֶךְ הָעוֹלָם, *Barukh ata Adonai, Eloheinu, melekh*
בּוֹרֵא פְּרִי הָאֲדָמָה. *ha'olam, boreh peri ha'adama.*

"Blessed are You, Lord our God, King of the universe, who creates fruit of the ground [*ha'adama*]."

If one mistakenly recited the blessing of *Ha'adama* over a fruit of the tree, he has fulfilled his obligation and need not correct himself and recite the blessing of *Ha'etz*. The reason is that the tree itself grows from the ground, and therefore its fruits are also considered to have grown from the ground. By contrast, in the opposite case, if one recited the blessing of *Ha'etz* over a fruit of the ground, he must correct his mistake and recite the blessing of *Ha'adama*. Therefore, if one is uncertain whether the correct blessing over a certain food is *Ha'etz* or *Ha'adama*, he should recite the blessing of *Ha'adama*, as he thereby certainly fulfills his obligation.

Other Foods: *Shehakol*

For all other foods and drinks, e.g., milk and dairy products, eggs, meat, fish, drinks, etc., one recites the blessing,

בָּרוּךְ אַתָּה אֲדֹנָי, אֱלֹהֵינוּ מֶלֶךְ הָעוֹלָם,
שֶׁהַכֹּל נִהְיָה בִּדְבָרוֹ.

Barukh ata Adonai, Eloheinu, melekh ha'olam, shehakol nihya (or: nihyeh) bidvaro.

"Blessed are You, Lord our God, King of the universe, by whose word all things [*shehakol*] came to be."

The blessing of *Shehakol* is a general blessing; therefore, if due to error or lack of knowledge one recited this blessing on fruit, pastry, or even bread or wine, he has fulfilled his obligation and does not recite another blessing.

Order of Precedence

If one has a variety of foods and beverages, such as cake, wine, fruit, vegetables, and fish in front of him, and he wishes to eat them all, he must recite all the blessings in order of importance, and eat each item immediately after its blessing. The most important blessing (apart from the blessing of *Ha-Motzi*, on bread) is *Mezonot*. Therefore, he should eat some of the cake first. After the cake he should recite the second-most important blessing, which is *Hagafen*, and drink the wine. Then he recites *Ha'etz* and eats the fruit, followed by reciting *Ha'adama* and eating the vegetable. Finally, he recites the blessing of *Shehakol* and eats the fish.

The Torah lists seven species for which the Land of Israel is praised: "A land of wheat and barley, and grapevines, and figs, and pomegranates; a land of oil olives and [date] honey" (Deuteronomy 8:8). As these fruits are of special importance, one who plans to eat ordinary fruits (apple, pear, plum, etc.) and also fruits of the seven species should recite the blessing over the fruits of the seven species. The order of the appearance of the seven species in the verse is also significant. The more closely a fruit follows one of the two mentions of the word "land" in the verse, the more important it is considered, and one would recite the blessing over that fruit rather than one of the others mentioned in the verse. Accordingly, this is the order of importance of the fruit of the seven species: olives, dates, grapes, figs, and pomegranates.

Blessing after Food

After eating or drinking, one recites a blessing known as the final blessing [berakha aharona]. One thereby thanks God for sustaining and nourishing us in His great kindness.

Quantity

After consuming food, one recites a blessing only if he ate at least an olive-bulk of food within four minutes: An olive-bulk, according to its halakhic definition, is greater than the size of the olives we have nowadays. The accepted ruling is that an average sized slice of packaged bread contains roughly three olive-bulks. Therefore, if one ate a third of a slice of bread, or a similar quantity of any other food, he must recite a blessing after eating the food. According to some Sephardic halakhic authorities, a slice of bread consists of only one olive-bulk. A blessing is recited after drinking at least a quarter of a *log* (86 cc, about two thirds of a cup) in the amount of time in which a normal person would drink that quantity when drinking to quench his thirst.

Below are the blessings to be recited after various types of food.

Bread: Grace after Meals

The blessing after a meal containing bread is called Grace after Meals, *Birkat HaMazon*, and it contains four blessings (as detailed below).

Baked Goods: *Al Hamihya*

The blessing after foods made from the five types of grain (other than bread) is called the *berakha ahat me'ein shalosh*, which means one blessing that is like three, as it contains the themes of each of the first three blessings of Grace after Meals. It is also recited after drinking wine or eating fruit of the seven species (grapes, figs, pomegranates, olives, and dates). The basic text of this blessing is identical in all cases, but its beginning and conclusion vary in accordance with the type of food or drink one consumed.

For Ashkenazim:

בָּרוּךְ אַתָּה אֲדֹנָי, אֱלֹהֵינוּ מֶלֶךְ הָעוֹלָם,

Barukh ata Adonai, Eloheinu, melekh ha'olam,

עַל חֲמֵשֶׁת מִינֵי דָגָן: עַל הַמִּחְיָה וְעַל הַכַּלְכָּלָה

After the five species of grain: *al hamiḥya ve'al hakalkala*

עַל הַיַּיִן: עַל הַגֶּפֶן וְעַל פְּרִי הַגֶּפֶן

After wine: *al hagefen ve'al peri hagefen*

עַל פֵּירוֹת מִשְׁבַעַת הַמִּינִים: עַל הָעֵץ וְעַל פְּרִי הָעֵץ

After fruit of the seven species: *al ha'etz ve'al peri ha'etz*

וְעַל תְּנוּבַת הַשָּׂדֶה וְעַל אֶרֶץ חֶמְדָּה טוֹבָה וּרְחָבָה שֶׁרָצִיתָ וְהִנְחַלְתָּ לַאֲבוֹתֵינוּ לֶאֱכֹל מִפִּרְיָהּ וְלִשְׂבֹּעַ מִטּוּבָהּ. רַחֵם (נָא) אֲדֹנָי אֱלֹהֵינוּ עַל יִשְׂרָאֵל עַמֶּךָ וְעַל יְרוּשָׁלַיִם עִירֶךָ וְעַל צִיּוֹן מִשְׁכַּן כְּבוֹדֶךָ. וְעַל מִזְבְּחֶךָ. וְעַל הֵיכָלֶךָ. וּבְנֵה יְרוּשָׁלַיִם עִיר הַקֹּדֶשׁ בִּמְהֵרָה בְיָמֵינוּ. וְהַעֲלֵנוּ לְתוֹכָהּ. וְשַׂמְּחֵנוּ בְּבִנְיָנָהּ וְנֹאכַל מִפִּרְיָהּ וְנִשְׂבַּע מִטּוּבָהּ וּנְבָרֶכְךָ עָלֶיהָ בִּקְדֻשָּׁה וּבְטָהֳרָה.

Continue: *ve'al tenuvat hasadeh, ve'al eretz ḥemda tova urḥava sheratzita vehinḥalta la'avoteinu le'ekhol mipiryah velisbo'a mituvah. Raḥem (na) Adonai Eloheinu al Yisrael amekha ve'al Yerushalayim irekha ve'al tziyon mishkan kevodekha ve'al mizbeḥekha ve'al heikhalekha. Uvnei Yerushalayim ir hakodesh bimhera veyameinu, veha'aleinu letokhah, vesamḥenu bevinyanah, venokhal mipiryah, venisba mituvah, unvarekhekha aleha bikdusha uvtahora.*

בְּשַׁבָּת: וּרְצֵה וְהַחֲלִיצֵנוּ בְּיוֹם הַשַּׁבָּת הַזֶּה.

On Shabbat: *Urtzeh vehaḥalitzeinu beyom haShabbat hazeh.*

בְּרֹאשׁ חוֹדֶשׁ: וְזָכְרֵנוּ לְטוֹבָה בְּיוֹם רֹאשׁ הַחֹדֶשׁ הַזֶּה.

On *Rosh Ḥodesh: Vezokhrenu letova beyom rosh haḥodesh hazeh.*

בְּרֹאשׁ הַשָּׁנָה: וְזָכְרֵנוּ לְטוֹבָה בְּיוֹם הַזִּכָּרוֹן הַזֶּה.

On Rosh HaShana: *Vezokhrenu letova beyom hazikaron hazeh.*

בְּפֶסַח: וְשַׂמְּחֵנוּ בְּיוֹם חַג הַמַּצּוֹת הַזֶּה.

On Passover: *Vesamḥenu beyom ḥag hamatzot hazeh.*

בְּשָׁבוּעוֹת: וְשַׂמְּחֵנוּ בְּיוֹם חַג הַשָּׁבוּעוֹת הַזֶּה.

On *Shavuot: Vesamḥenu beyom ḥag hashavuot hazeh.*

בסוכות: וְשַׂמְּחֵנוּ בְּיוֹם חַג הַסֻּכּוֹת הַזֶּה.

On *Sukkot*: *Vesamḥenu beyom ḥag ha-sukkot hazeh.*

בשמיני עצרת ושמחת תורה: וְשַׂמְּחֵנוּ בְּיוֹם הַשְּׁמִינִי חַג הָעֲצֶרֶת הַזֶּה.

On *Shemini Atzeret* and *Simḥat Torah*: *Vesamḥenu beyom hashemini ḥag ha'atzeret hazeh.*

כִּי אַתָּה אֲדֹנָי טוֹב וּמֵטִיב לַכֹּל וְנוֹדֶה לְךָ עַל הָאָרֶץ

Continue: *Ki ata Adonai tov umetiv lakol venodeh lekha al ha'aretz*

עַל חמשת מיני דגן: וְעַל הַמִּחְיָה.

After the five species of grain: *ve'al hamiḥya.*

על היין מחוץ לארץ: וְעַל פְּרִי הַגֶּפֶן.

After wine from outside the Land of Israel: *ve'al peri hagefen.*

על יין יבול הארץ: וְעַל פְּרִי גַפְנָה.

After wine from the Land of Israel: *ve'al peri gafnah.*

על פירות משבעת המינים: וְעַל הַפֵּרוֹת.

After fruit of the seven species from outside the Land of Israel: *ve'al haperot.*

על יבול הארץ: וְעַל פֵּרוֹתֶיהָ.

After fruit of the seven species from the Land of Israel: *ve'al peroteha.*

בָּרוּךְ אַתָּה אֲדֹנָי, עַל הָאָרֶץ

Continue: *Barukh ata Adonai, al ha'aretz*

עַל חמשת מיני דגן: וְעַל הַמִּחְיָה.

After the five species of grain: *ve'al hamiḥya.*

על היין מחוץ לארץ: וְעַל פְּרִי הַגֶּפֶן.

After wine from outside the Land of Israel: *ve'al peri hagefen.*

על יין יבול הארץ: וְעַל פְּרִי גַפְנָה.

After wine from the Land of Israel: *ve'al peri gafnah.*

עַל פירות משבעת המינים: וְעַל הַפֵּרוֹת.

After fruit of the seven species from outside the Land of Israel: *ve'al haperot.*

על יבול הארץ: וְעַל פֵּרוֹתֶיהָ.

After fruit of the seven species from the Land of Israel: *ve'al peroteha.*

"Blessed are You, Lord our God, King of the universe,"

After the five species of grain: "for the nourishment and for the sustenance"

After wine: "for the vine and for the fruit of the vine"

After fruit of the seven species: "for the tree and for the fruit of the tree"

"and for the produce of the field, and for the desirable, good, and spacious land that you willingly gave as an inheritance to our forefathers, to eat of its fruit and be satisfied with its goodness. Please have compassion, Lord our God, on Israel, Your people, on Jerusalem Your city, on Zion the home of Your glory, on Your altar and Your Temple. May You rebuild Jerusalem the holy city, swiftly in our time, and may You bring us back there, and gladden us in its rebuilding, and we will eat from its fruit, be satisfied from its goodness, and bless You for it in holiness and purity."

On Shabbat: "Be pleased to refresh us on this Shabbat day."

On *Rosh Hodesh*: "Remember us for good on this day of *Rosh Hodesh*."

On Rosh HaShana: "Remember us for good on this day of remembrance."

On a festival: "Gladden us on this (such and such) festival day."

"For You, God, are good and do good to all and we thank You for the land"

After the five species of grain: "and for the nourishment."

After wine from outside the Land of Israel: "and for the fruit of the vine."

After wine from the Land of Israel: "and for the fruit of its vine."

After fruit of the seven species from outside the Land of Israel: "and for the fruit."

After fruit from the Land of Israel: "and for its fruit."

"Blessed are You, Lord, for the land"

After the five species of grain: "and for the nourishment and for the sustenance. "

After wine from outside the Land of Israel: "and for the fruit of the vine."

After wine from the Land of Israel: "and for the fruit of its vine."

After fruit of the seven species from outside the Land of Israel: "and for the fruit."

After fruit from the Land of Israel: "and for its fruit."

For Sephardim:

בָּרוּךְ אַתָּה אֲדֹנָי, אֱלֹהֵינוּ מֶלֶךְ הָעוֹלָם,

Barukh ata Adonai, Eloheinu, melekh ha'olam,

עַל חֲמֵשֶׁת מִינֵי דגן: עַל הַמִּחְיָה וְעַל הַכַּלְכָּלָה

After the five species of grain: *al hamiḥya ve'al hakalkala*

עַל היין: עַל הַגֶּפֶן וְעַל פְּרִי הַגֶּפֶן

After wine: *al hagefen ve'al peri hagefen*

עַל פירות משבעת המינים: עַל הָעֵץ וְעַל פְּרִי הָעֵץ

After fruit of the seven species: *al ha'etz ve'al peri ha'etz*

וְעַל תְּנוּבַת הַשָּׂדֶה וְעַל אֶרֶץ חֶמְדָּה טוֹבָה וּרְחָבָה שֶׁרָצִיתָ וְהִנְחַלְתָּ לַאֲבוֹתֵינוּ לֶאֱכֹל מִפִּרְיָה וְלִשְׂבֹּעַ מִטּוּבָה. רַחֵם אֲדֹנָי אֱלֹהֵינוּ עָלֵינוּ וְעַל יִשְׂרָאֵל עַמָּךְ וְעַל יְרוּשָׁלַיִם עִירָךְ וְעַל הַר צִיּוֹן מִשְׁכַּן כְּבוֹדָךְ. וְעַל מִזְבְּחָךְ. וְעַל הֵיכָלָךְ. וּבְנֵה יְרוּשָׁלַיִם עִיר הַקֹּדֶשׁ בִּמְהֵרָה בְיָמֵינוּ. וְהַעֲלֵנוּ לְתוֹכָהּ. וְשַׂמְּחֵנוּ בְּבִנְיָנָהּ וּנְבָרֶכְךָ עָלֶיהָ בִּקְדֻשָּׁה וּבְטָהֳרָה.

Continue: *ve'al tenuvat hasadeh, ve'al eretz ḥemda tova urḥava sheratzita vehinḥalta la'avoteinu le'ekhol mipiryah velisbo'a mituvah. Raḥem Adonai Eloheinu aleinu ve'al Yisrael amakh ve'al Yerushalayim irakh ve'al har tziyon mishkan kevodakh ve'al mizbaḥakh ve'al heikhalakh. Uvnei Yerushalyim ir hakodesh bimhera veyameinu, veha'aleinu letokhah, vesamḥenu bevinyanah, unvarekhakh aleha bikdusha uvtahora.*

בשבת: הָרַחֲמָן הוּא יַנְחִילֵנוּ עוֹלָם שֶׁכֻּלּוֹ שַׁבָּת וּמְנוּחָה לְחַיֵּי הָעוֹלָמִים.

On Shabbat: *Haraḥaman hu yanḥilenu olam shekulo Shabbat umenuḥa leḥayei ha'olamim.*

בראש חודש: הָרַחֲמָן הוּא יְחַדֵּשׁ עָלֵינוּ אֶת הַחֹדֶשׁ הַזֶּה לְטוֹבָה וְלִבְרָכָה.

On *Rosh Hodesh: Haraḥaman hu yeḥadesh aleinu et haḥodesh hazeh letova velivrakha.*

בסוכות: הָרַחֲמָן הוּא יְזַכֵּנוּ לֵישֵׁב בְּסֻכַּת עוֹרוֹ שֶׁל לִוְיָתָן.

On Sukkot: *Haraḥaman hu yezakenu leishev besukkat oro shel livyatan.*

במועדים: הָרַחֲמָן הוּא יַגִּיעֵנוּ לְמוֹעֲדִים אֲחֵרִים הַבָּאִים לִקְרָאתֵנוּ לְשָׁלוֹם.

On intermediate festival days: *Haraḥaman hu yagi'enu lemo'adim aherim haba'im likratenu leshalom.*

לְיוֹם טוֹב: הָרַחֲמָן הוּא יַנְחִילֵנוּ לְיוֹם שֶׁכֻּלּוֹ טוֹב.

On festival days: *Haraḥaman hu yanḥilenu leyom shekulo tov.*

כִּי אַתָּה טוֹב וּמֵטִיב לַכֹּל וְנוֹדֶה לְךָ (אֲדֹנָי אֱלֹהֵינוּ) עַל הָאָרֶץ

Continue: *Ki ata tov umetiv lakol venodeh lekha al ha'aretz*

עַל חֲמֵשֶׁת מִינֵי דָגָן: וְעַל הַמִּחְיָה וְעַל הַכַּלְכָּלָה. עַל יְבוּל הָאָרֶץ: וְעַל מִחְיָתָהּ וְעַל כַּלְכָּלָתָהּ.

After the five species of grain: From outside the Land of Israel: *ve'al hamiḥya.* From the Land of Israel: *ve'al miḥyatah.*

עַל הַיַּיִן: וְעַל פְּרִי הַגֶּפֶן. עַל יְבוּל הָאָרֶץ: וְעַל פְּרִי גַפְנָהּ.

After wine: From outside the Land of Israel: *ve'al peri hagefen.* From the Land of Israel: *ve'al peri gafnah.*

עַל פֵּירוֹת מִשִּׁבְעַת הַמִּינִים: וְעַל הַפֵּרוֹת. עַל יְבוּל הָאָרֶץ: וְעַל פֵּרוֹתֶיהָ.

After fruit of the seven species: From outside the Land of Israel: *ve'al haperot.* From the Land of Israel: *ve'al peroteha.*

בָּרוּךְ אַתָּה אֲדֹנָי, עַל הָאָרֶץ

Continue: *Barukh ata Adonai, al ha'aretz*

עַל חֲמֵשֶׁת מִינֵי דָגָן: וְעַל הַמִּחְיָה. עַל יְבוּל הָאָרֶץ: וְעַל מִחְיָתָהּ.

After the five species of grain: From outside the Land of Israel: *ve'al hamiḥya ve'al hakalkala.* From the Land of Israel: *ve'al miḥyatah ve'al kalkalatah.*

עַל הַיַּיִן: וְעַל פְּרִי הַגֶּפֶן. עַל יְבוּל הָאָרֶץ: וְעַל פְּרִי גַפְנָהּ.

After wine: From outside the Land of Israel: *ve'al peri hagefen.* From the Land of Israel: *ve'al peri gafnah.*

עַל פֵּירוֹת מִשִּׁבְעַת הַמִּינִים: וְעַל הַפֵּרוֹת. עַל יְבוּל הָאָרֶץ: וְעַל פֵּרוֹתֶיהָ.

After fruit of the seven species: From outside the Land of Israel: *ve'al haperot.* From the Land of Israel: *ve'al peroteha.*

"Blessed are You, Lord our God, King of the universe,"

After the five species of grain: "for the nourishment and for the sustenance"

After wine: "for the vine and for the fruit of the vine"

After fruit of the seven species: "for the tree and for the fruit of the tree" "and for the produce of the field, and for the desirable, good and spacious land that you willingly gave as an inheritance to our forefathers, to eat of its fruit and be satisfied with its goodness. Have compassion, Lord our God, upon us, on Israel, Your people, on Jerusalem, Your city, on Mount Zion the home of Your glory, on Your altar and Your Temple. May You rebuild Jerusalem the holy city, swiftly in our time, and may You bring us back there, and gladden us in its rebuilding, and we will bless You for it in holiness and purity."

On Shabbat: "May the Compassionate One let us inherit a world that will be entirely Shabbat and rest for life everlasting."

On *Rosh Hodesh*: "May the Compassionate One renew for us this month for good and blessing."

On *Sukkot*: "May the Compassionate One let us merit to dwell in the *sukka* of the skin of Leviathan."

On intermediate festival days: "May the Compassionate One bring us to other festivals that are to come for us in peace."

On festival days: "May the Compassionate One let us inherit a time that is all good."

"For You, God, are good and do good to all and we thank You (Lord, our God) for the land"

After the five species of grain from outside the Land of Israel: "and for the nourishment and for the sustenance."

After the five species of grain from the Land of Israel: "and for its nourishment and for its sustenance."

After wine from outside the Land of Israel: "and for the fruit of the vine."

After wine from the Land of Israel: "and for the fruit of its vine."

After fruit of the seven species from outside the Land of Israel: "and for the fruit."

After fruit of the seven species from the Land of Israel: "and for its fruit."

"Blessed are You, Lord, for the land"

After the five species of grain from outside the Land of Israel: "and for the nourishment and for the sustenance."

After the five species of grain from the Land of Israel: "and for its nourishment and for its sustenance."

After wine from outside the Land of Israel: "and for the fruit of the vine."

After wine from the Land of Israel: "and for the fruit of its vine."

After fruit of the seven species from outside the Land of Israel: "and for the fruit."

After fruit of the seven species from the Land of Israel: "and for its fruit."

Other Food: *Boreh Nefashot*

After eating all other types of foods, including vegetables, fruits not from the seven species, foods whose blessing before eating is *Shehakol*, and rice, one recites the following blessing:

בָּרוּךְ אַתָּה אֲדֹנָי, אֱלֹהֵינוּ מֶלֶךְ הָעוֹלָם, בּוֹרֵא נְפָשׁוֹת רַבּוֹת, וְחֶסְרוֹנָן עַל כָּל מַה שֶּׁבָּרָאתָ (לכמה מקהילות אשכנז: שֶׁבָּרָא) לְהַחֲיוֹת בָּהֶם נֶפֶשׁ כָּל חָי. בָּרוּךְ חֵי (ויש אומרים: חַי) הָעוֹלָמִים.

Barukh ata Adonai, Eloheinu, melekh ha'olam, boreh nefashot rabot vehesronan, al kol ma shebarata (some substitute: shebara) lehahayot bahem nefesh kol hai, barukh hei (some substitute: hai) ha'olamim.

"Blessed are You, Lord our God, King of the universe, who creates the many forms of life [*boreh nefashot*] and their needs, for all that You have created (in some Ashkenazic communities: that He has created) to sustain the life of all that lives, blessed is the Giver of life to the worlds."

> **Further reading:** For more on the use of the phrase "Giver of life to the worlds" in reference to God, see *A Concise Guide to the Sages*, p. 8.

Even after merely drinking (a beverage other than wine) one recites *Boreh Nefashot*, provided that one has drunk at least a quarter of a *log* continuously. One generally does not recite a blessing after drinking hot drinks or alcoholic beverages as they are generally drunk slowly and not continuously.

A Meal with Bread

The Sages encouraged people to eat a meal every morning, called *pat shaharit*, "morning bread."

Animals First

The Torah states, "I will provide grass in your field for your animals, and you will eat and you will be satisfied" (Deuteronomy 11:15). Since the verse mentions the food of one's animals before one's own meal, the Sages derived that it is prohibited to eat before feeding the animals in one's possession.

Washing Hands before a Meal

Before eating bread, one must wash his hands, for reasons of both cleanliness and sanctity.

Daily Routine

The washing of hands is performed as follows: First one fills a cup with water. With the left hand, one pours water twice consecutively on the right hand, and then with his right hand does the same for his left hand. Some have the custom to pour three times in succession on each hand. It is best to wash one's hands with a copious amount of water, and this is considered auspicious for wealth. After washing hands, one rubs his hands together and recites the following blessing:

בָּרוּךְ אַתָּה אֲדֹנָי, אֱלֹהֵינוּ מֶלֶךְ הָעוֹלָם,   *Barukh ata Adonai, Eloheinu, melekh*
אֲשֶׁר קִדְּשָׁנוּ בְּמִצְוֹתָיו וְצִוָּנוּ עַל נְטִילַת   *ha'olam, asher kideshanu bemitzvotav,*
יָדָיִם.   *vetzivanu al netilat yadayim.*

"Blessed are You, Lord our God, King of the universe, who sanctified us through His mitzvot, and commanded us concerning the washing of the hands."

Upon the conclusion of the blessing, one dries his hands.

One who intends to eat less than the amount of an egg-bulk of bread should wash his hands in the normal manner, but without reciting the blessing.

📖 **Further reading:** The measure of an egg-bulk is twice the size of an olive-bulk; see the section entitled "Blessing after Food," p. 518.

A woman who is accustomed to removing her rings from her fingers when she kneads dough must remove the rings before she washes her hands for the meal, as they constitute an interposition, i.e., a separation between the water and her hands.

Blessings during a Meal

One must try to ensure that the blessing of *HaMotzi* is recited over the bread as close as possible to the washing of the hands. One should not cause an interruption between them by waiting a long time or through unnecessary talk that does not concern the meal.

At the start of the meal, one dips the bread in a little salt, among other reasons as a reminder that the offerings in the Temple were salted. Next, he recites the blessing of *HaMotzi* and partakes of the bread. This blessing renders one exempt from reciting a separate blessing for any of the other foods eaten at the meal. The reason is that almost everything one eats at the meal, including the main course and the side dishes, is considered subordinate to the bread.

An exception to this rule is dessert. This dish, which is not intended to satiate, and is therefore not part of the meal itself, is not subordinate to the bread. Therefore, one must recite a separate blessing for dessert, determined according to the particular dish he is eating.

Drinks consumed at a meal are also considered subordinate to the bread, so one does not recite a blessing over them. Wine and natural grape juice are exceptions, as due to their importance one recites the blessing of *Hagafen* over them, even during a meal. If one recited *Kiddush* over wine before the meal of Shabbat or a festival, or even merely tasted *Kiddush* wine before the meal, and then wants to drink wine during the meal as well, he is exempt from reciting another blessing over the wine, as the blessing over the wine of *Kiddush* also applies to the wine in the middle of the meal.

Manners and Etiquette

One should avoid speaking while his mouth is full, as this is a choking hazard. It is meritorious to speak words of Torah during the meal.

One should not stare at the face of a person who is eating, or at his plate, so as not to make him uncomfortable.

Grace after Meals

At the end of the meal one says Grace after Meals [*Birkat HaMazon*]. This blessing, which is recited after eating bread, encompasses all the other foods of the meal as well, including the dessert, drinks, and even the wine; one is therefore exempt from any other blessings after food for that meal. One should recite Grace after Meals in the place where he ate.

📖 Further reading: For more on Grace after Meals, see *A Concise Guide to the Sages*, p. 236.

During Grace after Meals, it is customary to leave any leftover bread on the table. After Grace after Meals one should try not to throw away leftover bread. If it is difficult to use these scraps as food for people or animals, they should be wrapped in a bag and only then thrown into the garbage, out of respect for the bread.

Before Grace after Meals, one pours water on the ends of his fingers, in order to cleanse them. This water is called *mayim aharonim*, "the final water," because it is poured at the end of the meal, in contrast to the washing of hands that is performed at the beginning of the meal.

Women are obligated to recite Grace after Meals. One should educate children to recite Grace after Meals, as one should educate them to perform all mitzvot.

Content of the Blessing

Grace after Meals consists of three blessings that are obligatory by Torah law:

(1) Blessing of nourishment: From the beginning of the blessing until "Blessed are You, Lord, who feeds all [hazan et hakol]." This is a blessing of thanksgiving for the food that God gave us.

(2) Blessing of the land: From "We thank You [Nodeh lekha]" until "Blessed are You, Lord, for the land and for the food [al ha'aretz ve'al hamazon]." This is a blessing of thanksgiving for the Land of Israel, the mitzva of circumcision, and the Torah.

(3) Blessing for Jerusalem: From "Have compassion [Rahem]" until "Blessed are You, Lord, who (in His compassion) will rebuild Jerusalem. Amen [boneh (verahamav) Yerushalayim. Amen]." This blessing requests that Jerusalem be rebuilt and the kingdom of David be restored.

The Sages added a fourth blessing to these three, which is called Hatov vehametiv, a blessing noting God's goodness. After this blessing it is customary to add a sequence of requests that all begin with the word HaRahaman, meaning the Compassionate One, which is a reference to God. For example, "May the Compassionate One reign over us," "May the Compassionate One grant us an honorable livelihood," and others.

The Laws of Zimmun

If three or more adult men ate bread together, they must recite Grace after Meals with a zimmun, an "invitation." A zimmun means that the diners join their blessings together, by means of one of the diners saying to the others, "Let us bless the One from whose food we have eaten." The others respond, "Blessed be the One from whose food we have eaten, and by whose goodness we live," and the one leading the zimmun repeats after them, "Blessed be the One from whose food we have eaten, and by whose goodness we live." Then each person recites Grace after Meals by himself.

According to the Ashkenazic custom, the one leading the zimmun says the entire first blessing (the blessing of nourishment) out loud, while the other diners recite the blessing quietly, in parallel to him. When the one leading the *zimmun* finishes the blessing, they answer "Amen," and then each continues Grace after Meals by himself.

When there are ten men present, the wording of the *zimmun* changes to include an explicit mention of God's name. In this situation, the one leading the *zimmun* says, "Blessed be our God from whose food we have eaten," the other diners answer, "Blessed be our God from whose food we have eaten, and by whose goodness we live," and the leader repeats what they said.

At a *zimmun*, any women who participated in the meal must also respond. Three women who ate together may recite Grace after Meals with a *zimmun* if they choose. Furthermore, if three women ate together with men but they want to have their own *zimmun* instead and participate in a *zimmun* alone, without the men, they may do so. If there are ten men present, which means that the *zimmun* includes the term "our God," the women join in and respond to the men's *zimmun* instead of having their own *zimmun*.

Blessings over Fragrances

Just as one recites blessings before eating or drinking, so too, one must recite a blessing before enjoying a pleasant fragrance. In these cases, too, the text of each blessing suits the type and origin of the aroma.

Types of Fragrance

When the source of the fragrance is from a tree, one recites the blessing,

בָּרוּךְ אַתָּה אֲדֹנָי, אֱלֹהֵינוּ מֶלֶךְ הָעוֹלָם,
בּוֹרֵא עֲצֵי בְשָׂמִים.

Barukh ata Adonai, Eloheinu, melekh ha'olam, boreh atzei vesamim.

"Blessed are You, Lord our God, King of the universe, who creates fragrant trees."

When the source of the scent is vegetation, one recites the blessing,

בָּרוּךְ אַתָּה אֲדֹנָי, אֱלֹהֵינוּ מֶלֶךְ הָעוֹלָם,
בּוֹרֵא עִשְׂבֵי / (לספרדים): עִשְׂבֵּי בְשָׂמִים.

Barukh ata Adonai, Eloheinu, melekh ha'olam, boreh isvei (Sephardim: isbei) vesamim.

"Blessed are You, Lord our God, King of the universe, who creates fragrant grasses."

If the fragrance does not fit either of the two categories above, such as if it is extracted from an animal, like musk oil, the blessing is,

בָּרוּךְ אַתָּה אֲדֹנָי, אֱלֹהֵינוּ מֶלֶךְ הָעוֹלָם,
בּוֹרֵא מִינֵי בְשָׂמִים.

Barukh ata Adonai, Eloheinu, melekh ha'olam, boreh minei vesamim.

"Blessed are You, Lord our God, King of the universe, who creates various spices."

If an edible fruit, or its peel, has a strong and pleasant scent, and one wants to enjoy its fragrance, he should first recite the blessing,

בָּרוּךְ אַתָּה אֲדֹנָי, אֱלֹהֵינוּ מֶלֶךְ הָעוֹלָם,
הַנּוֹתֵן רֵיחַ טוֹב בַּפֵּרוֹת.

Barukh ata Adonai, Eloheinu, melekh ha'olam, hanoten re'aḥ tov baperot.

"Blessed are You, Lord our God, King of the universe, who gives fruits pleasant fragrance."

Some say a slightly different version:

בָּרוּךְ אַתָּה אֲדֹנָי, אֱלֹהֵינוּ מֶלֶךְ הָעוֹלָם,
אֲשֶׁר נָתַן רֵיחַ טוֹב בַּפֵּרוֹת.

Barukh ata Adonai, Eloheinu, melekh ha'olam, asher natan re'aḥ tov baperot.

"Blessed are You, Lord our God, King of the universe, who gave fruits pleasant fragrance."

If one does not know the source of the pleasant fragrance, for example, whether it is from a tree or another plant; or if one smells fragrances from a variety of sources, mixed together, he recites the blessing, *Borei minei vesamim*, "Who creates various spices," as this is a general formula that covers all types of fragrances.

When No Blessing Is Required

One does not recite a blessing over a fragrance that is dispersed in order to counter an unpleasant odor, such as air freshener or perfumed soap for bathrooms. Likewise, no blessing is recited over synthetic aromas, which are produced in chemical processes from substances that are naturally odorless. One also does not recite a blessing if the source of the fragrance is not present, such as the case of a box that used to contain a fragrant fruit. This is termed "a fragrance without substance."

Daily Routine

Blessings of Thanksgiving and Praise

In addition to the routine blessings over daily pleasures, the Sages instituted blessings of praise and thanksgiving to God for less common experiences. The following are the more frequent of these:

Who Has Given Us Life [*Sheheheyanu*]

The most well-known blessing in this category is the *Sheheheyanu* blessing, instituted for those moments when one experiences joy in the wake of events that are not part of his daily routine.

בָּרוּךְ אַתָּה אֲדֹנָי, אֱלֹהֵינוּ מֶלֶךְ הָעוֹלָם,
שֶׁהֶחֱיָנוּ וְקִיְּמָנוּ וְהִגִּיעָנוּ לַזְּמַן הַזֶּה.

Barukh ata Adonai, Eloheinu, melekh ha'olam, sheheheyanu vekiyemanu vehigianu la'zeman hazeh.

"Blessed are You, Lord our God, King of the universe, who has given us life, sustained us, and brought us to this time."

On festivals one recites the *Sheheheyanu* blessing for the special day. Women recite this blessing when lighting candles for the festival, while men do so during the festival evening *Kiddush*. Likewise, before a mitzva that is performed at a special time, such as sitting in the *sukka*, lighting the Hanukkah candles for the first time that year, and reading the megilla on Purim, one recites *Sheheheyanu*.

If a person purchases or receives an item such as a new garment, jewelry, an important utensil, or a piece of furniture, and this brings him joy, he should recite the *Sheheheyanu* blessing. Since the joy is the decisive factor for this type of blessing, one does not recite the *Sheheheyanu* blessing when he buys something simple and mundane like a new undershirt, socks, a ladle, a stool, or the like, as these items do not bring one considerable joy.

In the case of fruit that grows at a certain season of the year and can be found in the markets only during this season, one recites the *Sheheheyanu* blessing when partaking of the fruit for the first time after its renewal in its season. Some first recite the blessing over the fruit, "Who creates fruit of the tree [*ha'etz*]," next recite the *Sheheheyanu* blessing, and then eat the fruit. Others recite the *Sheheheyanu* blessing before the blessing of *Ha'etz* over the fruit.

Daily Routine

Who Is Good and Does Good

When more than one person shares in an acquisition and its accompanying joy, they do not recite the *Sheheheyanu* blessing but rather the following blessing:

בָּרוּךְ אַתָּה אֲדֹנָי, אֱלֹהֵינוּ מֶלֶךְ הָעוֹלָם,   *Barukh ata Adonai, Eloheinu, melekh*
הַטּוֹב וְהַמֵּטִיב.   *ha'olam, hatov vehametiv.*

"Blessed are You, Lord our God, King of the universe, who is good and does good [*hatov vehametiv*]."

For example, if a couple bought a new home together, then when they enter their home to live in it or when they affix the *mezuzot*, they recite the blessing *Hatov vehametiv*. Additionally, at a meal where two types of wine are served, if the second is better than the first, one recites the blessing *Hatov vehametiv* before drinking the second wine.

Natural Phenomena

One who sees lightning in the sky recites the blessing,

בָּרוּךְ אַתָּה אֲדֹנָי, אֱלֹהֵינוּ מֶלֶךְ הָעוֹלָם,   *Barukh ata Adonai, Eloheinu, melekh*
עוֹשֶׂה מַעֲשֶׂה בְרֵאשִׁית.   *ha'olam, oseh ma'aseh vereshit.*

"Blessed are You, Lord our God, King of the universe, Author of creation."

One who hears thunder recites the blessing,

בָּרוּךְ אַתָּה אֲדֹנָי, אֱלֹהֵינוּ מֶלֶךְ הָעוֹלָם,   *Barukh ata Adonai, Eloheinu, melekh*
שֶׁכֹּחוֹ וּגְבוּרָתוֹ מָלֵא עוֹלָם.   *ha'olam, shekoho ugvurato maleh olam.*

"Blessed are You, Lord our God, King of the universe, whose strength and power fill the world."

If the lightning and thunder occur at the same time, one recites a single blessing, "Author of creation," over both of them.

One may recite the blessing over lightning or thunder only immediately after seeing or hearing it. If the amount of time that has passed since the event is sufficient for a person to say the three words *Shalom alekha rabbi* ("peace be upon you, my teacher"), one may no longer recite the blessing.

One who sees a tall and impressive mountain, such as Mount Hermon, Mount Tabor, or Mount Masada, recites the blessing,

בָּרוּךְ אַתָּה אֲדֹנָי, אֱלֹהֵינוּ מֶלֶךְ הָעוֹלָם, *Barukh ata Adonai, Eloheinu, melekh*
עוֹשֶׂה מַעֲשֶׂה בְרֵאשִׁית. *ha'olam, oseh ma'aseh vereshit.*

"Blessed are You, Lord our God, King of the universe, Author of creation."

Likewise, one who sees the Mediterranean or the Red Sea after not seeing them for at least thirty days recites the blessing "Author of creation."

By contrast, whoever sees the ocean after not having seen it for at least thirty days recites the blessing,

בָּרוּךְ אַתָּה אֲדֹנָי, אֱלֹהֵינוּ מֶלֶךְ הָעוֹלָם, *Barukh ata Adonai, Eloheinu, melekh*
שֶׁעָשָׂה אֶת הַיָּם הַגָּדוֹל. *ha'olam, she'asa et hayam hagadol.*

"Blessed are You, Lord our God, King of the universe, who made the great ocean."

If one sees a rainbow, he may glance at it briefly, but should not stare at it for a long time. When he sees it, he recites the blessing,

בָּרוּךְ אַתָּה אֲדֹנָי, אֱלֹהֵינוּ מֶלֶךְ הָעוֹלָם, *Barukh ata Adonai, Eloheinu, melekh*
זוֹכֵר הַבְּרִית, נֶאֱמָן בִּבְרִיתוֹ וְקַיָּם בְּמַאֲמָרוֹ. *ha'olam, zokher haberit, ne'eman bivrito, vekayam bema'amaro.*

"Blessed are You, Lord our God, King of the universe, who remembers the covenant, is faithful to His covenant, and fulfills His word."

The Wayfarer's Prayer

One who journeys between cities recites the Wayfarer's Prayer [*Tefillat HaDerekh*] to request protection against the dangers of the road. Some add additional verses tied to the theme of protection.

Which Journeys

In earlier generations, people would often journey from city to city on foot. The Sages established that one who walks a distance of about 4 km or more should say the Wayfarer's Prayer.

Nowadays, when intercity trips are generally undertaken in motorized vehicles, some still say the Wayfarer's Prayer on every journey between cities that is at least 4 km long. Others follow the practice that for short trips one recites the Wayfarer's Prayer without saying the name of God at its conclusion. According to this view, only when the trip lasts as long as the amount of time it takes to hike about 4 km, i.e., a ride of at least 72 minutes, does one recite the Wayfarer's Prayer with the name of God.

When to Recite

One should recite the Wayfarer's Prayer upon leaving the city, preferably as soon as he exits the inhabited areas. If one forgets to say it then, he can say it later on the journey.

One recites the Wayfarer's Prayer only once per day, even if he stops several times within one or more cities over the course of the journey. When one leaves a city and expects to return to that city on the same day, he adds the phrase "and return us in peace" to the text of the Wayfarer's Prayer. But if one will return only the next day, he does not add this clause; instead, he recites the entire Wayfarer's Prayer again on the following day.

Text

For Ashkenazim:

יְהִי רָצוֹן מִלְּפָנֶיךָ אֲדֹנָי אֱלֹהֵינוּ וֵאלֹהֵי אֲבוֹתֵינוּ, שֶׁתּוֹלִיכֵנוּ לְשָׁלוֹם וְתַצְעִידֵנוּ לְשָׁלוֹם, וְתִסְמְכֵנוּ לְשָׁלוֹם, וְתַנְחֵנוּ אֶל מְחוֹז חֶפְצֵנוּ לְחַיִּים וּלְשִׂמְחָה וּלְשָׁלוֹם. (וְתַחֲזִירֵנוּ לְבֵיתֵנוּ לְשָׁלוֹם). וְתַצִּילֵנוּ מִכַּף כָּל אוֹיֵב וְאוֹרֵב בַּדֶּרֶךְ וּמִכָּל מִינֵי פֻּרְעָנִיּוֹת הַמִּתְרַגְּשׁוֹת לָבוֹא לָעוֹלָם, וְתִשְׁלַח בְּרָכָה בְּמַעֲשֵׂה יָדֵינוּ. (לרבים יחד:) וְתִתְּנֵנוּ/ (ביחיד:) וְתִתְּנֵנִי (ויש אומרים תמיד: וְתִתְּנֵנִי) לְחֵן וּלְחֶסֶד וּלְרַחֲמִים בְּעֵינֶיךָ וּבְעֵינֵי כָל רוֹאֵינוּ, וְתִשְׁמַע קוֹל תַּחֲנוּנֵינוּ. כִּי אֵל שׁוֹמֵעַ תְּפִלָּה וְתַחֲנוּן אַתָּה. בָּרוּךְ אַתָּה אֲדֹנָי שׁוֹמֵעַ תְּפִלָּה.

Yehi ratzon milefanekha, Adonai Eloheinu velohei avoteinu, shetolikhenu leshalom vetatzidenu leshalom vetismekhenu leshalom vetanhenu el mehoz heftzenu lehayim lesimha ulshalom (if planning to return on the same day: vetahazirenu leveitenu leshalom). Vetatzilenu mikaf kol oyev ve'orev baderekh umikol minei puranuyot hamitragshot lavo la'olam. Vetishlah berakha bema'aseh yadeinu, vetitenenu (some rule that an individual substitutes: vetiteneni) lehen ulhesed ulrahamim be'einekha uveinei khol ro'einu, vetishma kol tahanuneinu, ki El shome'a tefila vetahanun ata. Barukh ata Adonai, shome'a tefila.

"May it be Your will, Lord, our God and the God of our forefathers, that You lead us toward peace, guide our steps toward peace, and support us in peace, and make us reach our desired destination in life, gladness, and peace (if planning to return on the same day add: and return us in peace). May You rescue us from the hand of every enemy and ambush along the way, and from all manner of punishments that assemble to come to earth. May You send blessing to our handiwork, and grant us (some say an individual says: grant me) grace, kindness, and mercy in Your eyes and in the eyes of all who see us. May You hear the sound of our supplication, because You are God who hears prayer and supplication. Blessed are You, Lord, who hears prayer."

For Sephardim:

יְהִי רָצוֹן מִלְּפָנֶיךָ אֲדֹנָי אֱלֹהֵינוּ וֵאלֹהֵי אֲבוֹתֵנוּ, שֶׁתּוֹלִיכֵנוּ לְשָׁלוֹם וְתַצִּילֵנוּ מִכַּף כָּל אוֹיֵב וְאוֹרֵב בַּדֶּרֶךְ, וּמִכָּל מִקְרֵה וּפֶגַע רָע. וְתַגִּיעֵנוּ לִמְחוֹז חֶפְצֵנוּ לְשָׁלוֹם. וְתִתְּנֵנוּ לְחֵן וּלְחֶסֶד וּלְרַחֲמִים בְּעֵינֶיךָ וּבְעֵינֵי כָל רוֹאֵינוּ. בָּרוּךְ אַתָּה אֲדֹנָי שׁוֹמֵעַ תְּפִלָּה.

Yehi ratzon milefanekha, Adonai Eloheinu velohei avoteinu, shetolikhenu leshalom, vetatzilenu mikaf kol oyev ve'orev baderekh, umikol mikreh ufega ra, vetagi'enu limḥoz ḥeftzenu leshalom. Vetitenenu leḥen ulḥesed ulraḥamim be'einekha uveinei khol ro'einu. Barukh ata Adonai, shome'a tefila.

Repeat three times:

וְיַעֲקֹב הָלַךְ לְדַרְכּוֹ וַיִּפְגְּעוּ בוֹ מַלְאֲכֵי אֱלֹהִים, וַיֹּאמֶר יַעֲקֹב כַּאֲשֶׁר רָאָם, מַחֲנֵה אֱלֹהִים זֶה. וַיִּקְרָא שֵׁם הַמָּקוֹם הַהוּא מַחֲנָיִם.

VeYa'akov halakh ledarko, vayifge'u vo malakhei Elohim. Vayyomer Ya'akov ka'asher ra'am: Maḥaneh Elohim zeh. Vayyikra shem hammakom hahu Maḥanayim.

שִׁיר לַמַּעֲלוֹת, אֶשָּׂא עֵינַי אֶל הֶהָרִים, מֵאַיִן יָבֹא עֶזְרִי: עֶזְרִי מֵעִם אֲדֹנָי, עֹשֵׂה שָׁמַיִם וָאָרֶץ: אַל יִתֵּן לַמּוֹט רַגְלֶךָ, אַל יָנוּם שֹׁמְרֶךָ: הִנֵּה לֹא יָנוּם וְלֹא יִישָׁן, שׁוֹמֵר יִשְׂרָאֵל: אֲדֹנָי שֹׁמְרֶךָ, אֲדֹנָי צִלְּךָ עַל יַד יְמִינֶךָ: יוֹמָם הַשֶּׁמֶשׁ לֹא יַכֶּכָּה וְיָרֵחַ בַּלָּיְלָה: אֲדֹנָי יִשְׁמָרְךָ מִכָּל רָע, יִשְׁמֹר אֶת נַפְשֶׁךָ: אֲדֹנָי יִשְׁמֹר צֵאתְךָ וּבוֹאֶךָ, מֵעַתָּה וְעַד עוֹלָם:

Shir lamma'alot: Essa einai el heharim, me'ayin yavo ezri. Ezri me'im Adonai, oseh shamayim va'aretz. Al yitten lammot raglekha, al yanum shomerekha. Hineh lo yanum velo yishan, shomer Yisrael. Adonai shomerekha, Adonai tzillekha al yad yeminekha. Yomam, hashemesh lo yakkekka, veyare'aḥ ballayla. Adonai yishmorkha mikkol ra, yishmor et nefshekha. Adonai yishmor tzetekha uvo'ekha me'atta ve'ad olam.

Daily Routine

"May it be Your will, Lord, our God and the God of our forefathers, that You lead us toward peace, and rescue us from the hand of every enemy and ambush along the way, and from any evil occurrence or mishap and make us reach our desired destination in peace. And grant us grace, kindness, and mercy in Your eyes and in the eyes of all who see us. Blessed are You, Lord, who hears prayer."

Repeat three times: "And Jacob went on his way and angels of God met him. When he saw them, Jacob said, 'This is God's camp,' and he named the place Mahanayim."

"A song of ascents. I lift my eyes up to the hills; from where will my help come? My help comes from the Lord, Maker of heaven and earth. He will not let your foot stumble; He who guards you does not slumber. See: the Guardian of Israel neither slumbers nor sleeps. The Lord is your Guardian; the Lord is your Shade at your right hand. The sun will not strike you by day, nor the moon by night. The Lord will guard you from all harm; He will guard your life. The Lord will guard your going and coming, now and for evermore."

Many have the practice to say various other verses following the Wayfarer's Prayer.

Various Topics

Mezuza

One of the 613 mitzvot of the Torah is that of placing a *mezuza* on one's door. The source for the command to affix the *mezuza* appears in two passages in the Torah that have identical wording: "You shall write them on the doorposts of your house, and on your gates" (Deuteronomy 6:9, 11:21). The Torah commands us to write those passages and affix them to the doorways of our homes.

The two passages in which the mitzva of *mezuza* appears are the first paragraph of *Shema*, beginning with the words *Shema Yisrael* (Deuteronomy 6:4–9), as well as the passage beginning *Vehaya im shamo'a* (11:13–21). These two passages, both of which are recited daily in the prayers as part of *Shema*, are the passages that are written on the *mezuza* parchment.

> Further reading: The full content of the passages of a *mezuza* can be found in *A Concise Guide to the Torah*, pp. 451, 462; for insights of the Sages on these sections, see *A Concise Guide to the Sages*, pp. 231, 236.

The text of the *mezuza* begins with the first verse of *Shema*: "Hear, Israel: The Lord is our God, the Lord is one" (Deuteronomy 6:4), which expresses our faith in the one and only God. It is followed by the commands to love God, to place His commandments upon our hearts, to teach them to our children, to speak about the Torah in the mornings and the evenings, and to affix *mezuzot* to our doorways. The passages end with the promise that if we follow these commandments, we and our children will merit long lives in the Promised Land.

A *mezuza* is placed on all the doorways of one's house so that when one enters and exits through them, the *mezuza* will be a constant reminder of the existence of the Creator and the requirement to love Him and to keep His mitzvot. That is why some people place a hand on the *mezuza* every time they pass through a door, and many even kiss it out of love for the mitzva.

The *mezuza* also serves as a sign that this is a Jewish home, under the protection of the Creator and Ruler of the world. Jews throughout the ages were careful to observe this mitzva, as they would affix *mezuzot* to their doorways even if they lived in hostile environments. The Sages also understood that the *mezuza* serves to protect the house and its inhabitants. This is alluded to in the name of God that is inscribed on the outside of the *mezuza* parchment, *Shadai*, which is interpreted as an acronym for the words *Shomer daltot Yisrael*, the "Guardian of the doorways of Israel."

Quality of the *Mezuza*

A *mezuza* can be of varying degrees of quality, dependent on several factors: the quality of the parchment, the beauty of the writing, and the personal attributes of the scribe who wrote it. The scribe must meticulously write each letter by hand according to its precise requirements. As this is easier to do when the size of the parchment and letters is larger, small *mezuzot* are usually of poorer quality than large ones. It is possible, however, for a small *mezuza* to be written with great precision, and in that case it will in fact generally be more expensive than a large *mezuza*, as its writing requires more painstaking effort to achieve the same level of accuracy.

The Parchment

The *mezuza* parchment must be made from the skin of a kosher animal, which has been tanned and processed with special intent to be used for the mitzva of *mezuza*. There are various levels with regard to the quality of the parchment. Some manufacturers coat the parchment with white lime wash, which facilitates writing on its surface. However, the lime makes the *mezuza* more susceptible to damage from moisture and deterioration over time. Furthermore, the lime can crack, which may cause damage to the letters. Therefore, one should avoid buying such *mezuzot*.

It is important to keep in mind that a *mezuza* printed on paper, even if the paper closely resembles parchment, is not valid for the mitzva. This is not a *mezuza* at all, and the residents of a house with such a *mezuza* do not fulfill the mitzva. Unfortunately, some distributors sell forgeries of this kind, and this is another reason to buy *mezuzot* only from a reliable vendor. The best way to obtain kosher *mezuzot* of superior quality is to buy them from a God-fearing scribe, with whom one is familiar and who is trustworthy, or from a store run by reliable, God-fearing people.

The Scribe

The *mezuza* is written by a scribe, known as a *sofer Stam*, "a writer of *Stam*," *Stam* being an acronym for *sifrei Torah* (Torah scrolls), *tefillin* (phylacteries), and *mezuzot*. This is a professional scribe who has studied this special art of writing, along with its *halakhot*, and is qualified to perform this holy task.

The scribe must be a trustworthy, God-fearing man. The fulfillment of the many *halakhot* of writing a *mezuza* depends on his integrity; since some of them depend on the intent of the scribe, no one else can know if he was in truth stringent about them and had the proper intent in mind.

Quill and Ink

The *mezuza* is written with a feather quill. Special black ink is used; the ink is made by a process that must also meet the requirements of a series of *halakhot*.

📖 **Further reading:** For an interesting explanation on why a *mezuza* must be written with a quill, see *A Concise Guide to the Sages,* p. 361.

The *Mezuza* Case

The completed *mezuza* is rolled up (preferably by an expert) from the end to the beginning, with the writing on the inside. Then it is wrapped, usually in plastic wrap, to guard it from weather damage, and placed in a protective case. The *mezuza* case has no halakhic significance, and therefore there are no rules about the material from which it may be made, or its shape. However, if a *mezuza* is affixed to the doorpost in a room where a married couple sleeps (and the door is on the outside of the doorpost), it should be in an opaque rather than a transparent case.

Two important points should be borne in mind:

(1) The *mezuza* case is merely an external covering, and at most it may be said to be an embellishment of the mitzva, but it is not the main mitzva object. The greater investment of one's money should be focused on the quality of the *mezuza* parchment.

(2) Some people mistakenly place the rolled parchment facing downward, which means that the *mezuza* is upside down. The *mezuza* must be affixed to the doorpost with the writing facing upward. An inverted *mezuza* is not valid and it is as if it is not there at all. If a *mezuza* was affixed upside down, it must be reset in the correct position.

Affixing a *Mezuza*

After one has acquired a good-quality *mezuza*, there are several *halakhot* regarding how and where to place it in the doorway of the house.

Placement of a *Mezuza*

The *mezuza* should be affixed to the doorpost, on the right side of the doorway as one enters the room. It should be placed on the bottom of the upper third of the doorframe, but it is valid if it is higher than that, as long as it is at least ten centimeters from the top of the doorpost.

The *mezuza* can be attached to the doorpost in any manner that holds it firm, such as with nails, screws, or glue.

Various Topics

There is a difference in custom between Ashkenazim and Sephardim about the positioning of the *mezuza* on the doorpost. According to the Sephardic custom, it should be set vertically along the length of the doorpost. The Ashkenazic custom is to place the *mezuza* on a slight diagonal, with its upper side tilted toward the inside of the room and the lower side angled outward; see illustration.

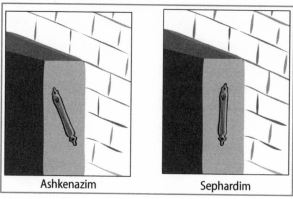

| Ashkenazim | Sephardim |

Position of a *mezuza*

Before affixing a *mezuza,* one recites the following blessing:

בָּרוּךְ אַתָּה אֲדֹנָי, אֱלֹהֵינוּ מֶלֶךְ הָעוֹלָם,
אֲשֶׁר קִדְּשָׁנוּ בְּמִצְוֹתָיו וְצִוָּנוּ לִקְבּוֹעַ מְזוּזָה.

Barukh ata Adonai, Eloheinu, melekh ha'olam, asher kideshanu bemitzvotav, vetzivanu likbo'a mezuza.

"Blessed are You, Lord our God, King of the universe, who sanctified us through His commandments, and commanded us to affix a *mezuza*."

When affixing mezuzot in several doorways in the house, one recites the blessing only once, before affixing the first *mezuza*, and this blessing applies to the other *mezuzot* as well.

Cases of Uncertainty

In certain situations, there may be a doubt as to whether there is an obligation to affix a *mezuza* in a particular doorway, or there may be doubt about its proper location. In such cases, a rabbi should be consulted.

The following are some examples of situations in which there is uncertainty as to the obligation of setting a *mezuza* or its location: when the lintel on top of the door is round rather than straight; when the door closes on the outside of the lintel rather than under it; when the doorway is particularly high; when there is not enough space for attaching a *mezuza* inside the door-way.

In all the rooms of the house, the *mezuza* is affixed on the doorpost to the right side as one enters the room, coming from the entrance of the house. If two rooms are open to each other such that a doorway can be accessed from either side and it is not obvious in which direction one is considered to be "entering" and in which direction one is considered to be "leaving," the determination is made based on the common flow of traffic. If the flow of traffic is equal in each direction, the *mezuza* should be affixed on the right side of the doorpost as one pushes the door open from one room to the other. In case of doubt, one should consult a rabbi.

Which Rooms?

The obligation to affix a *mezuza* applies to the main entrance of every residence, as well as the doorways to all the internal rooms that are used for residential purposes and whose size exceeds four square meters. This category includes bedrooms, storage rooms, balconies, courtyards, and stairwells.

No *mezuza* should be placed at the entrance to bathrooms.

Levels of Importance

The *mezuzot* on the doors of the house are all significant, but the *mezuza* that is affixed at the main entrance of the house is of special importance. There are two practical ramifications to this concept:

(1) If one cannot afford to buy superior-quality *mezuzot* for all the doorways, the *mezuza* for the main entrance is the most important and, therefore, it is worthwhile to invest in it before the others.

(2) There is a halakhic rule that in matters of holiness "one may raise up but not lower," i.e., one may promote an object of sanctity from an inferior to a superior position, but not vice versa. Therefore, one should not "demote" a *mezuza* by moving it from the main entrance of the house to one of its interior rooms.

Checking *Mezuzot*

Mezuzot should be taken down to be examined every three and a half years. Some people have them checked once a year, in the month of Elul. The examination should be performed by one who is well versed in the relevant *halakhot*.

If the *mezuzot* were found to be kosher, there is disagreement between halakhic authorities about whether to recite the blessing "to affix the *mezuza*" when returning them to their places. Each person should follow the custom of his community and the instruction of his rabbi. If a *mezuza* was disqualified and replaced, all agree that one must recite a blessing when affixing the new *mezuza*.

📖 **Further reading:** The full content of the passages of a *mezuza* can be found in *A Concise Guide to the Torah*, pp. 451, 462; for insights of the Sages on these sections, see *A Concise Guide to the Sages*, pp. 231, 236.

Kashrut

The *kashrut* of food, i.e., its acceptability to be eaten according to *halakha*, is one of the most distinctive characteristics of a Jewish lifestyle. The practice of *kashrut* occupies an extensive place in the written Torah, the Talmud, and the halakhic literature. The Torah itself presents a list of animals that one may eat and those that are forbidden for consumption (see Leviticus 11). Yet, in order to eat meat, it is not enough merely to know that it comes from a kosher species of animal; there are several other matters that must be addressed before one may eat it. *Kashrut* also applies to fruits and vegetables, which one may likewise eat only under certain conditions.

In general, the *halakhot* of *kashrut* can be divided into several parts, and their laws will be presented below accordingly.

Minerals: All minerals are kosher, that is, anything produced from inanimate materials (such as salts), by any manner of processing, is kosher and may be eaten.

Food from plants: The prohibition of *orla* applies to fruits, which means that it is prohibited to eat the fruits of a tree in the first three years after it has been planted. If fruits or vegetables are grown in the Land of Israel, one must separate *teruma* and tithes from them before they may be eaten. Questions of *kashrut* of fruits and vegetables grown in the Land of Israel also arise in the Sabbatical Year. Furthermore, it is important to distinguish between unprocessed fruits and vegetables, and those that people process through fermentation, cooking, and so on, with regard to which there are more potential *kashrut* issues.

Animal products: Only some species of animals are kosher. Every kosher-species animal (apart from fish) must be slaughtered in a prescribed manner, and one must remove the blood from the meat, as well as certain tendons and fats. Likewise, one must separate between meat and dairy products. The laws of *kashrut* include being careful not to eat insects or worms that can be found in fruits, vegetables, and fish.

The first part of this section lists the various types of permitted and forbidden foods. The second part focuses on the actual practice of keeping kosher: managing a kosher kitchen, kashering utensils (i.e., rendering utensils fit for use), eating in restaurants, and more.

Various Topics

Wine

Wine can present a unique problem. There is an ancient prohibition, alluded to in the book of Daniel, against drinking the wine of gentiles. This prohibition includes any wine that was not stored in a closed and sealed vessel and which was touched by a gentile. The reason for this prohibition is the concern that drinking the wine of gentiles might cause Jews to be tempted to assimilate into gentile culture and to intermarry.

📖 **Further reading:** On the dangers of overindulgence in wine in general, see *A Concise Guide to the Sages*, pp. 15, 141.

Wine of Gentiles

One may not drink wine made by gentiles. The same restriction applies to any beverage made by gentiles that is produced by refining or processing wine (cognac, brandy, champagne, and the like). It does not apply to other liquors that are not produced from grapes. Therefore, beer, apple cider, whiskey, vodka, and the like, can all be kosher even when produced by gentiles. Sometimes a problem can arise with regard to their consumption during Passover; see the section dealing with the *halakhot* of Passover.

If the wine underwent a process of cooking before a gentile touched it, no prohibition applies to it; this is the *halakha* with regard to pasteurized wine. If someone is hosting non-Jewish guests, he is advised to use cooked wine, or not to bring wine to the table at all, in order to avoid problems of *kashrut* and a possible uncomfortable situation.

There are alcoholic drinks that, while generally kosher, sometimes involve *kashrut* problems, such as a mixture of milk with vodka or liquor, a mixture of wine with whiskey, or moth larva that is found in certain types of tequila (mescal). It is recommended to consult a rabbi who specializes in *kashrut* or to purchase only products that have a reliable kosher certification.

Baked Goods

A basic question arises regarding all types of sweetened or seasoned baked goods: With what were they sweetened or seasoned, and which other ingredients do they contain? Even when the manufacturer is required by law to specify the ingredients of a product, the list in most cases will not include ingredients of minute quantities, and it also will not specify the manner of preparation of the product. Therefore, when buying such baked goods, one must make sure that they include the stamp of a reliable *kashrut* agency. Since it is impossible to know which ingredients are present in any product, and since a product can become non-kosher simply by being produced on non-kosher equipment, even plain bread requires kosher certification.

Bread of a Gentile

The Sages prohibited one to eat bread produced by a non-Jew. This prohibition was not applied to bread that is mass produced by a professional baker. However, bread produced in a private non-Jewish home is prohibited, even if one knows that the ingredients and equipment used were all kosher. Some are stringent and will not even eat bread baked in a non-Jewish bakery unless the oven was lit by a Jew.

Separating *Halla*

The commandment to separate a small piece of dough [*halla*] is one of the mitzvot assigned to Jewish women, who are usually the ones responsible for the running of the kitchen at home. Originally, *halla* had to be given to a priest, as it is one of the "gifts of the priesthood" to which they are entitled for their devotion to the Temple service. The source of the commandment is the following passage from the Torah: "Speak to the children of Israel, and say to them: When you come to the land that I am bringing you there, it shall be, when you eat from the bread of the land, you shall set aside a gift for the Lord. The first of your kneading basket you shall set aside a loaf as a gift; like the gift from the threshing floor, so shall you set it aside. From the first of your kneading basket you shall give to the Lord a gift for your generations" (Numbers 15:18–21).

Like *teruma*, *halla* must be eaten by the priest in a state of ritual purity. Since the destruction of the Temple, it is impossible to attain ritual purity, and so today one is not required to give *halla* to the priests. Still, the command to separate *halla* applies nowadays as well. It is performed in commemoration of the original, full-fledged mitzva, in anticipation of the coming of the messiah and the rebuilding of the Temple. The separation also reminds one that everything he owns comes from God.

Performing the Mitzva

It is best to separate *halla* from the raw dough. According to Ashkenazic custom, one separates an olive-bulk (about 27 grams) of dough. If one failed to set aside the *halla* before baking, it should be separated afterward, with the stipulation that the separation is also for any substance that has been absorbed in the walls of the oven and the sides of the baking pan.

Not all situations are subject to the separation of *halla*; see below for details. Before separating *halla* from dough that is definitely subject to the requirement of *halla*, one recites a blessing:

בָּרוּךְ אַתָּה אֲדֹנָי, אֱלֹהֵינוּ מֶלֶךְ הָעוֹלָם, אֲשֶׁר קִדְּשָׁנוּ בְּמִצְוֹתָיו וְצִוָּנוּ לְהַפְרִישׁ חַלָּה (יֵשׁ מוֹסִיפִים: מִן הָעִיסָה).

Barukh ata Adonai, Eloheinu, melekh ha'olam, asher kideshanu bemitzvotav, vetzivanu lehafrish ḥalla (some add: min ha'isa).

Various Topics

"Blessed are You, Lord our God, King of the universe, who sanctified us through His commandments, and commanded us to separate *halla* (some add: from dough)."

One then burns the *halla* in fire, outdoors or on the stove, wrapped in silver foil. It is not necessary to burn it immediately; rather, one may accumulate several pieces of *halla* and burn them together. One who finds it difficult to burn the *halla* may wrap it in plastic and discard it in the garbage.

The obligation to separate *halla* applies only when one prepares a certain minimum amount of dough. There are differing opinions regarding this amount. On a practical level, one should set aside *halla* without a blessing if the dough contains at least 1.230 kg of flour. According to Rabbi Hayyim Na'eh (one of the most expert halakhic authorities of recent generations with regard to halakhic measurements), a blessing is recited over the separation of *halla* if there is at least 1.666 kg of flour in the dough. Some recite the blessing only if the dough contains no less than 2.250 kg of flour.

It is prohibited to split a large batch of dough into smaller pieces for the purpose of exempting oneself from the obligation to separate *halla*.

Animal Products

This is a very broad category, and different laws apply to each type of animal.

📖 **Further reading:** The source for the *halakhot* of *kashrut* for animals can be found in *A Concise Guide to the Torah*, pp. 272, 468.

Invertebrates

All invertebrates are prohibited for consumption. The prohibition includes mollusks, snails, oysters, crabs, and all species of insects, spiders, arthropods, and many more.

There is one exception: In principle it is permitted to eat certain species of grasshoppers. In fact, eating grasshoppers was (and still is) accepted among the members of a few Jewish communities, particularly Yemenite and North African Jews. In other communities, however, the eating of any kind of grasshopper is avoided.

The prohibition against eating insects includes substances that come from their bodies. Nevertheless, it is permitted to eat the honey of bees. This permission, which can be traced to biblical sources, is based on the fact that the honey is not fully produced by the bees: It is essentially flower nectar that is broken down by an enzyme in the bee's saliva, and thereby turns into honey. Pure honey does not require kosher certification, provided that it is free of admixtures.

Checking for Insects

Considering the prohibition against eating bugs, one must carefully examine vegetables and grains in which various types of worms and insects are likely to be found. It is especially necessary to examine herbs, lettuce, cabbage, cauliflower, and dried fruits. One should seek guidance in how to ensure that one's vegetables and fruits are bug-free.

Leafy vegetables: Where available, it is best to purchase vegetables that have been specially grown in a manner that allows them to be relatively free of bugs, such as in the greenhouse system developed in Gush Katif. These vegetables are separated from the ground soil, which greatly reduces the incidence of bugs in the vegetables.

Sifting flour: Insects can often be found in flour and similar substances. The most common of these is the flour beetle. Proper pest control can prevent the insect from multiplying, but any insects that are already in the flour must be removed by thorough sifting.

Rice and beans: There can also be insects in rice and other grains. The usual sign for the presence of larvae is webbing and clumping. One must examine the grains carefully to make sure that they contain no insects. In the case of chickpeas and beans, it is recommended to perform the examination after they have been soaked in water and have swelled.

Amphibians, Reptiles, and Fish

Amphibians: Frogs, toads, and the like are all prohibited for consumption.

Reptiles: All types of lizards, snakes, and turtles are prohibited for consumption.

Fish: The Torah distinguishes between kosher and non-kosher species of fish: Fish that have fins and scales are permitted to be eaten, whereas fish without fins and scales are forbidden. This division overlaps to a large extent, though not absolutely, with the zoological division between Osteichthyes, bony fish whose skeletons are primarily composed of bone tissue and which are permitted for consumption, and Chondrichthyes, whose skeletons are made of cartilage rather than bone, most of which are predatory fish, and which may not be eaten.

Most fish that people eat are halakhically permitted for consumption. One can perform a simple test to see if a fish is kosher, by examining whether it has scales. A fish that has visible scales, which can be removed from its skin, is kosher.

Sharks, catfish, and eels are not kosher.

There are several species of fish whose status in Jewish law is unclear, and sometimes the practical question of whether one may eat them or not depends on the local custom.

The distinction between kosher and non-kosher fish, as with all animals, includes all their by-products, from fish oil to caviar. Some types of caviar are kosher while others are not; it depends on the fish from whose eggs the caviar is made. For example, one should not eat black Russian caviar, which is produced from the sturgeon, a non-kosher fish.

All other water creatures are prohibited for consumption, including, as noted, crabs and clams, and, of course, marine mammals, from seals to whales. All products produced from these marine mammals are prohibited as well.

Unlike animals and poultry, there are almost no halakhic problems with regard to kosher fish. It is permitted to kill fish in any manner, and it is permitted to consume their blood as well. The reason it is permitted to consume the blood of fish, unlike the blood of kosher birds and animals, is that the verse states: "And all blood you shall not eat in any of your dwellings, of bird or of animal" (Leviticus 7:26), with no mention of fish.

It is permitted to eat fish as part of either a meat or a dairy meal. Nevertheless, one may not cook fish and meat in the same pot, nor eat them together. Rather, one should take a short break between fish and meat dishes, by having a drink or something similar.

Poultry

There are many *kashrut* considerations pertaining to poultry, and each requires a separate discussion.

The first factor is the identification of permitted and prohibited birds. The Torah provides a list of non-kosher birds, but not all species in the list can currently be identified with certainty. Although the Sages provided certain signs of *kashrut* for various birds, in practice the number of species of birds that one may eat without concern is quite limited. These include certain common domestic birds: chickens, turkeys, geese, ducks, and pigeons.

After one has confirmed that the bird is indeed kosher, there are a few steps one must perform before it may be eaten. The first of these is slaughter.

Nowadays, the slaughter of birds is carried out by professional ritual slaughterers who have the appropriate certificate from an authorized rabbi, attesting to their knowledge of the *halakhot* as well as their practical skills. Apart from performing the act of slaughter itself, an expert must ensure that the bird is not afflicted with a wound or sickness that renders it a *tereifa*.[1] Furthermore, if something goes wrong during the process of slaughtering, the slaughter is disqualified and the bird is defined as a *neveila*, an unslaughtered animal carcass.

In summary, *halakha* permits the eating of kosher birds, provided that they are healthy and are slaughtered according to Jewish law.

Next, the bird must be "kashered," or rendered kosher, which involves removing its blood to the maximum extent, as the Torah prohibits consuming the blood of poultry and land animals. Kashering is performed by salting the meat and washing it in water. Today, most of the poultry and meat that is sold in supervised shops and markets which have kosher certificates has already been salted properly in the slaughterhouse or in an adjacent facility, and there is no need to do anything further to render it kosher.

> **Further reading:** The sources for the prohibition against consuming blood can be read in *A Concise Guide to the Torah*, p. 466.

Raw liver cannot be kashered by salting. Therefore, even if it is purchased in a kosher butcher shop, one must kasher it by sprinkling a little salt on it and roasting it on a fire to remove its blood. Then one should rinse it in cold water. If liver that has not been roasted in fire was cooked in a pot, it renders the pot non-kosher.

With regard to hearts, there are different opinions, and one should consult a rabbi.

Eggs: Eggs may be eaten only if they come from kosher birds or fish. The eggs of non-kosher birds and reptiles are prohibited.

---

1. *Tereifa* is a halakhic category that refers to an animal with an injury that will cause it to die within twelve months.

Most of the eggs sold today are non-fertilized, and they contain virtually no blood. Nevertheless, there can sometimes be blood in an egg, and this blood is prohibited for consumption. Therefore, it is advisable not to crack an egg directly into a pan or a dough; instead, it should be cracked over a bowl or a glass and the egg should subsequently be examined to ensure that it is free of blood. Only then may one use it in cooking.

Mammals: The Torah states that animals that chew their cud and have cloven hooves may be eaten, whereas animals that lack both or one of these characteristics may not be eaten. Among domesticated animals one may eat cattle, sheep and goats, while among the non-domesticated animals one may eat all types of deer and gazelles, which constitute a defined zoological family. All other mammals are prohibited, and from a halakhic point of view, there is no difference between the prohibitions of eating a horse, a camel, or a pig.

As is the case for birds, one must observe the laws of ritual slaughter and *tereifa* with regard to mammals. An animal that was not properly slaughtered, or which is classified as *tereifa*, may not be eaten.

There are more incidences of *tereifa* in mammals than in birds, and therefore, after their slaughter one must conduct a more comprehensive and thorough examination.

In this regard, there are those who are careful to eat only meat that is "*glatt*," literally "smooth," i.e., meat with regard to which no questions arose during its slaughter or subsequent examination, and which is therefore kosher according to all opinions.

📖 Further reading: For more on the various levels of *kashrut* and their meaning, see p. 573.

Other Prohibitions Involving Animals

There are other prohibitions that apply to the flesh of animals: the prohibition against eating specific fats, and the prohibition against eating the *gid hanasheh*, the sciatic nerve. There are professionals whose job is to remove these forbidden parts from the meat.

It is interesting to note that the ancient Chinese called the Jews who lived among them "the people who remove the nerve," as an acknowledgement of their religious observance.

📖 Further reading: This prohibition is in commemoration of our forefather Jacob's wrestling with the angel, which is described in *A Concise Guide to the Torah*, p. 81.

There are some communities in which the hind parts of the animal (where the sciatic nerve is located) are not sold as kosher meat, either due to a lack of familiarity with the *halakhot* of removing the nerve, or because of the great effort that this procedure entails.

The meat of the animal must be kashered (see above) after the slaughter, to remove all of its blood.

> 📖 **Further reading:** For more on eating meat and vegetarianism, see *A Concise Guide to Mahshava*, p. 122.

Milk and Dairy Products

A special status applies to milk produced by gentiles. Due to the concern that non-kosher substances might have been mixed into the milk in an attempt to reduce its cost, the Sages decreed that milk is kosher only if a Jew milked it from a kosher animal, or at least supervised its milking. This is known as *halav Yisrael* (sometimes spelled *cholov Yisroel*).

The Laws of Milking Performed by a Gentile

Certain halakhic authorities of recent generations have accepted the ruling that if there is organized governmental supervision of the dairy industry (such as the FDA in the United States), which protects consumers against fraud and deception in the agricultural industry, this guarantees that a product marketed as 100 percent cow's milk is indeed exactly that, and therefore, it is tantamount to a certificate of *kashrut*. In practice, this means that although no Jew supervised the milking, it is permissible to drink the milk.

There are many halakhic authorities who do not accept this innovation of permitting milk obtained without Jewish supervision. Therefore, many of those who are strict about matters of *kashrut* are careful to consume only *halav Yisrael*.

As for products made from powdered milk, many halakhic authorities are more lenient here, as in their opinion, the entire prohibition of milk from gentiles applies only to milk that is in its original form. But those who are especially stringent will be careful even with regard to powdered milk and will only consume products whose milk ingredients are all *halav Yisrael*.

The Prohibition of Cooking Meat in Milk

A piece of meat can be strictly kosher, and milk and its products might also be fully kosher, but if they are cooked together, not only will the meal not be kosher, but the utensils and dishes in which they were cooked will become non-kosher, and they must undergo a process to render them kosher once again. The separation between meat and milk is a central feature of a kosher kitchen.

📖 **Further reading:** For more on the prohibition of cooking meat and milk together, see *A Concise Guide to the Torah*, pp. 193, 225, 469.

Three Prohibitions Involving Meat

According to Torah law, it is prohibited to cook meat and milk together. It is also prohibited to eat meat and milk that were cooked together, or even to derive any benefit from meat and milk that were cooked together. Consequently, it is even prohibited to feed this mixture to one's animals or to sell it to a gentile.

Poultry

In the case of poultry with milk, only the middle of the three aforementioned prohibitions applies. That is, it is prohibited to eat poultry with milk. There is no prohibition against cooking them together, nor is it prohibited to derive benefit from the mixture. Consequently, it is permitted to feed such food to house pets or to sell it to a gentile. Nevertheless, the vessel in which it was cooked is considered not kosher.

Enactments, Customs, and Recommendations

Over the generations, in order to prevent confusion and error, the Sages have maintained that one should have separate sets of dishes for meat and dairy foods. Likewise, the Sages instituted that those participating in the same meal, or even if they are merely eating separate meals at a single table, should not eat meat and milk at the same time, unless they are eating on separate tablecloths or placemats.

The category of meat includes the meat itself, its soup, the sauce made from it, and any food that contains meat. In practice, one should be careful even regarding foods that have been cooked in a pot used for meat. For all these, one should use not only specific cooking pots and baking utensils, but also separate sets of dishes and cutlery.

In order to prevent mistakes, it is customary to have distinguishing marks to separate dishes and utensils used for milk or meat. It is also best to use different tablecloths for meat and dairy meals.

Furthermore, one should not wash meat and dairy vessels together after use. In many homes, two separate sinks are installed in the kitchen for this purpose, to avoid mistakes. In any case in which a dairy utensil was used for meat dishes or vice versa, it is possible that the utensil has been rendered non-kosher and is now prohibited for use. If one wishes to keep the item and continue using it, he must ask a rabbi how to kasher it.

📖 **Further reading:** For details, see the chapter on kashering kitchenware, p. 560. The source for the *halakha* of kashering kitchenware can be found in *A Concise Guide to the Torah*, p. 419; *A Concise Guide to the Sages*, p. 216.

This separation between meat and dairy applies to almost all kitchenware items. Special care should be taken with regard to earthenware, metal, and wooden products, as well as ceramics. It is permitted to use the same drinking glasses for meat and dairy meals (after they have been thoroughly washed, of course), but many maintain separate glasses nonetheless.

The use of items made of plastic materials raises many halakhic problems. To avoid situations of uncertainty, one must be very careful to use completely different utensils of this type for meat and dairy.

Waiting between Meals

In addition to the prohibition against eating meat and milk together, the Sages decreed that one must wait a certain period of time between eating meat and consuming milk and dairy products.

After eating a meat meal, it is customary in many Jewish communities to wait six hours before drinking milk or eating dairy products. According to various local customs, this waiting period is shorter.

By contrast, the waiting time after consuming dairy foods before eating meat is only half an hour, or an hour at most. It is recommended, however, to be strict to wait after eating hard cheese, meaning cheese that is aged for at least six months, as one does after eating meat. Some *kashrut* agencies post lists of cheeses in this category, which can be found online.

Foods that contain neither meat nor dairy products are called pareve (also spelled *parve*), meaning "neutral." These may be eaten with either meat or milk. It is worthwhile to clarify whether any given compound food is pareve by consulting with the individual who made it or by examining the kosher certification of store-bought items.

Cooking with Milk and Dairy Products

Managing a kosher kitchen requires the careful monitoring of milk and dairy products.

Of course, one may not cook meat with milk or butter, nor add milk to those side dishes that are served along with meat (e.g., mashed potatoes with butter or milk; quiche that contains cream or cheese). It is also prohibited to serve dairy desserts at the end of a meat meal.

One may cook vegetables or soup with dairy products, but this cooking must be performed in accordance with the dietary laws, as follows:

Cooking with milk and dairy products should be done using only dairy utensils, and the food must be served at a dairy meal. In other words, it is prohibited to cook such food using any pots, pans, knives, baking molds, or ovens that will be used for meat dishes. Similarly, one may not serve this food on plates that are used for meat meals, nor may one use cutlery that is used to eat meat.

In order to cook and bake dairy products, one must have a suitable set of cooking implements that will be used solely for dairy foods. Likewise, the serving dishes, e.g., plates, cups, and cutlery, should not be used for meat dishes.

Nowadays, there are suitable non-dairy substitutes for milk, butter, and cream, and these greatly expand the different culinary options without violating laws of *kashrut*.

An oven that is used for baking or cooking dairy should not be used to cook meat. It is ideal to have separate ovens for meat and dairy, but if this is not possible, one should consult a rabbi as to how best to use one oven for both meat and dairy.

Ready-Made Food and Eating in Restaurants

If one purchases ready-made or semi-prepared food, the potential for *kashrut* problems greatly increases. Therefore, it is very important to be careful to buy products that have certification from a reliable *kashrut* agency, and likewise to eat only in restaurants that have a valid certificate of *kashrut*.

Guidelines and Recommendations

When purchasing food products that have undergone some form of preparation (cooking, preservation, etc.), one must take into consideration that various *kashrut* problems can apply to the main product and to its additives. Likewise, there may be issues with the manner in which the products were prepared; for example, whether they were cooked in non-kosher equipment or by gentiles. Therefore, one must make sure that the product has certification from a reliable *kashrut* agency. In restaurants, one should check to make sure that the *kashrut* certificate is current and has not expired.

Due to the many problems in the field of *kashrut* supervision, it is recommended to rely only on known, reputable *kashrut* authorities. One should also prefer restaurants that are managed by religiously observant people, who can be expected to feel personally responsible for the *kashrut*

Various Topics

of the food that they serve their customers. A restaurant in which one can see a *kashrut* supervisor whose appearance and behavior indicate that he is a God-fearing individual is better than a restaurant with a certificate of *kashrut* on the wall, but which does not have a supervisor on site.

In some eateries, there are pictures of famous rabbis hanging on the walls, and there may also be charity boxes on the counter. Such religiously oriented items should not be viewed as an alternative to a proper *kashrut* certificate. Similarly, one should not rely on the word of the restaurant owner or the waiters, who state authoritatively that "everything is strictly kosher." Instead, one should ask them to present a certified and up-to-date document of *kashrut*.

Cooking by Gentiles

The Sages prohibited eating food that was cooked or baked by a gentile, even if all of its basic ingredients are kosher. There are two reasons for this prohibition: First, to prevent excessive socializing between Jews and gentiles, which might encourage intermarriage. Second, there is a concern that eating kosher items in a gentile's house could lead one to eat other foods there that are not kosher.

Details of the Prohibition

This decree of the Sages applies to foods prepared by gentiles by means of cooking, frying, or roasting. It is permitted to eat kosher food that has been prepared by a gentile by salting, smoking, or pickling.

Bread that was baked by a gentile is not included in this decree, but rather it is covered by the prohibition of a "bread of a gentile," which was discussed on p. 547. The same is true of wine whose production involved a gentile, and its *halakhot* are also detailed in the same section.

When one employs a gentile cook, a Jew must be the one to light the fire or turn on the electric cooker. Even so, Sephardim do not rely on this leniency and insist that the Jew must be the one to put the food onto the heat source. It is important to know that when a gentile cooks without the supervision and involvement of a Jew, even the utensils that he uses are rendered unkosher, and it is prohibited to use them for further cooking until they have been properly rendered kosher.

Travel Abroad

If one travels abroad, to a place where there is a Jewish community, but he does not know further details about the local *kashrut* arrangements, he should contact the community rabbi to obtain necessary information and guidance. In many locales around the world, one can contact the Lubavitch (Chabad) representative of that place.

In especially remote locations, where there is neither a Jewish community nor a Chabad House, one must either bring food along or make his own food from raw materials he can obtain there. Unprocessed fruits and vegetables may be eaten anywhere without hesitation. There is likewise no problem with plain, unflavored tea or coffee.

Managing a Kosher Kitchen

There are two main requirements for managing a kosher kitchen:

(1) Only kosher raw products may be used.

(2) Mixing dairy products with meat products must be avoided, and similarly, there must be a full separation between meat and dairy utensils. In a kitchen that has pareve dishes, which are neither meat nor dairy, they should not be mixed with other kinds of dishes. The following are some rules and guidelines on this matter:

Recommended Rules of Usage

Sinks: It is best is to install two sinks in the kitchen, one for meat dishes and the other for dairy dishes. If there is only one sink, one should not place dishes directly in the sink itself. Rather, he should place a rack on the bottom of the sink, to prevent the dishes from touching the sink itself. It is, of course, important to use different racks for meat and dairy dishes. One must also be careful not to allow the sink to fill with hot water while there are dishes in it, as this would cause the dishes to absorb substances from the walls of the sink. An alternative option is to have separate basins for the meat and dairy dishes and to put the relevant basin in the sink as needed.

Refrigerator: Since the food in a refrigerator is cold, there is no problem with using it for storing both meat and dairy products side by side. Cold dishes that are touching one another do not transfer their meat or dairy status to each other. Nevertheless, it is best to keep dairy products away from meat, in order to prevent a liquid milk product from splashing and coming into contact with the meat or the vessel that it is in, or vice versa.

Oven and baking: An oven can be used for cooking meat or dairy products, but it cannot be used for both. It is recommended to have two separate ovens, or at least two chambers in an oven that are entirely separate from one another. If one has only one oven, he should consult a rabbi about how best to use it for meat and dairy without violating the laws of *kashrut.*

Microwave: In principle, a microwave oven may be used for heating both meat and dairy products (separately, of course), if one is always careful to cover the food and make sure that there are no remnants of food on the rotating glass plate or on the walls of the microwave. In practice, it is hard to ensure that the microwave remains clean, and many people find it inconvenient to cover the food on a regular basis. If foods from both meat and dairy dishes splash onto the microwave's glass plate, it becomes completely non-kosher. Therefore, it is best to use a microwave oven exclusively designated for either meat or dairy foods. If one needs to heat up food of both types, the ideal solution is to have two separate microwave ovens.

Food processor, mixer, blender: As much as possible, these devices should be kept pareve, and no meat or dairy ingredients should be placed in them. In that case, one can use them to prepare dough, salads, and the like, which can subsequently be integrated into any meal, meat or dairy. If one nevertheless wants to use them for meat or dairy ingredients, it is recommended to have two separate devices.

Toaster: A device that is used for making cheese toasts, for example, may not be used for preparing sandwiches that will be eaten with meat. If a toaster is used for pareve bread only, it can be left as pareve and used for toasting bread for any type of meal.

Stove: There is no problem with using the same stovetop for meat and dairy, as even if the food were placed directly on the iron grate, it would burn completely. Nevertheless, it is best to take care when placing meat and dairy dishes at the same time on the stove lest food from one of the dishes splash onto the second type.

Dishwasher: One may not use the same dishwasher for both meat and dairy dishes. If one has only one dishwasher, he must decide whether it will be designated for meat or dairy, and then use it solely for washing that type of dishes.

For certain devices and under certain conditions, some authorities are lenient in this regard, and one should consult a rabbi.

Pareve kitchenware: In addition to dairy and meat dishes and utensils, it is a good idea to have pareve utensils, i.e., for various uses. A good example of this is a bread knife. It is also good to have a pareve knife for cutting fruits and vegetables. Such a knife is useful if, for example, one wants to cut half an onion or cucumber for a meat meal and leave the other half for a dairy meal. It is also advisable to keep a pareve pot or pan in the kitchen for making fish, which may then be eaten in either a meat or a dairy meal. It is best not to place these pareve utensils into the meat or the dairy sink together with dirty meat or dairy dishes. Likewise, one must be careful that they do not come into contact with hot meat or dairy foods.

Kashering Kitchenware

If a person who has not kept a kosher kitchen decides to make his kitchen kosher, it is essential to go through a process to render the used kitchenware kosher. This applies even to a situation in which only kosher-certified foods had always been used in the house. The requirement to kasher the items in such a case is due to the likelihood that meat and milk were mixed together.

The principles of the laws of kashering of kitchenware are straightforward, but their practical implementation can be quite complicated. Therefore, it is best to seek the advice and practical assistance of someone who is knowledgeable in these *halakhot*. Not every person, even if he is mitzva-observant and a scholar, is an expert in all the details of these laws. Only a rabbi who is thoroughly familiar with the *halakhot* involved can address the various problems that arise during the process. Nevertheless, it is important to be familiar with the main difficulties and their solutions in the field of keeping kosher, as this will help one avoid mishaps, and even could solve the simple errors that can occur in any home.

What One Must Know

For the purposes of the laws of kashering kitchenware, there are three factors that must be examined in order to categorize the various types of equipment:

(1) the material from which the kitchenware is made;

(2) the temperature at which one uses it;

(3) the manner of its usage, whether it is with dry or liquid substances.

Other relevant factors are: whether it is used with an implement that interposes between it and the food, or if it comes into direct contact with the food; whether it is used for cooking, frying, or baking.

It is generally not recommended to rely on memory regarding the usage of an item of kitchenware. Sometimes people will say, "We never used this utensil for non-kosher food," but they might be mistaken. Those who are insufficiently aware of the many *halakhot* of *kashrut* often do not realize what kind of problems can arise with regard to different foods. With that said, if one is absolutely certain that a specific pot was never used for cooking non-kosher food, for example, or if it was not used at all, this certainty can help him decide what should be done with it.

Before any kitchenware item can be kashered, it must be put aside and not used for twenty-four hours.

The question of the temperature of the item during its usage is a basic factor in many regards. Kitchenware that is used only to hold cold or room-temperature foods, and is never heated, does not require special kashering. Rather, it is enough to clean it thoroughly. This is the case, for example, for a container or bin in which one keeps bread or cakes, or a refrigerator or similar storage facilities.

By contrast, an item of cookware that is used with hot food does require kashering.

In the case of knives, including bread knives, even if they have not come in contact with hot foods, they require kashering. The same applies to containers in which one stores liquids such as wine and alcohol.

Regarding this matter, there is an important fundamental rule: Any vessel or utensil whose material and shape enable it to be kashered must be kashered by immersing it (or in some cases by rinsing it) in clean hot water, as explained below.

How Does One Kasher?

Before kashering a kitchenware item, one must clean it and make sure that it contains no food residue, stickers, rubber linings, and the like.

Next, one takes a large (kosher) pot and boils water in it. Once the water is boiling, one places the items that require kashering into this water. One dips it for a few seconds into the boiling water and then takes it out. After this action, which is called *hagala*, "purging," in the halakhic literature, the item is fit for kosher use.

In this fashion, one can kasher metal kitchenware, including many cooking implements and silverware.

With regard to kitchenware that is used at a high temperature with direct contact with food (without water), such as cookware used for roasting and frying, their kashering is similar to the manner of their use: Metal utensils which can be heated to become glowing hot should be put into a fire until they glow from the heat. For items for which this is impractical, such as many frying pans, they cannot be kashered. Ovens must be cleaned thoroughly, turned on or lit, and left burning at their highest temperature. After this process, they are fit for any use.

Earthenware dishes generally cannot be kashered, although in rare cases it might be possible to kasher them (one should consult a rabbi about this matter). It is generally advisable to discard them and buy new ones.

Wooden kitchenware items may be kashered by *hagala* in hot water.

Regular glass items, since they are very smooth and are not used at high temperatures (even in the case of drinking glasses, one does not pour boiling water into them), do not require *hagala*. One should rinse them thoroughly and then leave them to soak in water for a period of three days, changing the water each day.

Pyrex and the like, in which food is cooked directly, can be kashered by *hagala* (although there are many Ashkenazic halakhic authorities who are stringent and prohibit their further use).

It is customary to kasher enamel items by means of *hagala*.

In the case of products made of plastic materials that are used to hold only cold foods, it is enough merely to wash them. But if they are used to heat foods, one should not kasher them, but rather discard them.

A kitchenware item made of two different materials attached together requires thorough examination. One should be particularly careful to check pots or the like that are comprised of different parts connected by screws or gluing. In all such cases, it is appropriate to clarify each case individually by consulting a rabbi, as sometimes the item cannot be properly cleaned or kashered by *hagala*.

Most kitchenware items that have an electrical mechanism in some part of them require careful examination. Generally, they can be kashered by heating at their highest temperature, when they are completely empty, or by placing only water inside them. One must pay special attention to items that are used by means of pressure or which are used for spicy substances. A mixer requires a special inquiry in each individual case, although it can usually be dismantled, and each part dealt with separately.

Miscellaneous

The supplementary equipment that one uses when preparing or eating food also requires kashering by one method or the other. Following are a few examples:

Wooden or metal boards on which one customarily cuts food require thorough cleaning, and if possible, *hagala* as well.

Tables, on which food sometimes spills, should be cleaned well.

Dishwashers require cleaning and heating to the highest level, and some maintain that they cannot be kashered at all. It is therefore advisable to consult a knowledgeable rabbi regarding their kashering.

If one has dentures that can be removed from his mouth, they also require thorough cleaning and soaking in hot water.

The cooking surfaces in the kitchen, as well as washbasins for dishes, involve unique problems. If the kitchen countertops are made of metal or stone, they should be cleaned as thoroughly as possible to remove any dirt and food residue. Then one should pour on them water that continues to boil while it is being poured, e.g., from an electric kettle and the like. Here too, it is advisable to consult a rabbi who has expertise in the field.

Kitchen sinks present a separate problem. Today, many observant Jews install two separate sinks in the kitchen, one for meat use and one for dairy use, and thereby they avoid many problems. If this is not possible, the sink itself should be regarded as a surface that is not kosher, and one should make sure that no hot food comes into contact with it. As mentioned earlier, one can put in the sink a rack upon which to place utensils.

Usually when things are done in the right way, especially with the guidance of a qualified and experienced rabbi, the process of kashering a whole kitchen takes no longer than a few hours. This preliminary stage is essential to maintaining the *halakhot* of *kashrut*.

Between Meat and Dairy

After kashering the kitchenware, it is important to separate the items that are used for meat from those used for dairy, and to mark them in such a way as to prevent them from becoming mixed up. In any case of a mix-up between them, one must re-examine their status, and until the halakhic clarification has been completed, they must be set aside and not used.

As an aside, it is worth pointing out that there is a fundamental difference between the kashering of kitchenware all year long and the kashering of such items from *hametz* use prior to Passover. The process of preparing kitchenware items before Passover is more severe.

Further reading: For more on preparations for Passover, see p. 274.

Special Mitzvot that Apply in Israel

With regard to fruits and vegetables, there is a distinction between produce grown in the Land of Israel and produce grown elsewhere. All raw vegetables that grow outside Israel are permitted to be eaten, virtually without any concern for *kashrut* problems at all, other than the need to check certain vegetables for bugs, which will be discussed below.

The situation in Israel is different, as many commandments apply to produce that grows in the ground in Israel. As stated above, one must separate *teruma* and tithes from fruits and vegetables; the correct manner of this separation will be clarified below. In the case of fruits from a tree, one must make sure that the fruit is not *orla*, i.e., the fruit of a tree in its first three years of growth. Likewise, many problems of *kashrut* can arise in the Sabbatical Year, as detailed below. In Israel, it is recommended to purchase fruits and vegetables from a store that has proper *kashrut* supervision in order to avoid these *kashrut* complications.

As for cooked fruits and vegetables, they should be treated like all cooked foods, with regard to which the following *kashrut* matters can arise: cooking by gentiles; the status of the vessels used for cooking, and the various flavorings and additives used. All these issues will be dealt with below.

Teruma and Tithes

As stated, the obligation of *teruma* and tithes applies to fruits and vegetables that grow in the Land of Israel. Eating fruits and vegetables from which *teruma* and tithes have not been separated is prohibited. This is relevant even to consumers outside of Israel. If one purchases produce imported from Israel, one should ensure that it has a *kashrut* certification, or one should separate the *teruma* and tithes oneself.

One must distinguish between a situation in which it is known for certain that *teruma* and tithes have not been separated from the harvest (such produce is called *tevel*), and a case of uncertainty as to whether the requisite separations have been performed. In either case, one must set aside *teruma* and tithes. When there is a definite obligation to perform the separations, a blessing is recited beforehand. In a case of uncertainty, the separation is carried out without a blessing.

The process of the separation of *teruma* and tithes is somewhat complicated, but we will try to simplify it:

By Torah law, a Jew who lives in Israel must separate from the produce that he grew in his land certain portions for the priests and Levites, and another portion that he must bring to Jerusalem and eat there or give to a poor person, depending on the year. One must also pay special attention to the precise order of the separation.

Teruma gedola (literally, "the great offering"): When the Temple was still standing, approximately two percent of the crop was set aside and given to the priests. This portion, which is called *teruma gedola*, is sacred, and it was permitted to be eaten only by priests and their families, and even they could eat it only if they and the food were both in a state of ritual purity. Nowadays, when attaining ritual purity is not possible, *teruma gedola* may not be eaten, even by priests, so the produce that is separated as *teruma* is ultimately disposed of. For this reason, nowadays there is no need to be strict about the amount of two percent, which was established by the Sages in the time of the Temple, but rather one separates a minute amount for *teruma gedola*, in accordance with the basic requirement of Torah law. The separated produce should be not be destroyed directly, but should be set aside to rot of its own accord, or it should be wrapped respectfully in a plastic bag and thrown away in a trash bin.

The first tithe: After *teruma*, ten percent of the remainder of the produce is set aside and given as a gift to a Levite. This is called the first tithe. It is not considered a sacred food, and may be eaten by anyone.

The *teruma* of the tithe: The Levite is required to set aside ten percent of the tithe that he has received, and give it to a priest. This portion, amounting to one percent of all the produce, is called "the *teruma* of the tithe" and it, like *teruma gedola*, is sacred, and may be eaten only by priests in a state of purity.

Nowadays, the first tithe is not given to a Levite, but rather it is separated and left in the possession of the owner of the produce. By contrast, the *teruma* of the tithe must be treated like *teruma gedola*.

The practical implication of the above is that one must physically set aside slightly more than one percent of his produce. The one percent is the *teruma* of the tithe, while the additional minute portion is *teruma gedola*. This produce may not be eaten, but must be left to rot or discarded respectfully, as explained earlier.

Second tithe or the poor man's tithe: Afterward, one must set aside a third portion, which is either "the second tithe" or "the poor man's tithe." The status of this portion, which is ten percent of the remainder of the produce, varies in accordance with the cycle of the Sabbatical Year. In the first, second, fourth, and fifth years of the Sabbatical Year cycle, this third portion is designated as the second tithe. In the third and sixth years, it is designated as the poor man's tithe.

The poor man's tithe is meant to be given to the poor. This is only if it is known for certain that the produce has not been tithed before; in cases of doubt, the owner of the produce may keep the tithe for himself. As for the second tithe, it is desacralized by redeeming it onto a coin, as detailed below.

The total amount of separated produce in Temple times was therefore slightly more than twenty percent of the entire crop. In practice, nowadays one removes only a little more than one percent (aside from the poor man's tithe when relevant). This amount comprises *teruma gedola* (one percent) and *teruma* of the tithe (a minute amount), the only portions that may not be eaten.

Desacralization on a Coin

The obligation to bring second tithe produce to Jerusalem and to eat it there in a state of holiness and purity applied during the time of the Temple. In those days, if it was too difficult to transport that produce to Jerusalem, one was permitted to redeem the tithe onto money, which was then brought to Jerusalem and used to purchase food. This food assumed the sanctity of second tithe and had to be eaten in Jerusalem in a state of ritual purity.

One may partake of the second tithe in Jerusalem only when the Temple is standing. Now that the Temple has been destroyed, it is no longer permitted to eat second tithe produce, and the only remaining option is to redeem it and transfer its sanctity onto a coin. This money can no longer serve its original purpose of purchasing food in Jerusalem to eat in purity, so it retains its status of sanctity; see below for what one should do with it. For this reason, it is permissible nowadays to use for redemption a coin that is only a small fraction of the actual value of the tithe.

Procedure and Text of the Separation

The separation of *teruma* and tithes is an act that almost every person in Israel might have to perform at some point, and therefore it became necessary to formulate a fixed text and a standard procedure for the separation.

The procedure is as follows: One takes slightly more than one-hundredth (one percent) of each kind of produce from which one wishes to separate *teruma*, and puts it aside.

If one is dealing with produce about which it is known with certainty that *terumot* and tithes have not already been separated, one must recite a blessing before reading the text of the separation. In a case of uncertainty, one does not recite the blessing, but only the formula of separation itself. The blessing is as follows:

בָּרוּךְ אַתָּה אֲדֹנָי, אֱלֹהֵינוּ מֶלֶךְ הָעוֹלָם,
אֲשֶׁר קִדְּשָׁנוּ בְּמִצְוֹתָיו וְצִוָּנוּ לְהַפְרִישׁ
תְּרוּמוֹת וּמַעַשְׂרוֹת.

*Barukh ata Adonai, Eloheinu, melekh
ha'olam, asher kideshanu bemitzvotav,
vetzivanu lehafrish terumot uma'asrot.*

"Blessed are You, Lord our God, King of the universe, who sanctified us
through His mitzvot, and commanded us to separate *terumot* and tithes."

Then one recites the text of the separation: "The part that is more than one-
hundredth that is here (in the small portion that has been placed to the side)
is hereby teruma gedola, on the northernmost side (of that small portion).

"The remaining one-hundredth which is here, and another nine equal
parts on the northernmost side of the (main pile of) produce, is hereby the
first tithe. That one-hundredth (in the small, set-aside portion) which I previously made first tithe shall hereby be teruma of the tithe.

"And the poor man's tithe is hereby on the southernmost side (of the
main pile). And if it is the second tithe that is required, the second tithe is
hereby on the southernmost side." (The usage of the terms "northernmost
side" and "southernmost side" is to have a uniform text for the declaration.
In principle, one could separate the *teruma* and tithes from any side.)

If one knows for certain which tithe he is required to separate, the second tithe or the poor man's tithe, one mentions only that tithe.

If the produce is subject to the second tithe, one must redeem the
produce of the second tithe that he has designated as being on the southernmost side.

One takes a coin and designates it for this purpose. If one knows for
certain that the produce is subject to the second tithe, he recites a blessing
before the redemption:

בָּרוּךְ אַתָּה אֲדֹנָי, אֱלֹהֵינוּ מֶלֶךְ הָעוֹלָם,
אֲשֶׁר קִדְּשָׁנוּ בְּמִצְוֹתָיו וְצִוָּנוּ עַל פִּדְיוֹן
מַעֲשֵׂר שֵׁנִי.

*Barukh ata Adonai, Eloheinu, melekh
ha'olam, asher kideshanu bemitzvotav,
vetzivanu al pidyon ma'aser sheni.*

"Blessed are You, Lord our God, King of the universe, who sanctified us
through His commandments, and commanded us concerning the redemption of the second tithe."

Afterward, one recites the formula of the redemption of the tithe onto a
coin: "And it (the second tithe) and its [requisite addition of one] fifth are

hereby desacralized onto a *peruta*[2] within the coin that I have designated for the desacralization of second tithe."

If one is performing a one-time separation, one may desacralize the second tithe on a ten *agora* coin in Israel, for example, and then destroy it by beating it with a hammer or with pliers, in such a manner that prevents its further use.

One who expects to be separating *teruma* and tithes on a more frequent basis should set aside for this purpose a coin of a larger denomination, which may be used for many redemptions. Thus, if, for argument's sake, the value of a *peruta* is ten *agorot*, one can use a five-shekel coin to be used for redemption fifty times. When the value of the coin has been fully used up, one desacralizes it onto a smaller coin, which is subsequently destroyed. It is also possible to desacralize the coin onto food, for example, a tablespoon of sugar, and then dissolve the sugar in the sink.

Neta Reva'i, a Fourth-Year Sapling

The fruits of a tree that grew in the fourth year after the tree was planted are called *neta reva'i* and have the same halakhic status as second tithe produce. That is, they may not be eaten before they are desacralized onto a coin.

The procedure for this desacralization is as follows: One takes a coin and says: "The fourth-year produce that is here, and its [requisite addition of one] fifth are hereby desacralized onto a *peruta* within the coin that I have designated for the desacralization of fourth-year fruit."

For fruits grown in Israel, if one is certain that the fruit in question grew in the tree's fourth year, a blessing is recited before the redemption:

בָּרוּךְ אַתָּה אֲדֹנָי, אֱלֹהֵינוּ מֶלֶךְ הָעוֹלָם, *Barukh ata Adonai, Eloheinu, melekh*
אֲשֶׁר קִדְּשָׁנוּ בְּמִצְוֹתָיו וְצִוָּנוּ לִפְדּוֹת נֶטַע *ha'olam, asher kideshanu bemitzvotav,*
רְבָעִי. *vetzivanu lifdot neta reva'i.*

"Blessed are You, Lord our God, King of the universe, who sanctified us through His commandments, and commanded us to redeem [the fruits of] a fourth-year sapling."

In order to avoid the need to keep in one's house a collection of coins for the desacralization of second tithe and *neta reva'i* and to have to deal with the destruction of the coins, there are several "tithe foundations" in Israel,

---

2. A *peruta*, equal to the value of one-fortieth gram of silver, is the smallest amount considered to have monetary value in all matters of *halakha*.

known as Keren Ma'asrot, which handle all the requirements of the coins for their subscribers, so that they merely have to recite the above formula (with some minor adjustments).

After reciting the text, one takes the produce that he had placed to one side and leaves it out to rot, or respectfully wraps it in a plastic bag and discards it in the garbage.

One who wishes to avoid having to perform the separation of tithes himself should buy his fruits and vegetables only from a store that is under the supervision of a recognized and certified *kashrut* body that performs all the requirements of *teruma* and tithes for the produce that they sell.

Biur Ma'asrot, the Disposal of Tithes

In the fourth year of the Sabbatical Year cycle, each person must dispose of the tithes of the first, second, and third years of the cycle that are still in his possession and have not been transferred to their proper place. Likewise, in the Sabbatical Year, one must dispose of the tithes of the fourth, fifth, and sixth years. This disposal is performed on the day before Passover, or on the sixth day of Passover.

This disposal is achieved by separating all the requisite portions that have not yet been separated, and appropriately dispersing any remaining *teruma* or tithes in one's possession. On a practical level, for most people this simply means destroying any second tithe coins one may have in his possession.

If one is subscribed to a *Keren Ma'asrot* all of these activities are performed by the management of the foundation.

After performing these actions, some have the custom to read the following verses, which describe the disposal of the tithes and the related "confession" that was recited in the Temple:

כִּי תְכַלֶּה לַעְשֵׂר אֶת כָּל מַעְשַׂר תְּבוּאָתְךָ בַּשָּׁנָה הַשְּׁלִישִׁת שְׁנַת הַמַּעֲשֵׂר וְנָתַתָּה לַלֵּוִי לַגֵּר לַיָּתוֹם וְלָאַלְמָנָה וְאָכְלוּ בִשְׁעָרֶיךָ וְשָׂבֵעוּ: וְאָמַרְתָּ לִפְנֵי אֲדֹנָי אֱלֹהֶיךָ בִּעַרְתִּי הַקֹּדֶשׁ מִן הַבַּיִת וְגַם נְתַתִּיו לַלֵּוִי וְלַגֵּר לַיָּתוֹם וְלָאַלְמָנָה כְּכָל מִצְוָתְךָ אֲשֶׁר צִוִּיתָנִי לֹא עָבַרְתִּי מִמִּצְוֹתֶיךָ וְלֹא שָׁכָחְתִּי: לֹא אָכַלְתִּי בְאֹנִי מִמֶּנּוּ וְלֹא בִעַרְתִּי מִמֶּנּוּ בְּטָמֵא וְלֹא נָתַתִּי מִמֶּנּוּ לְמֵת שָׁמַעְתִּי בְּקוֹל אֲדֹנָי אֱלֹהָי עָשִׂיתִי כְּכֹל אֲשֶׁר צִוִּיתָנִי: הַשְׁקִיפָה מִמְּעוֹן קָדְשְׁךָ מִן הַשָּׁמַיִם וּבָרֵךְ אֶת עַמְּךָ אֶת יִשְׂרָאֵל וְאֵת הָאֲדָמָה אֲשֶׁר נָתַתָּה לָנוּ כַּאֲשֶׁר נִשְׁבַּעְתָּ לַאֲבֹתֵינוּ אֶרֶץ זָבַת חָלָב וּדְבָשׁ: (דברים יד, יב-טו)

"When you finish tithing all the tithes of your produce in the third year, the year of the tithe, and you have given it to the Levite, to the stranger, to the orphan, and to the widow, and they ate within your gates, and were satisfied. You shall say before the Lord your God: I have disposed of the consecrated from my house, and also I gave them to the Levite, and to the stranger, to the orphan, and to the widow, in accordance with all Your commandment that You commanded me; I did not violate any of Your commandments, and I did not forget. I did not eat from it during my mourning, and I did not dispose of it in a state of impurity, and I did not give from it for the dead; I heeded the voice of the Lord my God, I have acted in accordance with everything that You commanded me. Look from Your holy abode, from the heavens, and bless Your people Israel, and the land that You gave us, as You took an oath to our fathers, a land flowing with milk and honey" (Deuteronomy 26:12–15).

The Sabbatical Year

In the Sabbatical Year (every seventh year, in a recurring cycle), it is prohibited to plow, sow, and cultivate the ground in the Land of Israel. Vegetables grown in Jewish owned property in the Land of Israel during this time may not be eaten. By contrast, the fruits of trees that grew in this year may be consumed, but they have a sanctified status, and they are therefore subject to certain restrictions. This mitzva appears in several places in the Torah, the main one being toward the end of Leviticus: "The Lord spoke to Moses at Mount Sinai, saying: Speak to the children of Israel, and say to them: When you come into the land that I am giving you, the land shall rest a Sabbath to the Lord. Six years you will sow your field, and six years you will prune your vineyard, and you will gather its harvest. And in the seventh year, it shall be a sabbatical rest for the land, a Sabbath for the Lord; your field you shall not sow, and your vineyard you shall not prune. The aftergrowth of your reaping you shall not reap, and the uncultivated grapes of your vine you shall not gather; it shall be a sabbatical year for the land" (Leviticus 25:1–5).

Vegetables

All vegetables that grow during the Sabbatical Year in Israel in land owned by Jews are forbidden for consumption. Therefore, it is necessary to have a *kashrut* certificate for every food product containing produce from the Land of Israel, in order to ensure that they contain no ingredients that are problematic due to the laws of the Sabbatical Year.

The Chief Rabbinate of Israel conducts a sale of many of the fields in Israel to a gentile, for the duration of the Sabbatical Year, so that they may be cultivated during that year. This "solution" for the restrictions on agriculture during the Sabbatical Year is called in Hebrew *heter mekhira*, meaning "permission [granted] through sale [of the land]." Though accepted by some, there are many that do not rely on this *heter*, and are stringent not to consume vegetables that were grown during the Sabbatical Year by Jewish farmers.

Produce that is available in regular vegetable stores may at times not even be covered by the *heter mekhira*, but was possibly sown in absolute violation of the prohibitions of the Sabbatical Year. Consequently, even those who rely on the *heter mekhira* must check that the store has a certificate of supervision and *kashrut* from the Chief Rabbinate, in order to be sure that the goods in the store are permissible at least according to the *heter mekhira*.

One who does not rely on the *heter mekhira* must buy his produce during this year from stores that sell only products regarding which there is no concern at all that they are in violation of the Sabbatical Year's laws. Likewise, one must make sure that products that contain vegetable ingredients do not include produce of the Sabbatical Year. One must continue to be cautious in this regard for about a year after the Sabbatical Year, as the restrictions for Sabbatical Year produce can sometimes apply to preserved and processed food products sold even after the year has passed. This is relevant outside of Israel as well, for products imported from Israel.

The Sanctity of the Sabbatical Year

Vegetables that grew during the sixth year of the Sabbatical cycle but were picked in the Sabbatical Year have a sanctified status. Similarly, fruits that begin to grow during the Sabbatical Year also have a sanctified status. Such produce is said to have *kedushat shevi'it*, sanctity of the Sabbatical Year. They are permitted to be eaten but they are subject to several restrictions. They may not be traded or sold for profit. They also may not be treated in a manner leading to its destruction or degradation.

One may not discard the leftovers of Sabbatical Year produce into the garbage in the usual manner; this includes peels, if they are edible. Rather, they should be left to rot of their own accord and then discarded, or wrapped and sealed in a plastic bag and only then placed in the trash.

Ritual Immersion of Kitchenware

Another aspect of the *halakhot* of kitchenware items is the requirement to immerse them in a *mikva* (ritual bath). The *halakha* states that many types of kitchen items that were owned by a gentile, even if they were never used, must be immersed in a *mikva* in order for them to be permitted for use by a Jew. Obviously, a used implement that was in the possession of a gentile also requires kashering if one wants to use it. Even a new kitchenware item that was manufactured in a factory owned by a gentile, which does not need to be kashered, must be immersed in a *mikva* before using.

Different Kinds of Kitchenware

The *halakha* of immersion applies by Torah law to kitchen items made of metal. Earthenware and wooden products do not require immersion. Those made of glass do need immersion (by decree of the Sages). A blessing is recited over the immersion. Earthenware does not require immersion, but some have the practice to immerse ceramic dishes without a blessing, and one should consult his rabbi about this. Plastic does not require immersion, but there are those who immerse even plasticware without a blessing.

An item that requires immersion, whether new or used, must be brought to a *mikva* for immersion. Most ritual baths include a separate *mikva* for kitchenware only. This is the preferred situation for practical reasons, but is not absolutely necessary. It is permissible to immerse dishes and utensils in a *mikva* that is designated for people, but one should first consult the caretakers of the *mikva*. Using such a *mikva* for kitchen items requires great caution, since a broken piece of glass or a sharp utensil falling into the water is an obvious hazard for the people who come to immerse themselves in the *mikva*.

Immersing Kitchenware

Before immersing an item of kitchenware, one recites the following blessing:

בָּרוּךְ אַתָּה אֲדֹנָי, אֱלֹהֵינוּ מֶלֶךְ הָעוֹלָם, אֲשֶׁר קִדְּשָׁנוּ בְּמִצְוֹתָיו וְצִוָּנוּ עַל טְבִילַת כְּלִי ("כֵּלִים" אם מטבילים יותר מכלי אחד).

Barukh ata Adonai, Eloheinu, melekh ha'olam, asher kideshanu bemitzvotav, vetzivanu al tevilat keli (if immersing more than one item, conclude: al tevilat kelim).

"Blessed are You, Lord our God, King of the universe, who sanctified us through His commandments, and commanded us concerning the immersion of a utensil." If one is immersing more than one item, he concludes with the words "of utensils" in the plural.

Immediately after reciting the blessing, one should put the item briefly into the water, and while it is in the water, release his grip on it for a moment, so that the water completely touches it from all sides at once. Alternatively, he can pass it from one hand to the other while it is under the water.

Regarding kitchenware items that have an electric element which might be damaged if it is placed in water, it is advisable to consult a rabbi, as there are often solutions for such cases.

Various Types of *Kashrut*

The food market is flooded with a variety of *kashrut* certificates. This can prove quite confusing to the uninformed shopper. It is therefore important to understand that a *kashrut* certificate is like a seal of approval, attesting to the fact that a qualified body has supervised the *kashrut* of the product or the eatery. Sometimes one supervisory authority has more stringent requirements than another, so that the certification issued by that authority will meet higher standards. Unfortunately, there are also constant attempts to deceive the *kashrut* authorities, and therefore closer supervision ensures a higher level of *kashrut*.

Naturally, a better-quality certification also entails a greater expense, as strict supervision requires an expanded team of supervisors and more equipment to carry out the job.

Family Purity

One of the three commandments that are in a woman's purview is the mitzva of "family purity." (The other two mitzvot are the separation of *halla* and the lighting of Shabbat and festival candles.) Admittedly, the husband is involved as well, as maintaining the system of rules that is called "family purity" requires the full cooperation of both partners in a marriage. Yet, as this mitzva relates to physiological processes occurring in the woman's body, and because it is the woman who performs many of the practical actions involved in the fulfillment of the mitzva, the responsibility and the merit of its fulfillment belong to the woman. The kabbalistic literature provides a spiritual explanation for this: The power of the woman is greater than that of the man in everything that involves the spreading of sanctity and purity within the walls of the Jewish home.

The Torah states: "And a woman, if she has a discharge, her discharge from her flesh being blood; seven days she shall be in her menstrual state; anyone who touches her shall be impure until the evening" (Leviticus 15:19). It further states: "And to a woman in her state of menstrual impurity you shall not approach to uncover her nakedness" (Leviticus 18:19). The Torah applies a status of ritual impurity to a woman during the days of her menstruation, and prohibits a man from engaging in marital relations and physical intimacy with her.

We are taught to fulfill the commandments of the Creator because it is His will, not for personal benefit. Although one must fulfill any mitzva even without understanding its purpose, the Sages point out the observable benefit to marital and family life that results from the fulfillment of the mitzva of family purity. The Talmud states: "Rabbi Meir would say: For what reason does the Torah say that a menstruating woman is prohibited to her husband for seven days? So that when she becomes pure again, she will be as beloved to her husband as at the time when she entered the wedding canopy with him" (*Nidda* 31b). The strict observance of the *halakhot* of family purity and its requirement of separation preserves the freshness of marital life, protects the couple's relationship, and grants the entire family unit happiness and stability.

This section details the laws of family purity, including the *halakhot* concerning menstruation; the requisite *hefsek tahara*, which is the examination done by the woman prior to her transition from impurity to counting toward her immersion in the *mikva*; the counting of "seven clean days"; preparing for the *mikva*; and the immersion itself.

Menstruation

After every instance of blood emerging from a woman's womb, she must observe the *halakhot* of a menstruating woman [*nidda*]. Usually this occurs at the onset of the menstrual cycle, but there can be other cases of blood flow that render a woman a *nidda*. When the bleeding has stopped, and after the woman performs the *hefsek tahara* and counts seven clean days, she immerses herself in a *mikva*, and is thereby purified.

How Does a Woman Become a *Nidda*?

As mentioned above, the *halakhot* of *nidda* apply to a woman not only during her menstrual cycle, but after any emergence of blood from the womb, including birth or a miscarriage, God forbid. The Sages also included here the blood resulting from the rupture of the hymen.

Staying Apart

From the moment a woman is defined as a *nidda*, husband and wife are forbidden to have any physical interaction. This prohibition requires that the couple refrain from all intimate contact, including hugging, kissing, and any touching that expresses affection. The Sages added to the basic prohibitions those forms of touching that do not express affection as well, out of a concern that these could lead to forbidden contact. Examples of the kinds of contact forbidden by the Sages include any physical contact, sleeping in a shared bed, eating from the same plate, and even handing an item directly from one to the other.

It is important to note that in the event that one spouse requires physical help, due to illness or disability, etc., one should consult a rabbi about if and how this may be done.

In addition to forbidden contact, the Sages ordered that the couple should avoid cultivating an intimate atmosphere, such as conversation about intimate matters, which could lead to problematic touching. During this time, the relationship between the couple should transcend the physical dimension and become far deeper and truer. This is the time to love and respect one's partner because of who she or he is, while disengaging from the pleasures of the body. It is also an opportunity to develop one's longing for the partner and thereby increase the mutual attraction for the contact that can be enjoyed immediately upon the completion of the purification process.

Minimum Time

After the start of her menstrual cycle, the woman must wait for the complete cessation of the bleeding before the process of purification can begin. It is important to know that there is a minimum number of days that a woman must wait after the start of the bleeding until she can begin the purification process. That is, even if her bleeding stopped after just two days, she may not start the process of purification immediately. According to the Sephardic custom, the minimum number of days of menstruation impurity is four before beginning the purification process, while according to the Ashkenazic custom, one must observe a minimum of five days.

In exceptional situations such as, for example, if the woman is undergoing fertility treatments, a rabbi should be consulted about whether and how it is possible to bring forward the beginning of the purification process, in order to increase the time range for conception.

The Road to Purity

At the end of the menstrual cycle (on condition, as stated, that the minimum days have passed), the woman must examine herself to make sure that the bleeding has stopped completely. This initial examination [bedika], which is called the hefsek tahara, must be performed toward evening, before sunset.

Hefsek Tahara

A woman performs the hefsek tahara by means of a small white cloth, whose cleanness is checked in advance. It is known as a bedika cloth, or in Hebrew, an ed bedika, literally "an examination witness," because the examination serves as a reliable "witness" to the woman's status. Pre-made packets of these cloths can be obtained in ritual baths, and in Israel they are often available in pharmacies and supermarkets.

Before doing the hefsek tahara, the woman must wash herself well, so that no traces of blood are left on her body which might then appear on the bedika cloth and incorrectly prevent her from being purified. Afterward, she should take a bedika cloth, examine it on both sides to ensure that it is entirely clean, wrap it around her finger, and then insert the wrapped finger into the vagina and rotate it gently but thoroughly. This test enables her to affirm that the bleeding has stopped completely and that the area is entirely clean of blood. If she finds faint blood marks on the bedika cloth, these might be residues of an old blood flow and it is recommended for her to examine herself again a few minutes later with another bedika cloth. She may repeat the action yet again if it seems that there is a reasonable chance of achieving a clean bedika. If the other bedika cloths are also stained and in the meantime the sun has set, she has no choice but to postpone the implementation of the hefsek tahara to the following day.

To Know How to Ask

An important factor in maintaining the laws of family purity is knowing to approach a rabbi when necessary. The *bedika* cloths will often have stains, and in order to make a decision as to whether this is indeed blood or possibly some other secretion that does not confer ritual impurity, one requires halakhic knowledge and expertise. Consultation with a rabbi can save much confusion and aggravation.

It is highly recommended for each couple to choose a qualified rabbi to whom they can refer all problems in this field. Under no circumstances should the questions be considered unpleasant or embarrassing. The correct and healthy attitude toward this topic is the same as all mitzvot of the Torah. The rabbis involved in this practice are accustomed to such questions and they accept them respectfully and with patience.

Seven Clean Days

From the day after performing the *hefsek tahara*, the woman begins counting seven "clean days," on which she does not experience any bleeding. On each and every one of these days, she must examine herself in the same manner as for the *hefsek tahara*, with several differences. According to some opinions, she should not wash herself just before performing the examination. In addition, these examinations should be performed only once; she may not keep repeating them until the *bedika* cloth comes out clean. She performs the examination twice each day, immediately after arising in the morning, and before sunset in the evening.

Sometimes the count of "seven clean days" can be interrupted by the appearance of blood on a *bedika* cloth or a stain on an undergarment. In such cases, it is advisable to consult a rabbi and to follow his instructions. If a woman decides alone in cases of uncertainty, she might mistakenly be too lenient, but she might also be needlessly stringent. Both alternatives are problematic. If it is indeed blood, the woman will need to start the count of seven clean days over again.

In the night that follows these seven clean days, the woman immerses herself in a *mikva*.

Washing the Hair and Interposition

In preparation for immersing in the *mikva*, the woman must thoroughly cleanse herself in a way that ensures that there is no dirt or anything else on her body that might interpose between her body and the water of the *mikva*.

Before immersing in the *mikva*, the woman should take a shower and wash her body well, especially in places that are hard to reach, such as inside the ears and in folds of the body. She must remove any makeup from her face. She must also untie any braids, remove any foreign object (beads, rubber bands, etc.) from her hair, and wash and comb through all the hair of her head. Likewise, she must clean her nails and remove any polish or coating from them. It is also mandatory for her to brush her teeth, even though the *mikva* water does not enter the mouth. The immersion must be performed without any jewelry on the body (including earrings, bracelets, rings, and the like).

Mikva and Immersion

Immersion in the *mikva* is not like bathing, as it includes a spiritual dimension of purification and renewal. For this reason, it is important to pause for a moment before immersing, to relax and leave behind the daily stresses of life. The woman should perform the necessary actions calmly, while preparing herself for the reunion she will have with her husband in the evening.

Present at the ritual immersion in the *mikva* is a designated female attendant, called a *balanit* in Hebrew, meaning literally "female bathhouse attendant." This title is somewhat misleading, as her role is not limited to the technical operation of the *mikva*; rather, she serves as an instructor and guide in the purification process, while helping to ensure that the immersion is performed properly and without complication. It is important to be attentive to the instructions of the *balanit*, keeping in mind that there are often certain differences in prevailing customs between one *mikva* and another.

The immersion in the *mikva* is accompanied by a blessing:

בָּרוּךְ אַתָּה אֲדֹנָי, אֱלֹהֵינוּ מֶלֶךְ הָעוֹלָם, *Barukh ata Adonai, Eloheinu, melekh*
אֲשֶׁר קִדְּשָׁנוּ בְּמִצְוֹתָיו וְצִוָּנוּ עַל הַטְבִילָה. *ha'olam, asher kideshanu bemitzvotav, vetzivanu al hatevila.*

"Blessed are You, Lord our God, King of the universe, who sanctified us through His commandments, and commanded us concerning immersion."

The blessing should be recited after entering the waters of the *mikva*, when the entire body, apart from the head, is covered with water. The common Ashkenazic practice is to immerse once, then recite the blessing, and then to immerse again.

There are two dates in the year when immersion is forbidden and must be postponed for the following night: the night of Yom Kippur and the night of *Tisha BeAv*. The reason is that on these days it is prohibited to wash oneself, and it is also forbidden to engage in marital relations.

If the time for the immersion is a Friday night, all prior preparations must be performed before Shabbat, and the woman should arrive at the *mikva* at the start of Shabbat. The exact time for the immersion will be determined by the *balanit*.

When the night of immersion falls on a Saturday night, the woman should take a shower on Friday in preparation for the immersion, and then again on Saturday night, at which point she should perform the rest of the preparations for the immersion: washing the hair, cleaning her nails, brushing her teeth, etc.

Ritual Fringes
[Tzitzit]

One of the positive commandments of the Torah is the mitzva of *tzitzit*, ritual fringes. The verse states: "Speak to the children of Israel, and say to them: They shall make for themselves *tzitzit* on the corners of their garments" (Numbers 15:38). The obligation of having *tzitzit* applies to a garment that has four corners (see Deuteronomy 22:12); one attaches the *tzitzit* to each of these four corners. If a garment has fewer than four corners, or if one or more of its four corners are rounded rather than angular, the obligation of *tzitzit* does not apply to it. Over the course of time, the term *tzitzit* has come to refer to the entire garment that has *tzitzit* threads hanging from it, although technically the garment itself is called a *tallit*, literally, a "robe" or "shawl."

The obligation of *tzitzit* applies by Torah law only if one chooses to wear a garment with four corners; if one is not wearing such an item of clothing, he is not obligated to wear *tzitzit* at all. However, the Sages urged that every man should wear a garment of four corners, with the requisite *tzitzit*, in order to fulfill the mitzva. This can be either a *tallit katan*, a small garment generally worn under one's shirt, or a *tallit gadol*, a large prayer shawl. Women are exempt from this mitzva.

The reason for this mitzva is that by looking at the *tzitzit*, one remembers the mitzvot of the Torah and thereby avoids sin, as the Torah itself explains: "It shall be for you a fringe, and you shall see it and remember all the commandments of the Lord, and perform them; and you shall not rove after your heart and after your eyes, after which you stray" (Numbers 15:39).

This section discusses the *halakhot* of making and wearing a *tallit katan* and a *tallit gadol*.

The Fringes of the *Tzitzit*

Tzitzit consist of four specially prepared strings, which are inserted through a hole in each of the four corners of the garment so that they emerge from both of its sides, thereby doubling their number to eight. One of these strands is longer than the others, and it is called the *shamash*.

Windings and Knots

After the strings are threaded through the hole in the corner of the garment, they must be tied firmly with a double knot. The *shamash* is wrapped around the other seven threads several times, and then another knot is tied, and this is repeated another three times. There are various customs regarding the precise manner in which the *shamash* is wound around the other strings and in which the strings are tied together, and each person should follow the practice of his community.

The Times of the Mitzva

Since the main point of the *tzitzit*, as indicated by the verse cited above, is for the strings to be seen and to serve as a reminder, the mitzva of *tzitzit* applies only during the daytime, when they can be seen.

By Day

The obligation to wear *tzitzit* begins at the hour when there is sufficient daylight for one to recognize an acquaintance from a distance of two meters without artificial light. This is also the time of day when it becomes possible to distinguish between the white strings of the *tzitzit* and its sky-blue [*tekhelet*] strings. The timetables that list the daily halakhic times usually include the earliest time for each day when one may recite the blessing over the mitzva of *tzitzit*.

By Night

According to many halakhic authorities, the mitzva of *tzitzit* applies specifically by day. However, there is nothing wrong with wearing *tzitzit* at night as well. There are some authorities who hold that the mitzva applies even at night if one is wearing a garment that is worn commonly by day, and the mitzva does not apply to garments worn primarily by night, even if one wears them during the day. Accordingly, one who wears his regular garments of *tzitzit* at night would still be in fulfillment of a mitzva. Some people even go to sleep at night while wearing *tzitzit*, so as not to be separated from this important mitzva even for a moment.

As for wearing a *tallit gadol* at night, the kabbalists maintain that one should not wrap himself in a *tallit gadol* at night, whereas halakhic authorities have no objection to this practice. Each person should follow the instruction of his rabbi.

Once a year, on the night of Yom Kippur, it is customary for everyone to wear a *tallit gadol* even at the evening service.

    Further reading: For more on wearing a *tallit gadol,* see the section dealing with the *halakhot* of Yom Kippur, p. 167.

In any event, the blessing over the *tallit* or *tzitzit* may be recited only in the daytime, when one fulfills the mitzva according to all opinions.

The *Tallit Katan* and *Tallit Gadol*

The *tallit katan* is worn on the body under or over one's shirt. The *tallit gadol*, by contrast, is a large, rectangular cloth that is much larger than the *tallit katan*. One wraps himself in this *tallit* during the morning prayers.

Tallit Katan

One dons a *tallit katan* after rising from sleep. If this is already at the time when one can recite the blessing, he recites the following:

בָּרוּךְ אַתָּה אֲדֹנָי, אֱלֹהֵינוּ מֶלֶךְ הָעוֹלָם,
אֲשֶׁר קִדְּשָׁנוּ בְּמִצְוֹתָיו וְצִוָּנוּ עַל מִצְוַת
צִיצִית.

Barukh ata Adonai, Eloheinu, melekh ha'olam, asher kideshanu bemitzvotav, vetzivanu al mitzvat tzitzit.

"Blessed are You, Lord our God, King of the universe, who sanctified us through His commandments, and commanded us concerning the mitzva of *tzitzit*."

The blessing over the *tallit katan* and, likewise, the blessing over a *tallit gadol* (see below), must both be recited while standing, to show honor for the mitzva.

Many do not recite a blessing when donning a *tallit katan* if later that morning they will recite a blessing over a *tallit gadol*.

Tallit Gadol

The *tallit gadol* is the garment which a person wraps around himself for the morning prayer service. One wears a *tallit gadol* in order to honor the prayers with a special garment.

Who and When?

One wraps himself in the *tallit gadol* before donning the *tefillin* [phylacteries]. The custom of most Ashkenazic communities is that men begin to wear a *tallit gadol* when they get married. By contrast, for Sephardic Jews it is

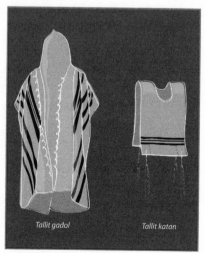

Tallit gadol   *Tallit katan*

Tallit gadol and *tallit katan*

accepted that one dons a *tallit gadol* from the time of his bar mitzva. Women are exempt from *tzitzit*, in accordance with the general rule that they are exempt from time-bound positive mitzvot.

The Manner of Wrapping

The manner of wrapping the *tallit* around oneself varies greatly from one community to another, and even from one family to another in the same community. One who was instructed by his father or knows his family custom should follow that practice. Likewise, one who was taught by his rabbi should act accordingly. But in general, the customs can be divided between Ashkenazim and Sephardim, as detailed below.

Before wrapping oneself in a *tallit*, it is customary to separate the strands of the *tzitzit* from one another and check that none are torn or missing. It is easiest to do this while the half-folded *tallit* is lying on one shoulder with all its fringes dangling forward. During this examination, some have the custom, especially among the Ashkenazim, to recite the following verses:

בָּרְכִי נַפְשִׁי אֶת אֲדֹנָי, אֲדֹנָי אֱלֹהַי גָּדַלְתָּ
מְאֹד, הוֹד וְהָדָר לָבָשְׁתָּ. עֹטֶה אוֹר כַּשַּׂלְמָה,
נוֹטֶה שָׁמַיִם כַּיְרִיעָה.

Ba'rekhi nafshi et Adonai, Adonai Elohai gadalta me'od, hod vehadar lavashta. Oteh or kasalma, noteh shamayim kayri'a.

"Bless the Lord, my soul. Lord my God, You are greatly exalted, You are clothed in splendor and glory. Enveloping with light as if with a cloak, He spreads out the heavens like a tent cloth" (Psalms 104:1–2).

Before wrapping the *tallit*, some have the custom to say a formula that begins with the words: *Leshem yihud*, "for the sake of the unification," which can be found in some prayer books.

Afterward, one holds the upper part of the *tallit*, which in most cases is adorned with an embroidered strip, with the *tallit* spread out in front of his face such that its outer side (the side that is visible from the outside while the *tallit* is worn, and which has the strip sewn onto it) is facing him, and in this state he recites the blessing:

בָּרוּךְ אַתָּה אֲדֹנָי, אֱלֹהֵינוּ מֶלֶךְ הָעוֹלָם,
אֲשֶׁר קִדְּשָׁנוּ בְּמִצְוֹתָיו וְצִוָּנוּ לְהִתְעַטֵּף
בַּצִּיצִית.

Barukh ata Adonai, Eloheinu, melekh ha'olam, asher kideshanu bemitzvotav, vetzivanu lehitatef batzitzit.

Various Topics

"Blessed are You, Lord our God, King of the universe, who sanctified us through His commandments, and commanded us to wrap ourselves in *tzitzit.*"

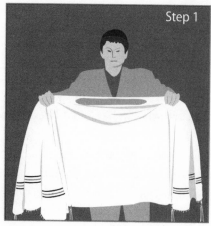 

Wrapping oneself in a *tallit*

Next, one turns the *tallit* around to behind his back, raises it over his head, and wraps it around himself.

As stated, there is a difference between Ashkenazim and Sephardim regarding the manner of wrapping:

Ashkenazic Custom:

According to the Ashkenazic custom, one places the *tallit* over his head, with its upper (decorated) edge covering the forehead to the level of the eyes. Some are strict that this upper edge should cover the eyes and even the whole face. Then one moves the four corners of the *tallit* forward, above the height of the elbows (see step 3 in the image), while the shoulders are also covered by the *tallit* together with the head, until near the elbows. Now one brings the four corners together and throws them backward, over the left shoulder. At this stage, some have the custom to cover their face with the *tallit,* while others, on the contrary, maintain that the face should remain visible (see step 4 in the image).

Wrapping oneself in a *tallit*: According to the Ashkenazic custom

One stands in this manner for a few seconds, while reciting the verses:

מַה יָּקָר חַסְדְּךָ אֱלֹהִים וּבְנֵי אָדָם בְּצֵל
כְּנָפֶיךָ יֶחֱסָיוּן. יִרְוְיֻן מִדֶּשֶׁן בֵּיתֶךָ וְנַחַל
עֲדָנֶיךָ תַשְׁקֵם. כִּי עִמְּךָ מְקוֹר חַיִּים בְּאוֹרְךָ
נִרְאֶה אוֹר. מְשֹׁךְ חַסְדְּךָ לְיֹדְעֶיךָ וְצִדְקָתְךָ
לְיִשְׁרֵי לֵב.

Ma yakar ḥasdekha, Elohim, uvnei adam betzel kenafekha yeḥesayun. Yirveyun mideshen beitekha venaḥal adanekha tashkem. Ki i'mekha mekor ḥayim, be'orekha nireh or. Meshokh ḥasdekha leyodekha vetzidkatekha leyishrei lev.

"How precious is Your kindness, God; men take refuge in the shadow of Your garment. They are sated by the rich fare of Your House; You give them to drink from the stream of Your delights. For the source of life is with You; through Your light we see light. Extend Your kindness to those who know You, and Your righteousness to the upright of heart" (Psalms 36:8–11).

After the wrapping, one arranges the *tallit* in its proper place, on the head and shoulders.

There are also several methods with regard to placing and arranging the *tallit* on one's body, and each person should choose the method he prefers. Most people wear the *tallit* this way: The two lower corners, together with the majority of the *tallit*, hang behind the head, covering one's back and legs.

Various Topics

The two upper flaps are placed on the shoulders, covering the front of one's chest, on either side of the neck, the right to the right and the left to the left.

Sephardic Custom:
According to the Sephardic custom, one also places the *tallit* over his head, with its upper edge covering the forehead to the level of the eyes. Then one moves the entire cloth of the *tallit* forward, so that both sides are dangling from the shoulders on both sides of the neck, two corners hanging from the right shoulder and the other two from the left shoulder (see step 3 in the image). Next, one takes the part of the *tallit* that is hanging on the right side and tosses it back over the left shoulder, so that it envelops the neck and chin, but not the eyes and the rest of the face (see step 4 in the image). Now one grasps the corners of the *tallit* that are hanging down from the left shoulder and throws them, too, behind the left shoulder (step 5 in the image).

One stands in this manner for a few seconds, and then arranges the *tallit* to its normal position, resting on the head and shoulders (see below) and recites these verses:

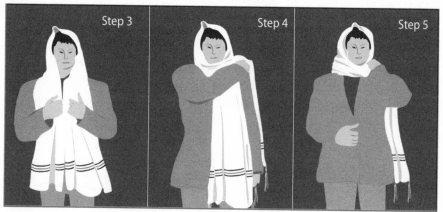

Wrapping oneself in a *tallit*: According to the Sephardic custom

מַה יָּקָר חַסְדְּךָ אֱלֹהִים וּבְנֵי אָדָם בְּצֵל כְּנָפֶיךָ יֶחֱסָיוּן. יִרְוְיֻן מִדֶּשֶׁן בֵּיתֶךָ וְנַחַל עֲדָנֶיךָ תַשְׁקֵם. כִּי עִמְּךָ מְקוֹר חַיִּים בְּאוֹרְךָ נִרְאֶה אוֹר. מְשֹׁךְ חַסְדְּךָ לְיֹדְעֶיךָ וְצִדְקָתְךָ לְיִשְׁרֵי לֵב.

Ma yakar ḥasdekha, Elohim, uvnei adam betzel kenafekha yeḥesayun. Yirveyun mideshen beitekha venaḥal adanekha tashkem. Ki i'mekha mekor ḥayim, be'orekha nireh or. Meshokh ḥasdekha leyodekha vetzidka'tekha leyishrei lev.

"How precious is Your kindness, God; men take refuge in the shadow of Your garment. They are sated by the rich fare of Your House; You give them to drink from the stream of Your delights. For the source of life is with You; through Your light we see light. Extend Your kindness to those who know You, and Your righteousness to the upright of heart" (Psalms 36:8–11).

There are those who add other verses, which can be found in some prayer books.

For both Ashkenazim and Sephardim, some have the custom to leave the top of the *tallit* on their head throughout the prayer service. Others do so only during the *Amida* prayer or perhaps also during the recitation of *Shema*. Another custom is that those who are not yet married do not place the *tallit* on their heads at all.

Various Laws

If one removed the *tallit* with the intention of wearing it again, as, for instance, if he goes to the bathroom in the middle of the prayers, he does not recite a blessing when he puts the *tallit* on again. But if he took off the *tallit* without intending to put it on again, or if the prayer shawl simply fell off his shoulders, he must recite the blessing once again when he puts it back on.

One wraps himself in a *tallit* before donning the *tefillin*.

In the case of *tzitzit* or a *tallit* that has become worn out, one must treat it with respect and not use the fabric for sewing other clothes. It should not be placed in the *geniza*, the repository for discarded religious items, together with holy books, but rather it may be wrapped in a double covering and discarded in the garbage.

The Sky-Blue Strings

It is a mitzva from the Torah to dye one (or according to some opinions, two) of the strings of the *tzitzit* a special sky-blue color. This color is reminiscent of the blue sky, which is in turn reminiscent of God in heaven.

Identifying the Dye

The sky-blue color was produced from the secretion of a certain sea-snail. The Talmud relates that this snail would emerge from the sea every seventy years (*Menahot* 44a). At a certain point, the snail stopped appearing on land and the tradition with regard to its identification was lost. Alternatively, the identity of the sea-snail may have been lost due to historical, political, or economic factors.

The use of sky-blue dye for the strands of the *tzitzit* ceased back in the period of the *geonim*, probably around 1300 years ago. In the absence of the sky-blue dye, it has been customary to wear *tzitzit* with just white strings, which is still a fulfillment of the mitzva. Starting from the nineteenth century, several attempts were made to reconstruct the original sky-blue color, while at the same time, a polemic arose over the correct identification of the snail and the extent to which we can renew the sky-blue dye of *tzitzit* nowadays. A leading voice for the opinion that the correct sea creature had been identified, and that the use of the sky-blue dye should be renewed, was the Radziner Rebbe, Rabbi Gershon Henoch Leiner, who claimed that it was produced from the cuttlefish. He was opposed by many of the halakhic authorities, who claimed that this dye should not be used, as they were not convinced it was produced from the correct source. Additionally, some argued that it is impossible to recreate this tradition nowadays, and that dyeing some of the strings contradicts the custom to wear only white fringes (whereas by strict *halakha*, the strings that are not sky-blue may be any color).

Later, Rabbi Y.I. Herzog, first Ashkenazic Chief Rabbi of the State of Israel, identified a different sea creature as the source of the sky-blue dye mentioned in the Torah. On the basis of his work and that of scholars who followed him, some people today wear sky-blue fringes produced from the *murex trunculus*. There are still some people who wear sky-blue fringes dyed in the manner prescribed by the Radziner Rebbe. The majority of the public still wears *tzitzit* with just white strings.

Tefillin
(Phylacteries)

The commandment to don *tefillin* is one of the most important of all the mitzvot. It has even been said that this mitzva is equal in weight to the entire Torah. It is also one of the three mitzvot that are called an *ot*, a "sign" of the connection between the Jewish people and God (the other two are circumcision and Shabbat). It is for good reason that a Jewish boy's acceptance of the responsibility of mitzvot is associated specifically with the donning of *tefillin*. This mitzva expresses the profound bond between the Jewish people and the Torah. By placing the *tefillin* on his body, a Jew subjugates himself to God, and accepts upon himself the responsibilities and obligations of his Jewishness.

The *tefillin* are placed on the arm, adjacent to the heart, and on the head, next to the brain. This symbolizes that by means of the *tefillin*, one serves the Creator of the world with both his head and his heart, which are the seats of the intellect and the emotions.

The *tefillin* consist of leather boxes that contain four passages from the Torah, which relate the story of the exodus from Egypt and tell of our commitment to the Creator who redeemed us, and our obligation to fulfill His commandments. Each of these passages includes the commandment to bind those Torah portions onto the arm and the head, as a sign and reminder of the close bond between us and God.

This section will examine the physical makeup of the *tefillin* from up close, while analyzing the *halakhot* of donning and removing them, as well as other laws relating to this central and important mitzva.

The Boxes, Passages, and Straps of *Tefillin*

Tefillin are comprised of three main parts: the written Torah passages [*parshiyot*], the boxes [*batim*] that hold them, and the straps [*retzuot*]. The passages are inserted into the boxes, which are connected to the straps with which one fulfills the commandment: "You shall bind them" (Deuteronomy 6:6), i.e., tie the *tefillin* on the arm and on the head. The *batim* are hollow boxes made of the hide of a kosher animal. They are processed in accordance with precise instructions. After the passages have been placed inside the boxes, they are sewn with string made of animal sinews, and then the leather straps are inserted through them, by means of which the *tefillin* are bound to the head and the arm.

The Form of the Boxes [*Batim*]

The boxes of the *tefillin* must be square. They should be made from the skin of a kosher animal and be dyed black.

The *tefillin* of the head and the *tefillin* of the arm are somewhat similar in external appearance, but in fact there is a major difference between them. Whereas the box for the head consists of four distinct compartments, with one Torah passage placed in each compartment, the box for the arm *tefillin* contains only one space, into which a single scroll of parchment, containing all four passages in sequence, is inserted.

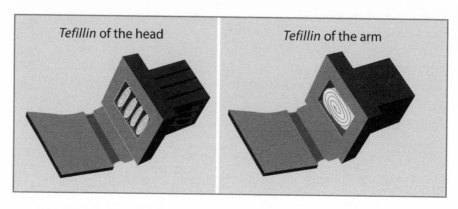

Tefillin of the head   *Tefillin* of the arm

The Torah Passages [*Parshiyot*]

The passages of the *tefillin* must be written by a scribe, with a quill and ink, on parchment. There are many halakhic requirements regarding the writing of the Torah passages. Accordingly, one must trust that the scribe is an honest and God-fearing man. Sometimes a scribe can make a mistake that disqualifies his work, and he alone knows that this has occurred and must make the painful decision to shelve the written passages over which he has toiled. After the writing, the passages are examined through a meticulous proofreading, in order to ensure that every letter was written correctly. Nowadays it is also common for a proofreading to be performed by means of computerized scanning, which ensures that there are no missing or additional words in the passages.

The first passage of the four is: "Sanctify to Me every firstborn" (Exodus 13:1–10), toward the end of which it is stated: "It shall be a sign for you on your arm and a remembrance between your eyes" (Exodus 13:9). The second passage is: "It shall be when the Lord will take you" (Exodus 13:11–16), which includes the command: "It shall be a sign upon your arm and an ornament between your eyes" (Exodus 13:16). The third selection is the *Shema* (Deuteronomy 6:4–9), which states: "You shall bind them as a sign on your arm, and they shall be for ornaments between your eyes" (Deuteronomy 6:8). Finally, the fourth passage is: "It shall be if you will heed" (Deuteronomy 11:13–21), which, near its conclusion, instructs: "And you shall bind them as a sign upon your arm, and they shall be as ornaments between your eyes" (Deuteronomy 11:18).

Rashi and Rabbeinu Tam

These four passages must be written in a specific order; otherwise the *tefillin* are invalid. Over the generations, disagreements arose over what the correct order should be. The leading opinions on this issue are those of Rabbi Shlomo Yitzhaki, known as Rashi, and his grandson, Rabbi Yaakov, known as Rabbeinu Tam. The *halakha* follows the opinion of Rashi, and these are the *tefillin* donned by the Jewish people in all communities around the world every day. Nevertheless, many people, after removing the standard (Rashi) pair, are scrupulous to don a second pair of *tefillin* that are made in accordance with the opinion of Rabbeinu Tam.

The Straps of the *Tefillin*

The *tefillin* straps are made of leather and they must be black. The minimum width of the straps is 9 mm. As for the minimum requisite length of the straps of the head *tefillin,* they should be sufficient to encircle the head of the person who dons them, and then they should hang down on both sides and reach his lower abdomen. The strap of the arm should be at least long enough to wrap around the arm, stretch it to the middle finger, and then twist it three times around that finger.

According to *halakha,* on the straps of the head and the arm *tefillin* must be knots with specific shapes, the tradition for these having been passed down by oral tradition. The knot on the arm *tefillin* is in the form of the Hebrew letter *yod.* In the case of the knot of the head *tefillin,* there is a dispute between the halakhic authorities as to the correct form. The two prevailing opinions are to tie the knot in the form of the Hebrew letter *dalet* or the final letter *mem.*

The *tefillin* straps are sacred, and therefore one must treat them with respect and be careful not to demean them by dragging them on the floor and the like.

Various Topics

In order to protect *tefillin* from damage and improper treatment, it is customary to place them in special plastic boxes, which are then inserted into a sturdy container or cloth or velvet bags or something similar.

Donning and Removing *Tefillin*

Donning *tefillin* is usually performed after wrapping oneself in the *tallit*. If one is not yet married and it is the custom in his community not to wear a *tallit* before marriage, he should don *tefillin* without a *tallit*. First one dons the arm *tefillin*, without wrapping the straps around his fingers, and then the head *tefillin*, after which he wraps the straps of the arm *tefillin* around his fingers. When removing the *tefillin*, one proceeds in the reverse order, first removing the head *tefillin* and then the arm *tefillin*.

The Arm *Tefillin*

One starts by donning the arm *tefillin*, which is wrapped around the arm of one's weaker hand. This is derived from the fact that the Torah states: "It shall be a sign upon your arm [*yadekha*]" (Exodus 13:16), with the word *yadekha* spelled with a *kaf* and a *heh* at the end instead of the expected final letter *kaf*. The Sages interpreted the apparently superfluous letter *heh* as an indication that the *tefillin* should be placed on the *keheh*, or weaker, arm. For right-handed people, this is the left hand, whereas for left-handed individuals, it is the right hand. Since the definition of left-handedness for this matter is complex (it depends on the precise use of one's hands, the extent of the tendency, etc.), it is best for a left-handed person to consult a rabbi about the arm on which he should place the *tefillin*.

According to the Sephardic custom, one dons the arm *tefillin* while sitting, whereas according to the Ashkenazic custom, it is done while standing.

One places the arm *tefillin* in the center of the upper arm, where it is next to the heart, and recites the blessing:

בָּרוּךְ אַתָּה אֲדֹנָי, אֱלֹהֵינוּ מֶלֶךְ הָעוֹלָם,
אֲשֶׁר קִדְּשָׁנוּ בְּמִצְוֹתָיו וְצִוָּנוּ לְהָנִיחַ תְּפִלִּין.

Barukh ata Adonai, Eloheinu, melekh ha'olam, asher kideshanu bemitzvotav, vetzivanu lehani'aḥ tefillin.

"Blessed are You, Lord our God, King of the universe, who sanctified us through His commandments, and commanded us to don *tefillin*."

Various Topics

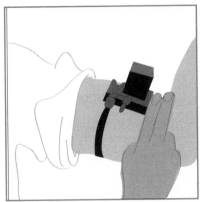

After concluding the blessing, one wraps the strap of the *tefillin* around the upper arm (see step 2 in the image) and then continues to wrap it seven times around the forearm (see step 2 in the image).

There are several different customs regarding the manner of wrapping the straps, and one should follow the tradition of his family or his community.

Step 1

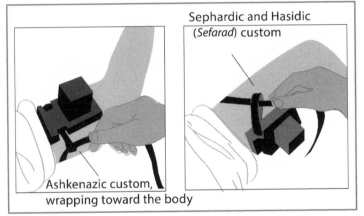

Sephardic and Hasidic (*Sefarad*) custom

Ashkenazic custom, wrapping toward the body

Step 2: Wrapping the *tefillin* straps of the arm

Ashkenazic custom   Hasidic (*Sefarad*) custom   Sephardic custom

Step 3: Ashkenazic custom; hasidic custom; one of the Sephardic customs

The Head *Tefillin*

At this point, one pauses and does not complete the wrapping of the strap around the fingers. Instead, he takes out the head *tefillin* and places it on his head, with the *tefillin* box positioned in the place where the hairs above the forehead grow, directly above the space between the eyes, and then recites the blessing:

בָּרוּךְ אַתָּה אֲדֹנָי, אֱלֹהֵינוּ מֶלֶךְ הָעוֹלָם,
אֲשֶׁר קִדְּשָׁנוּ בְּמִצְוֹתָיו וְצִוָּנוּ עַל מִצְוַת
תְּפִלִּין.

Barukh ata Adonai, Eloheinu, melekh ha'olam, asher kideshanu bemitzvotav, vetzivanu al mitzvat tefillin.

"Blessed are You, Lord our God, King of the universe, who sanctified us through His commandments, and commanded us concerning the mitzva of *tefillin*."

Immediately after this second blessing, one says:

בָּרוּךְ שֵׁם כְּבוֹד מַלְכוּתוֹ לְעוֹלָם וָעֶד.

Barukh shem kevod malkhuto le'olam va'ed.

"Blessed be the name of His kingdom's glory forever and ever."

The placement of the head *tefillin*

Sephardim and a small number of Ashkenazim recite only the blessing over the arm *tefillin*, with this single blessing applying to the head *tefillin* as well. In this matter too, each person should follow the tradition of his forefathers.

One fastens the loop of the head *tefillin* around the circumference of his head and positions the back knot in the indentation below the base of the skull.

One must make sure that there is nothing interposing between the *tefillin* and his body, in the case of both the arm *tefillin* and the head *tefillin*.

After positioning the head *tefillin*, one goes back and completes the donning of the arm *tefillin*: One twists the end of the strap three times around the middle finger and wraps the remainder around the palm. Some recite different verses while binding the straps on the finger and hand, and again, each person should follow the custom of his forefathers.

The Manner of Removing *Tefillin*

The *tefillin* should be removed in the reverse order of how they are donned. Once again, Ashkenazim remove the arm *tefillin* while standing whereas Sephardim do so while sitting.

The order of removing the *tefillin* is as follows: One unwraps the straps from the finger (some also loosen a few more wrappings from the hand at this stage), and then takes off the head *tefillin*, places it in its protective box, before completing the removal of the arm *tefillin*.

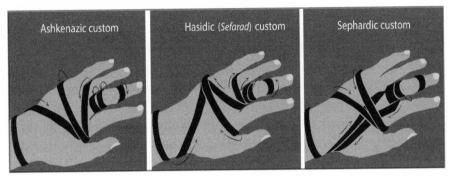

| Ashkenazic custom | Hasidic (*Sefarad*) custom | Sephardic custom |

Ashkenazic custom; hasidic custom; Sephardic customs

Various Laws

Every male from the age of bar mitzva is obligated to don *tefillin* every weekday. Young boys who are about to start donning *tefillin* should learn how to do so and practice a few weeks or months before their bar mitzva, according to their family custom. Women are exempt from the mitzva of *tefillin*, like other positive time-bound mitzvot.

📖 **Further reading:** For more on donning *tefillin* before bar mitzvah, see p. 39.

The mitzva of *tefillin* continues throughout the entire day. In the past, Torah scholars would indeed wear them from morning to evening. In our time, it is customary to don *tefillin* only for the morning prayers, removing them at the end of the prayer service. Some have the custom to don them again at other specific times during the day, such as for the afternoon service.

One who did not don *tefillin* in the morning should do so, with the recitation of the blessing or blessings, later in the day, until sunset. This mitzva is not dependent on the prayer service, and one fulfills it even if he dons the *tefillin* when he is not praying. Nonetheless, it is preferable to recite the entire morning service while wearing *tefillin*. If circumstances do not allow this, the most important thing is to recite *Shema* and the *Amida* prayer with *tefillin*.

The mitzva of *tefillin* is actually comprised of two distinct mitzvot: the head *tefillin* and the arm *tefillin*. Therefore, if one has available only one of

Various Topics

the two elements of the *tefillin*, or if for some reason he cannot don both of them, he should don the *tefillin* that he is able to wear.

Tefillin are sacred items, and therefore, one must maintain a clean body while wearing them. One may not take them into inappropriate places, such as the bathroom. One must also take great care that they do not fall onto the ground. If *tefillin* do fall, it is customary to fast for a full day or to donate to charity the cost of the meals of a full day, for atonement.

On Shabbat and festivals, one does not don *tefillin*. Some have the custom to wear *tefillin* on the intermediate festival days, while others do not do so.

One who dons *tefillin* every day does not have to examine them regularly, and the *tefillin* retain their presumptive status as kosher. Nevertheless, it is advisable to have one's *tefillin* checked once every few years, as weather conditions and other factors can damage the parchment and the letters that are written on it.

Tefillin that are not worn every day must be checked once every three and a half years.

It is a considered a virtuous practice to give one's *tefillin* to an expert for examination every year in the month of Elul.

Interpersonal Mitzvot

A considerable number of the 613 mitzvot of the Torah are interpersonal, that is to say, they regulate relations between people. Even a majority of the Ten Commandments, which can be understood as the outline of the entire Torah, are interpersonal mitzvot.

In a certain sense, transgressions of interpersonal mitzvot are more severe than sins against God. Whereas repentance atones for sins between a person and his Creator, as for "transgressions committed between man and his fellow...one is never forgiven until he gives to his fellow that which he owes him, and placates him" (Rambam, *Sefer HaMadda, Hilkhot Teshuva* 2:9).

This chapter discusses the obligation to love one's fellow Jew, the laws of slander and gossip, prohibitions of fraud, deception, theft, and robbery, as well as the obligations to return lost property, honor one's parents, prevent the suffering of animals, and more. The common denominator of all these topics is that they are interpersonal mitzvot.[1] The subsequent sections will deal with charity and the laws of interest.

The Prohibition Against Hating Other Jews

The Torah forbids one to hate others, as it is stated: "You shall not hate your brother in your heart" (Leviticus 19:17). Aside from obvious displays of animosity, this prohibition even includes hatred that is repressed and is not expressed outwardly. Several practical *halakhot* are derived from this commandment:

Not Holding a Grudge

If one feels hurt by something another person said or did, he should approach that individual, share his feelings, and even ask: "Why did you do that to me?" or "Why did you say such and such about me?" This obligation is learned from the verse: "You shall rebuke your neighbor" (Leviticus 19:17). In other words, one should be open with the other person and point

---

1. The obligation to refrain from causing unnecessary pain to animals does not fit easily into either the category of 'mitzvot between God and man' or that of 'mitzvot between one person and another.' As it is service of God by means of how we relate to other creatures, like interpersonal mitzvot, it will be addressed in this section.

out the severity of his actions. If the offender expresses sincere regret and asks for forgiveness, the victim should be gracious and accept the apology.

If one asked a favor from a friend and was rejected, and after a while the tables turned and the friend who refused him was in need of help himself, he should not hold a grudge against his friend and remind him: "When I asked for your help, you rejected me."

Judging Favorably

When someone sees a person doing something that could be viewed in two ways, one positive and the other negative, he must judge the other favorably and adopt the positive interpretation.

📖 Further reading: For more on judging favorably, see *A Concise Guide to the Sages*, p. 438.

Gossip and Malicious Speech

We are commanded to avoid any action that might harm others, including speech that is defined as "gossip" [*rekhilut*] and "malicious speech" [*lashon hara*]. The term *rekhilut* comes from the same root as *rokhel*, a peddler. Just as a peddler goes from place to place, offering his wares to passersby, so too, the gossiper goes from one person to another, transmitting information that might cause friction between people or harm them. *Lashon hara* means speaking unfavorably about others.

📖 Further reading: For more on *lashon hara*, see *A Concise Guide to the Sages*, pp. 145, 385.

One May Not Speak or Listen to Slander

Just as it is prohibited to speak maliciously of others, one may not listen to such speech; one must refuse to listen to negative reports about others.

Exceptions to the Prohibition of Malicious Speech

In certain very specific cases, the *halakha* permits giving or receiving negative information about others when that information will save someone from harm. For example, it is permitted to warn someone to avoid doing business with a dishonest person. This is permitted only when the negative information is verified and reliable; one may not state the warning in definitive terms.

If one is asked about another person, and the questioner requires the information in order to make important decisions, the one who is asked must tell the truth, even if it contains unflattering information. However, he must limit his remarks to dry and verified facts.

Further reading: For more on the value of truth, see *A Concise Guide to the Sages*, p. 384.

It is permitted to listen to negative reports about others if there is a positive benefit in it. For example, it is permitted to listen to an angry person if it will help him calm down, or to listen to both sides of a dispute if it can give one the ability to make peace.

If someone needs information about another person e.g., an employer who is considering whether to accept a person for a job, he may inquire about the candidate, and even listen to negative information about him. However, he should relate to the reports he receives with caution and skepticism, rather than accepting them as objective facts.

Fraud

The prohibition of defrauding others is mentioned in two places in the Torah. In one place, it is referring to monetary fraud [*ona'at mamon*], that is to say, unfair business conduct that causes financial loss to another. In the other place, the Torah is referring to verbal abuse [*ona'at devarim*], i.e., saying things that cause suffering to others or that deceive them.

A person must be honest and frank in his business dealings with others and must not conceal important details from them. For example, a salesperson should disclose any defects of a product to a potential buyer. Another example is that one must fulfill the terms of a contract, including delivering an object at the agreed-upon time.

Honoring One's Word

When two people agree verbally to carry out a certain transaction, and then one of them retracts his consent before it is completed, the other party does not have a legal claim against him. Nevertheless, the *halakha* states regarding one who retracts such verbal agreement that "the Sages are displeased with him." In situations like this, it is best to specify ahead of time that a verbal agreement does not go into force until the transaction is completed.

Misleading Advice

The Torah states: "You shall not place an obstruction before the blind" (Leviticus 19:14). The Sages explain this to mean that just as a blind person cannot see the path in front of him, so too, one is prohibited from misleading a person in areas where he has no understanding or knowledge. Accordingly, one who gives erroneous or deceptive advice to another has violated this prohibition.

Verbal Abuse

It is prohibited to cause another person grief through insulting or disparaging speech. For example, one should not use mocking nicknames or titles. This prohibition applies even to appellations that are commonly used. However, one violates this prohibition only if he uses the name or epithet with the intention of shaming the individual.

One May Not Cause Suffering

This prohibition is most severe when one shames someone in the presence of others, to the extent that the Sages compared this abusive act to bloodshed.

A husband must take extraordinary care with his wife's honor, and avoid causing her any suffering; this too is included in the prohibition of verbal abuse.

The prohibition of verbal abuse also includes bothering a salesperson in a store with questions about the quality and price of a product when the questioner has no intention of buying from that store. Nowadays, however, some businesses actually encourage buyers to come into their store and inquire about products even if they do not intend to purchase them, in the hope that they might still buy something, either during that visit or on another occasion. If this is the policy of the store, it is permitted.

Criticism Is Permitted

The prohibition against hurting others verbally does not apply to offering constructive criticism to a friend, as long as one does so with good intentions and knows that the other person is interested in what he has to say. Even then, one must voice the criticism in accordance with the *halakhot* of giving reproof.

Deception

Deceiving others is included in the prohibition of verbal abuse, and it is forbidden even when no actual lie or significant harm results.

Prohibited Deception

The following are examples of this prohibited kind of deception:

A person offers to help his friend, with the clear knowledge that his friend has no need for assistance; he does it just to create the impression that he was willing to help.

A person invites someone to stay at his home, knowing with certainty that the he will not agree to come.

However, if he really wishes to host his friend, he may plead with him even if is clear to him that the friend does not want to agree. If he indeed wants the friend to come, it is even permitted to invite him multiple times, even while knowing that ultimately the friend will not acquiesce, as this is a way of honoring the other person.

Theft and Robbery

It is prohibited to steal, as the Torah states: "You shall not steal" (Leviticus 19:11), and it is likewise prohibited to rob, as it states: "And you shall not rob" (Leviticus 19:13). The terms "stealing" and "robbing" both refer to taking something that belongs to another without his consent. The difference is that whereas a thief who steals items acts secretly and furtively, the robber transgresses in the light of day and in the presence of his victim. Following is a summary of the laws of theft and robbery.

Receiving Permission

One may not take money or an item belonging to another without his consent. This includes even an item of little value.

Any use of another person's property without his permission is considered theft, even if the one who used it subsequently returns the item to its original place and in its original condition. In order to use the property of another, one must first obtain explicit permission from the owner; one may not rely on the assumption that "he would obviously let me." This is the *halakha* even when the two people in question are good friends.

It is prohibited to hide the property of others for the purpose of intimidation or amusement, even if the one hiding the item makes no use of it and intends to return it immediately.

When One May Use Something without Permission

In the following two cases it is permitted to make use of property belonging to others, even without their explicit permission:

(1) When it is an item whose value is negligible and owners typically do not object to others taking or using it, for example, taking a single tissue from a box of tissues. This leniency applies only if the owner of the item is absent when the user needs the item. If the owner is there, one must ask for and receive his consent.

(2) When the user knows without any doubt that the owner of the item allows him to use it, and also that it is an item that will not diminish in value as a result of its use. This permission is likewise not all-encompassing, but

rather applies only on a case-by-case basis. One may not repeatedly and habitually take the item unless he receives explicit permission to do so.

Returning Stolen Property to Its Owners

One who robbed someone or stole something from him must return it to its owner, as it is written: "He shall restore the stolen item that he stole" (Leviticus 5:23).

Full Compensation

If the item was lost, damaged, or irreversibly changed its form, the thief must pay the owner its full value, established at the time that he took it.

It is prohibited to buy a stolen item from a thief or robber, as by doing so, the buyer is only encouraging him to continue his criminal behavior. If one purchased a stolen item, and the owner has not lost all hope of restoring it to his possession, the buyer must return the item to its owner.

Takanat HaShuk

If one innocently bought an item without knowing that it was stolen, and the owner of the item demands that he return it to him, the owner must pay the buyer the price that the buyer paid the thief. The owner of the item is then entitled to sue the thief to reclaim this payment. This *halakha*, which is called *takanat hashuk* (a provision ensuring the integrity of the marketplace), was established by the Sages in order to protect blameless people who bought stolen property from being taking advantage of by thieves.

If the owner of the item had already despaired of recovering the stolen object, and it was given or sold to a third party who did not know that it was stolen, that third party is exempt from returning it to its original owner even in return for payment. The owner of the item may of course still sue the thief to recover its value.

The Prohibition of Withholding Wages

In the past, it was customary to pay hired workers on a daily basis. When this is the case, the Torah establishes that this practice has the status of a law that is binding upon the employer, as it states: "You shall not keep the wages of a hired laborer with you overnight until morning" (Leviticus 19:13). It further states: "On his day you shall give his wage, and the sun shall not set upon it" (Deuteronomy 24:15). The meaning of these two verses is that if the laborer finished his work at the end of the day, the employer must pay him his wages before the next morning, and transgresses a prohibition if he delays payment. If the worker completed his work in the middle of the day, the employer must pay his salary before sunset.

Payment on Time

Nowadays, it is customary to pay salaried workers on a weekly, bi-weekly, or monthly basis as established by law or agreement. In many workplaces, a certain date of the month is set as the day of payment for the previous month's work. The prohibition against withholding wages applies in modern times as well: An employer must pay the salary at the end of the pay period, and if a fixed date has been agreed upon, he must abide by it.

If a worker was contracted to perform a job rather than being paid a wage calculated on a daily or hourly basis (this is common, for example, with electricians, plumbers, or dry cleaners), then once the worker has completed the work to the satisfaction of the customer, the customer must pay the worker on that same day, unless previously agreed otherwise.

The Obligations of the Employee

Corresponding to the employer's obligations, the worker also bears some responsibilities of his own.

Fairness at Work

An employee who has been hired to work for a certain number of days or hours must take care to make maximum use of the work time. He must make sure to eat and sleep properly, so that during the work hours he will be at his best and be as efficient as possible.

An employee must refrain from using his employer's property for his own personal needs. This prohibition does not apply, of course, to cases where the employee receives permission of his employer.

"You Shall Distance Yourself from Falsehood"

The Torah instructs us: "You shall not lie to one another" (Leviticus 19:11). Elsewhere in the Torah it is stated: "You shall distance yourself from falsehood" (Exodus 23:7). This verse teaches that telling a lie is something that must be avoided in and of itself, even if this is unrelated to the actual deception of someone.

When Is It Permitted to Depart from the Truth?

Nevertheless, there are cases in which it is permitted to deviate from the truth. In certain situations, it is even a mitzva to refrain from telling the truth. Examples of these cases include the following:

It is permitted to lie when telling the truth is apt to cause unnecessary friction between two people.

It is permitted to "adjust" the truth and present the facts in a somewhat inaccurate manner in order to spare someone from grief.

A humble person may conceal his knowledge or good deeds from those around him.

It is sometimes permitted to conceal the truth regarding intimate matters, in order to protect people's privacy.

Returning Lost Property

A person who finds a lost item is obligated to return it to its owner, as the verse states: "You shall not see your brother's ox or his sheep wandering, and disregard them; you shall return them to your brother" (Deuteronomy 22:1). The ox and sheep mentioned here are merely examples; the commandment is to return any lost item of minimal value. The Sages clarified the ways in which one fulfills this mitzva.

📖 Further reading: For a story of returning lost property involving Rabbi Ḥanina ben Dosa, see *A Concise Guide to the Sages*, p. 350.

Distinguishing Marks

If one knows who is the owner of an item that one has found, he is obligated to return it directly to him or to his home. If one does not know who the owner is, he must take an active role in looking for the owner by publicizing the item he has found. He should give only general information in his announcement, so that the owner can approach him and claim his loss by identifying it by its distinguishing characteristics. If the person who claims ownership over an item is only able to provide a general description (such as its color), that is insufficient, as it could easily be a guess while the item belongs to someone else. Knowledge of the precise location of the item is considered a distinguishing mark.

One Who Finds Money

One who finds money in the street may take it for himself and does not need to publicize it or seek its owner. The reason for this is that the person who lost the money has presumably despaired of recovering it, as he knows that all banknotes and coins are essentially the same and he will be unable to provide distinguishing marks in order to claim it.

Even if there is a name or phone number on the lost bill, this is not a clear sign that it belongs to that person, as money passes from hand to hand and it is impossible to know if this information was written by the last owner.

However, if there is a clear distinguishing mark on an item that was found together with the money, one must publicize his finding and return the money to a person who can identify this distinguishing mark. For example, if money was found in an envelope that contains a clear mark, or if it is a bundle of bills or coins, and the claimant knows the exact amount, or if the notes are tied with a rubber band that has unique features, these are all considered identifying marks.

Money in a Store

When a person finds money in a store and did not see who dropped it, then its status depends upon its location. If the money was found near the cash register or in another place where it can be presumed that it was dropped by the storekeeper, then it belongs to the store owner, and the finder must give the money to the person minding the store. If he found the money elsewhere in the store, he does not have to declare his finding, and may keep it for himself.

Cases Where One Should Not Touch the Item

When one notices an item in a public place and it appears that it was not lost but placed there deliberately, he must leave the item in its place.

If the finder is uncertain as to whether the item was lost or intentionally placed there, and the item is in a secluded spot from where it is unlikely to be stolen, he should leave it where it is.

If one finds a lost item and he is embarrassed to carry it with him, because he is a distinguished individual or because he is unaccustomed to carrying such items in public, he must honestly answer the following question: What would he do if the item he has found was his own? If he would overcome the unpleasantness and take the item with him, he must act likewise in order to return another person's possession. But if he would leave it in its place and move on without it, he is exempt from carrying the item to his home and from returning it to its owner.

The Obligation to Rescue

If a person sees that another person's property is being damaged (for example, it is on fire, being washed away in a flood, or being stolen by someone), he is obligated to try to rescue this property. This obligation also falls under the rubric of returning lost property.

Hospitality

One of the most prominent commandments in the category of interpersonal mitzvot is the mitzva of hospitality. The Sages praised this mitzva highly and said: "Hospitality accorded to guests is greater than receiving the Divine Presence" (*Shavuot* 35b). In other words, if (as it were) God Himself would come to visit a person, and at the same time, flesh-and-blood guests were to knock on the door, one must greet the human guests first and only then welcome God.

The Needs of the Guest

The mitzva of hospitality includes providing all the needs of one's guest, including food, drink, a comfortable bed, and of course, a warm and friendly attitude.

At the end of the visit, it is important to accompany a visitor on his way, for at least a few steps outside the house, in order to make him feel that he was a welcome guest from whom it is difficult to part.

The highest level of hospitality is fulfilled when one hosts a person who requires financial or emotional support, such as a lonely individual or a new immigrant. Yet even when one hosts one's own family, friends, or neighbors, he fulfills an important mitzva, the commandment of *ahavat Yisrael*, loving fellow Jews.

On Festivals and Celebrations

On Rosh HaShana, *Sukkot*, Passover, and *Shavuot*, it is a special mitzva to invite guests and celebrate the festival with them.

When making a family celebration, some people have the custom to invite several poor people or, alternatively, to make a donation to charity that would cover the cost of hosting several guests.

Visiting the Sick

It is a great mitzva to visit with and assist a person who is ill. The visit itself, along with the caller's display of empathy, can strengthen and encourage the patient, and can even assist in the healing process. This duty applies both when the patient is in his home and when he is hospitalized in a medical center where professionals are taking care of him and providing for all his needs.

Cheering Up the Patient

The role of the visitor is to cheer up the patient, and therefore, it is important to be encouraging and to radiate optimism and joy rather than fear and despair.

It is crucial that the visitor takes the true needs of the patient into consideration. Some patients need physical assistance, while others simply want to talk and hear words of encouragement. Sometimes a long visit will weigh heavily on the patient, whereas on other occasions, every additional moment of one's stay makes him happy. In any case, the *halakha* cautions a visitor against being a burden on the patient.

By Phone as Well

When it is not possible to visit an ill person, one can fulfill the mitzva by showing interest and offering one's good wishes through a phone call.

Prayers for the Sick

The mitzva of visiting the sick includes sending good wishes for the patient's recovery and praying for his well-being.

In synagogues, it is customary to recite the *Mi SheBerakh* prayer on behalf of the sick. The custom in some synagogues is for people to approach the *gabbai* (sexton) to tell him the names of the patients they know, using each patient's Hebrew name and the name of his/her mother (e.g., Moshe ben Sarah, or Hannah bat Aliza), so that the *gabbai* will include those names in the text of the prayer. In other places, the *gabbai* recites the general formula of the *Mi SheBerakh* prayer, pausing for a moment for anyone in the congregation who knows a sick individual to utter the name in a whisper.

Adding a Name

It is customary to add an additional name that expresses life or healing to the name of a person who has a life-threatening illness. For example, one might give a very sick man the additional name Ḥayim (meaning "life") or Refael ("God is a healer"). A woman could receive the name Ḥaya ("living"). The name is added in the synagogue, while standing alongside the Torah scroll (on Mondays, Thursdays, or Shabbat, when the Torah is read) using the *Mi SheBerakh* prayer, or by reciting a special text designed for this purpose.

Further reading: For more on visiting the sick, see *A Concise Guide to the Sages*, p. 402.

Consoling Mourners

The main purpose of the days of shiva, the seven-day period when mourners sit and receive consolations from relatives and friends, is for the mourners to remember and think of the departed. It is also important for them to come to terms with their loss and draw strength from those around them. Therefore, it is a mitzva to go to the mourners' house during the shiva, to comfort them and raise their spirits.

Attentiveness

The mitzva of consoling mourners is performed by the very act of coming to a house of mourning and sitting with them, as this conveys to them that the visitor cares and shares in their sorrow. Sometimes a mourner is overcome with grief and has no desire to talk. Therefore, the *halakha* states that when one enters the house of mourning, he must sit quietly and wait for the mourner to open the conversation. One does not greet a mourner, nor even inquire about his welfare (see the laws of mourning, p. 105).

The pace of the conversation and its topics are to be dictated by the mourner, and those who came to console must be attentive to his wishes. If they are familiar with facts and stories about the good deeds of the deceased, it is appropriate to relate them to the mourner.

When one has sat for a while and feels that his presence is beginning to weigh on the mourner, he should get up and leave.

How and When to Comfort

Before leaving the shiva house, one says to the mourner a standard formula of consolation.

The Sephardic custom is to say:

מִן הַשָּׁמַיִם תְּנוּחֲמוּ.   *Min hashamayim tenuḥamu.*

"May you be comforted from heaven."

Ashkenazim say:

הַמָּקוֹם יְנַחֵם אֶתְכֶם בְּתוֹךְ שְׁאָר אֲבֵלֵי   *HaMakom yenaḥem etkhem betokh*
צִיּוֹן וִירוּשָׁלָיִם (יש מוסיפים: וְלֹא תּוֹסִיפוּ   *she'ar avelei tziyon virushalayim* (some
לְדַאֲבָה עוֹד).   add: *velo tosifu leda'ava od*).

"May God console you among the other mourners of Zion and Jerusalem (some add: and may you know no further sorrow)."

The mourner responds: "Amen."

To this standard formula one may add personal words of comfort, in any wording or style.

Various Topics

Those who cannot come to the house of mourning may console the mourner by telephone or in writing.

One who did not console a mourner during the week of shiva may fulfill the mitzva to comfort him during the following period as well. For those who are mourning parents, the mourning period is for a year, whereas for those mourning siblings, spouses, or children, the mourning extends for one month from the date of the burial.

Honoring One's Parents

The mitzva of honoring one's parents is one of the Ten Commandments. In the text of the Ten Commandments, it appears in a brief, summarized form, which is expanded upon in other places in the Torah, and more so in the statements of the Sages. The Talmud (*Kiddushin* 30b) compares one's duty to honor and revere one's parents to the obligation to honor and revere God. It explains: " There are three partners in the forming of a person: the Holy One, Blessed be He, one's father, and one's mother." The parents provide the physical body, while God breathes in us the breath of life. The Talmud further adds: "When a person honors his father and mother, the Holy One, Blessed be He, says: I relate to them as though I dwelled among them and they honored Me as well."

Further reading: For more on honoring parents, see *A Concise Guide to the Sages*, pp. 41, 153.

Unconditional Respect

The mitzva of honoring one's parents applies mainly to providing physical assistance when the parents require it. It does not have to involve financial expense.

The obligation to help parents is all-inclusive, and it applies to each and every one of their children, single or married, those who live with their parents, and those have moved elsewhere.

Helping parents must be done in a dignified manner, with a full heart and a warm, sincere demeanor. Likewise, honoring one's parents is not conditional on their behavior or way of life.

Parents, for their part, should try not to make excessive demands on their children.

When There Is No Agreement

The mitzva of honoring parents applies only to matters that concern the parents' lives, and not those that concern the lives of their adult children. An adult has the right to an independent life, and he may make decisions concerning his private life even if these are inconsistent with his parents' wishes.

Various Topics

Helping One's Parents

When a person must choose between helping a stranger and helping his parents, the decision is clear: The parents come first.

If possible, one should try to live near his parents, in order to be available to help them in times of need.

If the parents do not require physical assistance but are interested in daily visits from their children for their pleasure, the children are not obligated to see them every day but should try to visit their parents as often as possible.

Financial Expenditures

Children are not obligated to support their parents financially, and if they do spend money on them, they are entitled to repayment from the parents' property.

Types of Honor and Reverence

Honoring one's parents is expressed not only in deeds, but also in one's manner of speech. One must address them with respect in both language and tone, and of course one may not display anger toward them nor insult them. This is the case even if the parents, for their part, do not show respect to their children. Furthermore, it is prohibited to demean or grow angry with one's parents, even in one's thoughts. We are obligated to think about them in positive terms.

One may not sit in the permanent seat of one of his parents at home (e.g., if the parent sits at the head of the table) or in the synagogue. This *halakha* applies even when the parents are not present at the time. If the children have received permission from their parents to sit in their place, it is permitted.

After the death of the parent, one is permitted to sit in his or her place.

When a father enters the room or is called up to the Torah reading in the synagogue, his sons must stand up. Some are strict about this and continue standing until the end of the reading of the passage of the Torah and the father's return to his seat.

If the parent foregoes his honor regarding standing up for him (when he enters the room or when he is called to the Torah), his sons are permitted to sit.

Children may not call their parents by their first names, but rather by "father" and "mother" and the equivalent.

It is prohibited to wake a father or mother from their sleep, even for an important reason, as one must avoid causing any type of suffering to one's parents. But if the child knows that the parent will later be upset that he was not woken, he should wake him up. Even so, it is better to ask someone else to wake up one's parent.

One must honor a parent even after his or her death, e.g., by speaking of him or her in a respectful manner, saying Kaddish on the anniversary of the death (yahrzeit), and giving to charity in his or her memory. Honest and commendable conduct on the part of children also shows respect for the memory of their late parents.

📖 Further reading: For more on honoring a parent after his death, see *A Concise Guide to Mahshava*, p. 29.

When Must One Listen and When Not

When a parent expresses his or her opinion on a given matter, his children must not express disagreement with him or her. Doing so is disrespectful of the parent.

If a parent asks an adult child to do something that involves the child's private life, the child must listen respectfully, but is not required to obey. For example, if the parents want their son or daughter to study a particular profession, the child may still pursue a different occupation. Although he is not obligated to obey his parents with regard to his private affairs, when one obeys his parents with regard to his private life, he has performed a mitzva.

With regard to choices that express one's values, like if a son wants to study Torah and his parents oppose it, he should not listen to them.

If the parents object to their son or daughter's choice of spouse, the child has no obligation to obey them. Of course, it is highly recommended to try to appease the parents and receive their consent, but each person has the freedom to choose his own future.

If the parents decide to boycott the wedding and demand that their other children do the same, the brothers and sisters need not obey. Attending the wedding is part of the mitzvah of: "You shall love your neighbor as yourself" (Leviticus 19:18), and whenever the honor of one's parents comes into conflict with a mitzva, one must obey the Torah.

Not Only Biological Parents

One must honor a stepparent and not only one's biological parents. When one respects the stepparent, he is, in effect, honoring his biological parent as well.

The mitzva of honoring parents also includes one's grandparents, in-laws, and even older siblings. There is a hierarchy: It is proper to respect all people. It is more important to respect the aforementioned family members. The honor of one's parents stands above all others and takes precedence.

📖 Further reading: For more on honoring one's parents, see *A Concise Guide to the Sages*, pp. 41, 153.

Honoring an Elderly Person and a Torah Scholar

The Torah states: "You shall rise before the graybeard, and show deference before the elderly (Leviticus 19:32). The basic meaning of the verse is that one must respect old people who have reached the age of a *zaken*, a "graybeard," which is seventy years old. In addition, the Sages extended the meaning of this verse to apply to Torah scholars as well, as they interpreted the word *zaken* (elderly) as an acronym for *zeh kana ḥokhma*, meaning: "this one has acquired wisdom." In other words, one must show deference and respect to people who have Torah knowledge.

Method of Honoring Them

When a wise or elderly person passes by where one is sitting, one must stand up in his honor. It is a mitzva to give one's seat to an old person and to extend a hand to help him walk.

The *halakha* of honoring Torah scholars comprises three ascending levels of respect: First, one must respect every Torah scholar; second, one must respect a scholar who has taught him Torah; third, one must be especially respectful of the Torah scholar who is also his primary teacher.

Respecting a Torah scholar is similar in some ways to honoring one's parents. Just as parents are partners in the creation of their child's material existence, and one is therefore obligated to honor them, likewise a scholar who teaches Torah becomes a partner in creating the spiritual life of the student. This is even more true if that person is his primary teacher.

The honor due to Torah scholars includes the obligation to stand up when they approach, not to sit in their permanent seat, to refrain from contradicting them, and not to issue a halakhic ruling in their presence.

Cruelty to Animals

King David wrote in the book of Psalms: "The Lord is good to all, and His mercy extends to all His creations" (Psalms 145:9). Since we aspire to resemble the Creator and adopt His virtuous qualities, we too must open our hearts and widen the circle of our compassion, to all of God's creatures, which includes not only people but animals as well. Therefore, it is a mitzva to ease the suffering of animals. For example, one must remove a heavy load from a donkey that is "crouching under its burden" (Exodus 23:5). Certainly, one may not actively cause unnecessary suffering to living creatures.

It is an even greater mitzva to have compassion on animals that assist people, such as a hen that lays eggs, a donkey that bears loads, or a dog that guards one's home.

📖 **Further reading:** For more on cruelty to animals, see *A Concise Guide to the Sages*, p. 435; *A Concise Guide to Mahshava*, p. 122.

Mercy for Animals

If an animal is laboring in the service of a person, one may not make conditions unreasonably hard for it. In the case of an animal working in a field, or carrying on its back food that it could eat as well, it is prohibited to prevent it from eating that same food while it is being put to work.

If one seeks to buy an animal, he must be certain that he is indeed capable of providing that animal with its food.

It is written in the Torah: "I will provide grass in your field for your animals, and you will eat and you will be satisfied" (Deuteronomy 11:15). Since the verse mentions feeding animals before eating one's own meal, the Sages ruled that one is prohibited from sitting down for a meal before feeding the animals that are in his care.

One who has compassion upon wild animals that are struggling to find food on their own, and feeds them himself, has fulfilled a mitzva, but there is no obligation to do so.

Milking

Milking animals is a labor that is prohibited on Shabbat by Torah law. The Sages even prohibited a Jew from telling a gentile to do this job for him. Nevertheless, when the animal suffers if it is not milked, the Torah requires that it be relieved by asking a non-Jew to milk it. If there is no gentile available, a Jew may milk the animal, but he must do so in such a manner that the milk is not collected in a utensil and instead goes to waste.

Carrying Animals on Shabbat

On Shabbat it is prohibited to pick up and carry an animal. According to some opinions, this prohibition does not include small house pets that are meant to be carried. When it is necessary to move an animal, one may encourage it to walk by pushing it. If this assistance is not enough and the animal must be carried, there are halakhic opinions that permit this as well, as long as one does not violate the labor of carrying in a public domain.

When There Is Human Need

Cruelty to animals should be avoided unless it serves an essential human purpose. Actions that provide benefit to a person (financial gain, saving expenses, physical relief, or even amusement, such as training and exhibiting talking parrots) do not violate the prohibition of cruelty to animals.

One may not take pleasure in the suffering of animals. The fact that certain people enjoy watching such spectacles does not mean that it provides a "human need," and it is strictly prohibited.

In cases where it is necessary to perform an action that entails animal suffering for the benefit of humans, such as conducting scientific experiments that are aimed at saving lives, it is permitted to do so.

One may kill a harmful and dangerous animal that poses a threat to people. It is also permitted to kill insects or other pests that spoil the cleanliness of one's house and negatively affect the quality of people's lives.

Hunting

It is permitted to hunt animals in order to eat them or make a living from selling them. Nevertheless, hunting and killing that is performed for pleasure and amusement alone are inappropriate and unseemly for a Jew. Fishing is permitted even for pleasure.

Charity

The Torah commands us to provide financial support for people who are unable to make ends meet on their own. There are numerous Torah sources for this obligation. For example: "You shall open your hand to him" (Deuteronomy 15:8); "you shall support him, stranger or resident alien, and he shall live with you" (Leviticus 25:35); "and your brother shall live with you" (Leviticus 25:36). There is also a verse from the Prophets, which presents this mitzva in a particularly illustrative manner: "Isn't it slicing your bread for the hungry and bringing the wretched poor home, when you see the naked, you clothe him, and you do not disregard your own flesh?" (Isaiah 58:7). The obligation to support the poor is also alluded to in the very word *tzedaka*, charity, which comes from the word for justice, *tzedek*. One who helps the needy performs true justice in the world.

This section will discuss various matters involving the mitzva of charity: how and to whom to give, how much one should donate, and giving charity on various special occasions.

> **Further reading:** For more on the different levels and preferences in the giving of charity, see *A Concise Guide to Mahshava*, p. 248.

Definition of *Tzedaka*

Each and every person is obligated to give *tzedaka*. This *halakha* applies to men and women, rich and poor people, the elderly and the young alike. Even very young children should be educated in the giving of *tzedaka*.

Every act of giving, even of the smallest sum, is a fulfillment of the mitzva of *tzedaka*.

Some people mistakenly think that one can perform the mitzva of *tzedaka* only by giving money to the poor. The truth is that helping a person find work and earn a living, or even aiding a businessperson in crisis so that he can stand on his own two feet again, are both considered to be the highest level of the mitzva of *tzedaka*. The most important and loftiest form of *tzedaka* is precisely that act that prevents someone from descending into a state of poverty.

Granting a loan to a needy individual is also included in the mitzva of *tzedaka*. In one sense, granting a loan is superior to a donation, as the person receiving the loan does not experience the humiliation of having to rely on a charitable gift.

How Much and When to Give

The proper and recommended way to fulfill the mitzva is to give some money to *tzedaka* each day. One can give it directly to a needy person or drop money into a *tzedaka* box. It is a common practice to keep a *tzedaka* box in the home, and when the box is full, the giver should transfer its contents to the charitable organization of his choosing. If the *tzedaka* box is the property of a particular institution, its contents must be handed over to that institution.

Many people also keep a *tzedaka* box in their car, and occasionally place money into it. The merit of the mitzva contributes to the safety of the passengers of the car.

It is advisable to give *tzedaka* before the morning and afternoon prayers, as this helps one's prayers to be accepted before the Holy one blessed be He. In the morning service, some have the custom of giving money to *tzedaka* while reciting the words: "Riches and honor are in Your gift, and You rule over all," in the passage starting: "David blessed."

Tithing One's Income

One of the mitzvot of charity in the Torah is the obligation every third year to set aside one-tenth of the produce one grows in the Land of Israel for the poor. Inspired by this mitzva, the Sages instructed, either as an outright obligation or a least as a recommended practice, that each person set aside one-tenth of his income (a tithe) for *tzedaka*. The Talmud promises the donor that giving the tithe will not lead to financial loss; indeed, the opposite is the case, as it will bring him blessings and increase his earnings. The Sages found an allusion to this in the verse: "You shall tithe [*asser te'asser*]" (Deuteronomy 14:22), which they interpreted as meaning: Separate tithes [*asser*] so that you will become wealthy [*shetitasher*] (*Shabbat* 119a).

The method of calculating the tithe is as follows: Employees should pay one-tenth of their net income. Those who are self-employed should allocate one-tenth of the net profits to *tzedaka* after offsetting business expenses. It is recommended to keep an orderly record of one's earnings and donations.

The giving of the tithe applies to anyone who has a regular income that is sufficient to cover their basic family expenses.

A person who has debts must first discharge his obligations. In the meantime, he should suffice with making a symbolic daily donation to *tzedaka*. Those who are financially secure are advised to set aside more than one-tenth.

One-tenth should be donated not only from one's salary or business profits, but also from money received as a gift, inherited, or in some other manner.

The tithe applies only to monetary income, but not to non-liquid gains. Likewise, it applies to real profits, after the deduction of business expenses, that may be used at the person's discretion for whatever he desires.

When one starts to set aside a fixed daily amount or a fixed monthly sum for *tzedaka*, it is appropriate to declare at the time that he does not intend to accept upon himself a vow to do so, so as not to obligate himself to continue with this donation if future circumstances make it difficult. It is also advisable to say at the outset that the sum may be used for any good purpose that will arise in the future, not only as a donation to the poor.

Recipients of Charity

There is a virtue to donating through trustworthy charitable organizations. Giving in this manner spares the poor person from shame, as neither the donor nor the recipient knows who has given to the other. If one discovers that a certain person is in financial distress and needs help, even if in general he would not be defined as poor, it is permitted to help him with one's tithe money. This should be done in a respectful manner, taking care that he not be embarrassed. For example, one can offer him a loan while privately deciding not to demand or even expect repayment unless the recipient is relieved of his distress.

The Poor of Your City Take Precedence

The Sages established that "the poor of your city take precedence" (*Bava Metzia* 71a). This means that the order of priority for giving *tzedaka* is based on the closeness of the relationship of the needy person to the giver: One should prioritize taking care of direct relatives (parental support of their adult children, single or married, is also included in the mitzva of *tzedaka*), followed by neighbors, members of one's community, city, and only then those in need who come from wider circles.

If an unfamiliar person comes forward and requests money, and one has no means of ascertaining whether he is truly in need or simply taking advantage, one should give him a small amount. However, if he asks for food, one must immediately provide him with food until he has had his fill, as such a request indicates genuine distress.

If the person is known to be a swindler or someone who uses the money that he collects for unsuitable purposes, one should not give him anything.

Tzedaka on Special Days

On Purim, there is a special mitzva called *matanot la'evyonim*, "gifts for the poor." The minimum amount that one should give is enough for the needy person to buy food for the Purim feast. This amount should be given twice, to two poor people. One can fulfill the mitzva of *matanot la'evyonim* by making a donation to an organization that undertakes to give the money to two needy individuals, who will receive it on the day of Purim itself.

Before Passover, it is customary in every Jewish community to conduct a campaign called *kimha depisha* or *maot hitim*, which means "flour for *matzot* on Passover." The aim is to increase the normal level of donations from the public in order to help the needy meet the many expenses of the approaching festival. One should follow a similar practice before every festival.

On Yom Kippur, *Shemini Atzeret*, the last festival day of Passover, and on *Shavuot*, it is customary to recite in the synagogue the *Yizkor* prayer for a father or mother who have passed away. On this occasion, the son or daughter should accept upon themselves to give some *tzedaka*, making a pledge "without making a vow" to give money in memory of the soul of the parent. This sum should be paid on the day after the festival.

Additional dates in the year on which one should give extra *tzedaka* include the whole month of Elul, which is a period of mercy and forgiveness, as well as fast days, such as the seventeenth of Tamuz and *Tisha BeAv*.

There is a custom for women to give *tzedaka* every Friday night before lighting the Shabbat candles, and similarly on the eve of festivals. Many women also give *tzedaka* before performing other special mitzvot, such as separating *halla* and immersing in a *mikva*.

Charity during the Life Cycle

It is proper to give additional *tzedaka* on one's birthday.

Some have the custom that for every important occasion, such as a wedding, bar mitzva, or circumcision, they invite a few poor people to attend the celebration or they donate a generous sum to the poor.

During the year of mourning for one's father or mother, one should try to give more *tzedaka* than usual. This mitzva helps the soul of the deceased. Similarly, in subsequent years one should give extra *tzedaka* on the anniversary of the death (yahrzeit), in memory of the deceased.

Interest

The prohibition against taking or paying interest appears several times in the Torah. For example: "And if your brother shall become poor, and his means fail with you... Do not take interest [*neshekh*] or increase from him; you shall fear your God... Your silver you shall not give him with interest, and with increase you shall not give him your food" (Leviticus 25:35–37). "Increase" is also a term denoting interest, which is called *neshekh*, as explained by Rashi (Rav Shlomo Yitzḥaki, the great eleventh-century commentator on the Torah), "because it is like the biting [*neshikha*] of a snake, as a snake bites by making a small wound in one's leg which the person does not feel, and suddenly it spreads and swells up as far as his head. Likewise, one does not notice the effect of interest until the interest accumulates and it costs him a considerable sum of money" (Rashi, Exodus 22:24).

The core prohibition of interest is that one may not lend money to a person with an advance agreement that the repayment will be higher than the amount of the loan. It does not matter if it is a one-time payment, e.g., a loan of $100 for which the debtor must pay back $125, or a loan paid in installments, e.g., a loan of $100 that must be repaid by the debtor in five monthly payments of $25 each instead of $20. Either way, the result is that the debtor pays $25 more than the sum he borrowed.

This chapter briefly presents the concepts involved in the prohibition of interest, and lists specific practices that are prohibited because they are either instances of interest or closely related to them.

The Prohibition of Interest by Torah Law

The prohibition of interest applies not only to the creditor but also to the debtor. In other words, it is prohibited to borrow money with an agreement to repay the debt plus interest. Likewise, a third party may not help others violate the prohibition of interest by, for example, serving as a guarantor or a witness to such a loan.

Various Laws Relating to Interest

There is no difference between a loan with interest given to a poor person and a loan of this type given to a rich person. The severity of the prohibition is the same in both cases.

The prohibition of interest applies specifically to loans between Jews. One is permitted to collect interest from non-Jews or pay interest to a non-Jew. The explanation for this is that taking interest is not inherently immoral, and therefore in transactions with gentiles it is permitted. The prohibition is in force only between Jews, and it expresses the extraordinary solidarity which the Torah seeks to nurture and preserve among our people.

Interest That Is Prohibited by Rabbinic Law

As indicated above, the prohibition against lending with interest is not rooted in natural morality. On the contrary, the ability to receive credit in exchange for money is often in the interest of the debtor. Likewise, as the creditor could have invested the money and earned profits from it, it is not fair that he should have to lend it without receiving any yield, especially when the debtor uses the money for his own business and earns profits through it. Because lending and borrowing with interest seems reasonable and is nevertheless prohibited, the Sages, in order to inculcate the seriousness of the prohibition, instituted a series of laws and prohibitions that extend the prohibition to additional cases by rabbinic law. Some of these are very far removed from the case of a loan with interest and are called *avak ribit*, literally "the dust of interest."

Avak Ribit

The Sages prohibited certain transactions because they are considered to be *avak ribit*.

Discounted advance payment on a sale: A seller may not tell a buyer: "The product costs $100, but if you agree to pay me now and receive delivery only in a month's time, you can have it for $90." However, it is permitted to reduce the price of a product in exchange for payment in cash, under the following conditions:

(1) the product is in stock;

(2) it has no fixed price;

(3) the seller does not expressly tell the buyer that the discount depends on the method of payment.

Delayed payment: The seller may not offer the buyer the option to pay later at a higher price. For example, he may not say: "If you pay me now for merchandise that I provide you now, the price will be $100, but if you pay me for it only after a month, the price will be $110." This is a common problem today in cases where payment is made in installments, where the seller sets the price of the item higher than if it was paid for up front. Nevertheless, if the product has no clear nominal value (referring not only to the price tag on the product, but to a uniform price over a wide cross-section of stores), and the seller does not explicitly state the terms to the purchaser, he may make his own calculation and ask for a deferred payment at a higher price.

Loans that are not in the local currency: A loan should be made only in the currency that is used locally. Since, as far as the *halakhot* of interest are concerned, prices are defined in terms of the local currency, the value of foreign currency fluctuates, raising the risk of a sort of interest on loans made in it. For example, if someone in Israel lends someone else $100 when the shekel-dollar exchange rate is four shekels to a dollar, and at the time of repayment the exchange rate has risen to four and a half shekels to a dollar, then when the debtor repays $100 in U.S. currency, he is repaying more (in shekels) than he borrowed.

In the past, when real estate prices in Israel were set in dollars, the dollar could also be treated as a local currency in Israel. Today, however, when the shekel is stable and prices are set in shekels, it is highly doubtful that the dollar can be considered a local currency.

Accordingly, it is prohibited to borrow in one type of currency and repay in another type of currency, e.g., borrowing in shekels and repaying in dollars, unless the amount repaid is fixed by the original value in local currency of the loan, which means that in effect it is a loan in shekels. For example, if one borrows 100 shekels and wishes to repay in dollars, one must repay 100 shekels worth of dollars in accordance with the exchange rate of the day of repayment.

Interest in partnerships: There are certain prohibitions of interest that apply to business partnerships. The main idea is that all business partners must be equally exposed to the possibilities of profit and loss. When one makes a transaction as part of a partnership, he must make sure that the deal is conducted in accordance with the principles of Jewish law.

Penalties: Many contracts include a penalty clause entailing fines for arrears in payments. Such a penalty may be problematic in terms of the *halakhot* of interest. The possibility to insert clauses of this kind certainly exists, but it must be done in accordance with halakhic guidelines.

Interest through speech, gifts, and advance interest: The prohibition of interest includes changing the relationship between the creditor and the debtor. The debtor may not provide the creditor with favors due to the loan and the relationship that prevailed between them before the loan must remain the same after the loan was granted. For this reason, the debtor is forbidden to praise or flatter the creditor, or relate to him or provide him with a service in a manner that he had not previously accorded him.

The debtor may not give the creditor gifts until after he has repaid the loan. It is likewise prohibited to give someone a gift because he hopes to borrow money from him in the future.

Taking advantage of the situation by the creditor: The creditor must also be careful to keep the relationship between the pair as it was before the loan, rather than taking advantage of the situation to submit various requests to the debtor that he would not have done previously. For example, if before the loan the creditor would not have felt comfortable asking the other to borrow his car, he should not do so after lending him money.

All the above cases are prohibited under the rubric of *avak ribit*.

Accommodations with the Need for Credit in a Modern Economy

Economic developments have led to an increasing need for the giving and receiving of loans, and for the providing of credit by various financial institutions. These institutions could not operate if they did not generate profits and they are an essential part a modern economy. Against this backdrop, various halakhic methods have been developed to enable a great number of transactions which, under normal circumstances, would be forbidden due to the various prohibitions of interest.

Economic Solutions

Below are several ways that the *halakha* has addressed the challenges posed by the prohibition of interest. There are other methods, but they are less accepted today.

Heter iska: This is a halakhic convention developed in order to structure business transactions in such a manner as to avoid violating the prohibition of interest. It is an agreement between the creditor and the debtor that turns all their loans into investment ventures. A loan covered by a *heter iska* is defined as partnership between the creditor and the debtor, in which they both share the profits of the transaction. The additional payment of the debtor, beyond the principal, is not defined as interest but rather as the distribution of profits.

Nowadays, all banks in Israel sign a *heter iska*, thereby enabling customers to borrow money from the bank without violating the prohibition of interest. It means that the additional repayment for a loan received from the bank is not interest, but rather a share in the profits of the transactions executed by the customer with the money the bank lent him. This agreement also applies to the reverse case, when the customer deposits his money in the bank and the bank gives him an additional amount to the principal at set intervals. This increment is not interest, but a distribution of the profits from the transactions performed by the bank over the course of this period with the customer's money.

If a private individual wants to lend money to another with an agreement that he will repay more than the principal, they must first sign a *heter iska*, as otherwise the creditor and the debtor will violate the prohibition of interest.

Some halakhic authorities maintain that a *heter iska* is permitted only for business purposes, and it should not be used for day-to-day matters. This includes an overdraft in one's bank account, for which the bank charges interest. These authorities claim that in order for a *heter iska* to be valid, there must actually be an investment whose profits can be divided between the creditor and the debtor. However, other halakhic authorities contend that it is permitted to use a *heter iska* regarding any loan and for any purpose, and it is generally accepted to rely on this lenient opinion.

Limited liability corporations: Some halakhic authorities have argued that a limited liability corporation is permitted to both borrow and lend with interest. Since the corporation has limited liability, i.e. that the shareholders are not responsible for the debts of the company if it goes bankrupt, the shareholders are not regarded as partners in the company. Rather, the company itself is an economic entity and the prohibition of interest applies to private individuals, not abstract entities. If this is the case, interest would be permitted in both loans from a bank and loans to a bank (savings). Nevertheless, almost no halakhic authorities are willing to rely upon this argument in practice and require that a bank or investment company (which sells bonds, which are essentially loans to a company) be a signatory to a *heter iska*.

Other authorities have argued that there is a difference between borrowing money with interest from a limited liability company and lending it money with interest (e.g. a savings account in a bank or a bond with a fixed return). In the former case, the debtor bears personal responsibility for the loan and therefore it is regarded as loan with interest, which is prohibited in the absence of a *heter iska*. However, when the corporation is the debtor (like when it issues a bond), since it has limited liability and no one has personal responsibility for the loan, there is no prohibition of interest. In any case, it is recommended that one ensure that there is a *heter iska* also in this case.

General Note of Caution

In any case in which uncertainty arises as to whether or not a loan might involve prohibited interest, it is recommended to consult a rabbi who has expertise in this field.

Glossary

Glossary

Adar – Month of the Jewish calendar, occurring during February/March.

afikoman – Part of the middle matza at the Passover Seder, which is set aside during *Yahatz* and eaten at *Tzafun*, after the meal.

aggada (pl. aggadot) – Rabbinic story meant to impart an educational lesson.

Al HaNisim – Lit. "for the miracles"; a paragraph added to the *Amida* and the Grace after Meals on Purim and Hanukkah, thanking God for the miracles He wrought on behalf of the Jewish people.

aliya – Subdivision of the weekly Torah portion; the honor of being called up to the Torah for the reading of such a subdivision.

Amen – A response to a blessing indicating agreement with it and belief in its content.

Amida – A prayer comprising nineteen blessings that forms the central part of the prayer service. Also known as *Shemoneh Esreh* (lit. eighteen), because its original formulation had eighteen blessings.

arava (pl. aravot) – Willow branch, one of the four species taken on *Sukkot*.

ark – Repository in the prayer hall for Torah scrolls.

Ashkenazim (adj. Ashkenazic) – Segment of the Jewish population; broadly, Jews of European descent.

aufruf – Yiddish for "calling up." In Ashkenazic custom, a groom is called up to the Torah on the Shabbat before his wedding. This is observed as a celebratory event.

Av – Month of the Jewish calendar, occurring during July/August.

bar mitzva, bat mitzva – When a Jewish child reaches maturity and becomes formally obligated in mitzva observance. For a boy this occurs at the age of thirteen, for a girl at twelve.

baraita – A tannaitic statement that does not appear in the Mishna.

Barekhu – An invitation by the prayer leader to the congregation to recite a blessing. This marks the beginning of the blessings before *Shema* and of the blessings recited when one is called up to the Torah.

bima – The table in the synagogue upon which the Torah scroll is placed for Torah reading.

Birkot HaShahar – Morning Blessings.

Blessings over the Torah – Blessings said as part of the Morning Blessings, thanking God for the Torah and requesting His assistance to cleave to it.

brit – Circumcision ritual in which the baby is given his name.

dreidel – A four-sided spinning top played with on Hanukkah.

Edot HaMizrah – A general term for Sephardic congregations or the version of liturgy they use in their prayer services.

eiruv – A solution instituted by the Sages with regard to Shabbat prohibitions against carrying between domains and against walking far out of one's town; commonly used to refer to one type of *eiruv, eiruv hatzerot*.

eiruv hatzerot – The symbolic joining of private domains belonging to different people, thereby allowing them to carry from one place to another on Shabbat. This is accomplished when food belonging to the different residents is placed in one location.

eiruv tavshilin – When Shabbat falls on the day after a festival day, one must set aside bread and a cooked dish for a Shabbat meal before the festival begins. This allows him to cook or to carry out other preparations for Shabbat on the festival.

eiruv tehumin – The placement of food in a particular location, which establishes that location as a person's Shabbat residence. This allows him to travel two thousand cubits, the maximum distance one may travel on Shabbat (see *tehum Shabbat*), from that new location, rather than from his home.

Elul – Month of the Jewish calendar, occurring during August/September.

etrog – Citron, one of the four species taken on *Sukkot*.

farbrengen – Gathering of Chabad hasidim that may include the teaching of hasidic ideas, the telling of stories, and the singing of songs, as well as refreshments.

Full Kaddish – An Aramaic prayer of praise of God that is recited in the synagogue service, often by mourners.

gabbai – The synagogue sexton, who oversees the services.

gebrokts – Yiddish term for matza that has come into contact with liquid. Many Jews of hasidic descent have a custom not to eat *gebrokts* on Passover.

gematriya – A system in which each Hebrew letter is given a numerical value. It often highlights connections, sometimes mystical ones, between words.

geniza – Storeroom or repository in a synagogue used for discarded, damaged, or defective sacred books, papers, and objects.

Grace after Meals – Blessings recited after eating bread. Known in Hebrew as *Birkat HaMazon* and in Yiddish as *Bentching*.

hadas – Myrtle branch, one of the four species taken on *Sukkot*.

haftara – A portion from the Prophets read after the Torah reading on Shabbat, festivals, and public fasts.

haggada (pl. haggadot) – The text that presents the order of the Passover Seder. It contains instructions for the different parts of the Seder, and includes the text traditionally recited as fulfillment of the mitzva to retell the story of the redemption from Egypt.

HaGomel – Blessing said by one who is saved from a dangerous situation.

hakafot sheniyot – The seven rotations taken with the Torah, accompanied by music and dancing, on the night following *Simhat Torah*. This is customary in some communities.

halaka – Ceremonial first haircut, given to boys at age three; means haircut in Arabic. The Yiddish term is *upsherin*.

halakha (pl. halakhot) – Jewish law.

halakhic hour – One-twelfth of the period of daylight, may be longer or shorter than ordinary hours.

Half Kaddish – A shortened version of the Kaddish prayer (see Full Kaddish) that is recited by the prayer leader at certain points in the synagogue prayer service.

halla (pl. hallot) – Braided bread eaten on Shabbat and festivals. The name derives from the mitzva of *halla*, which is to separate a piece of dough and give it to a priest. Nowadays, however, the dough is destroyed.

Hallel – A series of psalms of praise recited on festivals.

hametz – Leavened grain products, which are prohibited for consumption on Passover.

HaMotzi – The blessing before eating bread.

Hanukkah – Eight-day holiday in the winter commemorating the victory of the Hasmoneans over the Seleucid Empire and the rededication of the Temple. On each day candles are lit.

hanukkiya – Hanukkah menora, the eight- or nine-branched candelabrum on which Hanukkah candles are lit.

hasid – Literally, a pious person. A member of the hasidic movement founded by the Baal Shem Tov in the eighteenth century.

hasidic – Having to do with Hasidism.

Hasidism – Pietist, anti-elitist movement founded by Rabbi Yisrael Baal Shem Tov in the eighteenth century. Hasidism emphasizes the service of God in all of one's actions, especially through ecstatic prayer and celebration, and the connection to God through the intervention of a *tzaddik*, a saintly person. Within a generation, Hasidism also became an intellectual movement, applying kabbalistic thought to an individual's religious life.

hatan me'ona – The name given in Sephardic communities to the penultimate *aliya* to the Torah before concluding the Torah on *Simhat Torah*.

hatan Torah – Literally, bridegroom of the Torah. The person who receives the *aliya* for the reading of the last section of the Torah on *Simhat Torah*.

Havdala – The ceremony for concluding the Sabbath. The blessing is said over a cup of wine, and with a candle and sweet-smelling spices.

hazan – Prayer leader in the synagogue, cantor.

hevra kadisha – Burial society, responsible for both preparing the deceased for burial and the actual interment.

hitbodedut – Seclusion practiced by Breslov hasidim for personal communication with God.

hitbonenut – Deep contemplation or meditation on one matter until the person has a spiritual experience regarding that matter. *Hitbonenut* combines intellectual study and spiritual passion.

Hol HaMoed – Intermediate days of *Sukkot* and Passover. On these days certain activities are prohibited, but there is no general prohibition of performing labor.

Hoshana Rabba – The seventh day of *Sukkot*, called *Hoshana Rabba* due to the custom of circling the *bima* seven times in a procession while reciting prayers that begin with the word *hoshana*.

huppa – Literally wedding canopy; *huppa* also refers to the wedding ceremony as a whole.

Isru Hag – The day after Passover, *Shavuot*, and *Sukkot*.

Iyar – Month of the Jewish calendar, occurring during April/May.

Kabbala – The Jewish tradition of mystical theory and practice.

Kabbalat Shabbat – The prayer service said at the onset of Shabbat on Friday night, as instituted by the Sages of Safed in the sixteenth century.

kabbalists – Thinkers who make use of the traditions of Kabbala

Kaddish – Prayer praising God that is said at particular intervals during the prayer service. See Mourner's Kaddish, Half Kaddish, and Rabbis' Kaddish.

kasher – To render a pot or a utensil kosher, usually by immersing it in boiling water or by heating it directly.

kashrut – The theory and practice of ritually kosher food.

Kedusha – Literally, sanctification. In this prayer, said during the repetition of the *Amida*, Israel joins forces with the angels in sanctifying God.

keli rishon – Primary vessel (lit. "first vessel"). The vessel in which something is cooked, even after it has been removed from a heat source.

kelipa (pl. kelipot) – Literally, husk. The kabbalistic term for those elements of existence that are forces of evil that need to be removed.

ketuba – A marriage contract that guarantees the wife a certain sum of money in the event of divorce or her husband's death.

kezayit – Olive-bulk, a halakhic measure of volume that generally corresponds to the amount of food one needs to consume in order to fulfill a mitzva or be liable to punishment for a transgression. According to the most prevalent halakhic opinion, an olive-bulk is about 27 ml.

Kiddush – The blessing made over wine at the beginning of Shabbat and festival meals. The *Kiddush* said on Friday night includes a blessing consecrating Shabbat.

kiddush – Light meal at which *Kiddush* is said on Shabbat morning.

Kiddush Levana – The blessing said once a month at the appearance of the new moon. Usually said on Saturday night at the close of Shabbat.

kiddushin – The part of the wedding ceremony involving the groom giving the ring to the bride. Once *kiddushin* has been performed they are formally married.

kimha depis'ha – Aramaic for "Passover flour," also known as *ma'ot hittin* (lit. "money for wheat"). Charity given before Passover to enable the poor to buy food for the holiday.

kinnot – The liturgical poems that lament the destruction of the Temple and other tragedies, recited on *Tisha BeAv*.

Kislev – Month of the Jewish calendar, occurring during November/December.

kitniyot – Foods derived from edible seeds such as rice, beans, and lentils. These are not *hametz,* but are prohibited on Passover in the Ashkenazic tradition.

kittel – A white robe worn by many married men on Yom Kippur, Seder night, and other occasions.

kohen (pl. kohanim) – A person of priestly lineage, a descendant of Aaron.

kol hane'arim – The *aliya* on *Simhat Torah* in which all the children of the community are called to the Torah. An adult recites the blessing.

Kol Nidrei – The prayer said at the onset of Yom Kippur in which the prayer leader asks to nullify all the vows made in the community that year.

Lag BaOmer – The thirty-third day of the *omer*, the eighteenth of the month of Iyar. *Lag BaOmer* is the day of the passing of Rabbi Shimon bar Yohai and also, in many customs, the end of the mourning period of the *omer*.

Various customs of *Lag BaOmer* include lighting bonfires and visiting Rabbi Shimon's grave at Meron.

lehem mishneh – Two whole loaves of bread that are used for the blessing at the beginning of a Shabbat meal.

Lekha Dodi – Liturgical poem composed by Rabbi Shlomo Alkabetz that is traditionally sung on Friday evening during *Kabbalat Shabbat*.

lulav – Palm branch, one of the four species that are taken together on *Sukkot*. Often, *lulav* is used to refer to all four species.

Ma'ariv – The evening prayer.

maftir – The additional reading at the conclusion of the Torah reading on Shabbat, festivals, and fast days. The person who receives the *maftir aliya* also reads the *haftara*.

maggid – In Eastern Europe before the Holocaust, a *maggid* was a person who gave sermons and admonished the community, e.g., the Maggid of Koznitz.

mahzor – Prayer book for festivals, Rosh HaShana, or Yom Kippur.

Marheshvan – Month of the Jewish calendar, occurring during October/November.

mashgiah – (1) *Kashrut* supervisor; (2) In many yeshivot, the person in charge of the spiritual development of the students.

matanot la'evyonim – Literally, gifts to the poor. Giving a gift to at least two poor people is one of the obligations of Purim.

matza (pl. matzot) – Unleavened bread that is eaten on Passover.

matza sheruya – See *gebrokts*.

megilla – Literally, scroll; often refers to the book of Esther.

melakha – Productive, creative activity (lit. "labor"), which is prohibited on Shabbat.

melaveh malka – Literally, "accompanying the queen." The meal customarily served on Saturday night to acknowledge the end of Shabbat.

messiah – Literally, "the anointed one." The anointed king from the house of David who will appear at the end of days and rule Israel righteously.

mezuza (pl. mezuzot) – The scroll affixed to the doorposts of a Jewish home containing the verses beginning *Shema Yisrael.*

mikva – Ritual bath. Food utensils acquired from gentiles must be immersed in a *mikva* before being used. A woman immerses herself in a *mikva* a week after her menstrual period before she resumes relations with her husband. Some men have the practice of immersing themselves in a *mikva* either every morning or every week.

Minha – The afternoon prayer service.

minyan – The quorum of ten men required for public prayer and Torah reading.

mishlo'ah manot – Gifts of food given on Purim.

mishnayot – Plural of mishna.

mishteh – Feast, one of the mitzvot on Purim.

mitnagged (pl. mitnaggedim) – Opponents of Hasidism. The original *mitnaggedim* fiercely opposed the innovations of the Baal Shem Tov and his followers. Once Hasidism became established, the *mitnaggedim* became a competing ideological movement that was centered in the great yeshivot of Eastern Europe.

mitzva (pl. mitzvot) – Literally, commandment. Traditionally there are 613 commandments in the Torah. Mitzva is often also used more loosely to refer to any religious obligation.

mohel – One who performs a ritual circumcision.

molad – The moment when the new moon becomes visible. See *Kiddush Levana.*

Morning Blessings – Blessings said upon rising in the morning celebrating the beginning of a new day.

Mourner's Kaddish – Kaddish said by mourners, usually by children for a parent, commemorating and elevating the soul of the deceased. See Kaddish.

muktze – An item that may not be handled on Shabbat or festivals. An item is *muktze* either because it serves no purpose (e.g., sticks and stones) or because its purpose involves a prohibited action on Shabbat or a festival (e.g., a pen).

Musaf – The additional prayer service said after the morning service on Shabbat and holidays.

Musar – (1) A type of Jewish literature devoted to moral development and spiritual and psychological growth; (2) A movement begun in the second half of the nineteenth century by Rabbi Yisrael Salanter that emphasized moral reflection and self-improvement, often through the study of Musar literature.

Ne'ila – The closing prayer service on Yom Kippur.

Nisan – Month of the Jewish calendar, occurring during March/April.

nisu'in – The second part of the Jewish marriage ceremony, in which blessings are recited under the wedding canopy.

nolad – An item that has just come into being. This concept is used in various *halakhot*, including those of festivals.

nusah – Version of a prayer used by a particular community.

Nusah Sefarad – Version of the prayer service used by those of hasidic heritage.

Old Yishuv – Ultra-Orthodox communities that were present in the Land of Israel prior to the various waves of Zionist immigration in the nineteenth and early twentieth centuries.

omer – An offering brought from the new crop of barley on the sixteenth of Nisan; the period from the sixteenth of Nisan until *Shavuot*.

onen – An acute mourner, one whose close relative has died but has not yet been buried. An *onen* does not perform any positive mitzvot.

panim hadashot – Literally, a new face. In order to recite the seven blessings celebrating the bride and groom during the week following the wedding, there must be *panim hadashot,* a person who was not present at the wedding.

parasha – The weekly Torah portion.

pareve – Food containing neither dairy nor meat ingredients.

pe'ot – Sideburns. Jewish men are forbidden to remove their sideburns above about half the ear. Some hasidic groups have the custom of growing their *pe'ot* long.

pesik reisha – Performing an action that will unintentionally bring about the performance of labor on Shabbat or a holiday is permitted. However, if such an unintentional result will necessarily occur, the action is called a *pesik reisha* and is prohibited. For example, it is prohibited to open a refrigerator on Shabbat if that action will necessarily cause an incandescent light bulb to be lit in the refrigerator, even if one opened the refrigerator with no intention of turning on the light.

Pesukei DeZimra – The psalms said at the beginning of the morning service.

pidyon haben – Redemption of the firstborn, performed on firstborn sons of Israelite lineage on the thirtieth day of life.

pikuah nefesh – Saving a life. Saving a life overrides all mitzvot in the Torah except for the prohibitions against murder, illicit sexual relations, and idolatry.

prozbol – Legal transfer of the responsibility for the collection of one's debts to the court. *Prozbol* is performed during the Sabbatical Year in order to avoid the cancellation of those debts.

Rabbis' Kaddish – The Kaddish prayer that is said after studying Torah. It includes a passage praying for the welfare of Torah scholars and their students.

Retzeh – (1) The third-to-last blessing of the *Amida*, in which we pray for the renewal of the Temple service; (2) The addition to Grace after Meals for Shabbat.

Rosh Hodesh – The first of the month, which is a minor holiday. Jewish months have either 29 or 30 days. When the preceding month had 30 days, *Rosh Hodesh* is celebrated on the 30th day of the preceding month and the first of the new month. When the preceding month had 29 days, *Rosh Hodesh* is celebrated only on the first of the new month.

sandak – The person at a circumcision ceremony who holds the baby during the actual circumcision. To be *sandak* is regarded as an honor, often given to one of the newborn's grandfathers.

Sanhedrin – The High Court of the Jewish people, composed of 71 members. The Sanhedrin continued to exist after the destruction of the Second Temple for about 350 years.

seder – Literally, order; one of the six sections of the Mishna.

Seder – Ceremonial Passover meal in which four cups of wine are drunk, matza and bitter herbs are eaten, and those present read the haggada.

sefer Torah – Torah scroll, in which the entire Pentateuch is written by hand, using special calligraphy.

Sefira (pl. Sefirot) – The ten different manifestations of the Divine according to Kabbala. The *Sefirot* bear structured relationships with one another, and the relationships between them serve to explain every aspect of Being.

Sefirat HaOmer – The counting of the *omer*, the mitzva to count the days and weeks beginning on the second day of Passover and concluding on the day before *Shavuot*.

segula – An object or practice that serves as a favorable omen or a talisman for receiving some benefit.

sekhakh – Sukka roofing. Sekhakh must be made from a plant that is no longer attached to the earth and is not edible or any sort of utensil (and therefore is not subject to ritual impurity).

Selihot – Prayers, mostly composed as liturgical poems, that petition God for mercy and forgiveness. *Selihot* are said on fast days, during the days before and between Rosh HaShana and Yom Kippur, and on Yom Kippur itself.

Sephardim (adj. Sephardic) – Jews who trace their traditions and liturgy back to medieval Spain and Portugal. Today, most Sephardic families trace their more recent origins to Middle Eastern countries, from Morocco in the west to Iran in the east.

seuda shelishit – The third Shabbat meal.

seudat havra'a – The meal prepared for mourners upon their return from the funeral, by their friends and neighbors.

seudat mitzva – A celebratory meal held in honor of the performance of a mitzva, including a wedding, bar mitzva, circumcision, and *siyum*.

Shabbat (pl. Shabbatot) – Saturday. Shabbat is the day of rest and the *halakha* proscribes thirty-nine specific labors on that day.

Glossary

Shabbat Hatan – Literally, groom's Shabbat. On the Shabbat either immediately before or after a wedding the groom's family and friends gather to celebrate. The groom usually receives an *aliya* to the Torah.

Shaharit – The morning prayer service.

Shalom Zakhar – Traditional Ashkenazic ceremony in which family and friends gather on the Friday evening after the birth of a baby boy to sing, share words of Torah, and celebrate the birth.

Sheheheyanu – The blessing recited on the occasion of a new experience: when one makes a significant purchase, upon eating a fruit or vegetable that was previously out of season, the first time one performs a mitzva, and at the beginning of holidays.

Shekhina – The Divine Presence, the manifestation of God in the world. In kabbalistic thought, the *Shekhina* is identified with the *Sefira* of *Malkhut*.

sheloshim – The thirty-day period of mourning after the death of a close relative.

Shema – The verse "Hear, Israel: the Lord is our God, the Lord is one" (Deut. 6:4). It is a mitzva to recite the *Shema* (along with other verses) every morning and evening. The *Shema* is a declaration of one's acceptance of the yoke of Heaven and is the ultimate expression of a Jew's loyalty to and faith in God. As such it has often been recited by martyrs at their deaths.

Shemini Atzeret – The eighth day of the festival of *Sukkot*, which is in many ways a separate holiday, as the mitzvot of *Sukkot* such as *lulav* and *sukka* do not apply to it.

sheva berakhot – The seven blessings recited at a wedding and at subsequent meals made for the couple in celebration of their wedding in the following week.

Shevat – Month of the Jewish calendar, occurring during January/February.

shevut – Actions on Shabbat that the Sages prohibited beyond those prohibited by Torah law.

shiva – The seven-day mourning period observed after the death of a close relative.

Glossary

shofar – A hollowed-out ram's horn that is sounded on Rosh HaShana.

siddur – Jewish prayer book.

Simhat Beit HaSho'eva – The celebration of the drawing of the water, a celebration that took place in the Temple on *Sukkot* in honor of the water libation that was brought on that festival. *Simhat Beit HaSho'eva* has become a general term for a celebration held on the festival of *Sukkot*.

Simhat Torah – The last day of the festival of *Sukkot*. In Israel, *Simhat Torah* is celebrated on *Shemini Atzeret,* while in the diaspora it is celebrated on the following day. On this day the yearly cycle of Torah reading is completed and begun again.

sitra ahra – Literally, the other side. In kabbalistic thought, the *sitra ahra* is the metaphysical locus of the forces of evil.

Sivan – Month of the Jewish calendar, occurring during May/June.

siyum – A celebration marking the completion of the study of a talmudic tractate or some other significant work of Torah literature.

sukka – A covered booth (see *sekhakh*). On *Sukkot*, it is a mitzva to dwell in a *sukka* rather than in one's house.

Sukkot – The festival beginning on the fifteenth of Tishrei, in which we are commanded to dwell in *Sukkot* and to take up the four species. *Sukkot* lasts seven days, concluding on the eighth day with *Shemini Atzeret* and in the diaspora extending a ninth day with *Simhat Torah*.

Tahanun – A petitionary prayer recited on weekdays following the *Amida* in both the morning and afternoon services. It is the custom in Ashkenazic (and some Sephardic) synagogues to lean over and cover one's face with one's arm during this prayer.

tallit – A prayer shawl, a four-cornered garment with *tzitzit* that is worn by men during the morning service.

Tamuz – Month of the Jewish calendar, occurring during June/July.

tanna – A Sage of the period of the Mishna.

tefillin – Phylacteries, leather boxes containing scrolls upon which are written passages from the Torah. The boxes are attached to one's forehead and one's upper arm with leather straps. *Tefillin* are worn by Jewish men during weekday morning prayers.

Glossary

tehum Shabbat – The Shabbat limit, the maximum distance one may travel on Shabbat: two thousand cubits beyond one's place of dwelling, or in a city, from the city limit.

tena'im – Literally, conditions. The contract explicating the monetary commitments of both sides in a marriage and the consequences for each side if they do not go through with the marriage. In many communites today, this is not done at all or if it is, it is merely a ritualized formality.

tereifa – An animal that has a certain type of physical defect that renders it non-kosher. The most common type of defect is a hole in the lung.

Tevet – Month of the Jewish calendar, occurring during December/January.

Three Weeks – The three-week period between the Seventeenth of Tammuz and Tisha BeAv, a period of mourning for the destruction of the two Temples.

tikkun – A set text of prayers and readings from the Bible and from rabbinic and kabbalistic works, read on evenings when it is customary to study Torah at night. These occasions include *Shavuot, Hoshana Rabba,* and the eve of the seventh day of Passover. Each day has its own *tikkun.*

tisch – Literally, table. A gathering of hasidim around their rebbe, with singing and Torah discourses.

Tisha BeAv – The ninth day of the month of Av, which is the anniversary of the destruction of both the first and second Temples. as well as of other disasters that befell the Jewish people. *Tisha BeAv* is a day of mourning and a fast day.

Tishrei – Month of the Jewish calendar, occurring during September/October.

Tu BeAv – The fifteenth of the month of Av. It is a minor holiday in commemoration of an ancient practice recorded in the Mishna (*Ta'anit* 4:8) whereby young women would dance in the vineyards in search of a bridegroom.

Tu BeShvat – The fifteenth of the month of Shevat, known as the New Year for the trees. This date has halakhic significance in terms of the calculation of the year for the purpose of tithes. Many have the custom to hold special celebrations on this day.

tzaʾar baʾalei hayim – Causing unnecessary pain to animals. Not only is this forbidden, but one is also obligated to alleviate the pain of animals in one's possession.

tzadik (pl. tzadikim) – In general, a *tzadik* is a righteous person. In Hasidism, a *tzadik* is an extraordinary individual who has a special connection to God. Ordinary people can connect to God through a *tzadik*, either by becoming his hasidim, his followers, or by his acting as an intermediary for them.

tzedaka – Charity, or more generally, righteousness. *Tzedaka* is used specifically to denote monetary gifts to the poor.

tzedaka box – A small box into which people put small amounts of money for charity.

tzimtzum – Literally, contraction. The kabbalistic/theological principle that God "contracted" Himself in order to create a "space" for the universe to exist.

tzitzit – Ritual fringes that one is commanded to place at the corners of a four-cornered garment.

Wayfarer's Prayer – A prayer one recites when he travels between cities, to request divine protection.

Yaʾaleh VeYavo – The prayer inserted into the *Amida* and Grace after Meals on *Rosh Hodesh* and festivals.

yad soledet bo – The temperature at which one's hand spontaneously recoils from an item's heat. Used for *halakhot* of Shabbat and *kashrut*.

yahrzeit – The anniversary of someone's death. On that day Kaddish is recited by his or her children.

Yedid Nefesh – A liturgical hymn composed by Rabbi Elazar Azikri in the sixteenth century. In many communities it is sung at the beginning of Friday night prayers. It is also often sung at the third meal on Shabbat.

yeshiva – A traditional institution for Torah study. The focus of the curriculum is usually the Talmud.

yetzer hara – The evil inclination, the aspect of the human personality that desires to sin. In some contexts the *yetzer hara* is conceived of as a metaphysical force.

Glossary

yihud room – The room in which the bride and groom briefly seclude themselves following their wedding ceremony.

Yizkor – A prayer said in memory of the deceased. Usually said by his or her
children on the last day of each festival and on Yom Kippur.

Zeved HaBat – Celebration for the birth of a girl.

zimmun – The invitation to recite Grace after Meals, added when three men
(or three women) eat together.

A Concise Guide to Halakha

Rabbi Adin Even-Israel Steinsaltz

Steinsaltz Center

English Edition

Executive Director, Steinsaltz Center
Rabbi Meni Even-Israel

Editor in Chief
Rabbi Jason Rappoport

Executive Editor
Rabbi Michael Siev

Translator
Avi Steinhart

Editors
Rabbi Yaakov Blinder
Rabbi Yehoshua Duker

Copy Editors
Caryn Meltz, Manager
Dvora Rhein
Ilana Sobel

Hebrew Proofreader
Avichai Gamdani

Illustrations
Razia Richman
Eliyahu Misgav

Designer
Eliyahu Misgav

Typesetters
Rina Ben-Gal
Estie Dishon

Technical Staff
Adena Frazer
Adina Mann

Hebrew Edition

Halakha Advisor
Rabbi Ariel Holland

Senior Editors
Menachem Brod
Amechaye Even-Israel

Editor
Rabbi Zalman Ruderman

Research
Rabbi Yehoshua Meirson
Life Cycle
Rabbi Netanel Miles
Calendar Year
Rabbi Uri Gamson
Shabbat & Festivals;
Other topics
Rabbi Ad'el Kedar
Day to day;
Between Man and Man